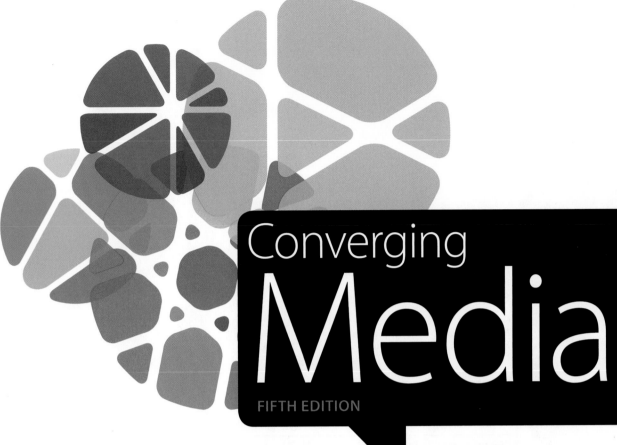

Converging Media

FIFTH EDITION

A NEW INTRODUCTION TO
Mass Communication

John V. Pavlik
RUTGERS UNIVERSITY

Shawn McIntosh
MASSACHUSETTS COLLEGE OF LIBERAL ARTS

New York   Oxford
OXFORD UNIVERSITY PRESS

Oxford University Press is a department of the University of Oxford.
It furthers the University's objective of excellence in research,
scholarship, and education by publishing worldwide.

Oxford New York
Auckland Cape Town Dar es Salaam Hong Kong Karachi
Kuala Lumpur Madrid Melbourne Mexico City Nairobi
New Delhi Shanghai Taipei Toronto

With offices in
Argentina Austria Brazil Chile Czech Republic France Greece
Guatemala Hungary Italy Japan Poland Portugal Singapore
South Korea Switzerland Thailand Turkey Ukraine Vietnam

For titles covered by Section 112 of the US Higher Education
Opportunity Act, please visit www.oup.com/us/he for the
latest information about pricing and alternate formats.

Published by Oxford University Press
198 Madison Avenue, New York, New York 10016
http://www.oup.com

Library of Congress Cataloging-in-Publication Data

Pavlik, John V. (John Vernon)
  Converging media : a new introduction to mass communication /
John V. Pavlik, Rutgers University ; Shawn McIntosh, Massachusetts
College of Liberal Arts. -- Fifth edition.
     pages cm
  Includes bibliographical references and index.
   ISBN 978-0-19-027151-0
1. Mass media. 2. Digital media. 3. Internet. I. McIntosh, Shawn.
II. Title.
  P90.P3553 2016
   302.23--dc23

                                    2015028062

Printing number: 9 8 7 6 5 4 3 2 1

Printed in the United States of America
on acid-free paper

To my wife, Jackie,
and my daughters,
Tristan and Orianna

—J.V.P.

To my parents,
Dennis and Kathie

—S.M.

Brief Contents

Contents

PART TWO   MASS-COMMUNICATION FORMATS

3 Print Media: Books, Newspapers, and Magazines   63

4 Audio Media: Music Recordings, Radio 97

5 Visual Media: Photography, Movies, and Television   125

Features

6 Interactive Media: The Internet, Video Games, and Augmented Reality   161

www.oup.com/us/pavlik

8 Journalism: From Information to Participation   227

9 Advertising and Public Relations: The Power of Persuasion   259

PART FOUR   MEDIA AND SOCIETY

10 Media Ethics   295

www.oup.com/us/pavlik

Features

11 Communication Law and Regulation in the Digital Age   323

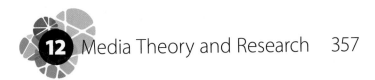

14 Global Media in the Digital Age   411

Converging Media provides extensive content on the twelve core values and competencies of the Accrediting Council on Education in Journalism and Mass Communications (ACEJMC). As a nationally elected member of the ACEJMC from 2004 to 2007, John V. Pavlik recognized that the ACEJMC-based learning goals provide a useful benchmark for assessing student learning. By covering the twelve core values and competencies, this text provides a strong foundation for students to become well-rounded journalists and experts in mass communication.

ACEJMC LEARNING GOALS	HOW *CONVERGING MEDIA* SUPPORTS
1. FREEDOM OF SPEECH: Understand and apply the principles and laws of freedom of speech and press for the country in which the institution that invites ACEJMC is located, as well as receive instruction in and understand the range of systems of freedom of expression around the world, including the rights to dissent, to monitor and criticize power, and to assemble and petition for redress of grievances.	• Regulation of journalism and mass communication in the digital age including libel and censorship (p. 328, 349) • Fairness (p. 344) • The public's right to know (p. 310) • Media systems around the world (p. 418)
2. HISTORY: Demonstrate an understanding of the history and role of professionals and institutions in shaping communications.	• Origins of photography, movies, television, and video games (p. 126, 128, 146) • History of journalism (p. 230) • History of advertising (p. 264) • History of public relations (p. 282) • History of media law and the regulation of electronic media (p. 325) • Early research on media effects (p. 359) • History of recorded music and radio (p. 99, 112) • History of print media (books, newspapers, magazines) (p. 66, 76, 89) • History of the Internet (p. 168)
3. GENDER, RACE, AND SEXUALITY: Demonstrate an understanding of gender, race, ethnicity, sexual orientation, and, as appropriate, other forms of diversity in domestic society in relation to mass communications.	• Effects of media and advertising on women and men (p. 377) • Role of women in the history of newspapers (p. 232) • Diversity in the newsroom (p. 254) • Minority newspapers (p. 232, 254)
4. GLOBAL SOCIETY: Demonstrate an understanding of the diversity of peoples and cultures and of the significance and impact of mass communications in a global society.	• Relationships among various global and local media sources (p. 424) • Cultural and socioeconomic impact of global media (p. 426) • "International Perspectives" boxes throughout (example, p. 70) • International theories of the press (p. 413) • Media in a global society appears as a theme in several chapters
5. THEORY: Understand concepts and apply theories in the use and presentation of images and information.	• Photography, movies, and television (p. 135, 147) • Grammar of media (p. 44) • Information overload in the digital age (p. 218) • Major media theories and research (p. 359, 370, 376)

ACEJMC LEARNING GOALS	HOW *CONVERGING MEDIA* SUPPORTS
6. ETHICS: Demonstrate an understanding of professional ethical principles and work ethically in pursuit of truth, accuracy, fairness, and diversity.	• "Ethics in Media" boxes throughout (example, p. 55) • Chapter on media ethics, including accuracy and the pursuit of truth (p. 295) • Chapter on communication law and regulation in the digital age (p. 323) • Fairness and diversity (p. 318)
7. CRITICAL AND CREATIVE THINKING: Think critically, creatively, and independently.	• "Convergence Culture" boxes throughout (example, p. 211) • "Media Matters" at end of chapters (example, p. 34) • Discussion Questions throughout • Critical-Thinking Questions in selected image captions (example, p. 335) • Foundations for critically examining media presented early in the text (example, p. 39)
8. RESEARCH: Conduct research and evaluate information by methods appropriate to the communications professions in which they work.	• Chapter on media theory and research teaches students to evaluate research methods and findings (p. 378)
9. WRITING ABILITY: Write correctly and clearly in forms and styles appropriate for the communications professions, audiences, and purposes they serve.	• Appropriate writing style for particular media and for the communities and purposes that media professionals serve (p. 243) • Importance of clear and accurate writing in news creation (p. 240)
10. EVALUATION OF WORK: Critically evaluate their own work and that of others for accuracy and fairness, clarity, appropriate style, and grammatical correctness.	• Media Matters and Critical Thinking Questions throughout the text encourage self-reflection in the form of spoken and written responses while promoting group discussion and peer evaluation of work.
11. NUMERICAL AND STATISTICAL CONCEPTS: Apply basic numerical and statistical concepts.	• Data for students to analyze about newspaper circulation and readership and advertising impact (p. 84) • Pricing structure of the recording industry (p. 106) • Figures and tables throughout apply numerical and statistical concepts (example, p. 73) • "US Media Giants" (pullout at the back of the book)
12. TECHNOLOGY: Apply tools and technologies appropriate for the communications professions in which they work.	• Social media (p. 191) • Interactive media (p. 161) • Role of mobile media, such as the iPad, in delivering video (p. 183) • Mobile media and digital books (p. 74) • Impact of touch screens on human–computer interface (p. 165) • Use of digital technology in journalism (p. 248) • Impact of digital technology and mobile media on advertising (p. 274)

Features

FIGURES

Preface

With the potential to strengthen or to undermine personal freedom, media convergence is a double-edged sword. Digital technologies, including mobile and social media, have empowered citizens to access, interact with, and generate content and stories around the world and on demand. In recent years, Twitter and similar services have helped citizens throughout the globe organize protests against government policy, oppressive regimes, and corporate malfeasance. At the same time, however, these powerful digital tools have enabled governments, corporations, and others to conduct sweeping surveillance of citizens and even international leaders around the world, as demonstrated by the epic Edward Snowden revelations and the more recent June 2015 WikiLeaks about the NSA spying on the last three French presidents.

Privacy may be little more than a memory in an age when ubiquitous high-definition cameras, big data analytics, and social media are generating massive databases with information on nearly every man, woman, and child around the globe. Even when we are not being spied on, we may be eagerly revealing too much about ourselves. As Alessandro Acquisti, professor of information technology and public policy at Carnegie Mellon University, observed in a 2013 *60 Minutes* interview with Lesley Stahl, "Most of us have fully identified, high-definition frontal photos of ourselves online." On Facebook alone, users have posted billions of photos of themselves, their friends, and their relatives. And Facebook's increasingly refined facial-recognition technology will continue to facilitate being tagged by friends and being tracked by those whose intentions may be less friendly.

The existence of such vast repositories of data, valuable for security and commercial purposes (such as individually targeted advertising), raises concerns for civil liberties, particularly the right to privacy and freedom of speech. Another related issue involves who has the right to own and control this information, especially with telecommunications companies and Internet giants contributing to the NSA's surveillance program.

Meanwhile, the digitization of media and the convergence of media formats and industries proceed unabated. Research indicates that we now spend more time using digital devices than we do with any other medium, including television. Digital content is more likely to be viewed on a tablet or a smartphone than on a laptop or desktop computer. Digital distribution is now the dominant format for music, television, and radio, whether delivered terrestrially, by satellite, or via the Internet.

Thanks to tablets and e-readers, the popularity of ebooks has surged. Following significant declines in print circulation, newspapers and magazines are experiencing growth in tablet, smartphone, and online distribution. Digital movies, television, and video-game distribution is now mainstream, with companies such as Netflix and Amazon producing and streaming their own original television shows. Tablets and other mobile devices are blurring the lines between Internet, movies, and television while allowing technology companies such as Google, Apple, and Amazon to challenge traditional media distributors.

Our engagement with media has also changed, becoming more active as mass and interpersonal communications converge. Anyone can broadcast a personal opinion on Twitter or via other social media; and increasingly, people do so while consuming traditional media such as television, posting comments and conversing about popular shows. Interactive media, especially video games, also constitute an increasingly popular form of entertainment.

Convergence is a worldwide phenomenon today. The globalization of media industries and distribution has produced a cultural convergence that, at worst, smothers various local perspectives in a homogeneous Westernized culture and, at best, enables different local voices to be heard. Diverse cultural viewpoints have also begun to influence the content of new Hollywood blockbusters and other forms of Western media.

Rarely has media usage so varied. Those who grew up in a pre-Internet era of mass communication may enjoy reading a printed newspaper over breakfast; digital natives may get their news from their Facebook feeds—if they get any news at all. The older group may have impressive collections of DVDs, CDs, and even vinyl; the younger group may trust the digital, online "cloud" with their favorite movies and music, accessible from any location or on their portable devices. One group may worry how increased product placement affects the type of shows produced; the other group may wonder what product placement is and why it matters. Some may feel that their romantic associations are nobody's business; others may publicly announce their relationship status, posting that and much more personal information on social-networking sites.

Interestingly, this media divide is often represented in the college classroom comprised of students who are digital natives and their professors who hail from an older mass-media tradition. Yet, just like the media discussed in this book, the two parties can converge, often across generations, to enrich their understanding of where media have been, where they are today, and where they are going. Each group can—and should—learn from the other.

Convergence is creating the kind of mass communication that audiences have long desired, tools that increase control over what they watch, read, or listen to and increase the ability to share their stories and their lives with others. But with that greater power comes greater responsibility and a greater need for us to understand how our media work and how they may affect our society and political systems. A double-edged sword does indeed cut both ways; which way it cuts depends largely on who is wielding it and how.

Converging Media, Fifth Edition: An Updated Introduction to Mass Communication

Change is a constant in the mass-communication industry, and in recent years this transformation has rocketed forward with surprising speed. Students are changing. The field is changing. The world is changing. Yet these changes go largely unnoticed in most textbooks. An introductory textbook should provide a foundation of knowledge for students learning a new field. But when the foundation sits on a bed of shifting sand, the introduction needs to be revised continually.

Converging Media: A New Introduction to Mass Communication embraces the metamorphosis of today's mass-communication system and examines the changes even as it prepares students for what comes tomorrow. This book represents the beginning of a third wave in mass-communication textbooks, building on the earlier waves of case studies and critical-cultural approaches. This new approach demands a more balanced and nuanced understanding of the role that technology and digital media have played in our mass-communication environment.

The fifth edition of *Converging Media* follows the class-tested formula of the previous edition by offering

- **A Fresh Perspective.** Through the lens of convergence, our book shows how different aspects of media are parts of a whole and how they influence each other. Digital media are not relegated to special features or an isolated chapter; they are integrated throughout every chapter. This better reflects the world as students live in it and prepares them to understand the changes that are taking place. This organization invites students and professors to engage in timely discussions of media within a larger framework of understanding traditional mass-communication topics.

- **Comprehensive Coverage of Traditional Media.** To understand the present, we have to study the past. We cover the development and historical influences of print and electronic media and the issues these media face today. The communication professions of journalism, advertising, and public relations are viewed from historical, societal, and career perspectives, giving students insights into how they interact and influence each other.

- **Unique Coverage of Social Media.** As the first introductory mass-communication textbook to devote a chapter to this emerging area, we place social media within a larger media and sociocultural context. Today's popular social media tools are given a historical context and are connected thematically to older online communication tools. Social media are such an integral part of the media mix for so many people that they must be covered in an introductory course, not introduced in an upper-division media and technology course.

- **Cutting-Edge Examples.** We have chosen examples that are diverse, interesting, and up to date. We have written *Converging Media* with students always in mind—understanding the changing world they live in today. Taken from popular media that are familiar and relevant to undergraduates, the examples illustrate how the landscape of media has evolved—and is still evolving.

- **Cultural Context.** Mass communication, media technologies, and convergence take place firmly within a sociocultural milieu that simultaneously affects and is affected by these forces. Understanding this cultural context is vital for a complete grasp of convergence and today's media environment. We emphasize the cultural influences and implications of media technologies while explaining how they work and how they were developed.

- **Emphasis on Ethics.** The book has a chapter devoted entirely to ethics (Chapter 10) and we continue to thread ethics-related discussions throughout other chapters, as appropriate (see Ethics in Media boxes). Students should learn that ethical considerations are tightly linked to a full understanding of mass communication and media. Ethics can also help guide us in the complex and often-confusing world of converging media, giving a basis for sound and humane decisions on media use, production, and new technologies.

- **International Perspectives.** A chapter on today's global media environment (Chapter 14) provides a broad perspective on media in various countries and the social, economic, and cultural effects of media globalization overseas and domestically. In the remaining chapters, we also highlight international perspectives in feature boxes and in the text itself. Through comparisons and contrasts, students obtain an appreciation for different media systems throughout the world and how they work.

Features for Students

We have kept features limited and focused on a few key areas that foreground interesting and relevant aspects of the content discussed in the book.

- **Convergence Culture** boxes showcase how media impact our social, political, and popular culture in sometimes-dramatic ways. Three are new to this edition, six updated.
- **Media Pioneers** boxes examine the careers of visionaries and leaders in the world of media both historically and in the contemporary scene. They feature individuals past and present who have made or are making media history. Subjects represent a diversity of past and present, media vocations, and cultural and ethnic backgrounds. This feature now appears in every chapter. Four are new to this edition, the rest updated.
- **Ethics in Media** boxes, appearing in select chapters, discuss timely issues related to ethical practices and issues in mass media. Three are new to this edition, five updated.
- **International Perspectives** boxes take a global perspective on chapter topics, showcasing how the use of media and technology and media industries are similar to or different from the U.S. context and why that is so. Two are new to this edition, six updated.
- **Timelines**, appearing in select chapters, provide a history, or even prehistory, of different media, such as newspapers, television, and social-networking site launches, giving the context for their development.
- **Media Matters** (formerly known as Media Quiz) encourage critical thinking about media-related topics.
- **Chapter Opening Vignettes** have been updated for currency where necessary, and seven have been completely revised and are new to this edition.
- **Discussion Questions** are now located throughout each chapter.
- **Further Reading** assignments round out each chapter.

Changes to the Fifth Edition

This fifth edition has undergone several changes to keep pace with the rapidly evolving world of media.

- **Coverage of New Issues.** Throughout the text, we have updated and expanded coverage of critical topics, including the convergence of interpersonal communication and mass communication, gamification, augmented reality, cybersecurity, and the third screen. Noteworthy chapter-specific changes include
  - **Chapter 1:** Discussion of digital natives and digital immigrants. Expanded treatment of the digital divide.
  - **Chapter 2:** Addition of a Media Pioneers feature. Extended analysis of concept of balance in journalism.
  - **Chapter 3:** Updated research on book readership, publishing, and sales, particularly ebooks, self-publishing, and Amazon. Extended treatment of newspaper chain acquisitions and mergers. Expanded discussion of online news sites, including recent competition presented by social media and citizen journalism. New Media Pioneers box.

- **Chapter 4:** Updated data on the record industry and radio programming. Expanded discussion of revenues and podcasts. Substantial revision and updating of Media Pioneers box.
- **Chapter 5:** Discussion of cord-cutters and cord-nevers.
- **Chapter 6:** Updated data on the video-game industry.
- **Chapter 7:** Updated discussion of Facebook, teen usage, and privacy norms. New timeline on social-networking sites, such as Instagram and Ello.
- **Chapter 8:** Updated information on the latest transformations in journalism production and business models.
- **Chapter 9:** Discussion of behavioral advertising and native advertising. Extended treatment of branding. New Media Pioneers feature.
- **Chapter 10:** Expanded discussion of dialogic social media. Addition of a Media Pioneers feature. New section on misrepresentation and plagiarism.
- **Chapter 11:** Expanded treatment of prior restraint and the First Amendment's application to social media. New content on the legality and future of advertising recreational marijuana on electronic media.
- **Chapter 12:** Updated and revised discussion of new directions in media research, along with the introduction of longitudinal and cross-sectional studies and random samples and sampling error.
- **Chapter 13:** Updated discussion of political campaign expenditures. Extended treatment of "going viral" and memes.
- **Chapter 14:** Updated discussion of the impact of social media on the public sphere, particularly concerns about cybersecurity. Expanded analysis of censorship in Asia and world press freedom in general.
- **Emphasis on Careers in Media.** In addition to the Media Pioneers feature, which presents the contributions and career foundations of innovators and leaders who have influenced and continue to shape the world of media, a new **Media Careers** section has been added to the end of each chapter (with the exception of Chapter 1). In it, we discuss relevant traditional and emerging career paths in the industry, helping students appreciate the full range of possibilities in communications professions.
- **Discussion Questions.** Formerly located at the end of each chapter, discussion questions that encourage critical thinking have been integrated throughout the chapter.
- **Further Reading.** The fifth edition includes new sources in each chapter.

How the Book Is Organized

Converging Media has the comprehensive mission of explaining not only the world of digital media and social media but also the basics of communication theory, ethics, and traditional mass-communication forms, while also assisting in the development of media-literacy skills. We do this using a class-tested, multipart structure.

PART 1: THE CHANGING MEDIA LANDSCAPE

Chapter 1 not only explains the multifaceted nature of convergence (and disputes over its definition) but looks at theories of communication in general to see how the nature of mass communication is changing. **Chapter 2** discusses media literacy, which helps meet students' need for solid critical-thinking skills in the twenty-first century's complex and fast-changing digital-media environment. Providing an early foundation in media literacy ensures that students will bring a critical perspective to the remainder of the book.

PART 2: MASS-COMMUNICATION FORMATS

Chapter 3 begins the exploration of traditional media with a discussion of the print industry and the digital dynamics to which it is now subject. **Chapter 4** explores sound—namely, the recording industry and radio. The recording industry has of course been at the forefront of changes that digital media have brought to their industry through sharing of music files. Radio is increasingly facing questions about its role as people come to expect music on demand. There are also more options for bands to promote their music, such as in video games and on television shows. **Chapter 5** looks at visual media—photography, movies, and television—and how each of these developed and influenced the ways that we see media. Photography is often ignored in books such as this but is an important aspect of the development of our media usage. Technological advances in photography not only led directly to motion pictures but increased the importance we place on visual media today. **Chapter 6** explores how interactivity and user interface have played fundamental roles in the development of the Internet and video games. The chapter also discusses gamification as well as the promise and perils of augmented reality.

PART 3: MEDIA PERSPECTIVES

Chapters 7, **8**, and **9** examine the way that digital and social media are changing traditional communication professions. **Chapter 7** provides an overview of social media, which is allowing the public to talk back to media producers and companies. Users of social media can also band together and create entirely new projects outside the traditional media professions. Journalism, the subject of **Chapter 8**, is probably the field most threatened by the digital democratization of news reporting. Yet it remains an exciting field to enter, precisely because of the importance of social media and journalism to democracy. Advertising and public relations, the subjects of **Chapter 9**, also confront drastic changes as advertisers face more fragmented audiences with greater media choices than in the past and as consumers migrate to mobile media use.

PART 4: MEDIA AND SOCIETY

Part 4 shows the broader social effects of media developments. **Chapter 10** treats media ethics, with an in-depth discussion of the issues each profession faces. We explore the unique dilemmas raised by digital technologies, including threats to privacy. **Chapter 11** explores legal and regulatory aspects of media, especially as related to the First Amendment. For students who are interested in better understanding media or who are considering a career in academia, **Chapter 12** introduces some major media theories and presents different types of research and the strengths and weaknesses of each. **Chapter 13** thoroughly examines politics and communication, an area that, in introductory books, is often confined to U.S. election coverage. **Chapter 14**, on global media, introduces the notions of the public sphere and public opinion and looks at the media's role in democratic and nondemocratic countries throughout the world. The globalization of media technology, industry, and content highlights international issues, including the digital divide, cultural imperialism, and cybersecurity.

Supplements

Adopters of the fifth edition of *Converging Media* will be pleased to know that Oxford University Press offers a comprehensive support package for both students and instructors, for all kinds of introductory mass-communication courses.

FOR STUDENTS

- The **Companion Website at www.oup.com/us/pavlik** offers a wealth of study and review resources, including learning objectives, summaries, chapter quizzes, flashcards, activities, discussion questions, suggested reading, and links to a variety of media-related websites.

FOR INSTRUCTORS

- **Ancillary Resource Center (ARC) at www.oup-arc.com**. This convenient, instructor-focused website provides access to all of the up-to-date teaching resources for this text—at any time—while guaranteeing the security of grade-significant resources. In addition, it allows OUP to keep instructors informed when new content becomes available. The following items are available on the ARC:
  - The **Instructor's Manual and Test Bank** provides sample syllabi, teaching tips, exercises, and test questions that will prove useful to both new and veteran instructors. The Instructor's Manual includes chapter overviews, learning objectives, detailed chapter/lecture outlines, discussion topics, and suggested activities for each chapter.
  - The comprehensive **Computerized Test Bank** offers over eight hundred exam questions in multiple-choice, short-answer, and essay formats, with each item classified according to Bloom's taxonomy and tagged to page and section references in the text,
  - Newly revised **PowerPoint-based lecture slides** highlight key concepts, terms and examples, and incorporate images from each chapter. With streamlined text, more visual support, and additional lecture tips in the notes section, these presentations are ready to use and fully editable to make preparing for class faster and easier than ever.
- **Course cartridges** for a variety of Learning Management Systems, including Blackboard Learn, Canvas, and Moodle, allow instructors to create their own course websites integrating student and instructor resources available on the Ancillary Resource Center and Companion Website. Contact your Oxford University Press representative for access or for more information about these supplements or customized options.

Acknowledgments

Creating a book such as this is very much a collaborative effort, and the authors have benefited greatly from the advice and wisdom not only of the reviewers but of those who adopted the first, second, third, and fourth editions of the book.

These adopters sometimes had to work hard to persuade colleagues and departments that *Converging Media* was the text to use to introduce students to mass communication. We can only hope that the argument is easier to make with this fifth edition as we witness a growing number of books about media convergence in the market.

We would also like to thank the adopters who wrote to us over the years asking when a revised edition would be published and who offered encouraging words about the usefulness of the book when there were still plenty of professors who were not convinced that a new approach to teaching mass communication was needed or who thought that only minor tweaks to curricula would do the trick.

John Pavlik truly appreciates the love and support of his family, especially his wife, Jackie, and his daughters, Orianna and Tristan. Shawn McIntosh is similarly grateful for the love and support of his wife, Naren, and his son, Altan, who is growing up in this evolving media world as a digital native.

We want especially to thank the editors at Oxford University Press with whom we worked: Toni Magyar, our editor; Maegan Sherlock, development editor; Marie La Vina and Paul Longo, editorial assistants; and David Jurman, marketing manager. They immediately understood and shared our vision of what this textbook should and could be to introductory mass-communication courses. Their insights and advice helped this book surpass our expectations. We also wish to thank Dr. Mary Ann McHugh, whose extensive editing and creative contributions have streamlined and updated much of the text. We are grateful for the fine job of Oxford's production group: production manager, Lisa Grzan; production editor, Marianne Paul; and art director, Michele Laseau. The copyeditor, Deanna Hegle, also helped clarify, simplify, and improve the book.

And last but certainly not least, we wish to thank the following reviewers for the detailed and insightful feedback on various parts of the book and instructor resources.

FIFTH EDITION REVIEWERS

Amelia H. Arsenault, *Georgia State University*

James Brancato, *Cedar Crest College*

Scott Brown, *California State University, Northridge*

Jennifer Fogel, *State University of New York–Oswego*

Shari Hoppin, *Troy University*

Jenn Mackay, *Virginia Tech*

David Magolis, *Bloomsburg University of Pennsylvania*

Andrea McDonnell, *Emmanuel College*

Andrew Nelson, *Loyola University New Orleans*

Stephen Swanson, *McLennan Community College*

FOURTH EDITION REVIEWERS

Joseph Abisaid, *Monmouth College*

Nathan Atkinson, *Georgia State University*

Jeff Boone, *Angelo State University*

Pennie Boyett, *Tarrant County College–Southeast*

Allison Butler, *University of Massachusetts–Amherst*

Elizabeth B. Christian, *University of New Haven*

Sara Drabik, *Northern Kentucky University*

Mara Einstein, *Queens College*

Jason Genovese, *Bloomsburg University of Pennsylvania*

Aimee Gillette, *Howard Community College*

Meredith Guthrie, *University of Pittsburgh*

Jeffrey B. Hedrick, *Jacksonville State University*

Mark Hungerford, *University of New Hampshire*

George Johnson, *James Madison University*

Hume Johnson, *Roger Williams University*

Tom Kelleher, *University of Hawaii–Manoa*

Vincent Kiernan, *Georgetown University*

Daekyung Kim, *James Madison University*

Derek Lackaff, *Elon University*

Ryan Lange, *Alvernia University*

David Magolis, *Bloomsburg University of Pennsylvania*

Rick Marks, *College of Southern Nevada*

Joy A. McDonald, *Hampton University*

Meaghan Meachem, *Lyndon State College*

Wendy Nelson, *Palomar College*

Pamela O'Brien, *Bowie State University*

Andrea Otanez, *Everett Community College*

Eun-A Park, *University of New Haven*

Richard D. Pineda, *University of Texas–El Paso*

Hilary Russo, *St. John's University*

Jessie M. Quintero Johnson, *University of Massachusetts–Boston*

CarrieLynn D. Reinhard, *Dominican University*

Karen A. Ritzenhoff, *Central Connecticut State University*

Kevin Tankersley, *Baylor University*

Anita J. Turpin, *Roanoke College*

Tammy R. Vigil, *Boston University*

Justin Walden, *Pennsylvania State University*

Jamie Ward, *University of Michigan–Dearborn*

Matt Weidman, *Widener University–Exton*

Ronald A. Yaros, *University of Maryland–College Park*

THIRD EDITION REVIEWERS

Lonny J. Avi Brooks, *California State University, East Bay*

Ovril Patricia Cambridge, *Ohio University*

Skye Dent, *Fayetteville State University*

Marie Dick, *St. Cloud State University*

Paul Glover, *Henderson State University*

Chandler Harriss, *Alfred University*

Myleea D. Hill, *Arkansas State University*

Hans Ibold, *Indiana University*

Daekyung Kim, *Idaho State University*

Viktoria Kreher, *Southern Illinois University, Carbondale*

Carole McNall, *St. Bonaventure University*

Robert M. Ogles, *Purdue University*

Ted Satterfield, *Northwestern Oklahoma State University*

Lauren Reichart Smith, *Auburn University*

Elyse Warford, *Georgia State University*

Scott Winter, *University of Nebraska–Lincoln*

SECOND EDITION REVIEWERS

Charles Apple, *University of Michigan–Flint*

Charlyne Berens, *University of Nebraska–Lincoln*

William R. Bettler, *Hanover College*

Joseph S. Clark, *Florida State University*

David Cundy, *Iona College*

James Ettema, *Northwestern University*

Michael Robert Evans, *Indiana University*

Thom Gencarelli, *Manhattan College*

Roger George, *Bellevue College*

Donald G. Godfrey, *Arizona State University*

David Gore, *Eastern Michigan University*

Margot Hardenbergh, *Fordham University*

Chandler Harriss, *Alfred University*

Karima A. Haynes, *Bowie State University*

Jeffrey B. Hedrick, *Jacksonville State University*

Tamara Henry, *American University*

Patricia Holmes, *University of Louisiana–Lafayette*

Seok Kang, *University of Texas–San Antonio*

Greg Lisby, *Georgia State University*

John Madormo, *North Central College*

Charles Marsh, *University of Kansas*

Stephen J. McNeill, *Kennesaw State University*

Olivia Miller, *University of Memphis*

James E. Mueller, *University of North Texas*

Robert M. Ogles, *Purdue University*

Selene Phillips, *University of Louisville*

Marshel D. Rossow, *Minnesota State University–Mankato*

Ted Satterfield, *Northwestern Oklahoma State University*

Randall K. Scott, *University of Montevallo*

Brad Schultz, *University of Mississippi*

Arthur L. Terry, *Bethel University*

Mina Tsay, *University of Kentucky*

FIRST EDITION REVIEWERS

Robert Bellamy, *Duquesne University*

Gerald Boyer, *Maryville University*

Mark Braun, *Gustavus Adolphus College*

Margaret Cassidy, *Adelphi University*

Steven Chappell, *Truman State University*

Joseph Chuk, *Kutztown University*

Vic Costello, *Gardner-Webb University*

David Gordon, *University of Wisconsin–Eau Claire*

Charlotte Kwok Glaser, *College of Notre Dame*

Colin Gromatzky, *New Mexico State University*

Steven Keeler, *Cayuga College*

Yasue Kuwahara, *Northern Kentucky University*

Dianne Lamb, *George Southern University*

Mitchell Land, *University of North Texas*

Jeremy Harris Lipschultz, *University of Nebraska–Omaha*

Arthur Lizie, *Bridgewater State College*

John Lule, *Lehigh University*

Thomas McPhail, *University of Missouri*

Anthony Olorunnisola, *Pennsylvania State University*

Kathleen Olson, *Lehigh University*

Ronald Roat, *University of Southern Indiana*

Marshel D. Rossow, *Minnesota State University–Mankato*

Andris Straumanis, *University of Wisconsin–Eau Claire*

L. Lee Thomas, *Doane College*

Max Utsler, *University of Kansas*

About the Authors

John V. Pavlik is a professor in the Department of Journalism and Media Studies at the School of Communication and Information, Rutgers, the State University of New Jersey. He is also faculty associate at the Columbia Institute for Tele-Information. Having published widely on the impact of new technology on journalism, media, and society, Pavlik has also authored more than a dozen computer software packages for education in journalism and mass communication. He is codeveloper of the situated documentary, a new type of digital storytelling using mobile augmented reality. He is former associate dean for research at Northwestern University in Qatar and a former senior fellow at the San Diego Supercomputer Center. He was the inaugural Fulbright Distinguished Chair in Media Studies in 2008 at the Academy of Fine Arts, Vienna, Austria. He received his PhD and MA in mass communication from the University of Minnesota and is a 1978 graduate of the School of Journalism and Mass Communication at the University of Wisconsin at Madison.

Shawn McIntosh is an assistant professor of digital journalism and communications in the Department of English/Communications at the Massachusetts College of Liberal Arts in North Adams, Massachusetts. He was a lecturer in strategic communication at Columbia University's School of Continuing Education, where he taught graduate courses in theories of persuasion, communication ethics, and digital media, and was an adjunct faculty member at New York University's School of Professional Studies, where he taught public affairs and research methods courses. He was an adjunct faculty member at Iona College, where he taught online journalism, website publishing, feature writing, and information visualization. McIntosh was an editor and freelance writer for ten years for various newspapers and magazines in the UK, the United States, and Japan. He has taught journalism and strategic communications in Latvia and Chile on Fulbright specialist awards. His research interests include social media, citizen journalism, and communication for social change. He received a BS in microbiology from the University of Idaho and an MS in journalism from the Graduate School of Journalism at Columbia University.

Converging
Media

SETH ROGEN   JAMES FRANCO

이 무식한 미국놈들을 믿지 마십시오

THE
ERVIEW

Mass Communication and Its Digital Transformation

A crude Seth Rogen comedy seems an unlikely candidate to spark an international incident that became a cause célèbre for free speech, increased fears about cyberwarfare, and led to U.S. sanctions against North Korea, but that is exactly what happened in the final months of 2014 and into early 2015. This curious chain of events also highlights—often unexpectedly—just how much digital media has transformed mass communication.

North Korea was vocal in its displeasure about the planned Christmas Day release of the comedy *The Interview* in which Rogen and James Franco play a pair of celebrity tabloid-show producers chosen by the CIA to assassinate North Korean leader Kim Jong-un.

On November 24, Sony Pictures, distributor of the film, learned that its computer systems had been hacked. In the days that followed, a string of embarrassing emails between executives and other sensitive corporate data, including early versions of screenplays and executive salaries, were leaked to the public. Sony and some cybersecurity experts, including those in the FBI, claim it was a North Korean group, while other experts remain doubtful.

On December 17, Sony announced the cancellation of the theatrical release of *The Interview* after receiving threats that movie theaters showing it would be blown up, an executive decision widely criticized as a blow to free speech. Another movie studio scrapped plans to make another anti-North Korean movie, and Paramount refused to allow the rerelease of *Team America: World Police*, the 2004 comedic movie by the makers of *South Park*. It too made fun of North Korea, and some theaters also wanted it to show on Christmas Day.

Less than a week later, Sony reversed itself and announced that *The Interview* would play in theaters that still supported this and be available for rent on video-on-demand (VOD). Just before New Year's, several cable and satellite companies announced deals with Sony to show *The Interview* for pay-per-view, on iTunes, Xbox Video, YouTube Movies, Google Play, and other on-demand services, long

LEARNING OBJECTIVES

>> Define convergence.

>> Discuss the main types of convergence and their implications for communication.

>> Explain the eight major changes taking place in communication today because of convergence.

>> Define mass communication.

>> Describe the basic theories of mass communication.

>> Identify the basic components and functions of the mass-communication process.

before the usual three-month window between theatrical releases and being shown on cable or DVD. Between December 24, 2014, and January 4, 2015, *The Interview* earned $31 million, making it Sony's number one online film.[1]

Several ironies make this fiasco worthy of its own comedy feature film. First, it was not government that threatened free speech but corporate interests, ranging from Sony Pictures itself to theater owners who refused to show the movie. Second, the United States issued more sanctions against North Korea in early January, even though cybersecurity experts were still debating who was actually responsible for the hack. Third, it was revealed that even when confronted with a legacy of artificial constraints from an earlier mass-communications era, convergence will prevail, especially where the possibility exists to release a film originally intended for movie theaters on home entertainment gaming systems or iTunes. Finally, a comedy critically reviewed as mediocre at best attracted many more viewers—and generated more income—than it likely would have.

The media of mass communication have long played a fundamental role in people's lives. The media inform, educate, persuade, entertain, and even—or perhaps especially—sell. Media can provide personal companionship and public scrutiny. They can shape perception on matters great and small. They can function in countless and increasing ways as extensions of one's self.

We will examine the nature of mass communication and how it is changing in the digital and social media age in a global village connected by electronic networks. Specific technological advances are producing widespread societal, cultural, and economic changes as journalists, public relations professionals, and advertising practitioners—in short, content creators and consumers of all kinds—face a new world of media symbols, processes, and effects.

Few communications technologies better encapsulate the fundamental aspects of convergence than two seemingly very different devices: the telephone and the television. We will first look briefly at the history and evolution of the telephone as a communications device because it touches on almost every important issue that we are dealing with today regarding the Internet and digital media. Furthermore, the phone continues to be at the heart of some of the most innovative changes taking place in how we communicate with each other and how we interact with the world and with media. At the end of the chapter, we will take a brief look at the television, how it continues to be at the forefront of convergence and how it is changing our relationship with the media.

> **DISCUSSION QUESTIONS:** Keep a media diary for a day of the media you consume (and create). Note the sources of your news, the types of online communication you use with friends and family, and the frequency you are on the phone (talking and texting). What did you learn from the diary?

Telephony: Case Study in Convergence

Although nowadays we may take the portability of our cell phones for granted, this mobility has important repercussions for a wide range of activities. First, we are no longer tied to a specific place when making or answering a phone call. The question "Where are you now?" when calling a friend on a landline need not be asked—your friend is obviously at home; otherwise, he would not have answered the phone.

By being able to communicate anywhere and anytime, you are able to coordinate with others with greater spontaneity than in the past. Prior to widespread use of cell phones, if you had a sudden change of plans (or change of heart) regarding a meeting with someone, you had very limited ways to let the person know you would not show up. Coordinating meeting times and places among several people in a group took much more effort and did not allow for last-minute changes. Also, consider how much more we use a phone we carry, as opposed to when you had to travel to the location of the phone (e.g., home, a phone booth). This makes us more likely to call or text to share information on the spot. It also can mean, however, that we are less likely to interact with those immediately around us as we communicate with distant others.

Our familiarity with the phone belies its revolutionary character from a communications standpoint. Before the phone, people could not talk directly to others whom they could not physically see. In an emergency, the only way to inform the proper authorities was to physically go where they were and let them know. The phone played a major role in changing our patterns of communication with each other and thereby changing social relations. But it was the telegraph, created more than thirty years before the telephone, that first revolutionized our speed of communication.

The telegraph was the first means of electronic communication, using a series of taps on a keypad that represented dots and dashes to spell out words. These signals were transmitted over telegraph wires connecting one location to another. Telegraph operators were specially trained to code and decode messages, and the result was a thriving new industry that grew during the mid- to late nineteenth century. This innovative form of instantaneous communication led to entirely new kinds of business enterprises, including personal messaging services and "newswire" services such as Reuters and the Associated Press.

Telephones adopted the principles discovered with telegraphy but allowed voice to be transmitted. Although Alexander Graham Bell is the inventor of record for the telephone in 1876, others were also working on how to transmit voice electronically through wires; and there is some evidence that Bell's invention may have borrowed liberally from existing patents of inventors trying to build similar devices. Still, after years of lawsuits, it was Bell who won out. This parallels the many suits and countersuits seen today as companies claim patent infringement on Internet or software inventions and technologies (e.g., Apple's $1 billion mobile-device patent infringement victory over Samsung in 2012).[2]

Regardless of who can claim credit for inventing the telephone, it was easier for the general public to use than the telegraph. Even so, it was not immediately thought of as an interpersonal communication device, largely because it was expensive and difficult to connect every single household to the telephone network. This parallels the "last mile" issue in twenty-first-century broadband, or high-speed, Internet connections coming directly into homes and touches on the importance of networks in our

As the telephone network spread, telephone lines started to clutter the landscape.

communication environment. It also highlights how seemingly obvious uses for new communications technologies become apparent only much later. How they may be used or adopted is very much an open question that relies not only on the technology alone but on a range of economic, social, and cultural issues at the time.

Despite the dramatic changes the phone would bring to communications, it was initially either ignored or thought of as simply a novelty. With subsequent technological improvements that made it easier to hear and to increase the number of voices that could be carried on a single wire, the telephone became more widely accepted. The ring of the telephone was a death knell for most telegraph companies, just as later media technologies rendered earlier technologies from which they were built obsolete and changed entire industries in the process.

Initially, especially in Europe, the telephone acted as a kind of early radio. Wealthy patrons paid a fee to listen to music performances that were sent along the wires, and some public venues would pipe in sermons or performances for their patrons.[3] For several years in Budapest, Hungary, Telefon Hírmondó delivered news over the telephone, with subscribers dialing in at certain times to listen to someone reading the news of the day. A similar service was also tried in 1911 in Newark, New Jersey, but lasted for only a few months before closing.

Delivering news over telephone wires therefore is not something new with the Internet, and it also shows a public desire for information and entertainment "on demand," long before video recorders or TiVo. What was still missing at that time was an economic model that could support a business such as telephone newspapers. This issue is commonly dealt with today by media companies that need to see a return on investments before they are willing to experiment with new ways of doing business.

The decision whether to make the telephone a government-run agency or a private enterprise was an important crossroad, and the choices made in Europe (government) differed from those made in the United States (private enterprise). Even into the twenty-first century, these choices have had profound repercussions for the actual and perceived development, use, and control of the Internet. And it continues to be the case that new technologies often inherit the baggage of political or social decisions made much earlier.

Leaving the early development of American telephone systems to private enterprise resulted in many incompatibilities among competing systems. Local telephone companies sold their own telephones, which would often not work with other telephone systems. This might have prevented a person from calling somebody who used a competing phone provider. The issue of compatibility between systems is still seen today in the form of competing computer operating systems, gaming systems, Internet browsers, and other electronic devices, including ebooks and tablet computers.

During the formative years of the telephone industry, the U.S. government sought to eliminate such incompatibilities in the phone network by granting one company, AT&T, a monopoly on the telephone system. This, too, had important repercussions for later developments in telecommunications. Just as the monopoly telegraph company, Western Union, had done in the late 1800s when it became apparent the telephone was a threat to its business, AT&T in the 1960s and 1970s tried to hamper the development of a new kind of network that would potentially hurt its business. The network needed to develop the Internet was not compatible with the AT&T system. Even though AT&T realized the new network was more efficient, the telephone company feared losing dominance and initially refused to adopt it.

Issues of government regulation and private enterprise, monopoly powers, and business interests at the expense of the public interest are still very much with us today. How much we pay for services, what companies charge and how they set up payment plans, and a variety of other business decisions are influenced by the laws and regulations that have been created, sometimes as a result of industry lobbying efforts.

Just as payment amounts and methods may influence how we use the telephone, social and cultural factors play an equally important role in determining whether a technology is adopted. Initially, people do not know how to act or interact with a new technology. Consider the classic story of the farmer, for example, who in the early days of the telephone went to town to place an order for supplies. The store clerk told him to place his order directly with the company over the phone, so the farmer dutifully wrote out his order, rolled it up carefully, and then jammed the rolled note into one of the holes of the phone handset and waited.

If this seems too silly to be true, recall your own reactions when you have to use a friend's phone or an unfamiliar TV remote control. The variety of functions seen in phones today stretches its very definition compared to even twenty years ago. Young people today in much of the world would consider a phone that does not take pictures or play video games or provide an address book a dinosaur. In short, the phone continues to evolve as a multifunctional communications device. The so-called smartphone connects us to our friends and to the world of information and entertainment through the Internet via almost 1 billion mobile applications (apps). It provides a nearly seamless interface between interpersonal and mass communication, as we access via a favorite app a review of a restaurant and then subsequently snap a photo of our meal to share via Instagram. We might even wirelessly post our own review on the spot, after which it can be seen by potentially millions of people worldwide.

Today's cell phones typically have a variety of functions that have nothing to do with the traditional functions of the phone.

All these aspects of the development and use of the phone—ranging from the technical, legal, and regulatory to the economic, social, and cultural—touch on the notion of media convergence. But as we will see, convergence is a debated concept and has multiple layers of meaning. As we explore this phenomenon, we will unpack its many layers and reveal how they encompass some of the most dramatic transformations taking place in communications today.

Three Types of Convergence

Convergence is known broadly as the coming together of computing, telecommunications, and media in a digital environment. It is important to study and understand convergence because what might first seem like wholly technological or media issues profoundly influence our economic, social, and cultural lives as well.

There is some disagreement among scholars over a single definition of convergence, an indication of the far-reaching consequences of the changes taking place in mass communication today. Indeed, many transformative forces for which we have still to develop adequate descriptions are in play, changes whose effects are

convergence

The coming together of computing, telecommunications, and media in a digital environment.

also uncertain. For now, the term "convergence" seems to come closest to encompassing many of these forces. Some argue that convergence has already occurred, and in many respects you could say that is true. But we believe that convergence is an ongoing and dynamic phenomenon that continues to shape the world of traditional media.

We can look at three main categories of convergence as in Figure 1-1 as ways to frame our understanding of the changes taking place today in the media industries: technological convergence, economic convergence, and cultural convergence. As you will see, these three categories actually overlap in many respects.

TECHNOLOGICAL CONVERGENCE

Perhaps the most easily visible aspect of convergence is the rise of digital media and online communication networks. Technological convergence refers to specific types of media, such as print, audio, and video, all converging into a digital media form. Such types of convergence are becoming increasingly apparent in news organizations, for example, where today's journalists often need to be able to tell stories in text, audio, video, and even interactive media.

FIGURE 1-1 Three Types of Convergence and Their Influence on Media

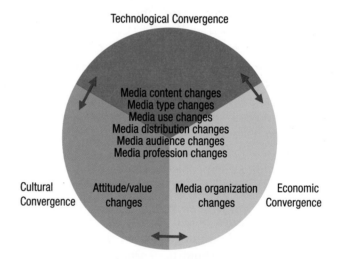

Digital media often change the very nature of their traditional counterparts and affect how we use and perceive them. For example, although you can look at an ebook on a Kindle as simply digital print, the fact is that a Kindle ebook alters the reading experience. One obvious way is that because of its storage capacity, you can easily carry many books in one device, allowing you to move back and forth between books or for cross-referencing passages quickly. Furthermore, you can change the text size to make reading more comfortable, look up words, annotate and index sections, and even purchase new books on the spot through a wireless Internet connection. Precisely because users can alter the look and size of the text they are reading, the notion of page numbers also becomes meaningless on a Kindle—much to the chagrin of students who realize they need to cite quotations taken from a book. You can even share your high-lighted passages with others, making book reading a collaborative experience.

Most of these activities, such as looking up a word you don't know in a dictionary, already occur with printed books. The significant difference, however, is that a single device now allows for all these actions, eliminating the need to carry a separate dictionary or permanently mark a book. Activities that used to be separate or cumbersome are now easier and folded into the media experience. Not simply a matter of convenience, these changes fundamentally alter how we interact with our media. We may be far more likely to look up a word on a Kindle than if we had to walk to the shelf to get the dictionary, for example. The music, television, and film industries, which we will look at in later chapters, provide other examples of how our media use changes thanks in large part to changes in technology.

Ebook readers such as the Kindle and the Nook have transformed the reading habits of people around the world, not to mention the book industry. **CRITICAL THINKING QUESTIONS:** How do you think ebooks are influencing the notion of books and reading? Are ebooks better or more useful than traditional books? Which would you rather read, and why?

This form of convergence, although highly relevant for today's communications professionals, is not the only way to think of convergence. The changes that come from new technologies also affect business models and established industries, which often see the upstarts as threats to their dominance. These fears can be valid, as sometimes these new companies become larger and more powerful than established ones. Google, founded in 1998, is a case in point. Because of the importance of networks in today's world, it is often advantageous for a company to control not only media content but the means of distributing that content through the networks, which is part of what economic convergence is about. In August 2015 Google itself announced that it would change its company name to Alphabet, with Google simply being one part of a corporation that exists in many other fields besides just media and technology.

ECONOMIC CONVERGENCE

Economic convergence refers to the merging of Internet or telecommunications companies with traditional media companies, such as Comcast with NBC Universal. Traditional media companies have grown fewer and much larger in the past fifty years through mergers and acquisitions, a process we define as **consolidation**, not convergence. Economic convergence occurs when formerly independent media enterprises further the success of one another because they fall under the same corporate umbrella. Entertainment companies may own news stations; large corporations traditionally outside of the media business, such as GE, may purchase media companies like NBC. This can result in conflicts of interest when corporate parents don't want some aspects of their businesses covered in the news or when a news outlet gives prominent coverage to a movie produced by a studio also owned by the corporate parent.

consolidation

A process whereby traditional media companies have grown fewer and much larger in the past fifty years through mergers and acquisitions.

Economic convergence also has important repercussions for the nature of the media, telecommunications, and computing industries. A telecommunications company that also owns a media company can speed the transmission of its own content and slow the content from competing companies, thus influencing customers to watch more of its own material. It could also control the type of content its customers see by blocking material from certain websites.

MEDIA PIONEERS
Steve Jobs

The cover of *Time* magazine on February 15, 1982, featured 26-year-old Steve Jobs as symbolic of America's risk takers, one who "practically singlehandedly created the personal computer industry." Jobs personalized his high-tech microprocessor devices by having form meet function with eye-catching yet minimalist designs that placed the digital world at the user's fingertips.

His singular talent was not necessarily for invention but for recognizing how to create what he envisioned from what was available and then finding talented people to do so. In 1979, at Xerox's PARC facility in Palo Alto, California, Jobs saw the future of personal computing—a graphic user interface operated by a mouse, the distinguishing feature of what eventually developed into the Macintosh computer in 1984.[4] Similarly, decades later, Jobs repurposed for the iPhone a lightweight, damage-resistant glass that Corning had created but never placed in production.

Not content to create devices that manipulated the existing world, Jobs changed the world so that people could better use the tools he created. The iPod (2001) did not introduce any radical new technology, but the accompanying creation of iTunes forever changed the music industry. Cellular technology was hardly new when the iPhone (2007) brought about a transformative convergence of telecommunications and the Internet. Unlike existing tablets, the iPad (2010) enveloped computing, telecommunications, digital publishing, and even television and movies.

Jobs ran his corporation as a closed system, convinced that only Apple could ensure the quality and integrity of its products. Although, for example, he encouraged anyone to develop apps for use on Apple's mobile devices, such apps are made available only with Apple's approval. Jobs's business model delivered Apple from near bankruptcy in 1997, and made it the most valuable company in the United States shortly before his death in 2011.[5]

Jobs was fond of saying he did not believe in giving customers what they wanted; he gave them what they did not know they needed.[6] In his mind's eye, that need was digital convergence made possible with smart devices that almost anyone could use and enjoy.

The Internet is not causing this type of behavior, as numerous historical examples exist of media owners censoring content or blocking public access. But what makes this issue more significant and prominent is the combination of consolidated media giants and ever larger audiences. Despite the explosion of channels and media content, our choices may be narrower than they appear. Consider the increasingly frequent temporary blackouts of channels as cable companies and media conglomerates fight over television licensing fees and let their agreements lapse. Over 3 million households on the East Coast missed the first two games of the 2010 World Series as Cablevision and Fox Networks fought over the terms of a new licensing agreement and Fox channels were suspended for Cablevision subscribers. In late 2014 and into early 2015, satellite provider DISH Network stopped carrying Fox News and Fox Business channels because of disagreements over licensing charges.

As both sides accuse the other of working in bad faith and both sides try to gain public sympathy through advertisements, websites, and social media, determining a winner in the court of public opinion is difficult. In a cultural shift, the relationship between the audience or public and media producers is also changing.

CULTURAL CONVERGENCE

Culture refers to the values, beliefs, and practices shared by a group of people. It may refer to a population at large, such as Americans, or to various subgroups within a larger group who may share certain ethnic, social, or professional traditions and practices, such as Irish Americans, video gamers, or corporate attorneys.

A powerful aspect of cultural convergence occurs through the globalization of media content when, for example, an HBO series such as *Sex and the City* becomes wildly popular among female office workers in Thailand; or when a Mexican telenovela, or soap opera, finds avid mass audiences in Russia. The popularity of such shows across a variety of nations speaks to some aspect they possess that foreign audiences identify with or aspire to, indicating that there may be more in common between a young professional woman in Bangkok and one in New York City than one might imagine. In the context of cultural convergence, a significant concern is the impact of global media on multiculturalism, or the diversity of culture, especially internationally.

But we can also look at cultural convergence from the perspective of how we consume, create, and distribute media content. The shift from an audience that was forced to be largely passive and silent, simply consuming content produced by large-scale media companies to a public that can now produce and share content

---

INTERNATIONAL PERSPECTIVES
Crying in a BMW

Television dating shows have become very popular in China, offering viewers a titillating mix of sharp tongues, attractive young women, discussions about sex, and rampant materialism. In the most popular show, *If You Are the One*, produced by Jiangsu TV, a female contestant won notoriety when asked by a bachelor if she would like to ride on his bicycle with him. She said she would "rather cry in the back of a BMW" than smile on the back of a bicycle.

Another female contestant told the panel that if anyone other than her boyfriend wanted to hold her hand it would cost the person $30,000.[7] These kinds of comments—combined with on-screen and offscreen scandals—have drawn the ire of China's television censors who claim shows like these are corrupting China's youth with vulgarity and crass materialistic values. As a result, some shows were canceled, and those that stayed on the air toned down the more flamboyant aspects of the programs.

The popular dating shows form part of China's burgeoning commercial television industry. When China's

state-run television allowed commercial stations in the 1990s, it may have created a dragon it cannot now fully control. Periodic attempts to set strict guidelines that discourage materialism among Chinese youth have had doubtful effect. In April 2012, Chinese media reported that several people were arrested for their involvement in a scheme in which a 17-year-old teenager donated a kidney because he wanted to buy an iPad and an iPhone.[8]

with others cheaply and easily is one of the major themes of this book and a crucial component of cultural convergence.

Although mass communication will continue, in the sense that media companies and others will continue to produce messages for large audiences, a significant trend involves more personalized and frequent messages tailored to the needs of individuals. Furthermore, what was traditionally considered interpersonal communication, such as email, can also be widely distributed by individuals through online networks, making the dividing line between interpersonal and mass communication increasingly hard to distinguish.

The ability of companies to better target people with personalized advertising and messages by tracking their online activities raises important issues of privacy, consumer rights, and media business economic models. Whether people will become more active in media production and more engaged in civic or political activities than in the past remains open to debate, with some scholars taking an increasingly critical look at how media corporations and companies in general are turning online public participation to their advantage. In one future, there is an engaged public who uses digital media and online networks to further interactivity and democracy prevails; and in another, there are established media conglomerates and other powerful economic forces that hijack public interests for their own ends. Such tensions and concerns will shape the nature of the Internet and digital media use far into the twenty-first century.

Digital technology has allowed more people to create professional-quality videos and other media content.

> **DISCUSSION QUESTIONS:** Discuss ways in which audiences can engage with each other through social media and with media organizations. Do you think this has made audiences more active? Why or why not?

Implications of Convergence

Whether an Internet-connected world will ultimately and fundamentally improve society is impossible to say; yet, for better and for worse, digital media have changed and will continue to transform the relationship between mass-communication industries and the public. Media organizations face many challenges, but so do media consumers as the nature of our media environment changes. Some general trends can be discerned that will provide a better perspective on how our digital-media use is changing our media world and, by extension, our social and cultural worlds.

Clearly, the changes brought about by convergence have had dramatic implications. Within the larger framework of the three types of convergence, these changes affect eight different areas, recurring themes addressed throughout this book:

1. Media organization
2. Media type
3. Media content

4. Media use
5. Media distribution
6. Media audience
7. Media profession
8. Attitudes and values

MEDIA ORGANIZATION

In the world that predated convergence, media content was created and published or broadcast on predetermined schedules by centralized media organizations in which a central unit or individual controls content production and distribution as well as marketing and other functions. A newspaper was printed and distributed daily or weekly; a television show appeared at a certain time on a certain day. The economics of the media system throughout most of the nineteenth and twentieth centuries heavily favored a mass-production model leveraging centralized control to produce efficiencies. Only large companies could bear the costs of content creation, production, marketing, and distribution.

Internet-based media can be less centralized, partly because many of the associated costs have been greatly reduced. Of course, movies, television shows, and many other types of mass-produced media still rely on the old production and distribution models; but now new marketing avenues on the Internet make it easier to mass distribute media products, as illustrated by the *The Interview* and Sony Pictures example at the beginning of the chapter.

Unlike public service media, most media companies throughout the world operate to make a profit. Advertising is one of the main sources of revenue for these organizations, and advertisers today are spending less in traditional media and more online. The gap is beginning to narrow, although many media companies are still not making up the difference with online advertising. This has increased the financial pressure, especially in print media, which, having seen the largest drop in advertising, has led to layoffs, reduced printing and pages of newspapers and magazines, closings, and buyouts of struggling companies.

Concentration of media ownership, or consolidation, was a growing trend even before digital media. Convergence is in some ways fueling media consolidation by leading traditional media giants such as Time Warner to join with a former online colossus such as America Online, giving rise in 2001 to the short-lived AOL Time Warner. In 2010, AOL, long jettisoned from Time Warner, bought one of the most popular blogs on the Web, *The Huffington Post*, yet another illustration of how the boundaries between traditional technology companies and media companies have blurred.

The trend is clear: Analog and digital media are rapidly being consolidated into the hands of a few very large, very powerful, and very rich owners, an economic structure referred to as an **oligopoly**. These media enterprises are increasingly likely to be part of large, global media organizations publicly owned and accountable to shareholders, whose main interest is the financial bottom line. When traditional telecommunications companies, such as Comcast, join with large media companies, such as NBC Universal, it gives the companies a tremendous centralized control over what access and content is available to media consumers, which is problematic.

oligopoly

An economic structure in which a few very large, very powerful, and very rich owners control an industry or collection of related industries.

Related to changes in media organization and structure are changes in the types of media or ways in which we get our media content. The seemingly insignificant decision to watch a television program on a TV on a specific day and time or on demand on a mobile device actually has significant consequences for media organizations, advertising revenues, and audiences.

MEDIA TYPE

Just what constitutes a television or radio receiver, or TV or radio programming, is in a state of flux. Once, it was simple. Radio programming was what a listener heard on a radio. Today, however, radio stations can transmit their programming via Internet or satellite and listeners can tune in via computers or smartphones. Moreover, these radio station websites can include images, graphics, text, and video, and listeners can choose what they want to hear or see when they want. The audience can sometimes even choose how they want to get content, such as watching the video, listening to the podcast, or reading the story. A growing number of print and radio reporters trained in digital video shooting and editing can now be "VJs," or video journalists, webcasting their stories visually.

Beyond decisions to either watch a video or read a story, defining media types entails consideration of vaster concerns such as media empires built on owning certain kinds of media and complex governmental laws that regulate different media industries and media ownership. In the United States, for example, print media enjoy more free-speech protections than the more tightly regulated electronic broadcast media, and cable providers are treated differently than broadcast networks. This raises the question of how text on the Internet should be treated—does it have the same First Amendment protections as its print counterpart because it is simply words? Or should it be treated as electronic media because it is delivered electronically? And now, as more people watch TV on mobile devices, what are the responsibilities of the Internet provider in all of this, as simply the channel and not the creator of the content itself? Many of these questions have yet to be settled.

MEDIA CONTENT

hyperlink

Clickable pointer to other online content.

Stories told in a digital, online medium can make connections with other types of content much more easily than in any other medium. This is done primarily through the use of **hyperlinks**, clickable pointers to other online content. Online interactive advertisements encourage visitors to click on the ads and go to the sponsor's website, or play a game, or take a survey. In entertainment programming, hyperlinked content allows a viewer to explore a story in a nonlinear narrative, whose outcome may be determined by the user's choice of links.

On-demand content has become increasingly popular. In the traditional media world, the publisher or broadcaster set the schedule for news, entertainment, and marketing information. Children growing up in an on-demand media world of YouTube, podcasting, and digital video recorders (DVRs) may not readily understand why the same options don't always exist while listening to the radio or watching a traditional television channel that has no on-demand features. The changes have happened so fast and been so extensive that new terms have been created to highlight the differences between a generation that has grown up with digital technologies and those that were born in the analog era. **Digital natives** are the postmillennial generation that have only known digital and social media, whereas **digital immigrants** are older generations that may also use digital media, but that generally have more trouble adapting in varying degrees to the digital media world.

Digitization, the process that makes media computer readable, is transforming both how and when media organizations distribute their content. Delivery no longer occurs solely through traditional channels but also via the Internet, satellites, mobile devices, and a host of other digital technologies. Increasingly, content is available twenty-four hours a day, with news organizations updating news continuously and for a worldwide audience.

Digital technology is similarly transforming the production cycle and process as illustrated by Figure 1-2. In fact, the transformation may be even deeper in terms of media-content production. Whether in Hollywood motion pictures, television shows or news, books, magazines, newspapers, or online, producing media content has rapidly become almost an entirely digital process. Shot with digital cameras and edited on computers, movies can be sent by high-speed Internet to digital movie theaters. Reporters working for television, radio, newspapers, or any other news operation capture their raw material with digital devices as well, editing their stories digitally. Even book authors typically compose on a computer, with digital words remaining the norm throughout the production process, being read on e-readers, smartphones, or tablets.

Digital media are challenging our understanding of media content as static or unchangeable. This is especially evident in a **wiki**, a website that can be edited by anyone. Wikis have grown in popularity, revealing the demand among Web users

digital native

A term coined in 2001 by author Marc Prensky for a member of a younger generation that has grown up with and is consequently very comfortable using digital media and adapting to rapid technological changes.

digital immigrant

An individual who grew up in the analog media era and who generally has more trouble adapting to new digital technologies, despite perhaps a desire to use and understand them.

digitization

The process that makes media computer readable.

wiki

Website that lets anyone add, edit, or delete pages and content.

FIGURE 1-2 "Media Iceberg"

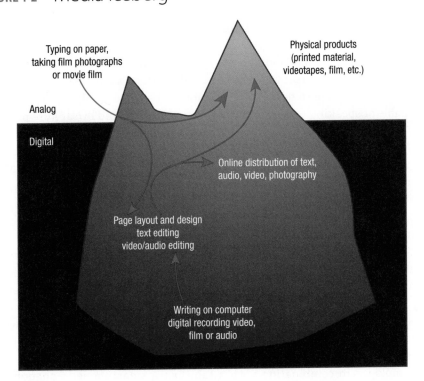

for such a function. The wiki owes much of its success to Wikipedia, where the stuffy and authoritative encyclopedia article became a collaborative hybrid of encyclopedia and breaking news updated by users.

Of course, content was never actually unchangeable; it just seemed that way. A book could be reprinted as a new edition, yet for most readers the changes between editions were practically speaking impossible to discern. An online book is a much more fluid and dynamic document, with discussion forums on book material incorporated into the contents, ongoing online discussions between the author and readers, and interactions among readers.

Similarly, mash-ups of existing media have become common thanks to digital editing tools for music and video. Any popular item produced from mass media (e.g., advertisements, movie trailers, music videos) has the potential of being quickly transformed into a number of user-generated parodies or send-ups, most done simply for the fun of creating something rather than for commercial gain. Consider the many mash-up videos of Canadian singer-songwriter Carly Rae Jepsen's 2012 smash hit "Call Me Maybe." Online discussions and mash-ups exemplify increasing audience interaction and participation, one of many changes in media use.

> **DISCUSSION QUESTIONS:** Discuss any media content you have created in the past week or so (such as posting pictures to social media, forwarding videos or stories, etc.) and what happened with that media. Who saw the content you posted, and did it reach a wider audience than you thought it would?

MEDIA USE

The pervasiveness of the media system, expanded exponentially by modern global satellite communications, entails unprecedented access to mass communication. Fewer and fewer places on the globe are truly isolated, even famously remote and physically inaccessible locations. In May 1996, climber and guide Rob Hall was trapped high on Mt. Everest for more than a day after a sudden storm hit. Facing certain death—unable to descend and unable to be rescued—Hall was nonetheless capable of speaking to his pregnant wife in New Zealand by satellite phone.[9]

A 24/7 media age, which had begun to emerge even before the advent of the Internet, has arrived. This environment has several implications for industries and for consumers, how we use media, and what we expect from them. Media companies have to find content to fill the time, and thus we are seeing more encore performances of hit shows or movies on channels like TNT, showing the same movie two or three times in a row and on multiple nights. This practice fills programming time while allowing viewers greater scheduling flexibility.

Portable media devices and flat-screen technologies mean that we can take our media with us and access them in previously inaccessible places. Video displays in elevators or at checkout registers are two examples of how advertisers are using technology to reach captive audiences. Playing video games or watching videos on smartphones make media even more ubiquitous. Research shows we live in a multiscreen world where the tablet has begun to replace the personal computer or laptop.[10] Although the TV is still the first screen or the most used, it is often employed in combination with a tablet or a smartphone, a phenomenon called "the third or fourth screen," depending on the relative position of the movie screen in terms of public use.

Pervasive mass communication means better access to entertainment, information, and news—in theory. It can also mean that media organizations can turn us into super-consumers of media of questionable social or civic value. One might, for example, question the value of viewing a lowbrow reality show on your mobile phone while riding the bus or spending hours at home watching funny cat videos on YouTube.

All the activities mentioned here are predicated on the broad assumption that individuals have ready access to computers, a broadband Internet (wired or Wi-Fi) connection, and the knowledge and skills to use them. Many in advanced, industrialized countries take these as givens, but these digital advantages are far from universal, even within developed countries.

Better Internet access has neither arrived equally to all nor allowed everyone to benefit equally from that access. People in lower socioeconomic groups in industrialized countries have lagged in almost every category of Internet access. The high cost of telecommunication services, including broadband Internet, keeps many from being able to develop the skills and knowledge that can help them participate fully in society.

Although still far behind dozens of other countries, the United States has been making slight gains in high-speed Internet penetration and affordability of available services, as well as Internet speed. In 2013, the United States ranked thirty-third in terms of Internet speed, trailing Canada, but in 2015 it had moved up to twenty-seventh, slightly behind Norway. Even so, Americans' average Internet speed was less than a third that of first-ranked Singapore.[11] (See Figure 1-3.)

In Switzerland, Secretary of State John Kerry and his team huddle around a tablet to watch President Obama announce from the White House a new agreement with Iran on its nuclear program. **CRITICAL THINKING QUESTIONS:** How important is a tablet or mobile device for your news consumption? Does digital portability help keep you better informed?

FIGURE 1-3 Average Consumer Download Speed by Country (2015)

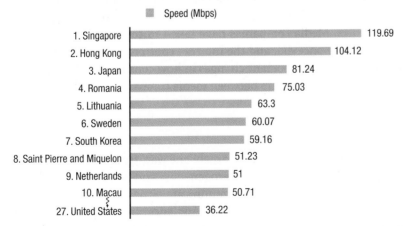

Source: Ookla Speedtest, Household Download Index, http://www.netindex.com/download/allcountries/

MEDIA DISTRIBUTION

Content is much more fluid, dynamic, and rapidly transmitted around the globe in an online environment. The expansive reach of global media and instantaneous communications is not without its perils, however, for events in distant places can have far-reaching repercussions. False rumors about political or company leaders can demonstrate the power and danger of rapid global communication. For instance, a fake tweet in spring 2013 from a hacked Associated Press account claiming President Obama had been injured in an explosion temporarily wiped out $130 billion in the stock market.

The Internet enables audiences around the world to participate in a dialog about global events and issues, bringing individuals separated by thousands of miles and various political and cultural boundaries into direct contact with each other. It is not clear what the net effect of this sea change in communication will be, but it is clear the foundation is potentially being laid for a more connected and engaged global public. Increased connectivity and engagement does not necessarily mean more rational discussion or civilized debate though, especially as people discover that what they may consider cultural common sense others may consider heresy. Consider the vitriol displayed in many discussion groups, even among people of the same culture but whose opinions differ.

Audiences are increasingly active in their communication with each other and with the creators of mass-communication content, a trend that can decrease corporate power as it increases consumer control. Through **viral marketing**, the online equivalent of word-of-mouth advertising, a popular website, product, or piece of content can rapidly reach millions of online users, all without corporate promotion or advertising dollars. The success of **peer-to-peer (P2P)** file-sharing programs demonstrates how an Internet audience can shift the balance of power from media organizations to consumers, even though those organizations created and provided that content in the first place.

Digital media make it easier than ever for the public to create and distribute media content, whether it is **user-generated content (UGC)** such as an original drawing done via illustration software, an animation or video, or a song sampled and mixed from current hits by famous recording artists. Writing and music have led the way in consumer-created content—especially music, where remixes of previously recorded (and copyrighted) material are common. This is not to say that the average person now has the same ability to produce and create a hit song as a major recording label, for most individuals lack the marketing and promotion resources that a recording label has at its disposal; but the basic capability of producing and distributing at least exists. Media companies have failed to control the channels of media distribution as they once did, and the Internet continues to threaten their business models. This has led to important changes in how consumers view and use content while changing the relationship between media companies and their audiences.

MEDIA AUDIENCE

Traditional mass communication is largely one way, from the sender of a message to the receiver. Relatively large, heterogeneous, and anonymous audiences have relatively few means by which to communicate either with each other on a mass scale or with the creators and publishers. Audiences in the age of convergence can now more easily and quickly communicate with each other and with those who create and publish mass-communication content via social media, email, online

---

viral marketing

Promoting a product, service, or brand online through word of mouth, usually via online discussion groups, chats, and emails.

peer-to-peer (P2P)

The basis of file-sharing services, a computer communications model and network whose computers are considered equal peers who can send, store, and receive information equally well.

user-generated content (UGC)

Content created by the general public for distribution by digital media.

CONVERGENCE CULTURE
User-Generated Content: Creativity or Piracy?

With the ease of copying and altering digital content, almost anyone can remake media content. Two or three popular songs from different artists can be combined into a new song; an artist's paintings can be manipulated digitally and mixed with one's own work. Is this kind of content creation original art, or is it copyright infringement because it relies on preexisting art owned by someone else? What are the ethical and legal obligations of the creator who uses others' works?

Some argue that previous works encountered by an artist will influence almost any creative endeavor and that digital content simply facilitates mash-ups. They argue that copyright—essentially a government-granted monopoly to the content creator (or owner of the copyright, as is often the case with recording labels where the artists don't own the copyright)—is anachronistic in the digital age and increasingly stifles creativity through steep licensing or copyright fees. Copyright reduces the amount of creative material in the public domain, thus reducing the pool of works freely available.

Yet copyright remains a cornerstone of media industries, a fundamental way for media companies to generate revenues. Most media industries, especially in entertainment, would be hard pressed to envision a world with no copyright that would still allow them to create the kind of content they do.

Creative Commons, a non-profit organization, has made a range of "copyleft" contracts for content creators that help ensure creative works remain in the public domain. Under the various contracts, content creators allow their content to be used by anyone for free but with certain stipulations, such as they must be credited or the content can be used only if it isn't sold. Another common stipulation within the community is that people using the content must allow it to remain free for public use.

Visit the Creative Commons website and click on the "Find CC-licensed works" link (under the Explore heading). Search for some content of interest, such as "hip hop" via SoundCloud (Music) or ccMixter (Music). What do you find?

---

forums, and other interactive media. In addition, they can create the content themselves and reach far larger audiences with less expense than was possible with traditional media. They are generally not anonymous because they can be tracked through user names or IP addresses.

Audiences aren't willing to wait for the evening news or the next day's newspaper for developments in a breaking story. They can get their information and entertainment from literally thousands of sources around the world. Audiences are no longer content to sit back and listen in silence to what the media report; they actively seek, relay, and question the most recent information on social media, blogs, instant messaging, and other informal communication channels. There have been cases of employees finding out about looming company layoffs through websites hours before the company officially announced its plans, and military family members learning of the death of a loved one in combat through social media before the military informed the family.

Digital media do not cause people to become active media producers, called "**produsers**" by some media scholars in an attempt to capture how we now use and produce (not just consume) content. Nevertheless, digital media provide people who are so inclined with ready tools to produce media far more cheaply and easily than with analog alternatives. Active audiences have two important implications for media companies: They may compete for the limited time of target audiences, and they may become more critical consumers of mass communication, which is relevant to media literacy, the topic covered in Chapter 2.

produsers

Audiences who no longer are simply consumers but also produce content.

As produsers, people learn to become more critical of the media and to raise questions about the quality of the news, information, and entertainment they receive. The channels available through interactive media let the public speak to a general audience and directly to traditional media producers, thereby imparting a sense of shared experience, even perhaps community, as people see that others may feel as they do; others also found a particular advertisement offensive or considered a certain show rather lame. An interactive public is more likely to be an active public, organizing and working together on common problems. Those who have developed trusting relationships through interaction are less likely to perceive themselves as anonymous faces in a crowd or isolated individuals who have no voice.

Risks accompany these changes, however. Actively choosing the media you want to see, hear, or read can narrow the scope of news or entertainment that you would the late Michael Dertouzos, former MIT Media Lab director called the tailoring of news to one's specific interests "The Daily Me." Some scholars worry that this phenomenon could fragment audiences into small groups of like-minded individuals who avoid interacting with other groups and who select only news and information that reinforces their beliefs and values. Although digital media can easily accelerate media fragmentation, a trend already evident in analog media, personalization and localization of news does have potential benefits by allowing the public to get the most relevant and engaging content for them as individuals while becoming better informed about current events.

MEDIA PROFESSION

Obviously, all the changes that convergence has brought to mass communication will also change the way communications professionals do their jobs. Just as digital media absorbed traditional print, video, and audio, divisions between print and electronic journalists, and between advertising and public relations practitioners, will fade. In addition to writing effectively, more newsrooms expect reporters to use video and audio to tell stories. To better reach and persuade audiences, those in advertising and public relations find themselves increasingly using tools that were previously the sole domain of the other profession.

To take advantage of digital media, new skills will have to be learned, and it will be more important than ever not to abandon the fundamental principles and ethics of each profession in the inexorable march toward the digital realm. This is no easy order given how corporate parents can exert pressure to blur the lines between news and entertainment or news and promotion.

Giving the audience a chance to respond to and interact with journalists as well as provide their own news coverage in the form of **citizen journalism** is another important development in journalism today. A mistake in a story can be publicly countered, corrected in the discussion section of the story, and then incorporated in a revised version. Citizens can provide news content or report on stories of relevance to their locales that big news operations may not deem newsworthy.

citizen journalism

The gathering and sharing of news and information by public citizens, particularly via mobile and social media, sometimes via traditional media.

ATTITUDES AND VALUES

Changes in audience interactions have had repercussions for companies in general and media companies in particular. People have come to expect a certain degree of transparency in their communications with each other and with leading organizations, including media organizations. A growing number of cases that exposed organizations deceiving the public have damaged their reputations. One such example involved Edelman, a global PR firm that financed the "Wal-Marting Across America" blog in 2006. The blog was ostensibly written by a couple traveling around the country who liked to park their recreational vehicle at Wal-Mart because of the free services offered to RVers. Of course, they had nothing but good things to say about Wal-Mart and its employees. When the truth was revealed that Edelman, whose client was Wal-Mart, was actually paying the couple, the ethics of such a blog, which failed to state who was funding it, were hotly debated.

Because most people on the Web do not physically make contact with each other and know one another only through their online interactions and communication, establishing a sense of trust has become crucial. A growing number of reputation systems aid users in this effort, such as rankings on Amazon or eBay and "karma points" on Slashdot, a popular technology news and discussion website. Managing an online reputation is serious business for companies as well as for individuals. Imagine the potential impact of bad reviews on eBay for someone trying to make a living by selling items on the site. Companies are also vulnerable and can fall prey to disinformation campaigns, which makes monitoring rival blogs and online discussions important.

Reputation and transparency rely on digital relationships founded on trust and respect. Media companies that do not realize this will suffer in the long run. For many, it means a shift in corporate policies or philosophies and a loss of the control they have enjoyed through much of the mass-communications era. Conventional wisdom among some executives is that employees are more willing to spend company time doing personal things, like shopping online, than they were in the past. But, on the other hand, companies, which also expect employees to stay longer at work or to answer business emails while at home or on vacation, must accept that the blurring of company time and private time is a large-scale trend.

The convergence of digital media has led to confusion over our traditional notions of privacy, both for individuals and for companies. Although privacy laws in a number of cases have clearly been violated, even by traditional standards, often what is acceptable or even legal and what is not is still a source of confusion. A person writing a blog, for instance, may consider it a private journal. So if a potential employer mentions inappropriate postings during a job interview, she may be angered by what feels like an invasion of her privacy. Similarly, information that always has been public but too cumbersome to retrieve, such as property deeds or police arrests, can now be easy to find online.

One component of privacy is alone time, and these moments have become increasingly rare in an age of pervasive media. Maintaining a sense of privacy can be difficult when we are getting barraged with updates from Facebook friends or receiving text messages. Some even argue that digital natives raised on social media have lost the ability to appreciate or even tolerate solitude, once a coveted commodity.

Wireless communication between devices, without the need for specific human direction—such as swiping a debit card at a supermarket checkout—makes it easy to establish a profile of a person simply through his electronic transactions over a short period of time. The ability to track consumers with such accuracy, especially on the Web and through mobile devices, means that we can personalize our media content; but it also means we have revealed much about our

ETHICS IN MEDIA
Interactively Mapping Gun Owners

On December 22, 2012, the Poughkeepsie (NY) *Journal News* published online an interactive map providing the names and addresses of all registered handgun owners in New York and Rockland counties. Although the Second Amendment to the United States Constitution protects citizens' right to bear arms, there has never been consensus about just what this right means. Recently, the enduring national debate about gun control or rights has intensified following a spate of shooting of schoolchildren, such as that in Newtown, Connecticut, in 2012; Sparks, Nevada, in 2013; Troutdale, Oregon, in 2014, and elsewhere—these, in addition to similar episodes of carnage on university campuses across the country.

When the *Journal News* published the names and addresses of thousands of legal gun owners, however, a vigorous debate ensued about gun owners' right to privacy and public access to personal information, even if such information was in the public domain. Within seventy-two hours of the publication of the interactive map, more than 1,700 comments about the map and its data had been posted on the *Journal News* discussion board. Both sides weighed in on the debate. One poster wrote, "LOVE the Gun License map! Excellent information to anyone concerned with who they live around!" Another wrote, "So should we start wearing yellow Stars of David so the general public can be aware of who we are?"

In the age before ubiquitous Internet access, government agencies centrally kept such public domain data and restricted access to limited groups or individuals with a

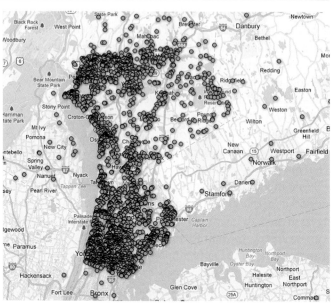

Mining public data sources, this interactive news map enables access to detailed personal information about gun ownership.

special interest and who were willing to physically go where the data were housed.

The convergence of data, the Internet, and digital devices has made it increasingly common for media organizations or others to post such personal information for all to see, from Poughkeepsie to Kathmandu. Is it ethical to make these data so easily and widely available for all? Should media make such personal information available if it helps foster more debate about important topics, regardless of ethical concerns?

behavioral targeting

Advertisers tracking individuals' web-browsing behavior to provide ads that closely match the topics of sites visited or searches made.

cookies

Information that a website puts on a user's local hard drive so that it can recognize when that computer accesses the website again. Cookies also allow for conveniences like password recognition and personalization.

personal habits and interests, not all of which we may wish to share with companies or advertisers who use that information for **behavioral targeting** in their advertising campaigns.

Mass-communication organizations can keep detailed and updated records on their audiences by tracking their paths within their websites through intelligent software agents and programs known as **cookies**. These allow a website to recognize when a previous user returns and to offer personalized content. Cookies provide invaluable information for media organizations to better understand an audience's media behaviors, preferences, and habits. Advertisers on websites also add cookies to your computer so they can track your browsing behavior as well. Surveillance is an increasingly powerful tool necessary to optimize content and to give advertisers a high return on their investment, even as it raises serious concerns about the erosion of privacy.

So far we have discussed how convergence has been changing the media industries and their business models, the issues communications professionals have faced with the advent of new technologies, the nature of the relationship between media producers and audiences, and legal matters that have yet to be addressed. You have gotten a glimpse of the powerful transformations taking place today in mass communications and the media and will see even more detailed examples in subsequent chapters.

But before we can move forward, we have to take a step back and look at what mass communication itself is and how media scholars theorize it operates. We will then be able to use these foundations to better understand the changes taking place today.

Mass Communication in the Digital Age

The traditional mass-communication model differs from other forms of communication, such as **interpersonal communication**, which is communication between two or more persons. Interpersonal communication often interacts and intersects with **mass communication**, communication to a large group or groups of people that remain largely unknown to the sender of the message.

INTERPERSONAL COMMUNICATION

Interpersonal communication is usually interactive, or flowing at least two ways, and tends not to be anonymous. Think of chatting with a friend or a small group. Responses are generally immediate, and the speaker or speakers will often adjust their messages based on the responses they receive. Interpersonal communication involves both verbal and nonverbal messages: not just what was said, but how it was said.

These same principles apply to live public speaking, even though this is a one-to-many model, and opportunities for audience feedback will be more limited than in a casual small-group setting. The speaker and the audience can communicate through a variety of nonverbal cues such as facial expressions, physical contact, or body language. If speakers see looks of boredom or audience members yawning, they can adjust their presentation accordingly in an effort to make it more interesting.

Interpersonal communication can also take place through a **medium**, or communication channel, such as the telephone, when texting or talking, or the Internet, when participating in a chat room or on a discussion board, for example. Note how the mediation limits some aspects of interpersonal communication compared to face-to-face interactions. Visual cues are absent either on the telephone or online (unless using a webcam), and meanings can be misconstrued in text messages (even those supplemented with emoticons). The online medium also blurs the line between interpersonal and mass communication, as a private email or text can be forwarded to many other people.

interpersonal communication

Communication between two or more individuals, often in a small group, although it can involve communication between a live speaker and an audience.

mass communication

Communication to a large group or groups of people that remain largely unknown to the sender of the message.

medium

A communication channel, such as talking on the telephone, instant messaging, or writing back and forth in a chat room.

Interpersonal communication takes place between two or more people, is interactive, and can happen face-to-face or through a medium.

MASS COMMUNICATION

Media of mass communication refer to any technological means of communicating between large numbers of people distributed widely over space or time. Ever since Johannes Gutenberg invented the Western world's first mechanical printing press in Germany in 1455, one general model of communication has traditionally characterized mass media, whose central features, as articulated by different theorists, are also outlined in Table 1-1.

According to this framework, media companies create content they believe the audience will want and distribute that content to an audience who has very few ways to provide immediate feedback. This premise has characterized all media of mass communication—books, magazines, newspapers, broadcast television or radio, cable or satellite TV, recorded music, or motion pictures. Digital media, however, are radically changing that model, as we will see throughout this book.

In the traditional mass-communication model, content creators play a fundamental role in society by representing and defining reality (consider the work of journalists or other communication professionals) or by creating fictional works to explain, interpret, or entertain (consider the work of artists, authors, and film auteurs). Authors and artists create stories about issues and events; they write books and articles; they create music or motion pictures; and then they publish, broadcast, or present their creations at set dates or times and in set locations.

Some mass-communications models, such as live television or radio, are **synchronous media**, which require the audience to be assembled simultaneously for the broadcast, transmission, or event. Others are **asynchronous media**, such as newspapers or magazines, for example, which do not require the audience to assemble at any given time. Audio and video recording devices let people

synchronous media

Media that take place in real time and require the audience to be present during the broadcast or performance, such as live television or radio.

asynchronous media

Media that do not require the audience to assemble at a given time, such as printed materials and recorded audio or video.

TABLE 1-1 Traditional Theories or Models of Analog Media

THEORY OR MODEL	MAIN FEATURES OR CHARACTERISTICS
General Mass Media	1. Communication flow is largely one-way, from sender or source to receiver or audience. 2. Communication is from one or a few to many (i.e., one or a few sources generate and distribute content to large, heterogeneous audiences). 3. Communication is anonymous (sources typically do not know their audiences, and audiences do not know the sources, except at a general level). 4. Audiences are seen as largely passive recipients of the messages distributed by the media, with little opportunity for feedback and practically no opportunity for immediate feedback or interaction with each other.
Shannon and Weaver Transmission Model (see p. 28)	Information source Transmitter Channel Receiver Destination
Schramm's Simplified Communication Model (see p. 29)	1. A source, who encodes 2. a message, or signal, which is transmitted (via the media or directly via interpersonal communication) to 3. a destination, where the receiver decodes it.

time shift and record a live concert or performance so that it can be watched anytime, thereby turning synchronous media into asynchronous media.

time shift

Recording of an audio or video event for later listening or viewing.

MASS COMMUNICATION AND CONVERGENCE

Digital media and online networks have blurred the line between interpersonal and mass communication. The media companies built on mass-communication models, despite facing many challenges in the digital era, are not disappearing anytime soon, and neither will certain fundamental aspects of mass communication.

What is changing, however, is the interplay between mediated interpersonal communication and mass communication: Interpersonal communication is capable of adopting some characteristics of mass communication, and mass communication is trying to adopt certain characteristics of interpersonal communication in an attempt to remain relevant to audiences. Let's examine some examples.

Email is considered a form of mediated interpersonal communication, yet as anyone who has had his or her inbox clogged with forwarded jokes from Aunt Gertrude can attest, it can also be broadcast to many recipients, following the one-to-many model typical of mass communication.

Despite their interpersonal tone and scope, some weblogs, or **blogs**, have become very influential among the public or among decision makers, with readership greater than many well-established mainstream publications. Blogs may allow immediate feedback or discussion from readers, who often must be registered to post feedback and are therefore not anonymous—thereby weakening two of the linchpins in the definition of mass communication. Yet it is hard to claim that the most popular blogs are not a type of mass communication because of the numbers of audience members reading them and the lack of interaction between the blog author and a respondent.

blog

Short for weblog, a type of website in which a person posts regular journal or diary entries, with the posts arranged chronologically.

Twitter also follows a blended mass-communication and mediated interpersonal-communication model, as people broadcast their tweets to thousands or even millions of followers, yet the followers can re-tweet and interact with each other and their followers.

The fragmented nature of audiences on the Web complicates attempts to define a "mass." Some websites have small but dedicated followings, while others have millions of visitors a month, reaching far more people than your typical local newspaper. Yet the local newspaper would traditionally be considered a type of mass communication, unlike a YouTube video such as "Charlie Bit My Finger—Again!," despite over 808 million views eight years after being posted and well over two thousand various remixes and spoofs.

It is important to remember that much of the interaction and conversation that occurs online does so because of the information and entertainment generated from mass communication. "Charlie Bit My Finger," for example, gave rise to a handful of fan clubs on Facebook (including a Mexican one). Consider a TV series like *Star Trek*, though, which ran for only three seasons in the late 1960s but continues to have a thriving fan subculture that consumes—and creates—content about the series and its actors, not to mention the various movies and television-series spin-offs from the original *Star Trek*. The daily mix of news, information, and entertainment that we consume through mass-communication channels gives us fodder for remixes, blogs, interactions with each other—and reactions to media producers who provide the content.

Functions of Mass Communication

Defining mass communication was once straightforward. The media were relatively stable and well known. The functions of mass communication in society were also relatively well understood and thoroughly researched. Studies by Harold D. Lasswell, Charles Wright, and others suggest that these functions have tended to fall largely into four broad categories.[12] These functions can be a useful lens through which to examine various forms of mass communication.

SURVEILLANCE

surveillance

Primarily the journalism function of mass communication, which provides information about processes, issues, events, and other developments in society.

In mass communication, **surveillance** refers primarily to journalism that provides information about processes, issues, events, and other developments in society. This can include news on the latest military activities, weather alerts, and political scandals. Aspects of advertising and public relations as well as educational communication can also employ surveillance.

One weakness in the surveillance function is that an excess of news about disasters, murders, or other unusual events can skew the audience's perception of what is normal in society. Receiving too much information on a particular topic can also promote apathy. Consider how media coverage of a scandal regarding a sports figure such as Yankees baseball player Alex Rodriguez can take on a life of its own and seem to continue forever until we are truly sick of seeing any more stories about A-Rod and athlete doping. Celebrity scandals may present more trivial examples, but skewed or apathetic responses to coverage of wars or disasters, especially in developing countries, are more significant and problematic.

Although surveillance is an important function of mass communication, repeated exposure to a story can have negative effects. After you hear about plane crashes in the media, are you more likely to worry about being in a plane crash?

CORRELATION

Correlation refers to the ways in which media interpret events and issues and ascribe meanings that help individuals understand their roles within the larger society and culture. Journalism, advertising, and public relations all shape public opinion through commentary, criticism, or even targeted marketing campaigns. Polls or surveys allow individuals to learn what others think about an issue and where their views fit within mainstream opinions. People may even shift their views or beliefs subtly to better align themselves with a desirable social group.

By correlating one's views with other groups or perceived notions of general public opinion, the media can help maintain social stability, although this function can be taken too far, and the media can thwart social change or block a full range of views from being disseminated to a mass audience. Interpretation can also tend to favor established business or elite interests over disadvantaged or minority groups, increasing the apparent credibility and authority of the dominant culture.

CULTURAL TRANSMISSION

Cultural transmission refers to the transference of the dominant culture, as well as its subcultures, from one generation to the next or to immigrants. This includes socialization, which the media perform by teaching societal rules and depicting standards of behavior. This function is especially important for children but also necessary for adults who may have immigrated recently to a new country with a different culture.

Not all aspects of cultural transmission are viewed favorably. It has been criticized for creating a homogenized culture that promotes mindless consumerism as a means to achieve happiness rather than imparting more humanistic, and ultimately more rewarding, values such as an appreciation of multiculturalism and diversity.

ENTERTAINMENT

The entertainment function is performed in part by all three of these activities (surveillance, correlation, and cultural transmission) but also involves the generation of content designed specifically and exclusively to entertain. Although some claim that this function helps raise artistic and cultural taste among the general populace, others disagree, arguing that mass media encourage escapism and promote lowbrow entertainment at the expense of high art.

Entertainment can also perpetuate certain stereotypes about various groups, wittingly or unwittingly. These can be especially hard to detect because they are often presented as part and parcel of a story line that makes oversimplified characters seem natural in context. For good and for bad, powerful cultural principles and symbols permeate entertainment, transmitting specific sets of values that can go unquestioned.

💬 correlation

Media interpretation ascribing meaning to issues and events that helps individuals understand their roles within the larger society and culture.

Wartime propaganda posters provide windows into how public opinion can be shaped.

💬 cultural transmission

The process of passing on culturally relevant knowledge, skills, attitudes, and values from person to person or group to group.

Cultural transmission is a function of mass communication sometimes criticized for promoting mindless consumerism.

DISCUSSION QUESTIONS: Consider your own use of social and digital media. What is the source of much of what you discuss with your friends online—does it come from news or politics or primarily entertainment sources such as television, movies, and music? What implications do you think your habits have for notions of the public?

Theories of Communication

Over the centuries, great thinkers have tried to define communication and understand it as a process. They have proposed a variety of theories in their attempts to explain it. One of the earliest communication theorists was the philosopher Aristotle, who in 300 BCE called the study of communication "rhetoric" and identified three primary elements within the process: the speaker, the subject, and the person addressed. He also identified three basic rhetorical appeals to persuade an audience: pathos, an appeal that excites emotions; ethos, an appeal that establishes the speaker's credibility; and logos, an appeal that relies on logic and reasoning. Aristotle's principal ideas laid an enduring foundation for communication research even today.

The need to enrich our understanding of communication from a theoretical perspective arose with the importance that mass communication began to have in people's lives, especially as electronic communication such as radio and television became so dominant.

TRANSMISSION MODELS

In 1949, scientists Claude E. Shannon and Warren Weaver formulated an influential model of communication.[13] Known as a transmission model of communication, it is closely related to communication theorist Harold Lasswell's famous question about media effects, which he posed in 1948: "Who says what in which channel to whom with what effect?" This model has allowed for many general applications in mass communication.

The Shannon and Weaver mathematical theory of communication is based on a linear system of electronic communication. The original formulation of the model included five main elements (see Figure 1-4). An information source formulates a message. A transmitter encodes the message into signals. The signals are delivered via a channel. A receiver decodes the signals, "reconstructing" the

FIGURE 1-4 Shannon and Weaver Mathematical Theory

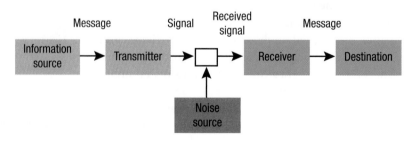

original message, which reaches its destination. The communication flow in this model is decidedly one-directional, from the sender to the receiver. The system has a limited capacity to provide feedback from the receiver to the information source: to acknowledge receipt of the message, to indicate whether the message has been understood, and to communicate the receiver's reaction. The communication process can be adversely affected by noise, or interference, from the environment, possibly by way of competing or distracting messages or even electrical interference.

The model clearly explains how a telephone works. The information source speaks (encoding a message); the phone (transmitter) transforms the sound waves into electrical impulses (the signal), which are sent over the channel (the tiny box in the center of Figure 1-4); and those electrical impulses are turned back into sound waves by the phone (receiver) at the other end of the line where they are heard and (one hopes) understood (decoded) by another person (destination). Noise is any interference anywhere along the way.

The Shannon and Weaver model is especially technological in its orientation and therefore limited in its utility for understanding traditional mass communication because it does not fully reflect the role of humans in the process—specifically, how meaning is created. Moreover, the advent of digital, networked communication media is greatly expanding the interactive nature of communication, making the limited feedback capacity of the model more problematic even by its own standards.

Adapting the Shannon and Weaver model and integrating concepts from Aristotle, pioneering communication scholar Wilbur Schramm in 1954 developed a **simplified communications model** in the book *The Process and Effects of Mass Communication*, as summarized in Figure 1-5.[14]

Significantly, Schramm envisioned understanding as an integral part of human communication. He also realized that another important aspect of the

simplified communications model

Developed by Wilbur Schramm in 1954 and based on the mathematical theory of communication. It includes a source who encodes a message, or signal, which is transmitted (via the media or directly via interpersonal communication) to a destination where the receiver decodes it.

FIGURE 1-5 Schramm–Osgood Model

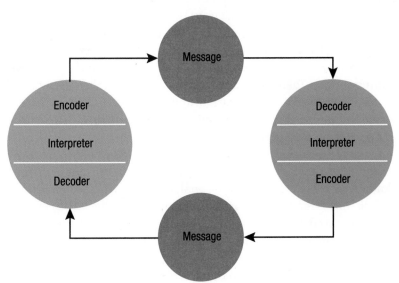

traditional communication model needed correcting: in human communication, mediated or not, communication is not a one-way process. Schramm wrote, "In fact, it is misleading to think of the communication process as starting somewhere and ending somewhere. It is really endless. We are little switchboard centers handling and rerouting the great endless current of information." As a result, Schramm and Charles Osgood developed a circular model of communication. The participants exchange roles of source/encoder and receiver/decoder.

However, even this model, based on certain concepts derived from the transmission model, has its limitations for some scholars. Conceiving of people as switchboards of information processing does not adequately explain how an advertisement may tug at our heart strings and evoke deep-ranging yet differing emotions in people or how people may see the same message very differently. For that we have to look at other theoretical traditions.

DISCUSSION QUESTIONS: Imagine a small classified ad on Craigslist that simply says "Baby shoes for sale. Never used." Explain the ad in terms of the transmission model, then consider how these six words may evoke thoughts or feelings with you. Does the transmission model of communication adequately describe your feelings as well?

CRITICAL THEORY AND CULTURAL STUDIES

A typical critique of transmission models of communication (made by others outside the critical-theory tradition as well as within) is that they treat communication as some kind of separate phenomenon independent of the people who are engaging in communication. Its technological orientation may explain an electronic signal well, but it falls far short when trying to explain the deeper meaning behind someone reading a morning paper. Defining humans as a type of switchboard center, as Schramm does, does not explain how media economics may influence what paper we are able to read or if we even have an Internet connection—nor does it help us better understand the ways in which power, identity, and a host of other factors affect how we make and share meaning through communication.

In contrast, **critical theory** is broadly influenced by Marxist notions of ideology, exploitation, capitalism, and the economy in understanding and eventually transforming society. There are many branches of critical theory, not all of which focus on media and mass communication, and they often disagree with each other on fundamental points. We will explore **cultural studies**, which tend to focus more on mass communication.

To understand a cultural-studies approach to the subject of communication, it is important first to see its intellectual heritage through the lens of critical theory and to know how it differs from traditional, or positivist, social science. Critical theorists criticize positivist researchers for applying physical science research methods inappropriately to human behavior. They do not agree that certain statistical techniques, and enough research, can uncover various "natural laws" of society and behavior.

Critical theorists not only claim that the process of scientific creation of "fact" is a social and variable process like any other (consider how Pluto has gone from

critical theory

A theoretical approach broadly influenced by Marxist notions of the role of ideology, exploitation, capitalism, and the economy in understanding and eventually transforming society.

cultural studies

An interdisciplinary framework for studying communication that rejects the scientific approach while investigating the role of culture in creating and maintaining social relations and systems of power.

being viewed as a planet to now being planetary object 134340), but they also refute that natural laws can be discovered to explain human behavior. They see the drive to predict and better control society as one more form of oppression. In short, critical theorists would say positivists ask uninspiring questions and get uninteresting—if not misleading—answers that largely describe the societal and cultural status quo as unproblematic.

Cultural-studies researchers join critical theorists in rejecting the positivist scientific approach. By utilizing a host of disciplines ranging from anthropology and sociology to political science and literary theory, they examine the symbolic environment created by mass media and study their role in culture and society. For these researchers, a television commercial can be a rich source of cultural codes and representations that tell us in subtle and not-so-subtle ways how we as members of society should act and think.

Communications scholar **James Carey** was a leading cultural-studies theorist who developed what he called a ritual view of communication. He claimed that "communication is a symbolic process whereby reality is produced, maintained, repaired, and transformed."[15] From this view, the act of reading a newspaper has less to do with receiving information than with participating in a shared cultural experience that portrays and confirms the world in a certain way. By reading the paper, we are actually participating in a ritual that produces and reproduces certain sociocultural norms played out through our actions and interactions with others.[16] The same dynamic can be said to take place with online media, such as posting photos on Flickr or texting a friend—you are not simply transmitting information but are sharing ways of doing things and ways of thinking that actually create the society we live in through our repeated actions.

Television: The Future of Convergence

We started this chapter by looking at the telephone, an example of a communication technology whose role in convergence you may not have considered. We will end by looking briefly at television, particularly at how convergence has shaped television today and how it will affect its future.

We will discuss the invention and development of television in Chapter 5 and focus here on the role convergence has played for this quintessential mass-communication technology. Television's dominance as a mass medium in the latter half of the twentieth century through to today means it has been much discussed, debated, and studied. Television has been blamed for everything from a decline in young people reading to a rise in societal violence. The impact of few mass-communications technologies has been as striking. Despite disagreement about the degree to which television may affect our culture and society, the belief that television has certain detrimental (or beneficial) effects has influenced everything from government regulation to the kinds of commercials and programming we see. The enormous popularity of television makes it a powerful instrument for teaching people culture and social norms—or at least idealized norms.

Television viewing habits changed with the advent of the remote control. Channel-surfing made it easy for people to later name and understand the process of Web surfing that occurs on the Internet. Digital video recorders (DVRs) also changed TV viewing habits. The use of **product placement** has grown in response

💬 James Carey

Communications scholar and historian who has shaped a cultural-studies approach to communication theory.

James Carey was one of the most influential media and communications scholars of the twentieth century.

💬 product placement

A form of advertising in which brand-name goods or services are placed prominently within programming content that is otherwise devoid of advertising, demonstrating the convergence of programming with advertising content.

to advertisers' fears that viewers fast-forward through commercials when watching recorded programming. Product placement shows a convergence of normal programming with advertisement content, often not recognized as such.

Over the years, television has been able to adapt to new methods of distributing content. Over-the-air broadcast towers used to be the primary way that people received their television signals; today cable and satellite systems are dominant. However, cable television systems were first created in 1948 so that viewers in areas where over-the-air signals could not easily reach could get television programming, long before most households had cable systems.

The first transatlantic satellite signal was sent in 1962, when television as a mass medium was still not even fifteen years old.[17] Entertainment, especially movies and sports programming, played a role in encouraging the growth of cable and satellite–cable partnerships in the 1970s.

In 1978, Ted Turner launched WTBS Atlanta as a national **superstation**, a local TV station that reaches a national audience by beaming its programming nationwide via satellite to local cable systems, which then transmit to local subscribers. In 1980, Turner employed the same technological combination to launch the first twenty-four-hour TV news network, the Cable News Network (CNN). Today, many countries use similar systems for their own national broadcasting. In a country like Indonesia, which has hundreds of islands, a cable system between islands is simply not practical. Using satellite to beam programming to local cable operators, who connect viewers in their areas with cable, has proven to be an economical solution.

Television is a major communications industry in its own right. But when it began as a mass medium in the late 1940s, its rapid rise in popularity was seen as a threat by the film industry, which blacklisted actors if they performed on television shows. It took several years for the film industry to realize that television could replace the second- and third-run movie theaters as a source of additional revenues for older films. The specter that the movie industry feared of mass audiences staying home and watching television instead of going out to the movies never materialized; people still went in droves.

Today, the tug-of-war between the movie industry and television for attracting audiences continues, even as some film companies own television channels through the process of consolidation. The latest battles have been taking place in the area of 3D, which used to be seen solely in movie theaters. Not only has 3D viewing technology for movies gotten better, but television screens have rapidly caught up; and now 3D television is also on the market.

Perhaps one of the biggest areas of convergence is the melding of the television and the personal computer or mobile device. Television is becoming more interactive, encouraging viewers to do things like vote for their favorite *American Idol* contestants (although still not through the television—they use mobile phones for that). At the same time, a growing number are watching television programming on their PCs, tablets, or smartphones. In the future, it may not matter much whether we think of television as merged with mobile device or mobile

superstation

A local TV station that reaches a national audience by beaming its programming nationwide via satellite to local cable systems.

device as merged with television; we will simply have a high-definition screen with which we can interact, accessing the Web or social media even as we watch our favorite programs.

DISCUSSION QUESTIONS: Consider watching the same film on TV, a PC, a tablet, or in a theater. List several ways in which these viewing experiences differ, and identify the relative advantages and disadvantages of each.

LOOKING BACK AND MOVING FORWARD

This book takes the premise that mass communication as we have known it is fundamentally changing, perhaps to the point where this term is no longer a relevant or accurate description of current communication. Convergence is, broadly speaking, the process where we are seeing these transformations take place on technological, economic, and sociocultural levels. Many of the ramifications of convergence will likely not be realized or fully known for years to come, while others seem to have had immediate and dramatic effects on our media landscape.

What we have today is a fascinating and confusing mixture of mass-communication industries and business models combining with various emerging digital technologies and communications practices that simultaneously threaten and hold great promise for traditional media companies and the communications professions. Issues of consumer privacy, of copyright, and of affordable access to the Internet, among other legal, regulatory, and ethical issues, have still to be worked out.

The public may finally have some say in the matter in the new digital media environment. Through communication tools that give the public unprecedented power to share information with each other and to "talk back" to those in power, people are able to connect and organize on any number of issues important to them, affecting policy changes through online and offline means. We have already seen the power of online organizing for various politicians in terms of getting donations and engaging young people in political campaigns. Will the Internet and other digital media flourish and produce a rich montage of diverse voices? Or will the emerging global media system be a homogenous blend of commercial banality where news and entertainment are little more than commodities that sit with equally insipid user-generated content? It is still an open question, but dealing responsibly with issues like these is the moral mandate of mass communication in the digital age. In this book, we hope to give you the tools to do so.

MEDIA MATTERS   THE NATURE OF "INTERMASS" COMMUNICATION

Even before the Internet era, scholars were asking how mass media and interpersonal communication affected each other.[18] Where is the dividing line between interpersonal and mass communication in your media world? Is the line disappearing?

1. How long have you had a Facebook page?
2. How often do you update or add content to the page, and what prompts you to do so?
3. How would you feel if your professor or a potential employer insisted that you friend them so they can see your page?
4. Are you starting to spend more time on social media sites other than Facebook?

Which ones? Why are you changing your usage patterns?

5. Are you typically on the Web or social media when you watch TV?
6. Do you often text or chat online with friends while watching the same program?
7. Have you ever uploaded music, videos, or other content to file-sharing sites?

According to World Internet Project research, chances are good that you have participated in many if not most of these activities.[19] This shows that the line between interpersonal and mass communication is a blurry one indeed.

FURTHER READING

Convergence Culture: Where Old and New Media Collide. Henry Jenkins (2008) NYU Press.

The Coming Convergence: Surprising Ways Diverse Technologies Interact to Shape Our World and Change the Future. Stanley Schmidt (2008) Prometheus Books.

Understanding Media Convergence: The State of the Field. August Grant, Jeffrey Wilkinson (eds.) (2008) Oxford University Press.

Media Organizations and Convergence: Case Studies of Media Convergence Pioneers (LEA's Communication Series). Gracie Lawson-Borders (2005) Lawrence Erlbaum Associates.

The History of the Telephone. Herbert Casson (2006) Cosimo Classics.

America Calling: A Social History of the Telephone to 1940. Claude Fischer (1994) University of California Press.

The History of Wireless: How Creative Minds Produced Technology for the Masses. Ira Brodsky (2008) Telescope Books.

Speaking into the Air: A History of the Idea of Communication. John Durham Peters (1999) University of Chicago Press.

Understanding Media Theory. Kevin Williams (2003) Oxford University Press.

Understanding Media Cultures: Social Theory and Mass Communication, 2nd ed. Nick Stevenson (2002) Sage Publications.

Theories of Communication: A Short Introduction. Armand Mattelart, Michèle Mattelart (1998) Sage Publications.

Communication Theories: Origins, Methods, and Uses in the Mass Media, 5th ed. Werner J. Severin, James W. Tankard Jr. (2001) Addison Wesley Longman.

Digital Disconnect: How Capitalism Is Turning the Internet Against Democracy. Robert W. McChesney (2013) The New Press.

What Will Be: How the New World of Information Will Change Our Lives. Michael Dertouzos (1997) HarperEdge.

CHAPTER PREVIEW

Media Literacy in the Digital Age

On February 9, 2014, Missouri football player Michael Sam announced in an ESPN interview that he was gay, paving the way for him to become the first openly gay player in the National Football League (NFL).[1] Although Sam made his announcement via traditional news media, including ESPN and *The New York Times*, the real national discussion about Sam's entry into professional football followed online in the social media arena. Twitter exploded with activity shortly after Sam's historic revelation. One example of a popular tweet welcoming Sam into the NFL world came from Richie Incognito, a pro football player who himself had been criticized for bullying another player by using homophobic slurs: "It takes guts to do what you did. I wish u nothing but the best."[2] Within hours, on February 10, 2014, users had retweeted Incognito's original posting 361 times and favorited it 299 times.

But Sam wasn't the first professional athlete to come out as gay. On April 29, 2013, Jason Collins, center for the Washington Wizards, also revealed his sexual orientation to an unsuspecting public. And more than twenty years prior, in 1981, Czech American tennis star Martina Navratilova made that aspect of her private life public, a similar announcement that prompted a vastly different reaction from the media.

"The media certainly roasted me," Navratilova told *Democracy Now!* "I had my share of, you know, 'Here's Martina's love nest,' or 'Good Versus Evil,' as one columnist headed a column about me playing against Chris Evert. So, it was pretty nasty, but, you know, you just kind of deal with it."[3]

Navratilova was pleased to see the positive coverage of Collins and surprised that the media wanted to discuss the issue. "I certainly didn't get an invitation to speak on *Good Morning America*, because it was, like, still a taboo subject," she said. "It was such a negative subject, it made headlines, but in a very bad way."

Comparing the varying reactions to these announcements across the years raises interesting questions about the role of media in our society. Did the media gradually help change our attitudes about gay rights, or did the media simply follow gradual changes in public opinion? What part might entertainment have played,

LEARNING OBJECTIVES

>> Define media literacy.

>> Explain how mediated and nonmediated communication differ.

>> Define the role of semiotics and framing in influencing our understanding of the world and media content.

>> Define media grammar and describe its various aspects in different media.

>> Explain how commercial forces influence media organizations and content.

>> Define media bias and its effects on media content.

>> Use basic media-literacy skills to improve your critical thinking when consuming media content.

including sitcoms such as *Will & Grace* that feature gay characters, in increasing our acceptance of gays?

Also consider how the media outlet itself may influence the acceptance of stories. If Collins had penned his essay in *The Advocate*, a prominent gay magazine, instead of a mainstream sports magazine such as *Sports Illustrated*, do you think other media outlets and the public would have been as receptive?

We live in a media society. Mass media surround and influence our world in a variety of ways. They entertain us, they inform us, and they sell us everything from household products to political candidates. Although we often tend to study media and mass communications as something separate from our culture, society, and lives, the fact is that media are just as real as the "real world."

Media are pervasive in modern life, making it more important than ever to understand how their messages may influence us. We must look critically at all media we receive and understand something about how media organizations work as businesses, how they fit into other aspects of society, and how they can influence culture and manipulate public opinion.

In this chapter, we explain some basic principles of media literacy in both non-digital and digital media while teaching you to analyze critically the media messages you encounter.

> **DISCUSSION QUESTIONS:** Compare news articles about Michael Sam and Jason Collins announcing they are gay with news coverage of Martina Navratilova's similar announcement. What differences do you see in how the stories were depicted, and what effect do you think such framing had on public opinion about homosexuality?

Education and Media

In school, we learn to read, write, and do arithmetic. We learn about history, other cultures, literature, science, and politics. We learn athletic skills and teamwork; we can even learn about art, mechanics, computer programming, and cooking.

But we also learn much from our daily and extensive interactions with media content—some may even argue that we learn more of practical value from daily exposure to media than to class content during a typical school day. The common component of the four functions of mass communication mentioned in the previous chapter—surveillance, correlation, cultural transmission, and entertainment—is that they essentially educate and inform us.

This raises a significant question: If media are so pervasive in our lives, why aren't we studying them in the same way that we study geography or biology, for example? Why can we take a class in high school on how to dismantle a car engine but not one that teaches us how to deconstruct our modern systems of media and mass communications?

The question highlights two interesting and related issues. First, it shows that education, like media, is not something separate from our lives. We are learning all the time, even when not in a formal academic setting such as a classroom or when doing homework. Second, given that we are learning all the time through our interactions with each other and with media content, we must strive to ensure that what we are learning is accurate and useful. This requires skills to examine where that learning is coming from and how it may be affecting our thought processes.

Educators have recognized a growing need to teach media-literacy skills to school-age children, starting as young as kindergarten or elementary school and continuing to high school graduation. Some countries, such as Canada and Australia, have taken the lead in media-literacy education, while the United States generally lags behind. This is changing, however, and a growing number of states, such as New Jersey, have implemented statewide media-literacy guidelines for K–12 schools.

What Is Media Literacy?

Being able to read a book, navigate a website or post a tweet, and recognize that a background music change signals a scary part of a movie are all types of media literacy. Some fall under what we would consider the traditional meaning of the term "literacy," and others can be classified as visual literacy or computer literacy. Media literacy encompasses all these skills and many more, and the various approaches to media education differ to some degree on what exactly media-literacy education should entail.

Media literacy can be defined as the process of critically analyzing media content by considering its particular presentation, its underlying political or social messages, and its media ownership or regulation that may affect the type of content we receive. Some approaches to media education emphasize media-creation skills as a way to examine our media critically, through either creative media projects or alternative media production such as recreating a popular commercial from a feminist perspective.

Developing media literacy is an ongoing process, not simply a goal. Even though you can never attain perfection, it is always possible to improve your media literacy and thus become a wiser media user. The importance of media in contemporary society makes it imperative that audience members think critically about media content to better control their actions and not be controlled by media messages. Learning new skills in creating media, such as taking courses on graphic design or video production, can help further your media literacy.

Media-literacy scholar W. James Potter talks about building "knowledge structures," ways to visualize developing one's level of knowledge on a given topic or topics.[4] If, for example, you have a basic understanding of the history of the World Wide Web, and someone claims to have been on Facebook since 2001, you can be confident that he or she is incorrect: Facebook was not created until 2004 (and then only for Harvard students).

Still, media literacy entails more than simply remembering historical facts. Media consumers should always question what they see, hear, or otherwise experience when receiving or interacting with mediated communication. Is a news story biased? Why is it even

media literacy

The process of interacting with and critically analyzing media content by considering its particular presentation, its underlying political or social messages, and its ownership or regulation issues that may affect what is presented and in what form.

Learning media-literacy skills has become even more important for students today.

news? Does a popular television show or video game encourage gender or racial stereotypes or antisocial behavior? What is an advertiser really trying to sell and to whom? These are just a sample of the kinds of questions critical media consumers should ask.

It is important to develop knowledge not just about the media but also about the larger social, political, and economic forces that influence media content, media production, and communication technologies in general. To that end, we must first step back and consider what a medium is. Then we will look at some of the concerns people have had over the years about the effects that media may or may not have on us.

What Makes Mediated Communication Different?

An enduring and fundamental concern about the media is that what we see and hear through mediated communication—the signs, symbols, and words from books, the Web, television, and radio—can somehow affect us in ways that non-mediated communication does not. This assumption has led to a large body of research on media effects, which we discuss in more detail in Chapter 12.

Some theoretical frameworks offer explanations of how we may make sense of the world through media and how the media messages we receive seem somehow natural.

SEMIOTICS

semiotics

The study of signs and symbols.

Semiotics, the study of signs and symbols, goes back in some form to Plato and Aristotle. Contemporary semiotics has been greatly influenced by Ferdinand de Saussure, the father of linguistics, and his notion of signs as having dual properties. These properties are the signifier, or the form; and the signified, or what the form represents (some semioticians propose a third component, an interpretant, between these two). For example, an image of a rose, the signifier, may signify any number of things, or signifieds, depending on the context (see Figure 2-1). An image of a rose on a Valentine's Day card may mean one thing, whereas a rose tattoo with blood-dipped thorns on the arm of a biker may mean something else entirely.

Context plays a major role in the audience's understanding of the signified, even when the signifier remains the same. The power of signs to affect our thinking should not be underestimated. René Magritte's famous painting of a pipe that also says "This is not a pipe" illustrates how we typically take the sign as reality. Most people, when shown his painting and asked what it is, will reply, "A pipe." But Magritte is absolutely correct: his picture of a pipe is not actually a pipe—it is simply a picture of a pipe.

We must also remember that in semiotics, "sign" does not simply refer to visual images but words as well. Words could be considered a more complex form of sign, for we have to learn that certain sounds carry particular meanings (which are entirely arbitrary). There is no logical reason that the color red is called "red" in English, "rojo" in Spanish, and "aka" in Japanese; all of these are simply linguistic conventions for those particular languages.

Ceci n'est pas une pipe.

Rene Magritte's famous "This is not a pipe" picture reminds us how we mistakenly understand the representation of something as the thing itself.

FIGURE 2-1 Semiotic Signifier and Signified

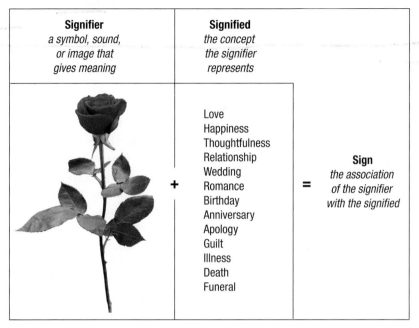

When Gertrude Stein said, "A rose is a rose is a rose," she was highlighting the semiotic principle that we subconsciously associate items, such as a rose, with imagery and emotions. A rose (the signifier) can mean many different things (the signified), depending on the context. Examining this relationship (the sign) deepens our understanding of the ways we generate meaning when we communicate.

Although this point may seem rather obvious, another semiotic insight is not quite so evident. Once we learn what certain sounds mean (or what certain visual images mean), we take what we have learned as natural and accept it largely without question. This fact makes the creation and use of signs extremely powerful because it not only influences our thinking but even directs certain behaviors. Think of what you do without question, for example, whenever you are driving and come to a stop sign.

Similarly, an indexical sign is visual but signifies something else to which it is not actually related except by association. Consider the image of a floppy disk in most software programs that indicates the "save file" function. Most computers in use today do not even have floppy-disk drives, yet we understand what the image has come to represent.

Some scholars argue that semiotics is the heart of communication. Noted semiotician and novelist Umberto Eco, in his book *A Theory of Semiotics*, asserts that "Every act of communication to or between human beings—or any other intelligent biological or mechanical apparatus—presupposes a signification system as its necessary condition." In other words, without a common understanding of what signs mean, whether they are visual or lingual, we would not be able to communicate.

Some knowledge of semiotics is required for a deeper understanding of the processes of communication and the production of meaning among people and in cultures. It is also especially important for advertising professionals who seek insights into how target audiences may receive various ad and branding campaigns.

FRAMING

framing

The presentation and communication of a message in a particular way that influences our perception of it.

"There would be tens of thousands of jobs created" if President Barack Obama approved the Keystone XL pipeline.
— *Anna Kooiman on Thursday, November 6th, 2014 in a segment on "Fox & Friends"*

FOX NEWS

THE ED SHOW 7/31/14
New Canadian pipeline, new environmental problems
Newly proposed "Sandpiper" pipeline could have serious environmental problems and implications for those living near the Minnesota Wetlands and Wild Rice Fields. Ed Schultz, Jane Kleeb and Steve Morse discuss. Duration: 8:04
msnbc

Fox News and MSNBC framed their coverage of the Keystone Pipeline quite differently, with Fox News emphasizing jobs—Keystone pipeline would create "tens of thousands of jobs"—and MSNBC focusing on the environmental impact: "New Canadian pipeline, new environmental problems."

echo effect

A phenomenon that occurs when people surround themselves with online voices that echo their own, reinforcing their views and the belief that those opinions are in the majority when in fact they may not be.

George Lakoff is a noted cognitive linguist who discusses the effects of framing on the public's perception of a range of social and political matters.

All forms of mass communication, including news, employ **framing**, which works in much the same manner as signs in semiotics. It relies on the notion that we classify, organize, and interpret things into certain schema, or frameworks, to simplify the complex. We have to do this just to get through the day; if we carefully considered and analyzed every message we received, we would never be able to leave the house in the morning. Instead, we take mental shortcuts with much of what we encounter, letting some things go unexamined as we carry on with our lives.

Frames act much like signs and symbols in semiotics: Once accepted, they appear natural and go largely unquestioned. They also shape our perceptions of people, places, issues, and events. Two words—"rights" versus "benefits"—provide a simple example of framing. If an Iraq War veteran is lobbying the government to obtain better health care and services for injuries, demanding veterans' rights has a different connotation than asking for veterans' benefits. The term "benefits" suggests something extra, a privilege perhaps not available to other people and therefore unequal or unfair. Arguing for veterans' rights, on the other hand, suggests something fundamental that is being with withheld.

Framing may sound simply like spin, but it is not. We all frame our world, and good communicators know how to frame debates in ways that favor their views and disadvantage those of opponents. A persuasive communicator who wins the framing battle also likely wins that particular debate. Pollster and political communications consultant Frank Luntz helps conservative politicians reframe words to persuade others. See Table 2-1 for examples.

Similarly, George Lakoff, UC Berkeley professor of linguistics and cognitive science, discusses liberal framing, often chastising Democrats for failing to employ persuasive depictions of controversial issues such as health care. See Table 2-2 for examples of liberal reframing. Note how some of these have successfully become the dominant term for the issue, just as some terms have for conservative frames.

Framing is of great consequence in today's world because of the ubiquity of mass-communication media. It is easy to see how this media coverage can shape our perceptions of the world, especially when "framed" conversations are intensified by the **echo effect**, a phenomenon that occurs when people surround themselves with online voices that echo their own, reinforcing their views and the belief that those opinions are in the majority when in fact they may not be. But, as we will see, concerns about media effects are not new.

TABLE 2-1 Reframing Political Issues for Conservatives

NEVER SAY	INSTEAD SAY
Tax cuts	Tax relief
Inheritance tax	Death tax
Undocumented workers/aliens	Illegal immigrants
Drilling for oil	Exploring for energy

Source: Frank Luntz, *Words That Work: It's Not What You Say, It's What People Hear.*

TABLE 2-2 Reframing Political Issues for Liberals

ISSUE OR CAUSE	DISCUSSED AS
Tax subsidies	Corporate welfare (Ralph Nader)
Gay marriage	Same-sex marriage
Tax increases for the wealthy	Paying a fair share
Abortion debate	Pro-choice or women's rights

Early Concerns of Media Effects

Over the last century, public concern has arisen about the possible effects of each new medium of mass communication as it has emerged. Questions have been asked about each medium's impact on culture, political processes, children's values and behaviors, and the like. In the 1920s, much of the public became worried about the depiction of sex, violence, and lawlessness in film. In recent years, questions have proliferated about how the Internet and video games may influence us, even perhaps altering how we think.

Such anxieties have a long history. In the 1800s, critics warned that newspapers caused juvenile crime. Moralists believed that the flow of sensational news stories about crime and vice would lead people to imitate such immoral behavior. In 1888, *Punch* magazine attributed Jack the Ripper's crimes committed in Whitechapel, a rough inner-city district of London, to "highly coloured pictorial advertisements."

Alarm about the effects of media on children has even deeper roots. We know that in ancient Greece, philosophers Socrates and Plato worried about the influence of literacy on children. Plato was especially apprehensive about the morally corrupting resonance of poetry, particularly allegorical tales such as Homer's *Battles of the Gods*, which he sought to ban.[5] In 360 BCE, Plato offered this reasoning:

> Children cannot distinguish between what is allegory and what isn't, and opinions formed at that age are usually difficult to eradicate or change; it is therefore of the utmost importance that the first stories they hear shall aim at producing the right moral effect.

> PLATO, *THE REPUBLIC*

It is hard today to appreciate the profound effect writing once had on society. No longer was a good memory prized as it was in a nonliterate oral culture, because memorization was not needed to store information. The form of storytelling changed with writing because repetitive phrases were no longer needed as memory prompts for storytellers, and the rhythm and cadences of what was written differed from what had been spoken.

Moreover, storytellers could lose control of their words in written form. Someone could take a person's words and twist their meaning, with no chance for an immediate response or perhaps any response at all. In fact, the author of a work had no way of knowing who might read it or when. Greek children sneaking off with a scroll of poetry to read in secret may seem comical; but in a fundamental sense, this is no different than kids today sneaking into an R-rated movie in the multiplex or surreptitiously removing the parental controls on the cable TV service or computer.

Plato's issues with writing as a new medium relate to its particular media grammar, knowledge of which is integral to the development of media literacy.

Media Grammar

media grammar

The underlying rules, structures, and patterns by which a medium presents itself and is used and understood by the audience.

First, a critical consumer of media messages must understand **media grammar**, the underlying rules, structures, and patterns by which a medium presents itself and is used and understood by the audience. Each medium of mass communication presents its messages uniquely. With media familiar through widespread use or exposure, we do not often think about the extent to which media grammar affects our perceptions—what we see and how we see it. In many respects, it becomes background in much the same way that semiotic signs become natural to us. Nevertheless, media grammar can have profound implications for our understanding of media content. We become more aware of it when we encounter a new medium whose rules we do not yet know.

Here, we will look briefly at the main forms of media, the basics of their particular grammar, and their potential effects on our perceptions and expectations.

PRINT MEDIA

Print media, partly due to their long history compared to other types of mass communication, have developed a very sophisticated media grammar. Everything about a book—its physical dimensions, the artwork on its jacket, the size and style of the typeface, whether it is hardcover or paperback, whether it contains pictures or not—conveys important messages to the potential buyer beyond the actual content. Within a book itself, several aspects of media grammar have evolved over the years. Spacing between words to aid reading comprehension is an early example, as are page numbering, tables of contents, indexes, and chapter headings. Many of these conventions we now take for granted actually took years to become widely adopted and standard in books.

Newspapers have their own types of media grammar that have also evolved over time and that continue to change. An obvious example is the number of color photos and graphics in newspapers today compared to forty years ago. Because space is limited in a newspaper, more graphics means less room for text. Many media critics and journalists have complained that this packaging of news into relatively short, easy-to-read units accompanied by splashy visuals does readers a disservice by not providing them with the necessary depth of information. Proponents of the trend argue that to compete with television and other visual media for audience attention, newspapers must present news in formats that accommodate readers' busy lifestyles.

Even without knowing the language, we can often recognize what kind of foreign newspaper we are viewing simply from the look of the publication. **CRITICAL THINKING QUESTION:** What visual aspects of the newspaper help us identify its type of publication and its type of target audience?

Most newspapers are organized into sections, such as sports, business, and local news. Not only do these help organize information so that readers can quickly find stories that interest them, but they also create parameters for what types of stories to expect. Sections also help define where certain advertisers prefer to appear in the paper, showing how media grammar can intersect with commercial interests.

Magazines use sophisticated graphic and design techniques, even more so than newspapers, and feature more long-form writing, often with just one or two articles per page and multipage pieces. Advertising often takes up a full page, and in some magazines it is hard to tell immediately if something is an ad rather than graphics at the beginning of a feature. Magazines combine certain elements of books and newspapers in their media grammar. Because of their length, they usually have a table of contents (many also have an advertiser index) that helps readers rapidly access specific articles. Like newspapers, magazines are often divided into subject-related sections within their topic areas.

Given that the grammar for print media developed over hundreds of years, we have adapted surprisingly quickly to the rise of electronic media, especially audio and, later, video.

RADIO AND RECORDED MUSIC

Radio and recorded music have their own grammar, one based only on sound. Radio uses a combination of audio techniques to achieve different ends. These include volume changes, multiple audio tracks, **actualities** (i.e., edited audio clips from interviews with people), sound effects, and **voice-overs**, all of which can be used to convey information, capture attention, or evoke a mood or scene.

Recorded music typically conforms to particular stylistic conventions, especially regarding length (less than five minutes a song) and music format. Popular music genres, such as hip-hop, rock, and country, have certain rhythms, lyrical styles, and sounds that make them clearly distinguishable. This underlying media grammar of specific categories or genres makes it easier to market and promote artists. Once again, we see how media grammar can interact with the economic interests of the media. Radio stations brand themselves by the genres they generally play, making it easier for audiences to pick stations that play music they like.

Still, putting music into genres such as this has its drawbacks. Someone with a sound or style that does not readily conform to a well-established genre may find it harder to get airplay because radio stations are reluctant to play something that does not fit nicely into their established formats. An artist may also find it difficult to get a recording contract in the first place, for a recording label will not want to sign someone it believes radios will not want to promote.

Even the apparently chaotic talk radio has a well-defined media grammar. It is one of the few traditional mass-communication formats to include frequent interaction between media producers or hosts and the audience. Despite its highly interactive nature, however, those who call in are obviously in a subordinate position, as they do not control how long they speak and can even be disconnected at any time.

actualities

Edited audio clips from interviews with people.

voice-over

An unseen announcer or narrator talking while other activity takes place, either on radio or during a television scene.

Rush Limbaugh is a conservative commentator, considered the father of today's politically oriented talk show format.

Although radio developed years before television became a mass medium, and some of the earliest television shows were taken directly from popular radio programs, media producers and audiences had already developed a fairly complex visual grammar, thanks in large part to the popularity of movies.

FILM AND TELEVISION

Film and television have much shorter histories than print, but they have developed an intricate media grammar based on editing, camera angles, lighting, movement, and sound.

In the early history of film, for example, most movies were only a few minutes long and either simply recorded daily activities or essentially filmed short stage plays. Filmmakers started producing more sophisticated story lines for their short films and introduced a technique unique to film at the time—crosscut scenes. By crosscutting different scenes to simulate events happening simultaneously in two different locations (think of the classic scenes of a train heading down the tracks and a woman tied to the tracks by the villain), filmmakers were able to tell much more complex and dramatic stories. Further, increasing the speed between crosscut scenes increased dramatic tension.

With many more such tools at their disposal, today's filmmakers are able to convey a lot of information, all through visual or audio techniques. Think of how we respond to background music and strong shadows in horror movies, or how we understand a dream sequence or flashback, or how we visually distinguish good from bad characters even before the plot or dialog has revealed their true natures.

The media grammar of television fiction employs many of the same techniques seen in movies, although television production budgets are, of course, much smaller than movie budgets. Consider the media grammar of an average sitcom— it is usually shot on a set, with perhaps less than half a dozen locations (almost always indoors), and the actors come and go as if on a stage. The camera is usually stationary, although multiple camera angles are used; and punch lines are reinforced by a **laugh track**, which in some sitcoms can be timed with almost clockwork precision (even if the line isn't particularly funny).

Other types of television shows have their own media grammars, such as game shows, soap operas, talk shows, and news. Television news, especially, has borrowed some elements of online media grammar—which had originally borrowed heavily from television for graphical user interfaces such as windows and digital video. Examples include multiple windows on the television screen showing different kinds of information and scrolling news tickers across the bottom of the screen giving updates.

In what has been dubbed geek-chic TV, *The Big Bang Theory*, the most popular comedy since *Friends*, follows the exploits of another group of friends, most of whom are nerdy scientists. This multi-cam sitcom prompts mirthful responses from its devoted and enormous TV audience with a prominent laugh track. **CRITICAL THINKING QUESTIONS:** With closed captions instead of volume on, watch an episode of your favorite sitcom that has a laugh track. Do you chuckle as readily without the auditory cues?

laugh track

A television sitcom device that generates prerecorded laughter timed to coincide with punch lines of jokes.

DISCUSSION QUESTIONS: Consider the media grammar of a popular film, focusing especially on how camera angles give the audience cues as to what to think and feel about the characters. Come up with as many different camera techniques and their possible meanings as you can and compare with other students' interpretations.

DIGITAL-MEDIA GRAMMAR

We may be thoroughly familiar and comfortable with the Internet and social media, but many people throughout the world have limited or no contact with the online realm, whose grammar is still developing. The Web of 2004 bears little resemblance to the Web today, and the Web will look even more different ten years from now.

Even with constant changes in the Web, certain elements of media grammar have been established. **Hypertext**, for example, is generally either underlined or otherwise set apart typographically or graphically from nonlinked text. More and more web designers are following an unwritten rule to have a website logo in the upper-left corner of the screen linked to the website's home page. Icons in the form of buttons, badges, and other symbols create a visual, interactive language that lets us interact easily with the content and inform others on our social networks what we are reading or doing. Other examples include more or less standardized icons for functions such as printing, opening a document, playing a video, emailing a document, and zooming in or out on maps.

The media grammar of digital media evolves with our communication devices. Today, we think nothing of swiping across the screen on our mobile phone to move to a new window or pinching the screen to zoom out. These kinds of touch-screen interfaces in turn affect the design and features of websites, further changing the look and feel of the Web.

The digital media grammar has adopted freely from traditional media forms that it has absorbed, but it has also continued to innovate and create new ways for us to interact with the media. For example, the shift from a point-and-click interaction with a mouse to touch-screen swipes and "pinches" to manipulate the content helps make us aware that there is nothing natural about how we use media today. The same principle applies to how the evolution of our current media system operates and how it has evolved, even though we are often so embedded in that system that it is hard to step outside of it and examine it critically.

hypertext

Text online linked by HTML coding to another web page or website or to a different part of the same web page.

Many websites share certain conventions that users have come to expect, such as a link in the top left-hand corner back to the home page.

Implications of Commercial Media

Even in open and democratic societies with a free press, economic factors and corporate decisions often influence what is and is not covered in the news and what kind of entertainment is created for the general public. Rarely do typical media consumers think of the commercial factors that shape the content they see every day, forces that affect everything from what types of entertainment shows are produced to what kind of news is reported.

These activities happen at the local, national, and international levels. At the local level, reducing the number of reporters at a news organization to save money can result in a noticeable drop in local coverage, such as coverage of area schools. The newspaper company may save money, but the public is poorer for the lessened coverage of local issues. A company that advertises heavily in a local newspaper may gain undue influence in the paper's decision as to whether to publish articles

MEDIA PIONEERS
Marshall McLuhan

International cultural icon and provocative media prophet Marshall McLuhan is known today less for a prolific body of writing than for a couple of prescient precepts so oft repeated they now border on the cliché. Yet the scholar who coined aphorisms as familiar as "the global village" and "the medium is the message" leaves a colorful pioneering legacy as a public intellectual few academics can claim.

"Academic" was nonetheless a profession the twenty-year-old undergraduate expressly rejected in 1930s Western Canada. As Terence Gordon explains, "He was learning *in spite of his professors* (emphasis in original), but he would become a professor of English in spite of himself."[6] After receiving a BA from the University of Manitoba, McLuhan went on to Cambridge University, where he finished another BA (1936), required to proceed to an MA (1939) and a PhD (1942). Following a period of agnosticism in his youth, McLuhan became a devout Roman Catholic (a conversion his Baptist mother had discouraged); and from 1946 until experiencing a stroke in 1979, he taught at St. Michael's College at the University of Toronto.

With spectacular sales of *Understanding Media: The Extensions of Man* (1964) came pop-culture fame, a degree of mainstream recognition arguably unprecedented for a North American academic. During the cultural revolution of the sixties and seventies, McLuhan counted iconic figures as diverse as then Canadian Prime Minister Pierre Trudeau and hippie guru Timothy Leary among those he influenced. Marshall advised Pierre on television appearances and allegedly inspired Tim's buzz phrase "turn on, tune in, drop out."[7] "Whatcha doin', Marshall McLuhan?" was a recurring line on *Laugh-In*, a popular TV comedy of the era. In 1969, *Playboy* made a serious attempt to answer such a question in a lengthy interview with McLuhan at home in the Toronto suburbs where he lived with his wife and several children. Woody Allen, in his 1977 tour de force *Annie Hall*, even cast McLuhan as himself in a cameo scene satirizing a pedantic and pretentious media professor.

McLuhan, however, was not simply famous for being famous. A rare visionary, he foresaw in the sixties, long before the Internet, a global village created by the movement from print to electronic media. And one of his most significant and enduring contributions to the yet undefined area of media literacy was a directive to look beyond the superficial content of the message and consider how the intrinsic, various, and complex effects of the medium—another message in itself—affect our perceptions.

In spite of, or perhaps because of, his arresting pronouncements and his celebrity status, the work of the Canadian media theorist has been denounced by some for dilettantism, cryptic rhetoric, and empirically unsubstantiated claims that unabashedly baffle, among other perceived flaws. McLuhan, characterizing his academic inquiries as "probes," remained apparently unfazed by critics, even wryly professing to share some of their confusion: "I don't pretend to understand it. After all, my stuff is very difficult."[8]

critical of it by threatening to withdraw its advertising. Or a newspaper publisher with other business interests in tourism or real estate, for example, may influence coverage by discouraging or even forbidding reports on certain crimes that may hurt these commercial ventures.

Such manipulation of content is not confined to small-town media outlets. In 1998, HarperCollins, a subsidiary of Rupert Murdoch's News Corporation, cancelled a book by Chris Patten, former British governor of Hong Kong. *East and West* was reportedly highly critical of China's policies, and Murdoch at the time was courting China to accept Murdoch's Star TV satellite and cable programs.

Similarly, a few years prior, he removed the BBC from Star TV when Chinese leaders expressed displeasure at the BBC's reports on the killings in Tiananmen Square in June 1989. More recently, accusations swirled about Murdoch's undue influence on the 2013 elections in his native Australia, where he controls 70 percent of the capital city news circulation. The publishing mogul was allegedly using his newspaper headlines and even front pages to promote his candidate and party of choice.[9]

These incidents are not meant to illustrate that Rupert Murdoch is particularly greedy or selfish; similar stories of corporate decisions influencing what we see or do not see can be told about all of the major media corporations and will be covered in more detail throughout the book, especially Chapter 10 on media ethics.

> **DISCUSSION QUESTIONS:** Would you be willing to pay an annual television licensing fee if television networks and cable companies promised to show fewer commercials? If so, how much would you be willing to pay? Would you pay more to see no commercials?

COMMERCIAL-MEDIA DEBATE

Media scholar Robert McChesney has written several books that reveal how corporate media have adversely affected the quality of communications content we receive and how media companies have lobbied the government to further their own corporate interests at the expense of the public interest. He claims that today's corporate media giants actually harm our democracy and political processes in a number of ways. These range from poor news coverage that does not challenge the status quo (especially when it comes to media companies' own business investments) to banal entertainment that dulls our senses and incessant advertising that implies happiness is found through consumerism—although, as we discuss later, most media outlets depend on that very advertising to exist.

Media scholar Robert McChesney founded Free Press to promote media reform and to weaken the power of corporate media giants.

According to McChesney, the commercial nature of mass communications underlies all mass media. And all would agree, regardless of political ideology, that it takes money to run a media organization. The question becomes one of where the money comes from—the commercial marketplace or public sources of funding.

Arguably, media companies are businesses just like any other; and a business that fails to turn a profit will fail to do right by its private owners or shareholders if it is publicly traded. In recent history, media businesses have been among the most profitable of any industry, with profit margins typically around 20 percent on an annual basis.

On the other hand, critics of our corporate media system argue that media companies are not like other companies, that their "products"—the signs and symbols that shape our culture and views of the world through the news and entertainment we consume—influence our thinking and behavior considerably more than other types of products. Therefore, media companies should be publicly funded so that they are not as beholden to the marketplace and the influence of market logic on media content.

Proponents of commercial media identify the profit motive as a key incentive for media companies to produce quality content that people will want to watch or

INTERNATIONAL PERSPECTIVES
Mobile Telephony in the Developing World

Despite the prevalence of the Internet and personal computers in the United States and other industrialized countries in Europe, South America, and the Asia-Pacific region, an even stronger competitor to the Internet and PC has emerged in the developing world—the mobile phone.

Mobile telephony can hold several advantages over the Internet in many developing countries. First, poor telecommunications infrastructures in these countries often make landline calls expensive and sporadic at best

for those who have phones. Without adequate phone lines, let alone consistent electric power, it is nearly impossible to depend on a PC or regular Internet service. Many of these countries do not have cable television wires, relying instead on satellite transmission of cable content, when allowed by the governments. In countries such as Malaysia, for example, owning a satellite dish is a crime.

Mobile telephones provide an easy and relatively cheap way to communicate, and text messaging allows further mass coordination so that the phone becomes part of a larger, ad hoc, mass-communication system. They also foster a sense of community among phone users. In Nigeria, for example, women generally run the various stalls in the urban market, coordinating prices with sellers in different locations by mobile phone. What's more, recognizing their common interests and grievances, these sellers joined together to try to alleviate some of the greater problems they faced.

Kenya's M-Pesa, a mobile payment system, has become the primary source of remittances by Kenyans in the city to relatives in the countryside. So popular is M-Pesa that its transactions comprise 31 percent of Kenya's gross domestic product (GDP).[10] M-Pesa was launched by mobile telecommunications company Safaricom, which has 19 million customers in Kenya, 15 million of whom use M-Pesa.

Africa's vast number of mobile phone users, estimated at 700 million or 70 percent of the African population, and the lack of bank access for many, means that mobile phone payments are a promising growth area.[11] It shows how technology and economics converge to help developing countries leapfrog rich industrialized countries in some areas.

As low-cost smartphones expand their reach in the developing world, and companies such as Google begin to deliver free, high-speed, wireless Internet service through its "Project Loon" using aerial balloons, mobile Internet becomes another compelling advantage to mobile media.

read. The Disney Company, for example, is among the most profitable of major publicly owned media companies in the United States. And it is recognized for its quality entertainment products, including award-winning motion pictures, recorded music, and television (it owns the ABC television network and ESPN, the most profitable channel on television).

Critics claim, however, that financial pressures can lead media companies, especially publicly traded companies, to focus on the short term with decisions such as cutting costs or laying off staff, actions that may increase near-term profits but decrease the quality of a product such as news coverage. These profits may be immediate but not sustainable.

Critics also assert that consumers actually have fewer choices than we believe when it comes to media content, thanks in large part to the concentration of media ownership.

> **DISCUSSION QUESTIONS:** Imagine a media system that is entirely publicly funded and government run. What problems might arise with such a system, and how might programming be different?

CONCENTRATION OF MEDIA OWNERSHIP

Economies of scale have financial incentives for most companies. Strictly speaking, economy of scale refers to the decrease in unit manufacturing cost that results from mass production. Media enterprises can reduce costs and increase profit by becoming larger and reaching a larger market with their content. Of course, just getting bigger doesn't necessarily translate into greater economies of scale, but it is the basic reason behind a fundamental trend in media over the past half-century. Successful media enterprises have acquired, either through purchase or merger, other media enterprises and have thereby grown in size and scope. Newspaper companies have bought other newspaper companies; radio-station groups have bought other radio-station groups. Cross-media enterprises have acquired other media enterprises, sometimes extending internationally as well. The result is a media system that is increasingly large, multifaceted, and global in ownership. These companies compete with other large media enterprises and across international borders.

Some critics have argued that despite the possible economies of scale, media conglomerates and media monopolies (i.e., when only one media organization serves the public or community) have a significant downside. Greater concentration of ownership, or fewer owners owning more media, results in less diversity of media voices and the possible silencing of minority and non-mainstream views—a disservice to the public.

In his book *New Media Monopoly*, Ben H. Bagdikian, one of the most vocal critics of concentrated media ownership, presents evidence that during the 1990s, a small number of the country's largest corporations purchased more public communications power than ever before. In 1983, the biggest media merger to date was a $340 million deal involving the Gannett Company, the newspaper chain that bought Combined Communications Corporation, whose assets included billboards, newspapers, and broadcast stations. In 1996, Disney's acquisition of

Despite News Corporation's split into two separate companies in 2013, one focusing on entertainment and the other on publishing, both are still independently in the top tier of media conglomerates based on company value.

Capital Cities/ABC cost $19 billion. In 2001, AOL's acquisition of Time Warner dwarfed even this deal at $160 billion.

Although we have not seen deals of this size in the 2000s and 2010s, acquisitions typically continue to occur in the billions of dollars. These include cable provider Comcast's acquisition of NBCUniversal from parent company General Electric for $30 billion in 2009 and completed in 2013; Google's purchase of YouTube in October 2006 for $1.6 billion; and the McClatchy newspaper chain purchase of thirty-two Knight-Ridder newspapers in March 2006 for $4.5 billion.

These large companies, Bagdikian contends, have built a communications cartel within the United States, a group of independent businesses that collaborate to regulate production, pricing, and marketing of goods. This cartel controls industrial products such as gasoline, refrigerators, or clothing. But also at stake are the symbols—the words and images—that define and shape the culture and political agenda of the country. In other words, a cable provider such as Comcast, which in many markets is the sole provider, now also controls the content from its NBCUniversal media properties. Bagdikian writes,

> Aided by the digital revolution and the acquisition of subsidiaries that operate at every step in the mass communications process, from the creation of content to its delivery into the home, the communications cartel has exercised stunning influence over national legislation and government agencies, an influence whose scope and power would have been considered scandalous or illegal twenty years ago.

Bagdikian further notes that 99 percent of the daily newspapers in the United States are the only daily in their cities. Similarly, all but a few of the nation's cable systems are monopolies in their cities. Most of the country's commercial radio stations are part of national ownership groups, and just a half-dozen formats (e.g., all news, rock, hip-hop, adult contemporary, oldies, easy listening) define programming. The major commercial television networks and their local affiliates carry programs of essentially the same type all across the country. Looked at from this perspective, the media do not offer the diversity in content that one would expect, even as the number of TV or radio channels increase.

This system is called a **media oligopoly**, a marketplace in which media ownership and diversity are severely limited and the actions of any single media group affect its competitors substantially, including determining the content and price of media products for both consumers and advertisers.

Nine diversified media giants dominate the media worldwide (see foldout section at the back of this book). Many of these international conglomerates are themselves part of a larger company comprising nonmedia business interests or contain in their financial portfolio significant nonmedia commercial properties and investments. They include a wide range of media or channels of distribution. Note that three of the nine started as computer or technology companies and that Google didn't even exist until late 1998.

Each of these nine companies is responsible for much of what we see, hear, or read in traditional media or interact with on the Web. Of course, these are not the only media companies in the world: McChesney identifies a "second tier" of about fifty large media companies operating at the national or international level, each doing more than $1 billion of business a year. Any of these second-tier companies, in and of themselves, can be considered a huge media power with an array of business interests, although their revenues pale in comparison to the big nine.

media oligopoly

A marketplace in which media ownership and diversity are severely limited and the actions of any single media group affect its competitors substantially, including determining the content and price of media products for both consumers and advertisers.

Becoming literate about the concentration of media ownership and consolidation of media companies into ever-larger companies does not entail simply learning the inside scoop on who owns what. As Bagdikian, McChesney, and other scholars have indicated, the power that these media wield has serious political, societal, and cultural repercussions. If much of the media we consume comes from a handful of large conglomerates, it raises questions about the role that **media bias**, how information may be skewed toward a particular viewpoint, might play in forming our views of politics, society, and culture.

> **media bias**
>
> A real or perceived viewpoint held by journalists and news organizations that slants news coverage unfairly, contrary to professional journalism's stated goals of balanced coverage and objectivity.

> **DISCUSSION QUESTIONS:** Consider your level of media diversity by listing the types of shows you watch, material you read, and music you listen to. Trace three different media in this list back to their corporate parents. Classify your tastes into genres, and compare with someone else to assess the diversity of your media consumption.

Media Bias

Both the left and the right claim that the media, especially the news, are biased against them; and both sides can cite various examples in the media, in scholarly studies, and in popular books that supposedly prove their points. If the media make neither side happy, then they must be doing something right, some might say. Still, this rather glib response to an apparent paradox circumvents the very real issue of media bias and how to recognize it.

Professional journalism has a strong culture of what used to be called "objectivity" but is now referred to as "fairness and balance," or the professional duty to cover an issue so that all sides are presented accurately and justly. This also

Daytime TV shows such as *The Talk* can sometimes introduce formerly taboo or controversial social subjects to the public's attention.

means that professional news reporting should not reveal a journalist's personal views.

We tend to think of the news as objective—a belief supported by its media grammar, particularly the camera angles, lighting, distance between the subject and interviewer, sound, and intercut scenes that all affect our perceptions. The "objective point of view" in television news interviews treats the viewer as an observer. Typically, the camera is kept still, with shots over the shoulder of the journalist interviewing a subject. Prior to the interview, the journalist instructs the subject never to look directly into the camera, a privilege reserved for the news anchor or field reporter, who often summarizes or concludes her report in this manner that establishes eye contact with the audience. This grammar encourages the viewer to see significant differences between subject and reporter, specifically, the latter's greater authority and objectivity.

Any notion of objectivity or even balance in news coverage has been challenged for a number of reasons. Many question its very possibility. This becomes especially problematic with news stories that feature various groups who may not self-identify the same way they are identified by news organizations. A framing bias could affect a journalist's choice of terms, defining someone as a "terrorist" rather than "rebel," for example. Because most news is about some type of conflict and because conflicts often involve a disagreement over basic facts or even definitions of terms, news organizations often get caught in semantic battles.

Another criticism of the balanced approach is that in striving for balance, news organizations can simply become stenographers for opposing sides, dutifully reporting what each side says but never providing any context for readers or viewers, thus depriving the audience of relevant information. According to this view, news organizations would serve the public better if they provided more openly partisan commentary and critique on news events rather than trying to pretend they are above the fray and simply reporting from a fair and balanced perspective.

Finally, some question whether balance, even if it were attainable, is always even a worthy goal. W. Lance Bennett in *News: The Politics of Illusion* argues that giving various positions equal consideration in a debate can confer on them equal legitimacy when this may not be the case, leaving readers and audiences confused about whose views are more credible. (Who knows? After all, both sides had equal airtime.) Many believe, for example, that challenging knowable and empirical realities on purely political grounds only muddies the waters of what should remain a scientific debate.[12]

Media scholars on the left claim that the media are not biased to favor liberals but actually skew toward promoting conservative or at least corporate-friendly ideologies. Eric Alterman, author of *What Liberal Media? The Truth About Bias and the News*, argues that the constant refrain from conservative commentators about the media's liberal bias has made many media outlets present more conservative views than they would have otherwise. When representatives of the political left are enlisted to provide an opposing perspective, they are often much closer to the center than some equally qualified experts who may be more liberal, thus shifting the debate to the political right.

Media scholars also cite many examples of pro-business and pro-government bias in news coverage, regardless of the political party in office. Some were highly critical of the complacency of news organizations during George W. Bush's

ETHICS IN MEDIA
When Media Report Rape Allegations

Bill Cosby is a widely known media figure and comedian who in 2014 at age 77 was planning to make a career comeback. Cosby had been a popular entertainer and media celebrity since at least the 1960s with his successful TV series, *I, Spy*; his children's animated series, *Fat Albert*; and in the 1980s, *The Cosby Show*.

Then, just as Netflix was planning a comedy special commemorating his 77th birthday and NBC television network had scheduled a new Cosby pilot project, reports began circulating in the media and social media about allegations that Cosby had sexually assaulted women many years before. Although the cases never went to trial, with a number being settled quietly out of court, rumors remained in the air. Then, in autumn of 2014, a video by emerging comedian Hannibal Burress referring to the rape allegations against Cosby went viral.[13]

After that, the story snowballed in the mainstream media and beyond, especially once an Associated Press video interview showed Cosby refusing to address the allegations and even asking the reporter not to show any portion of the interview where he had been asked to comment.[14] Cosby's scheduled appearances were canceled on a variety of programs from David Letterman's *Late Show* to Queen Latifah's daytime talk variety series. The cable network TV Land even axed reruns of the esteemed *The Cosby Show*.

Dozens of women have, as of this writing, come forward to renew their allegations of sexual assault. Through his

A firestorm of criticism in the media has engulfed Bill Cosby, allegations that may recast the legacy of one of America's most venerable comics. **CRITICAL THINKING QUESTIONS**: Conduct a Google search on the topic of sexual assault or rape and Bill Cosby. Watch the Hannibal Burress viral video that catapulted long-heard rumors into the limelight. Do these reports unfairly damage the reputation of a leading black man? Or do they finally give voice to women victimized by a rich and powerful celebrity? Should the media report on allegations that the legal system has not vetted?

lawyer, however, Cosby maintains that the charges are baseless and that the media are irresponsible to repeat such false accusations.

administration as Republican leaders made their case to invade Iraq, which turned out to have neither weapons of mass destruction, as the administration claimed, nor a role in the Al Qaeda attacks on September 11. They also point to coverage of the financial crisis in 2008 that left fundamental issues leading to the crisis largely unquestioned. If media organizations truly had a liberal bias, they say, then there would have been greater critical reporting on such events and more discussion about reforms rather than the considerable parroting of political and corporate elites that took place with few proposals for systemic changes.

Media bias occurs not only in news stories, however. Entertainment media play an important role in propagating stereotypes and demonizing certain behaviors. They can also normalize people and activities too. Popular daytime talk shows featuring formerly taboo subjects, ranging from transgender children to domestic violence, can help make discussion of such issues more acceptable, which can in turn lead to these subjects appearing on television shows or dramas, thus becoming even further embedded in our popular culture landscape.

Similarly, advertising can play a role in propagating certain stereotypes or in promoting cultural norms, which has drawn criticism from some groups. In 2013, a Cheerios ad depicting an interracial couple with their child generated thousands of complaints and negative comments in social media from those who considered the portrayal of a black husband and a white wife offensive. Children, on the other hand, saw nothing wrong with the commercial when asked.[15]

Understanding how media bias may affect our thinking and common-sense assumptions about the world is an important aspect of media literacy. Next, we will discuss how to develop media-literacy skills that improve our critical thinking.

> **DISCUSSION QUESTIONS:** For one day, note how many Facebook posts you see expressing conservative political views, how many presenting liberal views, and how many dealing with pop culture or entertainment. How might the results influence your views of the world and news?

Developing Critical Media-Literacy Skills

One assumption underlying criticisms of media bias and media effects is that the public is largely passive and accepts unquestioningly the media it consumes. However, audience research has shown that audiences can be quite active in interpreting and using media. Media-literacy skills help us become more engaged and aware media consumers and producers as we learn to think critically about what we receive and transmit.

We have looked at basic media-literacy skills in the form of understanding media framing and bias, as well as the role of media grammars. More advanced critical media-literacy skills help us question our fundamental assumptions about media and think about it in alternative ways.

Here, we provide a brief guide on how to think critically about media you encounter. These skills can be applied in varying degrees with any media, ranging from advertisements to movies, news, and even video games.

1. **What is the purpose of the media content?** Is the purpose to persuade, inform, or entertain? How might the media be working across these functions, perhaps in hidden ways? For example, an advertisement's main purpose may be to persuade you to buy a product, but it may also entertain and inform while doing so. A news story may be presented as primarily informative, but the nature of the story may also persuade audiences to adopt a new position or confirm their existing assumptions about the world.

2. **Consider the source of the media.** Is the news story coming from a media organization known for its political views on either the left or the right? If the source is not a well-known media company but a blogger, examine the types of organizations the blogger links to for a sense of his or her likely political views. Most websites and blogs link to other sites whose views reflect their own.

3. **Examine framing of media content.** How might the choice of words affect how media consumers perceive the information? How could

alternative words possibly change the overall impression of what was written? In news stories, who is interviewed, who is treated as an expert and what organizations do they work for, and how are they framed within the stories? Who is quoted earliest in the story, and who is quoted more often?

4. **What stereotypes are presented?** It takes practice to question stereotypes that appear so frequently they seem natural. One way to challenge your thinking about portrayals of other groups in the media is to consider what you would think if you or your group were portrayed that way. Would you agree with that representation or stereotype? Would you be offended?

5. **Question the media ecosystem.** Identify and question stereotypes as reflected in the media environment or community of channels both online and off (i.e., the media ecosystem). Think about whom the stereotypes help and whom they harm. Is a group or organization profiting in some way from promoting harmful stereotypes, and does the stereotyped group have the same access to media as the dominant group? If not, why not?

CONVERGENCE CULTURE
Dos and Don'ts When Evaluating Online Information

The Internet is full of hoaxes, cranks, scams, and cons. The up-to-the-minute, 24/7 nature of news online and via social media and its low-cost distribution make the Web an ideal place for misinformation to spread quickly because facts cannot always be quickly verified. Adding to the confusion are hacking attacks, such as the 2013 cyberattack on *The New York Times*'s website that prevented many users from accessing the site.[16] The cyberattack was carried out by the Syrian Electronic Army, which also attacked Twitter, disabling the social media outlet and posting false information.

How do you know when you are being fed a line when online?

- Check the About Us section of a website to get background information on who runs it. Do the site's operators identify their mission, their principles, and their sponsors, or do they seem evasive and unclear?
- Scan the sites they link to on a Useful Links page. Most websites link to others who share their views or similar beliefs.
- Compare the information on the website with similar stories on other websites, both from branded news names and from smaller sites. If a well-known or respected group has made an important and relevant announcement, the organization's website should post that information as well.

- Question the name of the organization that owns the website. Lobbying groups and other organizations trying to push a specific agenda will often adopt names that mask their true goals or cast them in a euphemistic light, or they will create front groups to hide behind. SourceWatch, a project of the Center for Media and Democracy, is one good website for learning more about the names behind the organizations that appear in the news.
- Do not immediately trust information that lacks a date somewhere on the page. Information that may have been accurate when first posted may well be out of date when you visit the site.
- Cautiously consider information you read from discussion groups, chat rooms, blogs, and tweets, even if the person posting claims to be an expert on the subject. Try to confirm the information with another source, and examine the speaker's academic or professional credentials through a quick Google search. As the famous *New Yorker* cartoon of a dog sitting at a computer talking to another dog said, "On the Internet, nobody knows you're a dog." In the Internet age, that dog could be just about anywhere or anyone in the world.

What kind of media might the stereotyped group produce if it had equal access to media production and distribution?

6. **Make the media.** Learning media production skills beyond writing is invaluable for media literacy as well as for the job market, especially for communications professions. Reconstructing a commercial, a music video, or even a news program from an alternative perspective is an excellent way to challenge your assumptions about the presentation of media and their messages.

MEDIA CAREERS

Careers in the media are in transition as jobs evolve and new occupations emerge. According to Alissa Quart, senior editor at *The Atavist*, one of the most important new media career paths is in the area of social justice. These journalists contribute to media literacy by researching and writing on the often complex topics of criminal justice, income inequality, and race, gender, and class. Reporting on these sensitive matters requires both a good sense of societal concerns and strong critical thinking skills. Leading media organizations such as *The New York Times* have recently hired inequality editors and reporters, and more such positions are in the offing around the nation and the world.

LOOKING BACK AND MOVING FORWARD

Media literacy is not a goal to reach but an ongoing process; skills can always be improved to become a better mass-media consumer, user, and participant. Media literacy involves thinking critically about the media and questioning how different media organizations may be biased in of their selection of stories, their coverage of stories, and even their choice of whom to quote in interviews or invite to speak in panel discussions.

Entertainment media also have biases and can propagate ethnic and gender stereotypes. We may be unaware of the commercial forces that shape the content, largely because we see the end product and not the processes behind the scenes that created the media product.

Consider how commercial forces may not always have the best interests of the public at heart, even when media companies claim they are serving the public or simply giving people what they want. Digital and social media present both an opportunity and a threat for the media and communication industries.

Longstanding corporations, institutions, and entire industries are being turned upside down by the digital revolution. Businesses built on analog technologies of production and distribution are trying to figure out how to adapt in the digital age. New efficiencies of creating and delivering content in a digital, networked environment are emerging throughout the world. Long-held, highly profitable business models based on analog technology are less viable in a digital marketplace. Changes in our media environment also create a greater need for media literacy, especially in the digital realm.

The problem of dealing with the enormous amounts of information available to us, **information overload**, affects everything from government agencies being able to act rapidly on intelligence they have gathered to workers being able to share relevant knowledge within companies.

Some say information overload has also affected the quality of students' work and even their basic understanding of how to research and synthesize information to create new ideas. Some college students submit research papers that are simply cut-and-paste pastiches of material taken from different websites—sometimes without even changing original font styles. Even students who realize that this is not actually the correct way to write a paper can have a hard time discerning trustworthy sources of information on the Web.

Some people claim that the constant interruptions typically seen in the workplace have hampered productivity and creativity, with tasks taking longer to complete than in the past and workers feeling less able to concentrate for the extended periods required to tackle complex problems. Email is a major culprit in information overload, but the rise of social media has no doubt contributed to today's frequent interruptions.

Nevertheless, the new digital world means new business opportunities. It means opening new markets formerly restricted by political, economic, and geographic boundaries. It means new storytelling formats that bring true interactivity to media. Whether these fresh opportunities will enhance media diversity remains to be seen. The continued concentration of media ownership suggests that the big media companies threatened by the digital shift are starting to regain control of the media environment.

The rise of user-generated content and social media directly challenges traditional media companies who commanded the public's attention throughout most of the twentieth century. The ways the public is creating media, often on nonmarket principles and simply for the joy of sharing and interacting with others, belie the notion that the public is as happy with its mainstream media content as media conglomerates would have us believe.

As some people are discovering, profits do not necessarily have to proceed from the sale of packaged media products such as bestselling books. Seth Godin, a noted author on Internet advertising and marketing, makes his books freely available for download on the Internet. What would appear to be the fast track to the poorhouse is Godin's successful strategy to get his books in the hands of many influential people, including business leaders and conference organizers, who then invite him (and pay him well) to speak at events and conferences.

Companies sustain their efforts to keep the public satiated with (and paying for) a never-ending stream of media content that maintains the primarily one-way flow of content from media producer to audience. Scholars such as McChesney doubt the Internet will become a transformational communication technology that can improve democracy and better engage citizens. Whether this occurs or not will depend largely on how media literate the public becomes and how well we develop our moral reasoning and ethical thinking to create the kind of society we want to live in, not just have to live in.

💬 **information overload**

The difficulties associated with managing and making sense of the vast amounts of information available to us.

Critics contend that Apple deliberately deleted songs from users' iPods if they had been downloaded from competitors' services.

MEDIA MATTERS   TESTING YOUR MEDIA LITERACY

You may consider yourself media literate and technologically savvy because you have grown up surrounded by traditional and digital media. But media literacy entails much more than being able to tweet or recalling all the movies in which your favorite actor has appeared. See what you know and what you can find out to determine some of what media literacy involves.

1. Consider a current popular movie that you have seen. Discuss some of its ethnic, religious, gender, or other stereotypes, and consider why they appear. Do they have any consequences for the groups stereotyped?

2. Working in a small group, describe your favorite genre of music (e.g., hip-hop, rock, country) without using the name of the genre, the titles of any songs, or the names of popular artists. Do not hum or imitate the music style. See who can figure out the genre first. Why do you think it was so hard for you to explain without explicitly naming the genre, the songs, or the artists?

3. What visual elements do you normally associate with television news? Compare your list with that of your classmates, and then discuss how and why you think these visual elements came to define the format called "news."

4. In what ways may an advertiser influence the news, if at all?

5. Do you consider information from a blog or tweet or via a mobile device more or less trustworthy than material found on an organization's website? Why do you think so? How do you decide what information to trust online?

6. Do a Web search for the top ten movies of the past year, and note what genres they fall into (e.g., action, thriller, romantic comedy). Why do you think some genres seem more popular than others?

7. Would you sign a petition in support of tort reform that limits the amount people can sue companies via frivolous lawsuits? What about a petition against the Corporate Immunity Act, which would prevent litigants from fully recovering the damages inflicted on them by corporate wrongdoing? What is the difference between these two?

FURTHER READING

Media Literacy, 6th ed. W. James Potter (2012) Sage Publications.

Approaches to Media Literacy: A Handbook, 2nd ed. Art Silverblatt, Jane Ferry, Barbara Finan (2009) M. E. Sharpe.

Digital and Media Literacy: Connecting Culture and Classroom. Renee Hobbs (2011) Corwin Press.

The New Media Monopoly. Ben H. Bagdikian (2004) Beacon Press.

The Political Economy of Media: Enduring Issues, Emerging Dilemmas. Robert W. McChesney (2008) Monthly Review Press.

Digital Disconnect: How Capitalism Is Turning the Internet Against Democracy. Robert McChesney (2013) The New Press.

The Problem of the Media: U.S. Communication Politics in the Twenty-First Century. Robert McChesney (2004) Monthly Review Press.

Jamming the Media: A Citizen's Guide to Reclaiming the Tools of Communication. Gareth Branwyn (1997) Chronicle Books.

Citizen Muckraking: How to Investigate and Right Wrongs in Your Community. The Center for Public Integrity (2000) Common Courage Media.

The Conquest of Cool: Business Culture, Counterculture, and the Rise of Hip Consumerism. Thomas Frank (1997) University of Chicago Press.

Convergence Culture: Where Old and New Media Collide. Henry Jenkins (2008) NYU Press.

New Media, Old Media: A History and Theory Reader. Wendy Hui Kyong Chun, Thomas Keenan (2007) Taylor & Francis.

The Filter Bubble: How the New Personalized Web Is Changing What We Read and How We Think. Eli Pariser (2012) Penguin Books.

The Wealth of Networks: How Social Production Transforms Markets and Freedom. Yochai Benkler (2007) Yale University Press.

Bodies in Code: Interfaces with Digital Media. Mark Hansen (2007) Routledge.

News: The Politics of Illusion. Lance Bennett (2012) Longman.

3

Print Media
BOOKS, NEWSPAPERS, AND MAGAZINES

A Justice Department announcement in April 2012 had several of the biggest book publishers shaking in their boots—and others shaking their heads.

A government antitrust suit accused Apple and five major publishers of colluding to set 2010 prices of ebooks so no publisher could undercut Apple. When Amazon's Kindle was practically the sole ebook reader, ebooks typically cost $9.99, a price that jumped to $14.99 after Apple's iPad, which could also perform the same function, debuted. The publishers—HarperCollins, Hachette, Macmillan, Penguin, and Simon & Schuster—settled with the government, while Apple has continued to fight the suit. In July 2014, however, without admitting wrongdoing, Apple agreed to settle a class-action lawsuit from states and consumers with a payout of up to $400 million dollars, subject to further appeals.[1]

Amazon controls about 67 percent of the ebook market worldwide.[2] An already tense relationship with publishers soured further when Amazon, formerly a retailer of ebooks, entered the publishing business and became a direct competitor. The government suit claims that publishers worked clandestinely with Apple to promote non-Kindle ebooks to break Amazon's near monopoly on ebooks through its Kindle reader.

Ironically, the antitrust suit actually strengthens Amazon's position, replacing a perceived monopoly with an actual one. A commanding position in ebooks allows Amazon to absorb losses on sales as it attracts more Kindle buyers and locks in the market. Yet supporters of the book-publishing industry, including many bookstore owners, are not persuaded that Amazon's monopoly is good in the long run, as competition provides incentive for such a company to continue to innovate and to maintain low prices.

At the heart of the matter here is a classic confrontation between a traditional business model—in this case, book publishing—and a bold new competitor that wants to encourage reading while adapting to new distribution methods and pricing models.

LEARNING OBJECTIVES

>> Describe the general functions of print media, and distinguish between books, newspapers, and magazines.

>> Trace the historical development of print media.

>> Explain current business issues affecting the industries for each print medium.

>> Outline the financial model for each print medium, including sales, circulation, readership, and distribution as well as the transition to digital business models.

>> Identify forces—including political, cultural, economic, technological—likely to affect the future of the print media.

Print media are arguably facing some of the biggest challenges from digital media, ranging from declines in advertising revenues to changing patterns of reading among the public. Print will continue, however, to play an important role in the media landscape—even when text is read in electronic form.

Representing the beginning of mass communication, print media originated in the typographical era of the Middle Ages. Mass forms of mechanical printing and typography contributed to sweeping social transformation in Europe, including mass literacy and the Renaissance. Adapting to such technological change challenged society—a recurring problem encountered by subsequent ages. In 1962, noted communication theorist Marshall McLuhan claimed the following about electronic media in *The Gutenberg Galaxy*, an observation that applies equally to the digital age: "We are today as far into the electric age as the Elizabethans had advanced into the typographical and mechanical age. And we are experiencing the same confusions and indecisions which they had felt when living simultaneously in two contrasted forms of society and experience."

McLuhan, among others, argues that the medium of the printed word has even changed the way we think. Reading lets us ponder. We can reread and rethink passages of written text, developing responses in ways simply unavailable with the spoken word. If, as scholars claim, the print format promotes critical-thinking skills and refined, logical arguments, it raises questions regarding the effects on our abilities to think logically and critically as we read less and consume more audio or video digital media.

> **DISCUSSION QUESTIONS:** Do the Internet and the digital media age constitute a media revolution as far-reaching as that brought on by the printing press? Identify some societal and technological similarities and differences between now and the mid-1400s to support your argument.

Functions of Print Media

Print media, in the form of books, newspapers, and magazines, serve many overlapping social functions. Among the most important are cultural transmission from generation to generation, the diffusion of ideas and knowledge, and entertainment.

TRANSMISSION OF CULTURE

Media, in all their forms, teach us the language, values, and traditions of a culture. Although not the sole means of transmitting culture, books, newspapers, and magazines convey what society considers right or wrong, acceptable or unacceptable. Reading often introduces immigrants and children to societal rules and norms. Ancient religious texts such as the Bible, the Koran, or the Torah have successfully imparted cultural mores and values for centuries.

DIFFUSION OF IDEAS AND KNOWLEDGE

Education in particular transmits culture, and books are central to lifelong formal and informal education. Textbooks and other works of nonfiction impart everything from philosophical theory to psychological self-help, teaching us not only how to do things but also how to understand and appreciate the arts, literature, history, contemporary society, and the social and natural sciences.

Newspapers and magazines inform us of and interpret the latest events so that we can make sense of the world. Here we read about recent foreign events as well as new discoveries, fashions, and trends. Special-interest magazines feature particular fields or hobbies, knowledge that helps us connect with others who share our interests.

ENTERTAINMENT

Sometimes we read for specific knowledge; sometimes we read for the sheer joy of it. The printed page can offer escape or diversion, allowing us to travel to exotic places or distant planets where we encounter fantastic creatures and memorable people. Popular books often become the basis for films or cable series, such as *Game of Thrones*. A film version of a favorite novel may disappoint, though, because the locations and characters fail to resemble what we originally imagined.

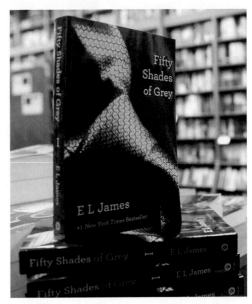

Comic books and picture books, providing young readers with some of their first adventures in reading, are designed to entertain. Short stories, nonfiction magazine articles, and books can both engage and inform, however. As their literacy skills develop, children advance to early reader books such as *The Cat in the Hat* by Dr. Seuss, chapter books such as *Charlotte's Web* by E.B. White, young-adult (YA) fiction such as *To Kill a Mockingbird* by Harper Lee, and nonfiction such as *The Diary of a Young Girl* by Anne Frank.

Accessing the thoughts of the ancients through their texts may allow us to find commonalities across centuries. Great literature can elevate our senses and make us feel new emotions as characters come to life. Readers who may not otherwise know or care about our legal system or our military intelligence can, nevertheless, learn much from legal thrillers such as *An Innocent Client* by Scott Pratt in the Joe Dillard series or military action stories such as *Tom Clancy: Support and Defend* by Mark Greaney, who is continuing the popular Jack Ryan series started by author Tom Clancy.

An enduring source of entertainment for young and old alike, some books subsequently become the basis for feature films. **CRITICAL THINKING QUESTIONS:** Think of movies you may have seen after reading the book. Were you pleased or disappointed with the film version? Why was this the case?

Still, some recent studies indicate a drop in this activity, with only 67 percent of Americans sixteen and older reporting that they read paper books, down from 72 percent in 2011. Meanwhile, ebook reading is growing rapidly, with almost half of readers under thirty saying they had read an e-book in the previous twelve months.[3]

Distinctive Functions of Books

Even before books existed in the form that we know today, compiling comprehensive knowledge in a single document was considered a vital, even sacred, endeavor. Historically, religious texts have shaped beliefs and worldviews so profoundly that wars continue to erupt over conflicting doctrine.

Staged book burnings attest to the social and cultural significance of books throughout history and right up to today. Consider, for example, the violent protests in Afghanistan after members of a Florida church burned copies of the

Islamic State militants have sought to purge cities they've invaded in Iraq and Syria of books, antiquities, and other artifacts that do not conform to their extremist interpretations of Islam.

Koran, the Muslim holy book, in March 2011. Some groups have burned books they believe corrupt children, including those widely considered classics. Texts have been banned for sexual content or political messages critical of the government. Although more common in the early-to-mid-twentieth century, this still occurs, as when Lebanon banned the controversial 2003 novel *The Da Vinci Code*.

Textbooks, although intended primarily to impart objective knowledge, can express values through omission as much as inclusion. Whether high school science textbooks should discuss both evolution and creationism is still a subject of heated debate in the United States. China and Korea censure Japanese history textbooks that either ignore or euphemize Japan's World War II military atrocities. Purported cultural values of books written to entertain can also stir controversy. The Harry Potter book series by J. K. Rowling has been criticized for not featuring stronger female characters in central roles and even for promoting witchcraft.

These examples demonstrate the book's enduring cultural relevance and authority in the digital age. Newspapers and magazines neither present the same sense of established knowledge and compiled wisdom nor allow for the unfolding of long or complex stories. The growing popularity of e-readers attests to the important role that books still play in our lives.

History of Books to Today

codex

Manuscript book of individually bound pages.

Since the Sumerians of 3500 BCE pressed marks into wet clay tablets, creating what some scholars consider the first book form, authors have been recording textual narratives. By 2500 BCE, writers in western Asia were using animal skins as scrolls, a more portable form than clay tablets. The ancient Egyptians wrote the *Book of the Dead* in 1800 BCE on papyrus. Between the first century BCE and the sixth century CE, the **codex**, a manuscript of bound individual pages, began replacing the scroll, establishing the modern book form. Book publishing continued to evolve through innovation and invention: block printing in China by 600 CE; movable copper-alloy type in Korea in 1234 CE; and the Western world's first mechanical printing press in Germany in 1455 CE.

MONASTIC SCRIBES

Until the invention of printing, books had to be laboriously copied by hand. In the Middle Ages, specially trained monks, or scribes, copied religious and classical works in monastic writing rooms called scriptoria. Largely dedicated to promoting the ideas of the Christian Church, many books in this era were written in beautiful calligraphy and were richly illustrated.

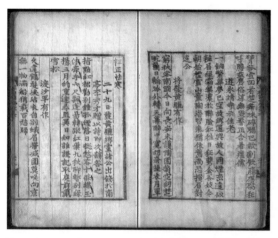

Korean copper-alloy type was the first printing to use metal plates, hundreds of years before Gutenberg's European press.

Early books were published in scroll format and then codexes. Until paper arrived from China via the Middle East in the later

Middle Ages, European scribes wrote on parchment or vellum made from treated hides of goats, sheep, or calves. Because copying and illustrating by hand were extremely time-consuming, and creating parchment was expensive, books were generally not widespread before the end of the Middle Ages.

JOHANNES GUTENBERG

The Christian Church grew in Europe along with the need for religious texts. In 1455 CE, this need inspired **Johannes Gutenberg** (1400–ca. 1468) to invent printing with lead, using movable type, and pressing oil-based ink on paper with a converted wine press.

Born to an upper-class merchant family in Mainz, Germany, Gutenberg met the silversmith Prokop Waldvogel in Avignon in 1444 who taught the craft of "artificial writing," as early printmaking was called. In 1450, Gutenberg formed a partnership with the wealthy Mainz burgher Johann Fust to complete his own printing invention and to print the famous **Gutenberg Bible**, or "forty-two-line Bible," whose 1455 publication is considered the beginning of mechanical printing.[4]

Despite the advent of new printing technology, the handmade tradition continued. Books were still bound by hand, and illustrators embellished printed pages with drawings and artistic flourishes to match the expectations for handwritten manuscripts. Combining a printing press with existing bookbinding technology enabled mass production at a fraction of the time and cost of an equal number of hand copies. Religious and cultural centers of Europe initially welcomed the printing press with enthusiasm.

Johannes Gutenberg

German printer credited with creating the first mechanical printing press in 1455.

Gutenberg Bible

Bible printed by Johannes Gutenberg in Europe in 1455, considered one of the first mechanically printed works.

The Gutenberg Bible, like most books of the period, had lavish hand-colored illustrations alongside the printed text.

Noah Webster is most famous for his dictionary, but he also published a grammatical textbook used widely throughout much of the nineteenth century.

💬 **dime novel**

First paperback form whose cost of ten cents made it accessible even to the poor.

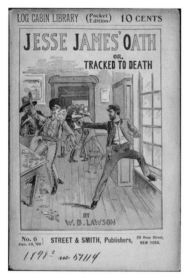

Dime novels, relatively affordable paperbacks that first appeared in 1860, made a range of tales accessible to an increasingly literate public.

BEGINNINGS OF MASS COMMUNICATION AND MASS LITERACY

Critical to the growth of Renaissance culture, the printing press spread scientific discoveries and religious beliefs—some of which challenged the authority of the Catholic Church. Many books copied by scribes, especially scientific works, were printed in Latin, effectively reducing readership to elites educated in the classics. Printers rapidly discovered that books and broadsheets printed in local common languages (the vernacular) found an eager audience as more common people learned to read. Books had left the quiet monastic scriptoria and entered the bustling commercial world of printmakers and the average person.

Despite this increase in printed materials from the Renaissance onward, literacy was not universal. Most Europeans and Americans remained illiterate until the nineteenth century. In colonial America, education was available largely to the wealthy, who could afford to hire and house private tutors for their children. Textbooks played a crucial role in the increased public education of the early 1800s that helped reduce illiteracy among the general population.

One of the first textbooks in America, the *New England Primer*, published initially circa 1690 by Benjamin Harris, introduced children to the English alphabet, the rudiments of reading, and basic Christian values. In 1783, Noah Webster, known today for *Webster's Dictionary*, wrote *A Grammatical Institute of the English Language*, a response to the popular textbooks imported from England that conveyed English cultural values. Known popularly as the "Blue Back Speller," Webster's textbook provided tutorials on language, religion, morals, and domestic economy. McGuffey Readers, first published in 1836, became standard reading books for schoolchildren throughout the nineteenth century.

Nineteenth-century textbooks, like modern ones, reflect contemporary social mores. Issues such as slavery and racism were not challenged. Today, textbook content on topics such as evolution and the Civil War is debated. To appeal to the widest cross section of society, textbooks tend to avoid controversial subjects, embracing perspectives and knowledge generally agreed on within the dominant group.

CHEAPER AND SMALLER BOOKS

Successful publishing has always been driven by wider distribution and lower production costs. The printing press and digital books—and all the trends in between—appeared as a result of these forces. Wider distribution of a popular book, usually one that entertains, is one way to make money; lower prices that make the book affordable for many is another. The dime novel and, later, mass-market paperbacks, satisfied both these criteria.

Dime Novels

Accessible to even the poor, the **dime novel** sold for ten cents, as its name suggests. In 1860, Irwin P. Beadle & Company introduced this first paperback book, which initially featured stories of Indians and nationalistic pioneer tales. Ann S. Stephens wrote the first dime novel, *Malaeska: The Indian Wife of the White Hunter*. Within a year of publication, *Malaeska* had sold more than three hundred thousand copies. By the 1870s, dime novels included melodramatic fiction, adventures, detective stories, romances, and rags-to-riches tales.

Mass-Market Paperbacks

In 1939, Robert de Graff's company, Pocket Books, introduced **mass-market paperbacks** in the United States, a line of plastic-laminated books adorned with its familiar kangaroo mascot, Gertrude, priced at twenty-five cents and sized small enough for a back pocket. The paperback revolution stemmed from offering books in places such as drugstores and supermarkets, a mass-distribution network alternative to established bookstores.

The post-World War II baby boomers, who became the students of the 1950s and 60s, were dubbed "the paperback generation." They were raised on Dr. Benjamin Spock's best-selling paperback *Dr. Spock's Baby and Child Care* and influenced by paperbacks such as J. D. Salinger's *Catcher in the Rye* and Kurt Vonnegut's *Slaughterhouse Five*.

Print-on-Demand

One interesting development in printing that began in the late 1990s is **print-on-demand (POD)**. High-quality color laser printing and binding machines can print a single book in a few minutes at a fraction of the traditional cost with tiny print runs that can make available and affordable books otherwise difficult or impossible to obtain.

POD enables writers to publish using low-cost printers and sell their paperbacks online or even in some bookstores. The combination of low-cost, digital, and online technologies has released a flood of POD and ebooks published by authors in recent years. In 2013, over 458,000 books were self-published, a 437-percent increase since 2008, with ebook publishing dropping slightly and print books rising 29 percent over the year before.[5] Industry watchers claim that this shows how the self-publishing industry is maturing and how printed books are still very relevant for self-published authors. A growing number of POD publishers, such as Xlibris, Virtual Bookworm, and Lulu Publishing, publish books for as little as $400, not including editing or other potential costs for an author.

In 2002, the Internet Archive (www.archive.org) formed a group dedicated to digitizing and archiving all kinds of media. In its first year, the Internet Bookmobile, a Ford minivan with a computer and a POD printer, toured U.S. cities giving people access to more than twenty thousand public domain books in its digital

mass-market paperback

Inexpensive, softcover books small enough for a back pocket and sold in bookstores, supermarkets, drugstores, and other public places.

print-on-demand (POD)

Publication of single books or tiny print runs based on customer demand using largely automated, nontraditional book-printing methods such as the color laser printer.

Brewster Kahle, Internet Archive founder, has built a vast digital library of more than 1 million public domain books, all available for free download to any Internet-connected computer or mobile device.

archive, all available in minutes and at a fraction of bookstore costs. The Internet Archive hoped it might prove a cost-effective option for libraries tasked with pursuing late books and reshelving them.

Ebooks

Ebooks offer various advantages over printed books, permitting us not only to read text but also to make electronic annotations and bookmarks and to search via an interactive table of contents or by keyword. In the late 1990s, major publishers, preparing for a surge in consumer demand, experimented with the online sale and distribution of ebooks. Despite a slowdown in the growth of self-published ebooks, mainstream publishers are still betting on the growth of the ebook market.

INTERNATIONAL PERSPECTIVES
Global Ebook Marketplace

While the American public has been hungry for ebooks since 2008, the digital appetite has been smaller internationally, where only some 20 percent of ebook sales occur. In European countries such as Germany, Spain, France, and Sweden, ebooks accounted for just 1 percent of total book sales in 2011. Two years later, according to Statista.com, the ebook market share in Europe rose to 4.5 percent, with a projection of 21 percent by 2017. In other parts of the world less economically developed and less literate, including much of Latin America, Asia, and Africa, ebook sales have been virtually nonexistent.

Yet some organizations, such as O'Reilly Media, report that ebooks are poised to take off globally. In Europe, sales of the Amazon Kindle have been rising as

Digital e-readers enable ebooks and other content to be displayed in a variety of languages and alphabets.

e-reader prices decline. In the United Kingdom, the 2010 arrival of the Amazon Kindle unleashed pent-up demand. Within nine months, ebooks were outselling hardcover print. In 2011, Amazon introduced the Kindle to Germany, France, Spain, and Italy. Apple reported in 2010 that sales of its Italian iBooks skyrocketed from 150 to 1,000 copies a day within the first four days on sale.

By 2013, demand had increased with the simultaneous release of most new ebook titles in multiple languages. In addition, geographical licensing restrictions had relaxed while navigating ebook copyright law—a complex dance among authors, agents, publishers and distributors—had become easier.

Ebook cost has dampened international growth, however. Outside the United States, the average price in 2010 of a newly published ebook was $14, plus taxes, compared to an American sticker price of $7.72. And in the potentially huge market in China, with one-sixth of the world's population, ebooks have been an especially tough sell. Many Chinese read on their phone using "online literature" platforms such as Cloudary where user-generated content dominates. Moreover, digital publishing, like publishing in general, is controlled by the government, which has entered the market cautiously.

Nevertheless, as these various and diverse challenges are met, the global demand for ebooks is expected to rise dramatically, particularly in Japan, South Korea, and China, with sales of nearly a billion total ebooks expected by 2016 in those three countries.[6]

The 2007 launch of Amazon's Kindle ebook reader was heralded as the latest technological breakthrough, a potential tipping point toward digital. Older Kindle models with 4 GB of memory can store up to 3,500 titles, according to Amazon; whereas the Kindle Fire, with 8 GB, can store 7,000 titles—along with allowing movie viewing, listening to music, and playing games. Penguin Random House, Simon & Schuster, HarperCollins, and other major publishers have embraced ebook readers such as the Kindle, the Sony Reader, and Barnes & Noble's Nook, making many more titles available digitally. Free sample chapters and other marketing techniques have promoted growth, as have improvements in hardware, such as screen clarity and greater storage. Popular tablets, including the iPad and Kindle Fire, have also expanded the market, blurring the distinction between an exclusively ebook reader and a multifunctional entertainment device that includes ebook functions.

Current Book-Industry Issues

In 2013, the book-publishing industry's annual worldwide value was $151 billion, the largest sector among media entertainment and publishing industries.[7] U.S. net revenues were $27.01 billion, essentially showing no growth from 2012.[8] Despite an enormous global market, tremendous consolidation of worldwide industry ownership has impacted the diversity of book titles and perspectives.

At least three significant trends affect book publishing. First, industry mergers and consolidation enable publishers to increase profit margins by reducing operating costs associated with warehousing, marketing, and sales. Increased size also means more leverage with dominant retail giants Barnes & Noble and Amazon.com in negotiations that include obtaining prominent display locations in bookstores and on the Web.

Traditional publishing companies, however, increasingly see Amazon as a competitor: partly because of its dominance in the independent publishing and ebook sectors, with 65 percent of the ebook trade, and partly because it insists on setting ebook prices lower than what traditional publishers would like to charge for some titles. Conflicts between publishers and Amazon arose because they could not agree on the percentage of sales that a distributor like Amazon should get; and Amazon's creation of a subscription model for ebooks, Kindle Unlimited, also challenged traditional methods of book sales (and authors' royalties, leading to many complaints among authors).

Second, the book-publishing industry is intertwined with global media and the entertainment industry. Increasingly, profits for the biggest publishers are derived from technology products and services, such as electronic databases and educational testing. Some books are published and subsequently adapted or licensed for film or TV and other entertainment sectors, such as video games.

Third, the emergence of online booksellers, ebooks, and on-demand printing is transforming sales and distribution, growth that renders an uncertain future for traditional brick-and-mortar bookstores and even the power of traditional publishers to set prices. Amazon.com, bn.com, and others are capturing a rising percentage of total book sales, even as they dominate ebook sales. Mega-bookstores such as Borders and warehouse shopping outlets selling discounted books were thought to have the needed economies of scale to compete with online enterprises. Yet in July 2011, Borders, the second biggest bookstore chain in the United States, closed all its stores after filing for bankruptcy several months earlier. Independent bookstores are also suffering. Even large ones like Portland-based Powell's have laid off employees, one of many changes implemented to cope with consumer change.

Based on annual revenue in 2013, Thomson Reuters, after acquiring news giant Reuters and selling its textbook division in 2007, is now third to Pearson, after second-ranked Reed Elsevier. This is a clear example of the way mergers and digital media are affecting the publishing industry, for Thomson earns the majority of its revenue from electronic databases and not printed books or journals. Thomson Reuters maintains headquarters in New York, but its parent corporation is actually in Canada.

McGraw-Hill Education is the top-ranked U.S. company, ranking tenth in the world in 2013, followed by Scholastic in eleventh place, and Wiley in twelfth. Only seven of the top fifty-six book publishers worldwide have their parent company headquartered in the United States, although several have joint Canadian/U.S. or European/U.S. ownership.[9] Overseas companies (Bertelsmann, based in Germany, and Pearson, based in England) jointly own familiar publishers such as Random House and Penguin, which merged in 2013.[10]

Sales and Readership of Books

For more than twenty years, the patterns of book sales have been unsteady. The industry has grown slightly overall, but total revenue has varied by a few

FIGURE 3-1   Book Publishing Products and Services Segmentation

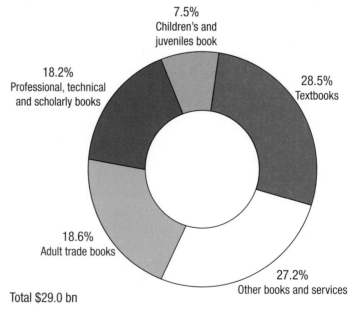

7.5%
Children's and juveniles book

18.2%
Professional, technical and scholarly books

28.5%
Textbooks

18.6%
Adult trade books

27.2%
Other books and services

Total $29.0 bn

Source: IBISWorld.com, 2015

FIGURE 3-2 Book Publishing Industry Revenue Growth, 2009–2014
(in billions of dollars)

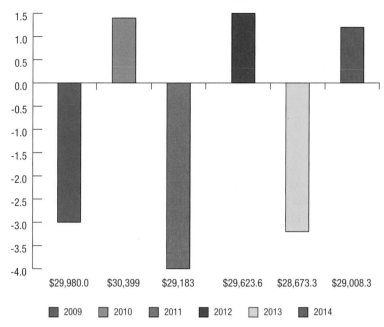

$29,980.0	$30,399	$29,183	$29,623.6	$28,673.3	$29,008.3

■ 2009   ■ 2010   ■ 2011   ■ 2012   □ 2013   ■ 2014

Source: IBISWorld.com, 2015

percentage points every year, and different categories sell well or poorly depending on the year.

Categories are the most important concept in book sales. Each has different markets and different strategies for reaching their audiences, and each is affected differently by economic and other factors. For example, during the most recent recession, sales of trade books, or books intended for general readership, fell because people had less disposable income. On the other hand, professional, technical, and scholarly books rose as a category, as businesspeople bought books to educate themselves rather than going to more expensive business seminars. Textbooks make up the largest portion of the publishing industry in terms of sales, followed by the category Other Books and Services, which includes religious texts and general reference works (about 10.6 percent), and other services, including digital publishing and design services for independent authors (16.6 percent). Figure 3-1 shows the different categories used by the book-publishing industry that make up its $29 billion in net revenues in 2014.

As Figure 3-2 shows, a slight downward trend has generally characterized revenue growth in the publishing industry, despite the increase in self-publishing

Ebooks have proven especially popular among youth.

Books like Suzanne Collins's *The Hunger Games* trilogy not only have proven hugely popular reading among the YA set but have also led to major motion pictures.

sales (which are not included in these statistics except for any revenues generated by publishers from their various support services to authors). Publishers actively seek potential bestsellers, as a single best-selling title can have dramatic effects on a publisher's revenues for the year. For example, the *Fifty Shades of Grey* trilogy in 2012 contributed to a 75 percent rise in operating revenue for publisher Random House, and a 22.5 percent increase in global revenue.[11]

Outlook for Books

The recession hurt the industry, and the growth of digital media has affected few enterprises as greatly as book publishing. Ebooks, accounting for only about 1 percent of total book sales in 2008 and then 22 percent in 2012, surpassed sales of hardcover books early in 2012—and ebooks had been outselling mass-market paperbacks on Amazon eighteen months before that.[12] Ebook sales, $859 million in 2012, are predicted to exceed $9.7 billion by 2016.[13]

Another area of tremendous growth has been audiobooks, both downloaded and physical. In 2013, for the second year in a row, titles published in this format more than doubled from the previous year, up from 16,309 to 35,713. Industry retail sales are estimated at $1.3 billion, with digital downloads accounting for 62 percent of net sales.[14]

Even as ebook sales increase, publishers seek new ways to generate more revenue more quickly. One growing avenue of revenue is services such as design and technology support to independent authors. What price consumers are willing to pay for ebooks remains a question, with different publishers trying different pricing structures such as offering older titles at deep discounts, around $2.99, and newer titles around $12.99 or more. In March 2011, HarperCollins Publishing announced that library patrons could check out an ebook only twenty-six times before the library must repurchase it. The disagreements between online sellers such as Amazon and the publishing industry are being closely watched, as the results could have dramatic effects on pricing of ebooks and greatly affect the publishing industry.

Reflecting remarkable media convergence are some series of books authored by women around the world that have captured immense YA readership and have been blockbuster movies or major television series. These include Stephenie Meyer's supernatural *Twilight* series and Suzanne Collins's *Hunger Games* trilogy. Famed for her Harry Potter series, J. K. Rowling has also written an adult novel, *The Casual Vacancy*, which premiered as a BBC TV miniseries in 2015.[15,16]

DISCUSSION QUESTIONS: Consider the "wish list" of books you would like to read over the summer or during break perhaps—what made you choose those books for your list?

Distinctive Functions of Newspapers

Portable and inexpensive, newspapers consist largely of words, photos, and graphics printed either daily or weekly on lightweight paper stock. Printing and distribution account for roughly 65 percent of production costs; the actual creation of the news, including reporters' salaries, accounts for only about 35 percent. "News" papers also consist largely of advertising, roughly 60 percent in the typical daily U.S. format.

The most important function of modern newspapers is surveillance—informing the public of important events—yet they also have correlation and entertainment functions. Opening and section front pages are typically all news, the most significant of which is placed "above the fold" on the top half of the page. As newspapers tend to serve communities defined by geographic, political, cultural, or economic borders, sections are generally organized by geography, including local, national, and international news; and topic, including business, culture, health, science, sports, and technology.

LOCAL NEWSPAPERS

The vast majority of U.S. newspapers serve local geographic communities (usually city based but with zoned suburb editions), monitoring their government, law enforcement, business, religion, education, arts, and other institutions. Some news, typically the product of larger news services such as the Associated Press and Reuters, is regional, national, or international. Local papers provide a legal record of the community's public communications, running obituaries and various announcements. Important in the local economic infrastructure, they also carry extensive advertising for community products, services, and businesses.

NATIONAL NEWSPAPERS

A few newspapers have emerged as truly national, with readership throughout the country. *The New York Times*, *USA Today*, and *The Wall Street Journal*, for example, each offer their own distinctive brand of news. *The New York Times*, the "paper of record" in the United States, also known as the "Old Gray Lady," offers especially strong coverage of international events and issues. The *Wall Street Journal*, bought by Rupert Murdoch's News Corp. in 2007, is the nation's leading newspaper covering business and finance. Many working in these industries also consider the *Journal* a must-read.

In 1982, newspaper mogul Al Neuharth launched *USA Today*, a strong mix of general-interest news featuring colorful graphics and easy-to-read sections, an overall design inspired by television. Prior to its launch, most newspapers were drab and filled with long columns of text. *USA Today* took ten years to become profitable; but in the meantime, it transformed the look and feel of most newspapers in the United States and many around the world.

Even more significant was its new economic model. Using then-new satellite communication technology, content was sent electronically to printing and distribution centers throughout the country, a cheaper method that permitted nationwide distribution for a daily paper, subsequently adopted by *The New York Times* and *The Wall Street Journal*.

FIGURE 3-3 Top 10 U.S. Newspapers by Circulation, in millions, 2014

Digital subscriptions

3255K	2294K	2149K	681K	673K	581K	477K	456K	443K	436K
2.3M	1.7M	1.6M	600K	530K	520K	500K	460K	430K	410K

Source: Cision.com, June 2014 (http://www.cision.com/us/2014/06/top-10-us-daily-newspapers/)

Japan's *Yomiuri Shimbun* has the largest circulation of any newspaper in the world.

Despite the relatively large circulation of the *Wall Street Journal* and *USA Today*, their circulation numbers are dwarfed by those of the world's largest dailies in Japan, the *Yomiuri Shimbun* (over 10 million), the *Asahi Shimbun* (8 million), and the *Nikkei Keizai Shimbun* (over 3 million). The coverage of the *Nikkei Keizai Shimbun* resembles that of the *Wall Street Journal*.

About 75 percent of the top 100 best-selling papers are in Asia, including the largest English-language newspaper, the *Times of India* (4 million). In the United Kingdom, the three top dailies are all sensationalist tabloids: *The Sun* (2 million), *The Daily Mail* (1.8 million), and the *Daily Mirror* (1 million). Each of these papers has seen steady declines in their circulations since 2008 when they had circulations of 3.2 million, 2.3 million, and 1.5 million, respectively. Most newspapers are seeing print circulations diminish as readers go increasingly online.

History of Newspapers to Today

News pamphlets or brochures, precursors to newspapers, were printed in Germany in the 1400s. From the early 1600s, newspapers or news sheets were printed in Germany, Holland, and England. As printers often faced government censors and even imprisonment, few publications had regular schedules. The first English-language newspaper published in what is today the United States was *Publick Occurrences, Both Foreign and Domestick*. Although it was published only once—on September 25, 1690, in Boston—more newspapers followed. The American colonial press took two forms: commercial papers and political papers.

THE COMMERCIAL PRESS AND THE PARTISAN PRESS

Merchants published the commercial papers. *The Boston Daily Advertiser* and the *Daily Mercantile Advertiser*, for example, reported on ship arrivals, departures, and cargo as well as weather and other items of commercial interest.

After independence and prior to the 1830s, most U.S. newspapers were affiliated with a political party or platform. Political parties sponsored *The Federal Republican and Daily Gazette*, for instance, which featured articles by often anonymous political figures. The partisan press, as it was called, did not subscribe to the modern principle of unbiased and impartial coverage and frequently and liberally borrowed news from other newspapers without attributing sources.

Publick Occurrences, although published only once, is considered the first newspaper in colonial America.

COLONIAL READERSHIP AND FINANCES

A subscription to either a commercial or a political paper cost eight to ten dollars per year or about six cents an issue. This was beyond the reach of the average worker, who made just eighty-five cents a day. Readership was largely limited to those who supported the political position of the paper and to society's well-educated, landowning, and affluent groups. By 1750, most colonists who could read had access to a newspaper, although the elite generally remained the literate class.

THE GOLDEN AGE OF NEWSPAPERS

In the 1830s, technological developments began to transform newspapers, ushering in a golden age of newspapers in America that lasted until about 1930, when radio began to dominate.

Prior to the 1830s, printing presses, powered by hand (and briefly by horses), could print only two hundred to six hundred one-sided sheets per hour, severely limiting circulation. But in the 1830s, the development of steam-powered presses producing up to four thousand sheets per hour on both sides made mass-scale printing possible.

Seizing the opportunity, publisher **Benjamin Day** launched the *New York Sun* on September 3, 1833. Instead of traditional subscriptions, newsboys in the streets sold the daily newspaper and its sensationalized stories for only one cent. The **penny press** truly offered news for the masses, reaching a circulation of eight thousand almost immediately and thirty thousand within three years, enormous success that astounded contemporary publishers. As with Gutenberg's printing press some four centuries earlier, news was no longer only for the political or commercial elite but for everyone.

A new marketing function also emerged with the penny press, which attracted large audiences and, consequently, businesses hoping to reach mass markets. The newspaper price did not cover printing and distribution costs, but the penny press began advertising medicines, entertainment, and jobs as well as items on which

 Benjamin Day

Publisher of the *New York Sun* who originated the penny press in 1833 by offering his paper on the streets for a penny.

penny press

Newspapers that sold for a penny, making them accessible to everyone. Supported by advertising rather than subscriptions, they tried to attract as large an audience as possible.

the commercial and partisan press frowned, such as theater, lotteries, and abortionists. Advertising became the primary revenue source in the modern business model.

Newspapers proliferated in the Golden Age, feeding the appetite for news in large eastern cities such as New York, Boston, and Philadelphia. Between 1870 and 1900, the U.S. population doubled, the urban population tripled, and the number of daily newspapers quadrupled. The 1880 U.S. Census counted 11,314 newspapers. Metropolitan newspapers sprouted throughout the nation, helmed by innovators whose names still resonate such as James Gordon Bennett, Horace Greeley, Joseph Pulitzer, William Randolph Hearst, and E. W. Scripps.

DISCUSSION QUESTIONS: Some journalism scholars are calling for newspapers to return to an era of partisan coverage, or to at least abandon the focus on objectivity that newspapers promoted throughout most of the twentieth century. Would you favor this type of coverage? Why or why not?

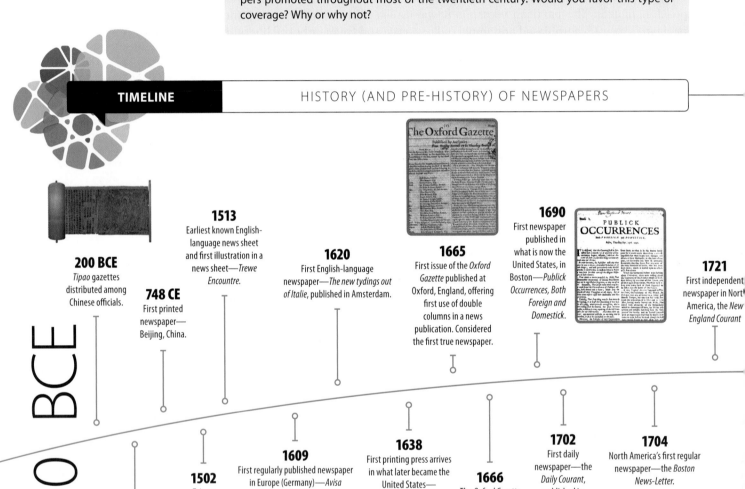

TIMELINE   HISTORY (AND PRE-HISTORY) OF NEWSPAPERS

200 BCE

200 BCE
Tipao gazettes distributed among Chinese officials.

748 CE
First printed newspaper—Beijing, China.

1513
Earliest known English-language news sheet and first illustration in a news sheet—*Trewe Encountre*.

1620
First English-language newspaper—*The new tydings out of Italie*, published in Amsterdam.

1665
First issue of the *Oxford Gazette* published at Oxford, England, offering first use of double columns in a news publication. Considered the first true newspaper.

1690
First newspaper published in what is now the United States, in Boston—*Publick Occurrences, Both Foreign and Domestick*.

1721
First independent newspaper in North America, the *New England Courant*.

59 BCE
Julius Caesar orders publication of first daily news sheet, *Acta Diurna (Daily Events)*—Rome.

1502
Zeitung ("newspaper") published in Germany.

1609
First regularly published newspaper in Europe (Germany)—*Avisa Relation oder Zeitung*.

1638
First printing press arrives in what later became the United States—Cambridge, Massachusetts.

1666
The *Oxford Gazette* becomes the *London Gazette* and is published continuously for more than 300 years.

1702
First daily newspaper—the *Daily Courant*, published in London.

1704
North America's first regular newspaper—the *Boston News-Letter*.

Current Newspaper-Industry Issues

After World War II, the urban society that had supported the penny press shifted to a more suburban population that spent considerable time commuting by automobile and relied more on radio, TV, and eventually the Internet. Tired suburban commuters preferred television for both news and entertainment in the evenings, driving afternoon papers into decline. Eventually, one paper or a morning and evening edition supplanted two or more competing dailies.

The **Newspaper Preservation Act of 1970** was intended to preserve diverse editorial opinion in communities where only two competing, or independently owned, daily newspapers exist. The two papers are ostensibly competitors but can sometimes be owned by the same company or work under a **joint operating arrangement**, or **JOA**, provided for by the Act. A JOA is a legal agreement that permits newspapers in the same market to merge their business operations yet maintain separate editorial operations. Today, nine cities in the United States are served by two or more major daily newspapers operating under a JOA, with eleven

Newspaper Preservation Act of 1970

Created in 1970 to preserve a diversity of editorial opinion in communities where only two competing, or independently owned, daily newspapers exist.

joint operating arrangement (JOA)

Legal agreement permitting newspapers in the same market or city to merge their business operations for economic reasons while maintaining independent editorial operations.

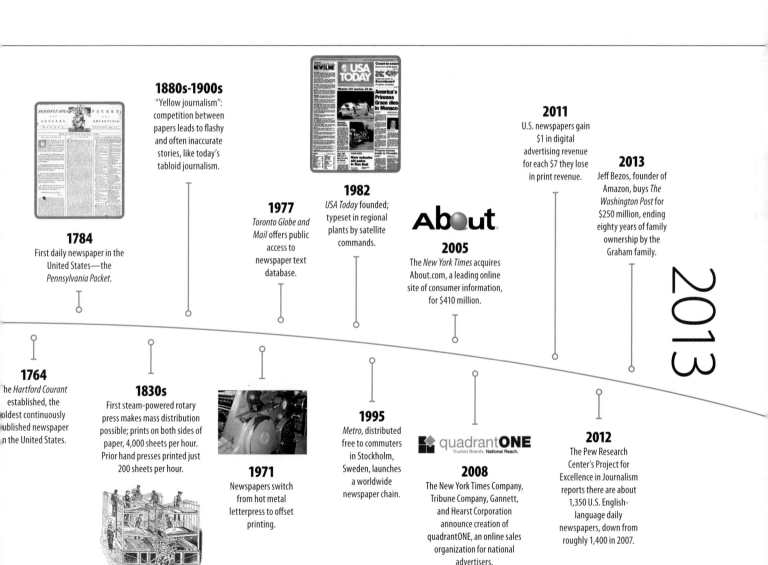

1880s-1900s
"Yellow journalism": competition between papers leads to flashy and often inaccurate stories, like today's tabloid journalism.

2011
U.S. newspapers gain $1 in digital advertising revenue for each $7 they lose in print revenue.

2013
Jeff Bezos, founder of Amazon, buys *The Washington Post* for $250 million, ending eighty years of family ownership by the Graham family.

1784
First daily newspaper in the United States—the *Pennsylvania Packet*.

1977
Toronto Globe and Mail offers public access to newspaper text database.

1982
USA Today founded; typeset in regional plants by satellite commands.

2005
The *New York Times* acquires About.com, a leading online site of consumer information, for $410 million.

1764
The *Hartford Courant* established, the oldest continuously published newspaper in the United States.

1830s
First steam-powered rotary press makes mass distribution possible; prints on both sides of paper, 4,000 sheets per hour. Prior hand presses printed just 200 sheets per hour.

1971
Newspapers switch from hot metal letterpress to offset printing.

1995
Metro, distributed free to commuters in Stockholm, Sweden, launches a worldwide newspaper chain.

2008
The New York Times Company, Tribune Company, Gannett, and Hearst Corporation announce creation of quadrantONE, an online sales organization for national advertisers.

2012
The Pew Research Center's Project for Excellence in Journalism reports there are about 1,350 U.S. English-language daily newspapers, down from roughly 1,400 in 2007.

2013

cities served by different newspapers under common ownership. Critics argue, however, that JOAs essentially permit monopolies.

Modern newspapers are still changing significantly, particularly with regard to the news and advertising content. Even leading newspapers are more likely to pander to popular taste to maintain circulation numbers. Departing from the editorial tradition (established after the penny press days) of selecting newsworthy topics regardless of general appeal, many newspapers are deferring to marketing polls and focus groups when setting standards for content, tone, and layout. To cut costs, many newspapers have closed international news bureaus and even statehouse news bureaus, relying instead on wire service news. Brightly colored photos and graphics like those pioneered in *USA Today* can, if properly executed, actually aid and enhance reading. Done poorly, however, they can trivialize the news and even confuse or mislead.

Newspapers have been experimenting with the electronic delivery of news to consumers since the late 1970s when newspapers such as the *Globe and Mail* (Toronto) allowed public access to their news databases. Yet most early efforts were not very successful in the days before widely available personal computers or Internet access. Reading text on computer screens was also very tiring.

Many newspapers view the Internet as a threat to their business model for subscriptions and advertising. Some have opted to reduce the days per week they print. Others, such as *The Christian Science Monitor* and the *Seattle Post-Intelligencer*, have eliminated paper format altogether. Most adaptations involve some combination of an expanded online presence and greater interactivity, including user-generated content, which begins to blur the traditional line between reporter and reader.

NEWSPAPER CHAINS

Another successful business model has relied on the newspaper chain. Traditionally, U.S. newspapers were owned by families, individuals, or political parties generally residing in the communities their newspapers served. In the twentieth century, both in the United States and globally, ownership became increasingly concentrated; and most newspapers today are part of a group ("chains") owned by a privately held or publicly traded company.

The newspaper business has historically been among the most lucrative enterprises, earning double the profit margins of other industry sectors. Profit margins in the 1990s were often in the range of 20 percent of gross revenues. Newspapers became a desirable target for investors. Large newspaper chains have successfully bought up smaller independent local or regional newspapers that faced shrinking audiences and advertising revenue as well as rising costs for newsprint and other necessary resources. Profit margins have narrowed drastically for newspapers, no longer making them investment targets. Some major papers, such as the tabloid *New York Daily News*, lose millions of dollars each year as they search for buyers.

Benefits of Chains

Chain resources are one of the benefits for smaller, struggling newspapers. This can be especially important in communities where a single advertiser accounts for considerable advertising revenue, a situation that may compromise the rigor of reporting on this company. Chains also offer shared resources for news gathering, especially when covering regional, national, or international stories—much as newspapers have benefited from a working relationship with the Associated Press.

Problems with Chains

Chains, especially those publicly owned and traded, can pressure local newspapers for higher profits. One common cost-cutting strategy is eliminating reporters and filling the news hole with wire service copy or material from the chain's other papers.

Chain-owned newspapers can weaken the connection between the local media and the local community. As cheaper wire service or chain-produced content squeezes out local reporting, people are forced to look elsewhere for local news. This sets up a spiral of decline—as readership drops, so do advertising profits, forcing more cost cuts either through fewer pages or reduced staff, making the paper even less relevant to readers.

LEADING NEWSPAPER CHAINS

From the beginning of the twenty-first century, an accelerated pace of chain mergers and sales transformed the business landscape. In 2006, for example, The McClatchy Company, the eighth-largest chain in the United States, paid $4.5 billion to buy Knight Ridder, the second-largest newspaper chain at the time, well known in the industry for its innovative expertise with new technologies. The industry continues to change dramatically with seemingly monthly acquisitions and mergers. In 2015, Apollo Global, a management company, was working toward purchasing Digital First Media, which only a year ago bought up Media News Group; and Gannett was poised to acquire ten of the newspapers currently in the Digital First Media portfolio once the Apollo deal went through. (See Figure 3-4.)

DECLINING NUMBER OF DAILY NEWSPAPERS

Since 1940, the total number of daily newspapers has dropped more than 21 percent, with about 1,350 dailies in the United States in 2013. In 2000, the number of morning dailies first exceeded, and has continued to exceed, the number of evening papers. Since 1940, the number of evening papers has decreased 51 percent, whereas the number of morning papers has increased over 100 percent, doubling since 1980 to 862 daily, with 525 afternoon daily papers in 2009. The number of Sunday papers has increased 65 percent since 1940, reaching a high of 917 in 2005 but falling to 900 by 2011.[17]

Sales and Readership of Newspapers

The printing press, newsprint, ink, press operators, delivery trucks and drivers, and maintenance of subscriber databases as well as various other non-news-related production and distribution costs make up roughly two-thirds of the overall cost of publishing a newspaper. That activities other than producing news account for most of the cost presents a considerable opportunity for digital newspapers.

Still, newspapers are having trouble adapting to the digital era. Readership, circulation, and advertising were continuing to diminish even before digital

FIGURE 3-4 Major Newspaper Chains in the United States

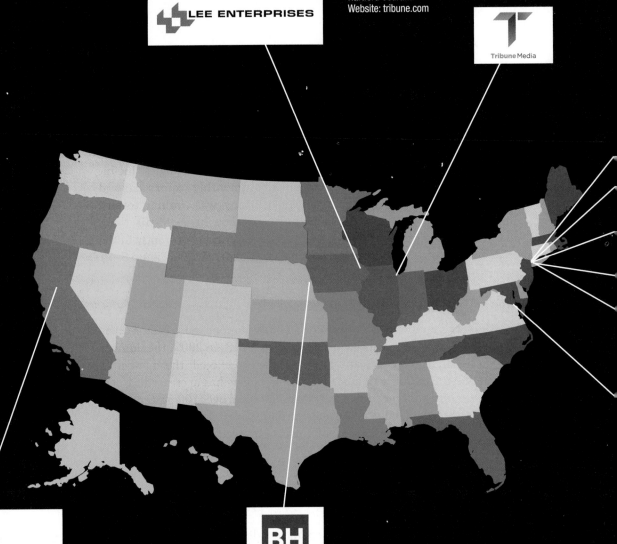

LEE ENTERPRISES (Davenport, IA)
A publicly traded company, Lee Enterprises owns some fifty daily newspapers in twenty-two states predominantly in mid-sized communities of the midwest and west. Based in Davenport, Iowa, Lee also publishes 300 weekly, classified, and specialty publications such as the *Southern Business Journal*. News properties include the following: *Sioux City Journal, Arizona Daily Star* (Tucson), *St. Louis Post Dispatch, Billings Gazette, The Bismarck Tribune, Lincoln Journal Star, Wisconsin State Journal* (Madison), and the *Albany-Democratic Herald* (OR).
Website: lee.net

TRIBUNE MEDIA COMPANY (Chicago, IL)
In 2014 Tribune Publishing was spun off from the Tribune Company to focus its print and companion digital properties in one company and its television and companion digital operations in another, Tribune Media, which owns forty-two TV stations. A top-five newspaper chain, the Tribune is one of the largest and oldest continuous newspaper organizations in existence, incorporated in 1847 with the founding of the *Chicago Tribune*.
News properties include the following: *Chicago Tribune, Baltimore Sun, Los Angeles Times, U-T San Diego, Orlando Sentinel,* and *Hartford Courant*.
Website: tribune.com

THE MCCLATCHY COMPANY (Sacramento, CA)
A publicly traded company, McClatchy is devoted almost solely to the newspaper publishing industry in the United States. Acquiring Knight Ridder in 2006, it then sold the *Minneapolis Star Tribune,* the *Anchorage Daily News,* and others, focusing on ownership in areas of fast growth. It owns twenty-nine daily newspapers in twenty-eight markets and a number of non-daily and online ventures.
News properties include the following: *The Sacramento Bee, Fort Worth*

BH MEDIA GROUP (Omaha, NE)
BH Media is a public Berkshire Hathaway company, the Warren Buffett-controlled conglomerate, ranked fifth largest in the world and first in the United States. Owning more than seventy newspapers and other titles across ten states throughout the south, midwest, and plains states, BH Media aggressively continues the purchase of many small community weekly publications in these areas.
News properties include the following: *Omaha World-Herald, Richmond Times-Dispatch, Tulsa World, Winston-Salem Journal,* and *The Roanoke Times*.

advance.net

ADVANCE PUBLICATIONS (Staten Island, NY)

Advance Publications is a private, family-controlled company, led by chairman and CEO Samuel I. "Si" Newhouse Jr., whose father founded the business in 1922. Advance owns thirty newspapers in some twenty-five cities from New York to Oregon, along with Condé Nast Publications, which operates twenty different print and digital magazines, including *Vanity Fair, Vogue, Golf Digest,* and *The New Yorker.* Advance Digital oversees a dozen local portal Internet news sites driven by its newspaper holdings.

News properties include the following: *The Plain Dealer* (Cleveland), *Times* (Trenton), *The Star-Ledger* (Newark), *The Times-Picayune* (New Orleans), *The Birmingham News, The Huntsville Times,* and *The Oregonian* (Portland).

Website: advance.net

The New York Times

THE NEW YORK TIMES COMPANY (New York, NY)

Although publicly traded, The New York Times Company has been controlled by the Sulzberger family since the death of Adolph Ochs, Times owner and publisher since 1896, his position being assumed in 1935 by his son-in-law, Arthur Hays Sulzberger. Focusing on its New York brand, in 2013 it sold the New England Media group, including the sale of The Boston Globe to John W. Henry, owner of the Boston Red Sox. *The New York Times* newspaper ranks third in the United States in daily circulation and readership.

News properties include the following: *International New York Times,* The New York Times Syndicate and News Service.

Website: nytco.com

HEARST *corporation*

THE HEARST CORPORATION (New York, NY)

Derived from the trust of famed publisher William Randolph Hearst, the Hearst Corporation is a private company set to dissolve only after all family members alive in 1951 at Hearst's death have passed on. The multimedia company features a diverse set of interests that includes ESPN, A&E Networks, and twenty-nine television stations, as well as fifteen daily newspapers, thirty-four weeklies, and hundreds of magazines worldwide, including *Cosmopolitan, Esquire, Good Housekeeping,* and *Popular Mechanics.*

News properties include the following: *Houston Chronicle, San Francisco Chronicle, Albany Times Union,* and *San Antonio Express-News.*

Website: hearst.com

News Corp

NEWS CORPORATION (New York, NY)

News Corporation is traded publicly but has a dual share structure permitting control by Rupert Murdoch, who also has substantial newspaper holdings in the United Kingdom and his native Australia. Its flagship U.S. newspaper, *The Wall Street Journal,* is among the top three newspapers in terms of daily circulation. The many services of Dow Jones and of Harper-Collins Publishers also form part of News Corps holdings.

News properties include the following: *New York Post, The Times* (UK), *The Sun* (UK), *The Daily Telegraph* (Australia), and *Barron's.*

Website: newscorp.com

digitalfirst MEDIA

DIGITAL FIRST MEDIA (New York, NY)

The second-largest newspaper chain in 2012, MediaNews Group was in 2013 subsumed along with Twenty-First Century Media by Digital First Media—managed by Aldon Global Capital, a hedge fund sponsor with holdings in many of the larger newspaper chains. To complicate matters further, in 2015 Digital First was in the process of being sold to Apollo Global Management, which in turn was poised to sell off certain newspapers to Gannett.

New properties include the following: *San Jose Mercury News, The Denver Post, Pioneer Press (St. Paul), Oakland Tribune, Press-Telegram* (Long Beach), and *New Haven Register.*

Website: digitalfirstmedia.com

GANNETT
It's all within reach.

GANNETT (McLean, VA)

Gannett, a publicly traded corporation, publishes daily newspapers in more than eighty communities across the United States and eighteen in the United Kingdom. By some measures, the most read daily newspaper nationally, USA Today, in combination with the others, makes Gannett the largest newspaper chain in the United States. Gannett also owns or services forty-six television stations in twenty-two states and D.C.

News properties include the following: *Arizona Republic* (Phoenix), *Detroit Free Press, The Indianapolis Star, The Courier-Journal* (Louisville), The Cincinnati Inquirer, The Tennessean (Nashville), *The Des Moines Register, Reno Gazette Journal,* and *Statesman Journal* (Salem, OR).

Website: gannett.com

Citizen journalism is often criticized for failing to meet professional standards. **CRITICAL THINKING QUESTIONS**: In what instances do you think that this criticism is justified? Identify two or three news stories that might have been told very differently or not at all had citizen journalists not documented events. How can you tell if this type of reporting is legitimate or not?

citizen journalism

The gathering and sharing of news and information by public citizens, particularly via mobile and social media, sometimes via traditional media.

readership

Number or percentage of newspaper readers.

circulation

Number of newspaper copies sold or distributed.

media. Shrinking circulation has made newspapers less appealing to advertisers, who have gone online—although not necessarily to the online newspaper.

One notable difference here is that the online newspaper sites compete directly with the leading national broadcast and cable television news. In fact, with growing calls for converged newsrooms and wider broadband access among the general public, newspaper websites increasingly feature audio, video, and multimedia.

Online newspaper sites also face direct competition on a number of other online fronts such as blogs, news aggregators such as Google News and Reddit, international news such as Al Jazeera, social media, and **citizen journalism**. A field that has exploded with the growth of digital media, citizen journalism broadens the scope of news content, increases the diversity of voices in the public sphere, captures compelling stories as they often unexpectedly unfold in real time, and reveals images that might otherwise have remained hidden. Despite its many benefits, trained journalists often view this particular brand of competition with skepticism for its lack of professional standards, most notably on the dimensions of veracity and objectivity.

CIRCULATION AND READERSHIP

Newspaper **readership** (number or percentage who read a newspaper) is larger than **circulation** (number of copies sold or distributed) because of "pass-along readership," readers who read the same copy. A growing U.S. population makes it appear that the number of newspaper readers has not decreased greatly. As a percentage, however, diminished readership and time spent reading are evident. Young readers are fewer than those between thirty-five and sixty-five. Yet despite this sharp decline in recent years, statistics indicate that the young are reading news online or on mobile devices in higher numbers than they were, with digital content often published by daily-newspaper parent organizations.

DISCUSSION QUESTIONS: Consider your campus newspaper. How often do you read it, and do you actively seek it out when it is published? How would you get information on the school and events if you did not have the campus paper?

ADVERTISING

Advertising generates close to two-thirds of U.S. newspaper revenue, with the rest from subscriptions. In other countries such as Japan, subscription prices are higher, and the revenue split is closer to 50–50. Since 2006, advertising revenue has fallen 48 percent, 26 percent in 2009, but only 6.3 percent in 2010. Online ad revenues, which grew quickly before 2008 and then declined slightly between 2008 and 2010, still fell far short of making up for the lost print ad revenues. Figure 3-5 shows that while print ad revenues have declined by more than half since 2003, online ad revenues have more than doubled—even though online ad revenues are still less than 18 percent that of print ad revenues.

CONVERGENCE CULTURE
Freesheets: Riding the Rails of Newspapers' Future?

It looked like a crazy idea, even back in 1995. At a time when newspapers were already struggling with rising costs and budget crises and just starting to understand the threat of the World Wide Web, Pelle Tornberg launched a free daily newspaper in Stockholm for subway commuters.

Designed to be read in fifteen minutes, the *Metro* was a colorful tabloid, with short articles on a variety of topics. Its target audience was an elusive yet lucrative readership for advertisers—the young, affluent, and urban—precisely the demographic that had largely stopped reading newspapers.

Now there are 210 free newspapers in fifty countries, with a total worldwide circulation of 40 million. The *Metro* chain of freesheets has expanded throughout Europe, Latin America, and Asia and into New York, Boston, and Philadelphia. They are now in a hundred cities in twenty countries and publish in eighteen languages.[18]

Free newspapers remain the fastest-growing segment of newspapers worldwide, although growth has slowed in some key markets. *The New York Metro* and its competitor, *amNewYork*, have been struggling to attain the kind of popularity seen in Europe. Even there, however, freesheets have had to close down in some cities.

Freesheets have shown themselves to be sustainable and popular, although environmentalists still protest this proliferation of printed paper, their concerns about trees

compounded by those about recycling that, they argue, uses harmful chemicals. The worldwide *Metro* chain claims to be the largest newspaper in the world. As tablet use rises, however, freesheet readers may transfer to paid-circulation newspapers; and the question remains whether reading freesheets will instill a lifetime habit of reading newspapers online or offline. The impact of electronic paper, or paper-thin flexible displays, now seen in Samsung's flexible OLED phone, may prove even more transformative.

FIGURE 3-5   Print Versus Online Ad Revenue (2003–2012) (in millions of dollars)

YEAR	PRINT	ONLINE	TOTAL
2003	$44,939	$1,216	$46,155
2004	$46,703	$1,541	$48,244
2005	$47,408	$2,027	$49,435
2006	$46,611	$2,664	$49,275
2007	$42,209	$3,166	$45,375
2008	$34,740	$3,109	$37,848
2009	$24,821	$2,743	$27,564
2010	$22,795	$3,042	$25,838
2011	$20,692	$3,249	$23,941
2012	$18,931	$3,370	$22,314

Source: Newspaper Association of America

As Figure 3-6 shows, advertising in all three main categories for newspapers—retail, national, and classifieds—has been down sharply since 2005. Sites such as Craigslist and eBay and services such as Groupon have siphoned away classifieds ads, down 75 percent since 2005, traditionally a large portion of newspaper advertising revenue. Job recruitment has fallen the greatest: Newspapers received revenues from recruitment classifieds of $8.7 billion in 2000 but only $760 million in 2011.

FIGURE 3-6 Newspaper Print Ad Revenue Declines (in billions of dollars)

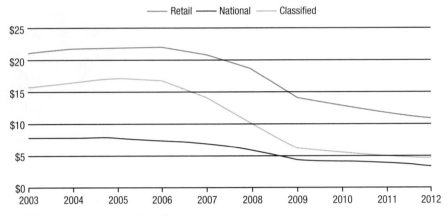

Source: Newspaper Association of America

Publishers generally believe that online advertising could continue to grow but will likely not be enough to support publications as print advertising did. Consequently, they are still exploring revenue options, especially the digital paywall in which readers must pay after receiving a certain number of stories for free. Although this seems to be working for big-name newspapers such as the *New York Times*, smaller newspapers that compete with hyperlocal citizen journalism sites for local readers' attention may have less success with this option.

Outlook for Newspapers

"The rumors of my death have been greatly exaggerated," once quipped Mark Twain, after reading his own obituary in a local newspaper. Can the same be said for newspapers?

We consider six major trends in light of this question. First, more newspaper executives are outsiders, with little appreciation or understanding of the industry's unique aspects. Second, digital subscription models progress slowly. Willingness to pay for digital subscriptions is often promoted through bundling with other incentives, such as receiving a Sunday paper or offering some stories for free. Third, understanding and measuring audiences has become increasingly critical in an online world where social media have made clicks or page views less relevant than they were only a few years ago. Fourth, local coverage is increasingly important (although staff reductions have made it harder to provide), some of which occurs on citizen journalism sites or with bloggers. Still, this coverage is typically not nearly as extensive as that of professional reporters covering local beats. Fifth, smaller but more numerous revenue streams need to be developed as

MEDIA PIONEERS
Ruben Salazar

On August 29, 1970, while riots stemming from a Chicano civil rights march raged in the chaotic streets, tear gas launched by a Los Angeles County Sheriff flooded the Silver Dollar Cafe and sent its occupants rushing out the back door—all except one unable to react, having been killed instantly by the direct impact of the tear-gas projectile. The victim was 42-year-old Ruben Salazar, a name unfamiliar to many Americans but a man who would soon become a martyr to many Chicanos. No charges were filed after a formal inquest, yet lingering questions about the circumstances of his death continue to enhance the Salazar mystique.

In a distinguished career cut tragically short, the most prominent Latino journalist of his day interviewed Robert F. Kennedy, Richard Nixon, Dwight D. Eisenhower, and Cesar Chavez, among other luminaries. Salazar, whose children were raised to speak only English at his Anglo wife's request, did not set out to become an activist, much less an icon in the burgeoning Chicano movement. A *Man in the Middle*, the apt title of a 2014 PBS documentary, Ruben was born to a conservative family of immigrants from Juarez and grew up in El Paso, where he majored in journalism at the University of Texas while working as a reporter and editor for the college newspaper.

Still, his early reporting revealed signs of the muckraking for which he would later be known. One of his first articles for the *El Paso Herald*, for example, described the notorious local jail, whose deplorable conditions he had experienced firsthand after feigning public drunkenness to get arrested. Subsequently, Salazar worked for the *Los Angeles Times* as a foreign correspondent in Viet Nam and in the Dominican Republic and as bureau chief in Mexico City. Salazar's later domestic reporting and columns exposed the many social injustices that Mexican Americans confronted in Los Angeles, such as inferior political representation, education, employment, and housing—a mission he also pursued as news director of KMEX, a Los Angeles Spanish-language TV station.[19]

A stamp issued by the U.S. Postal Service in 2008 commemorates this activist journalist's pioneering achievements. Ruben Salazar, in an era that had yet to appreciate or even invoke the value of diversity, embodied it in his relentless and principled pursuit of the complexities of professional and personal truths. An independent observer, a critical thinker, and a man of the people, he offered this metaphor on the dual cultural identity that informed his work: "The international bridge that connected Juarez and El Paso symbolized the division of my life. No matter which way I crossed this bridge, I could not leave either side behind."[20]

alternatives to traditional advertising and subscription-based models. Sixth, after the government bailout of the U.S. auto industry, advertising increased across all media channels. Relaxed restrictions on political advertising also greatly helped newspapers and other media.

Today's 24/7 news cycles mean newspapers must constantly update content. Other changes to meet audience needs may include interpreting or analyzing news events and more interactive multimedia; but these efforts could bring them into direct competition with news magazines, both print and digital, and make concepts like a weekly or even a daily newspaper obsolete.

Distinctive Functions of Magazines

Three factors clearly distinguish magazines from newspapers. First, magazines typically feature longer treatment of topics. Magazines gained popularity in the 1800s with serial novels, released one chapter at a time over many issues, or excellent short stories. Charles Dickens, author of *A Tale of Two Cities*, *A Christmas Carol*, and *Oliver Twist*, published many of his classics first as serials. Edgar Allan Poe also published most of his stories first in magazines. The circulation of *Lady's and Gentleman's Magazine* jumped from five thousand to twenty-five thousand the year Poe started writing for it, publishing *Murders in the Rue Morgue*, considered the first modern detective story, in the April 1841 issue. Many contemporary writers introduce their books with chapters or other excerpts in print or online magazines, or they create books from a series of magazine articles. Samuel Huntington's influential *The Clash of Civilizations* began as a 1993 magazine article.

Second, magazines are published at regular but less frequent intervals, most typically monthly, although weeklies and quarterlies are also common. Thus, this less time-sensitive writing tends to be more in-depth, analytical, interpretative, and creative.

Third, magazines have typically been published on higher-quality paper stock intended to be kept considerably longer than dailies. This paper is usually eight and a half by eleven inches. Certain magazine publishers, however, have reduced their size by a quarter or half inch, saving money on printing costs while maintaining advertising and subscription fees. Other magazines, such as *Rolling Stone* and *ESPN Magazine*, print on larger stock that stands out on crowded shelves.

A magazine tends to have a defined audience, without which attracting advertisers may pose a problem. (*Look* and *Life*, two general-interest magazines of the mid-twentieth century, are notable exceptions.) Magazines serve several important functions for their respective audiences and society, especially surveillance, correlation, entertainment, and marketing. Surveillance, the most basic function, is ordered by subject matter rather than geographic area. (Travel or regional-interest magazines are notable exceptions.) Most magazines cover specific topics such as science, health, or sports; some treat highly specialized topics such as doll collecting, harness racing, or scuba diving. Other magazines, such as *People* and *Entertainment Weekly*, aim largely or exclusively to entertain.

Many magazines have national, regional, or even international readership and distribution. The longer news stories found in major publications, such as *The Economist* and *Time*, can provide greater detail than newspaper articles. Higher-quality magazine paper can support exceptional photography and illustrations well suited to covering fashion, nature, entertainment, and science.

Almost all magazines serve a vital marketing function for a broad cross section of goods and services. Readers often spend more time perusing ads than reading content, especially with fashion magazines such as *Vogue*, *Glamour*, and *GQ*. These feature not only the latest designer news but also the hottest ads. Most magazines have developed tablet editions, sometimes adding audio and video content. Specific audiences are increasingly targeted by iPad magazines, such as *Cosmopolitan for Latinas* and *Uptown*, aimed at African Americans.

DISCUSSION QUESTIONS: Identify and describe which magazines you typically read, why you read them, and how you read them (print, digital, or some combination of both).

History of Magazines to Today

The early histories of magazines and newspapers are interwoven. Their technological, business (i.e., advertising), and journalistic/entertainment functions overlapped, and both helped spur the development of modern mass media. Not until 1731 did the first English-language periodical use "magazine" in its title: *The Gentleman's Magazine*, published in London. Benjamin Franklin published *Poor Richard's Almanack* in 1732, a predecessor of the modern magazine. In 1741 in Philadelphia, the first magazine was published in North America, the *American Magazine*, or *A Monthly View of the Political State of the British Colonies*. In 1811, the first newsweekly magazine, *Niles' Weekly Register*, was published.

In the nineteenth century, magazines helped a young America define itself and reach a nationwide audience. Newspapers were primarily metropolitan or local, while some magazines spoke to a national audience. Magazines such as *Harper's Weekly* also took the lead in developing sports journalism in the 1800s, reporting on, for example, the Schuylkill regatta in September 1876. Frank Leslie founded a variety of periodicals in this era, including one of the first influential newsweeklies, *Frank Leslie's Illustrated Newspaper*, launched in 1855. In 1871, he hired Miriam Florence Folline as editor of *Frank Leslie's Lady's Journal*. Frank's business went bankrupt in 1877; but after he died, in 1880, Miriam, whom he had married in 1874, took it over and skillfully restored its financial health. One of the wealthiest and most powerful women in journalism, she bequeathed some $2 million to the cause of women's suffrage.

In 1888, *National Geographic*, founded by the National Geographic Society, debuted, and it introduced color plates in 1906. Time Inc., founded by Henry Luce, bought humor and general-interest *Life* magazine in 1936 and made it into a weekly news magazine with a large format and excellent photography that produced many iconic images of the mid-twentieth century. Weekly publication ceased in 1972 due to dwindling circulation, but different iterations followed: a themed news magazine; a monthly news magazine; a Sunday newspaper supplement; and finally, in 2009, a website featuring many of its famous images. Focusing on its cable and film interests, Time Warner announced in 2013 it would spin off Time Inc. into a separate, publicly owned company. It currently owns several magazines, including *Time*, *Sports Illustrated*, and *Fortune*.

Just as the efforts of nineteenth-century newspaper publishers laid the foundation for posterity, so did the influential work of a number of important magazine journalists from the late nineteenth and early twentieth centuries. Among the most important were the **muckrakers**, dubbed so by a disapproving President Theodore Roosevelt because they pioneered investigative reporting of corrupt practices in government and business. "Muck" was the polite term for the manure, mud, and straw mixture found in stables. Notable muckrakers included Ida Minerva Tarbell, Joseph Lincoln Steffens, and Upton Sinclair (author of *The Jungle*). Lengthy investigations meant muckrakers often reported for magazines rather than newspapers. Muckraking investigative journalism served as a foundation for much of the long-form, investigative reporting seen today in a variety of leading news media, particularly quality public service digital initiatives such as *ProPublica*.

In the later nineteenth century, national magazines helped the growing United States establish a common sense of identity and culture.

💬 **muckrakers**

Journalists, particularly magazine journalists, who conduct investigative reporting on major corporations and government; they were dubbed muckrakers in the early twentieth century for the "muck" they uncovered.

Current Magazine-Industry Issues

In the 1940s and 1950s, television quickly drew national advertisers seeking large audiences. Consequently, general-interest magazines such as *Life* and *Look* saw their business base dissolve.

Magazine publishers, who had to adapt to survive, stopped publishing general-interest magazines in favor of specialized magazines on almost every conceivable topic, a move that attracted advertisers who wished to target specific audiences. Nearly eighteen thousand specialized magazines are now available in print, online, and on mobile devices.

Entrepreneur John H. Johnson recognized the unmet media needs of African Americans, founding *Ebony* magazine in 1945. His hometown high school in Arkansas City, Arkansas, was "whites only," so Johnson's family moved to Chicago, where he got his formal high school education. His mother funded his business by pawning her household furniture and giving her son $500 to start *Ebony*, which now has a circulation of more than 1.2 million. Johnson became a leading cross-media owner in the United States, with a book publishing company, a nationally syndicated television program, and two radio stations.[21] One of the first African Americans to appear on the Forbes 400 List, Johnson had an estate valued at $500 million on his death.

Magazines specialize in several major topic areas. In fact, Bacon's annual directory of magazines lists 225 market classifications. Ten of the most important, at least in terms of circulation, are news, fashion, women (with at least three major subgroups: middle-aged and older women, women under thirty-five, and teenage girls), families (especially aimed at parents of children under age twelve), sports (with some general interest but many specialized by sport), ethnic, medical/health, political, farm (*Farm Journal* alone has a circulation of 815,000), and lifestyles (type of home, region, cooking, etc.).

Sales and Readership of Magazines

Contemporary magazines, like all media, are increasingly subject to ownership consolidation and media concentration. The magazine industry did not suffer the same steep drops in circulation and advertising seen with newspapers during the recession. Nevertheless, it did suffer; and the recession claimed some notable victims, such as *U.S. News & World Report*, which stopped publishing in 2010 and went entirely online except for its college- and hospital-ranking issues. *Newsweek* also changed dramatically between 2007 and 2010, cutting staff and revising format to accommodate a revenue decline of 38 percent. Eventually, the Washington Post Company sold *Newsweek* to Tina Brown's *The Daily Beast*; and on January 4, 2013, it became a digital-only publication. In August 2013, it was sold to IBT Media.

Despite established magazines going to online-only editions, hundreds of new magazine titles are published every year. Most do not survive more than two years. The leading circulation magazines reflect general trends. Even the top print magazines, which target specific audiences and cover specialized subjects in depth and with quality, are not immune. Those with the largest circulation appeal to large and growing audience segments, such as aging baby boomers who are more likely to read a print format than younger people. However, young people are also

TABLE 3-1 Top Ten U.S. Paid-Circulation Magazines*

RANK	PUBLICATION	CIRCULATION
1	AARP®	22,837,736
2	AARPBulletin	22,183,316
3	Better Homes and Gardens	7,639,661
4	gameinformer	7,099,452
5	GOOD HOUSEKEEPING	4,315,330
6	FamilyCircle	4,015,728
7	NATIONAL GEOGRAPHIC	3,572,348
8	People	3,510,533
9	Reader's digest	3,393,573
10	Woman's Day	3,288,335

*Data as of June 30, 2014
Source: Alliance for Audited Media, 2014

proving to be avid magazine readers (although often in digital-only form), with 90 percent of college students saying they had read a magazine in the last month.[22]

Table 3-1 compares the top ten paid-circulation magazines in the United States in 1972 and 2014. The positions of both *AARP The Magazine* and *AARP Bulletin*, publications of the American Association of Retired Persons, reflect the fact that America's population is aging. In 1972, most of the magazines were either women's or general interest with subscriptions. In 2014, the top two magazines, both sent as AARP membership perks, have circulations far greater than the rest.

After years of slow but steady declines, the magazine industry is finally starting to see some growth, thanks to increased advertising and readership in digital editions, a trend the industry predicts will continue. This prediction is supported by specific magazine data in Table 3-2 that shows digital magazine sales, both subscriptions and single copies, are growing and, in many cases, vastly exceed newsstand sales.

Outlook for Magazines

The rise in popularity of tablets and other portable devices with relatively large screens and high resolution has helped increase reading activity, including longer-form content, compared to the laptop or PC era. Paragraph Shorts, an iPad app

TABLE 3-2 Digital Issues a Significant Portion of Magazine Sales

Average digital issue circulation for subscription and single copy sales

	2011		2012		2013		2014	
	SUBS	NEWSSTAND	SUBS	NEWSSTAND	SUBS	NEWSSTAND	SUBS	NEWSSTAND
The Atlantic	2,360	592	6,122	661	9,788	468	10,266	713
The Week	N/A	N/A	2,602	42	2,626	161	3,327	28
The New Yorker	27,372	1,953	51,157	799	73,802	8,837	80,153	9,956
The Economist	5,321	85	5,944	181	8,674	145	7,351	69
Time	N/A	N/A	N/A	N/A	44,938	5,259	49,191	16,001
The Nation	9,205	58	14,720	129	25,928	121	27,941	63
National Review	5,918	4,012	14,764	459	11,561	163	10,338	113
Fortune	N/A	N/A	N/A	N/A	9,107	4,821	11,666	9,105
The New Republic	N/A	N/A	3,374	110	6,788	170	7,992	118
Rolling Stone	15,190	519	19,976	674	24,121	2,349	28,913	23,506
Vanity Fair	11,171	7,132	43,351	3,604	60,820	18,018	62,746	17,530
New York Magazine	786	304	2,848	296	5,200	6,939	19,463	26,112
Bloomberg Business Week	18,334	171	36,911	53	37,423	727	54,004	2,725
Wired	17,629	10,076	73,066	3,423	86,178	16,843	75,369	20,870

Source: Alliance for Audited Media, AAM Audits and Publisher Statements. "News Use Across Social Media Platforms," Pew Research Center, Washington, DC (April, 2015) http://www.journalism.org/2015/04/29/news-magazines-fact-sheet/.
Note: National Review, Bloomberg and New York Magazine 12-month audits come out in June. 2011 data for Bloomberg Business Week, National Review, and New York Magazine are from the 6-month publisher's statements ending in December 2011. 2012 data for The New Republic are for 3 months ending December 2012; before 2012, The New Republic was not audited by AAM. Newsweek hasn't been audited since August 2013 and did not report digital replica copies for any of the years before. Forbes does not break out digital issues in AAM's statements.

launched in 2013, features short stories from publications around the world such as *The Paris Review*, *The New Yorker*, and *The Guardian*; and notables such as Ira Glass of PRI's (Public Radio International) *This American Life* narrate audio stories.

Although long-form narratives typically seen in magazines such as *The New Yorker* and the *Atlantic Monthly* must compete with a range of other content, including video or audio content, there appears to be a market for these types of stories, even if in primarily digital form.

Full-color pages and high-quality, glossy paper make print magazines both expensive to produce and environmentally unfriendly, even with recycled paper and vegetable inks. Visually enticing and readable magazine pages may also be their saving grace, though, as tablets improve and more magazines go digital. For now, high-quality print is still more readable than text on a similarly sized tablet screen, although the differences are rapidly narrowing, and digital offers multimedia and interactivity. Magazine ads, print or digital, can be works of graphic art, and the portability and relatively low cost of a magazine do not make consumers feel like they are making a major investment.

Certain magazines can also serve an important social function. Publicly reading the *New Yorker* imparts a very different impression of the reader than *Popular Hot Rodding* or *Guns & Ammo*. In fact, magazines considered prestigious can operate as subtle social markers simply by being displayed on the coffee table in the home or office, even if the magazine is never actually read.

It seems the public is willing to pay for an online subscription to a magazine perceived as the voice of authority in a specialized area. *Consumer Reports Online*, one of the few subscription success stories in the online-magazine world, has over 3 million subscribers who can access archived articles and reviews.[23] Enhancing this product is the Consumer Reports Mobile iPad app that allows subscribers to consult an authoritative source while out shopping.

The type of magazine content we see today may not change much, but the way in which we see it will. Despite several pressures, magazines continue to maintain some important advantages over newspapers as relevant print-based products. In the long term, however, print magazines will likely lose their relative importance, whereas better tablet screens, such as Apple's iPad high-resolution retina display, give magazines a new lease on life and a digital home.

Because of their highly visual nature, magazines are well suited for the tablet format.

MEDIA CAREERS

The title of book editor seems self-explanatory, but these professionals do much more than just edit (although they do that, too). Book editors are responsible for reading unpublished manuscripts submitted by authors and determining which ones may be most successful on the market. A book editor who successfully finds and shepherds a bestseller or two through the publishing process is well on the way to an impressive career in the book publishing industry.

Although one may imagine a successful book editor working in a global publishing house such as HarperCollins and hobnobbing with famous authors, thousands of smaller publishing companies, including academic and textbook publishers, offer rewarding careers (if not quite the same fame and glory). Editors can become knowledgeable about specialized academic areas, working with leading scholars in their fields to help them publish their books.

Good writing and editing skills are needed, of course, as well as a keen eye for detail and an understanding of the changing trends in the market. Liberal arts graduates, by training and interest, often make good editors, as they can draw from their knowledge on a range of subject matter while employing their critical thinking and writing skills.

LOOKING BACK AND MOVING FORWARD

In a media-saturated world of eye-catching multimedia and flashy graphics, gray, quiet, dull print seems like it will be less appealing to many. Indeed, some studies indicate a worrisome decline in reading among adults, especially young people. If print has improved our ability to think logically and rationally, that raises questions about how today's digital media may be affecting our thinking, adversely or otherwise. However, even with the proliferation of new media options, reading remains an important activity—some may say it could become even more important, especially if media literacy and critical-thinking skills decline.

From an economic perspective, media industries that have relied on printing on paper are facing grave challenges, not because the content has become irrelevant but because the packaging has changed. Just as scrolls eventually gave way to books and the form of writing also evolved, printed books are beginning to yield to digital formats that may produce equally revolutionary transformations.

Similarly, newspapers and magazines are facing drastic adjustments. There is nothing sacred or magical about the form of the modern newspaper (although for people who grew up reading newspapers it may seem so); and if papers are to survive, they may need to go digital—as some major newspapers are doing. This change is not simply one of form: it will alter the nature of the newspaper and likely even the nature of news itself because it allows print to converge with audio, video, and multimedia. Whether this reduces the importance of the written word or how it alters it in our minds remains to be seen.

Print published on paper will never disappear entirely, of course; sailboats did not disappear with the rise of steamships, nor did horseback riding with the invention of railroads and cars. But the changes that will inevitably occur will transform our society and culture. And the records that will be kept—most likely in written form, albeit stored digitally—will give future historians a rearview mirror that will reveal far more about us than we realize today.

MEDIA MATTERS   PRINT MEDIA

1. Do you prefer to read your textbooks in ebook format? Other than cost, do you notice any difference in how you read texts online compared to in print?

2. Where did you buy your latest book or ebook that was not a textbook?

3. What is the oldest book you own?

4. When was the last time you read a printed newspaper?

5. Compare the print version of your favorite newspaper with its digital version. Which format do you prefer, and why?

6. What do you feel are the greatest challenges facing print media in a digital age?

7. Do you subscribe to any magazines? Which ones? Do you prefer to read them on a tablet?

8. If you subscribe to a magazine, print or digital, describe how you typically read it. For example, do you read some sections first and jump around, or do you read it cover to cover? Do you read it over a month or soon after getting it? Are your reading patterns different in the print edition versus the digital? Why or why not?

9. What do you think the magazines you read regularly say about yourself as a consumer?

10. How do you think the major societal functions of books, magazines, and newspapers may change in the age of digital media?

FURTHER READING

A History of Reading. Alberto Manguel (1997) Penguin.

An Introduction to Book History. David Finkelstein, Alastair McCreely (2005) Routledge.

The Book: A Global History. Michael Suarez, H. R. Woudhuysen (2014) Oxford University Press.

Books: A Living History. Martyn Lyons (2011) J. Paul Getty Museum.

Preserving the Press: How Daily Newspapers Mobilized to Keep Their Readers. Leo Bogart (1991) Columbia University Press.

-30-: The Collapse of the Great American Newspaper. Charles M. Madigan (ed.) (2007) Ivan R. Dee.

The Vanishing Newspaper: Saving Journalism in the Information Age. Philip Meyer (2004) University of Missouri Press.

The Death and Life of American Journalism: The Media Revolution That Will Begin the World Again. Robert McChesney, John Nichols (2010) Nation Books.

The Magazine from Cover to Cover. Sammye Johnson, Patricia Prijatel (2006) Oxford University Press.

Magazines: A Complete Guide to the Industry. David Sumner, Shirrel Rhoades (2006) Peter Lang.

Pulp Culture: The Art of Fiction Magazines. Frank M. Robinson, Lawrence Davidson (2007) Collectors Press.

Newspaper Online vs. Print Ad Revenue: The 10% Problem. Scott Karp (2007) Publishing 2.0.

The Curse of the Mogul: What's Wrong with the World's Leading Media Companies. Jonathan A. Knee, Bruce Greenwald, Ava Seave (2009) Portfolio.

Just My Type: A Book About Fonts. Simon Garfield (2011) Gotham Books.

Audio Media
MUSIC RECORDINGS, RADIO

Taylor Swift is an award-winning musical artist whose popularity around the United States and the world has made her one of the most successful artists of the twenty-first century and kept her at the top of the Billboard charts. She is also at the center of the continuing revolution in the distribution and sales of recorded music. Swift stunned the music industry on November 3, 2014, when she pulled her entire music catalog from the online streaming music service Spotify.[1]

Swift has never endorsed free music and explained her logic in frank and plain terms: "Music is art, and art is important and rare. Important, rare things are valuable. Valuable things should be paid for." Some anticipated that Swift's new album *1989* would see a boost in sales as a result of fans not being able to hear it on Spotify. One anonymous music industry source attributes high sales to other factors, however: "There are reasons why you can sell 1 million units, but it's got nothing to do with not providing that album to Spotify."

Whatever the causes, predictions for the album's success, both critical and commercial, proved accurate. Not only did her fifth studio album receive industry acclaim, it topped iTunes sales charts in over 95 countries on its release and went on to sell well over 1 million units, 8.6 million albums worldwide as of February 2015. It became the highest selling release since 2002 and the top-selling album of 2014 in the United States. It also made Swift the first artist in music history to have three albums sell 1 million or more copies in the first week. In 2015, Swift, 25, became the youngest person to make Forbes's list of the world's most powerful women, ranked at number 64.

In February 2015, she received the International Federation of the Phonographic Industry (IFPI) Award, recognizing her as the most popular recording artist worldwide in 2014. Across all music formats including physical sales, downloads, and streaming, she led Billboard charts that featured artists such as Katy Perry, Beyoncé, Eric Church, Sam Smith, Ed Sheeran, Coldplay, and One Direction. Swift has managed to thrive in an industry where sales have long been in decline, and 2014 in general was no exception to the downward trend.[2]

LEARNING OBJECTIVES

>> Describe the nature and basic functions of the recording arts (i.e., music).

>> Discuss the history of the recording arts.

>> Describe how the recording industry works.

>> Identify the changes digitization, the Internet, and file-sharing services have brought to the recording-industry business model.

>> Describe the nature and basic functions of radio.

>> Discuss the history of radio.

>> Describe how the radio industry works.

97

Dr. Dre topped the list of musical money makers in 2014, with $620 million in earnings, much of it from Apple's acquisition of his music company, Beats. Second on the list is Beyoncé, who earned $115 million in 2014.

Regardless of form or format, listening to music remains a national pastime, second only to time spent watching television. People get their music via various media—on the radio through online, broadcast, cable, or satellite transmission, or on demand through personal mobile devices such as an MP3 player or smartphone. Music is often playing in the background as people go about their daily activities or engage with other media, such as video games or books. Couples often have "their" song that seems to speak meaningfully to their particular relationship (despite the fact that it was written for mass appeal), and many a teen has played air guitar in front of the mirror while dreaming of rock stardom.

Music is an essential element of movies and television, an audio cue to what to expect or feel in particular scenes. The low-pitched, menacing music in *Jaws* (1975) whenever the shark was going to strike heightened tension as viewers feared for its next victim. The theme became so famous that other movies reprised it as parody, and daily conversation is often similarly peppered with the musical "dun, dun, dun, dun ..." to suggest imminent trouble.

> **DISCUSSION QUESTIONS:** Is recorded music more important for teenagers than, say, people in their forties? Explain your answer.

The Recording Industry

Similar to other media-entertainment enterprises, a few very large firms (often subsidiaries of even larger media corporations) control the music industry. Because record labels do not profit from music that lacks strong mass-market appeal, styles tend to fit well-established genres, even to the point of being formulaic and homogeneous. This situation is improving, however, as online music distribution makes more diverse artists available to fans.

Distinctive Functions of the Recording Industry

entertainment

Providing or being provided with amusement or enjoyment.

cultural transmission

The process of passing on culturally relevant knowledge, skills, attitudes, and values from person to person or group to group.

Appealing to just about everyone, young and old alike, recorded music serves a variety of functions, primarily **entertainment** and **cultural transmission**. Education is an important form of cultural transmission. Children, especially, listen to recorded music, sometimes the same songs over and over, learning vocabulary, musical rhythms, and the pleasure of dancing. Musical tastes help people define themselves as members of a particular social group. Music can transmit culture both verbally and visually as fans adopt new expressions and emulate new styles that cross ethnic and socioeconomic boundaries.

Some argue that such cultural transmission has a potential dark side, however, a debate that intensified after the 1981 launch of MTV, whose twenty-four-hour format required scores of videos to fill airtime. Suddenly, how a band looked became as important as how they sounded. Hair bands became popular in the 1980s, groups such as Mötley Crüe, whose manes, makeup, and tight pants all played well on TV. New music channels found a home on cable in the 1990s, including channels devoted to diverse and specific genres such as heavy metal or country.

Artists may combine controversial lyrics with provocative video that critics argue send young, impressionable viewers socially unacceptable messages that may desensitize them to violence against women, for example, or promote Satanism. Research indicates that between 40 and 75 percent of music videos do contain sexual imagery, although it is generally mild and nongraphic. Sexism remains strong, however. Women are much more likely to be scantily clad, sexually objectified, and dominated by men.[3] With the rise of YouTube and other online video services, the debate has intensified, as an even broader array of potentially objectionable content is available on demand.

Although MTV, YouTube, or other sources of music video may not always represent the finest work of this commercial, profit-driven enterprise intended to entertain, the recording industry also produces music that rises to the level of true art. Whether the genre is jazz, opera, pop, or hip-hop, countless studio recordings have earned critical praise for their enduring cultural impact.

> **DISCUSSION QUESTIONS:** In what ways have MTV and the music video, whether online or via television, influenced the recording-arts industry and popular music?

History of Recorded Music

The recording arts developed in the 1870s, becoming the first medium of mass communication not based on print. They predated mass-media cinema at the turn of the century; and radio, invented in the 1890s, did not develop as a mass medium until the 1920s. In 1877, Thomas Edison patented his first "talking machine," the **phonograph**, using a tinfoil cylinder to record telephone messages. Edison held a monopoly in the recording industry for nine years until telephone pioneer Alexander Graham Bell and inventor Charles Tainter invented an improved audio-recording device, the **graphophone**, which used beeswax rather than tinfoil.

The Columbia Phonograph Company soon entered the picture with its own technology, selling recordings on wax cylinders that could be played on coin-operated machines. The Victor Talking Machine Company also launched the **gramophone**. Developed by inventor Emile Berliner, it used a flat disc rather than a cylinder to record sound.

Few dramatic changes occurred in music-recording technology over the first one hundred years. Even the mid-1950s creation of grooved vinyl long-play (LP) albums at 33 rpm (revolutions per minute), allowing playing times of forty to forty-five minutes rather than the two and a half minutes of the shellac 78 rpm albums, simply improved existing production processes and sound quality rather than revolutionizing them.

Electromagnetic tapes such as eight-track tapes, and later cassettes, created in 1965, actually provided poorer sound quality than LPs, but consumers were willing to trade audio quality for portability. Compact discs, developed in 1980, were the first conveyor of digitally recorded songs and the first real technological breakthrough in the recording arts since Edison's time. Not only can digital technology improve the sound quality of older recordings by removing unwanted noise such as pops and hisses, but it also allows for easy creation of "duets" by live and dead singers, such as the song "Unforgettable" by Nat King Cole and his daughter Natalie.

phonograph

First patented by Thomas Edison in 1877 as a "talking machine," it used a tinfoil cylinder to record voices from telephone conversations.

graphophone

An improvement on Thomas Edison's phonograph in recording audio, it used beeswax to record sound rather than tinfoil. Developed by Alexander Graham Bell and inventor Charles Tainter.

gramophone

Developed by inventor Emile Berliner, it used a flat disc rather than a cylinder to record sound.

It was a technological challenge to record sound on devices that would be easy for the public to use.

FROM TIN PAN ALLEY TO HOLLYWOOD

The history of recorded music involves both technology and artistry, physical changes in the material recording as well as cultural changes in the genre of music likely to be recorded. In the early days, much of the popular music in America was created in New York's historic Tin Pan Alley, an area in Manhattan on West Twenty-eighth Street between Broadway and Sixth Avenue, where music publishers had located close to theaters and vaudeville houses. Before record players became widespread, sheet music of songs heard in these venues was played at home. Existing for seventy years until roughly 1950, when radio and television became more important music promoters, Tin Pan Alley eventually became a generic reference to the music-publishing business that hired composers and lyricists on a permanent basis to write popular songs.

From George and Ira Gershwin to Cole Porter, many great composers were associated with the early days of Tin Pan Alley. Perhaps the artist most synonymous with the time is Irving Berlin, who achieved stardom in 1911 when his song "Alexander's Ragtime Band" became an international hit. He went on to pen such classics as "Blue Skies," "God Bless America," "White Christmas," and "There's No Business Like Show Business."

As Hollywood developed and motion pictures with sound emerged in the late 1920s and early 1930s, a recording industry also emerged in Los Angeles. The growth of musical recording and radio in the first half of the twentieth century enabled musicians and fans to hear many musical forms. A diverse array of black, Latino, Native American, Asian, and white artists created songs with audience crossover appeal that laid the foundation for much of popular music today, including rap and other formats.

ROOTS OF ROCK AND ROLL

The roots of rock and roll lie in a blend of musical forms, including blues vocalizations; gospel musical structures; urban rhythm and blues (R&B) instrumentals; and white western and "hillbilly" strains, or rockabilly. In the late 1940s and early 1950s, a combination of country artists, such as Hank Williams and Tennessee Ernie Ford, and R&B artists, such as T-Bone Walker, Fats Domino, B. B. King, Ruth Brown, and Muddy Waters, helped shape the character of early rock and roll.

From 1954 to 1959, rock and roll took off. Bill Haley and His Comets (western swing crossover), Ray Charles (gospel/R&B), Elvis Presley (rockabilly), Chuck Berry (R&B), Buddy Holly (rockabilly), and Ritchie Valens (Chicano rock) led the way. Popular rock vocal groups included the Platters, the Penguins, and Dion and the Belmonts as well as teen idols such as Frankie Avalon and Brenda Lee. Although much of the music owed its original inspiration to black artists, most of the commercially successful rock stars of the day were white.

This changed when Detroit's Berry Gordy Jr. started Motown Record Company in Motor City, Detroit, his hometown and a city with a historically large black population. Gordy was yet another black musician who had barely

The dog Nipper "listening to his master's voice" is a widely recognized symbol of what started as the Victor Talking Machine Company.

Irving Berlin was a noted composer of many of the twentieth century's most popular songs.

R&B performers Diana Ross & the Supremes were the most commercially successful Motown act and one of the most popular American vocal groups of all time, boasting twelve number-one pop singles on the Billboard Hot 100.

profited from his successful songwriting. With $700 borrowed from his sister and a makeshift studio in the basement, Gordy signed a kid off the street named Smokey Robinson and his backup singers, the Miracles, and started producing their music. The group quickly released a string of hits, and other successes followed when Gordy signed Diana Ross & the Supremes, Marvin Gaye, Stevie Wonder, the Jackson Five (with Michael Jackson), and many more talented black artists. By 1983, Motown was the largest black-owned company in the United States, with annual revenues of $104 million. Some thirty years after founding Motown, Gordy sold it to MCA Records in 1988.

In the 1960s, rock evolved to include Motown, as well as soul, "girl groups," surf rock, and folk. In addition to wielding musical influence, certain popular musicians also had great social and cultural impact, influencing trends and tastes, clothing and hairstyles. Folk artists such as Bob Dylan wrote songs that became anthems for social movements and shaped public opinion about the war in Vietnam, the environment, and civil rights. Reflecting his broad social influence and consummate artistry, in 1997, Dylan was nominated for a Nobel Prize in Literature.

The Who, who announced their 1982 tour would be their last, has continued to sell out arenas all over the world, with their 2014/2015 tour commemorating their 50th anniversary as a band.

REDEFINING ROCK

"The British invasion" redefined rock in the mid to late 1960s, with breakout groups such as the Beatles, the Rolling Stones, and the Who heightening its energy and popularity. Experimentation with drugs increased among youth in general

Rapper and entrepreneur Jay Z became the biggest artist to launch an album with an app, giving him the best opening-week sales of his career. In an unprecedented deal, Samsung purchased 1 million copies of *Magna Carta Holy Grail* for customers to download for free. This digital distribution method generated a new revenue stream along with a new set of problems, including piracy, server overload, and intrusive requests to access information on users' phones.

major labels

Universal Music Group, Sony Music, and Warner Music Group—the three biggest recording-arts companies, which control much of the music industry partly through their powerful distribution channels and ability to market music to mass audiences.

independent labels

Small companies that produce and distribute records. Not part of the three major-label corporations, they include those producing only one or two albums a year as well as larger independents such as Disney.

and rock musicians in particular. Some new strains emerged in rock, including psychedelic, jazz, and early heavy metal forms. A number of these early bands and artists, some of whom have even hit seventy, are still touring, much to the delight of legions of old and new fans alike, willing to pay top dollar for this opportunity. These living—and still performing—legends include groups who prematurely announced farewell tours decades ago.

In the 1970s, music moved from being socially conscious and experimental to highly produced and flamboyant. Glam rock bands flaunted dramatic makeup on stage, and sometimes off, as KISS did for many years. Disco appeared for a brief time in the mid-1970s, when punk also started, the latter being a response to the perceived overcommercialization of popular music. The 1980s saw the rise of heavy metal music, while pop bands such as Culture Club and Wham! sang blithely of love and infatuation. Rap left the urban streets for the mainstream in the late 1980s and early 1990s; while Seattle bands such as Nirvana, Soundgarden, and Alice in Chains developed a dark sound dubbed alternative or progressive rock.

Musical genres continue to transform and splinter as they wax and wane in popularity. Even older genres, such as swing, sometimes enjoy a short resurgence. Mainstream country music has come to sound more like country rock, for example, and some songs appear as crossover hits on both pop and country charts.

The Recording Industry Today

On the corporate side of recording, a handful of companies controlled the industry by 1909. Geoffrey P. Hull notes that although these companies experienced major changes, a three-way corporate oligarchy dominated the music industry until the 1950s, when a variety of notable industry-wide changes set in. These included greater competition due to the growth of rock and roll and diverse new recording labels such as Motown.

Like other media companies, record labels have been consolidating. In 1998, there were six **major labels**, and in 2004 only five, including Bertelsmann Music Group (BMG) and EMI. In 2008, Sony Music absorbed BMG; and in 2012, Universal Music Group acquired EMI. Now once again, three companies have oligarchical control, each a subsidiary of a larger media empire: Sony Music Entertainment, Warner Music Group, and Universal Music Group (UMG; see Table 4-1). UMG alone controls more than 25 percent of the worldwide market for recorded music. **Independent labels**—ranging from small local companies producing and distributing the music of only one or two artists to large labels such as Disney—have the majority of music titles, estimated at about 66 percent by SoundScan and the Recording Industry Association of America (RIAA), yet only about 20 percent of the sales.

Similar to book publishing, the vast majority of releases sell less than 5,000 copies per year, with only a handful of recordings, numbering in the hundreds, selling more than 250,000 a year. Yet these few, largely releases by major labels, account for over half the total sales volume. How do they manage to produce so many of the big hits? Some say they reap the rewards of producing and marketing

TABLE 4-1   The Major Record Labels and Their Main Subsidiary Labels

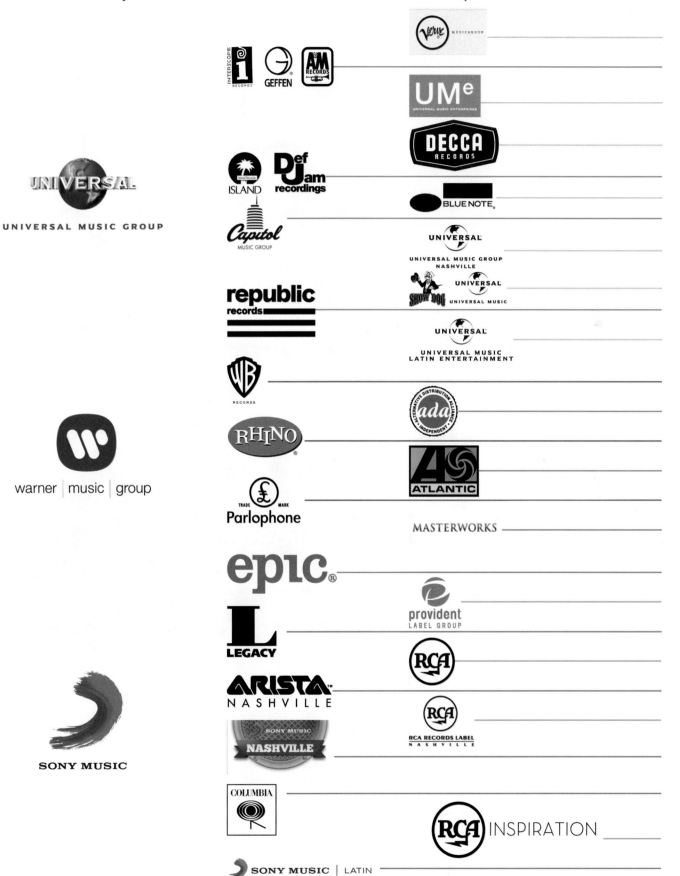

MEDIA PIONEERS
Amanda Palmer

When alternative rocker Amanda Palmer took a hiatus from the punk-cabaret duo The Dresden Dolls and decided to make her first solo album her way, she turned her back on her record label and turned instead, with open heart and empty hands, to her fans. The request? A relatively modest $100,000 to be raised on Kickstarter, one of several digital crowdfunding platforms employed by a growing number of artists. The response? An overwhelming $1.2 million—contributions from nearly 25,000 of the faithful, generated in a matter of weeks in 2012.

Depending on the amount of their pledge, fans would receive recordings in various formats or related artwork perhaps. And the most financially committed, many of whom met through Twitter or Facebook to pool together the requisite $5,000, could enjoy a private concert and house party with Amanda herself.[6]

Despite her newfound status as a Kickstarter sensation, a subsequent request directed at a different audience failed miserably. She quickly fell from Internet grace after attempting to recruit local musicians via her blog to play with her and her touring band The Grand Theft Orchestra for beer, hugs, and high fives. More controversy ensued the following year about a poem she wrote for alleged Boston Marathon bomber Dzhokhar Tsarnaev, deemed the worst poem ever composed in the English language by Gawker.com.[7]

Reactions to Palmer tend toward the extreme: a vibrant visionary to fans, an entitled egotist to critics. Regardless, her provocative and unapologetic resume in the art of asking, the title of a recent TED talk that she elaborated into a book, remains pioneering and eclectic. After graduating from Wesleyan College, she spent five years as a busker in Boston's Harvard Square, a living statue called the Eight-Foot Bride. Appreciative passersby would drop money in her hat, an activity that Palmer likens to fan funding of digitally recorded music through services like Kickstarter. In both cases, audiences need to step forward and provide direct support for artists they value.

Not surprisingly, given her philosophy and business model, Palmer is vocal about the "magic" of Twitter, which, as she observed in her TED talk, allowed her to "ask

instantly for anything anywhere"—a couch to sleep on, a piano to practice on, a home-cooked meal to savor backstage. And she waxed similarly effusive about the Internet in general as a means of connecting intimately and sharing freely: "Celebrity is about a lot of people loving you from a distance, but the Internet and the content that we're freely able to share on it are taking us back. It's about a few people loving you up close and about those people being enough."[8]

the best music from the best artists. Others say even marginal music from the major labels will dominate sales because of superior marketing.

Nevertheless, revenues have declined steeply since 2001, the beginning of the digital piracy era. In 2000, worldwide recorded music revenues were $36.9 billion. By 2013, global music sales were $15 billion (including synch revenues, payment for use of a song in another soundtrack, such as a commercial or TV show), down more than 55 percent, according to the IFPI, a London-based organization that represents the interests of the recording industry worldwide. The industry has struggled to stem the flood of free versions or mash-ups of songs found on file-sharing services, and the RIAA and IFPI claim that file-sharing services encouraging illegal downloads are to blame for the decline in sales. Other observers say the picture is more complex than that.

First, just under half (49 percent) of music sales globally in 2013 were still CDs, $7.3 billion of the total $15 billion, with worldwide revenues dropping 4 percent from 2012. CD sales declined 12 percent, or $1.9 billion, between 2010 and 2011 and hit a new low in 2014, down 20 percent from 2013.[4] Yet consumers are increasingly willing to buy songs online via iTunes and other services, and digital sales (online subscriptions and downloads) increased 8 percent, to a total of $7.7 billion in 2013, according to IFPI. Digital sales worldwide were almost half the total music sales; and in the United States, 51 percent of music sales were digital in 2013, up about half since 2009. Moreover, the purchase of entire digital albums, not just individual songs, was up more than 20 percent in the United States since 2010.[5]

More encouraging news for the music industry is the fact that global revenues from streaming and subscription services increased 51 percent in 2013, topping $1 billion for the first time. As CD sales drop, major retail chains such as Best Buy and Wal-Mart, where 65 percent of all CD sales occur, give them less floor display space. The waters are further muddied by exclusive distribution deals with major chains like Wal-Mart. In 2008, AC/DC's *Black Ice*, sold exclusively at Wal-Mart, was the fifth-highest-selling album of the year. Although sales of independent releases have also grown dramatically with the Internet and digital distribution, they continue to be low relative to most major labels, whose marketing resources and business model give them the competitive edge.

> **DISCUSSION QUESTIONS:** How many songs in your music library have you downloaded for free? How much would you have spent if you'd purchased each song for ninety-nine cents? How many downloaded songs from new artists persuaded you to purchase that artist's CD or to buy digital song or album downloads?

Recording-Industry Business Model

Throughout much of the twentieth century, the basic business model in the recorded-music industry involved creation, promotion, and distribution. These three main activities have not changed fundamentally, although some of their components have been altered in the digital age.

CREATION

Acting as gatekeepers, the major record labels sign talent and subsequently support these artists in the creation and recording of music. Because of their financial investment in the process, they have historically reaped the greatest financial rewards, with most artists receiving royalties of only around 10 percent of gross, or overall, sales.

Being signed to a major label does not mean that a struggling band has finally made it: Most releases sell fewer than 5,000 copies annually; only a handful sell more than 250,000. Of these sales numbers, 10 percent, about $2 per album sold, is not much income for a band.[9] For every Adele selling millions of albums, there are thousands of artists who sell only a few thousand indie or major-label albums and who never get airplay.[10]

PROMOTION

Promoting artists and their music is crucial to commercial success. Artists perform in concerts, for which additional royalties are received; but music gains exposure largely through radio, television, film, and, increasingly, video games, commercials, and mobile phone ringtones. In the past three decades, music videos have also been important.

Major labels get considerably more airtime than indies on radio, a primary promotional vehicle. Record labels traditionally provide radio and television programmers with free copies of recorded music and music videos in exchange for getting them played on their stations and channels. Unscrupulous programmers or disc jockeys in major markets have sometimes received cash, gifts, or other secret payments—**payola**—in return for increased airplay. Payola was very big in the 1950s until the Federal Trade Commission (FTC) ruled it unfairly stifled competition from smaller labels with fewer financial resources.

Payola, or "pay for play," reduces diversity on the air and is punishable today with fines or even imprisonment. Record labels have circumvented such restrictions, enforced by the Federal Communications Commission, by having artists give radio interviews in exchange for promotion, holding special events in certain markets, and giving away tickets or backstage passes in conjunction with the radio station.

DISTRIBUTION

Although recording formats have varied, the method of distribution has remained essentially unchanged. Record labels make copies from a master version and send the albums, tapes, or CDs to local retail outlets for sale to consumers. Online stores such as Amazon act much like their physical counterparts. Unfettered, however, by concerns about store display space, they can stock more CDs than retail stores, including CDs that are less popular. **Long tail** marketing and distribution allow businesses to succeed by selling a greater variety of items but fewer of each.

Another aspect of digital media and the Internet has been changing distribution much more radically. Consumers no longer have to buy a physical product. They simply download songs either through a subscription service or à la carte. Not only can the general public easily copy and distribute music, they can also create flawless copies with no loss in sound quality. Using widely available software, they can personalize content with mash-ups of multiple songs. These developments are affecting industry business models for music distribution profoundly.

payola

Cash or gifts given to radio disc jockeys by record labels in exchange for greater airplay of the label's artists or most recent songs. After several scandals in the 1950s, the practice is now illegal.

long tail

The principle that selling a few of many types of items can be as or more profitable than selling many copies of a few items, a practice that works especially well for online sellers such as Amazon and Netflix.

DISCUSSION QUESTIONS: Think of two songs that you particularly like from two different genres. Now imagine making a mash-up creatively combining elements of the two songs. What commercial potential might your new mash-up have, if any?

PRICING STRUCTURE

The pricing structure for recorded music is, of course, key in determining income for the label, the artist, and others in the distribution chain. In the 1970s, when vinyl LPs were the standard, list price (the consumer price) was about $6 (about $26 in 2012 dollars). In the 1980s, the compact disc was introduced, and CDs as a percentage of album sales gradually increased from just 22 percent in 1988 to 91 percent in 2001. List prices for CDs were about $19 in the early 1980s (about $39 in 2012 dollars), with wholesale prices about $12. Online album prices are somewhat lower, with typical prices for albums sold on iTunes at about $10 and even less on Amazon.com.

Over time, as production volume increased, production cost decreased; consequently, wholesale prices fell to about $10, with list prices at about $15 or often less with promotional discounts. Today, manufacturing costs for record labels are about $1 per CD, with artist and producer royalties about $2 per album (roughly 10–20 percent of the list price) and distributor charges about $1.50. Marketing costs (roughly 50¢) tend to be quite low because radio stations and music television provide most of the promotion for free. Thus, a label typically has a gross profit of $5 per CD sold. This admittedly simplified model still serves to illustrate how immensely the industry profits.

Music lovers around the world are using software like MiniMash to mix their own tunes from two or more songs by other artists.

Outlook for the Recording Industry

In 2015, Nielsen SoundScan and Billboard announced that music sales had decreased more than 10 percent between 2013 and 2014, continuing a steady decline since the early 2000s.[11] Instead, most artists generate the largest share of their revenues from touring and online streaming services. Once thought obsolete, vinyl sales also saw a slight uptick in 2014, but they make up only 3.5 percent of total recorded music sales. Revenue growth from streaming services is sustainable, some good news that suggests digital media, the bane of the music industry, may also be a boon.

DIGITAL RIGHTS MANAGEMENT AND ILLEGAL FILE SHARING

Critics argue that the music industry and major record labels have only themselves to blame for the general decline in music sales. Rather than embracing early on the potential of digital technologies and the Internet for generating new kinds of revenue streams, they resisted change in a number of ways that proved futile.

Security of copyrighted material remains a prime concern for record labels. Their past initiatives in **digital rights management (DRM)**, such as limiting digital copies of purchased music, have been viewed as heavy handed. Most DRM efforts with physical media like CDs have also proved unsuccessful because security codes have been quickly hacked. By 2009, none of the major record labels used DRM on their CDs, claiming the associated costs exceeded the gains.

digital rights management (DRM)

Technologies that let copyright owners control the level of access or use allowed for a copyrighted work, such as limiting the number of times a song can be copied.

DRM is far more common with online music, although not all online sellers use it. For downloaded music, DRM restricts either the types of devices that can play the downloaded song or the length of time the song can be played, or it limits access in some other way, such as requiring an ongoing subscription, as with Rdio. Generally, music services offering DRM versions of songs online have lower price points than non-DRM songs, which do not restrict formats or copying files between devices.

Since 2001, the recording industry has sued various file-sharing services and Internet service providers (ISPs), successfully shutting down and eventually bankrupting music file-sharing pioneer Napster. The RIAA even sued several thousand individuals for sharing files. Bad publicity ultimately made this practice untenable, though, and at the end of 2008, it opted to pressure the ISPs to cut those users off from the Internet rather than sue them individually.

Many ISPs have blocked access to file-sharing services because of the threat of lawsuits and the heavy load such sharing imposes, slowing down the networks even for users not sharing files. Universities, with their fast Internet connections and music-loving young masses, have been prime targets of the RIAA, which has pushed for special ethics education for new students to discourage the illegal file sharing of copyrighted works.

The recording industry has also been more aggressive in pursuing file-sharing services themselves. In late 2010, a four-year RIAA court case concluded with a federal judge shutting down popular file-sharing service LimeWire, with 50 million users monthly, after which BearShare, another file-sharing service, saw a sharp rise in users. As soon as one service closes, people apparently just seek out other existing or new services. Some proposed legislation, such as requiring digital security devices, supports industry efforts. Manufacturers, however, are resisting such directives, as are groups such as the Electronic Frontier Foundation (EFF), an advocate for citizen or consumer rights.

Electronic Frontier Foundation

The EFF is a not-for-profit organization that focuses on issues of privacy and developments in communications technologies.

NEW BUSINESS MODELS EMERGING

The music industry needs to develop new ways to sell music that match consumer interests and patterns of media use. To that end, two main business models seem to be emerging: downloads and subscription services.

Downloading music is hardly a recent activity. Not until the advent of Apple's iTunes in 2003, however, did the music industry finally succeed in getting consumers to pay for their downloads. Many in the recording industry, artists included, worried that à la carte song downloads would mean the death of the album, concerns that have proven to be largely valid. In the United States in 2013, there were 1.26 billion sales of individual songs online, seven times the volume of online album sales, which totaled just 118 million, according to data from Nielsen SoundScan. Added content such as behind-the-scenes footage, exclusive interviews, and games makes downloading an entire album appealing, but not sufficiently so for many consumers to justify the higher price of entire collections of

Giving consumers more choice in how they get their music has been a difficult adjustment for the major record labels.

songs. Although small compared to song and album downloads, downloaded ring-tones demonstrate how songs may be popular in a variety of formats, including those that normally would never have been considered mass media.

Subscription services, having grown remarkably in recent years, offer great potential for new types of revenue streams. Many subscriptions operate on a **freemium** model: some content is free, but a monthly subscription is required to take advantage of all the site has to offer. Different versions of the freemium model are currently being tested, such as advertising-supported content for the free service but no ads for the premium service. Other ways to distinguish the paid tier from the free tier include access to special content or songs that can be downloaded to other devices.

In North America, recent growth has made Slacker Radio and Pandora two of the biggest music-streaming and subscription services. Pandora has more than 75 million registered users, up from 25 million in 2008, and claims 500,000 paying subscribers. Sweden-based Spotify, launched in 2008 and the second most popular digital music service in Europe after iTunes, was available in the United States in July 2011, expanding the field of music-subscription competitors. Its revenues topped $1 billion in 2013. Also in 2013, Apple entered the field with its own streaming music service. As the names and functions of these services suggest, the lines have blurred between Internet radio and online music subscription services, making it hard to identify exactly where radio ends and downloading or streaming songs begins.

The recording industry is looking at working directly with ISPs, some of which offer their own branded music-subscription services to customers. They are also considering partnerships with mobile operators that will facilitate getting songs and music content from mobile devices.

> **DISCUSSION QUESTIONS:** What advice would you offer a record-label executive for creating a successful business model in the digital age?

What Is Broadcasting?

The term "broadcasting" originally referred to the practice of planting seeds by casting them broadly in a field rather than depositing them one at a time. In the early days of broadcasting as we have come to know it, wireless communications, initially only radio, provided point-to-point communication where telegraph lines were impractical or unreliable. Its main purpose was ship-to-ship or ship-to-shore communications for quick emergency transmissions. Subsequently, radio technology was developed to broadcast wireless messages widely to multiple locations. Dozens of years later, television allowed for the broadcasting of moving pictures as well as audio via wireless technology.

Broadcast technology works essentially the same way in both radio and television. A transmitter sends messages over a part of the electromagnetic spectrum to a receiver or antenna that translates the message to the radio or TV. The receiving device then decodes the audio or visual electromagnetic waves so that they can be heard or seen.

freemium

Subscriptions that provide some content for free but require a monthly subscription to take advantage of all the site has to offer.

Pharrell Williams's "Happy" was the number one streamed song worldwide in 2014.

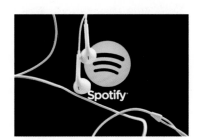

Streaming music service Spotify in 2014 had 50 million subscribers worldwide who streamed more than 8 billion hours of music.

broadcast

Originally a reference to casting seeds widely in a field that was subsequently applied to the fledgling electronic medium of radio and later television.

Radio

Early radios were often built to fit in with other living room furniture.

amplitude modulation (AM)

Radio carrier signal modified by variations in wave amplitude.

frequency modulation (FM)

Radio carrier signal modified by variations in wave length/ frequency.

Radio, the most widely available medium of mass communication around the world, is also the most heavily used medium in the United States: People listen to radio on average over 2.5 hours per day, although different types of research present disparate findings. For example, compared to observational studies, self-reports of radio usage tend to underreport radio listening greatly, likely because radio is often playing in the background while people do other things, even while they consume other media such as reading a book or going online.

At least 99 percent of all U.S. households have at least one radio receiver, similar to most industrialized countries. Even developing nations have relatively high radio penetration. Radio is less expensive to produce, transmit, and receive than television; radio receivers are highly portable—even wearable—and radio doesn't require literacy to understand. There are basically three types of radio broadcasting: **amplitude modulation (AM)**, **frequency modulation (FM)**, and satellite. Yet satellite radio, like so-called Internet radio, employs an entirely different method of delivering audio programming than traditional AM and FM radio. Both are "broadcast" in the sense that they reach mass audiences, but satellite's delivery makes it more akin to airplane audio programming than true broadcasting. Low-powered radio, often in the FM format, also varies from the general terrestrial broadcast formats. Less expensive to transmit, it has enabled many highly localized community radio stations to operate around the United States and internationally.

Distinctive Functions of Radio

Around the world, radio is a medium of news and entertainment. The low cost of both radio receivers and broadcasting has made it a particularly important and ubiquitous medium of mass communication in the developing world. Even in remote rural areas, it disseminates important information, such as agricultural instructions for easy, cheap, and rapid farming. Radio is also used globally as an emergency broadcast system for events such as severe storms, natural disasters, and military conflict, largely because of its portability and flexible power source. Radio receivers can operate easily for long periods on battery power alone.

In industrialized societies, radio has a broad array of functions, perhaps more diverse than any other of the traditional analog media. Talk radio provides information, debate, and even limited audience interactivity with listeners who call in. News programming offers breaking news as well as traffic and weather reports, school closings, and more. The broadcasting of recorded music for entertainment, the mainstay of commercial radio, benefits the public, artists, and the recording industry.

History of Radio

Radio boasts a remarkable history. Technically, economically, and programmatically, it has changed considerably since its early development, and it continues to

ETHICS IN MEDIA
Mashed-Up and Mixed-Up Musical Ethics

The aptly named "Blurred Lines" illustrates the challenges of ethics in media in the digital age. In 1977, legendary artist Marvin Gaye produced a sensational hit called "Got to Give It Up," a song that has remained familiar and popular over the years.

Four decades later, recording artist Robin Thicke produced the contemporary hit "Blurred Lines," which critics contend is little more than a digital rip-off of Gaye's masterpiece.[12] Thicke's song entered the musical charts in the summer of 2013 and quickly rose to the top of national and global markets, where it stayed for six weeks, selling more than six million copies and helping catapult Thicke to international fame.

Marvin Gaye died in 1984, tragically shot by his father in an apparent argument. His family now claims that Thicke essentially took the melody from Gaye's original hit and remixed it into the melody of "Blurred Lines."[13] Thicke has since admitted that he was high on drugs and alcohol when the new song was coproduced with international musical sensation Pharrell Williams and "T.I." Clifford Harris Jr. Thicke claims he cannot remember cowriting the hit and does not believe he would even have been capable of contributing to its creation. He also admits lying to the media at the time of the song's release about his part in writing the song.

Thicke and his musical partners also filed suit, defending their claim to having created "Blurred Lines" without stealing from Gaye's previous hit. They acknowledge a resemblance between the tunes, but claim the contemporary hit is tribute to Gaye, not theft. In March 2015, a jury disagreed, awarding the Marvin Gaye estate $7.3 million of the $25 million they sought in damages.

See if you agree with this view that the 2013 hit is a largely derivative mash-up of Gaye's classic song. Log onto YouTube, Vimeo, or another online music service and search

for both songs. Listen to "Blurred Lines" and "Got to Give It Up" and compare the melodies and the beat of each song. What is your conclusion? Does Thicke owe more than an apology to the Gaye family?

evolve in the digital age. The following discussion reviews the development of radio from its early days in the late nineteenth century to the early twenty-first century.

Heinrich Hertz

Demonstrated the existence of radio waves in 1885, setting the stage for the development of modern wireless communications. The measurement unit of electromagnetic frequencies was named for Hertz.

Guglielmo Marconi invented radio telegraphy, or the wireless telegraph, in 1899.

Granville T. Woods

Inventor of railway telegraphy in 1887, a type of wireless communication that allowed moving trains to communicate with each other and with stations, greatly reducing the number of railway collisions.

Guglielmo Marconi

Italian inventor and creator of radio telegraphy, or wireless transmission, in 1899.

Lee de Forest

Considered the father of radio broadcasting because of his invention that permitted reliable voice transmissions for both point-to-point communication and broadcasting.

WIRELESS TELEGRAPHY

Many inventors and scientists around the world were experimenting with radio technology around the same time. In 1884, German **Heinrich Hertz** began working with electromagnetic waves, and in 1885, he demonstrated the existence of radio waves. The measurement unit of electromagnetic frequencies was named for Hertz, whose work set the stage for the development of modern wireless communications, both fixed and mobile, a portion of which Americans have come to know as radio.

Another scientist experimenting with radio technology was African American **Granville T. Woods**, who in 1887 invented railway telegraphy that allowed messages to be sent between moving trains and a railroad station. This invention decreased railway collisions and alerted engineers to obstructions ahead on tracks.[14]

In 1899, Italian **Guglielmo Marconi** invented radio telegraphy. What he dubbed "the wireless," as it came to be called in much of the English-speaking world, made real-time audio transmission possible. Although transmitted in the form of Morse code dots and dashes without a wired connection, it might be deemed the first real radio transmission.

Kentucky farmer Nathan B. Stubblefield, called by some the *real* inventor of radio, created and demonstrated in 1892 a wireless communications device that could even transmit voice and music over a short distance, about five hundred feet. Stubblefield made his invention available to the Wireless Telephone Company, which proved to be a fraud. Because he never patented his device, he failed to reap the commercial rewards, dying tragically of starvation in 1928, alone and penniless on the dirt floor of a shack.[15]

EXPLORING RADIO'S EARLY POTENTIAL

The U.S. Department of Agriculture (USDA), recognizing radio's potential, financed Canadian Reginald A. Fessenden's early research for gathering reports and distributing them broadly. In 1901, Fessenden obtained a U.S. patent for his new radio transmitter with a high-speed electrical alternator that produced "continuous waves." His design is the basis for today's AM radio. In 1912, the USDA started transmitting weather reports by radio in telegraphic code.

VOICE TRANSMISSION

In 1906, Swedish-born inventor Ernst Alexanderson was among the first to build a high-frequency, continuous-wave machine capable of broadcasting the human voice and other sounds. An early radio station broadcast featuring a person's voice and a violin solo used his invention.

Although Italian Marconi and Canadian Fessenden did much of the early inventing work, American **Lee de Forest** developed a unique voice transmitter that proved reliable for both point-to-point radio communication and broadcasting; and by 1907, de Forest's company was supplying the U.S. Navy's Great White Fleet with arc radiotelephones for its pioneering around-the-world voyage. This feat helped establish de Forest as the father of radio, although, in reality, radio had at least three men who could claim that title.

RADIO BEFORE, DURING, AND AFTER WWI

Despite its evident practical uses, radio required improved technology to become a mass medium. With considerable financial support and direction from the U.S. military, research on the vacuum tube helped produce a reliable radio transmitter and receiver by about 1915. Using the perfected vacuum tube radio transmitter, de Forest's "Highbridge Station" 2XG introduced nightly broadcasts, a so-called wireless newspaper for amateur radio operators.

All this activity ceased when the United States entered World War I in April 1917. At this point, the U.S. government either took over or completely shut down all radio stations. For the duration of the war, private citizens could not legally own or operate a radio transmitter or receiver without special permission. The military continued to conduct research on radio technology and lifted radio restrictions when the war ended in late 1918. Regular commercial radio broadcasts

TIMELINE   MILESTONES IN EARLY RADIO-TECHNOLOGY DEVELOPMENT

1839

1907

1864
James Clerk Maxwell predicts the existence of electromagnetic or radio waves that use the conducting layer in Earth's atmosphere (i.e., electric waves can travel through the air).

1887
Granville T. Woods invents railway telegraphy, which allows messages to be sent between moving trains.

1893
Nicola Tesla demonstrates a wireless communications device.

1901
Reginald A. Fessenden obtains a U.S. patent for his new radio transmitter engineered to use a high-speed electrical alternator to produce "continuous waves." It will be the basis for amplitude modulation, or AM (medium-wave), radio.

1839
Carl Friedrich Gauss proposes the Earth's atmosphere contains a conducting layer.

1885
Heinrich Rudolf Hertz demonstrates the existence of radio waves based on Maxwell's prediction.

1892
Nathan B. Stubblefield creates and demonstrates a wireless communications device that can transmit voice and music.

1899
Marchese Guglielmo Marconi invents radio telegraphy, which he calls "the wireless."

1906
Ernst Alexanderson builds a working high-frequency, continuous-wave machine capable of transmitting a radio broadcast of the human voice and other sounds.

1907
Lee de Forest develops a reliable transmission technology for radio broadcasting of the human voice, for both point-to-point communication and broadcasts of entertainment and news.

began in 1920 when AM station KDKA of Pittsburgh, Pennsylvania, reported results of the Harding–Cox presidential election.

WIDESPREAD PUBLIC ADOPTION OF RADIO

In the United States in the early 1920s, roughly 6,000 amateur radio stations and 4,600 commercial stations run for profit had licenses. There were also some amateur enthusiasts who could be likened to computer geeks in the early days of personal computers and the Internet; but for most of the public, radio was still a novelty with limited application.

However, a sporting event on July 2, 1921, would help establish radio as a major medium of mass communication. People across the country were keenly interested in the heavyweight boxing title fight between champion Jack Dempsey and challenger Georges Carpentier. Radio networks did not yet exist, so only one station, a temporary long-wave station, WJY, broadcast the bout live, with technical support from the Radio Corporation of America (RCA), which, as a radio receiver manufacturer, wanted every American household to have a radio set (or two).

Broadcast organizers telegraphed a transcript of the commentary to pioneering station KDKA in Pittsburgh. It then broadcast the fight with a slight delay. With relatively few personal radio receivers, most listeners gathered in halls where local organizers, including volunteer amateur radio operators, set up receivers and charged admission to offset costs.

The evident breakthrough and promise of the new communications technology generated much media commentary, helping propel radio to mass-communication status. A broadcasting boom began after the Dempsey–Carpentier fight, with hundreds of radio stations springing up across the country, similar to the proliferation of Web servers in the mid- to late 1990s. Radio receivers were selling as fast as RCA and others could manufacture them. American Telephone and Telegraph Company (AT&T) began implementing programming for a national radio network in 1922 with flagship station WEAF in New York City, which quickly set the standard for the entire industry.

FM RADIO, EDWIN HOWARD ARMSTRONG, AND DAVID SARNOFF

Edwin Howard Armstrong

Columbia University engineering professor who invented FM radio transmission.

David Sarnoff

Head of RCA, he promoted the development of television as a mass medium yet blocked the development of FM radio for years because RCA produced and sold AM radio receivers.

In 1934, an important innovation in radio transmission technology occurred when Columbia University engineering professor **Edwin Howard Armstrong** (1890–1954) invented FM radio (and later, stereo FM radio) with his colleague John Bose. Armstrong completed his first field test on June 9, 1934, sending an organ recital via both AM and FM from an RCA tower on top of the Empire State Building to the home of a trusted old friend on Long Island. The FM organ came through loud and clear. The AM version had much more static.

Armstrong and **David Sarnoff** (1891–1971), head of RCA, had started out as friends, who both recognized the great potential of radio broadcasting. But FM radio threatened to destroy the RCA empire built on the mass sales of AM radios, or "radio music boxes." Once Sarnoff realized the magnitude of the invention, he blocked Armstrong by ordering RCA engineers to ask for more tests, lobbying federal regulators to deny Armstrong a license to test his invention, and even trying to obtain his patent. Armstrong responded as best he could, filing suit against RCA and many other radio companies infringing on the Armstrong FM radio patent.

Tragically, in 1954, Armstrong, who had never enjoyed commercial success in his life, committed suicide after long-running legal battles left him virtually penniless and his marriage broke up. Ironically, his many lawsuits were settled shortly after his death, leaving a fortune to his widow and the Armstrong Foundation. The story of Armstrong's invention and Sarnoff's machinations to protect the RCA business model mirrors some Internet developments in which legal wrangling or threatened business interests have prevented better technologies from prevailing.

For most of the first half of the twentieth century, AM radio listenership far exceeded FM. In the late 1970s, this shifted, and today FM listenership and stations are in the vast majority. FM radio ascended for a number of reasons, among them the inclusion of an FM dial in most car radios, changes in programming, and regulatory changes, combined with the fact that FM has less static.

CREATING A VIABLE BUSINESS MODEL FOR RADIO

Just as with the Internet, the question of how to make radio broadcasting a viable business would prove complex and controversial. Experiments with commercial sponsorship through the mid-1920s drew outspoken criticism of advertising on public airwaves. The controversy was exemplified in the May 1924 issue of *Radio Broadcast* magazine, which sponsored a $500 contest for the best essay on "Who Is to Pay for Broadcasting—and How?"

Eventually, a confluence of commercial interests, government decisions (sometimes influenced by commercial interests), and lack of coordination among advocates of publicly supported broadcasting made privately owned stations with on-air advertising the standard business model that continues to this day. Consequently, the engine that drives profits is audience size, especially among key demographic groups attractive to advertisers.

THE RISE OF RADIO NETWORKS

During the 1920s, the first commercial broadcasting networks were formed, initially as radio networks—affiliated radio stations in multiple cities all broadcasting a common core set of programming—and later as national television networks. Prior to the passage of the **Radio Act of 1927** and the creation of the **Federal Radio Commission (FRC)**, the predecessor to the **Federal Communications Commission (FCC)**, broadcasting was lively but haphazard. Numerous competing stations on the same or nearby frequencies often caused reception interference. Few regulations regarding transmitter power meant stronger signals could drown out weaker local transmitters. The FRC revoked thousands of radio broadcast licenses and instituted a system that favored fewer high-power stations over smaller but more numerous local low-power stations. This policy benefited large commercial companies over educational, religious, and small private broadcasters.

The National Broadcasting Company (NBC) was founded in 1926 when Sarnoff of RCA purchased New York station WEAF (now WNBC) from AT&T for $1 million. That same year, NBC bought WJZ (licensed to Newark, New Jersey, but transmitting in New York) from Westinghouse and thus created the first network.

CBS (Columbia Broadcasting Station) became the second network, first as the United Independent Broadcasters in 1927; and then, after going on the air with a partner, the Columbia Phonograph and Records Company; and finally becoming the

Edwin Howard Armstrong, inventor of FM radio, spent much of the latter part of his life battling companies that tried to squash FM radio because it threatened business models based on AM radio.

Radio Act of 1927

An act of Congress that created the Federal Radio Commission, intended to regulate the largely chaotic airwaves and based on the principle that companies had a civic duty to use airwaves, a limited public good, responsibly.

Federal Radio Commission (FRC)

Formed by the Radio Act of 1927, the commission, the precursor to the FCC, created a policy that favored fewer high-power radio broadcasting stations rather than more numerous low-power stations.

Federal Communications Commission (FCC)

Established in 1934, the principal communications regulatory body at the federal level in the United States.

CONVERGENCE CULTURE
NPR and PRI: America's Public Radio Networks

National Public Radio (NPR) debuted on April 19, 1971, with live coverage of the Senate Vietnam hearings; and a month later, it broadcast *All Things Considered*. A not-for-profit membership organization, NPR produces and distributes news, cultural, and informational programs, linking the nation's noncommercial radio stations into a national network. It broadcasts about one hundred hours of original programming each week, heard on more than 900 public radio stations nationwide by an audience of 25 million.[16] NPR.org reaches about 19 million visitors a month on its various digital platforms.

Public Radio International (PRI), established in 1983, produces and distributes additional public radio programming, such as *Marketplace* and Garrison Keillor's *A Prairie Home Companion*, to some 900 affiliate stations in the United States, Puerto Rico, and Guam and via SiriusXM satellite radio. PRI's international programs include *The World*, produced in collaboration with the BBC World Service and WGBH Radio Boston.[17]

Public radio distinguishes itself from commercial radio in a number of ways, including more extensive, impartial, and original audio news, especially long-form audio reporting as heard on *Morning Edition* and *All Things Considered*. NPR also offers extensive programming in classical and folk music, jazz, and opera, featuring a variety of live transmissions of the performing arts from theaters and concert halls. Evening programs include those that introduce listeners to classical music as well as to international musicians and unique musical styles.

Columbia Broadcasting System. In 1928, cigar maker Sam Paley bought CBS for $400,000, installing son William as head and moving network headquarters from Philadelphia to New York. Under William's longtime leadership, and later under that of his corporate heir, Frank Stanton, CBS maintained the number one position, describing itself as the Tiffany Network—although it was also called Black Rock, a reference in part to the black marble façade of its midtown Manhattan headquarters.

By 1935, fifty-eight of sixty-two stations nationwide were part of either the NBC or the CBS network. Not until the 1940s did ABC, a third commercial network, emerge.

CONSOLIDATION IN RADIO STATION OWNERSHIP

Throughout most of the twentieth century, radio ownership in the United States was relatively diverse. This was partly a result of federal laws preventing any one person or organization from owning more than twenty FM stations and twenty AM stations nationwide. Regulatory changes in 1992 and the passage of the Telecommunications Act in 1996 resulted in new FCC rules that eliminated such restrictions, although an owner must still be a U.S. citizen. Former FCC duopoly rules prohibited sole ownership, operation, or control of more than two AM and two FM stations in the largest markets. The combined audience share of the co-owned stations was also limited to 25 percent, with even further restrictions for smaller markets. Now the FCC permits a single entity to own substantially more in the same service market.

This shift in regulatory policy produced a trend in the 1990s and early twenty-first century toward increasing consolidation. Since the passage of the act, more than 4,400 radio stations have changed ownership, and the radio industry has become more of an oligopoly. For most of the first fifty years of radio broadcasting, radio was a small business; and owners, even if affiliated with a national network, were longtime residents of their station's town. Although this is still the case in many smaller towns, most stations in big cities have become part of a larger corporate entity.

Increasingly, groups now control eight or more stations in a single market, and the most powerful media groups own most of the large, highly profitable stations. Some support consolidation for a number of reasons, including increased efficiency; more economical, centralized production; larger budgets that permit greater programming experimentation and development; and better management. But critics argue that remote group ownership typically means less sensitivity to local concerns.

In the past few years, however, certain radio groups have been deconsolidating and selling some of their vast holdings. iHeartMedia, formerly named Clear Channel, sold almost half of its 1,200 radio stations and all of its 51 television stations since 2007, partly because of its intent to become a privately held company and partly because of FCC regulations. Despite these sales, iHeartMedia's stations and markets exceed that of the total number of the next three radio groups combined. In 2008, Cumulus Media, the second-largest radio group in 2011 in number of AM and FM stations owned, also went private. Although the move away from consolidation may seem like a good thing for the industry, the shift from publicly traded companies to privately held firms may also mean more business decisions based purely on the bottom line without consideration of the public role of radio stations.

> **DISCUSSION QUESTIONS:** Two major movements have shaped the development of radio: the shift early on from small, independent stations to large-scale, powerful commercial stations and the later shift from terrestrial radio stations to online personal radio stations. Identify some consequences of these changes, and explain which you personally consider most important.

The Radio Industry Today

Declining American radio revenues every year since 2006 has shown a reversal, with a 5.4 percent rebound in 2010 and another 1.2 percent increase in 2011 to $14.1 billion, according to BIA/Kelsey, a group that tracks and advises the radio industry. BIA/Kelsey projects over-the-air revenues for radio will reach $14.5 billion in 2014 and nearly $16 billion by 2018.[18] In addition, online radio revenues are also growing, and BIA/Kelsey expects them to be nearly $1 billion by 2018. The turnaround was in part due to a rise in digital revenues, which industry experts believe will continue to grow in the coming years. Today, there are approximately 10,000 commercial and 2,500 noncommercial radio stations in the United States, the latter group including NPR affiliates and college, community, and religious stations.

All U.S. stations are assigned call letters designating the station and their geographic location east or west of the Mississippi River. Stations east of the Mississippi have W as their first call letter, and stations to the west, K, although some exceptions exist for call letters assigned before boundaries were determined, such as KDKA in Pittsburgh. Under an international agreement issued at the London International Radiotelegraphic Conference in 1912, different countries were awarded different letters. The United States received KDA through KZZ.

Radio Station Programming

Radio grew in its early years to become a dominant medium of mass communication. Large audiences assembled to listen to individual programs during much of the first half of the twentieth century. But the rise of television in the years following World War II provided serious competition, a new media landscape to which radio, like magazines, adapted by specializing.

This specialization takes a number of forms, including program formats, the time of day for certain formats, and especially audience demographics. In radio, a day is broken up into different time segments called "dayparts." The 6 a.m. to 10 a.m. **daypart**, for example, is when most people listen to the radio as they get ready for work or school or during their commute. Accordingly, the programming emphasizes frequent news, traffic, and weather reports as well as some of the more outspoken talk radio shows such as *Imus in the Morning*.

Radio stations are organized by programming into dozens of formats that draw varied audiences.[19] Contemporary-hit radio, for example, attracts a much different audience than the country format—by far the most popular in the United States, with 2,014 stations, as Table 4-2 shows. The fastest growing format is Spanish language.

To reduce operating costs, more and more stations are relying on computerized automated systems that use remote DJs and set music. DJs ostensibly chattering and choosing songs in a local studio may never have even visited the city from where they are ostensibly broadcasting. Automated programming can cause problems during times of emergency. In 2002, for example, a train carrying ammonia derailed in Minot, North Dakota. Emergency services were in disarray, and power was out in many places. Yet, as there was no actual staff at the six Clear Channel radio stations (out of nine stations in the city), regular programming was not preempted with evacuation or safety information for concerned residents.

daypart

A segment of time radio and television program planners use to determine their primary audience during that time of day or night.

DISCUSSION QUESTIONS: List the techniques your favorite radio station uses to distinguish its music format and the station itself. Consider things such as sound effects, promos, and DJ style. Now find a station of a similar genre elsewhere in the country (via the Internet). Listen to it, and identify similarities and differences.

Outlook for the Radio Industry

Industry experts remain cautiously optimistic and predict slight growth in the future, thanks in part to an expected increase in digital revenues that, although large, will remain a fraction of overall revenues. Terrestrial radio stations will continue to exist and promote music, despite the rising popularity of music subscription services and downloadable music. Sales of stations to the top radio groups have been relatively steady in recent years, and further consolidation will likely continue. Radio groups are also buying music subscription services, such as iHeartMedia's 2011 acquisition of Thumbplay, which was not even a year old.

Slacker, Pandora, Spotify, and the like often promote their services as personal radio stations. Users can create and save their own playlists in "My Stations"

TABLE 4-2 Most Popular Radio Programming Genres

Genre	NUMBER OF STATIONS (United States)
Country	2,014
News/Talk/Information	1,497
Spanish	827
Sports	711
Classic Hits	665
Adult Contemporary	603
Oldies	77
CHR Top 40	575
Classic Rock	484
Hot Adult Contemporary	422
Religion	345

Source: "Leading radio formats in the United States in February 2013, by number of stations" Statista website, accessed November 26, 2014, http://www.statista.com/statistics/252230/top-radio-formats-in-the-us-by-number-of-stations/

or "Channels," names meant to evoke radio, whether on the desktop, mobile, or wearable device. Their on-demand nature, which actually makes them more like personalized audio programming than what has traditionally been considered radio, highlights the blurring of online music subscription services, downloadable audio, and traditional radio.

Podcasting and satellite radio are also affecting our perceptions of what constitutes radio. Most radio stations have websites where they promote their shows, provide extra content as podcasts, and let users listen live to shows. Proponents hype satellite as the future of radio while skeptics dismiss it as having an unsustainable business model.

PODCASTING

Increasing in popularity from 2004, podcasts are not identical to other downloaded or streaming formats. Although they are downloaded in one respect, the technology that interfaces with the user's computer differs from a direct file download. Podcasts are often episodic or belong to a series of related content, such as a news program or an investigative report. They are also easy to get and download, much like RSS (Rich Site Summary) feeds do with blogs, sending subscribers new content automatically.

Podcasts permit more flexible content delivery. Listening at the actual time of a certain report is no longer required, nor is visiting a website to download an audio file. Users can simply subscribe to receive podcasts and listen at their convenience on their computer or mobile device. Podcasts have proved popular not only for talk-based radio, such as NPR features, but also for sports and music. Harkening back to radio's earliest days, several companies in recent years are specializing in podcasting farm news, information on weather, commodity prices, and other news of agricultural interest. Easy and inexpensive to produce, podcasts could allow local radio news to be heard once again in communities where distant radio conglomerates now own stations.

Among the most popular podcasts to date is Serial, which debuted in 2014.[20] Produced by the creators of the public radio program *This American Life*, Serial offers a series of episodes that examine via in-depth reporting a true story told in audio narrative form. The first series, which reexamined the 1999 murder of a Maryland teen, generated a large following of more than 40 million people.[21]

SATELLITE RADIO

More akin to audio programming than to traditional broadcast radio, satellite radio uses digital signals broadcast from a satellite, beaming the same programming across a much wider territory than its terrestrial cousin. With up to seventy channels of CD-quality music in a variety of formats, and dozens of third-party news, sports, talk, and old-time radio programs (most of them commercial free as a subscription-based service), satellite radio has won a loyal audience of 24 million subscribers in the United States. And as with cable television, its subscription system entails fewer content restrictions.

Sirius Satellite Radio, which started out as CD Radio in the early 1990s, launched its satellites in 2000 and began broadcasting in 2002. When XM Satellite Radio launched soon after, the two companies competed vigorously in offering exclusive access to various sports channels, hosted music channels, and noted talk-radio hosts. In 2004, shock jock Howard Stern signed an exclusive five-year, $500 million contract with Sirius. Some media observers claimed this was a game changer that greatly enhanced the status of satellite radio. Others saw it as reminiscent of the wasteful spending of the dot-com boom of the late 1990s and argued that Stern would essentially disappear from the public eye (or ear) because of the smaller satellite radio audience.

Radio shock jock Howard Stern's move to satellite radio was hailed by some and criticized by others.

INTERNATIONAL PERSPECTIVES
Trusting in the Power of the Airwaves

Radio has proven to be a very important information source in developing countries, where spotty electricity service, government regulations, low education, and scant incomes have kept most people from owning a television, let alone a computer and Internet connection. Radios, however, are nearly ubiquitous, thanks in part to their portability, low cost, and ability to run on batteries or solar power or by hand cranks. Because radio does not require literacy, it has proven especially valuable in communicating with poor, often rural populations—such as in Southeast Asian, Latin America, and Africa—as a means of development and distribution of innovations such as new agricultural techniques or health advances.

UNESCO, the United Nations Education, Scientific and Cultural Organization, reports that 95 percent of the world's population has access to radio, about double the percentage that has Internet access.[22,23] UNESCO states that radio plays an especially important role in the developing world because of its ubiquitous presence, low cost, and reliability.

The implications of radio's capabilities are important for nongovernmental organizations (NGOs) and others working in the developing world, for they highlight how important it is for those from developed nations not to take for granted certain cultural assumptions about media and how they are used. For example, an award-winning print advertising campaign about disease prevention in the United States or Europe may not be understood or even seen by wide swaths of the population in a developing country, whereas a radio message could reach many more people who will perceive it as a reliable source of information.

Kenyan women listening to the radio.

In mid-2008, Sirius completed its acquisition of former competitor XM Satellite Radio and became Sirius XM Radio. The company almost filed for bankruptcy in early 2009—as large debts came due—but Liberty Media, owner of DirecTV, rescued it at the last minute, acquiring 40 percent ownership in the process. Sirius XM Radio continues its technological innovation, improving receivers and providing mobile phone apps, for example.

MEDIA CAREERS

Career paths in radio and the recording industry are among the most rapidly changing and unsettled in the media industry. Perhaps the most exciting opportunities involve entrepreneurial approaches. These career paths emphasize both digital savvy as well as a sense of innovation in how to produce popular audio-format programming that can appeal to an increasingly mobile and international marketplace. Listeners typically discover new music on the radio, often online; but the vast majority in the important demographic of young listeners from age 12 to 24 use YouTube to watch videos and keep up to date with the latest hits.[24]

A few serious fans may turn their passion for music into a career as a DJ at a radio station or nightclub. Disc jockeys who cater special events such as weddings or fundraisers need to be familiar with various types of music. Others may specialize in a particular genre. Regardless, DJs need to be sensitive to the musical tastes of their particular audience because their success depends on the ability to develop a loyal following of radio listeners or club hoppers. Sometimes disc jockeys transition to careers in the record industry, although for most, spinning remains only a part-time gig.

LOOKING BACK AND MOVING FORWARD

Radio is still an evolving medium, with many forms of delivery including traditional terrestrial broadcasting, online distribution, and satellite transmission via Sirius XM Radio. Future radio delivery may not lie in the heavens, but it will undoubtedly be grounded in certain consumer behaviors and desires readily apparent across all media, especially with music.

Although transmission and hardware will continue to change, radio itself—or, more accurately, the delivery of audio content to a mass audience—seems destined to remain an important form of mass communication. This is largely because radio, almost alone among mass media, allows people to engage easily in other activities while listening. No matter how advanced or portable media technology becomes, we cannot watch TV or read a book or newspaper while driving safely, for example. The shift to an on-demand and participatory media environment will become more significant. Satellite radio has signaled this shift, along with the various music subscription services or personal radio stations.

Services such as Pandora, Slacker, and Spotify may well represent the future of radio: a highly personalized system that not only responds to your musical tastes but uses special algorithms and collaborative filtering to suggest new artists who play similar styles of music. These changes may so drastically alter how radio stations think of their programming that the term "radio" may technically become obsolete or come to mean something very different.

Business models or ways of creating, promoting, and distributing music are still in transition. Although advances in technology improved both the sound quality and portability of recorded music, basic business policies endured. Innovative musicians are using digital crowdfunding to underwrite their own musical enterprises, circumventing the traditional record labels.

There are two main schools of thought about the state of the music industry today, which also apply to other entertainment media such as television and film. One camp claims that the music industry has only itself to blame for not adapting earlier to the digital repercussions for established business models. Rather than initiating bullying lawsuits, record labels should focus on developing alternative revenue streams, some of which already have growing sales such as digital downloads of à la carte songs, music subscription services, and ringtone sales.

The second school of thought explains diminished sales as the consequence of file sharing, viewed as theft, pure and simple. So although the interest in music remains as strong as ever, new revenue sources are still far from making up for losses of recent years, a drop-off that the industry blames on illegal practices that hurt not only corporations but also artists who rely on royalties to survive.

MEDIA MATTERS   THE REVOLUTION WILL NOT BE TELEVISED; IT WILL BE MASHED UP

1. Have you ever bought a vinyl LP?

2. Have you ever bought a song online?

3. What media device do you typically use to listen to music?

4. (T/F) Revenue from digital music (mostly downloads and subscriptions) surpassed CD revenue for the first time in 2012.

5. Where is the dividing line between radio stations that have call letters starting with K and those starting with W?

6. What is the most popular music format for radio stations?

7. Why is radio called "the wireless" in other English-speaking countries?

8. (T/F) Satellite radio does not have the same restrictions regarding content as broadcast radio stations.

9. Do you pay to subscribe to one or more music subscription services such as Pandora, Slacker, or Spotify?

10. How much would you be willing to pay per month to listen to commercial-free radio?

ANSWERS: 4. True. **5.** Mississippi River. **6.** Country music. **7.** Because it was perceived as a wireless form of telegraphy. **8.** True.

FURTHER READING

All You Need to Know About the Music Business, 8th ed. Donald Passman (2012) Hal Leonard Corp.

The Business of Music, 10th ed. William Krasilovsky, Sidney Shemel, John Gross, Jonathan Feinstein (2007) Billboard Books.

The Future of Music: Manifesto for the Digital Music Revolution. David Kusek, Gerd Leonhard (2008) Berklee Press.

Appetite for Self-Destruction: The Spectacular Crash of the Record Industry in the Digital Age. Steve Knopper (2009) Free Press.

The Listener's Voice: Early Radio and the American Public. Elena Razlogova (2011) University of Pennsylvania Press.

Empire of the Air: The Men Who Made Radio. Tom Lewis (1993) Harper Perennial Library.

Hello, Everybody! The Dawn of American Radio. Anthony Rudel (2008) Houghton Mifflin Harcourt.

Sound Business: Newspapers, Radio, and the Politics of New Media. Michael Stamm (2011) University of Pennsylvania Press.

Censorship: The Threat to Silence Talk Radio. Brian Jennings, Sean Hannity (2009) Threshold Editions.

Something in the Air: Radio, Rock, and the Revolution That Shaped a Generation. Marc Fisher (2007) Random House.

Right of the Dial: The Rise of Clear Channel and the Fall of Commercial Radio. Alex Foege (2009) Faber and Faber.

World Radio TV Handbook 2013: The Directory of Global Broadcasting. WRTH editors (Jan. 15, 2013), WRTH.

Radio Content in the Digital Age: The Evolution of a Sound Medium. Angeliki Gazi, Guy Starkey, Stanislaw Jedrzejewski (2011) Intellect/University of Chicago Press.

Visual Media
PHOTOGRAPHY, MOVIES, AND TELEVISION

Tristan is an undergraduate at Rutgers University. Like many college students, she doesn't watch much TV in the conventional sense. Between classes, work, and sorority life, she doesn't have much time left over; and she doesn't have a TV set in her apartment or a cable or fiber TV subscription. That doesn't mean she misses all her favorite shows, though, like *The Walking Dead* and *Bob's Burgers*. She uses her mobile device to log on to any of several mobile video services and watches online and on demand.

Americans love their TV and movies, but how they get that content is changing dramatically. Whereas broadcast television once dominated the TV viewing landscape, cable, fiber, and satellite TV entered the mix in a big way in the latter part of the twentieth century. Online viewing, particularly via mobile digital devices, has become the new TV and movie viewing platform of the twenty-first century.

Increasingly, people multitask when interacting with media, texting friends or tweeting while watching, say, *American Idol*. Soon a show without interactivity will seem like a relic. In 1953, interactivity meant a child viewer drawing a bridge on wax paper overlaid on the TV screen, as with CBS's *Winky Dink and You*, the first regularly scheduled interactive TV show.

Television advertisers are also developing new ways to watch us as we watch TV. Cable and satellite companies record our viewing behavior, information used with other demographic data gleaned from our daily transactions to match viewer profiles with specific advertisements. In the future, you and a friend may be watching the same program and texting each other about it but receiving different advertisements. This may feel Big Brother *1984* to you, but television advertisers are simply trying to do what Internet advertisers have been doing for some time now: target ads to specific consumer behavior.

LEARNING OBJECTIVES

>> Explain the role photography has played in our visual culture and its continued importance within mass communication.

>> Describe the impact of technological changes on the film and television industries.

>> Explain how business models and structures have influenced the film industry.

>> Describe the development of television from its origins to digital TV.

>> Explain the differences between terrestrial, cable, and satellite broadcasting and what they mean for viewers.

>> Describe the implications of the convergence of telecommunications companies and content companies.

Photographs, television, and movies shape our world, with journalism, entertainment, and art highlighting the importance of the visual in our lives. The photographic lens has long defined the linear narrative of visual storytelling, and recent changes with digitization allow visual media to render and create realities even more vividly. The past hundred years of filmmaking still provide the foundation for digital videographers as they explore working with more portable equipment and more sophisticated editing tools and effects.

Changes resulting from online consumption of video, film, and television are not yet fully understood, but already for many the Internet is a more significant source of imagery than is television. Sources of video content online include the popular YouTube and many similar video-sharing sites. **Cord-cutters** are increasingly common among those who once relied on a cable or other connection to get their TV, whereas **cord-nevers** are those who have known only mobile or wireless Internet-delivered TV.

Photography

Long important to mass communications, still images, or photographs, continue to perform two main functions: **surveillance** and **cultural transmission**. Photos and other images can verify factual claims. Whereas words might provide the narrative, photos confirm its truth, whether it involves a purported plane crash, an extramarital affair, or a mass grave in a war-torn country. Despite the possibility of being digitally doctored, photographs are still one of the surest ways to support facts. They transmit culture by what they show, how they show it, and which emotions they stir. At a glance, a photograph can tell a story or convey information quickly while engaging and entertaining.

> **DISCUSSION QUESTIONS:** Have digital film and television made photography less relevant? Why or why not? How do you explain the popularity of the "selfie"?

HISTORY OF PHOTOGRAPHY

The principles involved in creating photographs had been around hundreds of years before photography was invented. The earliest recorded use of a **camera obscura**—a dark box or room with a small hole that allows an inverted image of an outside scene to be shown on the opposite inner wall—is in the writings of Leonardo da Vinci, who explains how a camera obscura can aid drawing scenery, moving a sheet of paper around until the scene comes into sharp focus for tracing.

The other important element, understanding how light can affect certain chemicals, was also known for hundreds of years. Although some scientists could produce photographs with various light-sensitive chemicals, they had no way to make the images permanent. In June 1827, Joseph Niépce, using an asphalt-like material that hardened after exposure to light, created a picture, although it was unclear and required eight hours of exposure.[1]

After the death of Niépce, his partner, Frenchman **Louis Daguerre**, unveiled in January 1839 the **daguerreotype**, a method of creating a positive image on a

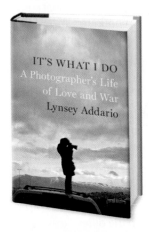

Lynsey Addario published a memoir in 2015 that documents her life as a war photographer, a calling she has pursued while pregnant and even after having being kidnapped—twice.

metal plate, with a reduced exposure time of thirty minutes or so.[2] Advances occurred over the next one hundred and fifty years in exposure time, image quality, and color photography. As cameras became more portable and user friendly, their popularity increased with the general public. And the Internet and wireless communications made it possible to share photos instantly with friends, family, or the entire world.

In the early days, when specialized knowledge was still required, **Mathew B. Brady** was highly acclaimed for his Civil War photos and portraits of famous people, many of whom are best known to us today through his work. Historians have criticized Brady for sometimes arranging his subjects, including battlefield corpses, for dramatic photocomposition purposes, a practice considered unethical in modern journalism. Nevertheless, Brady and other photographers helped the public see the conflict in the Civil War through the lens of the press, the first war documented by means of photography.

Early photography was not limited to journalism. Notably, Eadweard Muybridge used it for scientific documentation. His famous photo series was the first to document how a horse runs. Such applications help us see things that the human eye alone cannot. Today, scientific images of the heavens and of the microscopic alike captivate us. Some are even considered visual art.

daguerreotype

Photograph created by exposing a positive image on a metal plate.

Mathew B. Brady

Nineteenth-century photographer acclaimed for his Civil War images and portraits of famous people.

The Civil War was the first war to be documented by means of photography.

PHOTOGRAPHIC INDUSTRY TODAY

The photography industry, like the more prominent film and television industries, has experienced great change. Consider the impact of digital cameras. Only ten years after film sales peaked in 1999, Kodak announced it would stop making Kodachrome color film. Despite efforts to capitalize on the shift to digital by selling digital cameras and photo printers, Kodak continued to lose money and declared bankruptcy in January 2012. Fujifilm, headquartered in Tokyo and the world's largest photographic company, has also seen business diminish, but it integrated digital technology more effectively into its business model and has a range of popular digital cameras as well as inkjet and laser photo paper.

Today, professional photographers have more powerful cameras than ever before, and digital cameras allow anyone to take professional-quality pictures without manual camera adjustments.

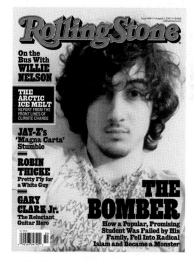

Rolling Stone magazine received heavy criticism over this cover photo of Dzhokhar Tsarnaev, convicted and sentenced to death for setting bombs that killed three people and injured scores more at the 2013 Boston Marathon.
CRITICAL THINKING QUESTIONS: Do aspects of the photograph seem to glamorize Tsarnaev? If so, which ones? Would another photograph, from a different angle or with a different expression, provoke the same reaction? Do you think reactions would be different to a cover photo of Tsarnaev on *Time* or *U.S. News and World Report*?

Movies

Still images were to mass media of the mid-nineteenth century what motion pictures were to the twentieth. At the end of the nineteenth century, activity could be recorded for the first time. More important for the movie industry, technology could not only re-create reality but *create* it.

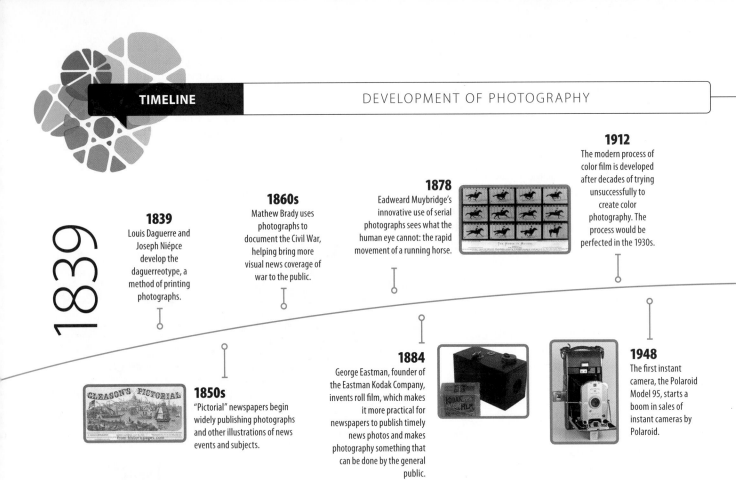

1839

1839
Louis Daguerre and Joseph Niépce develop the daguerreotype, a method of printing photographs.

1860s
Mathew Brady uses photographs to document the Civil War, helping bring more visual news coverage of war to the public.

1878
Eadweard Muybridge's innovative use of serial photographs sees what the human eye cannot: the rapid movement of a running horse.

1912
The modern process of color film is developed after decades of trying unsuccessfully to create color photography. The process would be perfected in the 1930s.

1850s
"Pictorial" newspapers begin widely publishing photographs and other illustrations of news events and subjects.

1884
George Eastman, founder of the Eastman Kodak Company, invents roll film, which makes it more practical for newspapers to publish timely news photos and makes photography something that can be done by the general public.

1948
The first instant camera, the Polaroid Model 95, starts a boom in sales of instant cameras by Polaroid.

The primary function of motion pictures is to entertain, with millions enjoying the sweeping epics, slapstick comedies, romance, action, and adventure of feature-length films. However, as with much entertainment, cultural transmission is also important. Many fans and critics alike consider cinema more than simple entertainment, a serious visual art form comparable to painting, sculpture, or architecture, with a history of important social influence. Still, most commercially produced motion pictures in the United States are intended to make money, only occasionally rising to the level of serious art.

Some cable television channels are devoted almost exclusively to films—such as the Independent Film Channel, Turner Classic Movies, American Movie Classics, Home Box Office, Cinemax, and Showtime—in addition to the frequent (and repeated) showing of movies on commercial and cable channels such as TNT. This means films remain part of the entertainment landscape long after leaving theaters. Yet, despite competition from other media, predictions that movie theaters would close as people stayed home watching television have proved unfounded.

Thomas Alva Edison

His inventions included the electric light, the phonograph, and the Kinetoscope. Edison's lab in Menlo Park, New Jersey, had over sixty scientists and produced as many as four hundred patent applications a year.

History of the Movie Industry

In 1891, **Thomas Alva Edison** (1847–1931) created the Kinetoscope, a "peep-show" precursor to the motion picture viewer. Yet Edison's failure to patent this technology permitted two French brothers, Louis Lumière (1864–1948) and

1991
Kodak, after developing variations of digital camera systems throughout the mid-1980s, releases the first professional digital camera system.

1999
The peak of sales of roll film. After 1999, sales of roll film drop an estimated 25 to 30 percent per year as more consumers buy digital cameras.

2013
Oscar-winning director Malik Bendjelloul even used his iPhone to finish shooting his movie when he ran out of money for 8 mm film.

1994
The Apple QuickTake 100 camera is the first consumer-level digital camera that allows connection with a home computer system via a serial cable. Kodak, Casio, and Sony release similar cameras in subsequent years.

2009
Polaroid announces the end of production of instant-film products, a consequence of the emergence of digital imaging.

2012
Smartphone cameras such as those in the iPhone 5 and the Samsung Galaxy S III are of such high quality, with 8-megapixel resolution and network connectivity, that many consumers use them as their main photographic device.

2013

Auguste Lumière (1862–1954), to patent a more portable camera, film-processing unit, and projector in 1895, a suitcase-sized single device that allowed shooting in the morning and footage that could be processed in the afternoon and projected for an audience in the evening. On December 28, 1895, the Lumières debuted their process to a paying audience at the Grand Café in Paris, showing a series of ten 15- to 60-second glimpses of real scenes recorded outdoors. Soon the rage all over France, the Cinématographe was clearly based on Edison's machine but could show motion pictures to many simultaneously.[3]

Failing to recognize their invention's potential, the Lumières reproduced daily life rather than telling a story. Louis felt that the novelty of viewing moving images on a screen that could be seen by walking outside would eventually wear off. This mindset differed from that of other film pioneers, such as Edison and Georges Méliès, who saw that film could change reality as well as replicate it.

SILENT ERA: NEW MEDIUM, NEW TECHNOLOGIES, NEW STORYTELLING

Adding sound to film was not technologically feasible in the beginning. Silent films could more easily cross language barriers than their "talkie" descendants because their few words, usually presented as text on the screen, could easily be translated into the local language.

ETHICS IN MEDIA
The Photojournalist's Dilemma: Immersion in Conflict

Vice News has emerged since its launch in December of 2013 as a pioneering enterprise in reporting the news without the traditional filter of mainstream media. Vice News reporters have used wearable technologies such as Google Glass and Livestream to deliver video news in real time from around the world to audiences everywhere. Editors at Vice News subscribe to a model of journalism called the "Immersionist" school. Many in the news industry and academy view these methods as the antithesis of traditional news reporting by diving deeply into stories and not attempting to provide coverage of a wide array of topics.

In 2014, Vice News used Google Glass to transmit via the Internet real-time video reports via Livestream for hours on end. Reporters using Google Glass delivered largely unfiltered footage of protests in Istanbul, Turkey; Montreal, Canada; and Ferguson, Missouri.[4] Providing narrative audio to accompany this raw coverage, these video streams gave viewers extraordinary depth of reporting on breaking news.

Critics, however, contend that such unfiltered reporting may fail to provide the critical perspective needed to put events into meaningful context. Reporters, critics claim, need to maintain a certain level of healthy skepticism to avoid being manipulated by organizers of events.

Video journalists and photojournalists sometimes struggle with critical questions such as these, and a core part of the answers deal with journalism ethics. The Society of Professional Journalists code of ethics states that a reporter's first responsibility is to the truth, a difficult objective to achieve when covering conflict. This is especially true in war, where, as Phillip Knightly observes, truth is the first casualty. Does a photo or a video tell the truth? Can they do so, even with an appropriate caption or narration? What about the rights of the subject of the photo or video?

Perhaps just as important are the ethical consequences of trauma for the reporter witnessing such atrocities.[5] In the theater of war, photojournalists and their news organizations have an ethical mandate not only to report the truth but to recognize and try to minimize harmful health consequences. Post-traumatic stress syndrome (PTSD) can manifest itself in the form of nightmares, flashbacks, and judgment errors. PTSD occurs in more than a quarter (28.6 percent) of war correspondents, about the same rate as among combat veterans and higher than among police officers.

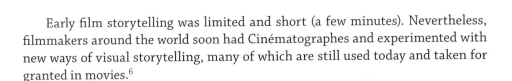

Early film storytelling was limited and short (a few minutes). Nevertheless, filmmakers around the world soon had Cinématographes and experimented with new ways of visual storytelling, many of which are still used today and taken for granted in movies.[6]

Méliès and Griffith

Unlike the Lumières, Frenchman Georges Méliès (1861–1938) used the medium to conjure and create illusions. He was the first to make objects suddenly appear, disappear, or change. Among the most memorable was his celluloid transformation of a carriage into a hearse. Méliès pioneered innovative special effects, including the first double exposure (*La Caverne maudite*, 1898), the first split-screen shot (*Un Homme de tête*, 1898), and the first dissolve (*Cendrillon*, 1899).

Méliès notwithstanding, many silent films were little more than novelties. But by the 1910s, the medium began to evolve into an important storytelling vehicle. *Birth of a Nation*, American D. W. Griffith's 1915 controversial classic, was the first major full-length film to introduce many innovative cinematic techniques such as crosscutting (parallel editing) to portray battle scenes. He often depicted the action in one set of shots moving from right to left while another moved left to right.

Murnau, Flaherty, and Eisenstein

Innovation in filming, lighting, editing, and storytelling continued throughout the silent era. In 1922, German director F. W. Murnau (1888–1931) created *Nosferatu*, an unforgettable adaptation of Bram Stoker's Dracula tale that helped develop the language of film. Also in 1922, American Robert Flaherty (1884–1951) directed *Nanook of the North*, the first great documentary film. This depiction of the life of an Eskimo whaler is still shown in college anthropology courses. Flaherty edited the film in New York after living among the Eskimos for six months while filming.

Russian filmmaker Sergei Eisenstein (1898–1948) pioneered fast cuts between scenes, similar to the editing commonly seen in music videos. Until then, most filmmakers kept the camera stationary, confining scenes to the picture frame. In 1925, he released *Battleship Potemkin*, a silent depiction of the 1905 revolt in Odessa by Russian sailors. A famous editing sequence, "The Odessa Steps," intercuts shots of trapped townspeople with shots of czarist troops firing on the crowd, an emotionally charged scene imitated in homage in several films including Brian De Palma's (1987) *The Untouchables*.

> **DISCUSSION QUESTIONS:** Camera-equipped drones are rapidly emerging as important tools for motion-picture storytellers, with the BBC in 2014 using a camera-equipped drone to create a documentary and other videographers using this innovative technology. If these silent film directors had benefitted from access to this new technology, how might they have used it to tell their stories differently?

SOUND AND COLOR

Although technology had to some degree revolutionized movies, sound and color were needed to fully recreate what people saw and heard. By the turn of the nineteenth century, several alternative but complex and cumbersome methods of producing color motion pictures had been developed, such as hand tinting or hand coloring scenes. Around 1920, a system used a beam splitter with a prism to divide light entering the lens, capturing the different colors on alternating frames. This produced the first successful feature-length color films in the 1920s.

Technicolor Motion Picture Corporation, founded in 1922, became the standard for color motion pictures for the next three decades. Among the earliest Technicolor films were *The Black Pirate* with Douglas Fairbanks in 1925 and *Gone with the Wind* and *The Wizard of Oz* in 1939. Not until the 1950s did color films, captured without prisms, beam splitters, or alternating frames, become more common.

Breaking with the contemporary norm, *The Artist* in 2011 was both in black and white and silent. It won five Oscars, including Best Picture.

Sound was easier. Even the earliest silent movies were not wholly silent. Live pianists, actors, and even entire orchestras added sound during showings. Actors sometimes accompanied showings, talking about their roles and answering audience questions before or afterward. In 1896, a paying audience saw the first sound film short in Berlin.

In 1927, Al Jolson starred in *The Jazz Singer*. This first commercially successful "talkie" was not a sound movie by contemporary standards. It contained little dialog but had subtitles and recorded music played back, a technology soon replaced by the superior sound-on-film systems (i.e., an optical soundtrack). In 1925, the first motion picture to synchronize sound was produced, more as a technical experiment than as a commercial endeavor.

By 1929, recording and playing back sound synchronously with the image had become more practicable. Very few silent films were made after this time, with the notable exceptions being those by Charlie Chaplin in the 1930s and *The Artist*, a

TIMELINE SELECTED MILESTONES IN EARLY MOTION PICTURES

1898

1934

1915
Louis Daguerre and Joseph Niépce develop the daguerreotype, a method of printing photographs.

1922
Robert Flaherty, director. *Nanook of the North*, the first great documentary.

1925
Sergei Eisenstein, director. *Battleship Potemkin*, a silent film known particularly for its editing sequence "the Odessa Steps."

1927
Al Jolson, actor. *The Jazz Singer*, the first commercially successful motion picture with sound.

1934
MGM, motion picture company; Maureen O'Sullivan, actress. *Tarzan and His Mate* reveals a scantily clad Jane and a prolonged underwater nude scene, contributing to a public backlash and the strict enforcement of the Hays morals code in movie content.

1898
Georges Méliès, director. First double exposure (*La Caverne maudite*), an advance in special effects.

1919
Oscar Micheaux, director. *Birth of Race*, African American response to the racial stereotypes portrayed in *Birth of a Nation*.

1925
Technicolor Motion Picture Corp.; Douglas Fairbanks, actor. *The Black Pirate*, among the first successful color major motion pictures.

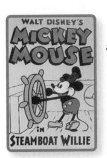

1928
Walt Disney, animator, voice, director. Disney's first animated hit, *Steamboat Willie*, introduced Mickey Mouse.

1932
Walt Disney, director. *Flowers and Trees*, the first color cartoon.

2011 French film shot in black and white that won three Academy Awards including Best Picture.

Some silent-era stars could not adapt either because of heavy foreign accents or unappealing voices. Screenwriting and filming changed dramatically, as stories were written for the spoken word rather than visual effect. Slapstick comedy was out, and witty one-liners and joke telling were in. Because of cumbersome microphones, cameras also became more stationary; and experimentation with moving cameras, innovative editing, and interesting camera angles became less common. Although there were winners and losers with the development of sound, the industry itself was unfazed by technological change. In the words of Al Jolson, "You ain't heard nothin' yet."

HOLLYWOOD MOVIE MOGULS

The United States motion picture industry began on the eastern seaboard, especially New York City, the center of entertainment, with its Broadway and vaudeville theaters. Thomas Edison's laboratories were also nearby, in New Jersey. Soon after, the powerful movie moguls of the early 1900s created Hollywood, where better weather permits year-round film production. Actors, producers, and directors relocated, and a split developed between theater (and, later, television) in New York and film in Hollywood. Most television shows are now filmed in Hollywood studios as well, where the U.S. movie industry is securely based. A number of regional centers for movie production also exist, including Toronto and Vancouver, Canada. Let's consider some Hollywood movie moguls active in the first half of the twentieth century.

Warner Brothers

Born in Poland (except for Jack), the Warner brothers, Albert (1884–1976), Harry (1881–1958), Jack (1892–1978), and Sam (1887–1927), founded a movie studio in 1923 that left a lasting mark on the industry. In 1903, Harry hocked his family's delivery horse to buy a used Edison Kinetoscope projector with which the brothers created a traveling movie show in Ohio and Pennsylvania. In 1905, they opened a small theater, then moved into film production and distribution. They launched "Warner Features" in St. Louis, Missouri, and then Warner Brothers Studio in California.

Sam Warner's "canned vaudeville" propelled the studio to a leadership position. In 1927, *The Jazz Singer* launched the new era of motion pictures with sound, the first of many classics during the powerful studio system, including *Captain Blood* (1935) and *Casablanca* (1942).

Walt Disney

Born in Chicago, Walter Elias Disney (1901–1965) expressed an early interest in drawing and enrolled in the Kansas City Art Institute in 1915. With forty dollars in his pocket, Walt left Missouri in August 1923 for Los Angeles, where his older brother, Roy, lived. Combining their meager resources and borrowing $500, the brothers set up shop in their uncle's garage and soon began making animated films.

In 1928, their first hit, *Steamboat Willie*, introduced Mickey Mouse, who talked and sang, featuring Walt's own voice but very little of his own skillful animation.

Walt Disney was a pioneer in animation and entertainment and a talented animator in his own right.

Thus, a star that made Disney a household name was born. In 1937, Disney's first full-length feature animation, *Snow White and the Seven Dwarfs*, broke all box office records. In the next five years, Disney also produced *Pinocchio*, *Fantasia*, *Dumbo*, and *Bambi*. During World War II, most of the Disney facilities produced special government work, including propaganda films for the armed services. Walt opened Disneyland in Los Angeles in 1955 and Walt Disney World in Orlando in 1971.

Always on the technological cutting edge, Disney introduced Technicolor with the 1932 animation *Flowers and Trees*. Part of the Silly Symphonies series, this first color cartoon won Disney his first Oscar. Also a pioneer in television, he produced his first programs in 1954, including the popular *Mickey Mouse Club*, and was among the first to offer color programming with *Walt Disney's Wonderful World of Color* in 1961. Disney won forty-seven Academy Awards, more than anyone else, and seven Emmys.

Samuel Goldwyn

Born in Warsaw, Poland, Schmuel Gelbfisz (ca. 1879–1974) died Samuel Goldwyn in Los Angeles, having emigrated from England in 1899. He produced *The Squaw Man* in 1914, directed by Cecil B. DeMille, and his production company became the foundation for Paramount Pictures, eventually built by Adolph Zukor. In 1916, he joined forces with the Selwyn brothers and cofounded the Goldwyn Pictures Corporation.

In 1924, his company merged with Louis B. Mayer and Metro Pictures to become Metro-Goldwyn-Mayer. Although his "Leo the Lion" trademark endured, Goldwyn was ousted and created an independent film company, which produced such classics as *Wuthering Heights* (1939), *The Pride of the Yankees* (1942), *The Best Years of Our Lives* (1946), *Guys and Dolls* (1955), and *Porgy and Bess* (1959).

Marcus Loew

Marcus Loew (1870–1927) ran a nickelodeon theater in the earliest days of movies, expanding his holdings over the next several years to create Loew's, a movie chain of luxurious theaters, and getting involved in making movies as well. In the 1920s, he merged his Metro Pictures, Samuel Goldwyn's Goldwyn Picture Corporation, and Mayer Pictures, creating Metro-Goldwyn-Mayer (MGM) Pictures. Unlike the other moguls, he preferred New York, his birthplace, and did not move to Hollywood.

Louis B. Mayer

In 1907, Louis Burt Mayer (1885–1957), perhaps the most famous and feared movie mogul, renovated a rundown movie theater in Boston that he parlayed into the largest chain in New England. In 1917, he funded Louis B. Mayer Pictures with great profits from his showing of *Birth of a Nation*. He became vice president of MGM in the 1920s and is credited with creating the Hollywood studio star system. In 1927, Mayer teamed with Douglas Fairbanks Sr. to form the Academy of Motion Picture Arts and Sciences.

DISCUSSION QUESTIONS: Could a group of new digital filmmakers revolutionize the industry and dominate movie production and distribution like the early Hollywood movie moguls? Why or why not?

Hollywood Star System

For the first several years, actors' and actresses' names did not even appear in the movie credits. Then shrewd studio heads cultivated fan interest, creating personas for popular stars, complete with false histories to market them better, a practice that continues today to some degree. Paramount Pictures (1912), Columbia Pictures (1920), Metro-Goldwyn-Mayer (1924), Warner Brothers (1923), and 20th Century Fox (1935) all held long-term contracts with star directors and actors.

During this era, stars were unable to seek their own contracts for individual films but could be loaned to another studio, often in exchange for other stars. They were also expected to be highly productive, sometimes starring in five or six films a year. Warner Brothers' Humphrey Bogart starred in forty films between 1934 and 1943. *Casablanca* was just one of four he made in 1943. Many films of this era, including *Casablanca*, were not great works of cinematic art but popular entertainment for studio profit.

People often saw these films for the stars they had come to know and for the characters they often represented. Gary Cooper, star of *Mr. Deeds Goes to Town* (1936) and *Meet John Doe* (1941), was known as a tall, awkward, humble man of integrity—the quintessential American, the strong, silent type. Jimmy Stewart played the same kind of person, immortalized in Frank Capra's holiday classic *It's a Wonderful Life* (1945).

Citizen Kane has been hailed as one of the greatest films of all time.

The studio star system and long-term actor contracts ended in the late 1940s with the confluence of several forces. First, in 1948, the U.S. Supreme Court divested studios of their theater empires because of monopolistic practices revealed in *United States v. Paramount Pictures*. **Independent films**, those produced outside the major studios, could then be shown in theaters and became financially viable. Independent producers were also able to rent large studios on a per-project basis and benefit from their extensive distribution networks while the studios welcomed the additional income. Studios productions still had an advantage, however. Booking their films in blocks made it cheaper for a theater to show several popular studio films than to take a chance on a single independent film.

independent films

Films made by production companies separate from the main Hollywood studios.

Second, the rise of television reduced theater audiences, especially for second- or third-run films. Although studio heads once threatened to blacklist any actor who moved to television, this ban was soon lifted as big names such as Bob Hope and Lucille Ball gave the new medium star power. Conversely, actors like Clint Eastwood who became popular on TV transitioned successfully to film. Today, many actors move from popular shows such as *Saturday Night Live* or situation comedies to movies.

THE DIRECTOR AS AUTEUR

Following WWII, French film critic André Bazin introduced the notion of the filmmaker as author, or **auteur**. Although some early filmmakers, such as D. W. Griffith and Sergei Eisenstein, could be seen as auteurs, in the intervening years,

auteur

Director as storyteller.

Japanese director Akira Kurosawa had a film career over fifty years and influenced such filmmakers as Steven Spielberg, George Lucas, and Francis Ford Coppola.

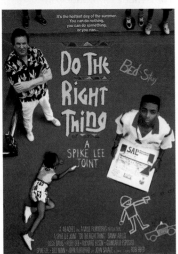

Spike Lee often makes films that tackle controversial or sensitive topics related to race, discrimination, and society.

filmmaking in the United States became a more collaborative, corporate enterprise—a trend promoted by Hollywood's studio system.

The 1950s French New Wave directors were probably the most influential auteurs. Important directors included Jean-Luc Godard (*Breathless*, 1959), Louis Malle (*Zazie dans le métro*, 1960), and François Truffaut (*The 400 Blows*, 1959). These directors used camera techniques that were innovative for their day, such as the now-common handheld cameras and freeze frames.

One of the most influential international film auteurs was Japanese director Akira Kurosawa, some of whose early films were remade by others as Westerns. *Seven Samurai* (1954) became *The Magnificent Seven* (1960) starring Yul Brynner and Steve McQueen; and in 1964, Sergio Leone remade *Yojimbo* (1961) as *A Fistful of Dollars*, starring Clint Eastwood. Two characters in the classic *The Hidden Fortress* (1958) are said to be the models on which director George Lucas, a great admirer of Kurosawa and Japanese cinema, based C-3PO and R2-D2 in *Star Wars* (1977). Kurosawa also borrowed from the West for *Throne of Blood* (1957) and *Ran* (1985), based on Shakespeare's *Macbeth* and *King Lear*, respectively.

Important American filmmakers have also contributed to the auteur movement. Among them are Blake Edwards, who directed *Days of Wine and Roses* (1962), and Stanley Kubrick, who directed *2001: A Space Odyssey* (1968), *Dr. Strangelove* (1964), *Full Metal Jacket* (1987), and *Eyes Wide Shut* (1999). Other notable contemporary American film auteurs are Martin Scorsese, whose films include *Taxi Driver* (1976), *The King of Comedy* (1983), and *The Age of Innocence* (1993); David Lynch, who made *Eraserhead* (1977), *Blue Velvet* (1986), and *Wild at Heart* (1990); and Spike Lee, who often makes movies that deal with race relations or controversial issues (*Do the Right Thing*, 1988), depictions of historical people and events (*Miracle at St. Anna*, 2008), and documentaries (*When the Levee Broke: A Requiem in Four Acts*, 2006).

TECHNOLOGICAL INFLUENCES ON MOVIE GENRES

Modern cinema comprises a variety of types, or **genres**. One basic distinction is between nonfiction, or documentaries, and fiction, by far the dominant type. Rarely shown in American multiplex cinemas, documentaries, if released theatrically at all, are shown in mostly urban art-house theaters to limited audiences. Notable exceptions have been the documentaries of Michael Moore, who created *Bowling for Columbine* (2002), *Fahrenheit 9/11* (2004), and *Sicko* (2007), all of which had theatrical releases.

Among the most familiar and popular genres of fiction film are action/adventure, comedy, romance, science fiction, suspense, historical, horror, Western, fantasy, musical, biography, and drama. In many cases, there are subgenres, such as crime drama, and some films cut across two or more genres, such as romantic comedy.

Technology has always influenced filmmaking and film genres from the days when short reels allowed films of only five minutes or less, which hampered the creation of complex stories, to the development of synchronized sound, which made the cameras stationary and changed movies from action- to speaking-oriented styles.

Today, digital technologies allow filmmakers to design and populate entire realistic worlds. George Lucas, of *Star Wars* fame, was at the forefront of spectacular computer-generated special effects, although critics charge these were sometimes at the expense of storytelling and character development. Digital technology has allowed for more realistic animation, and studios such as Pixar are using the less labor-intensive new technology to produce animated feature films—although it is still questionable how much money is saved after the costs for high-end computer systems to generate special effects are factored in. James Cameron's *Avatar* (2009), which he waited for more than ten years to make until the technology could match his vision of the film, cost over $300 million. As the first film to gross over $2 billion worldwide, the heavy investment more than paid off. Such was not the case for the effects-heavy *Green Lantern* (2011), which cost $200 million to make and may have topped out at only $260 million in worldwide ticket sales.

New technologies also affect what movies are popular. High-tech gadgetry in our daily lives and today's fast-paced media environment have parallels in many recent science fiction and technology-oriented movies. Slower-paced, character-driven movies based on historical events appeal less to younger audiences. Plots can also be interpreted differently because of changes in technology. A suspense movie made in the 1980s in which tension is created by the main character's difficulties in finding a public telephone would likely make young viewers today wonder why the character doesn't simply use her or his cell phone or borrow someone else's.

> **DISCUSSION QUESTIONS:** Technological limitations kept film reels short, so only a few minutes of footage could be shown at a time. In what ways could current technological limitations hamper our ability to tell stories through the Internet? How could storytelling be enriched?

genres

Topical categories.

Documentary maker Ken Burns has a special effect, the Ken Burns Effect, named after his technique of panning and zooming from a still image; it is built into most digital video-editing systems, including iMovie, Openshot, and Final Cut Pro. **CRITICAL THINKING QUESTIONS:** What do you think of filmmakers using the Ken Burns Effect? Is it effective, or does it show a lack of originality?

OTHER ENTERTAINMENT SOURCES FOR MOVIES

Movies have always relied heavily on other media as sources for stories. Some of the earliest films were nothing more than filmed stage plays, including Shakespearean dramas. Others were based on popular novels or stories, as are many movies today.

Successful original movies would sometimes inspire a TV series, such as *M*A*S*H* (1970), itself based on a novel; the subsequent television series of the same name ran from 1972 to 1983. Although it still occasionally occurs, such as with *Terminator: The Sarah Connor Chronicles*, today movies are equally likely to derive their inspiration from popular TV series, video games, cartoons, and even the Web.

Although *The Amazing Spider-Man* (2012) and *The Dark Knight* (2008) were hugely successful, many movies created from TV, comics, or video games have been less so. The past several years have seen a spate of movies based on popular television sitcoms, cartoons, and comic book characters: two *Addams Family* films (1991, 1998), *The Beverly Hillbillies* (1993), two *Brady Bunch* movies (1995, 1996), two *Scooby-Doo* movies (2002, 2004), and movies based on superheroes—the

The *Prince of Persia: The Sands of Time* is one of the few examples of successful movies that were taken from video games.

Fantastic Four, Iron Man, Thor, Captain America, the Incredible Hulk, and several Batman releases. The venerable Superman even made a return appearance in *Man of Steel* (2013).

Undercover Brother (2002), a parody of blaxploitation films of the 1970s, was one of the first movies derived from an animated Web series on a site called Urban Entertainment. A bidding war started among studios for the movie rights—showing how studios are mining the Web for story ideas. The Web also allows studios to gauge public interest through viral marketing efforts.

Studios have tried to cash in on the popularity of some video games and characters such as *Super Mario Bros.*, *Tomb Raider*, and *Resident Evil*. *Super Mario Brothers* (1993) did poorly at the box office, but *Lara Croft: Tomb Raider* (2001), although critically panned, did well enough to spawn a sequel in 2003.

DVDS AND STREAMING

Lower production costs for videotape created new opportunities for filmmakers who would not otherwise make feature films. Yet the movie industry strongly resisted the introduction of consumer videocassette recorder models in the 1970s, even suing VCR manufacturer Sony for encouraging illegal copying, copyright infringement that they claimed would ruin the movie business. This of course did not happen; and in fact, video (and now DVD) sales and rentals are double the revenue of box office receipts.

Two changes have radically altered the video market. First is the move from videotapes to DVDs, which provide more portability, better video and audio quality, and extra features unmatched on videotapes. Digital video also allowed low-budget directors to shoot professional-quality footage at a fraction of actual film cost. Editing and other postproduction work can also be done on computers or dedicated editing workstations. In only a few years, videotapes were replaced by DVDs, which in turn are slowly being replaced by the Blu-ray format, which offers even better sound, picture quality, and storage.

How people rent or buy video has also changed. Netflix, created in 1997, has transformed the video rental business by letting consumers use their broadband connection to stream movies and other video content on demand. The established video-rental model had involved going to a store, choosing a movie, and returning it within twenty-four or forty-eight hours to avoid late fees. DVD-rental kiosks, such as Redbox, have also made DVD rentals easier and more convenient; but by 2014, the DVD rental business itself had become obsolete.

Without expensive store rentals and other overhead costs, Netflix can maintain a larger, more diverse inventory. By November 2014, Netflix had 50 million subscribers worldwide paying about $8 a month for unlimited viewing of movies and other video content and about $13 a month for ultra-high-definition video.[7] Meanwhile, Blockbuster, king of video rentals in the 1990s, filed for bankruptcy in 2010.

Many industry experts believe that DVDs will eventually go the way of videotapes because of the popularity of subscription streaming services like Netflix, Amazon Prime, and Hulu Plus. These services forego any physical product, as consumers simply stream movies to their devices and watch them.

The trend can be seen clearly when looking at DVD sales versus streaming revenues in 2012. DVD sales still accounted for most of the revenues, $8.5 billion, but dropped 5.5 percent compared to the year before; whereas subscription streaming revenues rose to $2.3 billion from $1.6 billion.[8] By 2013, Netflix alone had generated $4.7 billion in annual revenues in the United States from its subscription services.

Much of the movie industry is not happy with the trend toward subscription streaming services, partly because they fear digital piracy and partly because profit margins are much higher on DVD and Blu-ray sales than digital streaming.

Netflix is flexing its international streaming distribution muscle as illustrated by the global company's 2014 original series *Marco Polo*, budgeting $90 million for production of the first season of 10 episodes.

Movie Industry Today

Today's motion picture industry contrasts significantly with the vertically integrated entertainment companies that owned not only the means of production but also the distribution system (i.e., the movie theaters). The Supreme Court's antitrust decision of 1948 forced studios to sell their theaters, and today much more power rests with the artists making the films, especially directors and high-paid actors and actresses.

The major studios have adapted to changing conditions and still frequently decide which movies to make and promote. Given the high costs, including several million dollars spent in marketing and specialized technical knowledge, it still requires large organizations like the movie studios to bring everything together.

Like other media industries, major studios are part of much larger media conglomerates. (See Table 5-1.) The major studios make movies under a variety of subsidiary production companies, some of which are quite large in their own right. Although lacking vertical integration, they still benefit from sister companies. For example, a Paramount picture may appear on CBS news (both owned by Viacom), or a Pixar picture on ABC news (both owned by Disney), or a 20th Century Fox picture on Fox News (both owned by 21st Century Fox).

A motion picture costs on average over $70 million, although movies often top $100 million, especially with special effects or big Hollywood stars. Marketing costs can add another $30 million to $50 million. Production, the largest single expense category, is usually about 25 percent of the total budget, including set construction, filming on location, film copies for distribution, and crew salaries. Almost all workers, from actors to screenwriters to cinematographers to carpenters, belong to unions that have standard salary rates and rules.

A filmmaker typically approaches a movie studio with a script, which may be original but is often adapted by a screenwriter from a novel or real-life story. A studio will often demand changes, sometimes major revisions, before agreeing to bankroll and distribute a movie. Creative differences may arise that can kill projects before they start or force filmmakers to seek support from other major or independent studios. The movie *Rain Man* (1988), starring Tom Cruise and Dustin Hoffman, was almost never made because studio executives demanded an action-packed chase scene involving Hoffman's autistic character.

Once a project has finally been approved and the actors' contracts and schedules agreed on, shooting can begin. This can take several weeks or even months, depending on schedules and other issues. After shooting, the filmmaker is still looking at several more months of postproduction work and editing hours and hours of footage into movie length. This too can produce creative differences, as studio executives may demand a happier or otherwise different ending based on early audience feedback. Deleting or even reshooting or shooting entirely new

TABLE 5-1 Ownership Among Major and Subsidiary Film Studios

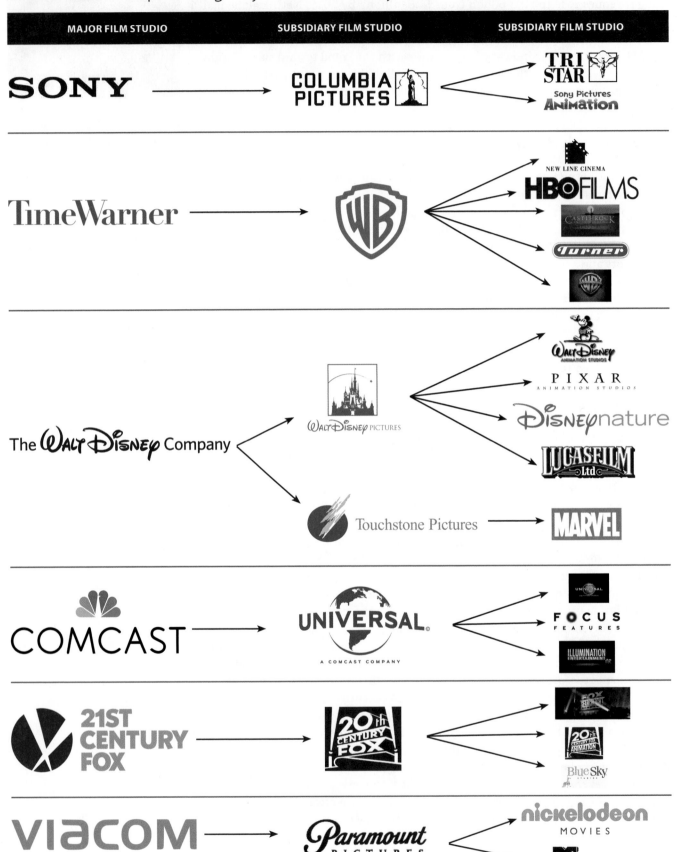

MAJOR FILM STUDIO	SUBSIDIARY FILM STUDIO	SUBSIDIARY FILM STUDIO

MEDIA PIONEERS
Kathleen Kennedy

With a career spanning more than three decades as producer of more than 60 major films distinguished by over 120 Academy Award nominations, Kathleen Kennedy advanced through the celluloid ceiling with digital force. As Sally Field told the CinemaCon crowd in April 2013 when presenting Kennedy with the Pioneer of the Year Award, "In an industry that is not and has not been female friendly, . . . Kathy has beaten those odds the only way a woman can—by being so much better than most everyone else."[9]

This is high praise—wholly supported by an extensive, diverse, and distinguished filmography that includes *Raiders of the Lost Ark* (1981), *E.T. the Extra-Terrestrial* (1982), *The Color*

Purple (1985), *Back to the Future* (1985), *Who Framed Roger Rabbit* (1988), *Jurassic Park* (1993), *Schindler's List* (1993), *Twister* (1996), *The Sixth Sense* (1999), *Persepolis* (2007), *The Diving Bell and the Butterfly* (2007), *The Curious Case of Benjamin Button* (2008), *The Adventures of Tintin* (2011), *War Horse* (2011), *Lincoln* (2012), and *Star Wars: Episode VII—The Force Awakens* (2015). As of 2014, Kennedy's films have grossed over $11 billion worldwide.[10]

One of Hollywood's most successful producers, male or female, Kennedy still flies under the radar with remarkable grace and characteristic modesty. She attributes her success in part to luck and good timing; others point to her astute judgment, formidable work ethic, empathy with cast and crew, and diplomacy when liaising between directors and studios.

Kathleen grew up in Redding, California, and graduated from San Diego State University with a BA in film. Her identical twin, Connie, is an executive producer at Profile Studios, a virtual production company for film and games that specializes in interactive storytelling. Her younger sister, Dana, is also a media professional, an Emmy-winning broadcast journalist, former news anchor, and talk show host.

Kennedy became Steven Spielberg's assistant on *Raiders of the Lost Ark*, after which she, her husband Frank Marshall, and Spielberg formed Amblin Entertainment in 1982. Ten years later, Kennedy and Marshall created their own production company. In 2012, George Lucas, with whom she had also collaborated over the years, selected her to become president of Lucasfilm. Kennedy is also a member of the Board of Governors and Board of Trustees of the Academy of Motion Pictures Arts and Sciences (AMPAS).

Having closely observed and embraced dramatic technological change in her stellar career, she maintains that the essence of great film—great storytelling—remains the same while the tool chest has expanded. "We've talked a great deal about the role that filmmaking technology has played in creating the Star Wars saga," says Kennedy. "We're incredibly excited to find ways to combine state-of-the-art visual effects with the practical approaches that were instrumental in making the original films so iconic; we plan to use everything in the toolbox to continue the Star Wars story."[11]

scenes may be required. The Ridley Scott classic *Blade Runner* (1982) is one of the most famous cases in which the studio required a reworking of the director's ending to make it more upbeat. Of course, several versions were later released, including a "director's cut" that more closely adhered to Scott's vision. Musical scores, dubbing, and voice-overs are also added during postproduction.

DISCUSSION QUESTIONS: Discuss new ways movie theaters might be able to use their large screens and space to show digital film not only from big-name moviemakers but from local artists as well. How might this affect the local movie theater and its role in the community?

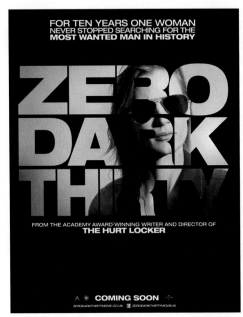

Oscar-nominated 9/11 picture *Zero Dark Thirty* stirred up controversy for Sony Pictures when victims' families complained that the movie's producers had not obtained their permission to use audio recordings, although in the public domain, of actual victims of the World Trade Center disaster. **CRITICAL THINKING QUESTIONS:** Although these voice recordings are in the public domain, do you think it is ethical for a commercial movie to use them without obtaining permission of the families of the victims or paying them royalties? Why or why not?

Marketing and Distribution for Movies

Marketing and distribution, often key to a movie's success, are quite expensive. A movie that debuts in one thousand theaters nationwide, however well attended, simply will not earn as much as one that fills half the seats in over three thousand theaters. Major studios can still distribute a movie more widely than independent film companies can. The Internet, however, has proven a valuable means of distribution due to its low cost and its potential to build audiences over time and space. A growing number of websites provide an extensive selection of independent and short films online.

The main channel for marketing movies is TV advertising. Heavy advertising occurs two weeks before release because it is nearly impossible for a movie to become popular after poor attendance following release. Much research, effort, and expense go into creating appealing movie trailers and packaging to reach the right target audience. Although studios advertise in other outlets, such as newspapers, radio, and billboards, almost 60 percent of spending is on network- and cable-television advertising. For some movies, such as *Paranormal Activity*, the Web and word-of-mouth are important, but these and social media are still a small but growing part in the overall marketing mix.

Movies have a regular pattern of exhibition "windows," places where they are shown that help increase revenues. When studios were at their strongest, they could control theatrical releases at what were deemed "first-run" theaters and then, after appeal faded there, second-run theaters. Movie studios determined which theaters were first-run and second-run and had agreements that assured theaters of exclusive showing privileges within a certain geographic area for a certain amount of time.

The usual exhibition windows for movies start with domestic theatrical release, then proceed to international release, video-on-demand (VOD), pay cable channels (HBO, Showtime, etc.), network or cable TV, and then syndicated TV. Each window has a specified time, and the windows generally do not overlap. Recently, however, likely blockbusters have been released simultaneously in the United States and select countries worldwide. Successful movies may get released to video earlier than usual to take advantage of theatrical residual popularity; or, if deemed not worthy of theatrical release, it gets the "straight to video" label and heads directly to DVD or on-demand distribution. VOD will probably become first after theatrical release, even though today it often appears simultaneously with the video release.[12]

Movie-Industry Business Model

A seemingly simple business model—get as many people as possible to pay to watch a movie—becomes more complicated when considering the varied ways to watch movies today other than in the theater and how important box office popularity is to attracting viewers in later exhibition windows. Increasing the complexity are the other means by which studios can generate revenue, including licensing deals, product placement, and promotional tie-ins.

Despite competition from a number of other forms of entertainment, movies continue to be highly popular. *Guardians of the Galaxy*, one of the most popular films of 2014, grossed over $333 million domestically.

The independent film *Napoleon Dynamite* (2004), for example, cost $400,000 and grossed $46 million worldwide. Because movies are so expensive to make and market, however, most lose money. High cost and high risk mean Hollywood studios seek safety in blockbusters, with their usual spate of sequels and generally formulaic stories and characters.

Audiences have been declining steadily over the past several years even as U.S. box office revenues have continued to rise, thanks to increasing ticket prices of about 5 percent a year and 3-D movies, which can charge about $3 more than non-3-D.[13] In 2013, gross U.S. box office revenues were at an all-time high at $10.92 billion, even though 2013's overall audience of 1.36 billion was down substantially from 2002's record 1.6 billion, when total box office receipts were less than $10 billion.[14]

U.S. box office revenues are not nearly as important from a financial standpoint as they used to be because international sales are often greater today. DVD rentals and sales are usually the biggest money generator for movies, long since surpassing box office revenues. Sales have dropped in recent years, though, as consumers rent rather than buy movies, increasingly through VOD services such as Netflix or cable operators.

Licensing deals can also generate revenue. With popular movies such as the *Toy Story* series, the studio receives royalties for licensing the rights to make toys, blankets, pajamas, and other goods based on the characters. Yet more caution has been exercised in recent years because these deals turn out poorly if a movie does not succeed at the box office. Promotional tie-ins, such as those with fast-food chains, can generate revenue as they generate interest in the movie. **Product placement**, using or showing real-life products in a movie, can also create revenue, although the overall amount is small compared to box office sales or video rentals.

product placement

A form of advertising in which brand-name goods or services are placed prominently within movie content that is otherwise devoid of advertising, demonstrating the convergence of programming with advertising content.

Outlook for the Movie Industry

Digitization has had profound effects on the movie industry, some of which are already being seen in the industry itself and in theaters. Amazing special effects using digital technology can far surpass previous efforts. As computer power increases, computer-artist and programmer skills improve, rendering surfaces like snow, skin, and fur more realistically.

Movie studios also save through digital-film distribution. It cost up to $2,000 to produce, duplicate, and ship one forty-pound celluloid film print to a movie

The Croods, a DreamWorks animation released in 2013, is created from 250 billion pixels, making it one of the highest-resolution movies ever.

theater, and most studios shipped prints to three thousand theaters nationwide if they hoped for a blockbuster. That means $6 million just in distribution costs for a major film.[15] A digital film, on the other hand, is simply sent over satellite or through broadband to a movie theater. In addition, endless perfect copies can be made, just as with other digital media, eliminating the need to receive even more prints when film breaks or loses its quality after repeated showings.

One obstacle to the movie industry's adoption of digital distribution, despite potential savings, has been concerns over piracy. The studios have watched the music industry's battles with file-swapping services such as Napster and realize that they are prime targets for similar practices. Nevertheless, the year 2013 seemingly marked the end of celluloid-film distribution to theaters in major markets.[16] Some industry experts estimate that digital distribution saves movie studios $600 to $800 million per year. By 2015, more than 80 percent of theaters around the world are expected to receive movies digitally via satellite.[17]

Assuming that the movie industry does eventually adopt digital technology at all levels of production, the moviegoer will likely see great improvement in picture quality (including 3-D) and sound as well as movie availability. More independent films may show in major theaters because the theaters and studios will not be banking on the same large audiences to break even because production and distribution costs will be lower.

Television

According to the Kaiser Family Foundation, children between eight and eighteen spend more time (6.5 hours a day on average) in front of some kind of screen—TV, computer, cell phone—than engaged in any other activity except sleeping. And more time is devoted to television than to any other medium. The average viewer today who lives to be seventy-five will have spent eleven years watching TV.

Many critics think television is mindless entertainment that does nothing for social skills and physical fitness. Others point to quality content, educational television, news, and cultural programming. Today's interactive television can even get the couch potato off the couch and physically active.

CONVERGENCE CULTURE
3-D Movies: What Will Be the Impact?

Movie studios have long been promoting 3-D movies as the Next Big Thing, but this time several noted directors are also cheerleaders, including Steven Spielberg, Peter Jackson, and James Cameron, all of whom have released 3-D movies. Some proponents even claim that 3-D will revolutionize cinema in the same way that sound revolutionized the early film era.

Many mainstream movies are now released both in conventional format and in 3-D. In 2014, blockbuster 3-D films such as *The Hobbit: The Battle of the Five Armies* and *Guardians of the Galaxy* offered high-quality immersive viewing experiences. Among the most commercially successful 3-D movies of 2014 was *Godzilla*, which had box office receipts of $200 million in the United States. With increasingly lucrative ticket prices, it's not surprising that moviemakers are turning increasingly to the 3-D format. Dozens more 3-D formatted movies are scheduled for 2015 production.

Blu-ray DVDs for home viewing are also available for a vast array of films. Titles in 2014 include *Gravity*, *The Hunger Games: Catching Fire*, and *Exodus: Gods and Kings*, all in 3-D.

3-D movies still require special glasses. Viewing quality, however, has improved dramatically in recent years, and these movies have become so important that writers now adapt scripts to incorporate 3-D effects. "You build sequences differently when you know things have to pop out and jump at you," says Kieran Mulroney, a script writer for Warner Bros.' *Sherlock Holmes* sequel, as reported in the *Los Angeles Times*.[18]

The next generation of 3-D movies will likely be even more popular because viewers may no longer need special glasses to enjoy special effects (which also incorporate surround sound). Like previous technological advances, the spread of 3-D will probably change the movie experience in unforeseen ways. Beyond 3-D is 4-D, movies and theaters that incorporate physical or tactile experiences and other

sensory components in the storytelling. For instance, the 4-D theater at the Bronx Zoo in New York City in 2014 showed moviegoers *Ice Age 4-D*. It not only featured 3-D video but put viewers in seats that moved as part of the story, simulating the movement of an earthquake; and in dramatic fashion, viewers were sprayed actual mist from a sneezing dinosaur, much to the delight of the author's 9-year-old nephew.

Terrestrial, or over-the-air broadcast TV, has traditionally been the norm, but today more than two-thirds of homes get TV via cable or satellite. Moreover, most households watch DVDs or VOD via television. Consumer recording devices for television were an important development, allowing the audience to **time shift**, that is, watch a program any time after the original broadcast rather than be held hostage by a broadcaster's scheduling.

Time shifting helped tilt the balance of power toward the audience in choosing media content—a trend that will continue as TV switches to a digital format. As with radio, digital media will complicate the very definition of television, especially as TVs take on more interactive programming and converge with computers and mobile devices. A Slingbox permits viewers to **place shift**, that is, access video via the Internet originally delivered digitally to the home.

time shift

Recording of an audio or video event for later listening or viewing.

place shift

Viewing TV from anywhere using the Internet to access video originally delivered digitally to the home (or another location).

Via a Slingbox, a viewer can use the Internet from anywhere in the world to place shift her or his television viewing.

The widespread use and content range of television help it serve its entertainment, surveillance, correlation, and cultural transmission functions. More U.S. households have televisions than telephones—about 97 percent have at least one TV—and it is the most influential mass-communication medium. More Americans get their news from television than from any other source, making its surveillance function preeminent. More Americans get their entertainment from television than from any other mass medium as well. Entertainment programming plays an important role in the cultural transmission of new trends and social norms.

Only one development has caused a drop in TV viewership—the Internet. Despite this, TV is still number one in most populations' media use. However, a 2009 Kaiser Family Foundation survey found that young people increasingly watch TV content that is not live, including DVDs, VOD, and television programming on computers or mobile devices.

Television became a mass medium providing a common set of experiences much faster than film, music, and radio, displacing radio, which had supplanted national magazines. Although more channels and audience fragmentation may reduce this effect, television continues to shape attitudes on a variety of social and cultural issues.

History of Television

cathode-ray tube (CRT)

Device in older televisions and computers using electron beams to transmit images to the screen.

Most TV sets and computer displays traditionally used a **cathode-ray tube (CRT)**, conceived in 1859 by German mathematician and physicist Julius Plücker. British chemist William Crookes built the first functional CRT in 1878. In 1873, British telegrapher Louis May discovered that selenium bars exposed to light conduct electricity. Some consider this the basis of photoconductivity, a critical foundation for the electronic transmission of visual and audio information. In 1881, British inventor Shelford Bidwell transmitted silhouettes using selenium in his "scanning phototelegraph," an electrical method that contributed to the development of modern television.

SEEING THE LIGHT: THE FIRST TELEVISION SYSTEMS

In 1884, German inventor Paul Nipkow developed a concept for mechanical television that used a rotating disk. In 1923, Scottish inventor John Logie Baird created Baird Television, the first mechanically scanned television device to profit from sending pictures through the air. Some consider Baird's thirty-line TV the first high-definition TV for its many more lines of resolution and finer visual detail.

In 1927, Philo T. Farnsworth transmitted the image of a dollar sign across his San Francisco apartment using his scanning-beam and synchronization-pulse technologies. This was the first electronic wireless transmission of an image, the initial step toward electronic television. His first "broadcast" transmitted images from a Jack Dempsey/Gene Tunney fight and scenes of Mary Pickford combing her hair (from *Taming of the Shrew*).

MODERN TELEVISION TAKES SHAPE

Much better image resolution was needed for television to advance. The CRT screen, with its greater number of scanned lines, afforded a better picture. In 1939,

Philo T. Farnsworth transmitted the first wireless electronic image, the first step toward electronic television.

David Sarnoff demonstrated 441-line TV technology at the New York World's Fair that drew national and international attention. That same year, the National Broadcasting Company (NBC) began regularly scheduled broadcasts to only four hundred sets in the New York area, development interrupted by the beginning of World War II. There were just seven thousand receiving sets and only nine stations in the United States in early 1946. By 1949, ninety-eight stations existed in fifty-eight markets. In 1950, 3.88 million households had television, 9 percent of the total 43 million.

By 1948, there were four commercial television networks: NBC, CBS, ABC, and DuMont (this last network failed in 1955). By the end of 1955, TV households numbered 30.7 million, 64.5 percent of U.S. households; and U.S. advertisers were spending more than $300 million on TV time. By 1960, 45.7 million U.S. households (87.1 percent) had at least one television set.

Color television broadcasting debuted in 1951 with a live CBS telecast from Grand Central Station in New York. Unfortunately, only twenty-five receivers could accommodate the technology, while the 12 million existing black-and-white sets displayed a blank screen. In 1953, color broadcasting launched in the United States when the FCC approved a modified version of an RCA system compatible with existing screens. Color television was only the next step in the ceaseless effort to present sharper and better pictures.

PROGRAMMING AND GENRE INFLUENCES

Much early TV programming came directly from radio, where talented actors and comedians such as Jack Benny adapted their routines for television. The influence of stage and film also lent much to early television. Dramas sponsored by Hallmark began in 1948, migrating among CBS, NBC, and ABC for over sixty years before running on Hallmark's own channel. Westerns from both radio and film were particularly popular, and although Hollywood studios initially resisted, bringing film to television provided yet another revenue source.

Considerable original programming occurred in the forms of hosted children's shows, variety shows, situation comedies, sports, and news talk shows. From this diversity emerged a more formal organizational division of programming: entertainment, sports, and news.

The 1950s, often referred to as the golden age of television, featured many critically acclaimed commercial successes. An entire postwar generation grew up with the children's show *Howdy Doody*; the first filmed TV sitcom, *I Love Lucy*; the radio carryover classic Western *Gunsmoke*; Jackie Gleason's *The Honeymooners*; Rod Serling's *Twilight Zone*; and *The Tonight Show*, among so many others. *The Ed Sullivan Show*, debuting in 1948 as *Toast of the Town*, established the variety format and often attracted half of all viewing households. In 1964, 73 million viewers nationwide tuned in to see the Beatles on that show.

The Ed Sullivan Show helped establish the variety show format and introduced many new artists to the American public.

Pushing the Programming Envelope

By the 1970s, significant program developments were afoot. Standard one-dimensional genres were infused with more complex, realistic characters and story lines. In 1977, ABC launched its twenty-six-hour miniseries *Roots*, based on the novel by Alex Haley, the final episode of which remains the third-most-watched TV program in history.

The Public Broadcasting Service (PBS) began broadcasting in 1970, inheriting programs from National Educational Television, a noncommercial network founded in 1954. Most famous among these was *Sesame Street*, arguably the most influential TV program for children, which has run continuously since 1969. Operating as a not-for-profit corporation owned by member stations, PBS has often been the home for commercially unviable programming in the arts and sciences, consistently winning more television awards for high quality than commercial television and cable networks combined.

Monday Night Football, started in 1970, became a cultural mainstay and led to more sporting events broadcast outside of the traditional weekend slot, producing greater revenue opportunities for sports franchises. Some sports, such as basketball, even changed their rules to promote a faster-paced and more exciting game.

All in the Family, the highest-rated program of the 1970s, introduced controversy into the situation comedy genre with its bigoted character, Archie Bunker. Its success encouraged others to explore many contemporary social and civil rights issues, although many more simply repackaged popular genres such as police dramas, mysteries, and science fiction.

In 1980, producer Stephen Bochco introduced a new genre of gritty police drama on NBC. *Hill Street Blues* featured several prominent characters, all with various story lines, and a realistic, often-chaotic quality that added dramatic elements of a soap opera. He continued to develop the genre in the 1990s with ABC's popular *NYPD Blue*.

Cable Comes of Age

Music Television, or MTV, debuted in 1981 as a cable channel with its first music video "Video Killed the Radio Star." The title proved prophetic. Having dramatically changed music promotion, MTV continued to introduce innovative, although not always culture-enhancing, programs such as *The Real World*, *Jackass*, *The Osbournes*, and MTV's most-viewed series ever, *Jersey Shore*. MTV exemplified a sea change in television programming from one-size-fits-all on the networks to a fragmented and specialized approach on cable or satellite channels devoted exclusively to travel, sports, and even specific sports such as golf or soccer, movie classics, television classics, cartoons, science, science fiction, home improvement, crime, animals, law, and history.

MTV, or Music Television, became such a part of youth culture after it debuted that teens who were once labeled "Generation X" were also called the "MTV Generation."

Several cable channels began to develop their own dramatic programming, occasionally attracting more viewers than many network shows. Despite being in only about 28 million homes, a third of those with network television and non-premium cable channels, the fourth-season premiere of HBO's hit mob series *The Sopranos* on September 15, 2002, attracted 13.4 million viewers, the most-watched show in its history. HBO had already been making original feature films; but original, critically acclaimed series such as *The Sopranos*, *Sex and the City*, *Big Love*, *Boardwalk Empire*, and *Game of Thrones* are making the networks finally take notice of cable. The FX channel, also generating buzz with cutting-edge programming, attracted 5 million viewers for the premiere episode of its police drama *The Shield*.

Reflecting the growing Latin American population in the United States, in the 1980s the Reliance Capital Group launched the Spanish-language network Telemundo Group. Cable and satellite television support channels that target ethnic groups while also offering access to some programming from their home countries. Today, usually for an additional monthly fee, many subscribers can get cable channels in Russian, Chinese, Japanese, Hindi, Tagalog, and Arabic, among other languages.

Critics of network television programming say the networks have only themselves to blame for large-scale defections to cable channels, in particular a risk-averse corporate culture that encourages copying popular programming rather than innovating. Cable TV programming can be more innovative and edgy because it is unfettered by FCC content restrictions on network profanity or partial nudity. Another factor that works against networks is their need to attract as large an audience as possible to charge higher rates for commercials, something that subscriber-based channels such as HBO do not have to consider.

Filling the Days

A staple of early television was the soap opera, so named because, first on radio and then on television, its principal advertising was for household products aimed at the daytime serial's primary audience, homemakers. Indeed, Proctor & Gamble produced both soap and soap operas, notably *Guiding Light*, the longest-running TV soap at nearly sixteen thousands episodes between 1952 and 2009; *As the World Turns* (1956–2010); and *Another World* (1964–1999). One by one, the soaps have died as more women entered the workforce and audiences shrank. Soaps have lost a quarter of their audience since the 1980s. No new English-language soaps have been introduced since the 1990s.

Many fans wax nostalgic over the loss of favorite soaps, pointing out that they set important new standards for daytime television by discussing topics like abortion and illegitimate pregnancy. Not all are gone. *Days of Our Lives* and *General Hospital* remain daytime fare. Full-length episodes of *Guiding Light* are still available at CBS's website. Telenovelas, Spanish-language soaps with passionate and sometimes-violent tales, are still popular on Spanish-language TV, although they typically run only for a few months or years by design. Soap operas introduced some of today's biggest movie and television stars including Morgan Freeman, Kelsey Grammar, Tommy Lee Jones, James Franco, Amanda Seyfried, and Brad Pitt.

Exceedingly popular in commercial television's first full decade was the game or quiz show, a format that had been successful in radio as well. By the end of the 1958 TV season, there were twenty-two network quiz shows, one of every five shows. As it happened, many were rigged; and after a public scandal and subsequent congressional investigation involving the popular *Twenty-One*, new rules for regulating game shows emerged.

An even cheaper format, the talk show, has largely replaced daytime game shows. *Dr. Phil*, *Jerry Springer*, *Rachael Ray*, and *The View*, for example, have assumed much of the role that soaps used to play in bringing controversial issues to the public arena.

Filling the Nights

The popularity of the prime-time game show was revived when ABC's *Who Wants to Be a Millionaire* became a ratings leader after its debut in 1999. Like *Survivor*, it

Born in Colombia, Sofia Vergara stars on one of the most popular shows on American television, *Modern Family*, and is the highest paid actor on television.

was a copy of a European show, reversing a long trend of European television's emulating successful American game shows. Although its success was relatively short lived, lasting only three years, the show helped spawn a number of other prime-time game shows. Despite the rapid rise and fall of some of these, others that air before prime time have enjoyed greater longevity, such as *Jeopardy!* and *Wheel of Fortune*.

Prime-time network programming is now dominated by dramatic series, reality shows, and situation comedies, with occasional made-for-TV movies or broadcasts of popular movies that have already appeared in theaters. The latter have become less important, however, as many viewers now choose to see uncut movies without commercial interruptions on DVD, cable, or satellite.

Sports

Some of the biggest television events involve sports. The Super Bowl, for example, annually draws one of U.S. television's largest audiences. Every four years, the World Cup, the quadrennial soccer tournament, draws large worldwide television audiences. Television commentator Les Brown explains how sports constitute a near-perfect program form for television, "at once topical and entertaining, performed live and suspensefully without a script, peopled with heroes and villains, full of action and human interest and laced with pageantry and ritual."[19]

Sports provide an ongoing venue for technical experimentation. Instant replay debuted in the 1963 Army–Navy football game, and slow motion replay came shortly thereafter. Not only do these now-standard techniques enhance viewing, they have become tools to assist officiating in certain sports, although not without occasional controversy. The rise in popularity of poker-tournament shows has been attributed in part to miniature cameras that allow viewers to see what hands players are holding as they place their bets.

Although sports events still populate the major networks, Disney's ESPN has become the dominant sports channel, drawing an industry-high $6 billion in annual subscriber fees. Yet it faces growing competition, including Al Jazeera's two twenty-four-hour sports channels (focused on soccer) and Rupert Murdoch's newly launched Fox Sports, a twenty-four-hour sports channel featuring NASCAR races, major league baseball and football games, soccer, and more.

Media play a role in determining what types of sports get promoted (and thus which ones get lucrative corporate sponsorships). The popularity of extreme sports and types of fighting besides boxing, such as mixed martial arts, has risen. Generally, slow-paced or highly individualistic sports fare less well than

Soccer is one of the most widely watched sports worldwide.

faster-paced events or exciting team sports. One notable exception is golf, likely due to its upscale demographic attractive to advertisers.

Professional wrestling blends sports and entertainment. World Wrestling Entertainment (WWE) combines the physical showmanship that has long defined professional wrestling with ample doses of sexuality and character-driven story lines—complete with crooked bad guys who cheat popular wrestlers of their rightful titles.

Reality Shows

It may be surprising to learn that reality shows have roots in the earliest days of television. Game shows like *Truth or Consequences*, whose contestants performed wacky stunts for prizes, or Alan Funt's *Candid Camera*, a classic prank show, were very popular in the 1950s and 1960s. In the 1980s, shows like *COPS* and *America's Funniest Home Videos* (AFV) debuted, and they continue to air today. *AFV* is a precursor to the kind of **user-generated content (UGC)** often uploaded to YouTube or other video websites.

Reality shows became much more popular beginning in 2000 after *Big Brother* and *Survivor* were both hits in the United States. Today, *American Idol*—which can trace its lineage (including home audience voting by phone) directly back to popular talent-search shows of the 1940s, such as *Arthur Godfrey's Talent Scouts*—remains a top-rated show and has launched singing careers for several of its finalists and winners.

Reality shows are a versatile genre. Home improvement channels have capitalized on the format with shows like *House Hunters* and *Property Virgins*, and lifestyle channels have had success with shows such as *Extreme Makeover* and *The Biggest Loser*. Practically any situation, real or fantasized, can be adapted to this format, and viewers enjoy watching both "regular" people and celebrities in various challenging situations.

Reality television is profitable for television networks because production costs are much lower than that of scripted programs with actors, sets, and writers paid union wages. The format has proven popular in Europe and Asia, making licensing deals appealing. In addition, many reality shows earn extra money through product placement. Watch an episode of *The Biggest Loser* and count how many times brand-name products are mentioned during the show.

Despite their name, few of these shows actually capture "reality." Through postproduction editing techniques and loose direction regarding how to act or what to say, the shows present a contrived narrative that may bear little resemblance to the participants' experiences at the time. Although reality shows have made some people celebrities, they also routinely subject participants to public ridicule.

> **user-generated content (UGC)**
>
> Content created by the general public for distribution by digital media.

Reality shows remain very popular despite the fact many do not truly capture any "reality" with which most viewers would be familiar.

DISCUSSION QUESTIONS: How many reality shows do you watch? Categorize them according to their genres, such as documentary style, reality legal programming, reality competition, social experiment, and hoaxes. Do you think certain genres have more redeeming social or educational value than others, or is there good and bad to be found within each category?

DIGITAL TELEVISION: PREPARING THE WAY FOR CONVERGENCE

The video and audio of the electronic television's display terminal has evolved since its early years. Long before the digital revolution in 1973, NHK (Japan Broadcasting Corporation) began research on analog **high-definition television (HDTV)**, demonstrating Hi-Vision in 1981, which had much higher resolution, sharper color, a wider aspect ratio, and superior audio. In 1990, an American company, General Instrument Corporation, proposed all **digital television (DTV)**, which became the global standard for next-generation TV. Note that HDTV can be digital, and digital TV can be HDTV, but the two were not always synonymous.

Since June 2009, all television broadcast signals in the United States were switched to digital. DTV enables the convergence of computing, television, and telecommunications that makes new storytelling techniques possible as well as linking to **multicast** (multiplex), simultaneously transmitting multiple channels of compressed content or the same content but at different times. DTV is another step toward converging TVs and PCs or other digital devices (e.g., tablets).

THE RISE OF FLAT-PANEL DISPLAYS

Large-screen, flat-panel, high-definition displays have changed the television-viewing experience. They bring near-theater-quality sound, color, and picture clarity to living rooms, sometimes in 3-D and all while saving space. Two main types of flat-panel displays have gradually overtaken CRT television: liquid crystal displays (LCDs) and plasma displays. Seen in digital alarm clocks, laptops, and tablet computers, LCD screens also use much less power than the traditional CRT display. At the end of 2007, LCD outsold CRT sets worldwide for the first time. In 2008, they became the majority of sets sold, at just over 50 percent, and their sales continue to grow.

LCD technology originated in the late nineteenth century and was developed throughout the first half of the twentieth century, yet the first LCD was created only in 1972. Defying earlier beliefs that LCD screens could be no larger than forty inches, television manufacturers have ramped up production of large-screen LCD television sets.

Plasma displays, created around the same time as the early LCD screens, appeared to have a number of advantages over LCDs in terms of picture quality, viewing angle, and screen size. With LCDs now nearly matching the size of plasma displays, however, and with LCD costs generally lower, plasma screens, as well as projection TV, have become less popular for large-screen, HDTV viewing. In some public areas, such as sporting arenas, very large screen displays using light-emitting diode (LED) technology are preferred.

Smart-screen TVs are another type of flat screen making significant inroads. These advanced TVs feature touch and gesture control and speech recognition, capabilities that enable interaction with programming as well as intuitive

high-definition television (HDTV)

Modern television technology that produces a much higher-resolution image, sharper color, a wider aspect ratio, and superior audio. Ultra-high definition is next-generation TV with even higher resolution video. 4K TVs can display video at 4,000 lines of resolution, compared to the 420 lines of standard definition TV.

digital television (DTV)

Television system in which all information broadcast by cable or through the air is in digital, or computer-readable, form.

multicast

Simultaneous transmission of multiple channels of compressed content or the same content but at different times.

interfaces for channel navigation and more. They also support video chat and other functions typically available on network-connected PCs or tablets. Next-generation displays have begun to incorporate curve-LED displays combining ultra-high-definition video with immersive 3-D viewing experiences that no longer require the viewer to wear stereoscopic glasses yet still create the feeling of a virtual presence within the video stream.

Television Distribution

Screen-image quality matters little if there is no way to mass distribute content—thus the early importance of television networks, derived directly from the existing national radio networks. Television programming is distributed in three primary ways: broadcasting, cable, and direct-to-home satellite. The Internet may catch up, however. It has rapidly become a fourth important medium, as more people watch clips of shows or entire programs online.

First Lady Michelle Obama's appearance on the 2013 Academy Awards television broadcast was digitally altered by Iran's semiofficial news agency Fars to cover her chest and shoulders, conforming with Iranian restrictions on images of the female body in media. **CRITICAL THINKING QUESTIONS:** Do you agree with Fars' decision to alter the First Lady's appearance digitally to conform with local conservative religious views? Why or why not?

BROADCAST TV

Broadcasting (terrestrial wireless) is the traditional means of over-the-air TV distribution for networks, affiliates, and local stations. ABC, CBS, and NBC were all originally radio networks; and Fox, launched in 1986, became the fourth national network, owned by News Corp. The broadcasting networks dominated television viewing until the 1980s when cable and satellite TV made program and audience fragmentation inevitable. Today, about 15 percent of U.S. households receive terrestrial signals on their primary TV set, but broadcast programs are also carried on cable and satellite TV. In fact, the three traditional commercial networks still have a cumulative monthly audience reach of 65 percent.[20]

CABLE TV

Many think cable TV was invented in the 1980s. But the first systems, **community antenna television (CATV)**, were built noncommercially in Mahoney City, Pennsylvania, and Astoria, Oregon, in 1948. In these communities, over-the-air reception was nonexistent or poor due to hilly terrain or distance. A nationwide cable system did not begin expanding rapidly until the 1970s, when local cable systems grew from about two thousand in 1970 to more than four thousand in 1980.

In the 1980s, the government began deregulating the industry, permitting companies to buy cable television systems nationwide. Early cable giant Tele-Communications, Inc. (TCI), now a subsidiary of AT&T Broadband, took advantage of deregulation, spending $3 billion for 150 cable companies across the United States. By the end of the decade, 50 percent of U.S. households were wired for cable TV.

community antenna television (CATV)

Cable television developed in 1948 so communities in hilly or remote terrain could still access television broadcasts.

SATELLITE TV

Direct broadcast satellite (DBS) emerged in the United States in the 1990s as a serious competitor with traditional terrestrial broadcast and cable television. Although already a viable commercial television alternative in Europe, sustained efforts to launch DBS in the United States had failed until the 1994 launch of DirecTV.

Prior to that, most direct-to-home satellite systems required expensive, large three-meter dishes. DirecTV and other 1990s DBS entrants introduced inexpensive, compact eighteen-inch dishes that could be installed without professional help and whose subscription price rivals that of cable. With its 20 million subscribers, DirecTV ranks second only to cable multiple system operator (MSO) Comcast in terms of subscribers, while rival Dish Network, with 14 million subscribers, ranks third.

Television Industry Today

Television station ownership has continued to consolidate since the passage of the 1996 Telecommunications Act. The 35 percent rule now permits groups to own stations that nationwide reach up to 35 percent of television households and to own two stations in major markets.

There are more than ten thousand local cable systems and two satellite distributors, yet consolidation in the video-distribution industry has resulted in a relatively few companies—roughly six hundred MSOs—controlling cable television and satellite TV for more than 90 percent of American subscribers. As Table 5-2 shows, the top multichannel video programming distributors have nearly three-quarters of all cable TV subscribers.

Between 2008 and 2014, Comcast lost more than 2 million subscribers and second-place Time Warner more than five hundred thousand, a decline especially notable in urban areas where the telephone companies, such as Verizon and AT&T, offer fiber-optic services.[21] The top 13 cable MSOs continued to lose subscribers in 2014, with some 150,000 subscribers cutting their cable cord in the third quarter of the year, the worst quarter in the history of cable TV.[22] Of course, companies like Comcast have at the same time gained new broadband Internet subscribers: 315,000 in the third quarter of 2014, for a total of some 21.6 million.[23]

CABLE SYSTEM STRUCTURE

The typical cable system features a tree-and-branch architecture. A headend, or main office, is the center, with fiber or coaxial cable trunk lines, feeder lines, and drops to end users. The 1990s move from analog to digital technology entailed upgrades costing most cable companies millions or billions of dollars not only to improve and expand channel capacity but to add interactive features, such as two-way capacity (e.g., for program ordering), cable modems, and set-top box converters for high-speed Internet. In 2014, more than 80 percent of American households subscribed to pay TV at an average basic subscription cost of $123, an annual increase of 9.4 percent since 2011.[24]

TABLE 5-2 Top Multichannel Video-Programming Distributors in the United States, 2014

CABLE/SATELLITE MSO	NUMBER OF SUBSCRIBERS
Comcast	22,376,000
DIRECTV	20,203,000
dish	14,041,000
Time Warner Cable	11,030,000
verizon FiOS	6,505,000
COX / Blue Sky	6,067,000
at&t U-verse	5,533,000
Charter COMMUNICATIONS	4,296,000
CABLEVISION	2,715,000

Source: Leichtman Research Group, Inc. accessed March 1, 2015, http://www.leichtmanresearch.com/press/111414release.html.

SATELLITE VERSUS CABLE

DBS offers more than three hundred digital programming channels, compared to nearly two hundred for cable. Subscriptions are usually cheaper than cable, even basic cable, but installation costs are involved with satellite dishes and other equipment.

The greatest DBS problem is its lack of a full local array, important for local news, weather, and other programming. Despite great channel capacity, they cannot carry every local station, only those in the largest markets, which require subscribers to pay a fee.

Cable companies have been strongly criticized for increasing monthly subscription costs and poor customer service. Most areas have only a single cable provider, although this is changing in some urban or heavily populated areas. Cable companies are introducing more services—such as VOD, DVRs, and video gaming—to compete with satellite and the Internet.

Television-Industry Business Model

Business models vary with television-signal delivery. Traditionally, terrestrial broadcasting networks relied primarily on selling advertising, one-minute or thirty-second ads, taking up between sixteen and twenty-two minutes of an hour-long program.

Advertising revenues generated network profits and subsidized the development of new shows. They also created a culture among networks very similar to that in Hollywood—a risk-averse mindset that sought hit television shows to attract the largest audiences, which meant more lucrative commercial spots. This promoted a copycat trend as other networks scrambled to emulate hit shows the next season.

The importance of tracking audiences led to the Nielsen ratings, a way to measure how many people in various markets were watching a particular show. As Nielsen ratings became the yardstick of success, small drops in viewership could have profound consequences, such as moving shows to different days or time slots or canceling them completely.

Founded in the 1920s by Arthur Nielsen for radio-audience measurement, the system relies primarily on two means of data collection. First is the diary of self-reported TV-watching behaviors. Second is the Set Meter, a digital device that automatically collects viewership data from TV sets. Set Meter data are combined with viewing data collected by individual "people" meters as well. In 2013, Nielsen announced it would begin collecting data about viewership from DVRs. Ratings are calculated by dividing households viewing a program by the total number of TV households. So a rating of 25 would mean one-quarter of all TV households (estimated by Nielsen at 116.3 million in 2014) watched a particular program. Nielsen reports ratings by demographic group as well, collecting its most detailed and comprehensive data four times a year during "sweeps." Nielsen data show a continuing trend of declining viewership of live TV, with the average American watching 4 hours and 32 minutes of live TV each day, 12 percent less than in 2013.

Cable's fragmentation of audiences made the Nielsen ratings a less accurate measure. Even hit cable shows usually have smaller audiences than low-rated network shows. Like satellite, cable services are typically offered in tiers, varying program packages at varying rates. The main cable services are basic, premiere channel, and per program, either pay-per-view or VOD. The FCC requires basic service, the minimum level, to include all local over-the-air television broadcast signals and all public, educational, or government-access channels. Basic cable channels air commercials even as they charge a monthly subscription fee. Smaller audiences mean lower advertising rates, however.

Premium cable subscribers get commercial-free content on various bundles, including HBO, Cinemax, and Showtime as well as specialized and foreign-language channels. Additional monthly fees can range anywhere from $4.99 to $16.99 a month. Pay-per-view services include fights or other sporting events, usually for around $50, while the increasingly popular VOD costs anywhere from $2.99 to $16.99 to download a movie. Some services offer free on-demand content along with paid programming. VOD services will continue to grow, especially as networks, cable, and satellite compete with online television services and services like Netflix.

NCIS became the world's most popular TV drama in 2013 as it entered its twelfth season. It also boasts two spin-offs featuring stories set in Los Angeles and New Orleans. **CRITICAL THINKING QUESTIONS:** What accounts for the international appeal of NCIS? Identify a number of popular series with spin-offs. Do you think the spin-offs proved as popular as the originals? Why or why not might this be the case?

An alternative to advertising and subscription-based models is public broadcasting. In the United States, PBS, a private, not-for-profit corporation owned by member stations, depends on a combination of annual federal appropriations, corporate sponsorships, and private viewer contributions. Different yet is the British Broadcasting Corporation (BBC). Started in the United Kingdom in 1936, it receives an annual fee collected by the government as a broadcasting tax levied on all TV and radio receivers.

DISCUSSION QUESTIONS: If you had to restrict your viewing to only one of the following for a month—network television, premium cable, or video on demand—which would it be and why?

Outlook for the Television Industry

The switch to an entirely digital television signal in the United States in 2009 freed up some areas of bandwidth used by analog while allowing broadcasters and cable operators to offer new products, including VOD and other interactive services. More significantly, it signaled another step toward an exclusively digital media world.

Although cable and satellite operators have had to adjust to digitization changes, network television has arguably been most affected, as audiences are drawn to other viewing options such as edgier or more innovative cable shows. And as audiences shrink, so do advertising revenues.

Networks are experimenting with online viewing, such as with Hulu.com, founded in 2007. Co-owned by NBCUniversal, News Corp., and Providence Equity Partners, Hulu was easily able to expand content from subsidiary companies Fox, NBC, Sony Pictures Television, Warner Brothers Television, and others. The networks have also made a notable effort to have online streaming video of a distinctly superior quality to the videos found on YouTube. These programs sometimes have embedded advertisements. To watch full episodes, users must pay a monthly fee to Hulu Plus. The subscription model of Hulu Plus is yet one more example of how media companies are realizing that old business models are untenable and that if they do not do something online, other upstart companies will.

Some companies, such as Netflix, Amazon, and Microsoft, are producing pilots (the first-run test shows of new TV series) and even entire original series for online distribution. Series produced for digital distribution on Netflix include *House of Cards*, *Hemlock Grove*, and *Orange Is the New Black*. And the fourth season of cult classic *Arrested Development* was also a Netflix exclusive. With Amazon Fire TV, subscribers to Amazon Prime can watch more than 200,000 movies and video and other content including music on demand via the Internet.

In 2015, HBO Now launched Internet streaming of its original programming and movies in an exclusive partnership with Apple, a convergence of media and technology that should appeal to a generation of cord-cutters and cord-nevers. The streaming service costs $14.99 a month, and its April debut coincided with a new season of *Game of Thrones*, HBO's most popular series.

MEDIA CAREERS

Entertainment is serious business at home and abroad, a dynamic field in a state of constant growth. The U.S. entertainment industry generates billions of dollars, revenue accrued in domestic and international markets. Rewarding careers in the visual arts of photography, film, and television are too numerous to list. Identifying the specific path that you would most like to pursue is an important first step.

The most high-profile positions, for the few who attain stardom, are in acting; but actors would be nowhere without talent behind the scenes in the major professions of casting (both locations and people), art, camera and lighting, costuming and makeup, special effects, production, directing, and writing. Numerous career options exist within each of these categories.

Media jobs in the television and movie industry also include creative opportunities for reporters and publicists. These positions require both skill in multimedia production as well as an understanding of social networking media and a strategic appreciation of the changing nature of TV and film in the increasingly interactive, mobile, and on-demand global marketplace.

LOOKING BACK AND MOVING FORWARD

Deregulation and the passage of the Telecommunications Act of 1996 paved the way for mergers and consolidation in the cable industry in recent years. Cable TV now offers consumers bundled packages of telephone, cable television, and Internet service. Verizon, traditionally a telecommunications company, has begun offering more regions in the United States direct-to-home fiber-optic lines, FiOS, a service whose popularity has contributed in part to the decline in cable subscribers.

Cord-cutters and cord-nevers are increasingly turning away from cable and other traditional pay TV services and toward broadband Internet services, wired and wireless, to access and watch VOD, live and interactively. If consumers use a cable provider for their telephone service, which rules apply—cable TV regulations or phone regulations? Why should an email sent over telephone wires be treated differently, from a legal perspective, than an email sent via cable? This goes to the heart of the so-called network neutrality debate roiling broadband policy makers.

From both a production and a distribution point of view, digital has presented a challenge to industries stretching back to the nineteenth century. Consumers have been increasingly empowered as both creators and distributors of their own movies and photographs. Reduced prices and their convergence with the Internet via mobile devices such as the tablet and the smartphone have made digital cameras ubiquitous.

Increasingly, TV viewers are holding another digital screen, such as a tablet or a smartphone. Multiscreen viewing, a trend likely to increase, was evident with Super Bowl XLIX. More than two-thirds of viewers were also using a handheld device and sending 24 million tweets, often interacting via social media with friends or family.

This century will continue to reshape the visual storytelling of photographs, television, and motion pictures in an increasingly public and participatory environment of social media and interactive technology. These changes in media production and consumption also present various problems, however, including the impact of such transformations on privacy and cultural transmission.

MEDIA MATTERS   EYE-Q TEST

1. (T/F) The principles used in photography were known for hundreds of years before the first photograph was ever made.

2. Was your first camera digital? Of the many ways that digital photography has revolutionized picture taking and distribution, which do you consider most important and why?

3. Is it an invasion of privacy to take a picture or shoot a video of the front of your house without your permission and post it on the Internet?

4. Why did some of the earliest film pioneers, such as the Lumière brothers, believe film to be a novelty that would be a short-lived fad?

5. Keep a diary for a week of the television shows you watch, how long you watch them, and how

(TV, computer, VOD, a mobile device, etc.). What patterns do you see, and what implications do they have, if any, for your media consumption?

6. If you live to be seventy-five, how many years of your life will have been spent watching television?

7. What is the most common way Americans get television signals—over-the-air broadcasts, cable, satellite, or online?

8. Are you a multiscreen viewer? It what ways does this media habit detract from and enhance the viewing experience?

9. When did all television signals in the United States convert to digital format?

ANSWERS: **1.** True. **3.** No. **4.** Because they took film of people doing everyday activities, and they felt the novelty of watching such things on screen would soon wear off. **6.** eleven years. **7.** Cable (but closely followed by satellite, and with Internet-delivered video growing rapidly). **9.** June 2009.

FURTHER READING

American Photography: A Century of Images. Vicki Goldberg, Robert Silberman (1999) Chronicle Books.

Film Art: An Introduction, 8th ed. David Bordwell, Kristin Thompson (2008) McGraw-Hill Higher Education.

Hollywood! A Celebration. David Thomson (2001) DK Publishing.

The Film Snob's Dictionary: An Essential Lexicon of Filmological Knowledge. David Kamp, Lawrence Levi (2006) Broadway Books.

Film: A Critical Introduction, 2nd ed. Maria Pramaggiore, Tom Wallis (2007) Allyn & Bacon.

The Film Encyclopedia: The Complete Guide to Film and the Film Industry, 6th ed. Ephraim Katz (2008) Collins.

The Business of Television. Howard Blumenthal, Oliver Goodenough (2006) Billboard Books.

The Columbia History of American Television. Gary Edgerton (2009) Columbia University Press.

Dangerous Lives: War and the Men and Women Who Report It. Anthony Feinstein (2003) Thomas Allen.

The Inventor and the Tycoon: A Gilded Age Murder and the Birth of Moving Pictures. Edward Ball (2013) Doubleday.

Movies: Discovering Careers. Facts on File (2012) Ferguson Publishing.

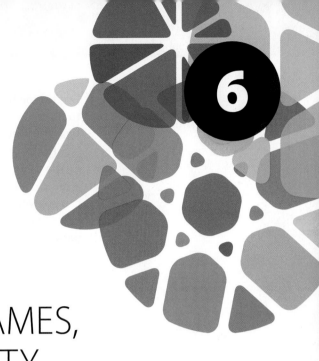

Interactive Media
THE INTERNET, VIDEO GAMES, AND AUGMENTED REALITY

Former college journalism student Palmer Luckey has emerged as a digital media trailblazer at the ripe old age of twenty. Taking his idea for a virtual reality headset to the crowdfunding website Kickstarter in 2012, Luckey quickly amassed some $2 million in funding, enabling him to create a working prototype. That captured the attention of another wunderkind, Mark Zuckerberg, founder of social media giant Facebook, who then acquired Luckey's virtual reality enterprise, Oculus Rift, investing 42 billion in the startup.[1] Moving rapidly toward the consumer media marketplace, Oculus Rift signals the arrival of fully immersive and interactive media.

Although it did not achieve the same start up acclaim as Oculus Rift, there was another unusual hit in 2014: the latest version of the game *Minecraft*. Created in 2009 for the PC, the game's simple and blocky graphics belie the complexity of the game, as players can literally interact with every element in the game world.

If visually *Minecraft* resembles video games from the 1980s and early 1990s, its sales figures reflect the popularity of video games today. *Minecraft* has sold more than 10 million copies for the PC and more than 54 million across all platforms.[2] And like today's social games, *Minecraft* has multiplayer options that allow people to compete against each other. A comparison of the seemingly disparate *Minecraft* and Oculus Rift reveals one thing in common—YouTube. Gamers across all platforms record and share their play online to create helpful video reviews and tutorials for others. They, too, discuss user-created modifications—mods—to the game.

Fans have also created scene-by-scene video presentations of their experience playing *Minecraft* using the Oculus Rift. Wearing this headset, gamers can play *Minecraft* within a completely immersive environment. Characters are rendered and edited just like in video or film. These YouTube mods have impressive viewing numbers approaching a million or more.

A *Minecraft* movie is apparently in the offing, and a wide variety of *Minecraft*-themed video parodies can be found on YouTube, ranging from Katy Perry to Coldplay, when they aren't being shut down for copyright infringement claims by the artists or their producers. This illustrates cross-fertilization between old and interactive media and some of the problems that accompany the hybridization.

LEARNING OBJECTIVES

>> Define the elements of interactivity.

>> Explain the importance of interactivity in terms of modern media.

>> Describe the historical development of user interfaces, the Internet, and the World Wide Web.

>> Explain how digital distribution empowers audiences to act as distributors themselves.

>> Describe why user interface is important to mass communication.

>> Explain how emerging trends will affect user interface and the way we use media.

>> Discuss relevant similarities in today's video-game industry with older media.

>> Explain what augmented reality is and how it can be used by media and other companies.

>> Identify some of the ethical issues related to interactive media.

Digital media transformed mass communication by allowing audience members to interact with content, with media producers, and with each other. Interactivity has had sweeping implications for all aspects of media and communication.

In the past, audiences were largely recipients of news and entertainment from media producers. Newspapers, magazines, and books had limited distribution and a restricted amount of news or information. Likewise, radio and television stations covered only specific geographic areas (as local stations still do). Although cable and satellite expanded the reach of television, viewers were still generally passive. A publisher or broadcaster sent media content to a large audience that could do little to influence the experience, short of not watching or reading at all.

Today, the audience can choose not only the type of content and media source but, in many cases, how, where, and when to engage with it. People can watch a video clip of an interview aired on television the previous day, download its full text transcript to read later on a mobile device, or get the audio podcast. Rather than trying to decipher unclear lyrics by listening over and over to a song, people can go to any number of song-lyrics sites and learn the actual words. Furthermore, audiences can easily distribute content to each other through email, blogs, Facebook, Twitter, and other social media. Interactivity has produced dramatic changes in the public's relationship with media. Its power to engage and involve users also raises new ethical issues, which we explore in this chapter.

In this chapter, we will focus on two main arenas where interactivity is most readily apparent: the **user interface (UI)**, which enabled the development of the Internet itself and the burgeoning video-game industry, and the emerging field of augmented reality, which promises to further change our media usage.

user interface (UI)

Junction between a medium and the people who use it.

Interactivity Defined

Interactivity, a crucial aspect of digital media, has been defined in many ways. According to media and Internet scholar Sheizaf Rafaeli, it is "the condition of communication in which simultaneous and continuous exchanges occur."[3] In other words, interaction involves two or more parties communicating through an ongoing give and take of messages.

For our purposes, we will define interactivity as having the following elements:

interactivity

For digital-media purposes, it consists of three main elements: (1) a dialog that occurs between a human and a computer program, (2) a dialog that occurs simultaneously or nearly so, and (3) the audience has some measure of control over what media content it sees and in what order.

1. A dialog that occurs between a human and a computer program (this includes emails, online chats, and discussion groups; at either end of the communication flow, a human interacts with a computer program—the Internet is simply the channel).

2. The dialog affects the nature or type of feedback or content received, changing as the dialog continues.

3. The audience has some measure of control over media content and the order in which it is seen (getting personalized or localized information, magnifying an image, clicking on a hyperlink, etc.).

These three components include almost all the activities that characterize our interaction with digital media and distinguish it from our interaction with traditional media. Some may consider changing television channels interactive, but the viewer is unable to engage in dialog with the television and cannot alter the nature of a program on a particular channel. The level of interactivity involved in

changing channels with a remote is simply not the same as that which characterizes Internet use.

In a dialog, both parties adjust their messages in response to feedback, thus
changing the nature of subsequent messages. Consider a simple example: You are
eager to share a funny story with a friend, but observing that he looks depressed,
you ask what is wrong rather than launching into your narrative. The feedback you
received altered your message. If you had sent a letter instead, the story would
have been conveyed as originally intended regardless of his state of mind.

The same thing happens in an interactive media environment, not only between users but between computer programs and users. Someone reading a news
story may click on a hyperlink for an unfamiliar name, taking that reader to another website that describes the person, which in turn may lead to other interesting links. This essentially changes the story for that particular user, who may have
a very different sense of it than someone who read the same story but did not click
on those links.

Similarly, two people may have very different impressions of the same story
after typing in their zip codes to get personalized or localized information or after
viewing a multimedia slideshow of the story as opposed simply to reading text or
listening to it on the radio. Traditional media devices do not permit switching,
such as moving from a printed newspaper story to audio.

> **DISCUSSION QUESTIONS:** Consider the differences between immediate interactivity,
> such as pushing a button or discussing on IM, and delayed interactivity, such as email or a
> discussion board post. How does the change in time affect conversations and relations?

Interactive Media Versus Mass Media

Interactive media can present information in a way that encourages users to learn
and explore. Online quizzes, surveys, and games appear in many places on the Web,
ranging from news sites to interactive adver-
tising, although many such items could be considered gimmicks. A far more important aspect
of interactive media is how it changes the
media experience for users. The dialogic nature
of interactive media can personalize our relationship with content and make it more relevant and compelling. We engage not only with
media but also with others through discussion
forums, online chat, instant messaging, emails,
and social media—interactivity that may further increase content relevance.

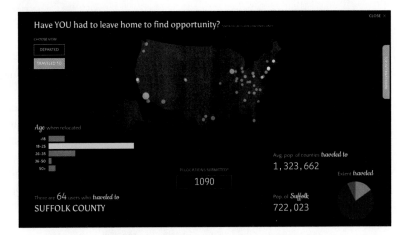

Interactive media also change our concepts
of narrative and what makes a story. The control
typically enjoyed by producers in traditional
media could well be a thing of the past in an interactive media environment. Users may have
less patience with long, complex stories and be

A web-based documentary on a dying county in West Virginia, *Hollow* allows visitors
to explore different narrative arcs through video interviews with some of the residents
who still live there. **CRITICAL THINKING QUESTIONS:** In what ways do interactive
narratives empower the audience? What kinds of challenges do journalists face when
creating this kind of interactive narrative?

more inclined to take hyperlinked detours. Users on varied narrative routes may wind up in different places because choices made during many video role-playing games may determine the ending. A growing number of interactive documentaries illustrate the significance of storytelling via varied narrative routes. Among the best examples are the award-winning *Hollow: The Story of a Dying County in West Virginia*;[4] *Fort McMoney: An Interactive Game Based on An Oil Boomtown*;[5] *Le Mystere de Grimou-ville: A Mystery in a French Community* (requires French);[6] and *Inside Disaster Haiti*.[7]

Interaction is important for media companies in other ways. Companies can see who commented on a particular story, how many visitors it had, how long they stayed, and where they went next. This knowledge can influence editorial content as publishers seek larger audiences. A type of story that gets more page views may tempt publishers to produce more of such pieces.

The ability to interact with the media and share one's specialized knowledge has embarrassed some news organizations, as readers point out errors or bias in news stories. Although newspapers have long published corrections, lag time, space limitations, and editorial control over what receives an official correction

INTERNATIONAL PERSPECTIVES
The Internet of Babel

It is easy for Americans, especially, to forget that not everyone speaks English, even as a second language. To date, language has generally not been a major issue on the Internet, largely because Internet users have tended to be well educated and able to communicate in English even if it is not their native language.

As Internet use spreads among people throughout the world, English will lose its dominance. In 2014, Mandarin (Chinese) was the most widely spoken language in the world, with one billion speakers. English is the second-most widely spoken, with 508 million speakers worldwide. Although the number of English speakers on the Internet grew about 300 percent between 2000 and 2014, that is dwarfed by the more than 1,000 percent growth in the number of Chinese speakers during the same time. Only Russian, with 1,825 percent growth, and Arabic, with 2,501 percent growth, showed comparably huge leaps in the number of Internet users.[8] Even so, Arabic speakers made up only 3.3 percent of total Internet users and Russian speakers 3 percent. Together, the top ten Internet languages (in order: English, Chinese, Spanish, Arabic, Portuguese, Japanese, Russian, German, French, and Malaysian) make up more than 82 percent of Internet users worldwide.

As languages other than English proliferate on the Internet, conflicts between different groups can increase. For example, when large numbers of Brazilians joined the social-networking site Orkut, they spoke among themselves in Portuguese, making English speakers feel left out. Monolingual English speakers could be missing opportunities to get information and communicate with others.

Although translation programs are improving, they still cannot compare to a good human translator. Still, hope remains for the monolingual English speaker as a growing number of free or low-cost language-teaching sites, such as Busuu and Duolingo, make it easier than ever to learn a foreign language. Even better for some, a growing number of volunteer translators are willing to fill in the gaps that computer translations miss.

has limited usefulness. In an online, interactive environment, readers can see comments and corrections from users along with the story.

The ability to learn what others may be saying about a particular news story or type of media content greatly democratizes our information environment. It helps us understand others as a community, albeit perhaps a specialized or temporary one. Yet it also threatens the traditional balance of power between media organizations and the audience. But before we address these issues, let's take a look at the feature that enables interactivity—the user interface.

Historical Development of User Interfaces

So familiar a feature is the user interface (UI), the junction between a medium and a user, we rarely give it a second thought and tend to forget that everyday practices initially had to be learned. Computers, because of their relative complexity, have more UI issues than traditional media. Even something as simple as navigating with a mouse can be challenging for a computer novice, let alone the functions of right-clicking and double-clicking.

Digital media have enabled a more active audience, one familiar with word processing, browsers, email, and so forth. The interface has helped shape these uses while empowering users, functions critical to the future of mass communication. Media content is essentially wasted if users cannot find a given website and access the desired information. The user interface should be intuitive and natural yet appropriate to the medium and customizable in content.

> **DISCUSSION QUESTIONS:** Give the address of a familiar website to a partner, and without looking at the screen, instruct the partner to complete certain tasks on the site. How difficult is it to explain the user interface or certain functions when you cannot look at the site and do it yourself? Why do you think this is so?

TELEVISION INTERFACES

Before the development of the computer, we did not generally employ the term "user interface." This is because traditional analog media were not designed to be interactive, and the equivalent of the user interface was generally unchanging. Turning a dial or pushing a button to receive content was an easy task to master. The development of the electronic user interface has both technological and social dimensions, getting people accustomed to using new technologies in a mass-communication context. Had the public not been familiar with television, it might not have been as ready to adapt to the Internet and computers.

Technological improvements in computer monitors, often now called displays, once they became the standard interface with computers, have largely been driven by the desire for more of the qualities that we have come to expect from television screens, such as color, a screen of certain dimensions, and crisp images. Although computer makers originally borrowed from television in creating monitors, television has returned the favor in borrowing from the online world of screen windows, scrolling text or tickers, and multiple items on various topics on a single screen. This is especially evident in newscasts.

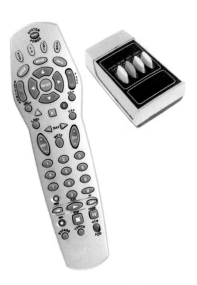

Remote controls have grown increasingly complex as we have gained more functions and channels on our television sets.

The TV remote control is not only one of the most important transformational technologies in television but also often the source of friction between the sexes and among family members. The first TV remote control was introduced in 1950.[9] Zenith introduced the Lazy Bones, a remote control connected by a wire to your TV set. In 1955, Zenith introduced the Flash-matic, the first wireless TV remote, which used a flashlight to change channels. The following year, Zenith's Space Command used ultrasound to change channels but also had the unintended consequence of disturbing household pets. Most modern TV remote controls use infrared technology.

The remote control altered viewing habits, as viewers could now easily toggle back and forth between channels, or channel surf, avoid commercials or uninteresting segments in programs, or simply watch multiple sports events.[10] Frequently changing channels could be considered a simple form of **multitasking**. Remote controls changed our media behavior in subtle yet important ways, preparing us for **human–computer interactions**.

INTUITIVE INTERFACES

Because computers and humans use different languages, some kind of interface, or "translator," is needed to allow communication between the two. The ideal, intuitive interface can be figured out quickly and easily; it should seem natural on first use.

In the earliest days of computing, the user interface was anything but simple. Usually, only the inventor or a highly trained specialist could operate a computer, interact with it, or access information contained within it. Data were entered on punch cards, often requiring hundreds of cards to represent even a simple piece of information, such as a series of numbers or names. The output of a computer analysis was typically printed on paper, which might take many minutes or even hours with a slow dot-matrix printer. If computers were to be more useful, they needed not only to become more powerful but also to develop a better interface for both the input and output of information. Even today, improvements and refinements continue to be made in the intuitive interfaces discussed next.

Keyboards

The first typewriters, developed in the 1870s to make writing faster, had keyboards arranged alphabetically, but it turned out this was a poor design because some keys were used more often than others and, if typed too quickly, would jam together. Christopher Latham Sholes developed the QWERTY keyboard (after the first row of letters in the upper-left-hand corner of the keyboard) in which the most frequently typed keys (such as "a" and "t") are spread far apart, slowing down the user and thus discouraging jamming.

Jamming became a nonissue with the invention of electric typewriters, but the QWERTY legacy endured, which explains why August Dvorak's keyboard, created in the 1930s and designed for maximum typing efficiency, was never adopted. His keyboard allows users to type more than three thousand words without reaching with their fingers. The standard QWERTY keyboard can be reprogrammed to the Dvorak layout easily with free software, but most people have never even heard of it.

Computer Mouse

In 1968, Douglas C. Engelbart invented the computer mouse, made of wood and used with a companion keyboard. His inspiration was a now-classic article in the

multitasking

In a computer environment, doing several activities at once with a variety of programs, such as simultaneous word processing, spreadsheet, and database work while conducting real-time chat through an instant-messenger service.

human–computer interaction

Any interaction between humans and computers, either through devices such as keyboards, mice, and touch screens or through voice recognition.

The Dvorak keyboard is much more efficient for typing than the standard QWERTY keyboard, greatly increasing typing speed and accuracy.

July 1945 edition of the *Atlantic Monthly* by Vannevar Bush titled "As We May Think." It discussed how the computer could be a desktop tool. Engelbart's mouse enabled the easy manipulation of computer data by pointing and clicking as desired. Although a major development in the evolution of the intuitive interface, the computer mouse may also become an artifact of computer history with the rise of touch-sensitive screens on computers and mobile devices.

Touch Screens

In 1974, the Control Data Corporation (CDC) introduced PLATO (Programmed Logic for Automated Teaching Operations), the first computer system to have a touch-sensitive video display terminal.[11] Before tablet computers and smartphones, ATMs were the most common example of touch-sensitive screens. Despite greatly facilitating human–computer interaction, touch-sensitive interfaces have certain drawbacks: the need to be within reach of the screen, which means large screen sizes would bother our eyes; and extremely small screen sizes, such as on smartphones, that limit interaction, just as with keyboards. This problem was resolved to a large extent with tablets that provide tactile feedback during typing.

Natural Input Methods

The first computer that could accept natural handwriting with an electronic stylus was sold in 1979, although it could not translate into computer-readable text until almost twenty years later. Among the most natural or intuitive user interfaces, as well as the most elusive, are computer voice recognition and speech synthesis. A hallmark of science fiction for generations, they are gradually becoming integral to the computing and mobile phone environment. For example, users can now get phone audio responses to questions they ask of Siri (Apple) or Google Now (Android). Speech recognition is not without its weaknesses as well. Imagine, for example, the cacophony in a library if everyone input information or notes in their computers via voice.

GRAPHICAL USER INTERFACES

Three developments helped make desktop computers capable of full multimedia: first, the development of greater computing power and increased storage capacity;

graphical user interface (GUI)

Computer interface that shows graphical representations of file structures, files, and applications in the form of folders, icons, and windows.

The highly anticipated Apple Watch, an iPhone-compatible smartwatch available in a number of models, colors, and price points, debuted in April 2015 to mixed reviews. Fashion meets function in the latest digital innovation from Apple, but the learning curve for navigating the small, new interface may be steep.

second, the addition of audio and video; and third, the creation of a graphical user interface. The foundation for the modern **graphical user interface** (**GUI**, pronounced GOO-ey) was created, like many other computer innovations, at Xerox Palo Alto Research Center (PARC). Debuting in 1974, Xerox's Alto, a computer with a graphical user interface navigated with a mouse, never caught on with the public. However, Apple Macintosh computers' implementation of GUI revolutionized human–computer interaction, followed several years later when Microsoft's Windows implemented a graphical user interface for its operating system.

The graphical user interface for personal computers and, later, the Web, enabled digital media to compete vigorously with traditional mass media. Educating and entertaining in ways unimaginable with analog, it not only changed how the audience accessed and utilized information, potentially transforming passive media consumers into active media users, it also changed how media organizations created, produced, and presented stories. Businesses seeking to reach the growing number of consumers online resulted in the commercialization of the World Wide Web, whose history is inextricable from that of the graphical user interface to which we now turn.

Historical Development of the Internet and the World Wide Web

Expensive computers often large enough to take up entire rooms in the organizations or institutions that owned them originally ran machine-specific languages and programs. They could not communicate with one another prior to the creation of the Internet, whose foundations were laid in 1969 when the Defense Advanced Research Projects Agency (DARPA) launched the Advanced Research Projects Agency Network (ARPANET). The first national computer network connected

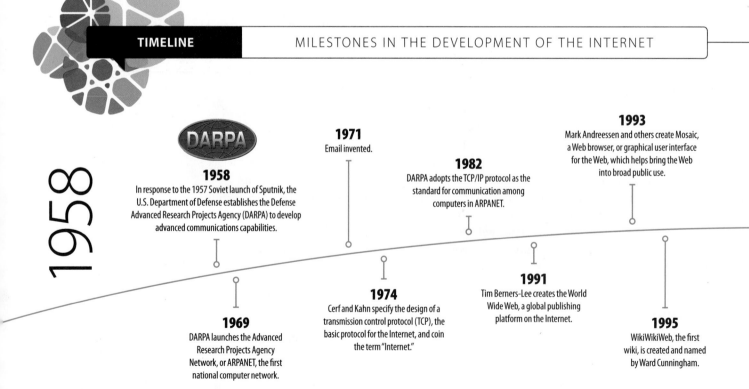

TIMELINE   MILESTONES IN THE DEVELOPMENT OF THE INTERNET

1958

1958
In response to the 1957 Soviet launch of Sputnik, the U.S. Department of Defense establishes the Defense Advanced Research Projects Agency (DARPA) to develop advanced communications capabilities.

1969
DARPA launches the Advanced Research Projects Agency Network, or ARPANET, the first national computer network.

1971
Email invented.

1974
Cerf and Kahn specify the design of a transmission control protocol (TCP), the basic protocol for the Internet, and coin the term "Internet."

1982
DARPA adopts the TCP/IP protocol as the standard for communication among computers in ARPANET.

1991
Tim Berners-Lee creates the World Wide Web, a global publishing platform on the Internet.

1993
Mark Andreessen and others create Mosaic, a Web browser, or graphical user interface for the Web, which helps bring the Web into broad public use.

1995
WikiWikiWeb, the first wiki, is created and named by Ward Cunningham.

many universities around the country for advanced, high-speed computing applications and research. Still, computers could not yet transmit information easily via the network because there was no "common language" or protocol, a set of rules that facilitate communication between parties who normally speak different languages.

The next important development was email, which "kind of announced itself," said Ray Tomlinson, the computer engineer who invented it in 1971. The *Guinness Book of World Records* claims the first email message he sent was QWERTYUIOP— the keys on the third row of the keyboard. And, according to Tomlinson, the symbol @ ("at") was the obvious choice for the symbol to separate the names of individuals from their machines: "As it turns out, @ is the only preposition on the keyboard. I just looked at it and it was there. I didn't even try any others."[12]

Electronic mail was a significant advance, but clearly something more robust was needed, a simplified, common language in which computers could speak to each other and by which they could send and receive large amounts of data.

INTERNET PROTOCOL

In 1974, Vinton Cerf and Robert Kahn introduced the term "Internet" and specified the design of a **Transmission Control Protocol (TCP)** as part of its main protocol. Jonathan Postel, as a graduate student at UCLA, outlined along with Cerf certain key principles of today's Internet protocols (IP).

Although the exact date when the Internet officially started is difficult to pin down, in 1982, the Defense Department adopted TCP/IP as the basis for the ARPANET, requiring universities that wanted to remain in the network to follow suit. Moreover, at this time, researchers began defining an "internet" (lowercase *i*) as a connected set of networks using TCP/IP, and the "Internet" (uppercase *I*) as a set of connected TCP/IP internets.[13]

Transmission Control Protocol (TCP)

A part of the main protocol for the Internet that allows computers to easily communicate with each other over a network.

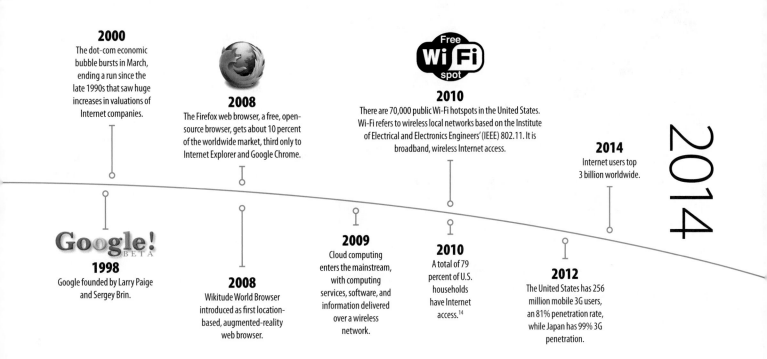

1998
Google founded by Larry Paige and Sergey Brin.

2000
The dot-com economic bubble bursts in March, ending a run since the late 1990s that saw huge increases in valuations of Internet companies.

2008
The Firefox web browser, a free, open-source browser, gets about 10 percent of the worldwide market, third only to Internet Explorer and Google Chrome.

2008
Wikitude World Browser introduced as first location-based, augmented-reality web browser.

2009
Cloud computing enters the mainstream, with computing services, software, and information delivered over a wireless network.

2010
A total of 79 percent of U.S. households have Internet access.[14]

2010
There are 70,000 public Wi-Fi hotspots in the United States. Wi-Fi refers to wireless local networks based on the Institute of Electrical and Electronics Engineers' (IEEE) 802.11. It is broadband, wireless Internet access.

2012
The United States has 256 million mobile 3G users, an 81% penetration rate, while Japan has 99% 3G penetration.

2014
Internet users top 3 billion worldwide.

2014

WORLD WIDE WEB

💬 **Hypertext Transfer Protocol (HTTP)**

A protocol that enables the standardized transfer of text, audio, and video files, as well as email, from one address to another.

💬 **Hypertext Markup Language (HTML)**

A coding format that describes how information should look on the Web.

Tim Berners-Lee created the World Wide Web to make it easier for people to find information online.

For its first decade, Internet activity required knowledge of a variety of arcane commands and terminology, and its principal users were academic and government researchers. In 1991, Tim Berners-Lee, a British researcher at CERN, a physics laboratory in Switzerland, invented the World Wide Web (WWW), altering the Internet's limited, specialized nature and opening it up to a much wider group of users. Berners-Lee created **Hypertext Transfer Protocol (HTTP)** that enabled users to connect to other Web pages or sites whose content is displayed and formatted with **Hypertext Markup Language (HTML)**.

As a global electronic-publishing medium accessed through the Internet, the World Wide Web fostered the most fundamental shift in human communication since the printing press five centuries earlier. It enabled inexpensive many-to-many communication over distance and time while making computer use easier for many nontechnical people. The next development would further lower the barrier and increase Internet access for the masses.

GRAPHICAL WEB BROWSERS

The creation of graphical Web browsers helped even nontechnical people navigate the Internet. Formerly, most information online was text based. A graphical Web browser brings multimedia, such as images or icons and other visual tools, to the Web interface, making it more user friendly. In 1993, Marc Andreessen, then at the National Center for Supercomputing Applications (NCSA) at the University of Illinois at Champaign–Urbana, created a graphical user interface called Mosaic. Although GUI browsers Viola and Erwise were also created in 1992, by the end of 1993, Mosaic had become the best-known Web browser.

In 1996, Microsoft created Internet Explorer (IE) to compete with Netscape (formerly Mosaic and then called Netscape Navigator). Because Microsoft offered Internet Explorer for free and eventually bundled it with the Windows operating system, IE became the dominant browser in only four years, with 75 percent usage, compared to Netscape's 25 percent. By 1999, at its peak, IE had 99 percent of the browser market. AOL bought Netscape that year and announced in 2007 that Netscape would be discontinued.

Firefox, an open-source browser created by the Mozilla Foundation and launched in late 2004, presented the first serious competition for Internet Explorer. By early 2015, without advertising or marketing, Firefox had captured about 10 percent of the browser market, most of it from IE. Google's browser Chrome, debuting in late 2008, had about 16 percent of the browser market by early 2013, declining about 1 percent from earlier highs. At the same time, IE was down to 56 percent.[15]

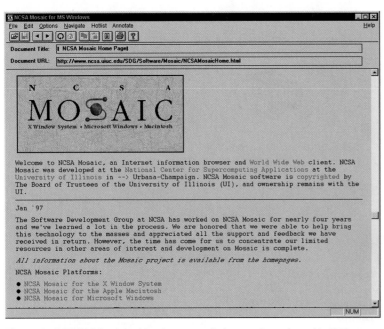

The original GUI Web browser, Mosaic, was revolutionary when released in 1993.

BROADBAND

A crucial element for online communication to reach its full potential as a mass medium is **bandwidth**. This coaxial or fiber-optic cable of varying capacity is perhaps more readily understood metaphorically as a pipe that delivers data (rather than water) to your home. Tapping the large data pipe, or "fat pipe," directly allows data to flow at high speeds; through thin pipes, data arrives at a trickle, no matter how fast the personal computer.[16]

Without high-speed, or **broadband**, connections, most people cannot receive audio or video in real time or of the same quality as television or radio. Broadband Internet behavior differs considerably from dial-up connection activity. Broadband users are more likely to produce and distribute media content, and their online expenditures are more than double.

Broadband connections also allow us to receive vast amounts of verbal and visual information from a variety of global sources that increase our knowledge as they broaden our cultural horizons. The inability to access the same information as others can become a serious disadvantage in terms of education or career possibilities. In the United States, broadband telecommunications costs can be high, which means that the lower end of the socioeconomic scale spends proportionately more for what many see today as a basic necessity.

DISTRIBUTION DYNAMICS

Even for people who may not be interested in creating original media content or who have no computer programming skills, today's broadband speeds and extensive networks accelerate the distribution of content. Consider, for example, a photograph from a local online newspaper. A user can easily copy the picture to his or her local drive, separate from the article it accompanies (it is also easy for the user to manipulate the photo, but for our discussion here, that is not important). She or he could then share the digital photo via Facebook, Twitter, or Google+ with, say, two hundred people.

Assume that only half of those two hundred people send it to two hundred other people. Within two "generations," over twenty thousand people could see the photo, all within a matter of minutes after it was originally sent and at virtually no cost to the senders. Distribution no longer depends on sending content from a central location to a passive audience. Rather than accessing media content from central servers, users can keep it on personal computers with large hard drives for storage and make it available to others on the Internet. Many localized distribution points have replaced a few centralized distribution points, creating the basis for **peer-to-peer (P2P)** applications, such as popular music-sharing services.

bandwidth

The carrying capacity and speed of telecommunication networks that determine how much information can be sent and how fast it can travel over the networks.

broadband

A network connection that enables a large amount of bandwidth to be transmitted, which allows for more information to be sent in a shorter period of time.

Mobile broadband Internet access gives Americans high-speed connectivity anywhere, anytime.

peer-to-peer (P2P)

The basis of file-sharing services, a computer communications model and network whose computers are considered equal peers who can send, store, and receive information equally well.

DISCUSSION QUESTIONS: See how the Internet can track you. Do a search on Amazon for a product that you would never purchase; then over the following days track what types of ads you see on different websites. How long does it take for the ads to revert back to topics that are actually more relevant to you?

FIGURE 6-1 Client/Server and Peer-to-Peer Networks

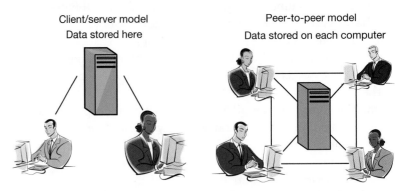

A client/server network relies on a server to provide content to people on the network, and content on a P2P network exists on various individual computers and is shared among them.

Decentralization of distribution means a loss of control for media companies because a single company cannot dictate what every single PC among the public may or may not distribute. This translates into potential lost revenues because copies are made and shared among millions of Internet users without any payment to the copyright holders. This is precisely what is happening with music online. The music industry's concern stems from the fact that each member of the public who uses file-sharing applications becomes a potential distributor of content merely by having certain files others would like to download. No one has to send anything.

File-sharing services using P2P networks started making the news in late 1999 primarily because of the rapid rise in popularity of Napster, a program created by eighteen-year-old Northeastern University student Shawn Fanning. Napster let Internet users easily share MP3 files, a compression format for digital music. College campus networks slowed as millions of students downloaded and shared music, and the music industry discovered just how active audiences could be when empowered by digital distribution.

Napster's centralized servers made it an easy target to shut down through legal action. But other file-sharing services that do not rely on centralized servers have been nearly impossible to bring to court, partly because they are based overseas or frequently move their server locations.

Streaming files can also be shared on a P2P network in various ways without a centralized server. **Swarming** with BitTorrent, perhaps the most popular file-sharing protocol on the Internet today, allows users who would otherwise have to pay high server and bandwidth costs to distribute large video and music files easily. Its general operating principle encourages sharing dynamics: the more content a user shares, the more content that user can access. Internet TV services such as Joost used similar swarming techniques to share streaming video files.

P2P networks serve other purposes as well, from distributing computing projects to creating an information network impossible to censor or shut down. Should a central company server go down, the content will likely remain available. As long as someone with the material is online, it can be downloaded. This ready availability demonstrates an interesting intersection between technological convergence and cultural convergence, as more people become accustomed to sharing files with one another.

swarming

The process used by some P2P systems in which multiple downloads of the same file are temporarily coordinated to accelerate the downloading process.

Video Games

Of the numerous interactive ways to use the Internet, which is the most popular? Recently, video games and social media have surpassed email in measures of Internet activity, although it is worth noting that more messages are still sent via email than through the U.S. Postal Service, and email marketing remains a cost-effective form of advertising for many companies. Online video gaming has exploded thanks to the graphical user interface, which revolutionized, if not wholly created, the industry. Advances in graphic capabilities helped video games grow from a computer-geek pastime to a huge business on par with, if not surpassing, other forms of entertainment media.

Played on computers or other electronic devices with graphic capabilities, video games—whose content is often borrowed freely from movies, television shows, and other areas of pop culture—demonstrate convergence in action. In turn, some popular games, such as *Lara Croft: Tomb Raider* and *Resident Evil*, have spawned movies. And **machinima**, a whole new genre created by video-game enthusiasts, takes cross-fertilization even further with 3-D animated movies modeled after video-game scenarios and characters.

Many game-related websites have active discussion groups in which fans of a particular game help each other with questions; complain about aspects of the game; compose cheat codes; provide hints for finding special bonus treasure; and even create **mods**, modifications to games. This ardent dedication, the envy of many other media companies, may court other dangers, however, such as addictive behavior.

Video sales have eclipsed U.S. domestic movie box office receipts since 2001. Increasingly, we see commercials for upcoming games that look like movie trailers. Technology, in the form of the video-game consoles, and content, in the form of popular game titles, have been closely intertwined as the industry, games, and technology continue to evolve with the rise of social and mobile gaming.

machinima

A combination of *machine* and *cinema* that uses 3-D animation techniques and characters from popular video games to make movies.

mods

Short for "modifications," user-created code changes that alter how video games are played or look.

Machinima App on Xbox One represents a new generation of video games that feature cinema quality video production.

Historical Development of Video Games

For a relatively new medium and industry, video games have seen many transformations in the past forty years. Companies have come and gone while certain titles, such as *Pac-Man* and *Super Mario Bros.*, became part of popular culture. Whole new ways of playing games have developed at the cutting edge of user interface and human–computer interactions.

Dating the birth of video games is difficult. In the 1950s, computers programmed to play checkers and chess, for example, could be found in university laboratories or government agencies but were far beyond what any average consumer could ever afford or use. Here, we consider only some of the major developments in popular video games.

In 1972, Atari released the arcade version of *Pong* (a home version was released in 1975), and Magnavox released the sports-related home video game *Odyssey*, which could be played on the television. Coin-operated arcade games and home

TIMELINE   MILESTONES IN THE DEVELOPMENT OF VIDEO GAMES

1962
The first computer-based video game, *Spacewar!*, is created by MIT student Steve Russell.

1972
The Magnavox Odyssey is launched, the first home video-game console.

1979
Milton Bradley's Microvision is the first handheld game console, grossing $8 million in its first year of release. Limited games, small screen, and lack of industry support led to its downfall in 1981.[17]

1983
Nintendo releases the Famicom in Japan, released as the Nintendo Entertainment System (NES) in the United States two years later, starting the third generation of video-game consoles.

1988
Sega Genesis is released, starting the fourth generation of video-game consoles.

1994
Sony releases the PlayStation, a console that uses discs instead of cartridges, the fifth generation of video-game consoles.

1962

1972
The arcade version of *Pong* is created and quickly becomes popular.

1977
Atari releases the Atari 2600, the most successful video-game console of its time, starting the second generation of video-game consoles.

1980
Pac-Man, developed by Namco and designed by Toru Iwantani, will become one of the most influential video games of all time.

1985
Nintendo releases *Super Mario Bros.*, which sells 10 million copies by the end of the year and became the game that defined "platforming." Until 2008, it was the overall best-selling video game.[18]

1989
Nintendo releases Game Boy, the first handheld video-game player since the ill-fated Microvision, selling 110 million units worldwide.

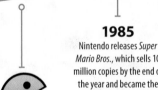

1999
Sega releases the Dreamcast, a console that pioneered online gaming and began the sixth generation of consoles.

video games with consoles and controllers competed for players in the early days.

Arcade games initially had the advantage. The first generation of video-game consoles was simply the games themselves; if a customer wanted to buy a different game, then that person had to buy a different console. The "Golden Age" of video arcade games spanned the early 1980s to the early 1990s, fading once console games became as powerful as arcade games and could play the same games with the same quality. Consequently, there are fewer video arcades today. Those that do exist emphasize immersive simulation games, such as racing cars, space battles, and first-person shooters.

The second generation was developed in 1977 with Atari's release of the first cartridge-based video-game console, the Atari 2600 VCS, which allowed players to play different games

Early gamers still fondly remember the iconic Atari 2600 VCS, the first game console that let players change game cartridges.

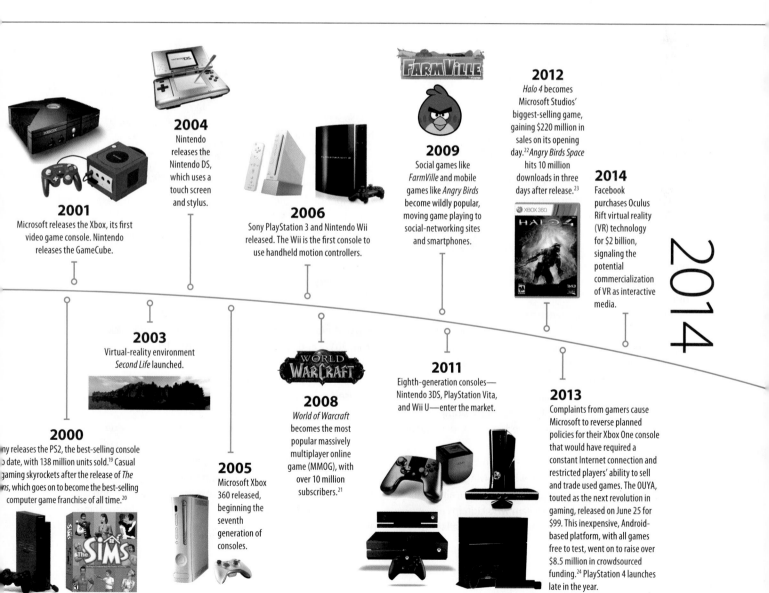

2001
Microsoft releases the Xbox, its first video game console. Nintendo releases the GameCube.

2004
Nintendo releases the Nintendo DS, which uses a touch screen and stylus.

2006
Sony PlayStation 3 and Nintendo Wii released. The Wii is the first console to use handheld motion controllers.

2009
Social games like *FarmVille* and mobile games like *Angry Birds* become wildly popular, moving game playing to social-networking sites and smartphones.

2012
Halo 4 becomes Microsoft Studios' biggest-selling game, gaining $220 million in sales on its opening day.[22] *Angry Birds Space* hits 10 million downloads in three days after release.[23]

2014
Facebook purchases Oculus Rift virtual reality (VR) technology for $2 billion, signaling the potential commercialization of VR as interactive media.

2014

2000
ny releases the PS2, the best-selling console o date, with 138 million units sold.[19] Casual gaming skyrockets after the release of *The ns,* which goes on to become the best-selling computer game franchise of all time.[20]

2003
Virtual-reality environment *Second Life* launched.

2005
Microsoft Xbox 360 released, beginning the seventh generation of consoles.

2008
World of Warcraft becomes the most popular massively multiplayer online game (MMOG), with over 10 million subscribers.[21]

2011
Eighth-generation consoles—Nintendo 3DS, PlayStation Vita, and Wii U—enter the market.

2013
Complaints from gamers cause Microsoft to reverse planned policies for their Xbox One console that would have required a constant Internet connection and restricted players' ability to sell and trade used games. The OUYA, touted as the next revolution in gaming, released on June 25 for $99. This inexpensive, Android-based platform, with all games free to test, went on to raise over $8.5 million in crowdsourced funding.[24] PlayStation 4 launches late in the year.

by switching cartridges. Games such as *Space Invaders*, *Combat*, and *Breakout* became very popular and helped make the Atari the dominant console game until the early 1980s when toymaker Mattel released a different system, starting one of the first console wars, which still occur today.

In 1985, Japanese playing-card company Nintendo released its Famicom (a shortening of "Family Computer") console in the United States as the Nintendo Entertainment System (NES). An 8-bit console, it ushered in the third generation of more powerful consoles, with better graphics and more processor power. Popular games such as *Super Mario Bros.* and the *Legend of Zelda* made NES the best-selling console in video-game history. In 1989, Nintendo released Game Boy (GB), a hugely popular mobile player.

The 1990s and 2000s saw console makers Nintendo, Sega, Sony, and later, Microsoft competing heavily as they developed increasingly powerful gaming systems and struck deals with game-developer companies for exclusive title rights. The fourth, fifth, and sixth generations of game consoles were largely delineated by either the shift from cartridges to disc-based consoles or the ever-increasing console power from 8- to 16- to 32-bit systems.

 MEDIA PIONEERS
Super Mario

In the world of video gaming, no one has achieved the fame or fortune of Mario, the carpenter turned plumber turned Super Mario, the king of platform gaming. His story is intimately connected to that of the industry itself, from his 8-bit beginning to his most recent 128-bit incarnation. Yet, whereas the technological world he inhabits has changed considerably over the past three decades, Mario remains largely the same unlikely-looking hero from his early days. His mischievous mustached face, along with his paunchy physique and blue-collar outfit, defies the handsome-hero stereotype but remains curiously compelling to young and old alike.

Many celebrities experience a modest debut, and Mario is no exception. He was introduced to the public in the 1981 arcade game *Donkey Kong* as Jumpman, a carpenter who contends with an escaped gorilla while leaping barrels and scaling a construction site to rescue a captive maiden. After a name and career change, Mario starred as a plumber battling creatures in the sewers of New York City along with his twin brother, Luigi. *Mario Bros.* proved a success despite the great video crash of 1983 to 1985.[25]

In 1985, *Super Mario Bros.*, featured on the Nintendo Entertainment System and credited with reviving the industry, offered some new characters and a new setting, although a rather familiar plot involving a villain who kidnaps a damsel.[26] Rated the number one video game of all time by

G4, *Super Mario Bros.* has sold over 40 million copies.[27] It remains the biggest seller in the Mario franchise, which has expanded to more than 100 games[28] selling over 500 million copies.[29] Mario games have appeared on nearly every new Nintendo console. Hit series include *Mario Kart* (e.g., *Mario Kart 7* from 2011); *Mario Party* puzzle games (e.g., *Mario Party 3DS*); *Paper Mario* role-playing games (e.g., *Paper Mario: Sticker Star* from 2012); and sports games, including *Mario & Sonic at the Sochi 2014 Olympic Games* and the 2015 *Mario vs. Donkey Kong* for the Nintendo Wii U. In 1993, *Super Mario Bros.* was released as a major film, although it did not translate well to the big screen with human actors.

Mario's enduring popularity in a fickle market is due not only to his winning personality. His new games often offer technological, artistic, and gaming features that satisfy the most avid players while continuing to draw new fans. Despite his displays of athletic prowess at the Olympics, don't expect Mario, who claims he and his brother can fix anything if there's spaghetti involved, to lose any weight.

Sony's PlayStation, launched in 1995, used CDs rather than cartridges, making games cheaper. More powerful consoles also allowed for 3-D graphics. PlayStation 2 (PS2), launched in 2000, could function as a DVD player as well and became the most popular console of its time.

In 2001, Microsoft released Xbox, the company's first console. Although sales lagged behind Sony's and Nintendo's consoles, one of the most popular game titles, *Halo: Combat Evolved*, was available only on the Xbox. Mobile gaming systems continued to evolve as well, with the Nintendo DS and PlayStation Portable released in 2004 and 2005, respectively.

In late 2005, Microsoft released the first of the so-called seventh-generation game consoles, the Xbox 360, which had an even more powerful processor. In late 2006, however, Nintendo leapfrogged ahead again and released the Wii, a seventh-generation console that included handheld motion controllers. Wildly popular for the 2006 holiday season, it quickly sold out in stores. It wasn't until late 2010 that Microsoft released its own motion-sensing input device for the Xbox 360, Kinect, which used the player's body motion as a "controller" and followed certain voice commands.

The motion sensors in the Wii and Kinect have radically changed how players interact with games. No longer do players simply sit and press buttons with their thumbs (although many still do). Rather, game players can run in place, exercise, dance, do yoga, and even fight as the video game captures their motions in real time.

The next generation of consoles, such as Xbox One, PS4, and Wii U, have added or improved on capabilities such as voice commands and face recognition.

In another dramatic change, more gaming systems are shifting to online-only modes, forgoing discs. Online services like Steam, Xbox Live, and UPlay allow gamers to play their games from any console or computer, and they facilitate easy downloading of updates and even player mods. These services require a broadband connection, however, and Xbox One's attempt to move their services entirely online drew complaints about restricting players' use of games.

Eighth-generation video-game consoles give users an immersive and interactive experience.

DISCUSSION QUESTIONS: Discuss a video game you loved to play as a child or young teenager. What made you like it so much? What made you finally stop playing it? How may your answers to either of these questions relate to material discussed in this chapter regarding user interface and the nature of the video-game industry?

Types of Video Games

There are as many video games as there are genres, which many games freely mix and match. As Table 6-1 shows, some of the most popular genres are sports, action, racing, role playing, simulation, and shooter. Genres help set parameters on content and game-play dynamics.

Table 6-1 shows other points of interest. First is the prevalence of tried-and-true titles, especially Nintendo's Mario franchise. Note also the general

TABLE 6-1 Best-Selling Video Games (to 2014)

RANK	GAME		YEAR	SALES
1	Nintendo: Wii Sports		2006	$81.2M
2	Nintendo: Super Mario Bros.		1985	$40.2M
3	Nintendo: MarioKart Wii		2006	$33.7M
4	Nintendo: Wii Sports Resort		2006	$31.6M
5	Nintendo Game Boy: Pokémon		1996	$31.4M
6	Nintendo Game Boy: Tetris		1999	$30.3M
7	Nintendo DS: Super Mario Bros.		2006	$29.1M
8	Nintendo: Wii Play		2006	$28.7M
9	Nintendo: Duck Hunt		1984	$28.3M
10	Nintendo: Super Mario Bros. Wii		2009	$26.8M
11	Nintendo DS: Nintendogs		2005	$24.5M
12	Nintendo Game Boy Color: Pokémon		1999	$23.1M

RANK	GAME		YEAR	SALES
13	Nintendo: Wii Fit		2007	$22.7M
14	Nintendo DS: MarioKart DS		2005	$22.5M
15	Nintendo: Wii Fit Plus		2009	$21.2M
16	Play Station 2: Grand Theft Auto San Andreas		2004	$20.8M
17	Super Nintendo: Super Mario World		1990	$20.6M
18	Nintendo DS: Brain Age		2005	$20.0M
19	XBOX360: Kinect Adventures!		2010	$20.0M
20	Nintendo Game Boy: Super Mario Land		1989	$18.1M

Source: VGChartz Game Database, http://www.vgchartz.com/gamedb/

dominance of Nintendo, claiming the top fifteen titles and eighteen of the top twenty. Many Wii games are also on the list.

Computer users continue to engage in massively multiplayer online games (MMOGs), such as *Aces High,* and massively multiplayer online role-playing games (MMORPGs), such as Activision Blizzard's *World of Warcraft.* In this kind of game, players create characters and participate in online quests or missions. They work with other players in real time using chats and text messaging to join teams, fight with or against one another, and gain treasure or experience through battling monsters. Console video-game makers see this area as one with great potential and have been moving to establish their own MMOGs. Examples of this with first-person shooters are multiplayer versions of games like *Call of Duty* and *Far Cry 3* in which players can either work together in teams or simply participate in free-for-all online combat.

Most MMOGs and MMORPGs use either a subscription model or some variation of a freemium model in which people can play for free but have limited access to the game world or to character development. Many games have also developed in-game economies in which more advanced players can sell or barter items. Some people use real money to buy virtual items that will help them in the games. In China, some enterprises pay people to play and acquire items that can then be sold on auction sites.

DISCUSSION QUESTIONS: Discuss what types of video games you enjoy and their genre or genres. What makes those games fun for you? Which is your favorite, and why? Do you enjoy online games or those played on mobile devices?

Video-Game Industry

Video games sold strongly in the 2000s. Sales did not dip until the recession in 2008. In 2014, U.S. sales of video-game titles and hardware were $10.54 billion, down from $16.998 billion in 2011.[30] As in prior years, big-name titles sold well. The top two titles in 2014 were Activision's *Call of Duty: Advanced Warfare*, which sold 5.8 million units in the United States, and the company's *Destiny*, which sold 3.8 million units. Third place went to Rockstar's *Grand Theft Auto V*, which sold 3.3 million units. Small game studios are having increased success, though, as titles such as *Papers, Please* have captured gamers' interest.

For much of the history of the development of video game titles, many small, independent video-game publishers coexisted with Japanese giants like Nintendo, Sega, and Konami. From the late 1990s and especially in the past several years, there has been rapid consolidation among video-game publishers throughout the world, much as in book publishing and the recording industry previously. Large video-game publishers may develop their own games internally, but often they either contract game development to studios or buy the developer companies outright and run them as subsidiaries.

Today, except for the odd hit, such as *Minecraft* from independent developer Mojang, most games come from subsidiaries of a handful of larger game-publisher companies, some of which themselves may be subsidiaries of global media companies. The largest gaming company by revenue is Japan's Nintendo. Activision Blizzard, formed by a merger in 2008 of popular game publisher and developer Activision and Vivendi Games (itself a part of NBCUniversal), is the second largest. Some of the company's popular titles in the separate Activision and Blizzard divisions include the *Warcraft* series, *Call of Duty*, the *Tony Hawk* franchise, and *Skylanders Giants*.

Electronic Arts (EA), founded in 1982, is one of the oldest and largest video-game publishers and developers, third after Nintendo and Activision Blizzard. EA's well-known titles include many popular sports titles, such as the *Madden NFL* and the *FIFA* series, along with popular action and combat series such as *Crysis* and *Mass Effect*.

Ubisoft, based in France, is Europe's largest independent game-development company and the third largest in the United States. Its popular titles include the *Assassin's Creed* series, *Far Cry*, and the *Tom Clancy* series of games. ZeniMax Media, a U.S. company, has acquired several well-known smaller developers in recent years including Bethesda Softworks, maker of the popular fantasy role-playing *Elder Scrolls* titles.

In recent years, social and mobile games have grown rapidly. In 2009, Zynga launched *FarmVille* in 2009 on Facebook. Playable on a browser or a mobile device, it had 69 million users within a year—a tremendous growth rate when compared to storied game franchises like the online *World of Warcraft*, which has 7.4 million subscribers. **Social games** can coexist easily on popular sites like Facebook and encourage players to recruit new participants from their network of friends.

social games

Online or mobile games that are played in real time with others or that encourage simultaneous group playing.

CONVERGENCE CULTURE
Is Playing Video Games Bad for You?

Some psychologists claim video-game addiction is on the rise. People have collapsed and died after playing video games for days without eating or sleeping. In South Korea, a couple found their 3-year-old daughter dead after returning home from a twelve-hour gaming session at an Internet cafe where they played a virtual-life game similar to *Second Life*. Twenty-six-year-old Xu Yan died in 2007 in Jinzhou, China, after reportedly playing online games continuously for two weeks during the Chinese lunar New Year holiday.[31]

The social aspects of massively multiplayer online role-playing games (MMORPGs) have been blamed for teen suicides, such as the 13-year-old Chinese teen in 2004 who, after playing *World of Warcraft* thirty-six hours straight, left a suicide note that he wanted to be with his heroes in the game. Others have taken online betrayals or thefts of virtual magic weapons or equipment seriously enough to kill themselves or physically hurt others. Children have become violent when not allowed to play games, and children and adults have skipped school or work to play.

Researchers still do not entirely understand the nature of video-game addiction, although they assume it stimulates the same dopamine receptors that affect other types of psychological addictions such as gambling. Games, especially role-playing games, also have powerful escapist aspects.

Research from 2009 conducted by the Centre for Addiction and Mental Health in Toronto, Ontario, on 9,000 students from grades 7 to 12, shows about one in ten school-age children spends seven or more hours a day in front of a computer screen. An even greater portion of children this age report having a video-game addiction problem. With the growth of mobile gaming on smartphones and tablet devices, screen time has only increased, as has the likelihood of addiction.

Mental health experts say signs of addiction include the following:

- Inability to stop the activity or playing much longer than anticipated
- Neglect of family and friends
- Lying to employers and family about activities
- Problems with school or job
- Carpal tunnel syndrome
- Dry eyes
- Failure to attend to personal hygiene
- Sleep disturbances or changes in sleep patterns

Psychologists believe that online games are addictive in part because they give people who feel like they do not fit into regular society a chance to interact easily with others and to redefine themselves. Other studies have shown that video games, especially character-driven games that encourage a range of activities and exploration, can help people experiment with new identities and new ways of seeing themselves, which in turn can help them in real-life social situations. A 2014 study shows that video-game play can actually influence the physical development of the brain.[32]

Two 2011 studies from Colorado State University report the potentially positive effects of the popular multiplayer online game *World of Warcraft*. These studies find that game players can get involved in the game to the extent that they block out their external environment. Researcher Jeffrey Snodgrass reports such "absorptive experiences" can be positive and provide mental health benefits.[33]

Recent research has indicated that a family can bond by gaming together while improving communication among family members. **CRITICAL THINKING QUESTIONS:** Have you ever played a board game with your family? A video game? Why or why not might this be the case? Which video games do you think your family might enjoy most as a group activity?

The huge number of players for games like *FarmVille* means an attractive audience for advertisers, generating a revenue stream that enables Zynga to keep the game free. The information on user behavior that Zynga collects is also a potential gold mine for marketers. Advertisers could use this in combination with other demographic or behavioral data to create highly targeted ads.

The industry, however, is still volatile. After much hype regarding the value of Zynga, experts questioned its business model. When their relationship with Facebook ended in March 2013, a huge revenue stream was lost; and in June 2013, the company announced it was laying off one-fifth of its workforce and closing some of its U.S. offices.[34] Despite Zynga's troubles and uncertain future, social games remain a large-scale and growing part of the industry.

Trends in Video Games

Some experts initially thought that the video-game market would be limited to males in their teens or younger. Yet research has shown that when the first young people who grew up with home-console video games in the 1980s and 1990s reached their twenties and thirties, they kept playing; and females were playing in greater numbers. The growth in tablet computers has increased the popularity of social and mobile gaming.

Today, game publishers tend to release games on multiple platforms. Previously, each console had specific games exclusively, leading to tough decisions for

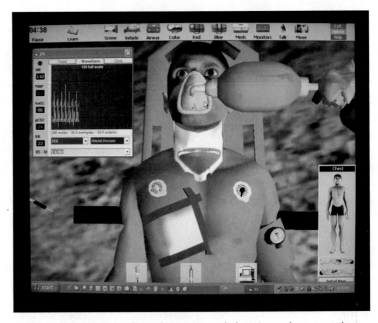

Video games are increasingly used in settings to help train or educate people, providing simulations that other media simply cannot.

consumers regarding which console to buy. The statement "Content rules" applies especially to video games, for a handful of popular titles and series make up a large portion of the revenues. In 2014, industry experts wondered if the drop in American sales for traditional industry segments was due in part to the lack of new titles or popular sequels. As industry consolidation continues and game-development costs rise—with budgets sometimes in the millions of dollars—companies will tend to stick with tried-and-true "blockbuster" series. But online and mobile gaming are likely to see significant growth as mobile devices and Internet-connected consoles are used to play against live opponents around the world. This may reduce the number of new or innovative genres or games in traditional arenas.

Those outside the industry see potential for other settings, such as education. **Serious games**, or applied games, educate players about history or politics, for example, while they entertain. The U.S. Army used video-game training for officers deployed in Iraq, putting them in tense situations requiring quick decisions. Emergency workers and city planners may practice their skills in simulated real-world situations and see the results of certain decisions. Video games have helped some in nursing homes stay mentally sharp and get mild exercise with a Wii, for example.[35]

serious games

Games created to be fun and educational that use game dynamics to instruct players on topics.

Gamification

Gamification, in general terms, is the use of game-like mechanics and thinking in a nongame setting, earning points or rewards, for example, for responding to a survey or writing a product review. Such techniques are not new to the Internet: Consider how you earn points when using some credit cards or how Boy Scouts earn merit badges. Online media provide many opportunities for gamification, including encouraging social competition or community recognition of achievements.

gamification

The use of game-like mechanics in nongame settings, such as earning points, badges, or rewards for performing certain actions.

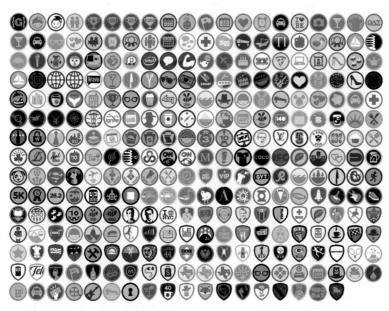

Badges are typically used in gamification to help give users incentives to participate in a site or perform certain actions.

Whereas the term itself was coined in 2010, the principles of gamification emerged earlier as ways of better engaging people in mundane tasks. Because we often compete with each other and like to be rewarded, recognized, and generally admired, a growing number of sites have integrated various tools to encourage us to do exactly that. I may earn a badge for answering questions from other users on a site. Some badges may be harder to obtain than others, encouraging me to write more reviews or edit more articles. Displaying my badges to others in the community may encourage others to want more. Sites may encourage voting, which creates competition among ideas or proposals and interaction among users.

Such techniques have promoted the growth of many popular sites. The location-based social-networking site Foursquare uses badges and titles to encourage frequent check-ins, increasing the site's usefulness for everyone as more people participate.

Gamification techniques can be seen in many fields, including marketing, customer service, and education. Sites like Khan Academy and the language-learning site Duolingo employ gamification to enhance learner engagement. Duolingo users learn parts of a foreign language in modules that unlock other modules and earn digital gold coins as they complete lessons. Gamification has critics, however, who claim that it fosters unnecessary competition, discourages collaboration, and creates a false sense of satisfaction in earning badges for relatively trivial actions.

Augmented Reality

Augmented reality overlays digitized information onto what we see in the real world, adding information that would not otherwise be visible to us or including additional information about what we are viewing. Augmented reality differs from and will likely have a greater impact on our lives and media than **virtual reality**, the replacement of the real world with a digitized, virtual one, a mainstay of science fiction stories hyped in the late twentieth century.

Thanks to television sports, we are already familiar with augmented reality. Sports scores, player stats, the yellow first-down line in football, and other extra information shown throughout games can all be considered limited augmented reality. True augmented reality overlays information onto real-world, context-specific scenarios personalized to each user.

For example, a person with an augmented-reality, head-worn display could be looking at the ruins of an ancient Greek amphitheater. The display could overlay any number of visuals, such as what it would have actually looked like in its day. Augmented reality could be useful for tourism in other ways, providing visual cues for public transit or pop-up restaurant reviews.

This idea is not new. In the late 1960s, computer scientist Ivan Sutherland created the first head-worn computer display, with limited graphics and computing power. Since the 1970s, researcher Steve Mann has been experimenting with various head-worn, augmented reality displays. Columbia University professor Steven Feiner, a pioneer in augmented reality, has been creating various augmented-reality prototypes since the early 1990s.

Augmented reality appears most frequently online for advertising and on consumer product websites. The augmented dressing room on a site like Tobi.com allows shoppers to upload pictures and "try on" a variety of dresses overlaid on the photo. You can vote yes or no or even forward the picture to friends. Taking augmented

virtual reality

The replacement of the real world with a digitized, virtual one, a mainstay of science fiction stories hyped in the late twentieth century.

augmented reality

Digital overlays of information on a screen that correspond to what is being looked at in the real world through the screen.

reality one step further is Bodymetrics, a company that installs a dressing booth in department stores that scans the body and then shows your "virtual self" in 3-D with different types of clothes, eliminating the need to actually try on each outfit.

These are just the first steps in augmented reality, whose true potential as a media interface lies in its personalizing a viewing experience depending on location and context. We see some simple examples of this with mobile phones that can overlay some information, such as map directions, when used as a camera viewfinder.

First available to testers in 2012, Google Glass more closely approaches the vision of Mann and Feiner for augmented reality. It lets people access a variety of information regarding what they are observing. A user could ask for sushi restaurants in the area and receive visual cues about restaurants around the corner or blocks down the street. Or a person could access historical photos to see what the neighborhood looked like one hundred years ago. If a landmark looks familiar, a user could ask which movies have used the landmark and get short clips of the movies, perhaps bookmarking them for later viewing.

Because the glasses can take pictures and shoot video, wearers could secretly record what they are seeing. For that reason, several Las Vegas casinos have already said they will not allow people wearing them into the casinos. The glasses also invite judgments about the "cool" versus "geek" factor. A popular Tumblr blog, *White Men Wearing Google Glass*, pokes fun at the Silicon Valley tech types wearing the glasses. Such representations may deter sales. On January 15, 2015, Google announced the end of the public phase of Glass development, although it would continue to develop wearables as an internal research program.

Samsung is one of many companies around the world that have introduced augmented reality head-worn displays to access the Internet through immersive media.

DISCUSSION QUESTIONS: Some contend that secretly recording conversations or activities, even when the acts recorded occur in a public space, is a violation of privacy. State and defend your position on the matter.

Ethics of Interactive Media

The power of interactive media to engage and involve consumers of media content raises many ethical issues. Some of these are amplified issues with traditional media; others are largely new. Some touch on age-old concerns regarding free speech, the role of advertising in society, and trust.

Interactivity requires faith in others because users must trust those they deal with on the Web. Face-to-face communication includes cues and mannerisms that help us establish trust with others, but online we rely on words and the results of our interactions.

Consider what would happen if you were in a chat room discussion with a number of members over the course of several days, greatly enjoying the discussions and the feeling that you have met some interesting, like-minded individuals. Then imagine your sense of betrayal if you learned that one or more of the participants was actually a computer program that gave context-specific responses to human posts. Your trust in that chat room—and perhaps all chat rooms where you did not know the individual participants personally—would likely be broken.

Trust between people is similarly relevant because we expect (or hope) that others will respect our views even if they disagree with us and that they will debate in civilized ways. Most people know how disruptive an obnoxious poster can be to a discussion group, spouting incendiary views simply to draw a reaction. **Trolling** degrades the quality of the discussion and wastes time.

Complaints about advertising's influence have also intensified in an interactive environment. At the forefront of this are video games for children created by companies, such as toy manufacturers, that feature their products prominently in the games. Because of the high level of engagement in video games, critics worry that unaware young users are absorbing hidden commercial messages.

Violence in video games is also a major concern to certain groups claiming that the game interactivity influences children more than simply passively watching violence on television. This is one reason the Entertainment Software Rating Board (ESRB) was created for video games and mobile apps. Similar to the movie-rating system, it ranges from EC (early childhood) to A (adult only). Ratings correspond to levels and realism of violence, sexual content, and strong language.

Behavioral targeting also raises ethical issues. A website tracks your browsing or search behavior and then delivers relevant advertisements. After looking at travel sites, you may get ads for deals on your Facebook page or see travel ads appearing on other sites for several days afterward.

trolling

Posting deliberately obnoxious or disruptive messages to discussion groups or other online forums simply to get a reaction from the participants.

behavioral targeting

Advertisers tracking individuals' web-browsing behavior to provide ads that closely match the topics of sites visited or searches made.

> **DISCUSSION QUESTIONS:** Identify some instances where you have encountered trolling. Is trolling more likely to occur on certain sites? What has been your response to such behavior? Explain your reaction.

MEDIA CAREERS

Careers in interactive media represent a growing opportunity, especially for anyone with an entrepreneurial spirit. Most notably, innovators with a new idea for an interactive media enterprise, such as a new app or a video game, may develop an idea for a digital media prototype and then perhaps solicit funding on a crowdfunding website. Another possibility in interactive media is as a player. Professional video-game playing is on the rise, and an increasing number of colleges even offer scholarships to students who show potential and skill at video-game play. With the growth of augmented and virtual reality, a new career pathway has also emerged for students interested in creating content for those platforms, especially with VR cinema companies such as Jaunt.

And jobs also exist for those who write creatively, particularly in the genres of fantasy and sci-fi. Screenwriting and storyboarding skills are also an asset. Game developers come up with a concept; writers develop compelling settings, plots, characters, and dialog that bring their concept, an imaginary world, to life. Writers need not be programmers, but they need to be familiar with the latest in video technology and passionate about gaming. Competition is fierce not only for players but also for candidates in this job market, which makes networking an even more important activity for those hoping to break into the industry.

LOOKING BACK AND MOVING FORWARD

With the convergence of computing, telecommunications, and media, technological changes can affect media and mass communication powerfully. Increased computer-processing power created better opportunities for a graphical user interface that made computers much more accessible to the average person, which expanded audiences online. Advances in technology will likely further alter our interaction with computers in unforeseeable ways, yet some general patterns in the following broad categories are evident: easier accessibility, more immersive media environments, and seamless or fluid interfaces. The video-game industry is leading the way in these fields because the very success of games depends on how enjoyable and playable they are.

Like traditional media, the video-game industry has consolidated. As with Hollywood movie studios, companies show a strong propensity for producing "blockbuster" game titles. The video-game industry now rivals Hollywood in terms of total revenue, with $64 billion earned in 2014. Video game industry revenues are expected to top $100 billion worldwide by 2018, potentially making it the largest media segment of all.[36]

Wireless handheld devices such as mobile phones and tablet computers are now commonplace. They raise important user-interface questions for content on small screens, such as how people can input information naturally yet privately. Geography and location matter because most devices have GPS receivers. From a user-interface perspective, this means that maps will become increasingly important as graphics-layered information on-screen. Map-based GUIs can provide everything from information on the nearest restaurant, including reviews, to local points of cultural or historical interest.

Accessing media content will be increasingly easy, but accessing the content one wants when and where one wants it may be harder than ever unless sound principles in user-interface design are applied to search-and-find functions.

A variety of forms of immersive media are emerging and expanding in the online environment. These include 3-D visualizations, virtual reality, 360-degree photography and video, and augmented reality. Immersive media environments can provide experiences unlike those encountered in traditional media or even in the typical digital-media environment, providing new opportunities—and new challenges—for user interfaces.

Interfaces that change to suit our informational and entertainment needs will gradually replace largely static web pages. We will not necessarily have to "go to" a website to get information; rather, we may have some version of the Web on a wearable computer and interact with the screen through voice commands or even eye movements. Wearable computers capable of recording do raise privacy issues, among other ethical and social concerns.

It is important to remember that the online environment with which we are familiar is not simply one in which we receive a variety of media content in different forms, although that continues to be a large part of it. It also includes various ways to communicate directly with media producers, other audience members, and one's social network. Our user interface helps us receive the kind of information and entertainment we want and easily communicate and interact with others. Interactivity is one of digital media's central and distinguishing features.

MEDIA MATTERS   ENGAGING WITH INTERACTIVE MEDIA

1. Define "interaction" in your own words. How might your definition explain the difference between using the Internet and watching a television show or buying something at a vending machine?

2. Visit a website or download a mobile app for a magazine or newspaper in a language that you do not know. From only visual cues, try to locate specific information such as movie reviews. How well did the common language of user interface and navigation guide you?

3. Gamification is a growing trend, with many websites and mobile apps offering rewards such as points or badges to encourage users to interact more with the site and one another. What potential disadvantages do you see with the gamification trend, if any?

4. Some critics say that video games are addictive. What behavior do you believe indicates such addiction?

5. Video games have been developed for a wide variety of educational settings, for example, training engineers and emergency workers in simulations. If video games can teach positive qualities and skills in such situations, do violent video games teach violent behavior? Defend your response.

FURTHER READING

Understanding Media: The Extensions of Man, reprint ed. Marshall McLuhan, Lewis Lapham (1994) MIT Press.

Bias of Communication, reprint ed. Harold Innis (1991) University of Toronto Press.

A History of Modern Computing. Paul E. Ceruzzi (1999) MIT Press.

Interface Culture: How New Technology Transforms the Ways We Create and Communicate. Steven Johnson (1999) Basic Books.

The Rise of the Image, the Fall of the Word. Mitchell Stephens (1998) Oxford University Press.

About Face 3: The Essentials of Interaction Design. Alan Cooper, Robert Reimann, David Cronin (2007) Wiley.

Designing with the Mind in Mind: Simple Guide to Understanding User Interface Design Rules. Jeff Johnson (2010) Morgan Kaufman.

Don't Make Me Think: A Common Sense Approach to Web Usability, 2nd ed. Steve Krug (2005) New Riders Publishing.

The Ultimate History of Video Games: From Pong *to* Pokémon—*The Story Behind the Craze That Touched Our Lives and Changed the World*. Steven Kent (2001) Three Rivers Press.

The Video Games Guide: 1,000+ Arcade, Console and Computer Games, 1962–2012, 2nd ed. Matt Fox (2013) McFarland.

Reality Is Broken: Why Games Make Us Better and How They Can Change the World. Jane McGonigal (2011) Penguin.

1001 Video Games You Must Play Before You Die. Tony Mott (ed.) (2010) Universe.

Replay: The History of Video Games. Tristan Donovan (2010) Yellow Ant.

The Google Story: Inside the Hottest Business, Media, and Technology Success of Our Time. David Vise, Mark Malseed (2006) Delta.

Planet Google: One Company's Audacious Plan to Organize Everything We Know. Randall Stross (2008) Free Press.

Click: What Millions of People Are Doing Online and Why It Matters. Bill Tancer (2008) Hyperion.

Augmented Reality: Theory and Practice. Dieter Schmalstieg, Tobias Hollerer (2014) Addison-Wesley.

The Innovators: How a Group of Hackers, Geniuses, and Geeks Created the Digital Revolution. Walter Isaacson (2014) Simon & Schuster.

The Impact of Social Media

Justine Sacco, a 30-year-old senior director of corporate communications at IAC, tweeted several jokes about travel on her way from New York City to visit family in South Africa. At Heathrow Airport in London, she wrote "Going to Africa. Hope I don't get AIDS. Just kidding. I'm white!" None of her 170 Twitter followers responded; and she got on the plane, blissfully unaware of how that tweet would change her life.

Eleven hours later, upon landing in Cape Town, she learned from a friend's text that @justinesacco had become the number one trending topic on Twitter—and not because of her sense of humor. The editor at Valleywag (essentially a gossip blog) was forwarded her tweet by someone, retweeted it to his 15,000 followers, and posted it on the Valleywag site. From that, a public backlash and shaming of Sacco began.[1]

Within weeks, she lost her job at IAC while being continually hounded by the media and receiving death threats online, even after she issued a written apology that attempted to clarify she was not racist and had simply been trying to offer social commentary about the bubble of white privilege.

Sacco's case follows a pattern similar to that of others whose various transgressions have provoked publicly shaming through social media—name-calling, death threats, and invasions of privacy, sometimes followed by termination of their employment. In early 2013, a woman at a conference overheard an off-color joke, found it offensive, snapped the jokester's picture with her phone, and tweeted her displeasure at yet another example of sexism in the technology field to her nearly 10,000 followers. The next day, the man was fired—and, subsequently, so was she. Once the man posted his story online, she received death threats, had her home address publicized, and was eventually dismissed after denial-of-service attacks on her company's website, which the organization was told would continue until she was fired.

Just as the rapid speed of communication among the public on social media has intensified the ability to publicly shame people—even for minor transgressions—the same dynamics can be a force that accelerates good works and enhances positive feelings. Consider the Michigan mother who created a "Happy Birthday Colin"

Facebook page asking people to send her 11-year-old son birthday greetings. The page quickly went viral, generating over 10,000 messages, cards, and letters for Colin, who has a condition similar to Asperger's that makes it difficult for him to make friends. *Good Morning America* decided to enhance his special day as icing on the cake, so to speak, by hosting a surprise birthday bash in Times Square that featured the Rutgers marching band and a subsequent trip to Disneyworld.[2]

The tools and capabilities of social media have existed since the earliest days of the Internet, but not until the past few years has their potential been realized by businesses, including media companies. Many of the changes have been driven from the ground up rather than by traditional media companies, a fact that empowers social media and often threatens traditional business models. Social media have altered roles and working practices in journalism, public relations, and advertising.

The rise of social media has also brought some ugly social issues to the fore. The potential harm and perhaps prevalence of such negative behaviors as bullying have increased because of social media, with dozens of cases reported just in the past few years of young people committing suicide because of cyberbullying. Of course, racism and bullying did not originate with social media. However, because it makes such bad behavior more public, social media do raise new issues and can make the behavior seem more common.

Defining Social Media

Social media continues to be defined and redefined by scholars, professionals, and the press. Finding a description on which everyone agrees is difficult, partly because the tools for social media change with advances in technologies, and popular sites or trends touted as The Next Big Thing seem to lose popularity almost as quickly as they enter the limelight. Nevertheless, we can examine the elements underlying some commonly used definitions and then apply these to the realm of mass communication.

According to John Jantsch, author of *The Duct Tape Marketing* blog, social media can be defined as "the use of technology combined with social interaction to create or co-create value."[3] He keeps the definition concise because his readers are busy marketing professionals. PR professional and social media expert Brian Solis defines social media as "a shift in how people discover, read, and share news and information and content. It's a fusion of sociology and technology, transforming monologue (one to many) into dialog (many to many)."[4] In other words, social media represent a convergence of mass communication and interpersonal communication. Anvil Media, a search-engine marketing firm, provides a definition derived from sociology: "An umbrella term that defines the various activities that integrate technology, social interaction, and the construction of words and pictures. This interaction, and the manner in which information is presented, depends on the varied perspectives and 'building' of shared meaning, as people share their stories, and understandings."[5]

These definitions all mention the intersection of technology, social interaction, and information sharing, seemingly simple elements that will continue to transform many aspects of mass communication. Before looking at them in more detail and exploring how they are changing mass communication and media industries, we will examine how social media differ from traditional media.

DIALOGIC COMMMUNICATION

Traditional media use a broadcast, or monologic, model of one-to-many communication, whereas social media employ a more dialogic model of many-to-many communication. Of course, this does not mean that mass-media audiences prior to the Internet never spoke with one another—there were fan clubs, letters to the editor, and a variety of ways to interact. The flow of communication, however, favored the broadcaster sending a message to many people simultaneously, with audience members having limited means to share their thoughts with each other on a mass scale.

Consider how a viewer in the 1970s might have been able to share his reactions to the previous night's episode of a popular yet controversial situation comedy like *All in the Family*. If he watched with friends or family, he could of course comment during or after the show. He might also discuss the program at the office the next day. If, however, a viewer felt particularly strongly about a racist remark made by the character Archie Bunker and felt that others should know how offensive the remark was, options to communicate these feelings to a broad audience were limited, expensive, and generally did not generate dialog.

He could write a letter of complaint to the network or the FCC, with no guarantee that he would hear from either. He could write a letter to the editor of the local newspaper; but even if published, it would reach a limited audience of only the paper's readers (and specifically those who read the letters to the editor that day). He could purchase an advertisement in the newspaper, which might get more attention than a letter to the editor, but that would be expensive, or the paper might choose not to accept such an ad. Or he could create a flyer, make photocopies, and hand them out or mail them to people, which would be both expensive and time-consuming.

If the viewer was persistent (or persuasive) enough or if he attracted enough supporters and perhaps held a demonstration or march, his crusade might get picked up as a news story in the local paper or television, thus perhaps attracting more people to his cause. Although at first glance this would seem to be a kind of many-to-many form of communication, consider the mechanisms by which it occurred—his message was communicated primarily through mass-media channels. Furthermore, it is unlikely that he would have had the resources—either time, money, or media attention—to carry out a campaign like this in the first place.

Now let's look at what a viewer would do circa 2015. Let us say that a racist comment made by Peter, the father, on the animated Fox show *Family Guy* offends a viewer. Her first public complaint is likely not a letter to the FCC or the Fox network but a tweet from her Twitter account, perhaps even with a hashtag that helps others easily find tweets on the topic. Or perhaps she weighs in on the discussion board of the show's website. Or maybe she goes to any number of other discussion groups or fan sites devoted to *Family Guy* and comments there.

Perhaps she finds within a couple of days that someone who shares her views has created a mash-up video of such stereotypes found on various prime-time shows or in the news. The video is uploaded to YouTube, where it gets viewed

Today audiences are able to express their displeasure with shows through a range of social media outlets, including showing excerpts of the shows themselves.

Clay Shirky, a writer, consultant, and NYU professor, examines the social and economic effects of Internet technologies.

hundreds of thousands of times within a couple of weeks. It may appear on a news aggregator site such as Reddit, getting even more views and generating further discussions among YouTube viewers both for and against the position conveyed in the video. Or she may create an online petition on a site such as Change.org, asking people to boycott the show or write letters of complaint to the network. If the video is viewed enough times or talked about enough, or the petition gets enough signatures, then mainstream news organizations may cover the story, amplifying public interest and discussion even more.

What is notable in this latter example is that, except with the original source material, traditional mass-media organizations are not involved (until perhaps later in the process), yet far more members of the public may be affected in a very short time than would have been the case in the 1970s—or even the 1990s. More importantly, our viewer may never even consider writing a letter to the editor of the local newspaper or to the FCC. A complete media ecosystem can be created and sustained through social interaction using tools that social media provide. Mainstream media may still play a role, of course, but they do not have to be involved like in the past.

This follows what new-media scholar and NYU professor Clay Shirky calls a "publish, then filter" model.[6] Traditional media industries such as news are based on a "filter, then publish" model of information. From a vast universe of possible information, specialists or professionals (editors, music producers, etc.) select their content, making decisions based partly on the limitations of their medium, such as time limits in TV news or space limits in print media.

This material—the news in a newspaper or the bands promoted by a major record label or MTV—is then distributed to the general public. The public is likely completely unaware of all the other possible types of information it could have received. Media business models have been built on this way of controlling and disseminating information, and even entire professions have made this model an essential part of their professional identities. An example is journalism, commonly described as necessary for a healthy democracy because of its role in informing the public and monitoring the government. Journalists function as gatekeepers, professionals with special access to the halls of power and unique skills and training that presumably give them the ability to decide what information should be disseminated to the public.

Yet, as seen in the "publish, then filter" model, prevalent in social media, many of these professional assumptions are being challenged, as are the business models. If the public can connect directly with the vast universe of information out there and find what is relevant through a combination of social networks, ratings systems, and online discussions, then what functions do organizations that restrict the flow of information to the public serve?

This is not to say that traditional mass media are no longer important or powerful. The media serve an important **agenda-setting** function in that they provide us with much of the material that we talk about, even if they do not necessarily tell us what to think. The media also tend to amplify events through their coverage because they generally have larger audiences than the majority of social media sites, even though traditional media audiences continue to fragment. In addition, much of what is talked about on social media derives from entertainment or news content created and distributed by traditional media organizations.

DISCUSSION QUESTIONS: Consider the traditional "filter, then publish" model and the "publish, then filter" model. What do you think are some of the biggest weaknesses of each type? Can you think of certain types of media that may be better suited to one type over the other? Why?

SOCIAL PRODUCTION

Another fundamental difference with traditional media is the collaborative aspect of social media that threatens established media business models used throughout much of the twentieth century and into this one. Most people cannot afford to start a newspaper or create a radio or television station. Digital media and the Internet greatly reduce costs for creating and distributing media content widely, to the point that they are well within the reach of many.

Collaborative, or participatory, media trace their roots to the **free and open-source software (FOSS)** movement. This type of participatory or social production contrasts sharply with the standard profit-making business models that rely more heavily on proprietary licensing agreements and intellectual property protections to protect products. To understand the difference, think LibreOffice versus Microsoft Office or Wikipedia versus *Encyclopaedia Britannica*. As the name suggests, the FOSS movement wants software to be freely available and the source code open to anyone to make modifications and improvements.

Although not always free in the sense of "no cost," this movement was informed by a strong spirit of keeping the information freely available to anyone and letting everyone share in the benefits. Commonsense theories of human behavior suggested that nobody would work hard on a project to only have others benefit greatly from it. Yet without the collaborative efforts of a good number of computer programmers and engineers committed to sharing information and knowledge freely, the backbone of the Internet would not exist. No company would have spent the resources to create the structure needed, especially when there was no clear way to profit from it.

The open-source model did indeed work. The Apache web server program, the Linux operating system, and the LibreOffice software suite are all open-source developments that continue to play significant roles in computing today. Some countries have adopted LibreOffice for all government agencies, a mandate that raises the distinct possibility that other institutions will follow suit to diminish compatibility issues.

Computing and media companies operating with mass-communication business models are not sitting idly by, however, while a new and different media ecosystem based on collaboration, interaction, and sharing emerges. Some companies have incorporated open-source software into their own product lines. IBM experienced a larger and swifter increase in revenues than expected after switching to Linux. Oracle simply purchased the MySQL database system, reneging on a promise to keep it truly open source.

free and open-source software movement (FOSS)

A movement that wants software to be freely available and the source code open to anyone to make modifications and improvements.

Dear Mr Branson,

REF: Mumbai to Heathrow 7th December 2008

I love the Virgin brand, I really do which is why I continue to use it despite a series of unfortunate incidents over the last few years. This latest incident takes the biscuit.

Ironically, by the end of the flight I would have gladly paid over a thousand rupees for a single biscuit following the culinary journey of hell I was subjected to at the hands of your corporation.

Look at this Richard. Just look at it:

I imagine the same questions are racing through your brilliant mind as were racing through mine on that fateful day. What is this? Why have I been given it? What have I done to deserve this? And, which one is the starter, which one is the dessert?

You don't get to a position like yours Richard with anything less than a generous sprinkling of observational power so I KNOW you will have spotted the tomato next to the two yellow shafts of sponge on the left. Yes, it's next to the sponge shaft without the green paste. That's got to be the clue hasn't it. No sane person would serve a dessert with a tomato would they? Well answer me this Richard, what sort of animal would serve a dessert with peas in?

I know it looks like a bhaji but it's in custard Richard, custard. It must be the pudding. Well you'll be fascinated to hear that it wasn't custard. It was a sour gel with a clear oil on top. It's only redeeming feature was that it managed to be so alien to my palette that it took away the taste of the curry emanating from our miscellaneous central cuboid of beige matter. Perhaps the meal on the left might be the desert after all.

Anyway, this is all irrelevant at the moment. I was raised strictly but neatly by my parents and if they knew I had started dessert before the main course, a sponge shaft would be the least of my worries. So let's peel back the tin-foil on the main dish and see what's on offer.

Social media have altered the power dynamic between consumers and producers. Consumers can now force a response from companies when they review or complain about a company's products.

Open-source software, which allows anyone to access its source code and is often free, demonstrates how successful social production can be. **CRITICAL THINKING QUESTIONS:** Do you favor open-source software models such as LibreOffice? Had you developed the software yourself and had a proprietary interest in it, would your opinion differ?

distributed computing

Individual, autonomous computers that work together toward a common goal, typically a large, complex project that requires more computing power than that of any individual computer.

Microsoft chose to compete more head-to-head with LibreOffice's predecessor OpenOffice, offering libraries and other public institutions free computers—loaded with Microsoft software, of course.

The success of the open-source model also raised the question that if it works for software, then why can't it work for entertainment, journalism, advertising, public relations—or any kind of content and knowledge production? Collaboration on such an unprecedented scale is seen with projects such as Wikipedia in part because of our powerful and cheap computers. Large-scale projects can be broken down into small components, making them easy for people to do and allowing individuals to contribute when and how they choose.

In what is called **distributed computing**, any number of volunteers can assist a project without inconveniencing themselves because the program works in the background. The free computing power amassed through the various users is much greater than any research project could afford. The website also informs people of progress, thereby engaging the public in a field they might otherwise have ignored. Examples of projects using the power of distributed-computing networks include seeking cures for diseases such as cancer, working on models of global warming, using protein-folding programs to test for new drug combinations, and even searching for extraterrestrial intelligence (SETI).

We see this culture of collaboration and openness in a range of media production today, ranging from crowdsourced news sites to reviews of everything from movies to restaurants to consumer products. Mainstream media companies encourage citizen reporting, letting the public send raw video footage or photographs from breaking news events, which may be aired after being vetted by editors and a show's producers.

We also see a combination of nonmarket principles of collaboration with market forces in crowdfunding sites like Kickstarter (see the Media Pioneers box in Chapter 4). People propose projects or goals and ask the community to donate money to their cause. If the financial goals are met within the allotted time, then the project is funded. Its creators often inform the funder community of progress and sometimes give them samples of the finished project, such as a video or CD.

This gradual change in our online culture, in the ways we freely help each other or simply use our computers to advance the general common good, demonstrates how technological and economic factors have altered our assumptions about people acting selfishly or not helping others.

Distributed computing combines the excess computing power of many computers to perform operations that not even supercomputers could perform alone.

DISCUSSION QUESTIONS: Have you ever made a decision to see a movie, buy music or a book, or go to a particular restaurant based on user reviews? If so, do you think that you have an ethical obligation to also contribute reviews that could guide others? Why or why not?

What Is "Social" About Social Media?

Cultural norms may have changed, but media have always had a social component. From the earliest days of print, people read aloud and in groups. In the 1930s and 1940s, families congregated around the radio to listen to their favorite programs; and people came together to listen to music, dance, and socialize. Even television, a medium maligned as passive and isolating, often has important social aspects, as families and friends get together to watch and discuss shows and sporting events. Some of HBO's most popular original series, such as *The Sopranos*, generated what became known as "water-cooler buzz," or discussions among workers about a show the day after it aired, which in turn created more interest among people who hadn't seen the show.

How are social media more "social" than traditional media? This is an important question. If traditional media are no less social than what is being touted as a revolutionary, transformative new kind of media, then it would follow that Web 2.0 and all the talk about it is just the latest hype about new technology.

The Center for Social Media in the School of Communication at American University identifies five fundamental areas in which people's media habits are changing: choice, conversation, curation, creation, and collaboration.[7] These five components provide an excellent framework for understanding social media better.

CHOICE

The public has far more media choices than in the past and far more options of media styles and genres than ever before. Even so, thinking of the public or audience primarily as passive consumers of media ignores the variety of ways people can interact and find the media content they want. Through search engines, recommendations from friends (often known only from online interactions), RSS feeds, and, of course, traditional media channels, people today are generally more proactive in getting the type of content they want.

Note that "more choice" does not necessarily mean "better quality." Simply because there are many more options does not mean that the quality of content people may find is going to be better. Greater choice, however, does mean that more media types and channels are competing with each other to attract the attention of the audience. This alters the production, promotion, and marketing of media and even what types of content may be created in the first place.

CONVERSATION

From the earliest days of the Internet, conversation was important, and it continues to be a defining characteristic of social media. Discussion groups, Usenet, email, IM, and Twitter have been or continue to be important tools that enable people to communicate easily with each other on a scale and in ways not possible with traditional media. Companies have had their reputations tarnished or enhanced because of online conversations, unknown artists have become famous through them, and funny or embarrassing moments caught on a video recording have made some people instant (if short-lived) celebrities.

Comcast has learned the hard way about the power of social media. In 2006, a customer posted a video on YouTube of a Comcast technician sleeping in the customer's home while waiting on hold—with Comcast—for over an hour. In 2008, Comcast was ranked at the bottom of the American Customer Satisfaction Index, and hundreds of customers contributed their complaints to the website ComcastMustDie.com. As part of its efforts to improve customer service, Comcast started monitoring blogs and online conversations and discussing customer concerns directly in the online forums. Many companies follow online discussions about themselves, but Comcast took an extra step in often responding to bloggers and engaging in conversation with them. Today, their actions are considered a prime example of a company improving through listening to its customers.

Many companies have discovered that their brands and corporate images are not what they claim in traditional advertising or public relations efforts but what the customers say they are. The focus on conversation is one other example of the shift from a lecture to a dialog between companies (including media companies) and the public.

CURATION

With so many options available today, how can people find the kind of media content they like? The traditional gatekeepers of information and knowledge, such as media professionals and librarians, are finding their roles changing in the social media environment. One major change is a shift from a "gatekeeping" model to what Australian media scholar Axel Bruns calls a "gatewatching" model in which people act as their own filters, classifiers, and reviewers.

Classifying content happens through an activity such as **tagging** or creating **folksonomies** of definitions. This helps bring some order to the vast array of content out there, and it helps in searches. An important difference in tagging is that people are not waiting to hear from an authority on how to classify terms, such as a librarian would do—they are doing it themselves. Sites such as Instagram, Flickr, Facebook, and YouTube have all encouraged tagging among users, which makes the content more searchable and helps users recognize relations among terms they may never have seen before.

News aggregation site Reddit is an example of how curatorial activities can enhance a site's relevance for everyone. Users vote either positively or negatively on stories that have been submitted, and stories with the highest percentage of positive votes get pushed to the front page. This creates a natural hierarchy of content, where typically material deemed most relevant or interesting to the Reddit community becomes more visible to other users of the site, even if they do not vote on stories themselves.

The online environment lends itself to a curatorial mode of contributing to the social media space. It is fairly easy to tag something with terms, or to write a one-paragraph review of a book or movie, or to write a few lines about a product recently purchased. It is also much easier to find, and publicize, fault with something. Online reviews have become increasingly important in consumers' decisions on items ranging from household goods to media products.

tagging

Using searchable keywords to define a piece of information, file, image, or other type of digital media in a nonhierarchical system.

folksonomies

Collection of tags created by users that provide metadata (data about data) regarding information.

Reddit users participate by voting for or against stories, pushing the most popular content to the front page of the site.

CREATION

The digital-media tools that facilitate the creation of content have played a major role in the rise of user-generated media content. Cheaper communication technologies allow more people to create media, whether it is the printing press in Renaissance Europe or the high-speed Internet in the twenty-first century. The ability to distribute content cheaply and easily to a mass audience, along with the chance to interact with others, is probably the most crucial aspect of how the Internet is transforming mass communication. Without this ability, the media landscape today would look vastly different. It could even be said that social media as we know them now would not exist.

Simply because the tools are readily available to create media does not, of course, mean that everyone will start producing great works of art. Most people, in fact, will be satisfied consuming media and not creating anything, and there will be far more amateurish or poor-quality content online than high art. Yet even if only a small percentage of the people online create and share content, the pool of media content will be larger than that in the traditional media world because of the sheer numbers of people online.

Creating content is not without its challenges. As noted elsewhere in this book, intellectual property laws are being challenged by a digital culture that sees nothing wrong with borrowing freely from existing media to create something new. Furthermore, many people online have come to expect a variety of media content for free. Rather than encourage creativity, as intellectual property laws were meant to do, more restrictive laws may have the opposite effect by removing creative material from the public domain. Nevertheless, content creators should be compensated for their work.

COLLABORATION

The willingness to collaborate on a common good for no personal monetary gain is perhaps one of the biggest surprises one encounters when examining social media. It is one thing to spend hours creating an app with the hopes of copyrighting it for licensing or offering it for money, but quite another to do so and provide it to the Web community for free use or to provide open access to your project and invite others to work on and improve it.

A number of cases of collaboration extend from the online realm to offline, especially in organizing people around politics or social movements. In fact, the most successful uses of online tools in political campaigns have included ample opportunities for people to socialize in real-world settings as well. This was the lesson the Howard Dean campaign learned in 2004 from looking at Al Gore's failed presidential campaign in 2000. Gore's campaign used online media primarily as another media channel, asking for donations and alerting users about issues and appearances. Dean used online tools to encourage supporters to get together in person and act, generating millions of dollars for his campaign in the process.

Although Dean eventually dropped out of the presidential race, Obama's presidential campaigns applied and further refined these lessons. In recent years, organizations such as Sunlight Labs and Code for America have partnered with government agencies and other organizations to host civic hackathons, bringing coders and others together to work jointly on finding solutions to common government problems. One example of this is Boston's Citizens Connect app, which

Civic hackathons, in which coders and others gather over one or two days to work on computing solutions for government or civic issues, have become increasingly popular in recent years.

lets Boston residents easily report various civic issues such as potholes and track the progress of the problems getting fixed.

In some ways, the realization that people need real-world socializing to complement their online socializing harkens back to the earliest days of social media, long before that term was applied. In fact, the need to meet, interact, and discuss was an impetus for the earliest online communities, many of which are precursors to today's social media tools and are still widely used today.

> **DISCUSSION QUESTIONS:** Which of the five ways in which our media use is changing (choice, creation, curation, conversation, or collaboration) do you think is the most important? Why?

Types of Social Media

Smartphones and tablets have made it easy for people to keep up with social media or online news at all times.

In 1980, France launched its videotext service, text delivery over the air or by cable for presentation on television screens or other electronic displays, known then as Teletel and later as Minitel. Ahead of its time, Minitel was one of the most successful, early interactive online information services before the Web. Minitel worked because the government subsidized it and provided every home with an access device. Its biggest problem turned out to be the emergence of the World Wide Web, which quickly outclassed the stand-alone Minitel communication terminals. Despite these drawbacks, there were still 10 million Minitel users in 2009, yet France Telecom finally closed the Minitel service in June 2012.

Many of the tools we now commonly associate with social media were used before social media became an Internet phenomenon. Even the pre-Web Minitel had what it called its "blue rooms," adult-oriented chat rooms, the only part of the

INTERNATIONAL PERSPECTIVES
Social Networks of Influential Languages

Just like people, it turns out that languages can also be mapped via social networking principles to reveal which networks are the most extensive and most important.

In social networks, a hub is someone or something that has many other connections to others, essentially acting as a communications or information focal point. One study on the influence of various languages that appeared in the *Proceedings of the National Academy of Sciences* by researchers at MIT, Harvard, Northeastern University, and Aix-Marseille University looked at three separate communication networks: books, tweets, and Wikipedia articles. They examined the output of all three networks done in various languages and mapped their translations to other languages to determine which tended to be most translated, thus reaching more people.

It is perhaps no surprise that English was a central hub, making it the best language to spread your message to other languages in all three networks, even though it is only the third most widely spoken native language, with 5 percent of the global population. A few other languages, such as French, Spanish, Russian, and German, worked as intermediate-level hubs in much the same way as English, except on a smaller scale. This means that even though the actual number of native speakers of some of these languages may be relatively small, books, tweets, and Wikipedia articles tended to get translated to and from these languages at a disproportionately high rate.

Chinese, Hindi, and Arabic—which combined have nearly a quarter of the world's population of native speakers—all had fewer connections in the networking map, meaning works written in these languages got translated to and from other languages far less than the number of native speakers would otherwise indicate.

What does this mean for native English speakers studying a foreign language? At least in terms of tapping into global conversations and knowledge and spreading your message, it may be better to study a language such as Spanish or German than Chinese or Arabic.

---

service that generated a significant revenue stream. The use of modern social media grew significantly with Web-related advances that facilitated creating and sharing content. Other differences include the rapid growth of the Web audience and the increase in broadband Internet connections that enhance user experience. Wireless Internet capabilities have also expanded access to social media.

Here, we will look specifically at how some social media tools have developed and been used over time. In most cases, people have found ways to subvert the tools to their own ends, making the service less useful for everyone. In response, communities have created social norms and rules of behavior along with punishments for transgressions.

EMAIL

Email, or electronic mail, was one of the first uses of the Internet and until 2008 was the most popular Internet activity. In 2010, email moved down to third place, following social-networking sites and online gaming.[8] Email can be overlooked as an element of social media, but its ease of use, prevalence, and capacity to send messages to more than one person make it a powerful communication tool.

Although email is an exchange of messages via telecommunication between two people, an individual can easily create a mailing list and send out a single message to multiple people, in a sense broadcasting the message. This capability has caused more than a few red faces, as anyone can attest who has been on a mailing list in which one member made disparaging remarks about another member, thinking the response was going only to an individual and not to the entire list.

Mailing lists differ from discussion boards in that messages posted get sent directly to subscribers' email inboxes rather than to an online location that a member must visit to read the messages. **Listservs** are automated mailing-list administrators that allow for easy subscription, cancellation, and delivery of emails to subscribers. Many organizations use them to keep their customers or supporters informed of the organization's activities or special deals.

The principles that allow for easy creation of mailing lists are also responsible for what many consider the scourge of email—**spam**, unsolicited email advertising. Spam, once rare and considered extremely bad form in the early days of the Internet, is now all too common. Computer programs comb the Internet and find email addresses on websites and social media, "harvesting" them to a central location that a spammer can then use to send messages or sell the list of emails to other companies.

A battle continues between spammers and companies creating software to block spam. Automated filtering software often removes much of the spam but may also inadvertently remove desired messages. Spam clogging the Internet and inboxes reflects the downside of being able to share content easily. Lowered costs of distribution on the Internet have helped create online communities and given the public a chance to distribute media content on a par with established media companies, but it has also made it easier for individuals and companies to abuse that distribution system, making it less valuable for all. Legislators are fighting back, however, with increasingly stringent antispam laws that penalize spammers.

The antispam legislation and better spam-blocking software seem to have had an effect. In 2010, an estimated 78 percent of all emails sent were spam. In 2014, 64 percent of all emails sent were spam, according to Symantec, with over half consisting of sex and dating topics and nearly 40 percent on pharmaceutical topics. Because of improved antispam technology, most spam gets blocked before reaching our inboxes. Spain is the number-one source of sent spam, followed by the United States, the previous spam leader, according to Symantec.

listservs

Automated mailing-list administrators that allow for easy subscription, cancellation, and delivery of emails to subscribers.

spam

Unwanted mass emailing from advertisers.

Although spam remains a problem, clogging inboxes and costing companies millions of dollars, antispam technologies and laws have reduced the amount of spam in recent years.

DISCUSSION BOARDS AND WEB FORUMS

Today, most online discussions boards are on Web-based forums that provide a variety of user-friendly tools to create and post discussions. Users can easily follow conversational threads on different topics or search for archived material. The precursor to Web forums was **Usenet**, created in 1979, which even today provides thousands of discussion boards, each separated by categories called newsgroups. Members of Usenet, the first file-sharing service, posted files to a newsgroup to share with subscribers, group members who could then download and save the files on their computers.

Usenet has decreased in popularity, especially with the rise of the Web and the association of the service with pornographers, who used it to send large files. Several Internet service providers (ISPs) either have blocked Usenet servers entirely or allow access only to certain newsgroups within the major categories. Despite its decline in popularity, Usenet presaged many of the principles seen today in social media, including decentralized servers, encouraging communication between users, and enabling users to find others with similar interests in niche categories.

Discussion boards are a vital form of mass communication on the Internet. Their format and asynchronous nature (i.e., not requiring users to be online at the same time) allow for relatively lengthy expositions on topics written whenever convenient for the person sending the message. They also provide value even to members who do not post messages but simply read what others are writing, a practice called **lurking**. Some discussion-board creators encourage newcomers to lurk for a while to become familiar with the tone and type of topics before posting messages of their own.

Because public discussion boards are easily searchable on the Web, they provide useful information on a range of specialized topics. People with similar questions can find helpful advice on any number of issues long after the initial discussions take place. One of the earliest online communities, created through discussion groups, is still thriving today. The WELL (Whole Earth 'Lectronic Link) began in 1985 and continues to promote high-quality and interesting discussions among its members, many of whom are noted intellectuals, artists, authors, and creative thinkers. The WELL's policy of requiring real names rather than user names has, according to some, enhanced discussion and fostered a strong sense of community among its members. Now owned by the Salon Media Group, publisher of *Salon* magazine, it charges members $15 a month, one of the few online communities that has successfully charged members simply for discussions.

CHAT ROOMS

Like discussion groups, chat rooms are usually divided by topic, ranging from highly technical computer issues to pop stars to sex. Chat rooms differ from **instant messaging**, which also takes place in real time, in that instant messaging usually involves an online conversation between two people or a few at most.

Because chat rooms are synchronous, occurring in real time, media organizations can use them to promote special guests online and let the audience "speak" to them, much like a radio station having a musician visit and take listeners' calls.

Chat rooms are not without their own unique communication problems. They can often be chaotic, much like trying to talk to someone across the room at a crowded, noisy party. It can be difficult to tell who is being addressed, although some chat rooms have general rules and guidelines posted for proper behavior. Although messages may be sent in real time, the fact that they must be typed inevitably slows down the give-and-take that occurs during spoken conversations. Some chatters can monopolize the conversation as well or repeatedly post the

Usenet
One of the earliest discussion forums in use today in which participants discuss topics in categories called newsgroups.

lurking
Only reading what others write in online discussion boards but not contributing to the discussions.

instant messaging
Often abbreviated IM, a form of real-time communication through text typed over a computer network.

scrolling

Simply repeating the same message in a chat room, which quickly draws the ire of other participants.

blog

Short for weblog, a type of website in which a person posts regular journal or diary entries, with the posts arranged chronologically.

same message, a practice called **scrolling**, which quickly draws the ire of other chatters in the room.

The video instant messaging service Snapchat, launched in 2011, has become very popular, with an estimated 700 million videos and photos sent each day, according to Snapchat. The unique characteristic of Snapchat is the automatic deletion of photos and videos after recipient viewing.

BLOGS AND MICROBLOGS

Blogs, or weblogs, are an individual's web pages of short, frequently updated postings arranged chronologically, much like a series of diary entries or journal pages. Blogs can contain thoughts, links to sites of interest, rants, or whatever the blogger wants to write about. The earliest blogs go back to 1994, although technological limitations made it more cumbersome to update posts then.

The role that technology plays in social media is clearly evident with the rise of blogs. Not until 1999 did blogs start increasing in popularity, largely due to new software tools that made blogging easier and did not require knowledge of HTML code or programming. Blogger.com, created in 1999 and bought by Google in 2003, is one such tool that makes creating, posting, and sharing a blog easy even for nontechnical people. WordPress is another very popular blogging platform that offers free blog hosting.

Some blogs, such as *BoingBoing* and the *Huffington Post*, have readerships in the millions and an influential agenda-setting function much like mainstream media. When a blog becomes popular and attracts many readers, responding to most of the comments or discussions becomes impossible for the blogger. In this way, blogs tend to develop the characteristics of traditional broadcasting or publishing models of information or news.

David Karp founded the popular microblog site Tumblr, which has surpassed WordPress in popularity and was purchased by Yahoo in 2013.

News organizations were slow to adopt blogs as part of their media offerings, seeing them as a threat or something that might detract from their credibility. In 2002, Steve Olafson, a longtime journalist for the *Houston Chronicle*, was fired for having a pseudonymous blog in which he criticized local politicians. Today, many big news organizations operate blogs and expect their reporters or columnists to blog regularly.

Although the blog's element of authenticity is vital to conversation or true dialog, its raw, honest, and unfiltered quality often becomes problematic in the business world. Excessively polished blogs or those that simply repeat public relations platitudes are unlikely to generate respect or develop a following. Adopting a more natural, conversational tone with the public and responding to their comments have been difficult for companies accustomed to carefully controlling their public messages.

Blogs have also moved from their text roots to include video, audio, and multimedia, an example of how users are creating content by mixing and matching different media types to make something new. Blogs also play an important curatorial role, as some become popular because the blogger finds the best and most compelling ideas and makes relevant comments about that content, which helps the blog's readers find information of interest to them and to understand it within a larger context.

As their name suggests, microblogs work much the same way as blogs, but the format and technology encourage shorter posts and content. Today, perhaps the most popular microblog is Twitter, which allows only 140 characters to be sent at a time, or tweeted. Launched in July 2006, Twitter has 302 million active users with 500 million tweets sent per day.[9] Many people have started using Twitter as a kind of curatorial news service, following people who tend to find new or interesting stories.

Some studies have shown that only about 10 percent of Twitter users contribute over 90 percent of the content.[10] That a relatively small percentage of people contribute a disproportionate amount of content is important to remember when considering how media-usage habits are changing. Just because the audience can now create and distribute content easily does not mean everyone will—the vast majority of people seem perfectly happy as consumers of media content.

Tumblr, another popular microblogging service, allows for easy uploads of text and multimedia content. Founded in 2007, the name derives from "tumblelogs," the original term used for microblogs before the latter name became more widely used. In May 2013, Yahoo bought Tumblr for $1.1 billion; in May 2015, Tumblr hosted over 237 million blogs and over 111 billion posts, surpassing popular blogging platform WordPress.[11]

Chinese microblogging site Sina Weibo ("weibo" means microblog in Chinese), founded in 2009, has been likened to a Chinese version of Twitter, even though it functions more like a Twitter/Facebook hybrid. Although still popular, with over 500 million users, it has suffered because of competition from free messaging and voicemail service WeChat, launched in 2011, which quickly gained nearly 300 million users and continues to rise in popularity.[12]

Many of the most popular social-networking sites offer microblogging services as well, although these are often called something like "status updates." Regardless of the name used, updating friends in your social network while out and about is essentially a type of microblogging.

WIKIS

Wikis have become more widely known, thanks to the phenomenal success of Wikipedia, the collaborative encyclopedia created entirely by volunteers that quickly came to rival the scope and accuracy of established encyclopedias. Like most of today's social media tools, the roots of wikis go back much further. A **wiki**, which means "quick" or "speedy" in Hawaiian, is essentially a web page that anyone can edit. In 1994, Ward Cunningham created the first wiki, WikiWikiWeb, designed for easy sharing of information among computer programmers. He took his wiki public in 1995 and asked developers to improve on it.

In 2001, Wikipedia used a version of a wiki system for its new encyclopedia that encouraged anyone to contribute and edit. This was a drastic change from traditional encyclopedias, the epitome of the gatekeeper media model of authoritative, unidirectional communication to a silent and passive audience.

Today, a variety of wikis are used for different purposes, especially in education. Corporate wikis encourage knowledge sharing among groups, especially when offices are far apart. One important aspect of wikis is the ability to see the

WIKIPEDIA
The Free Encyclopedia

Wikipedia is an excellent example of what can be created online by many people collaborating for free.

wiki

Website that lets anyone add, edit, or delete pages and content.

MEDIA PIONEERS
Jack Dorsey

A century and a half after Samuel Morse's initial telegraph transmission—What hath God wrought?—Twitter and its 30-year-old creator, Jack Dorsey, would tweet "just setting up my twttr" "inviting coworkers." And thus a radical one-to-many communication medium was launched that would crisscross the globe in ways the one-to-one telegraph system never could, yet in a similarly concise textual form. Almost as fast as you could tweet "The Next Big Thing," Twitter was it. Social media quickly embraced downsized expression of 140 characters or less, immediate and entertaining status updates from close friends and distant celebrities, as well as more serious broadcasts from journalists, politicians, activists, and even revolutionaries.

Elegantly simplified responses to complex problems characterize Dorsey's pioneering achievements. When, for example, an artisan friend lost a $2,000 sale because his small business could not justify the costs associated with credit card transactions, Dorsey conceived of and created a tiny card swipe reader that could plug into an iPhone or iPad, instantly making any small operation capable of meeting the costs of handling such sales. This concept and device formed the basis for Square, his foray into the world of seamless retail transactions.

Dorsey, described by one colleague as "a first-rate strategist, a first-rate designer, and a first-rate technologist"[13] and by another as "a technologist with the soul of an artist,"[14] is a dynamic entrepreneur with a holistic concern for his staff and for society. Operating in downtown San Francisco, he has led coworkers on excursions through the city during the day. Not merely a stroll by places of interest, these Friday outings became a commitment to cleaner streets, a project announced in this tweet from Jack: "Tomorrow morning at 11a Pacific we're going out & picking up trash for 30 minutes. Join us (equipment provided): 5th & Natoma. #cleanstreets."[15]

Dorsey's efforts to make our public communication more democratic, our business transactions more efficient, and our world cleaner will no doubt extend beyond his enterprises with Twitter and Square. In 2013, he joined the board of directors for the Walt Disney Company, and he has also expressed a desire to be mayor of New York City someday.

editing history of any particular page and to revert to an earlier version if needed. This function keeps an automatic archive of editing changes identifiable by users. In combination with discussion or talk pages associated with each article, it provides a ready way for participants to discuss and debate points.

What would seem like a major weakness of wikis—the freedom for anyone to change any content on a page at any time—has actually turned out to be their strength. Low barriers to creating content or adding special expertise a user may have make participation easy. Although not without its share of trolls, people who purposely vandalize Wikipedia entries by inserting false or nonsensical information, the Wikipedia community has shown a remarkable ability to police the vast and growing content on the site. Wikipedia has been able to avoid major disruptions of vandals, thanks partly to technology but mostly to the norms and rules the Wikipedia community has created over time, an example par excellence of how collaborative work and social media transform media audiences and operate on principles different from traditional media economic models.

Nevertheless, Wikipedia has had growth pains. In August 2009, it announced the need for more restrictive editing rules and page "lock" or "protect" to prevent further editing, a move away from its original freewheeling days. Even earlier, Wikipedia had blocked any changes from ISPs originating from either house of Congress because politicians' aides were continually changing politicians' entries to make them look better, breaking the Wikipedia community norm of neutral point of view (NPOV).

SOCIAL-NETWORKING SITES

The various social-networking sites have become perhaps the most visible face of social media. What distinguishes these sites from other types of social media is that in some manner they show users connections in their social network.[16] The ability to visualize and share one's social network while allowing others to tap into that map by contacting other people in the network has become an incredibly powerful tool.

Although today Facebook or LinkedIn seem to get all the attention, the first social-networking sites were actually created several years before, and some are still around. Classmates.com, founded in 1995, and SixDegrees, starting in 1997 and closing in 2001, are two early examples of social-networking sites. Classmates.com, as its name suggests, focuses primarily on putting people back in touch with former classmates from college, high school, or even grade school.

Reconnecting with old friends or creating friendships has proven to be a powerful force for establishing social-networking sites. Friendster, launched in 2002, was the first social-networking site with features similar to those of Facebook and LinkedIn. With the rise of MySpace and, later, Facebook, the popularity of Friendster rapidly waned in the United States but remained strong in Asia. Relaunched as a social-gaming website under new ownership in 2011, Friendster is still popular in some Southeast Asian countries.

The case of MySpace shows just how chaotic the business of social-networking sites can be and how easy it is to lose the trust of users when not considering the audience. Launched in 2003, MySpace became the most popular social-networking

Forbes ranked the cofounder, chairman, and CEO of Facebook number 16 on their 2015 list of billionaires. Mark Zuckerburg's net worth at that time was $35.4 billion.

site in 2006, only to lose that position in 2008 to Facebook. In 2005, News Corp. purchased MySpace and its parent company, Intermix Media, for $580 million. In June 2011, News Corp. sold MySpace for $35 million—a fraction of its original value—to Justin Timberlake and Specific Media, an advertising network. In mid-June 2013, MySpace launched a new version of the site, deleting without warning all the material users had on the old version of MySpace. This raised a huge outcry among users, many of whom had lost years of messages with past loved ones, blog entries, and games that they had purchased on the site.

In late 2003, Facebook began as a project within Harvard University called Face-mash, a version of the website Hot or Not. It launched as a social-networking site under its current name but available only to Harvard students in early 2004. A few months later it opened to other Ivy League schools and then expanded to include all college students. The next year, it accepted high school students and then companies; and in 2006, it opened to anyone thirteen or older, rapidly over-taking MySpace as the most popular social-networking site thanks to these

TIMELINE   SOCIAL-NETWORKING SITES

1995
Classmates.com launches to help users find friends from school, work, and the military.

1997
A social circles network, SixDegrees opens but closes four years later.

1999
AsianAvenue and BlackPlanet are created to target specific communities.

2002
Originally conceived as a social networking site, once-popular Friendster becomes a social gaming platform in 2011 after experiencing a decline in most markets. Created in Malaysia, it remains popular in Southeast Asia.

:::myspace

2003
Networking continues to specialize with the launch of LinkedIn (a professional site), Couchsurfing (a hospitality exchange site), and MySpace (a social site focused on music). Friendster turns down a $30 million buyout offer from Google, considered one of the biggest blunders in Silicon Valley.

2004
Facebook is created for Harvard students. Animal-themed Dogster and Catster become available. Orkut, owned and operated by Google, opens but closes ten years later. Image and video hosts Flickr and Vimeo launch.

You Tube

2005
YouTube enters the video-sharing competition. Ning is founded, allowing users to create custom social networks. Facebook expands to include high school networks. News Corp. buys MySpace, a hugely popular site with young people, for $580 million.

2006
Text-based Twitter launches. Facebook opens to corporate networks in early 2006 and to everyone late in the year. Google buys YouTube for $1.65 billion.

1995

expansions. By March 2015, Facebook claimed to have 1.44 billion active monthly users worldwide, which makes it the largest social-networking site in the world.

Facebook's rapid rise in popularity led to frequent media reports of potential buyouts from larger media companies, such as Microsoft. Despite these reports, Facebook launched its initial public offering (IPO) in May 2012, the largest in Internet history, valued at its peak at $104 billion.

Although Facebook remains the most popular social-networking site, two different reports in 2014 caused some alarm at Facebook and among investors. Both reports stated that fewer teens were using Facebook than in previous years, down to 88 percent in 2014 from 95 percent in 2012.[17] Most companies would not worry about such a small dip, especially with so many users, but some wonder if the decline could be the beginning of a long-term trend in which the coveted teen market moves elsewhere for their social-networking needs.

The launch of Google+ in June 2011 was Google's effort to compete with Facebook. Despite Google's dominance as a search engine and its growing number

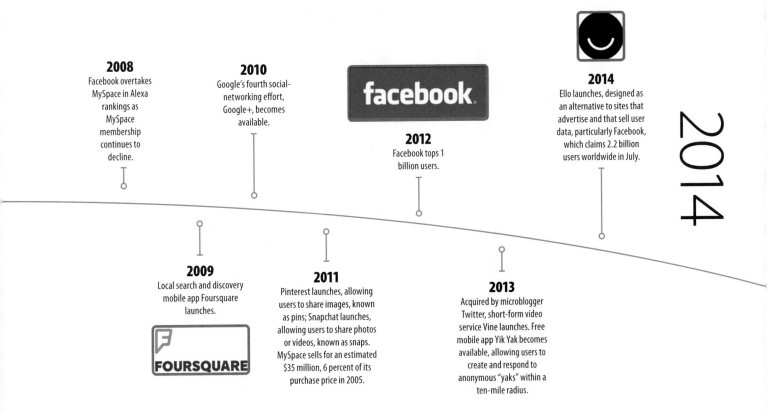

2008
Facebook overtakes MySpace in Alexa rankings as MySpace membership continues to decline.

2010
Google's fourth social-networking effort, Google+, becomes available.

2012
Facebook tops 1 billion users.

2014
Ello launches, designed as an alternative to sites that advertise and that sell user data, particularly Facebook, which claims 2.2 billion users worldwide in July.

2014

2009
Local search and discovery mobile app Foursquare launches.

2011
Pinterest launches, allowing users to share images, known as pins; Snapchat launches, allowing users to share photos or videos, known as snaps. MySpace sells for an estimated $35 million, 6 percent of its purchase price in 2005.

2013
Acquired by microblogger Twitter, short-form video service Vine launches. Free mobile app Yik Yak becomes available, allowing users to create and respond to anonymous "yaks" within a ten-mile radius.

of online services, Google+ remains far behind in terms of active users, with only about 9 percent of Google+'s 2.2 billion profiles having posted anything on Google+, according to one analyst.[18]

Many other social-networking sites have sprung up since 2003, some focusing on professional interests, such as LinkedIn; topic interests, such as Dogster; media or image sharing, such as Pinterest, Flickr, and Instagram; and location-based interests, such as Foursquare and Loopt. Launched in late 2014 with ninety people on its network, Ello, whose manifesto promises never to sell advertising or user data, claimed less than a year later to have millions of followers. Some have described Ello as the anti-Facebook, a moniker supported by the defection of many

TABLE 7-1 Most Popular Social-Networking Sites*

RANK	SITE	UNIQUE VISITORS
1	facebook	900,000,000
2	Twitter	310,000,000
3	LinkedIn	255,000,000
4	Pinterest	250,000,000
5	Google+	120,000,000
6	tumblr.	110,000,000
7	Instagram	100,000,000
8	VK	80,000,000
9	flickr	65,000,000
10	Vine	42,000,000

Source: *eBizMBA*, http://www.ebizmba.com/articles/social-networking-websites.
*As of May 1, 2015

CONVERGENCE CULTURE
Are We Really Separated by Six Degrees?

We've all met someone with whom we realized we share a coincidental mutual friend or a similar experience, such as attending the same school or belonging to the same fraternity or sorority. For scientists who study social networks, these amazing coincidences are precisely what make social networks important.

The number and type of our social connections can greatly affect our opportunities in life. If we have a robust social network of people who likewise have robust social networks (not identical to ours), then we are better able reach people in those other networks through our friends. For example, if I want a publisher to consider my novel, knowing an editor at the publishing house who can recommend the manuscript may help it get serious attention.

A popular pop-culture theory claims that everybody in the world is connected by no more than six degrees, or six links in a network. The number of connections or links between you and the U.S. president is theoretically no more than six. The notion that everyone in the world is separated by no more than six degrees gained public attention through a "small world" experiment conducted by psychologist Stanley Milgram in the 1950s. Milgram sent copies of letters to people in the Midwest and asked them to send the letter to the person they thought would most likely be able to forward it to a certain lawyer living in Boston. Out of the forty-two letters that reached the lawyer's home, the average number of links was nearly six, although the range was quite large.

Although Milgram never used the term "**six degrees of separation**," it was popularized in a 1984 play of the same name that also referenced his experiment. The notion became even more widespread with "Six Degrees of Kevin Bacon," a game that calculates the degrees of separation of various actors from Kevin Bacon. This can easily be done through the Oracle of Kevin Bacon website, which uses the Internet Movie Database as its source.

Surprisingly, even long-dead actors are connected with Kevin Bacon or with famous people who are not professional actors but who have appeared in documentaries or movies. This makes sense if you consider the actors gathered on a movie set as a **small world**, a social network of tight connections, people who get to know one another while filming and then get to know a large number of other actors, who then go on to make other movies with different actors.

Although finding an actor or actress separated from Bacon by more than even five degrees is difficult, he is actually not the most connected Hollywood actor. Both John Carradine and Robert Mitchum had far more connections than Bacon. If you know someone listed in the Internet Movie Database, then you can see that person's Bacon number and simply add one more (your link to that person) to see how closely connected you are to Kevin Bacon.

---

members of the LGBT community from FB to Ello due to safety concerns about Facebook's requirement for real names on user profiles.

In addition to seeking out social news about friends on these networking sites, many seek out local and world news about events and issues. According to a 2014 Pew study, social media are reshaping news, especially on Facebook, a pathway to news for 30 percent of the general population, most commonly about entertainment. Sixty-two percent of Reddit users get news from the site, yet this translates to only 2 percent of the general population. (See Figure 7-1.) Users are less likely, though, to follow current events as they unfold on Facebook, unlike Twitter, where many turn for breaking news.

six degrees of separation

Notion that everyone in the world is separated from all other individuals by at most six additional nodes in a social network.

small world

Tight-knit social network with many strong ties.

FIGURE 7-1 Social Media as a Pathway to News: Facebook Leads the Way

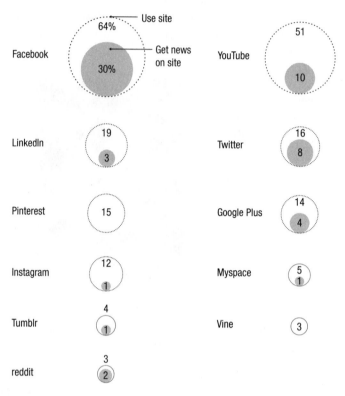

Percent of U.S. adults who use each social networking site and percent of U.S. adults who get news from each social networking site

Note: The percent of U.S. adults who get news on Pinterest and Vine each amount to less than 1 percent.

Aug. 21-Sept. 2, 2013

Source: "News Use Across Social Media Platforms," Pew Research Center, Washington, DC (November, 2013) http://www.pewresearch.org/fact-tank/2014/09/24/how-social-media-is-reshaping-news/

Pew also found that reading news on these sites does not necessarily promote sharing opinions about what was read. A 2014 Pew survey on social media and the spiral of silence, for example, discovered that people were less willing to discuss the NSA-Snowden story on the public forum of social media than in person. If, however, Facebook users felt their followers or online community agreed with their position, they were about twice as likely to join a FB discussion group on the topic.

Producers and Produsers

Throughout most of the twentieth century, media companies used technology to address audiences as masses. How many viewers a television show could boast determined advertising rates. Magazine and newspaper ads were priced according to their circulation. Records and movies were made according to which ones would likely draw the biggest audiences or sales. It didn't matter if most subscribers to a newspaper did not read the whole paper—in fact, there was no way to measure easily whether they even read it; claiming a certain circulation was enough. It was irrelevant if most of a television show's viewing audience went to the refrigerator during commercials.

All this began to change with the Internet and social media. Now companies could track audience behavior with more detail than ever before, all without installing special tracking devices, asking the audience to fill out forms or a keep a diary, or other intrusive measures. They could see what audiences were watching and doing when they interacted with media. Such tracking produced massive amounts of data and raised the problem of how to analyze such large data sets. This growth in **big data** has spawned entirely new businesses to tackle the data, figuring out what is relevant and what is not, and discovering ways to visualize and explain the data so that they can be used.

 big data

A collection of data sets too large for traditional analytic techniques to sort, analyze, and visualize.

What media companies saw when looking at the data did not make them happy. Nor did it make advertisers happy. A website could claim to get 2 million page views a month, but the same technology that let them state that with accuracy also told advertisers that only a fraction of 1 percent of the viewers clicked on their banner ads, and an even tinier portion acted as desired by buying a product from the advertiser's website.

Further, the kind of fragmentation of audiences already seen to some extent with the rise of specialized magazines and cable television channels accelerated with the Internet. Businesses that relied on mass audiences were now able to better watch their audiences, but unfortunately, they were watching those audiences shrink.

Although many more media choices for people caused much of the audience fragmentation, at least part of it was also due to the fact that audience members could now talk to each other and create their own media content. Even worse, they could talk back to traditional media producers in a public forum such as the Web. That might help some shows become hits, but it also meant that negative sentiment from the public could keep potential viewers away.

If audiences were active, then advertisers wanted to see the audience actually do something useful for them, like buying their products or at least visiting their websites or registering to get email newsletters. New technologies enabled companies to track and record all these kinds of activities, but they also created a need for new kinds of measurement metrics that could capture the dynamics of audience interaction more accurately.

As discussed in Chapter 1, some of the biggest changes taking place among the three types of convergence have to do with how media are being used differently and the implications for media-company business models that assumed a passive audience. Traditional audiences were seen largely as passive consumers by the mass-media companies that created content to sell to them. The audience might consume media in the form of programs, books, or music, or buy products advertised through various media channels.

Of course, people were not as passive as that relationship would indicate; but until the Internet, and especially social media, the chances for people to choose, create, and "talk back" to producers were extremely limited. Now, however, people have the tools to talk back, and many are doing so. What's more, they are not only

Media scholar Axel Bruns uses the term "produsers" to describe today's audiences as both consumers and producers of media content.

produsers

Audiences who no longer are simply consumers but also produce content.

talking back but simply ignoring the traditional producers and talking to each other. Audiences are shifting from simply being consumers of media content to what media scholar Axel Bruns calls **produsers**,[19] although others use the term "prosumers" or just "users."

This complex relationship dynamic is not easily defined. "Prosumer" still seems to emphasize consumption, almost like a professional consumer or kind of über-consumer. Similarly, "user" does not capture the sense of creation or production, an important element of the social media landscape.

Consumption in one form or another still predominates. Not everyone is (or wants to be) a producer of media content. But to contribute to the larger conversations taking place—to add something, however small, that helps create a greater whole—is easier than ever before. Posting a link to a worthwhile website or blog that others on a discussion board may have never heard of is a form of media production, collaboration, and knowledge sharing that should not be downplayed as nonproductive or unimportant, especially on a large scale.

Furthermore, people do not have to contribute to feel like they are part of a community; it may be enough for many to see that others feel the way they do, connecting them to something larger. We see this sense of activism and community in some of the mass protests that have taken place, especially in countries such as Egypt during the Arab Spring. Social media help people realize there are others—sometimes many others—who share their thoughts and feelings while providing informal media channels to express views publicly and to organize actions.

REPUTATION, RATINGS, AND TRUST

The change in audiences from consumers to produsers has had a powerful ripple effect, not only on business models but on many social factors. In the traditional-media world, we could rely on certain established brands to give us certain things. The *Wall Street Journal* or the *New York Times* delivered a kind of content that the *National Enquirer* did not, and we learned what to expect.

Today, that has changed. Although the traditional brands still (for the most part) retain their meanings for us, it is more difficult than ever to determine whether to trust information from unknown sources. How do we know that the Amazon book review we are considering was not written by someone paid for a glowing assessment or by the author's mother? How do we know that a Wikipedia entry about a prominent figure was not posted by some avid fan, highlighting only positive information and ignoring past scandals? How do we know that the blog about childhood diabetes is not the work of a pharmaceutical company trying to promote their drug?

These and other issues are all extremely important in today's media world; hence the importance of critical thinking and media literacy. Issues of trust and reputation become vital in figuring out what information we can believe. Ratings systems that rank the usefulness of a review or comment help us make that decision. But the question also arises whether the raters are trustworthy or not. This is where social networks can be useful, for we generally trust friends or people we have let into our social networks and are more likely to listen to what they say or recommend. This is one reason **word-of-mouth marketing** (or buzz marketing) has become so important for advertisers. Ratings systems as a measure of gauging trust will develop and become more important in our social media landscape, but some thorny ethical and legal questions have arisen as well.

One big legal concern is figuring out who owns user-generated content on social media sites. If someone decides to write a book based on discussions taken from a site such as The WELL, using extended passages of actual discussions, is this a breach of copyright? How should the poster be compensated, if at all? Is permission needed to use the post or an excerpt of it? If so, how much is fair use and how much is an infringement of intellectual property? These are just some of the issues that social media sites will have to wrestle with in the future.

word-of-mouth marketing

Marketing that takes place among customers through discussions with one another.

> **DISCUSSION QUESTIONS:** What policies should be adopted regarding content on discussion forums? Should the people who post own the content they have posted, or should the site hosting the content own it—or should it be there for the taking by anyone? Explain your reasoning and identify who should be responsible for content that is libelous or potentially harmful.

PRIVACY

Norms for privacy are also changing. For many people older than Millennials, making so much of one's life public through posting photos, discussing one's thoughts or desires on a blog, or sharing other highly personal information online feels strange. There is a sense that much of that is nobody else's business or that information should be shared only with a select group of people one knows and trusts.

This "living publicly" generally does not seem to bother Millennials, yet many feel their privacy has been invaded when they learn that an employer is raising questions about material found on a social-networking site. Most employers today do Google searches of job applicants and examine social-networking profiles if they can, making decisions about who will be called for an interview accordingly. Some potential employers even insist on access to applicants' Facebook profiles. The goofy profile picture of you partying at your college may be hilarious to your friends on Facebook but not so amusing to a potential employer trying to gauge how you may represent the company.

Facebook has landed in hot water frequently over its policies that invade users' privacy or that threaten to do so. In 2012 Facebook revealed that more than 83 million of their accounts might be fake, news that apparently caused company stock to drop to new lows. In an effort to address this security issue (and presumably any attendant financial fallout), Facebook later began enforcing its policy of real names for user profiles to promote identity "authenticity," deactivating accounts with names they deemed fake. Unfortunately, this did not make the FB community safer for all its members. To the contrary, this move heightened the dangers for individuals in certain vulnerable or at-risk groups who rely on anonymity for security, most notably the LGBT community and survivors of domestic abuse. Some Native Americans argued this policy has also hurt them, resulting in the deactivation of accounts with real or legal names that did not appear to meet Facebook standards.

A program launched in 2010 called Instant Personalization allows sites such as Yelp, Pandora, and Microsoft Docs to access what Facebook defines as public information (your name, your picture, your gender, your location, your friends, and all your likes) unless you opt out of it. However, even if you do opt out, if a friend has not opted out, then these sites may still access your information through the friend. Pandora uses the information on music likes, for example, to recommend songs to you based on genre similarities. Although some people may like this easy personalization, others see it as an invasion of privacy.

In 2012, Facebook paid a $20 million settlement in a class action lawsuit for using users' Likes in their Sponsored Stories features without first getting their permission. The settlement affected 125 million Facebook users. Facebook was also threatened with a lawsuit for putting users' photos in ads without permission. In 2014, Facebook made it easier to change its notoriously confusing privacy settings and made some minor moves toward improving users' privacy.

There are many temptations for companies such as Facebook and Zynga, the maker of FarmVille (which tracked Facebook users even when they left Facebook, before the relationship between Facebook and FarmVille ended), to invade users' privacy by tracking their online behavior. The data collected are immensely valuable to marketers trying to figure out how best to tap certain markets—especially the lucrative eighteen-to-thirty-four demographic. For many companies, the wealth of data on user behavior they can obtain—and sell—is simply too great to resist, even if it is an invasion of privacy. Facebook jealously guards the data it collects on its members, working out deals with advertisers to provide them with the kind of information they want.

The online advertising industry has been promoting a "do not track" option for users, which would let users state they do not want their online interactions tracked by advertisers. However, while the industry claims to promote such a system, they are also attempting to make the option nonbinding and therefore essentially ineffective.

Companies that are bought by other companies or that go out of business have databases of registered users and online activity that could provide very valuable information. When users registered with a site, however, they likely did not consider that their personal data and on-site behavior might at some point end up in the hands of a different company with less stringent privacy policies.

Now that anybody can essentially be a publisher with her or his own website, private individuals can more easily and unwillingly be thrust into the public eye. With the ubiquity of camera phones and small video cameras, revenge porn, in which former partners post nude or sexually explicit photos of their exes, has been a growing problem. Although still not illegal in many states, twenty-seven states have either passed or introduced laws making revenge porn illegal; and some members of Congress have promised to write a bill to make it illegal nationwide.

What ethical principles should media companies and the general public follow in deciding whether to post or publish material? Companies often have professional codes of conduct or codes of ethics, but no such general code yet exists for the public publishing content. Journalists often cite the public's "right to know" as a guiding principle when weighing ethical issues regarding publishing a story damaging to someone. Yet it is hard to say that the right to know outweighs someone's right to privacy when publishing a nude picture of an ex-girlfriend or when making defamatory claims about someone on a blog. The law tends to protect social-networking sites and websites, not holding them liable for what members post on the sites, which gives the sites little incentive to police their content.

Despite the valid concerns raised about privacy here, we can see that anonymity can be even more damaging in some cases. The Yik Yak app lets people post comments anonymously within a ten-mile radius. Yik Yak has caused problems at universities, as students have been victimized by vicious comments, and some students have used it to share test answers with other sections.

> **DISCUSSION QUESTIONS:** Consider your own time spent on Facebook. Have you found yourself using it less than you used to? Why? What are you using to stay connected instead of Facebook?

TRANSPARENCY

Even supposedly tech-savvy companies leading the social media revolution seem regularly to make blunders similar to traditional-media companies regarding the new audience dynamics, as the Facebook Sponsored Stories example shows. Companies creating faux viral videos or fake grassroots blogs, a practice called **astroturfing**, are often punished in the court of public opinion once their machinations are exposed. Sudden shifts in privacy policies, either unannounced or announced inadequately, have produced similar audience backlash.

💬 **astroturfing**

Creating a movement controlled by a large organization or group designed to look like a citizen-founded, grassroots campaign.

Facebook learned this the hard way in early 2009 when a change in their privacy policy, which had been made a few weeks earlier but went unnoticed by the general public, stated that Facebook would own the rights to user-generated content on the site, including posted photos. Publicized by a consumer interest group, the change elicited immediate and immense outrage, including a threat by the Electronic Privacy Information Center (EPIC) to file a complaint with the FTC.

Facebook quickly reversed the policy and created a group of users to discuss future privacy-policy changes—apparently to little avail, given their subsequent privacy problems just a few years later. Other companies should note these actions and reactions, emblematic of the shifting power dynamic between companies and the public. It would have been far better had Facebook created such a group in the first place rather than only after receiving complaints. Further, Facebook's own customers used the very tools that helped make Facebook so popular to organize against the company.

The need for transparency is becoming increasingly important with social media—a fact that individuals and organizations forget or ignore at their peril. Yet transparency often undermines corporate strategy making and

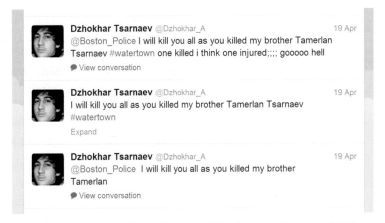

During the manhunt that followed the Boston Marathon bombings in April 2013, someone created a fake Twitter account for the suspect Dzhokhar Tsarnaev. The account posted threatening messages to the police. It was exposed as fake, but not before being retweeted, picked up by police scanners, and reported on by the media. Such fakes can cause harm by diverting police attention and resources during a crisis.

planning because companies do not want to reveal secrets to competitors. Even when business strategy is not involved, what seems like harmless jokes sent by email between colleagues can damage reputations and brands if those emails appear on the Web.

Fake Twitter accounts can be quite funny, but they have also caused a great deal of confusion when it becomes unclear if an account is fake or not. Phweeters (phony tweeters) have also crossed the lines of good taste when falsely reporting deaths, such as in 2009 when someone faked a journalist's Twitter account and reported the death of Cincinnati Bengals wide receiver Chris Henry twelve hours before he actually died after falling off a truck. Some news organizations picked up the tweet and reported it as news without first checking the validity of the account.

On July 4, 2011, Fox News claimed its Twitter account had been hacked when a tweet falsely reported that President Obama had been assassinated. A little over a month earlier, Representative Anthony Weiner (D-NY) claimed that his Twitter account had been hacked when one of his followers received lewd pictures of a man in boxer shorts. In Weiner's case, however, it turned out that he had actually been taking indecent pictures of himself and sending them to some followers he was flirting with online. The subsequent scandal forced Weiner, who is married, to resign.

Transparency is starting to be built into some ratings and review systems. Reviewers can state how long they have had a product, for example, which helps readers gauge if the glowing review is about a product just out of the box or one that has been used for a while.

The balancing act between privacy, transparency, and mining the rich databases of compiled data from user interactions will continue to affect social-networking sites. As a struggle about the rights of consumers versus business interests, it raises this question: Who will watch the watchers? As we will see next, that is not the only struggle we face in a social media world.

Social Media: The Good, the Bad, and the Ugly

Every new medium has its share of detractors, and the complaints over the ages are surprisingly similar. Real or perceived damage to youth ethics, attitudes, and beliefs is one typical complaint, as is how the new media make us dumber. The Internet and social media have not been immune to this, nor have other digital media, such as video games.

ARE SOCIAL MEDIA MAKING US LESS SOCIAL?

In this book, we have discussed various ways that people have been able to become more involved in media production and collaborate with each other on any number of issues, ranging from traditional politics to social activism. However, a deeper consideration of how we use social media raises questions. Are all your "friends" on Facebook really your friends? How do you differentiate between Facebook "friends" and friends you actually regularly see or talk to? Using the term "friend" to refer to people one has never talked to directly or met face to face stretches the definition of the word and can produce problems.

Consider what happens when friendship becomes romance online. In January 2013, the website Deadspin broke a story that tarnished not only mainstream sports news organizations but the reputation of one of college football's biggest stars. Notre Dame linebacker Manti Te'o was a media darling throughout the 2012 college football season, especially with his heartbreaking story about his girlfriend getting injured in a car accident and then later dying of cancer.

The only trouble was, there was no girlfriend. It was all an elaborate hoax played on Te'o, although when exactly he learned of the hoax and how long he kept silent about it remain open questions. The mainstream sports news journalists, perhaps to cover their own embarrassment at not doing adequate research, accused him of concocting the story to win sympathy. It seemed to defy belief that someone could claim a person was a girlfriend when their only communication was online.

By expanding our ability to communicate and be social even when not actually present, social media have made developing and maintaining relationships more complex, especially romantic relationships. The issue has entered pop culture, as seen by MTV's show *Catfish*. The show arranges meetings between people in relationships who have communicated only online. A **catfish** is someone who fakes an online profile, usually to get someone else to fall in love with the fake persona.

 catfish

Someone who fakes an online profile, usually to encourage another to fall in love with the false persona.

 ETHICS IN MEDIA

Cyberbullying: New Twists on an Old Problem

Bullying is, unfortunately, not a new problem, and it is hard to prove that the rise in popularity of social media has increased its frequency. What these communication tools have done, however, is make bullying more public and reduce bullies' inhibitions by offering anonymity. At the same time, social media have increased public awareness of how widespread bullying actually is and how damaging it can be to a young person's self-esteem.

Hurtful words formerly spoken in a school hallway can now be written down and posted on social networks, encouraging other nasty comments, as this story from a 12-year-old Colorado girl demonstrates:

> I posted a picture of myself on Instagram and people started commenting these awful things like "Eww ur so ugly" "Why don't you go kill urslef everyone would be happier that way" And I KNOW these people … they go to my school. I cried for a good 2 hours. But this wasn't the first time this has happened on all my pictures at least 3 people say something like that. I'm never going on Instagram again. I wish I could disappear so I don't I have to go to school.[20]

Many stories are similarly heartbreaking. Secrets can be exposed and broadcast to hundreds of peers in an online social network rather than simply whispered to a few close friends. Other types of cyberbullying are more subtle. Sending frequent text messages or making repeated phone calls is a type of harassment every bit as damaging and anxiety producing as more blatant forms of bullying.

Some teens have killed themselves after being bullied on social media. Education experts understand that social media are not causing the bullying, but they are giving teens and others a much wider platform to show the worst sides of human nature as they struggle with forming their identities, building relationships, and learning to communicate in the modern world.

The MTV reality show *Catfish* helps people in online relationships find out if their partner is who he or she claims to be.

Scholars have recently asked hard questions about how we actually use social media. For example, a 2011 study looked at how college students defined the term "hooking up" and found no consensus among students as to what it meant, other than it involved some sort of face-to-face, as opposed to exclusively online, encounter.[21] Hooking up could mean everything from simply meeting for drinks or dinner to kissing to intercourse. What's more, the ambiguity of the term was thought to preserve some sense of privacy that helped give women the same kinds of power that men normally enjoy in our society.

In her book *Alone Together: Why We Expect More from Technology and Less from Each Other*, MIT Professor Sherry Turkle examines how in many ways technology has separated us from one another. It gives us the illusion of greater connections and communication but actually makes us emotionally lazy and able to disengage from relationships easily. According to Turkle, young people are not the only ones to blame. Parents may send harmful social signals to their children by being physically but not emotionally present as they continually check their mobile phones and respond to texts or messages. In 2012, one company executive, tired of the barrage of emails, banned all internal emails for one week, forcing people either to meet face to face or to phone each other. He noted that he was better able to focus on big projects without the constant, distracting interruption of email.[22]

A Pew Research Center study in 2014 revealed that 67 percent of Internet users in the United States say that online communications with family and friends have strengthened their relations, with only 18 percent saying it has weakened them. Whether this is actually the case, or a matter of self-delusion along the lines of what Turkle has found, continues to be a matter of great debate.

DISCUSSION QUESTIONS: Download an app like Checky, which counts how many times you check your phone or tablet a day, and compare your numbers for the past few days with your classmates. What, if anything, does this tell you about how much you rely on your phone?

ARE SOCIAL MEDIA MAKING US DUMBER?

Scholars have looked at the effect of the Internet and social media on our levels of knowledge and ways of thinking. A growing body of evidence suggests that despite the unprecedented breadth and depth of information available on the Internet, today's young people are more ignorant than ever before about subjects such as politics or history. Many seem to feel that they do not need to remember information because they can always find it online.

In the book *The Dumbest Generation*, Emory University English professor Mark Bauerlein chronicles case after case and numerous studies that indicate American teens and young adults today demonstrate a worrisome lack of intellectual curiosity and a dearth of knowledge about the world in general. They spend much of their time on social media, mostly communicating about mundane issues with each other and making sure they keep their circles of friends. They have far more knowledge of pop culture than of politics, and they see nothing wrong with the belief that pop culture is more important than politics.

Bauerlein states that less than 30 percent could say what Reconstruction was, and in 2008, when the book came out, less than a quarter could identify Dick Cheney, vice president at the time.

While Bauerlein highlights some bleak findings about social media and political apathy, social media has also driven some recent political participation among young voters. As we will see in Chapter 13, Barack Obama's 2008 and 2012 presidential campaigns used social media to build and coordinate a nationwide volunteer network. Strong support among previously unengaged young people played an instrumental role in Obama's victories.

A more significant concern is whether heavy Internet and social media use are physically rewiring our brains and making us think differently. A 2007 UCLA study that examined the cognitive differences between heavy and light multitaskers found that heavy multitaskers—those who typically had multiple web browser tabs open, who frequently checked status updates, and who posted updates themselves—performed more poorly on memory and task tests than the light multitaskers.

Exploring these instances further, subsequent studies supported the early evidence that social media use makes it harder for people to concentrate on longer or more complex tasks and that social media users tend to get distracted more easily by trivial matters and not understand or remember more important material. The "always-on" nature of social media and mobile devices creates anxiety when away from social media and a need to always "be present" by commenting to others when connected.

A 2014 study titled "The Invisible Addiction: Cellphone Activities and Addiction among Male and Female College Students" found that college women reported spending an average of ten hours a day on their cell phones, while college men spend an average of seven and a half hours a day. The most frequent activity is texting, taking nearly 95 minutes a day, followed by emailing at 49 minutes a day and checking Facebook at 39 minutes a day.

The public has a world of information at its fingertips through the Internet, yet ironically, people often squander their greater communicative power on pop culture trivia and an incessant need to keep in contact with others. The discovery of information online does not necessarily equate with the acquisition of knowledge, and in fact, we may express less interest in actual learning because we feel that we can always just look something up.

People who have difficulty focusing their attention and who lack interest in politics may have difficulty acting as informed citizens of a democracy. A perpetually distracted public is easily led—and misled—because people lose the ability to think critically and question (or even recognize) abuses of power.

Growing research shows that heavy social media users are less able to concentrate and tend to get distracted by trivial issues. Yet social media also connect people with the wider world and can enhance self-esteem.

The fact that we may not always use social media wisely does not mean that social media themselves are bad. They can be used to learn more about the world or to improve one's skills, such as with online training and free or low-cost online courses. They can help us socialize, organize, create, and collaborate in ways never before seen, just as they can isolate and alienate if used to excess or inappropriately.

MEDIA CAREERS

With the rise in popularity of social media, companies of all kinds—not just media companies—have realized they too need to be where their customers are. Although companies often continue to see social media as simply another media channel, savvy organizations understand that social media bring their own ways of speaking and acting that differ from traditional media channels in which companies essentially controlled their messages to a largely silent (and presumably passive) audience.

Two new job titles have been created that did not exist several years ago, and the level of confusion as to what each does is emblematic of the ever-changing and chaotic world that is social media. Social media managers are responsible for the brand on social media; they join in social media conversations, respond to comments, create content, and generally act as the brand itself. They are also involved in strategizing and planning for the brand through various social media, whose performance they also analyze.

Community managers, on the other hand, are responsible for advocating for the brand on social media, trying to reach people who are not familiar with it. A community manager develops a persona as an individual, not as the brand itself, and promotes the brand through social media conversations. Much of a community manager's time is spent simply participating in conversations online about the brand and monitoring blogs or other social media sites where the brand is being discussed. Both job types are well suited to graduates in English and communications, given the emphasis on communicating to others in a natural and conversational way.

LOOKING BACK AND MOVING FORWARD

Like much of new media, social media actually have firm roots and influences in many aspects of old media, although in this case the term "old" refers more to the earliest days of PCs and the Internet than to radio, TV, or print media. Even so, the changes that social media have brought in a relatively short time have enduring implications for culture, business, and society that researchers are only beginning to explore.

One of the biggest changes, discussed throughout this book, is the difference in the relationship between media producers and consumers. Even without the large marketing and promotion budgets of major media companies, average people have been able to create content that has been seen, heard, or read by millions or even tens of millions of people worldwide.

Thanks to social-networking sites, the networks formed through online communication have become ever more visible and empowering. Numerous projects have demonstrated what can be accomplished when many work willingly together, efforts that can benefit even greater numbers of people. Wikipedia is one such project.

Perhaps even more significant over the long term, however, is how social media have encouraged people to create and share knowledge structures, not just knowledge. Sometimes-heated discussions in forums expose participants to different viewpoints and attitudes. People in collaborative projects must come to some sort of understanding or agreement, thus modifying what is written to satisfy everyone. Although such exposure may not change our beliefs, it may broaden our perspective and make us more willing to accept other positions.

Curation, such as tagging information or reviewing products or media content, also allows us to share knowledge structures or ways of looking at the world. Providing information about information can reflect worldviews just as accurately as direct comments on a discussion board. A user who tags a photo of fighting in Syria as "genocide" may suddenly see connections to other photos with the same tag and learn of past incidents elsewhere.

Following the actions of many users who are collaborating without even knowing it by using automated systems can yield amazing results. One example is Google flu trends, which uses aggregated data of search terms in the popular search engine to predict flu outbreaks up to two weeks earlier than traditional methods.

Of course, the social media tools available are only as good as the way they are used. Arguably, a community of sorts exists around even frivolous sites, but its value to all but a few may be questionable. Simply because we now have the tools does not mean we will always use them productively or efficiently.

Media companies are struggling to adapt to the world of social media, with mixed success. Companies not willing to give up control of their messages are having more difficulty than those receptive to engaging in the conversational chaos that is social media. Of bigger concern to companies, though, is how to earn revenues from all this incessant chatter, conversations often based on content the companies have spent money to create.

There are no easy answers to this question. Popular social-networking sites are sitting on a gold mine of user data gleaned simply from the interactions and behaviors of active users, data that advertisers are quite willing to pay for to better target consumers. However, the high degree of surveillance we have today does raise important questions about user rights and privacy. Some industries may find it easier to adapt to or to shape the social media landscape in ways that benefit them, while others may be facing a future in which their profession or industry as currently practiced is barely recognizable in ten or twenty years.

MEDIA MATTERS HOW CONNECTED ARE YOU?

1. Estimate how much time you spend per day on social media, via mobile phone, computer, or tablet. Which device do you typically use for social media? Do you use social media more or less often than your friends?

2. What is the longest time you have been without access to social media? How did you feel when you were not connected? Did your patterns of social media use change afterward?

3. Some researchers have claimed that social media use has made us more isolated, not more social. Agree or disagree with this assertion, and defend your argument.

4. When considering a movie, TV series, or book, would you be more persuaded by a review from the *New York Times*, Rotten Tomatoes, your school paper, or a Facebook friend with whom you have interacted only casually once or twice? What factors would influence your decision?

FURTHER READING

Social Media: A Critical Introduction. Christian Fuchs (2013) Sage.

Socialnomics: How Social Media Transforms the Way We Live and Do Business, 2nd ed. Erik Qualman (2013) Wiley.

Wikinomics: How Mass Collaboration Changes Everything. Don Tapscott, Anthony Williams (2008) Portfolio.

The Wealth of Networks: How Social Production Transforms Markets and Freedom. Yochai Benkler (2006) Yale University Press.

Infotopia: How Many Minds Produce Knowledge. Cass Sunstein (2006) Oxford University Press.

Here Comes Everybody: The Power of Organizing Without Organizations. Clay Shirky (2008) Penguin Press.

Cognitive Surplus: How Technology Makes Consumers into Collaborators. Clay Shirky (2011) Penguin Press.

How Open Is the Future? Economic, Social & Cultural Scenarios Inspired by Free & Open-Source Software. Marleen Wynants, Jan Cornelis (eds.) (2005) VUB: Brussels University Press.

The Wisdom of Crowds. James Surowiecki (2005) Anchor Press.

Perspectives on Free and Open-Source Software. Joseph Feller, Brian Fitzgerald, Scott Hissam, Karim Lakhani (eds.) (2007) MIT Press.

The Wikipedia Revolution: How a Bunch of Nobodies Created the World's Greatest Encyclopedia. Andrew Lih (2009) Hyperion.

Wiki Government: How Technology Can Make Government Better, Democracy Stronger, and Citizens More Powerful. Beth Simone Noveck (2010) Brookings Institution Press.

The Future of Ideas: The Fate of the Commons in a Connected World. Lawrence Lessig (2001) Random House.

Remix: Making Art and Commerce Thrive in the Hybrid Economy. Lawrence Lessig (2008) Penguin Press.

Blogs, Wikipedia, Second Life, and Beyond: From Production to Produsage. Axel Bruns (2008) Peter Lang.

Big Data: A Revolution That Will Transform How We Live, Work, and Think. Viktor Mayer-Schonberger, Kenneth Cukier (2013) Eamon Dolan/Houghton Mifflin.

Audience Evolution: New Technologies and the Transformation of Media Audiences. Philip M. Napoli (2010) Columbia University Press.

Groundswell: Winning in a World Transformed by Social Technologies. Charlene Li, Josh Bernoff (2008) Harvard Business School Press.

Tribes: We Need You to Lead Us. Seth Godin (2008) Portfolio.

Six Degrees: The Science of a Connected Age. Duncan Watts (2004) W. W. Norton.

Cyber Bullying: Protecting Teens and Adults from Online Bullies. Samuel McQuade III, James Colt, Nancy Meyer (2009) Praeger.

To Save Everything, Click Here: The Folly of Technological Solutionism. Evgeny Morozov (2014) Public Affairs.

Alone Together: Why We Expect More from Technology and Less from Each Other. Sherry Turkle (2012) Basic Books.

The Dumbest Generation: How the Digital Age Stupefies Young Americans and Jeopardizes Our Future (Or, Don't Trust Anyone Under 30). Mark Bauerlein (2009) Tarcher.

The Shallows: What the Internet Is Doing to Our Brains. Nicholas Carr (2011) W. W. Norton.

THE

8

Journalism
FROM INFORMATION TO PARTICIPATION

S ocial and digital media continue to transform the world of journalism as an increasingly prominent vehicle for quality news and information. In 2010, ProPublica was the first not-for-profit online news operation awarded a Pulitzer Prize.[1] In April 2012, the *Huffington Post* became the first commercial news website and blog to win.[2] Founded by Arianna Huffington, Kenneth Lerer, Andrew Breitbart, and Jonah Peretti, the *Huffington Post* launched on May 9, 2005, as a fully digital, U.S.-based, for-profit operation. It provides original news, online commentary, and aggregated content from other sites on a wide spectrum of subjects including politics, business, entertainment, lifestyle, culture, and comedy.

The *Huffington Post* received a Pulitzer for national reporting for an original series on wounded veterans. In "Beyond the Battlefield,"[3] experienced war correspondent David Wood explores "the challenges that severely wounded veterans of Iraq and Afghanistan face after they return home, as well as what those struggles mean for those close to them." Debuting online, the ten-part series was subsequently expanded and republished for Kindle and iBook.

The *Huffington Post* has evolved and matured since its introduction as largely an alternative to conservative online news such as the *Drudge Report*. In February 2011, AOL acquired the site for $315 million,[4] and founder Arianna Huffington became editor-in-chief of The Huffington Post Media Group. The *Huffington Post* effectively integrates social media both for reporting and for engaging citizens in an online news community. Every story encourages readers to follow and participate on Facebook, Twitter, Google+, and more.

Upon the death of Venezuelan president Hugo Chavez in 2013, the lead story on HuffPost featured a one-inch-tall headline in bold red—"He's Dead"—evoking sensationalist papers of a century ago. Yet the story also exhibited distinctly modern, digital features. A "scroll-over" of Venezuelan President Hugo Chavez's picture below the banner headline provided a "quick read," a paragraph summary of highlights. Clicking on the photo or text below accessed the entire story, with multimedia and

LEARNING OBJECTIVES

>> Describe journalism and its role in mass communication and society.

>> Outline important historical developments in journalism that affect how it is practiced today.

>> Discuss journalism today, including different types, and the effects of convergence.

>> Outline legal and ethical issues in the practice of journalism, particularly ethical issues in the digital world.

>> Explain some aspects of the business of journalism and how they affect the practice of journalism.

>> Examine how convergence is affecting business models and careers in journalism.

interactivity options. Readers could see the total number of social media shares to Facebook, Twitter, Google+, and email as well as thousands of comments on HuffPost Social News. Comments were polarized: for example, "Chavez will live forever in the hearts and minds of his people. The boorish comments of the great unwashed will not survive the night." And, "It is about time this man died, too bad it was not at the end of a rope. And the only thing he cared about was himself."[5] Within a few hours, a new blue headline appeared, "Life After Hugo," linking to a story speculating on the future of Venezuela. Clearly the digital era offers journalists new opportunities both to react to a developing story and to engage with their audience. Along with opportunities come new challenges.

Based in the United Kingdom, *The Guardian* in 2014 won a Pulitzer Prize for Public Service for its ground-breaking reporting both online and in print of the revelations of the secret surveillance program carried out digitally by the U.S. spy agency, the National Security Agency (NSA). The Pulitzer was awarded as well to the *Washington Post*, which was an international partner in the public service reporting project. This reporting demonstrated the central role that digital journalism now plays in a contemporary, globalized media age.

News organizations walk a thin line between providing a vital public service and thriving, or even surviving, as a business. Serving the public good does not preclude pandering to baser tastes for financial gain, and news organizations run as commercial enterprises have been accused of becoming too cozy with powerful business and political interests. Some believe the purpose of journalism is to "comfort the afflicted and afflict the comfortable." How well it is fulfilling these roles as public advocate and watchdog remains a topic of debate on print editorial pages, online discussion boards, and call-in talk shows. This should be viewed as a sign not of the profession's inherent failure but, rather, of its enduring importance in the digital age, where it is not enough simply to inform. Journalism today also needs to encourage public participation, as attested to by the rise of citizen journalism and hyperlocal news.

In addition to mobilizing the public, news is integral to three of the four main functions of mass communication: **surveillance**, **correlation**, and **cultural transmission**. To a lesser extent, journalism also serves the entertainment function. And because news consumption or participation is not a civic duty, many will engage only if it is an enjoyable leisure activity.

surveillance

Primarily the journalism function of mass communication, which provides information about processes, issues, events, and other developments in society.

correlation

Media interpretation ascribing meaning to issues and events that helps individuals understand their roles within the larger society and culture.

cultural transmission

The process of passing on culturally relevant knowledge, skills, attitudes, and values from person to person or group to group.

What Is News?

"Man Bites Dog," an oft-cited headline in introductory journalism classes, suggests that news becomes news when it is extraordinary. Reporting does indeed embrace the unexpected. But most news is largely predictable a day, a week, a month, or sometimes years in advance. Consider the types of news stories about any annual event, such as advice on holiday shopping or what the stars will be wearing to this year's Oscars—a glance at news archives will likely uncover a very similar story the previous year and the year before that. Stories that affect the public interest also clearly constitute news: fires, accidents, recent discoveries, and corporate or political corruption, for example. Several issues arise when examining the nature of news.

First is the frequent complaint that news dwells too much on the negative—crime, accidents, wrongdoing, and so forth. Although positive news, such as human-interest stories or new business openings, may also be criticized as public relations pieces that do not adequately address significant concerns, negative pieces may send a distorted message that things are worse than they actually are. A focus on events rather than trends amplifies this problem. Although the overall annual crime rate may be falling, coverage of particular crimes, especially sensational ones, will still be pervasive. Trends are not as readily accommodated by the narrative structure of journalism that tends to rely on people, what they did or had done to them, and the consequences. Trends involve data, which journalism has not historically presented effectively, although this has improved with the growth of data-driven reporting and effective graphics, supplemented by individual cases to illustrate a trend.

Critical media consumers understand that diverse people and particular forces, notably advertising and public relations, influence and manufacture the news. It doesn't just happen. Historian and Pulitzer Prize–winning author Daniel Boorstin describes what he calls **pseudo-events**, events staged to attract media attention and influence news coverage, such as press conferences, marches, and rallies. Story selection depends on various factors, including other events that day, the type of news organization, and even the political views of the owner in some cases.

On a **soft news day**, when editors consider the day's events not especially newsworthy, they will air programming or include human-interest stories. A flood in a distant country killing hundreds may appear on a "World News Brief" page on a slow news day but be omitted if there is important local news. How do editors decide that a popular local high school athlete killed in a traffic accident is more significant than five hundred killed overseas? They try to determine what is of most interest to their readership. Journalists have an **agenda-setting** function, meaning their news choices influence what the public will deem important and discuss.

Despite its strong public service mission, journalism is nevertheless subject to economic realities. Without significant audiences and substantial advertising revenues, most newspapers and news magazines, whether print or digital, would cease to exist, as would television and radio news programs. Most newspapers and magazines actually have more space devoted to advertising than to news. The Internet has challenged many of journalism's traditional business models, and falling advertising revenues for traditional media outlets have still not been outweighed by the gain in Internet advertising.

Let's examine the history of journalism as both a profession and a business, particularly how technological change has driven innovation.

pseudo-events

Events staged specifically to attract media attention, particularly the news.

soft news day

A day in which not much has happened that is newsworthy, entailing the addition of features with less real news value, such as human-interest stories.

On slow news days, editors are more likely to include features or photos that have little true news value.

agenda setting

Media's role in deciding which topics to cover and consequently which topics the public deems important and worthy of discussion.

DISCUSSION QUESTIONS: Think about the predictability of much news. What stories or story topics (e.g., elections, holidays, a follow-up to a story that broke yesterday) are cyclical or predictable in some fashion? Look at today's news and see how many stories you can find that fall into this category. Are there more or fewer than likely occurred out of enterprise or investigative reporting or as a result of some unpredictable occurrence (e.g., a natural disaster)?

The Historical Development of Journalism

The history of journalism has been synonymous with print, with the **penny press** and mass distribution of newspapers in the early nineteenth century producing a sea change in its theory and practice. To fill pages, editors, who had previously relied largely on "news" proffered by citizens or gathered by a small staff (as well as liberally copying from other newspapers, often without crediting the sources) now had to hire reporters who actively pursued stories.

Newsboys helped mass distribute penny papers by selling them throughout cities.

Articles were also typically organized chronologically, regardless of the relative importance of the information, and the opinions of editors or publishers (often the same person) mixed freely with other editorial content. No thought was given to presenting all sides of an issue fairly. With the penny press's need to attract as many readers as possible, however, publishers decided to concentrate more on sensational crimes and events than on their personal opinions. And to maintain objectivity or at least the appearance of such, editors began publishing their points of view exclusively on the "editorial" page, a tradition the Western press maintains today to guide public opinion on important matters, such as candidates for office. **James Gordon Bennett**, who founded the *New York Herald* in 1835, introduced, in addition to editorial commentary, a financial page and public-affairs reporting, more staples of modern journalism.

Also important to the development of modern journalism were minority newspapers. Among the earliest was *El Misisipí*, the first Spanish-language newspaper in the United States and first published in 1808 in New Orleans;[6] followed by the first Native American newspaper, the *Cherokee Phoenix* (1828), and the first African American daily, the *New Orleans Daily Creole* (1856). Frederick Douglass, an American statesman, abolitionist, and former slave, was also a journalist who published an antislavery paper, the *North Star*. These minority voices introduced the value of diversity to journalism while promoting more nuanced and balanced alternative perspectives.

NEWS VALUES AND THE ASSOCIATED PRESS

News continued to evolve, shaped by the democratization of politics, the expansion of the market economy, and the growing impact of an entrepreneurial middle class. One reason news became more impartial—a core value in journalism known as **objectivity**—was the emergence of the news wire service in the 1840s. In 1846, publishers of six New York newspapers organized the **Associated Press** (AP), in large part to take advantage of the telegraph, a high-speed communications medium too expensive for any single newspaper to afford. Gathering news for half a dozen papers with varying political viewpoints meant AP reports had to be politically neutral; and by the dawn of the twentieth century, these dispatches were virtually free of editorial comment.

Still based in New York, the AP provides textual, audio, and video news, photos, and graphics for its not-for-profit members' cooperative, including 1,500 newspapers and 5,000 radio and television news operations. Members provide much of the AP content, which in turn any member can use. It employs 3,200 people (two-thirds of whom work as journalists) in over 280 locations worldwide.[7]

The AP maintains the highest standards in journalism, having received fifty Pulitzer Prizes, including thirty for photos. As their website states, "More than 30 AP journalists have given their lives in this pursuit of the news. 'I go with Custer and will be at the death,' AP reporter Mark Kellogg wrote before Custer's final stand against the Sioux. And so he was."[8]

In addition to objectivity, the AP embodies at least four other core journalistic values. Foremost among these is a commitment to *truth* and *accuracy* in reporting. Quotations should be kept in context and reported accurately. Corrections that improve public understanding should be published when errors are detected. AP reporters, like all professional journalists, are committed to the *integrity* of the news. They do not plagiarize, or copy, work. They avoid conflicts of interest. Business reporters, for instance, must divulge their financial interest in a company and abstain from reporting on it. Much of this involves a commitment to the value of *ethics*, the moral basis for news. The AP tries to shield the identity of victims of sexual assault. AP reporters do not misrepresent themselves to get a story. They do not pay sources for an interview or a photo, a standard that certain tabloid and television news operations reject. Source attribution is also an AP ethical mandate. Anonymous sources, who erode credibility, can be used only when the material is information and not opinion or speculation and is vital to the news report; the information is not available except under the conditions of anonymity imposed by the source; and the source is reliable and in a position to have accurate information.[9]

DISCUSSION QUESTIONS: Find an AP article on a major event or significant person and compare its treatment of the topic to that of another news organization. What similarities and differences did you observe? Did the AP demonstrate a greater commitment to its core values?

PULITZER AND HEARST: THE CIRCULATION WARS, SENSATIONALISM, AND STANDARDS

Although objective reporting soon became the AP norm, not until well into the twentieth century did most newspapers adopt this model. Throughout the last half of the nineteenth century and the early twentieth century, **sensational journalism**, news that exaggerated or featured lurid details and depictions of crimes or other events, dominated content. Two of the greatest newspaper titans

sensational journalism

News that exaggerates or features lurid details and depictions of events to increase its audience.

MEDIA PIONEERS
Mary Ann Shadd Cary and Ida B. Wells

Mary Ann Shadd Cary

During the 1800s, as immigration increased and minorities began to identify as groups with shared interests and concerns, various minority or ethnic newspapers appeared in the United States. These papers served the needs of niche audiences, including Native Americans, African Americans, Jews, and immigrants whose native language was not English.

Among the most notable minority newspapers of the day was the *Provincial Freeman*. Founder, writer, and editor Mary Ann Shadd Cary observed in her paper that "self-reliance is the fine road to independence," a principle that her life strikingly exemplified. Shadd Cary was the first African American woman to edit a weekly newspaper and to publish in North America. She was also the first woman publisher in Canada. In addition, she was a teacher and a lawyer, only the second African American woman to earn a law degree.

Born a free black in 1823 in Wilmington, Delaware, Mary, the eldest of thirteen children, fled with her family to Windsor, Canada, after the Fugitive Slave Act, threatening the freedom of free northern blacks and escaped slaves,

was passed in the United States in 1850. In response to a vigorous campaign to deter runaway slaves from escaping to Canada, Mary wrote a forty-four-page pamphlet, "Notes of Canada West," outlining the opportunities for blacks in Canada.

Building on the success of this widely read publication, Mary established the *Provincial Freeman*, a weekly newspaper targeting blacks, especially fugitive slaves. She reported on a variety of important topics, among them lies being spread in the United States that African Americans in Canada were starving. Shadd Cary's father had worked for an abolitionist newspaper called the *Liberator*; after her husband's death in 1860, Shadd Cary returned to America, where she taught and wrote for the newspapers *National Era* and *The People's Advocate*.

Ida B. Wells was another important African American female journalist in the nineteenth century. Born a slave in 1862, six months before the signing of the Emancipation Proclamation, Wells spent her adult life fighting racism, especially the lynching of African Americans. She wrote for the religious weekly *The Living Way* and for various African American newspapers, including *Free Speech and Headlight*. She was elected secretary of the Afro-American Press Association in 1889.

Ida B. Wells

of this era were **Joseph Pulitzer**, publisher of the *New York World*, the *St. Louis Post-Dispatch*, and other papers, and **William Randolph Hearst**, publisher of the *San Francisco Examiner* and the *New York Journal*.

Joseph Pulitzer

Born in 1847 in Budapest, Hungary, Joseph Pulitzer emigrated to the United States in 1864, serving in the Union army during the Civil War. After moving to St. Louis in 1868, he became a reporter for a German-language paper. Pulitzer purchased the bankrupt *St. Louis Dispatch* in 1878, later merging it with the *Evening Post* to create the *St. Louis Post-Dispatch*. In 1883, he bought the *New York Post* and then the *New York World*.

Embroiled with fellow newspaper mogul Hearst in the circulation wars of the 1890s, Pulitzer used abundant illustrations, a racy style, and colorful headlines to promote the *New York World*. He wanted a focus on city news, compelling stories—humorous, odd, romantic, or thrilling—and accurate writing with attention to detail. By the early 1890s, the *World*'s circulation had risen to three hundred thousand by mixing sensational photographs with good, solid reporting, "crusades" against corrupt politicians, support for increased taxes, and civil service reform, for example.

Color comics in the Sunday papers were another of Pulitzer's most successful innovations. Although not the first newspaper cartoon, *The Yellow Kid*, a comic strip drawn as busy, single-panel illustrations, contributed much to the format many today take for granted.[10]

Joseph Pulitzer was a Hungarian immigrant who founded a newspaper empire in St. Louis and New York.

Featuring brash and vulgar antics on the backstreets of the fictional Hogan's Alley, *The Yellow Kid* was in some ways a late-nineteenth-century precursor to the crude kids of *South Park*, who debuted during more recent competition for television ratings. *The Yellow Kid* quickly became a central figure in the circulation battles when Hearst lured creator and cartoonist Richard Felton Outcault away from the *World*. Referring to the Kid's famous yellow shirt, critics coined the term **yellow journalism** to describe the sensational style of the of Pulitzer and Hearst newspapers.

After the four-month Spanish-American War in 1898, Pulitzer abandoned the sensational style that had helped build his brand, developing a vision of journalistic excellence outlined in a 1904 article for the *North American Review*.[11] Investigative stories that ran in his papers were instrumental in the passage of antitrust legislation and regulation of the insurance industry. This emphasis on public service journalism and accurate reporting remains a cornerstone of the annual Pulitzer Prizes, which he bequeathed along with an endowment for the Columbia University Graduate School of Journalism after his death in 1911.

Joseph Pulitzer

American newspaper magnate whose publications competed vigorously with those of Hearst. After 1900, Pulitzer retreated from sensational journalism, favoring instead more socially conscious reporting and muckraking. He founded the Pulitzer Prizes, annual awards for outstanding journalism.

William Randolph Hearst

American newspaper magnate during the late nineteenth and early twentieth centuries whose newspapers across the United States were noted for sensational journalism and political influence.

yellow journalism

Style practiced notably by publishers Pulitzer and Hearst during the late 1890s in which stories were sensationalized and often partly or wholly fabricated for dramatic purposes.

William Randolph Hearst

William Randolph Hearst, the son of a self-made multimillionaire miner and rancher in northern California, studied at Harvard; and at the age of twenty-three, in 1887, became proprietor of his first newspaper, the *San Francisco Examiner*, payment his father had received for a gambling debt. In 1895, the younger Hearst acquired the *New York Morning Journal*; he debuted the *Evening Journal* a year later, enticing away many of Pulitzer's best reporters and editors with higher pay while increasing his chain nationwide to include the *Boston American* and *Chicago Examiner*, as well as *Cosmopolitan* and *Harper's Bazaar*.

William Randolph Hearst's newspapers often had sensational coverage that helped give rise to the term "yellow journalism."

Circulation increased tremendously as the paper attracted readers with colorful banner headlines, splashy photography, and, some say, fabricated news. Hearst was often criticized for his sensational tactics, later immortalized in the now-defunct *News of the World*, a print tabloid newspaper in Orson Welles' cinematic masterpiece *Citizen Kane*. Historian Ernest L. Meyer characterizes his work as inflammatory:

> Mr. Hearst in his long and not laudable career has inflamed Americans against Spaniards, Americans against Japanese, Americans against Filipinos, Americans against Russians, and in the pursuit of his incendiary campaign he has printed downright lies, forged documents, faked atrocity stories, inflammatory editorials, sensational cartoons and photographs and other devices by which he abetted his jingoistic ends.[12]

Nevertheless, his 1933 editorial guidelines articulate news standards that resonate today: "Make the news thorough. Print all the news. Condense it if necessary. Frequently it is better when intelligently condensed. But get it in." In 1945, six years before his death at age eighty-five, he established the Hearst Foundation, which today provides important support for journalism education and other concerns, including health and culture. His ornate 130-room mansion, San Simeon, nicknamed Hearst Castle, was built in the 1920s and still stands as a California landmark.

THE RISE OF ELECTRONIC JOURNALISM

Newspapers began to suffer in the 1920s with the ascent of radio, which, supported entirely by advertising, offered news more quickly and for "free." And when television began broadcasting news in the late 1940s and early 1950s, newspapers' waning star was eclipsed. News was and still is an important part of how television fulfills its federal mandate to serve the public interest.

Television network news divisions in New York produced many of the early news programs. In 1947, NBC debuted *Meet the Press*, a made-for-TV news conference where journalists queried various newsmakers, often government officials. Until his untimely death in 2008, Tim Russert had been the longest-serving host of what has become the longest-running series on network TV. In the 1950s, NBC introduced the first early-morning network news show. Host Dave Garroway and chimpanzee sidekick J. Fred Muggs offered a decidedly entertaining approach that the *Today* show still maintains.

Murrow and News in TV's Golden Age

Setting the standard for television news during its golden age in the late 1940s and the 1950s was distinguished journalist **Edward R. Murrow**, who first achieved fame with dramatic radio news broadcasts from London during World War II. Murrow produced the popular television programs *See It Now* and *Person to Person* at CBS News.

Murrow's comments on television at the Radio-Television News Directors Association (RTNDA) meeting in 1958 ring equally true today for the Internet: "This instrument can teach, it can illuminate, and, yes, it can inspire. But it can do so only to the extent that humans are determined to use it to those ends. Otherwise it is nothing but wires and lights in a box." In *TV Guide* the same year, he offered another caveat: "Television in the main is being used to distract, delude, amuse, and insulate us."

Edward R. Murrow was a noted radio and television journalist in the earliest days of television.

Edward R. Murrow

A radio and, later, television journalist and announcer who set the standard for journalistic excellence during TV's golden age.

Changes in Television News

Interesting visuals on which television news relies can often dictate the selection and sequence of stories in a newscast. Perhaps because of its visual nature, television news has always catered to our entertainment needs, evident as far back as the early days of *Today*. Moreover, time constraints of less than thirty minutes or an hour to cover local, national, and international news, business news, sports, and weather constrict feature length.

The introduction of video cameras transformed television news. **Electronic news-gathering (ENG) equipment** allowed journalists in the field to capture and send videotaped news by satellite to the network, where it could be edited and broadcast much more quickly than film. This process has influenced the nature of video storytelling. The late CBS news veteran Bud Benjamin called it "NTV," the video-journalism equivalent of "MTV," with rapid-paced cuts and strong entertainment values.

The rise of twenty-four-hour news channels means a much larger **news hole** to fill and consequently much lower standards for what stations deem newsworthy. Coverage of events that would not otherwise reach a televised audience is not necessarily a bad thing, but often this material simply promotes or entertains. The prurient entertainment quality of much TV news was particularly evident in the weeks of almost nonstop coverage of the 2013 Jodi Arias trial, for example, a lurid case in which a woman charged with first-degree murder of her boyfriend testified on the stand about their often-bizarre sexual exploits.

electronic news-gathering (ENG) equipment

Tools such as video cameras and satellite dishes that allow journalists to gather and broadcast news much more quickly.

news hole

Amount of total space available after advertisement space has been blocked out, typically in newspapers.

In 2013, the launch of Al Jazeera America brought well-funded new competition from the Middle East to U.S. 24-hour cable and satellite TV news.

Foundations of Journalism

Professional, mainstream journalism is still practiced largely conventionally. Reporters cover events and write stories, and editors select what stories to assign and whether they appear, depending on the available pages for print news, which in turn depends on advertising revenue. Even digital-first news media (in which news is reported first in digital format before going to traditional channels) are constrained by screen size and audience attention spans. Digital technology does not change the fact that reporters need to visit places and interview people. Nor does digital technology replace an experienced editor's judgment about what makes a good story and how it should be edited.

To understand which aspects of journalism have already changed and which will likely change more with convergence, we must first consider some of the foundations of journalism.

THE HUTCHINS COMMISSION AND *A FREE AND RESPONSIBLE PRESS*

In 1947, what became known as the Hutchins Commission published a landmark 133-page report on the American press, *A Free and Responsible Press*. Written by Robert Maynard Hutchins and a dozen other leading intellectuals, this report of the Commission on Freedom of the Press argued that the public has a right to information that affects it and that the press has a responsibility, even a moral duty, to present that information because of their constitutionally guaranteed freedom. The commission indicated that the government, the public, and the press could all take steps to improve the functioning of a healthy press. These included government recognition of the same constitutional guarantees for all media, not just print.

The commission recommended that agencies of mass communication finance new, experimental activities in their fields and that members of the press engage in rigorous reciprocal criticism. The commission called on the public to create academic-professional centers for advanced communications study, research, and publication. Among the first such centers was the Media Studies Center, founded by the Freedom Forum in 1984, nearly forty years after the report. The commission also encouraged schools to exploit the total resources of their universities to ensure that their students obtain the broadest and most liberal training. Finally, the commission proposed the establishment of an independent agency to appraise and report annually on press performance. A National Press Council failed, however, although a similar idea has had marginal success in some states.

SEPARATION OF EDITORIAL AND BUSINESS OPERATIONS

Dubbed the "separation of church and state" in newsroom parlance, this basic principle entails that news coverage not be influenced by business decisions or advertisers, a separation intended to be reflected in page layout that clearly distinguishes between advertising and editorial content. At the *New York Times* headquarters, business and editorial staff even take separate elevators to their offices to avoid potential contact.

Yet many media critics complain that this separation has eroded in recent years as publishers and large media corporations increasingly let commercial concerns influence editorial content. A blatant example was when the owner of the *Los Angeles Times* demanded a special "news" section on the Staples Center, without explicitly informing staff that Staples both sponsored and approved the content. A more insidious example involves management layoffs that hamper original local reporting and force the paper to rely on cheaper but perhaps less relevant wire service news.

Advertorials are designed and written to look like news content but are in fact paid advertisements.

FAIRNESS AND BALANCE IN NEWS COVERAGE

Fairness and **balance** in news coverage have increasingly replaced objectivity, a goal that has been questioned in recent years. Critics argue that reporter bias cannot be avoided, and to claim objectivity in a given situation simply masks partiality. Even if the reporter has no strong personal opinion when writing a story, subsequent editing and placement in a newspaper or news broadcast can still reflect bias. Unintended biases can also inform an editor's choice of assignments and a reporter's choice of sources.

"Fairness" and "balance" mean equal and just consideration of all sides of a topic. This does not mean equal space, however. Support for a fringe candidate from a small group of fifty people, however vocal, would not receive the same amount of coverage as a popular candidate from a major political party. A journalist must consider factors such as contextual importance and source validity or authority.

fairness

News reporting on all relevant sides of an issue that allows representatives of those various sides the same coverage.

balance

Presenting sides equally and reporting on a broad range of news events.

DISCUSSION QUESTIONS: Look at the front page of your favorite newspaper app or website and assess the placement of stories and photos. What reasons might account for such placement? How would moving a story onto the front page or from the front to another page change your impression of its importance?

FRAMING THE NEWS

frame

Structure or angle given a news story that influences reader understanding covering the event.

Traditional news media often decide how they will **frame** a story before the reporting is completed and sometimes before it has even begun. Forcing facts to fit a preconceived frame is one of the biggest threats to fairness and balance. Yet this tendency cannot be wholly avoided, partly because it makes writing a news story easier and faster and partly because it helps us make sense of the world. Journalists, who often believe their work simply reflects reality, may not even aware be aware of their frame.

This can create problems, especially when treating more ambiguous and complicated situations that tend to defy simple framing. Consider, for example, the media's tendency to demonize, reducing complex events and people to "good" and "bad" and reporting accordingly. Depending on one's loyalties, a "terrorist attack" could also be described as "armed resistance."

DISCUSSION QUESTIONS: Discuss a current event in the news and how it is framed. How does this framing affect the way the topic is being covered? Suggest frames that may allow for more balanced, complete coverage.

EXPERT SOURCES

Another problematic issue related to framing is the use of expert sources to enhance story credibility, sources that by and large are white and male. A September

INTERNATIONAL PERSPECTIVES
Covering Islam

Framing in the news occurs everywhere, but it is arguably most prevalent in coverage of international news. In the 1980s, when Japanese companies were buying American companies, the American media often depicted the trend in warlike terms such as "invasion." This was echoed in recent years as China gained economic might and has wanted to buy American companies, such as Smithfield Foods, America's biggest pork producer; yet similar language is not seen when a Canadian or British company buys an American company.

Due partly to the terrorist attacks on September 11, 2001, Islam has largely been framed in the U.S. media as a monolithic religion advocating violence and repression of human rights, argues scholar Edward Said in his book *Covering Islam*.

Said says that the inaccurate depictions of Islam are created by a complex web of media that rely on self-proclaimed "Islamic experts" who pontificate on the Middle East and who often equate fundamentalism with Islam, even though Judaism and Christianity face similar fundamentalist movements.

The depictions feed into a nationalistic "us-versus-them" mentality that is similar to the anti-Communist fervor during the Cold War. Not only do these inaccurate portrayals of Muslims hurt our ability to see them on equal or humanistic terms, they provide a cover for repressive regimes that use Islam as an excuse for their policies.

Framing, in other words, paints over a complex reality and, more importantly, shapes our reactions and beliefs to the new reality that it creates. This in turn can affect how we interact with the groups that have been framed and can perpetuate negative stereotypes and discrimination.

2012 study found that particularly underrepresented are Latinos, a population that has more than doubled since 1990, comprising approximately 17 percent of the total population. Yet expert Latino voices are almost never heard in American English-language news media. In 2006, only 2 percent of the U.S. experts who appeared on PBS *NewsHour* were Latino, and President George W. Bush's Attorney General Alberto Gonzalez himself constituted 30 percent of those appearances. A 2014 investigation by Columbia University's Center for the Study of Ethnicity and Race revealed network TV to be even worse, with less than 1 percent of all stories on the nightly news programs highlighting Latinos.[13]

"Individuals of either sex, any age, and all races can be heard from on the network news, as long as they are not wielding power or offering expertise. The networks' 'golden rolodexes' of expert consultants are badly in need of updating," observes Andrew Tyndall, who directed a study called *Who Speaks for America? Sex, Age and Race on the Network News*.[14]

From Event to Public Eye: How News Is Created

News is regularly required to fill the scheduled evening TV broadcast, the morning paper, or the weekly news magazine. Like an accordion, news can expand or contract with the day's events, but only to a limited degree. And whether anything of import occurs today, networks will still air at least a thirty-minute newscast (twenty-two minutes, after subtracting time for commercials). Sometimes, during a major breaking news event—such as the September 11, 2001, World Trade Center and Pentagon attacks—they expand to an hour or even to continuous coverage.

In the past thirty years, hard news has yielded to lighter fare. In 1980, one of three front-page news stories dealt with government or public affairs, including international events, compared to just one in five today. In 1980, only one in fifty front-page daily newspaper stories featured celebrities, popular entertainment, and related subjects. Today, it's one in fourteen, not including the various teasers and blurbs promoting other parts of the paper. Television news is following print trends, with shorter stories and reduced coverage of politics and government. Forty percent of local TV "news" is now weather, sports, and traffic reporting.

This dramatic and inexorable shift has occurred for a number of reasons. One is an increasingly competitive environment in which newspapers vie with electronic entertainment media for audiences. Also important are changing ownership structure and business models. The resulting staff cutbacks in the past two decades have been substantial and wrought other changes, including the closure of foreign bureaus. News media are struggling to reinvent themselves in an online, digital age. Although TV is still the number one news source for most Americans, Pew Research found that as of 2013, nearly half of Americans turn daily to digital news sources, especially via smartphones and tablets.[15]

Regardless of news format, news techniques of gathering, reporting, and presenting information to the public, although refined over the years, have changed surprisingly little. Certain variations exist among print, broadcast, and online journalism; but the basics, which we look at now, remain largely the same.

Sometimes during protests or demonstrations, people act up when they see TV news cameras.

beat

Reporter's specialized area of coverage based on geography or subject. Common beats in large or medium-sized newspapers include education, crime, and state politics.

GATHERING THE NEWS

The AP publishes for members a daily listing of upcoming events, such as important court cases, demonstrations, and press conferences. Most journalists or their assignment editors refer to the AP daybook at night for tomorrow's story ideas, and the daybook remains a good predictor of the next day's news. Some media critics claim that much news is actually manufactured by media organizations aided and abetted by public relations news releases or video news releases (VNRs) and that press conferences, awards ceremonies, and the like are staged solely to attract public and press attention.

Although news about pseudo-events or based on publicity releases may well be "manufactured," the fact is that journalists must rely heavily on certain sources to stay informed. Reporters also develop sources when covering a **beat**, an area originally structured by geography, much like a police officer's, but now largely defined by subject, such as education, city hall, the state capital, or science. Beats facilitate the cultivation of valuable sources and access to newsworthy developments. Small hyperlocal news sites, which cannot afford specialized reporters, often have general-assignment reporters who cover a range of topics.

Moreover, the media spotlight tends to create more news. A big story such as a natural disaster or a U.S. presidential election resonates through the entire system. Yet even an unusual movie advertising campaign, for example, may trigger more stories about the campaign and its impact on the film's success, which in turn generate more publicity, making the movie more popular and more newsworthy. Some news filters up through the media network. A story in a local paper may be covered by a regional television station where a reporter for a national publication sees it and brings it to the national stage.

PRODUCING THE NEWS

Once a story has been assigned or selected and the raw material gathered, the reporter has to make sense out of all the interviews, background facts, video, and so forth, shaping these into a compelling story. Yet few journalists have the luxury of putting a story aside for a week to ponder word choice or polish prose. And if the story is breaking news, the reporter will have even less time.

In meetings usually several hours before deadline, newspaper editors decide which stories are most important and where they will be placed in print or online; these spaces are blocked out (advertising space has been blocked out first), an arrangement subject to change in the event of breaking news.

Editors look for logical weaknesses, errors, and gaps in stories, often asking reporters to get more information. Fact checkers research stories for accuracy and sometimes have to replace TKs (meaning "to come") with information they have sought out. Copyeditors correct writing and in-house style errors. In larger news organizations, headline and caption writers create apt headlines and photo captions to fit the space allotted. In smaller news outlets, a journalist may wear a number of these hats.

CONVERGENCE CULTURE
Platypus Journalism: The Future, or Evolutionary Dead End?

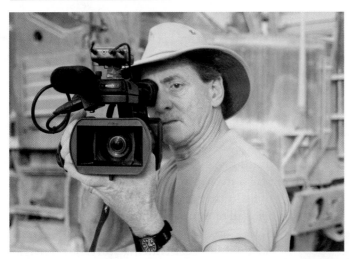

With thirty years of experience, Bill Gentile is one of the foremost practitioners of backpack journalism, using small, affordable digital cameras as well as online digital editing and distribution platforms to work effectively as a solo journalist. **CRITICAL THINKING QUESTIONS:** What impact do you think backpack journalism has on news reporting? Does it produce better stories? Why or why not?

News organizations have been slow to realize how drastically digital media are changing their business and the nature of the profession itself, but the grave consequences of this change in the form of lost advertising revenues, lower readership, and job cuts have made this situation impossible to ignore.

As news organizations scramble to reinvent themselves in the digital news environment, one new model of the future of journalism has seemed particularly appealing: a single correspondent in sole possession of all the tools to report, produce, and file stories from the field. Newer, cheaper digital tools, such as wireless Internet connections and more powerful computers, could enable journalists on the road to shoot video, record audio, write a story, and possibly create an interactive multimedia graphic. This scenario appeals to management, for one reporter would now be doing the work of at least three. Some early experiments in one-person news operations seemed promising, such as Kevin Sites's reporting for *Yahoo! News* from a number of global hotspots.

By 2013, the required gadgetry had been dramatically streamlined and mainstreamed. Today, most journalists routinely go out into the field equipped with a smartphone or tablet device or wearable camera not only connected to the Internet wirelessly but also capable of capturing audio and video, doing online research, editing stories in multimedia format, and filing them from the field or posting them directly to a digital-first news site. The reporter can also use social media to facilitate audience engagement.

The model has been mocked, however, as "platypus journalism" or "Inspector Gadget journalism," with critics arguing that journalists cannot do the same in-depth coverage when juggling all the tech gadgets as they could if they focused on one medium, such as writing or video. Critics claim the future of reporting more likely lies in some form of **crowdsourcing**—utilizing raw data gathered from the public—and citizen reporting rather than a one-man band of technology gadgetry. In this model, journalists may act more as curators than news gatherers for some types of stories, directing the flow of data feeds and choosing and interpreting accurate and relevant information to create compelling stories.

Design and page-layout artists create digital versions of copyedited articles in a page-layout program such as Adobe InDesign or online via WordPress. Proofreaders check for errors; after an editor approves an issue, it is sent to the printer, formerly as negative photographs of page hard copies but now entirely as digital pages received electronically.

TV camera crews and reporters usually return to the station to edit footage shot on location and to add voice-overs and graphics. Because time is so critical, news segments are rehearsed and edited down to the second. Breaking or international news is reported live from location, often broadcasting via satellite. Advances in mobile, digital technology have made it increasingly practical to do

crowdsourcing

Using raw data gathered from the public and citizen-journalists to help create a news report.

nonlinear video editing from the field and then transmit a completed video package or story wirelessly, even high-resolution, broadcast-quality material.

Digital video technology has reduced the requirements for shooting broadcast-quality video to a single cameraperson and a reporter, but producing a television news package still involves more technically than writing a print story. Many print news operations now have converged newsrooms. At TimesCast from the *New York Times*, for example, reporters produce digital video versions of stories they are working on for the paper, mobile apps, or the Web.

At a TV station, the producer and reporter decide what to edit and how the story will be put together, usually working with video editors or other technicians who carry out their instructions. Some news anchors also have a role in editorial decisions, whereas others simply deliver the news.

DISTRIBUTING THE NEWS

The goal of both print and electronic news distribution is the same: to attract as large an audience as possible, which means a higher advertising rate and more income for the media organization. To that end, newspapers and magazines use colorful or dramatic photos on their front pages or covers, often featuring what the editors have decided is the most enticing story. Some magazines may send press releases about particularly noteworthy stories in the next issue, with the hope that other media outlets will report on these and generate more sales. Particular stories can be syndicated and appear in other print-media outlets.

In 2015, Jon Stewart announced his departure from the satirical news show *The Daily Show*, disappointing legions of fans, particularly college students, who stayed on top of current events with his program.

Print media are distributed through subscriptions and newsstand sales. Subscribers are more valuable to media organizations because they represent a stable revenue base and provide mailing lists that can be sold or rented to other organizations. Material costs for print media, ranging from paper to ink to delivery trucks, can be quite high.

Television stations have short teasers during commercial breaks throughout the evening, usually a provocative question such as "Could the food you are eating be dangerous? Find out at eleven." To keep people watching, stories that served as bait typically appear later in the program, as does the weather. Networks transmit national news shows to affiliate stations, sometimes with time slots available for additional local news content. They also send video feeds of international and national news coverage.

Whether produced originally for print or broadcast, most news is also packaged for digital distribution direct to the consumer. Most news organizations, even those with traditional news products, are committed to digital-first publication to get their stories out to the public quickly before the competition does. Moreover, most if not all news media today engage audiences via social networking. Through a combination of Twitter, Facebook, YouTube, Google+, and more, they share news stories and invite readers to share, expanding their audience and the digital dialog on news. Editors who complain about news aggregators such as Google using their material for free still benefit from the increased online traffic.

Types of Journalism

Much serious questioning of journalism took place during the widespread challenging of societal norms in the 1960s. Leading reporters such as James "Scottie" Reston of the *New York Times* and Paul Anderson of the *St. Louis Post-Dispatch*, perceiving the limits of objective news reportage, developed **interpretive reporting** that attempted to situate the facts of a story in a broader context. Although critics argue that this approach represents life's complexities no better than does objective reporting, interpretive reporting opened the door to a variety of new styles, including New Journalism, literary journalism, and advocacy journalism.

> **interpretive reporting**
>
> Reporting that places the facts of a story in a broader context by relying on the reporter's knowledge and experience.

New Journalism developed in the 1960s and 1970s during a period of great social, political, and economic upheaval in the United States that included both the Vietnam War and the Watergate scandal. Reporters striving to capture the spirit of these complex times and explore current social issues, such as the drug culture, often used literary techniques such as point of view, description of characters' emotions, and first-person narrative. Truman Capote, Tom Wolfe, and Norman Mailer were three prominent authors associated with New Journalism, a style that critics charged blurred the line between fact and fiction.

The roots of literary journalism go back to muckraking, although this modern form does not always tackle social problems with the same fervor. Literary journalism stays closer to true, observable narrative, and its pace may be slow, with frequent, lengthy digressions. Because of standard article length and topic, literary journalism generally does not deal with breaking news, although such events may inspire subsequent stories. John McPhee employs immersive reporting, solid research, and excellent writing to create literary journalism. Other practitioners include Joan Didion, James Fallows, and Robert Kaplan, all of whom write on a range of issues, including foreign affairs and politics.

Another descendent of the muckrakers, one that maintains its critique of society and commitment to political and social reform, is advocacy journalism. Prominent practitioners include Gloria Steinem (founder of the magazine *Ms.* and a leader of the women's movement), Pete Hamill (one-time editor of the *Daily News* in New York), and Nicholas von Hoffman. Much of early environmental journalism was advocacy journalism.

ALTERNATIVE JOURNALISM

Alternative journalism, or, as it was often called, radical journalism, departed considerably from the traditions of objective reporting. Its roots go farther back to radical and socialist UK newspapers published in the nineteenth century to express workers' united voice and shared sense of injustice. Some radical papers had large circulations in their heyday, comparable to popular traditional papers. But because advertisers wanted neither to attract the working-class market nor to be associated with radical political movements, these papers struggled to stay afloat or ended up toning down their political rhetoric.

As an outlet for stories not seen elsewhere, alternative journalism often purposely defied professional conventions, in both tone and topic, much as New

The *Indypendent* is a print and digital newspaper published by the Indymedia group in New York.

Journalism did decades later. Despite alternative journalism's fringe status throughout most of the twentieth century, some of its material would make its way into the mainstream. Magazines such as *Mother Jones*, *The Progressive*, and *The Nation* straddle the gap between radical and conventional. And alternative urban weeklies with edgy, contrarian coverage often geared to a younger audience, such as the *Boston Phoenix* and the *Houston Press*, exemplify the genre.

Alternative journalism was given a new lease on life in 1999 during the World Trade Organization protests in Seattle when an ad hoc group of protesters, who felt the mainstream press was misreporting or underreporting, created their own independent media movement. Indymedia quickly spread worldwide with the growth of the Internet. Although most Indymedia groups remain small, their decentralized structure and open publishing systems facilitate the contribution of stories by people who may not otherwise get involved in journalism. Indymedia NYC publishes professional-quality newspapers along with maintaining a robust website.

> **DISCUSSION QUESTIONS:** Describe the potential pitfalls of one of the alternative journalism types and how these may be avoided or overcome—if possible.

PUBLIC JOURNALISM

Public journalism, or civic journalism, developed in the early 1990s in response to dissatisfaction with media treatment of social and political issues and concern about the apathy and cynicism among the general public this coverage possibly fostered—including an increasing distrust of journalists. Originating with longtime and respected professionals, public journalism takes a less radical approach that expands the watchdog role of the press while engaging the citizenry more actively in news creation and discussion. Public journalism strives for more nuanced reporting that avoids framing stories in terms of conflict and extremes.

Various newspapers experimenting with public journalism have reported a higher level of readership trust in the press as well as some signs of increased civic participation and awareness of social and political issues. Some critics argue these efforts are insufficient to break down the barrier between professional journalists and public audiences; others claim they represent little more than boosterism, or advocacy. Partly because of this criticism from peers as well as citizens, public journalism has waned in recent years. Later studies in communities with papers that followed public-journalism principles noted no significant increase in political awareness or public participation.

In the digital world, however, public journalism has thrived in the form of ProPublica, the first digital-only, not-for-profit news organization to win a Pulitzer Prize. Known for its investigative reporting and enterprise journalism, ProPublica has produced extensive interactive and multimedia public service coverage of critical topics like the impact of Hurricane Katrina on doctors at a hospital cut

off by floodwaters. ProPublica has also partnered with more than ninety news organizations, including the *New York Times*, *USA
Today*, and Salon.com, to extend its reach and
capabilities. It also features an ongoing collection of watchdog reporting titled, in
homage to the past, MuckReads. In addition,
ProPublica provides interactive tutorials on
digital reporting techniques, such as using
Google Docs as a news-gathering tool.

Debates on public journalism have also
been an entree to further discussion of the
challenges professionals face in the early
twenty-first century with the rise of citizen
journalism.

CITIZEN JOURNALISM

The Internet and social media have accelerated the growth of citizen journalism, a broad
field encompassing everything from blogging
to Slashdot to more formal ventures that emulate professional journalism in important
aspects, such as Allvoices, OhmyNews,
Meporter, Examiner, and Wikinews. Some
scholars even include consumer product-
review sites as a form of citizen journalism.

With the 2003 U.S. invasion of Iraq, the U.S. military introduced a new approach
to managing journalists in the theater of war by requiring all 775 reporters and
photographers to be embedded, meaning attached to military units. **CRITICAL
THINKING QUESTIONS:** How does the practice of embedding journalists affect the
quality of news reporting? Does being embedded help or hinder journalists' pursuit
of the truth?

Unlike advocacy or alternative journalism, citizen journalism is usually not
associated with an explicitly political or radical agenda, and its driving force
has been citizens rather than professional journalists, as in public journalism.
Consequently, mainstream journalism has been more willing to welcome these
efforts, even if cautiously. Many news organizations, CNN's iReport, for example, have tried to cultivate their audiences as sources of raw news footage. Other
news organizations, notably newspapers, have adopted a more integrated and
thorough approach in which citizen-journalists post news and stories on a
stand-alone website or mobile app, perhaps partially cobranded with the newspaper, which publishes the best stories in a weekly edition. Still other organizations have conducted training sessions for citizen-journalists, teaching them
interviewing, reporting, and writing skills. Mainstream critics claim that citizens are being used as unpaid reporters to fill holes in local news coverage resulting from staff cutbacks. AOL's Patch, for example, employs a model in which
thousands of unpaid citizen reporters cover more than 1,000 communities
across the United States under the direction of hundreds of professional AOL
editors.

The track records of original citizen-journalism sites vary. OhmyNews, a
South Korea-based site that operates much like a traditional news organization
with paid editors and a hierarchical editing structure, has had mixed success. Although very popular and financially strong in South Korea, the English-language
website version lost money and had to shut down, as did the Japanese OhmyNews.
In 2005, citizen-journalism advocate Dan Gillmor launched Bayosphere to cover

Wikinews is a citizen-journalism site that users can edit, as they can with Wikipedia.

the San Francisco Bay Area, but seven difficult months later he largely abandoned the project for practical and economic reasons.

Citizen-journalism sites all emphasize participant conversation and interaction. As gatekeeping becomes gatewatching, and the line between the professional practitioner and the audience blurs, the journalist's privileged position as arbiter of the news is undermined. The role of citizen journalism during the Arab Spring of 2011 illustrates the potential impact of such reporting. Videos uploaded to YouTube and reports provided via mobile social media proved pivotal in quickly getting out to the world firsthand eyewitness accounts from Tahrir Square and elsewhere.

Despite the great potential to increase citizen engagement on local, national, and international levels, citizen journalism lacks a business model to promote sustainability and support paid reporters and editors. Nevertheless, it signals a shift toward more interactive citizen participation. As NYU journalism professor Jay Rosen observes, "Journalism should be a conversation, not a lecture."

DISCUSSION QUESTIONS: Go to a citizen-journalism site such as Wikinews and compare its news coverage with that of mainstream news sites. How are they similar, and how are they different?

AN INTERNATIONAL PERSPECTIVE

There is nothing sacred about the inverted-pyramid structure of news stories or the emphasis on fairness and balance. Most Americans do not realize that journalism can be practiced in various ways because any experience they might have with foreign news is likely limited to the English-language BBC, whose treatment resembles American coverage.

An examination of news styles, from Europe to Asia and the Middle East, reveals a remarkable diversity in the writing, editing, and even selection of news.

"Je suis Charlie" ("I am Charlie") became a motto for freedom of speech and the press in the wake of the Charlie Hebdo massacre. **CRITICAL THINKING QUESTIONS:** How did religious leaders of different faiths respond to this particular massacre and to the general practice of religious satire? Do you agree or disagree with their positions and beliefs?

Reporters' opinions and feelings may be more prevalent or obvious in ostensibly factual news accounts. Since the Arab Spring, for instance, the volume of news sources from the Middle East has expanded. Some new voices present a narrative of sympathy for Arab suffering and popular rage against U.S.-backed Arab governments, such as the ousted Hosni Mubarak in Egypt.

In many countries, journalists still face censorship or licensing restrictions that naturally shape the kind of news produced. Journalists in many monarchies, from Norway to Jordan, for instance, are prohibited from publishing anything that might be deemed critical of the royal family. Dubbed "lèse majesté," meaning "injured majesty" in Latin, these laws often carry stiff penalties for infringements, including prison sentences and harsh fines. In such environments, journalists may act more like government stenographers, simply recording meetings and events that the state deems important to publicize, with a state-approved editorial voice.

For instance, a Muscat, Oman, court in 2012 sentenced four bloggers to jail for allegedly insulting the Sultan. Such penalties can have a chilling effect on journalism, even in a hot desert climate. As seen in early 2015 in Paris, objections to press coverage can even take the form of violent assaults on journalists. On January 7, 2015, Muslim extremists attacked a Paris publication, *Charlie Hebdo* (or Charlie Weekly), known for its satirical coverage of Islam, killing at least a dozen persons. Such terrorist attacks pose a threat to free and independent journalism everywhere.

Journalism in the Digital World

Mainstream news organizations have not always been quick to adopt new digital resources. Busy work schedules and corporate reluctance to subsidize professional training and development have contributed to this resistance. Clearly, journalists recognize the value of the Internet. And mobile devices, especially the multifunction smartphone, soon became a second vital device in the digital reporter's toolkit. Some organizations are experimenting with far more radical digital innovation. Pew reports that as of 2013 "a growing list of media outlets, such as *Forbes* magazine, use technology by a company called Narrative Science to produce content by way of algorithm [computer], no human reporting [writing] necessary."[16]

At present, however, journalists confront a more pressing threat than the computer algorithm. The increased power of human audience members to communicate with journalists and with one another in a public forum, whether as a citizen-journalist or simply as a participant on a blog, is undermining the journalist's traditional role of authority and gatekeeper. Now online readers can point out, quite publicly, when a journalist errs. News sites have found that if they do not provide a discussion forum, readers will simply go elsewhere to discuss stories and point out mistakes.

As Table 8-1 illustrates, four of the top ten global news sites in July 2013 were based on print publications and three on television news networks or partnerships. Three originated online: *Google News* and *Yahoo! News* are essentially news aggregators, publishing stories composed by other outlets. The *Huffington Post* has developed acclaimed original reporting. The large online audience for news, although a good thing, presents challenges for the news industry in the form of increased competition and decreased advertising revenues.

Digital platforms such as tablets and smartphones are also breathing new life into long-form journalism and nonfiction storytelling. *The Atavist* app features original text and multimedia nonfiction as well as award-winning magazine or book-length material from a variety of sources. Partners publishing via *The Atavist* include the *Wall Street Journal*; the *Paris Review*; and TED (Technology, Entertainment and Design), a not-for-profit organization that shares provocative ideas. In one such TED story, the nonfiction tale *The Sinking of the Bounty*, Matthew Shaer investigates the tragic sinking of the ship used in the 1962 movie "Mutiny on the Bounty."

Advances in technology that have threatened traditional business models continue to change the role of digital news in overall patterns of media use. We can observe certain trends, however, that help us predict the future of online journalism in public news consumption.

NONTRADITIONAL SOURCES

There are two types of nontraditional news sources: traditional outlets not typically viewed by the public and nonjournalism sites such as blogs and discussion groups. Reading an Indian newspaper online or viewing an Al Arabiya newscast to see how they cover a story exemplifies the former. The growth of the Internet and mobile media has made it substantially easier for the public to access these alternative news voices. Even looking at UK media coverage of international issues

TABLE 8-1 Top Global News Sites

RANK	TITLE	UNIQUE VISITORS
1	YAHOO! NEWS	175,000,000
2	Google news	150,000,000
3	THE HUFFINGTON POST	110,000,000
4	CNN	95,000,000
5	The New York Times	70,000,000
6	FOX NEWS.com	65,000,000
7	NBC NEWS	63,000,000
8	Daily Mail	53,000,000
9	The Washington Post	47,000,000
10	theguardian	42,000,000

Source: eBizMBA, http://www.ebizmba.com/articles/news-websites

can often be a valuable and educational experience for Americans, especially English-only speakers, who often receive a fairly narrow range of international news. A high degree of media literacy is especially helpful when assessing news sources and potential biases of alternative media.

Social movements and activism inform the perspectives of certain Native American newspapers. *Akwesasne Notes* originated in 1968 partially in protest against a government-mandated toll on a bridge the Mohawks used to travel from one part of their reservation, or Nation, to another. The production of news in the United States in other languages, particularly Spanish, continues to flourish as the U.S. population becomes more diverse. American Spanish-language TV and online news media generally subscribe to the values and practices of mainstream English-language journalism but feature much greater international coverage.

Some news sources, such as *The Daily Show with Jon Stewart*, *The Colbert Report*, *Last Week Tonight with John Oliver,* and *The Nightly Show with Larry Wilmore*, featured satire, typically of politics or of mainstream news media. Although the creators and hosts of these kinds of programs do not call themselves journalists, their viewers often admit getting much of their daily "news" from these enormously popular shows. Viewers, often young and highly educated, appreciate the less mainstream, commercial, and parochial mindset that characterizes these programs.

Nontraditional digital news sources increasingly view themselves as content providers unfettered by traditional publishers and gatekeepers. NBA.com, for example, publishes extensive news accompanied by video clips. Why would viewers go to CNN or ESPN when they can go straight to the source? Tweeting allows users to write and control their own personal narratives. Subscribing to an influential person's Twitter account or blog can also point people to news that they would otherwise not discover. Celebrity tweets or blog posts often become news stories themselves.

As personal control over one's own narrative increases, however, professional objectivity and critical evaluation tend to decrease. You are unlikely to find, for example, an exposé on NBA.com about the league's financial wrongdoing. Still, NBA.com will meet the needs of people who do not care about such news and simply want basketball scores and information on the latest trades.

ONLINE USER HABITS

Online media use differs from traditional use in a number of ways. First, users are generally more active, visiting multiple websites for information. In addition, most prefer to skim material rather than read at length. Shorter attention spans mean greater competition to attract attention to a particular news story. Stories often feature less text and more interactive graphics or multimedia. Whereas top news sites might attract large numbers of viewers, these viewers don't stay for long. Viewers spend on average only eighteen minutes a month, about half a minute a day, on *Yahoo! News*, for instance. NYTimes.com is a site considered especially "sticky" because paid subscriptions are generally required, and the quality of journalism is high. However, its visitors stay an average of only nineteen minutes a month, the equivalent of spending only thirty-five seconds a day with a paper for which you pay a daily newspaper subscription. USAToday.com keeps visitors an average of only nine minutes a month, twenty seconds a day. The stickiest site, CNN Digital Network, keeps its visitors thirty-five minutes a month, about a minute a day. Overall, these numbers suggest that the digital news experience may lack depth.

Readers accustomed to receiving regular news alerts via text and social media may visit a website or news app only when an alert pops up. This pattern fuels a 24/7 news cycle, forcing newspapers to publish frequent updates to keep up with the competition and capture at least a moment of a frenzied multitasker's attention. Digital tracking of developments throughout the day allows broadcasters to plan accordingly for evening newscasts that offer both fresh material to viewers who are already familiar with a story and sufficient background for those who are not.

Users who want not only essential facts but also context eagerly follow links accompanying stories to related stories or other websites. Story mentions and links on popular websites can end up generating massive volume that crashes a smaller news site's web server—the **Slashdot effect**, named for a frequent occurrence on this very popular technology news site. From a business standpoint, though, media organizations want visitors to remain on their site. This raises the question of what hyperlinks to provide and how to provide them so that users are encouraged to linger or to explore and return.

Slashdot effect

When a smaller news site's Web server crashes because of increased traffic after its mention on popular websites, named for a frequent occurrence on the very popular technology news site Slashdot.org.

PERSONALIZATION

The Internet allows users to personalize content, ranging from news on local weather to favorite sports teams to stock portfolios. Personalization, an engaging feature unique to online or mobile media, is transforming the way journalists write or produce stories. For example, a standard version of a story can be enhanced with database information on a user's online behavior, location, or stated interests.

Personalization is not without its downside, however. Personalized versions of the news may omit other important information without even identifying such omissions or changes. Highly personalized "Daily Me" news digests may also narrow people's range of interests to such an extent that they have difficulty talking about other topics.

CONTEXTUALIZATION

Users able to access a reporter's raw material will still want someone to provide necessary context and interpretation. They prefer not to read an entire political speech or government report, for instance, to determine what, if anything, is important. Although users, for example, may be able to find an interactive map indicating the frequency and type of crime in their neighborhood within the past year, most crime-mapping sites do not provide any context. Users will not learn from mapping sites whether crime rates are increasing or decreasing or what happened to people charged with those crimes. Ideally, a site could provide all this information, along with links to past news stories on specific crimes and other relevant information.

Mash-ups like this one signal an emerging form of media content blended from multiple images.

Mash-ups that combine geographic data overlaid with editorial content are becoming increasingly popular and easy to create. The real estate site Zillow, for example, lets users see house locations, estimated values, asking prices, and final selling prices.

CONVERGENCE

Increasingly, video, audio, and interactive graphics supplement and enhance online text; similarly, text can enrich primarily video stories by providing greater depth and context and different access to information. Truly interactive multimedia experiences that allow the user to stop or replay segments at will, skip familiar information, and learn background information as needed clearly distinguish online journalism from print predecessors.

Technology has changed not only how news is produced and presented but how it is gathered. Digital and video cameras have made photography and videography much easier for journalists, so much so that a single reporter can easily video-record interviews or events for a multimedia news story. Voice of America radio journalists, having been trained in digital-video shooting and editing, can enhance their online stories with video. Other news organizations, such as the BBC, are training many of their journalists in video techniques. Convergence requires journalists to be competent, if not necessarily expert, with the range of tools in the digital toolkit.

ETHICS IN MEDIA
Maintaining Standards in the Digital Age

One of the challenges of digital convergence is maintaining the highest ethical standards in journalism and media when conditions are changing constantly and rapidly. Journalists and other media professionals often have to operate quickly with fewer resources to support their efforts and decisions and where digital technology has sometimes laid hidden ethical traps.

Widespread protests erupted in August 2014 after a police officer in Ferguson, MO, shot and killed unarmed black teenager Michael Brown.

One such instance occurred during coverage of the ongoing social movement inspired by events in Ferguson, Missouri.

In August of 2014, an unarmed black man, Michael Brown, age 18, was involved in an interaction on the street with police officer Darren Wilson. A struggle ensued and Brown was shot and killed. Widespread protests erupted shortly after objecting to police violence against black men, not only in Ferguson but across the nation.

Covering the event and subsequent protests, on November 30, 2014, the *New York Times* ran online a digital photo of the home of the police officer at the heart of the controversy. *Times* policy normally prohibits publication of a home address of a law enforcement officer, especially during an ongoing situation. But encoded in the digital image were the precise geographic coordinates of the officer's home, giving anyone with some digital savvy the ability to extract the address.

The *Times* quickly retracted the photo in response to objections, but the Internet genie is not easily put back in the digital bottle. Once on the Web, the photo was widely accessed and distributed, and the officer began to receive death threats linked to his home address.

The *Times* claims the release of the home address was an inadvertent mistake, and it no doubt was. But the bigger question is whether in the age of digital connectivity and Big Data, news and media organizations in general need to take their ethics game to an entirely new level to maintain high ethical standards.

The Business of Journalism

The early years of the twenty-first century have been challenging for the media, particularly news organizations. Companies that predicted new business opportunities in convergence, such as the former AOL Time Warner or Bertelsmann, invested greatly in developing media services that never made a profit. Those that adopted a more cautious approach see even fewer reasons to invest in new media technologies. Nevertheless, even executives who have been burned say that they simply moved too quickly and that change will inevitably occur.

Advertising revenues have steadily declined for the past several years, profoundly so in print media; and, although growing, online advertising still comprises only a fraction of overall revenues. These losses, combined with a recession that began in December 2007, have strained news organizations severely. In 2008, the American Society of News Editors (ASNE) found that the newspaper industry had suffered its largest drop in thirty years, with a 4.4 percent workforce decrease from 2007. Jobs continue to be cut, although more recently at a reduced rate.

In a 2011 ASNE survey, newspaper editors cited three main challenges: (1) how to maintain quality writing and editing despite staff and budget cutbacks, (2) how to adapt roles and workflow processes rapidly to the 24/7 newsroom, and (3) how to take advantage of mobile media to generate revenue opportunities and reach more readers. The spread of the digital metered paywall as introduced by the *New York Times* in March 2011 signals a likely direction for the twenty-first-century business model. In 1997, the *Wall Street Journal* became the first major newspaper to require users to pay for digital content. However, until the *New York Times* adopted a limited version of this model, few followed suit.

Not only are layoffs common, but entire news bureaus are closing down. In 2000, Cox newspapers had thirty correspondents in Washington, DC, to cover the inauguration of President George Bush. In 2009, it closed its Washington bureau. Some news organizations have taken what are considered even more drastic steps. In 2009, the respected *Christian Science Monitor* and the 146-year-old *Seattle Post-Intelligencer*, a Hearst paper, opted for digital rather than print editions. A growing number of newspapers have reduced their print publication schedule to three times a week, publishing only digital news the remainder of the week. These trends will continue with newspapers, especially as tablet computers become more popular.

SALARIES

Salaries for journalism professionals vary with the medium (television is the highest paid, print media the lowest, digital in between); location or market (the larger the market, the higher the pay); position (ownership, higher management, or celebrity status correlates positively with pay); experience; and a variety of other factors, including sex (men are generally paid more than women, as unfair as that may be). Because salaries and overall compensation vary so widely—from $15,000 a year to many millions of dollars—crude averages are relatively meaningless.

In general, network television offers the highest salaries for midlevel producers. National magazines and newspapers pay fairly well, whereas papers in mid- and small-sized markets pay poorly relative to similar-level jobs in public relations,

FIGURE 8-1 Salary Range for Journalists by Experience

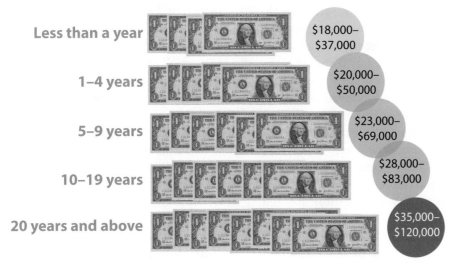

Less than a year	$18,000–$37,000
1–4 years	$20,000–$50,000
5–9 years	$23,000–$69,000
10–19 years	$28,000–$83,000
20 years and above	$35,000–$120,000

Source: Payscale.com

for example. Internet media salaries are good, and stock option plans made a few journalists instant millionaires when the companies went public. Many more, however, missed that gravy train in the dot-com bust.

DIVERSITY IN THE NEWSROOM

American newsrooms have been slow to change. In 1950, African American journalist Marvel Cooke (1903–2000) was hired as a reporter and feature writer for the *New York Daily Compass*. She was the only woman and the only black person on the paper's staff and among the first blacks to work for any white-owned daily newspaper.

The ASNE regularly conducts a survey on employment in U.S. daily newspapers. The numbers of minority and women hires have fallen short of mirroring the percentages found in the general population and fall shorter still when it comes to management. Because of layoffs and hiring freezes throughout the newspaper industry in recent years, the percentage of minority employees has actually risen slightly, to just over 13 percent. Industry watchers worry that the persistent dominance of white males in newsrooms skews news coverage toward material that appeals to them, content that does not reflect the communities of readers or viewers accurately. A 2012 *Extra!* study found that on the opinion pages of the *New York Times*, the *Washington Post*, and the *Wall Street Journal*, Latinos had less than 2 percent of the bylines. None of these papers even had a Latino staff columnist. In more than a year of political book reviews on C-SPAN or the *New York Times Book Review*, not one of the 432 authors, reviewers, or interviewers was Latino.[17]

Bob Butler, reporter at KCBS radio, is president of the National Association of Black Journalists, 2013–2015.

MEDIA CAREERS

The employment outlook for journalists in the digital age is generally not good, largely a reflection of the state of the overall economy and related budget and staff cutbacks. After a decade of strong employment and business growth, the twenty-first century got off to a troubled start that hit media and technology companies especially hard. Still, research from the University of Georgia on employment trends in journalism and media fields showed a slight uptick in 2011 and 2012 that stalled in 2013. Although the 2013 launch of Al Jazeera America provided new employment opportunities for some two hundred journalists, it was not enough to offset the overall stagnant job market for journalists. Moreover, salaries are flat, as data from the University of Georgia's annual survey shows.[18]

Still, these are exciting times for journalists, especially those with an entrepreneurial and innovative spirit. Online and mobile journalism, still in their infancy, will play an increasingly prominent role, and possibilities remain for journalists in traditional print, radio, and television if they are willing to adopt new methods and approaches utilizing the digital tools available. Even in traditional newsrooms, journalists now need a wide variety of digital skills and a solid understanding of online and mobile media's unique characteristics. Today's journalists must be as comfortable telling a story through an interactive, multimedia graphic as they are through a traditional text narrative. They may not need the same depth of technical knowledge as programmers or Web designers, but they need to be able to converse intelligently with them as stories are produced. In addition to strong writing and storytelling skills, contemporary journalists will benefit from knowing how to use spreadsheets, statistics, databases, code, algorithms, and social media to craft stories from complex raw information, such as Twitter feeds on breaking news events.

No specific college major is necessarily best for journalists, although most have degrees in the humanities or social sciences or journalism itself. A double major in journalism and the natural or physical sciences, or business is a great advantage for journalists specializing in those fields. Yet regardless of undergraduate major, a focus on writing, editing, and storytelling is crucial for a successful career. Students working at a college newspaper or digital news operation have the opportunity to experience this profession firsthand and publish stories, valuable clips that news organizations will expect job candidates to supply.

LOOKING BACK AND MOVING FORWARD

Today's 24/7 news cycle and recent budget and staff cuts mean less time to polish the final product and increased dependence on other sources to provide news. Yet despite its various perceived weaknesses and evident challenges, news remains the bedrock of journalism in its mission not only to inform the public of significant events but also to provide important context that helps people better understand these events.

The Internet and digital media are transforming journalism, change that the profession initially resisted rather than embraced. Consequently, many news organizations, especially newspapers, have only recently begun trying to figure out ways to live in the digital world. As advertisers go elsewhere to find audiences, news media are left scrambling to stay afloat and adjust to new realities. Foremost among these is a shift toward audience participation, now considered crucial to the practice of journalism and key to a truly healthy democracy.

Despite all this turmoil, the employment picture for journalism graduates has brightened. Rapid industry change has created new jobs for candidates with "the right stuff" for the convergent newsroom, where professionals no longer declare themselves to be a either a print journalist or a broadcast journalist. The former may be expected to shoot or record multimedia with a digital-video camera or audio recorder. Similarly, the latter are being asked to write text stories to accompany video. The convergent journalist, although not an expert in every type of media, is comfortable with various technologies and with social media.

Although increasingly important, technical expertise alone does not guarantee a successful career. Internalizing and practicing the values of journalism, especially a commitment to truth, accuracy, and fairness, is still paramount. Quality writing and compelling storytelling, especially if enriched with multimedia, are also essential. Whereas knowing how to use certain multimedia tools, such as basic image editing, is required, knowing which digital tool to use and when is even more important.

Journalism has always been fundamentally concerned with knowledge creation and management. Good reporters have extensive files of sources and contacts they can turn to when they need to know something quickly, and they have developed a sense for discerning good information from bad. In the world of convergent journalism, this ability becomes even more important. With the proliferation of potential sources for information, the public needs to hear trusted editorial voices that can identify and interpret who and what is reliable and significant and why. More than any other media professionals, journalists are equipped to serve this function, perhaps in closer collaboration with citizen-journalists or in new story-telling formats that invite audience participation.

MEDIA MATTERS   A NOSE FOR NEWS

1. (T/F) The FCC must license broadcast journalists, unlike their mobile news counterparts.

2. How would you define "news" in one sentence?

3. What publisher was the model for Orson Welles' classic movie *Citizen Kane*?

4. What two values have begun to replace the goal of objectivity in journalism today?

5. What is a pseudo-event, and how does it relate to news?

6. How has digital-first publishing affected journalism?

7. (T/F) Some of the most popular news websites now are citizen-journalism sites.

8. How does a 24/7 news cycle affect news organizations?

9. (T/F) Employment trends show signs of improvement in many news organizations.

10. On average and other things being equal, including years of experience and media market size, who makes more money—a journalist or a PR professional?

ANSWERS: 1. False. **3.** William Randolph Hearst. **4.** Fairness and balance. **5.** An event created to attract media attention, such as a press conference. **7.** False. **8.** A bigger news hole to fill, shorter and continuous deadlines, and changes in roles and work-flow processes. **9.** True. **10.** PR professional.

FURTHER READING

The Elements of Journalism: What Newspeople Should Know and the Public Should Expect. Bill Kovach, Tom Rosenstiel (2001) Three Rivers Press.

Slow News. Peter Laufer (2011) Sironi Editore.

News About News: American Journalism in Peril. Leonard Downie Jr., Robert G. Kaiser (2002) Knopf.

Breaking the News: How the Media Undermine American Democracy. James Fallows (1997) Vintage.

Custodians of Conscience. Theodore Lewis Glasser (1998) Columbia University Press.

Why Democracies Need an Unlovable Press. Michael Schudson (2008) Polity.

The Vanishing Newspaper: Saving Journalism in the Information Age. Philip Meyer (2004) University of Missouri Press.

The Death and Life of American Journalism: The Media Revolution That Will Begin the World Again. Robert McChesney, John Nichols (2011) Nation Books.

Digitizing the News: Innovation in Online Newspapers. Pablo Boczkowski (2005) MIT Press.

Convergent Journalism: The Fundamentals of Multimedia Reporting. Stephen Quinn (2005) Peter Lang Publishers.

Convergent Journalism: An Introduction. Stephen Quinn, Vincent F. Filak (2005) Focal Press.

The Elements of Online Journalism. Rey Rosales (2006) iUniverse.

We the Media: Grassroots Journalism by the People, for the People. Dan Gillmor (2006) O'Reilly Media.

Losing the News: The Future of the News That Feeds Democracy. Alex Jones (2011) Oxford University Press.

Page One: Inside the New York Times and the Future of Journalism. David Folkenflik (2011) Public Affairs.

Literary Journalism. Norm Sims, Mark Kramer (1995) Ballantine Books.

Tell Me No Lies: Investigative Journalism That Changed the World. John Pilger (2005) Thunder's Mouth Press.

The News Sorority: Diane Sawyer, Katie Couric, Christiane Amanpour—and the (Ongoing, Imperfect, Complicated) Triumph of Women in TV News. Sheila Weller (2014) Penguin Press.

Advertising and
Public Relations
THE POWER OF PERSUASION

9

ositioning a company, product, or person is a challenging core activity in public relations (PR); crisis response to a position in peril, an onerous one. Untoward events that swiftly sully a carefully cultivated image test the mettle of even the most seasoned and accomplished PR professionals. For high-profile figures, whose every move is scrutinized by fans and critics alike, damage control can prove especially problematic. And when the documented missteps of a politician, actor, or athlete surface in the media and go viral, as is so often the case in our digital age, a crisis can quickly escalate into a disaster whose effective management may offer the only hope for salvaging reputations and careers.

Enter or, rather, exit Ray Rice, from an Atlantic City elevator, dragging his apparently unconscious fiancé, Janelle Palmer, by her shoulders. Naturally, a witness recorded the horrific incident, and naturally, TMZ, a media outlet that traffics in Hollywood scandal and gossip, broke the news, complete with damning footage. As NFL training camps started in the summer of 2014, when conversation on sports and social media typically turns to early predictions about winners and losers, the spotlight shone brightly instead on the disgraced running back for the Baltimore Ravens and the disgraceful NFL reaction to a shocking video that provided seemingly incontrovertible evidence of abuse.

The initial NFL response appeared woefully insufficient, an assessment supported by a subsequent recording released in September (again by TMZ). The NFL commissioner claimed to have no prior knowledge of this second video that showed Rice knocking his fiancé unconscious in the elevator, and the leading rusher for the Ravens, who had initially only been suspended, was promptly fired.[1]

It was too little, too late, for most. The reputation of professional sports has long suffered for failing to satisfactorily address acts of domestic violence committed by its players. And the handling of the Ray Rice situation was no exception. The management of this crisis did not succeed in improving relations with a skeptical and outraged public, leaving the NFL with a metaphorical black eye.

LEARNING OBJECTIVES

>> Describe the overview of strategic communications.

>> Explain the theoretical foundations of advertising and public relations.

>> Describe the purpose and form of advertising and public relations.

>> Outline the history and structure of the advertising and public relations industries.

>> Identify various new types of advertising and PR strategies with digital media.

>> Examine the impact of digital technologies on advertising and public relations.

Antidomestic-violence activists felt compelled to take matters into their own hands, featuring a physical black eye to a powerful effect on social media in an effort to pressure NFL advertisers. Cover Girl had launched a "Get Your Game Face On" campaign portraying female fans sporting jerseys and makeup in the various team colors. A digitally doctored Ravens image dramatically transformed the model's look and the ad's message. Beneath the purple eye shadow appeared a huge reddish black eye, an image that quickly became a meme, often with the hashtag #Goodellmustgo.[2]

Cover Girl did not withdraw its NFL sponsorship, nor did NFL commissioner Roger Goodell resign. Nevertheless, this digital grassroots movement succeeded in increasing public awareness and meaningful dialog about domestic abuse.

Many diverse forces shape mass-communication media. Among the most important are advertising and public relations (PR), types of strategic communications linked by an emphasis on persuasion as well as a big-picture view informed by research. In this chapter, we examine the nature and history of these two essential media industries and their adaptation to the age of digitization and convergence.

Advertising has traditionally been the method by which companies or stores reach a mass audience, utilizing the distribution system newspapers or electronic media outlets have created. Public relations has typically involved managing the public persona or reputation of a company, also typically through media outlets and their mass-distribution networks.

In a digital, networked world, however, almost anyone can distribute information cheaply. It would seem that companies could now eliminate advertising costs by contacting audiences directly. Although true to some extent, the practice is less prevalent than one would think. Companies may have expertise in their fields, but they do not always understand how best to persuade their target audiences or how to best produce media content. The expertise of strategic-communications professionals is often needed to reach audiences with powerful, persuasive messages and to create an enduring brand or company image.

Advertising, the most prevalent form of media content, is paid for by a for-profit or not-for-profit organization, a political campaign, or a wealthy individual. Advertisements, whether in print, on broadcast radio and television, on billboards, online, or via mobile devices, provide much of the basic financial revenue that pays for the creation and delivery of media content. Two-thirds of most newspapers and magazines are filled with advertisements (not including advertising inserts). Even though most television programming time is devoted to content rather than commercials, consider the number of times the audience sees the same commercial during the course of a program, what advertising media planners call "frequency of exposure." Studies have shown that children tend to remember commercial jingles and catchphrases better than basic facts about U.S. government or history.[3]

PR has become increasingly important for all types of organizations and for famous individuals. Historically, many organizations have sought to influence media content and thus public opinion. Positive media coverage can increase

News conferences or other scheduled PR announcements intended to attract favorable publicity are examples of earned media.

knowledge of a company while enhancing its image and credibility. Contemporary public relations uses social media to engage the public or stakeholders in timely and interactive discourse in ways that were not possible in the mass-communication era.

Unlike advertisements, public relations material is not purchased content but rather **earned media**. A staged event or press release may become the basis of a news story. Awards ceremonies or news conferences, for example, suggest article ideas to journalists. Public relations professionals generate favorable publicity for clients and ensure that any potentially damaging information is framed in the least harmful way. During crisis communications situations, such as the disastrous 2010 BP oil spill in the Gulf of Mexico, PR people work to mitigate negative press coverage.

Most news media depend on the PR function of corporate, government, or not-for-profit organizations for information in various forms such as scheduled announcements, research studies or reports, corporate financial statements, interviews with executives and employees, and so forth. One measure of the effectiveness of PR is how many news outlets publish or air material based on what the organization has produced.

Strategic Communications

Central to a range of fields, including advertising, PR, and internal or corporate communications, strategic communications aim to persuade an audience to think or behave as the communicator wishes. Part of what makes this task challenging is knowing which media channel will be most effective for delivering a particular message to a particular audience. Some companies, for example, have been heavily criticized in the media for delivering notices of layoffs via emails rather than face to face—or even worse, employees hearing about layoffs in the media before they are informed from management.

Research on persuasion has identified various types of appeals, ranging from presenting scientific evidence to celebrity endorsement to attractive colors in the company logo. Perhaps the most important factor in successful persuasion is the audience, or, more accurately, knowing and understanding the audience, what they think and feel, their likes and dislikes, and many other factors about them. A large direct-email campaign, for example, does little good if your audience communicates primarily through text messaging or Facebook. Of course, audiences are evolving. Digital, networked media increasingly enable the public to be active participants in a dialog rather than merely passive receivers of messages from large organizations.

Strategic communications attempt to persuade target audiences to act in a certain way. Perhaps you want them to change their behavior by quitting smoking or eating more healthfully. Or maybe you want them to donate to a cause, email their senator, vote for a political candidate, buy your product (or buy more of your product), or maybe just "Like" you on Facebook. What kind of message will most likely persuade people to take the desired action? Will a personalized message be most effective, or will an advertising campaign on TV or online be the best way to reach and convince them? How should the message be crafted, and what tone should it convey? Can it be done in such a way that encourages people to send the message to others in their social network?

💬 **earned media**

Favorable publicity prompted by a public relations source rather than advertising, such as a news conference, an event, or a press release; the opposite of paid media, such as advertising or product placements.

The U.S. television industry holds its annual TV upfronts in May, when the industry pitches upcoming new shows to advertisers.

Strategic communications increasingly use social media to reach their audience. Companies like Dunkin Donuts use their Facebook pages to highlight pictures of their customers.

Advertisers carefully consider a range of factors to make ads as persuasive as possible.

💬 rhetoric

One of the ancient arts of discourse that focuses on the art of persuasion.

These concerns apply equally to an executive proposing company expansion to the board of directors as to a company launching a new product or a not-for-profit seeking more volunteers or donors. Here, we will focus on advertising and PR and leave internal corporate communications aside, but the principles are largely the same in terms of the need to know your audience and what will best influence them.

PERSUASIVE COMMUNICATIONS

The most effective campaigns use persuasive techniques that encourage audiences to agree with the persuader's point in an apparently natural or commonsense way. Audience members may have started out thinking one thing before being exposed to the message, but afterward think differently, often feeling like they came to the conclusion themselves. Unlike coercion, in which people are forced to change because of a real or perceived threat, persuasion often involves people freely persuading themselves. We may think of persuasive communications as a modern phenomenon that developed along with the rise of mass communications. Its roots go back, however, to at least the time of the Greek philosophers and their study of **rhetoric**, the art of persuasion.

Rhetoric was one of the three classical areas of learning that any educated person should know, along with logic and grammar. Despite strong objections by the likes of Socrates, Plato, and Aristotle, who valued truth, the Sophists, a group of Greek philosophers focused entirely on rhetoric, taught whomever could pay them and saw the truth as largely unimportant, something even perhaps in the eye of the beholder: the most important aspect of an argument was whether it was persuasive. Rhetoric remains a foundation of politics, business, and life. In an age when more people than ever can speak publicly, the ability to persuade and make your voice heard above other voices becomes even more vital.

At least two dozen major modern scientific theories of persuasive communication and audience decision making help explain or provide models of persuasion that guide the media campaigns of advertising and public relations. Most such theories include certain assumptions about how our thoughts and emotions affect our behavior. These can be broadly categorized as follows:

1. People's behavior and actions are somehow linked to their cognitions about the world, which generally include attitudes, beliefs, and values, as well as their general knowledge and social influences.

2. How people process information about the world (thinking deeply about issues or only looking at superficial cues) affects what messages they find most persuasive.

3. A persuader's credibility, authority, and attractiveness all can contribute to successful persuasion, although which is most effective depends on the type of message and audience.

One theory of note takes a different viewpoint. The **theory of cognitive dissonance** claims that we act first and then rationalize or create reasons for our behavior afterward to make our actions consistent with self-perceived notions of who we are. This theory helps explain a range of otherwise puzzling behaviors, such as why freshmen subject themselves to humiliating hazing rituals to join a fraternity or sorority to which they become intensely loyal.

theory of cognitive dissonance

Theory of persuasion that states we act first and then rationalize our behavior afterward to make our actions consistent with self-perceived notions of who we are.

THE ROLE OF MEDIA IN PERSUASION

Because people can only experience so many things directly, media are the obvious means by which the public becomes aware of a product or an issue. Getting an advertisement on national television seen by millions simultaneously may have a certain effect, but mere awareness is not enough. Too often, marketers assume that once people know about their merchandise or cause, they will want to buy it or participate. This is not the case. Awareness is only the first—and in many ways, the easiest—step in the process of persuasion.

Still, the media often have their own kind of credibility. An appearance on national television may confer on someone an air of authority as an expert. You are more likely to watch a YouTube video received from a trusted friend than from someone you do not know. So effective are the media in creating and establishing fame that many celebrities are now known simply for being celebrities and not for being singers, actors, or another kind of talented performer.

Jade Goody used her fame as a reality TV star in the UK to publicize the need for women to test for cervical cancer, from which she eventually died.

Although the **direct effects model** of media influence has been largely disproved, we still believe that media can influence the public in certain ways. From this assumption, it follows that media-based communications campaigns can be strategically designed to produce the attitude and behavior shifts that persuaders desire.

direct effects model

Model of mass communication that claims media have direct and measurable effects on audiences, such as encouraging them to buy products or to become violent.

Advertising

advertising

An ancient form of human communication designed to inform or persuade members of the public with regard to some product or service.

Advertising is an ancient form of human communication whose modern incarnation features typically sponsored or paid-for commercial messages designed to inform and persuade others to buy a good or service, accept a point of view, or act in some fashion desired by the sender. Print and electronic media that developed around this advertising model are in the business of selling mass audiences to advertisers. From an advertiser's perspective, the media exist primarily as the means to gather an audience. Communications professionals, while recognizing some truth in this view, would counter that media content must still be interesting, useful, or entertaining to attract an audience.

Media organizations determine how much they can charge advertisers for space in their print or digital publication or airtime on their station based on the number of audience members reached or delivered to the advertiser. In broadcasting, this number is the **rating**. In print and online media, it is the **CPM**, or **cost per thousand** audience members. The online model is still evolving, however; and CPM may include the cost per thousand page views or unique visitors to a site, a Web page, or a mobile app. In **performance-based advertising**, also used online, advertisers pay for results only, such as actual "click-throughs" to the advertiser's site rather than total page views. One of the largest areas of online advertising has become **search-engine marketing**, discussed in more detail later.

Advertising rates vary according to the size and quality of the target audience. In radio, for example, the most expensive time to purchase advertising is "a.m. and p.m. drive time" when audiences are at their peak as drivers commute to and from work. An advertiser for a youth-oriented product may choose to show its commercial on prime-time MTV rather than a late-night network slot because, although smaller, the audience is a better fit for their product. A media outlet whose audience is upscale and has disposable income would generally be more appealing to an advertiser than an audience without much spending power.

rating

Used in broadcast media to explain the number of households that watched a particular show.

cost per thousand (CPM)

Standard unit for measuring advertising rates for publications based on circulation.

performance-based advertising

Any form of online ad buying in which an advertiser pays for results rather than paying for the size of the publisher's audience or the CPM.

search-engine marketing

Paying for certain keywords to show up high in rankings in a search engine, such as Google or Bing.

THE HISTORICAL DEVELOPMENT OF ADVERTISING

In its earliest form, advertising was conducted as face-to-face, word-of-mouth communication in which buyers and sellers negotiated and bartered for goods and services. In ancient Egypt, papyrus advertisements were posted in common, public areas. The printing press gave rise in the fifteenth century to advertising in mass-communication settings, usually in the form of posters, flyers, or broadsheets. Broadsheet advertisements were a popular technique to attract people to emigrate to the New World. Colonists in the eighteenth and nineteenth centuries could obtain information, from where to buy groceries and patent medicines to when a ship was sailing.

By the mid-1800s, ads had become a mainstay for U.S. firms marketing products and services, designed to stand out more prominently from surrounding

MEDIA PIONEERS
Madam C. J. Walker

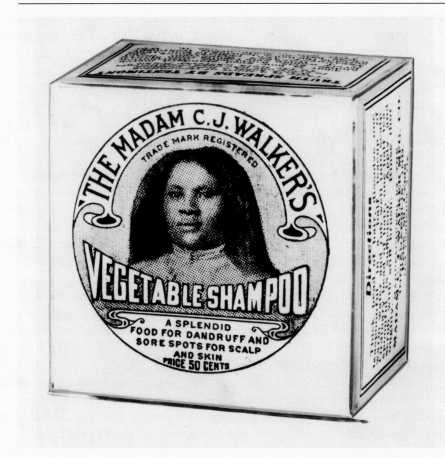

Born on a Louisiana cotton plantation in 1867 to former slaves, Sara Breedlove became the first female African American self-made millionaire in the United States. At the time of her death in 1919, she was also the richest African American woman. She made her fortune creating and effectively promoting her own line of beauty and hair products for black women through her company, the Madam C. J. Walker Manufacturing Company, using the name by which she was known.

Walker's ads were distinctive and effective for several reasons, including their sensitive and attractive portrayals of black women, with Walker herself often serving as the model. At the time, most other ads targeting black women used whites to sell the products or featured unfavorable, stereotypical depictions of African Americans. Walker's ads encouraged sales of the product lines and invited readers to apply to be a local company representative, much like Avon today.

Madam Walker was not just a pioneer of advertising but also a champion of social causes. After the East St. Louis Race Riot of 1917, which resulted in the deaths of an estimated two hundred blacks, Walker joined in a national effort to pass legislation making lynching a federal crime. Walker was also a philanthropist and an inspiration to others, especially women. In one of her many lectures, she once said, "I want to say to every woman present, don't sit down and wait for the opportunities to come . . . you have to get up and make them."

editorial content. Individuals also advertised their unique services. In 1856, publisher Robert Bonner ran the first full-page advertisement to promote his own literary paper, the *New York Ledger*.[4] At this time there were no standards in advertising, and medicinal advertisers often made extravagant and untrue claims about a product's curative powers.

The early twentieth century saw the number of mass-produced and packaged goods expand along with the automobile industry. Today, the automobile industry is the largest advertiser, followed by retail, business, and consumer services.

Advertising for cigarettes and other tobacco products grew during the twentieth century, but not without criticism. In 1919, the magazine *Printer's Ink* warned against "an insidious campaign to create women smokers" in reaction to the portrayal of women smoking in cigarette ads.

Advertising Agencies

Early advertisers bought newspaper space and targeted local audiences primarily. Not until the 1860s did ads appear in nationally distributed monthly magazines. Among the most successful early sellers of newspaper advertising space was Volney B. Palmer, who created both the first advertising agency in 1841 and the long-standing business model for the industry, providing his advertising clients with circulation data and copies of the ads in addition to deducting an **ad-agency commission** from the advertising publication fee as compensation for his efforts.

When the penny press lowered the cost of purchasing a newspaper to a penny from six cents, advertising had to make up for the lost subscription revenues, and the advertising business grew quickly. By the 1860s, there were more than twenty advertising agencies in New York City. When N. W. Ayer & Son, founded in 1869, bought Palmer's firm, the trend toward consolidation began. Ayer built on Palmer's basic media-billing model, which charged clients a fee for placing ads in newspapers and magazines, and he established a standardized ad-agency commission: 15 percent of the total media billings. This agency also set the standard for creative services, with some of the most famous ad slogans of the twentieth century including the De Beers tagline "A diamond is forever"; AT&T's "Reach out and touch someone"; and Camel cigarettes' "I'd walk a mile for a Camel." In 2002, parent group Bcom3 reluctantly retired the venerable Ayer name.

The new electronic media in the twentieth century drew heavily on the resources of the advertising industry, which used radio and television effectively to promote a wide variety of products and services throughout the United States and internationally. Television quickly surpassed print media as the main vehicle for reaching a national advertising market. Online advertising is today the fastest-growing segment, second in volume only to combined cable and broadcast TV advertising. In 2013, for the first time ever, online advertising surpassed broadcast TV advertising. Mobile advertising and video continue to be large and show strong growth.

Commercial Television

Because three of the four early TV networks were affiliated with the radio networks, questions arose: not about whether to support television through advertising, as had been the case originally with radio, but about the best way to do it. Commercials quickly became a mainstay on television. The year 1948 established an early high-water mark for advertising, with 933 sponsors buying TV time. Considering the relatively small number of television sets sold at the time, this indicates how eager advertisers were to reach mass audiences in the new medium.

Variety reported in 1957 that during a typical week, viewers saw 420 commercials totaling five hours, eight minutes. In the early days of television, the names of advertisers, who often sponsored whole shows, were included as part of the title, such as *Texaco Star Theater*. The not-for-profit Television Bureau of Advertising, founded in 1953, responded to the emergence of television as the leading medium for advertising with a variety of tools and resources.

---

ad-agency commission

A percentage amount of the cost of an advertisement taken by the advertising agency that helped create and sell the ad.

Tony Schwartz created "The Daisy Spot," a TV commercial that aired only once as a paid spot but is considered by many the most influential commercial of all time.

One of the most talented advertising professionals in the audiovisual realm was Tony Schwartz, who died in 2008 and whose career spanned most of the twentieth century. A master of implied messages, he became famous for "The Daisy Spot," a 1964 advertisement considered among the most powerful political ads ever aired.[5] It cleverly suggested that Republican presidential candidate Barry Goldwater would likely get the United States embroiled in a nuclear war.

Commercial developments continued to reshape the TV landscape. In the 1960s, ABC extended the station break between programs from thirty to forty seconds to increase profits, and other networks soon followed suit. Within a few years, standard commercial lengths reached one minute. By 1971, networks increased profits further by cutting the length from sixty seconds to thirty without reducing rates a corresponding 50 percent. Networks began the practice of advertising "piggybacking," running messages for two related products from one company in the same one-minute commercial. In 1969, New York's WOR-TV became the first station to air an **infomercial**, a thirty- or sixty-minute program of exclusively commercial content.

Also in 1969, the U.S. Supreme Court applied the **Fairness Doctrine** to cigarette advertising, giving antismoking groups equal air time to reply to tobacco commercials. In 1970, a congressional ban on radio and TV cigarette advertising took effect, costing the broadcast business roughly $220 million in revenues. The hard-liquor industry voluntarily banned TV advertising for sixty years, and initial attempts in the early 2000s to advertise hard liquor drew heated criticism. Despite public disapproval, advertising continued; and today, such commercials, often targeting an audience in their twenties or early thirties, can frequently be seen during prime time.

Internet

Although today we are accustomed to a range of advertisements on the Web, the Internet began as a resolutely noncommercial space, created with taxpayers' money by engineers and computer scientists motivated more by its potential for expanding communication and knowledge than by profit. The first email marketing message, commonly called **spam**, after the processed meat (whose inspiration

infomercial

Also called "paid programming," a thirty- or sixty-minute television show that seeks to sell a product and that usually involves a celebrity spokesperson and customer testimonials.

Fairness Doctrine

Adopted by the FCC in 1949, it required broadcasters to seek out and present all sides of a controversial issue they were covering. It was discarded by the FCC in 1987.

spam

Unwanted mass emailing from advertisers.

was a Monty Python sketch that uses the term), was sent on May 3, 1978, by DEC, a now-defunct computer maker to all of four hundred people on ARPANET, the precursor to the Internet. In 1994, immigration lawyers Canter and Siegel sent an email advertisement to over six thousand on Usenet. Prompting harsh backlash from the online community, this event is now widely held to be the start of the commercialization of the Internet, although seemingly quaint in comparison to the billions of spam messages sent worldwide today.

The first advertisements on the Web appeared on *Hotwired* in 1994, the online version of *Wired* magazine. *Hotwired* offered space on the website to fourteen advertisers in the form of the now-familiar **banner ad**. However, because online connection speeds were slow in 1994, the ads could not be large graphics and remained fairly small, with HTML text primarily. Today, increased bandwidth allows for multimedia ads, and advertisers are considering new types of advertising, including increased use of video, to further attract the consumer's attention.

THE RISE OF BRANDING

Branding, a process intertwined with the growth of advertising, creates in the consumer's mind a clear identity for a particular company's product or trademark. Derived from the Old Norse word "brandr," branding means literally "to burn" and came to mean burning a mark or brand into a product.[6] Branding via advertising developed in the 1890s and early 1900s as companies sought to distinguish their products in an increasingly cluttered and competitive marketplace. With little differentiation among similar products in terms of what they provided or the ingredients they contained, the only way to appear different was to present a memorable brand, or identity, to consumers.

To establish a brand's uniqueness, a catchy slogan and distinctive visual identity are created and then advertised across multiple media, with frequent exposure to the desired audience segment or target group. Among the first to do this successfully was Campbell's soup, which featured the artwork of Grace Weidersein in 1904 depicting "The Campbell's Kids," images that appear in its advertising to this day. Another highly successful campaign was launched in 1970 to promote Coca-Cola, whose "I'd Like to Teach the World to Sing" commercial became an instant hit. The popular song even sold a million records.

Brands are especially powerful tools to help distinguish among very similar competitors. Although Pepsi has traditionally been behind Coke in sales, in the 1970s, Pepsi's double-blind taste test (neither the tester nor the person running the test knew which was Coke or Pepsi) found, surprisingly, that more people preferred the taste of Pepsi over Coke if they did not know the brands. The subsequent advertising campaign touting this increased Pepsi's sales while Coke sales declined.

This prompted Coke in 1985 to introduce a new, sweeter formula—New Coke—which was soundly rejected by loyal Coke drinkers. Within three months, the company reintroduced and rebranded original Coke as Coca-Cola Classic, deciding to call the new formula Coke II. Ironically, after the reintroduction of the original Coke, sales outpaced both the new formula and Pepsi. By the mid-1980s, Coke II was only sold in the United States and Canada; and by 2002, it was discontinued entirely. The whole episode is considered a cautionary tale for marketers about branding and about fierce consumer loyalties that may not be apparent from typical market research.

banner ad

Original form of advertising on the Web, it appears across the top of a website.

branding

Process of creating in the consumer's mind a clear identity for a particular company's product, logo, or trademark.

Some products highlight their name to enhance brand recognition, whereas others are easily identified simply by their logo.

So hugely successful are some advertising campaigns that their brand names become synonymous with the product itself. Many consumers consider "Kleenex" (introduced in 1924) simply the generic name for facial tissue and "Xerox" generic for photocopy. This can be both good and bad for the advertiser. Consumers with extremely high brand-name awareness who go shopping for a particular product whose name has come to represent generic alternatives may actually end up buying another brand.

Brands are almost always trademarked. Companies can sue for trademark infringement, claiming that the copycat brand is stealing business by confusing consumers and perhaps hurting the company's reputation with inferior products. Companies may protect their brands zealously, such as when Coca-Cola forced a small café in a remote town in Yunnan Province, China, to change its name from Coca-Cola Café. Companies also attempt to associate themselves with a more famous brand by using a similar logo, colors, or name, such as the cheap electronics maker Coby, whose font is similar to Sony's, and the Northeast-based, urban fast-food chain Kennedy Fried Chicken.

Protecting a brand is not only about enforcing intellectual property. As much as 70 percent of a company's value may be in its brand rather than in its physical property, such as factories and products. Table 9-1 shows the estimated brand valuation of some major companies. "Buying the brand" can be a strong incentive in company mergers.

Branding is important to individuals as well, says personal-branding guru Dan Schawbel, author of *Me 2.0: Build a Powerful Brand to Achieve Career Success*. According to Schawbel and dozens of leading technology thinkers he has interviewed, creating a strong personal brand will help define and differentiate the new employee from the competition. Brands will become even more important in the digital age, especially in media industries.

In 2014, a federal appeals court upheld a decision in favor of 5-hour Energy for trademark infringement. 6 Hour Energy Shot (note this brand does not use hyphens in their name) has since been rebranded and relabeled as 6 Hour Power.

TABLE 9-1 Top Six U.S. Companies by Brand Valuations

COMPANY	2014 BRAND VALUE ($ MILLION)	BRAND CONTRIBUTION TO MARKET CAPITALIZATION OF PARENT COMPANY (%)
(Apple)	118,863	18
Google	107,439	30
Coca-Cola	81,563	44
IBM	72,244	45
Microsoft	61,154	16
(GE)	45,480	18

Source: "Best Global Brands, 2014," *Interbrand*, 2014, accessed June 10, 2015, http://www.bestglobalbrands.com/2014/ranking/

Celebrities fiercely guard their brands, likenesses, and even their names from infringement by others. In 2008, Curtis Jackson—aka 50 Cent—sued Taco Bell for using his stage name, a registered trademark, to promote its value menu. In 2014, an Indiana corporation that owns the likeness rights and other intellectual property related to the James Dean estate sued Twitter for allowing a user to create the account @James Dean without their permission. *Keeping Up with the Kardashians* sisters Kendall and Kylie have filed to protect "Kendall and Kylie," as well as "Kendall & Kylie."

DISCUSSION QUESTIONS: Consider both a familiar and an unfamiliar industry or category (e.g., cars, entertainment companies, airlines, hotels). Name three brands within each category. How did you become familiar with the brand, through direct use or only through advertising?

CONVERGENCE CULTURE
MMORPG, FPS—and IGA

In-game advertising (IGA) has been growing rapidly, both in dollars spent by advertisers and in the volume of ads themselves. IGA, advertising that occurs inside either online or stand-alone video games for desktop or mobile devices, is distinct from advergaming, games produced only to advertise a product.

In-game advertising debuted in 1978 in *Adventureland*, which included an ad, in essence a product placement, for the company's next game, *Pirate Adventure*. In 1991, Penguin biscuits inserted the first commercially sponsored IGA for its product in *James Pond: CodenameRoboCod*.

IGAs can be static or dynamic. A static ad is typically shown as a display in the background, much like an in-game billboard. For example, an Adidas billboard appears in *FIFA International Soccer*. It might also appear during a pause in game play while a game is loading. If a static IGA is integrated deeply, the player may have to view or interact with the ad to complete the game. Static IGAs cannot be changed once a game is produced and distributed.

As the popularity of online games has grown, so has the placement of dynamic IGAs. Advertisers can update these ads remotely, inserting newer versions over time. Such IGAs can be tied to specific campaigns or marketing offers. President Barack Obama's 2008 campaign inserted dynamic IGAs in several Xbox games.

Some companies offer free versions of games with IGAs, such as *Age of Conan*, whose embedded enticements lure gamers to purchase the premium version. Mobile games have increased not only the prevalence of IGA but greatly added to game and in-app purchases as well.

Research suggests IGAs have mixed value. A 2009 study showed that 80 percent of gamers could correctly recall a product advertised in IGAs, and 56 percent viewed advertisers favorably if an IGA allowed them to play for free.[7] A 2010 study indicated that only 36 percent of gamers could correctly identify products promoted in IGAs in car-racing games.[8] Most gamers dislike IGAs that distract them from game play itself.[9]

Ads for the candy company Chupa Chups appear in the background of the video game *Zool*.

SELLING PRODUCTS, SELLING IDEAS

Advertising techniques such as branding can sell more than products or services; they can sell images, ideas, political candidates, or lifestyles. **Social marketing** applies the lessons learned from years of advertising activities and theories of persuasive communications to encourage the public to transform behaviors positively through **public information campaigns**.

Efforts to change attitudes can be an uphill battle, however. First, behaviors that social marketers seek to change, such as drinking or smoking, often involve powerful physical addictions or psychological perceptions (teens may think it's cool to drink or smoke). Second, determining which advertising channels and types of messages will be most effective for the targeted group can be difficult. Third, ethical questions sometimes arise when it comes to which group is deciding what exactly constitutes a "pro-social" message and why other groups may not be targeted. Finally, assessing the success of a social-marketing campaign is problematic, for its effects will generally not be immediately seen, and larger sociocultural forces may influence how the target audience interprets the message.

Some social-marketing campaigns will use **fear appeals** to shock people into changing behavior. Television ads, for example, feature smokers who have had surgery for throat or mouth cancer or show graphic images of automobile accidents caused by drunk driving. Fear appeals can be tricky, however. Graphic images may offend some while not being effective for young people who think "that will never happen to me."

An effective social-marketing campaign for the National Crime Prevention Council used the tagline "Take a bite out of crime" and featured a cartoon dog, McGruff, dressed as a detective. A series of **public service announcements (PSAs)** covering a range of crime-related issues were widely aired on different media channels. Various surveys indicated a high awareness of the campaign and its anticrime points by adults and children, accompanied by a rise in crime-prevention measures like special locks on doors and windows and security lights.

Today, a digital McGruff offers advice on an interactive website, online safety games, and videos about how to use the Internet safely, not to mention an app to help parents safeguard their children's Internet activity, including social media filters. Ironically, the actor who played McGruff the Crime Dog evidently did not learn much from his character. In 2014, he was sentenced to sixteen years in federal prison for drug and weapons charges. Nevertheless, the uncorrupted animated version of the crime-fighting canine, who celebrated his 35th birthday in 2015, lives on online.

Social-marketing campaigns play an important role in educating people in developed and developing countries about a range of issues to prevent disease and to raise the general standard of living, including safe sex and proper sanitizing techniques to ensure clean water and untainted food. Because of high illiteracy rates and limited access to mass media in some regions, such campaigns must use visual symbols in powerful yet easily understood ways.

ADVERTISING CHANNELS

Advertising takes a variety of media formats or channels, including some important types that we may not normally consider mass communications.

social marketing

Advertising and marketing techniques that persuade people to change bad or destructive behaviors or adopt good behaviors.

public information campaign

Media program funded by the government and designed to achieve some social goal.

fear appeal

Advertising technique that attempts to persuade the audience by scaring them, such as antismoking ads that show disfigured former smokers.

public service announcement (PSA)

Advertising-like message from an organization with a worthy purpose that ostensibly benefits the public and for which the media donate time or space.

Creating persuasive messages can be especially difficult in countries with low literacy rates.

Each channel has certain characteristics that influence how advertising is implemented and how its effects are measured. The type of product or service being advertised helps determine which audience to target, and certain channels are more effective at reaching certain types of audiences. Here we will look at some of the traditional advertising channels, all of which are still in use, after which we will consider how online and digital advertising are changing these.

Print Media

In newspapers and magazines, commercial messages come in either of two forms: **classified advertising** or **display advertising**. Classifieds appear together in a special section posted by individuals and organizations to sell specific goods or services. Because customers pay by the word or pay a rate up to a certain word limit, messages are usually short and use abbreviations. Despite their small individual size, their large numbers in most papers used to comprise a significant portion of advertising revenue. Most newspapers now put their classifieds online to compete with other online classifieds, auction sites, and discount sites such as Craigslist, eBay, Groupon, and Living Social—sites that have largely decimated the classified advertising revenues of most newspapers.

Display ads are much larger, anywhere from one-eighth of a page to a full page or occasionally foldouts with multiple pages. They often contain images or other graphic elements that help them stand out. Costs vary by size, color, and location (back-cover placement is usually the most expensive). Publishing companies create a **rate card** of the various costs, which may be negotiated by those who advertise multiple times in a highly competitive market. An **advertorial**, a display ad created to look like an actual article in the publication, usually has tiny print on the top or the bottom of the page that says "paid advertisement."

Electronic Media

Despite decreased commercial time and fragmented audiences, advertising costs in electronic media, which can command larger audiences than print, are generally high compared to those for print media. Even large-circulation magazines of over a million readers reach a relatively small audience by network-television standards. Radio or television commercials, "spots," typically run for thirty seconds. Infomercials are paid programming in which a product is demonstrated and promoted for purchase, often with endorsements from a celebrity or satisfied consumers, who are typically paid or otherwise compensated. Pleased "customers" are often professional actors.

Subliminal advertising, a subject of controversy for some time, supposedly flashes messages or images briefly to produce an unconscious effect on the viewer. Despite no firm proof that subliminal advertising has any effect at all, it is illegal, and no advertisers have ever admitted to its use.

Another way advertisers attract attention is through **product placement**—products displayed or used by characters in television programs or movies. Product placement has become more important since the arrival of the digital video recorder (DVR), which allows viewers to skip commercials. Critics argue that most viewers do not notice that a product is being advertised, while proponents say this is exactly what makes it an effective technique. Perhaps the most famous case of successful product placement occurred with the blockbuster movie *E.T.* After M&M's refused to allow their famous candy product to be E.T.'s snack of choice,

classified advertising

Advertising traditionally found in print media, especially newspapers but also in some magazines and now increasingly online, that consists of messages posted by individuals and organizations to sell specific goods or services.

display advertising

Advertising in print media that usually consists of illustrations or images and text that can occupy a small section of a page, a full page, or multiple pages.

rate card

List of advertising rates by size, placement, and other characteristics, such as whether ads are black and white or full color. Frequency discounts are also usually offered, and the listed rates are usually negotiable, especially for large advertisers.

advertorial

Display advertisement created to look like an article within the publication, although most publications have the words "advertisement" or "paid advertisement" in tiny print somewhere nearby.

subliminal advertising

Persuasive messages that have supposedly unconscious effects on the audience, such as an image or word flashed almost imperceptibly on a screen.

product placement

A form of advertising in which brand-name goods or services are placed prominently within programming or movie content that is otherwise devoid of advertising, demonstrating the convergence of programming with advertising content.

Product placement has become a more widely used advertising technique since the arrival of the DVR, which allows viewers to skip commercials.

filmmakers opted for Reese's Pieces, a new candy whose sales shot up as the film became a global hit.

DISCUSSION QUESTIONS: In the first report about subliminal advertising, a drive-in movie owner in New Jersey claimed that after flashing subliminal images of soft drinks and popcorn during a movie, sales increased. What other factors might explain the increase in sales?

Outdoor

Outdoor advertising on billboards, taxis, buses, and bus stops, among other places, bombards the public. Store signs are among the oldest forms of public advertising, although their reach is limited to passersby. Even brand-name clothing effectively makes the wearer a walking advertisement—paid for by the consumer who purchased the clothing! Increasingly, municipalities are allowing corporate sponsorship of public vehicles and spaces to help shore up government budgets. Low-power video monitors with advertisements accompanied by news content appear in new public spaces, such as above cash registers and in elevators.

Interactive floor-based displays in airports or malls react to activities like footsteps, creating interesting games that people can play and others can watch—all the while engaging with an advertisement. Interactive outdoor advertising will continue to grow as technology such as face recognition is incorporated into street-level

outdoor advertising

Billboards and other forms of public advertising, such as on buses or taxis.

The Federal Trade Commission allows puffery in advertising, exaggerated advertising claims that "reasonable" audiences would not likely perceive as facts.

billboards, enabling the real-time display of messages customized to each passing pedestrian.

Direct Mail

Direct mail marketing, commonly called "junk mail" by recipients, advertises everything from lower insurance rates to credit card offers to pleas to donate to various charities or subscribe to magazines. Some companies make it appear that you have been specially selected or won a lottery and need to send in the material ASAP to claim your prize.

Many organizations rent their subscriber lists on a per-thousand basis; the more detailed the demographic data, the higher the cost. These lists become effective tools in the hands of advertisers who send targeted messages. List owners often seed them with false names to ensure that list renters are only using the list one time. Some savvy citizens use similar techniques to determine who is selling their name. Subsequent mailings in your pet's name, for example, could help identify the culprit.

Telemarketing involves phoning people at home, typically intrusive and annoying calls that many actively screen with voicemail or caller ID. These sales pitches are highly scripted, complete with prepared responses to a range of anticipated answers. The Telephone Consumer Protection Act of 1991 lays out strict guidelines on the times telemarketers may call and requires companies to remove people who request such removal from call lists. Some states have implemented "Do Not Call" registries that serve the same purpose. Exempted from the act, political campaigns may contact those registered on the do-not-call list, even on their cell phones.

ADVERTISING IN A DIGITAL WORLD

Traditionally, 70 percent or more of commercial-media revenues come from advertising, an economic foundation being transformed by digital technology. Advertisers have a greater capacity to track consumers and identify the most effective advertisements. They are also discovering that many traditional advertising techniques do not work well on the Web. Changes in technology and in online user behavior complicate the picture further.

Cookies

Web experiences, compared to other media, can be personalized for the user, a key aspect for both advertisers and media-content companies. Almost all websites leave a **cookie**, a small text file loaded onto a computer that identifies specific users who visit a site and where they go afterward. Cookies and Web analytics are able to tell what page someone came from before arriving at a page with an ad and how long the person spent on that page. They can "remember" visitors who return and can determine their computer operating system, their Web browser and, often, their approximate location.

Cookies not inserted by the content provider are called third-party cookies, like those advertisers place in ads. These cookies can both track and customize advertising messages as well as engage in "cookie pricing." Travel sites, for instance, will sometimes nudge up ticket prices if a pattern of browsing behavior reveals a traveler highly motivated to get a particular route. Cookies are just one

cookie

Information that a website puts on a user's local hard drive so that it can recognize when that computer accesses the website again. Cookies also allow for conveniences like password recognition and personalization.

of the new, unique advertising techniques. Still, some of the "old" digital media remain remarkably effective.

Email Marketing

Until the rise of social media sites such as Facebook and Twitter, email was the most used application on the Internet; and despite spam, it continues to be an incredibly powerful tool for advertising. Like direct mail, email can reach highly targeted audiences who, better yet, have the choice to **opt in** to receive emails, showing their willingness to hear from certain companies.

Email also has the advantage of being cheap to produce and send, especially if the message is text only, without any design or graphics. Free email advertisements are also lucrative for the companies that offer this service, such as Yahoo! Mail, Hotmail, and Gmail. Google uses software that scans each email sent via Gmail, analyzes the text, and inserts ads it deems most relevant to the topic.

Banner Ads

In the early days of the Web, most online advertising tended to follow the traditional advertising formats—particularly the display-ad model commonly found in print. Banner advertising, online ads spanning the top of a page like a banner, could be clicked on to visit the advertiser's website. Today, there are a variety of shapes and sizes of banner ads, including tower ads that take advantage of the tendency for users to scroll down. Such ads may also contain interactive quizzes, video, or other animation.

Studies tracking consumers online, however, indicate that banner ads have a very low **click-through rate (CTR)**, meaning a low percentage of users—in this case, an average of 0.06 percent—actually click on them. These disappointing numbers caused advertisers to doubt their effectiveness and seemed to stall the budding online ad industry.

Pop-Ups and Video

Initially viewed as the salvation for online advertising, pop-ups can be **interstitial ads** or **superstitial ads**. Interstitial ads have proven unpopular because users must close the ad browser window to see the website they originally wanted. To get around this, some ads take up most of a page rather than the whole screen. Perceived as less obtrusive, superstitial ads have become more widespread. These ads crawl across a screen or appear in a corner and can be created with a variety of multimedia programs and effects.

Ads in videos have grown quickly in recent years. It became clear that online users did not want to watch a standard thirty-second commercial before a short video, so online videos tend to be ten or fifteen seconds at most and sometimes give users the option to click off the ad after only five seconds. Sites such as YouTube have tried overlays at the bottom of screens, like those that promote upcoming shows on network television, and these have also made their way to mobile apps.

Classifieds and Auction Sites

Online classifieds have been able to take a large chunk of newspaper revenue because they offer several advantages. First, there is little or no need to squeeze text to fit within some predefined word and cost limit. Second, geographic

opt in

When consumers choose to receive mailings or marketing material, usually by checking a box on a website when registering for the site.

click-through rate (CTR)

Rate at which people click on an online advertisement to access more information.

interstitial ad

Online advertisement that opens in a new window from the one the user was in.

superstitial ad

Online advertisement that covers part of the existing screen or moves over part of it without opening a new window.

A human assists the computer algorithm "comparison engine" at FindTheBest, a privately held research company that allows users to research, filter, and compare more than 2,000 topics.

limitations are no longer an issue as long as what is being advertised can be shipped or mailed. This vastly increases the potential audience. Craigslist and other online classifieds websites have been immensely successful for many traditional businesses as well as for small entrepreneurs, who can generate national or international business online with very little overhead or infrastructure cost.

Auction sites have also become popular for many of the same reasons, starting with eBay, founded in 1995. Seller rating and review systems, easy online payment methods, and a high volume of sellers and buyers have created a thriving marketplace, especially useful for small businesses or those working from home. Many unusual items have come up for sale on eBay, including the case of a British man who in 2008 put his entire life—worldly possessions, job, and even friends—up for sale after a bitter divorce. The winning bid was about $380,000, considerably short of what he was asking.[10]

Search-Engine Ads

Advertising with popular search-engine sites such as Google, Bing, and Yahoo! has become one of the most important vehicles for advertisers in recent years. The two main methods of search-engine advertising—search-engine optimization (SEO) and search-engine marketing (SEM)—are unpaid and paid forms of advertising, respectively, yet their goal is the same: to appear as the first entry in a search-engine search.

SEO techniques involve website design, keywords, and links. SEM advertisers either pay a search-engine company for a sponsored link, usually clearly labeled as such (with a colored panel or the words "sponsored links"), or buy keywords sold at auction, paying the search-engine company a set amount every time its site is clicked on when that search term is used. These search engines and other digital media utilize algorithms or computer programs to aid in rapidly targeting ads, tracking consumer online behavior, and more, although a human assistant often makes the process more nuanced.[11]

Mobile Advertising

The dramatic growth of mobile media since 2000 has altered the advertising landscape fundamentally. The volume of text messaging, especially among the young, exceeds that of voice calls. With an estimated 2 billion smartphone users worldwide by 2016 and 1 billion tablet users worldwide by the end of 2015, mobile has emerged as a powerful new advertising channel. Facebook has been especially successful at inserting mobile ads between entries on newsfeeds that get users' attention without annoying them.[12] Google announced in mid-2015 that it had changed its search-engine algorithms so that mobile-friendly websites would show up higher in the rankings.

Five trends characterize the mobile advertising marketplace. First, the geo-location capability of mobile technology increasingly enables advertisers to customize messages to the consumer's location. Second, mcommerce, or mobile commerce, is growing rapidly and targeting consumers with real-time messages updated to their current mobile purchases. Consumers out shopping, for instance, use their mobile device to aid in comparative shopping and even price bargaining. Third, real-time mobile billing (RTB) is facilitating a new advertising pricing system optimized by mobile demand. Fourth, as mobile broadband access rises, video ads gain traction even on mobile devices. Fifth, ads tied to in-app downloads such as mobile games have increased greatly, with consumers seemingly willing to accept ads for free apps.

Behavioral Advertising

Behavioral advertising tracks user behavior and then inserts banner ads on similar topics on subsequent websites visited, which is why, after shopping for items on a site like Amazon, you start to see ads for the products you looked at on websites you visit later. Advertisers claim it offers users more relevant Web ads, but many consider this an invasion of privacy.

Although the behavioral advertising industry has outlined various principles and procedures in attempts to self-regulate, consumer groups and the government have found fault with this rapidly expanding area of advertising. Some companies do not stop tracking online users even after they have opted out. Another problem has been the use of Flash cookies that secretly reinsert a cookie even after the user has cleared her computer of all cookies. Coming years will likely see tensions increase between advertisers and government and consumer watchdog groups regarding best practices and consumer safeguards.

Viral Marketing

Some of the most successful advertising online is unaided by advertising agencies or expensive marketing campaigns. **Viral marketing**, sometimes called buzz marketing, guerrilla marketing, or word-of-mouth (WOM) marketing, promotes a product, service, or brand through natural online channels; people spread a message because they want to, not because they are being paid to. Humorous or strange videos often work best for this; but such videos, whose appeal is often their unpolished, amateurish quality, are not always a good fit for all brands.

Predicting content that will actually go viral is difficult. The ALS Ice Bucket Challenge, in which people challenged three friends to video themselves dumping a bucket of ice water on their heads, or donate to the ALS Association, became wildly and unexpectedly popular in the summer of 2014, especially in the United States. According to the ALS Association, it received over $100 million in July alone, and several other ALS organizations also saw large increases in donations during the latter half of the year.

Native Advertising

One of the largest growth areas in advertising for online publications is native advertising of several different but related types, including sponsored posts on Facebook or Twitter. Basically, native advertising (sometimes called content marketing) is the online version of the print advertorial. In other words, the editorial

viral marketing

Promoting a product, service, or brand online through word of mouth, usually via online discussion groups, chats, and emails.

The ALS Ice Bucket Challenge became wildly popular on social media in the late summer of 2014. **CRITICAL THINKING QUESTIONS:** ALS recently managed to raise a significant sum of money through donations, but do you know what ALS stands for or what its symptoms are? Have you followed any progress in research on ALS since then? Do you consider the Ice Bucket Challenge a success?

staff of the site or a marketer produces advertising content made to appear like actual content within the publication.

One type of native advertising is indicated by the small "sponsored by" or "promoted by" tags in pieces that usually have attention-getting headlines about celebrities or odd news events. Many large online publications have adopted some form of native advertising, including *The New York Times*, *Time*, *Forbes*, and *The Atlantic*. In 2013, *The Atlantic* was rebuked for how it handled a self-congratulatory piece sponsored by the Church of Scientology. The article itself was of poor quality, and *The Atlantic* later admitted to also deleting negative user comments it elicited.

DISCUSSION QUESTIONS: Consider articles on sites or suggested posts you may have clicked on in Facebook or other social media. How many of these did you recognize as sponsored content, or did you care? What are the dangers of blurring the lines between editorial and advertising content?

THE ADVERTISING BUSINESS

Worldwide ad spending for 2015 is estimated to be $578 billion, up from $546 billion in 2014, according to eMarketer.[13] Table 9-2 estimates advertising spending by medium to 2015. According to this forecast, in 2015, television still sits atop the media food chain, with about 40 percent of total ad dollars. Since 2011, TV's share of ad dollars remains relatively constant, while the relative position of the other media shift significantly. Newspapers see their relative share decline by

TABLE 9-2 Share of Global Advertising Expenditure (%)

MEDIUM	2011	2012	2013	2014	2015
Newspapers	19.9%	18.1%	16.3%	14.5%	13.0%
Magazines	9.3%	8.5%	7.8%	7.2%	6.6%
Television	39.4%	39.6%	39.5%	38.8%	37.7%
Radio	7.0%	6.9%	6.8%	6.7%	6.6%
Cinema	0.6%	0.6%	0.6%	0.6%	0.6%
Outdoor	6.7%	6.8%	6.8%	6.8%	6.7%
Internet	17.1%	19.5%	22.3%	25.5%	28.8%

Source: ZenithOptimedia, *Advertising Expenditure Forecasts*, September 2015

some 20 percent, from 20.3 percent in 2011 to less than 16 percent in 2015; and magazines by some 25 percent, from 9.4 percent in 2011 to 7.3 percent in 2015. Radio dips almost 10 percent, from 7.1 percent in 2011 to 6.6 percent in 2015. Outdoor drops about 5 percent, from 6.7 percent to 6.3 percent between 2011 and 2015. Bucking the downward trend is cinema (ads that run before a movie starts), which sees a 20 percent increase, from 0.5 percent to 0.6 percent between 2011 and 2015.

The big winner, however, is Internet advertising, which grows more than 45 percent between 2011 and 2015, from 16.1 percent to 23.4 percent of global advertising spending. Spending on Internet advertising is today greater than newspaper advertising spending and greater than outdoor, cinema, radio, and magazine ad spending combined. Internet ad spending, including $42.6 billion worldwide for mobile ($18.9 billion in the United States), continues to rise, and industry experts believe it still has lots of room for rapid growth. Although advertisers are of course looking to advertise across media or channels, the fact is that an increase in ad spending in one medium, such as the Internet, generally means a decrease elsewhere, such as in newspapers. This has made it especially challenging for the main player in the advertising world today, the advertising agency.

ADVERTISING AGENCIES

Advertising agencies perform many important functions, creating and selling advertising while linking various media with the many companies seeking to sell a product or service. The more than five hundred advertising agencies in the United States, which collectively employ more than seventy thousand people, have four main areas of operation:

1. *Creative*: copywriters and creative and art directors producing advertising content

2. *Client management*: account executives working with clients

3. *Media buying*: media planners and buyers determining and purchasing media time or space, the area that has traditionally produced agency revenues

4. *Research*: researchers collecting and analyzing media data on consumer characteristics and purchase behaviors

A number of Internet-original firms emerged in the late 1990s. Some have survived as boutique or specialized firms, but many have been bought by larger agencies for their interactive expertise. This follows the trend toward consolidation seen with traditional advertising agencies that still dominate the field. Today, much larger advertising and media-services companies own most of the world's leading advertising agencies, and ninety of the top one hundred firms have international operations. Most of these firms operate both advertising and public relations enterprises. These full-service companies handle all aspects of the communications business, from campaign planning to creative execution and media buying.

Table 9-3 presents data on the world's five largest advertising and media-services firms, ranked by their estimated revenue in 2014, and some of their biggest advertising and public relations subsidiaries, which are themselves often

INTERNATIONAL PERSPECTIVES
Hair-Raising Subway Billboard Ad Gets Noticed

Subway commuters in most major cities take the plethora of billboards on walls and platforms for granted, perhaps making a mental note of an upcoming film they'd like to see but, for the most part, ignoring the ads.

To help a billboard ad stand out from the crowd, advertisers have been incorporating interactive technologies to draw greater attention to otherwise static billboards. One notable example occurred in Stockholm, Sweden, where the pharmacy brand Apotek equipped

platform billboards to sense when trains were approaching the platform (for commuters on the platform, the wind coming before the train alerts them to an arrival).

The image on the billboard was a photo of a young woman with a full head of hair. As the train approached and the wind kicked up, the model's hair suddenly started to blow around wildly, seemingly in response to the train. Then the words "Make your hair come alive" and the brand name came on screen. The ad, which can be seen on YouTube, garnered international attention—along with surprise from commuters who suddenly saw a billboard with a moving image.

Later in the year a similar ad appeared on Stockholm's subway platforms, except this time instead, the wind blew off a wig off the model, revealing her bald head. This ad for a cancer charity was also a successful attention getter.

Different kinds of interactive billboards can be used to far different effect. A 2013 ad for *The Curse of Chucky* looked much like any other film poster at a bus stop in Brazil until the lights began to flicker and Chucky smashed through the fake glass of the poster box wielding a fake knife. The terrified occupants of the bus stop, however, appeared not to immediately comprehend that they had suddenly become part of an outrageous publicity stunt and were being chased not by the world's most deviant doll but by a small actor made up as Chucky. All the horror, both scripted and apparently genuine, was recorded, of course, and can still be seen on YouTube. As if simply waiting at a bus stop at night isn't creepy enough.

global operations. In 2013, Omnicom and Publicis planned to merge to form the world's largest advertising agency, but nearly a year later the deal was abruptly called off. Tokyo-based Dentsu, although a global player in terms of size, is typically not considered one of the "big four" of advertising agencies, as it focuses primarily on Japan, where it dominates the advertising industry.

TABLE 9-3 World's Five Largest Advertising and Media-Services Companies

AGENCY	MAJOR SUBSIDIARY GROUPS	HEADQUARTERS	WORLDWIDE REVENUES, 2014 ($ BILLION)
WPP	YOUNG & RUBICAM GROUP; group*m*; Ogilvy; JWT; GREY	London, United Kingdom	19.0
OmnicomGroup	DDB°; BBDO; TBWA\; FLEISHMANHILLARD	Netherlands, operational offices in New York, United States, and Paris, France	15.3
PUBLICIS GROUPE	Starcom; Starcom MediaVest GROUP; Leo Burnett; SAATCHI & SAATCHI	Paris, France	9.6
IPG	McCANN; FCB; LOWE	New York, United States	7.5
dentsu	dentsu DENTSU EAST JAPAN INC.; dentsu DENTSU WEST JAPAN INC.; Dentsu Digital	Tokyo, Japan	6.0

Source: http://adage.coverleaf.com/advertisingage/20150504?pg=71#pg72

Public Relations

Just as advertising agencies straddle the advertising and media worlds, public relations firms straddle the worlds of companies wishing to enhance their reputations and of media organizations that can widely distribute company messages and publicity. Unlike advertisers, however, public relations agencies do not pay media companies to place content. Rather, these professionals attempt to persuade important gatekeepers, such as editors, journalists, or influential bloggers, that information about their client is sufficiently newsworthy to be published or broadcast.

Public relations firms are ideally positioned to understand some of the new interactive dynamics in today's world of social media. Increasingly, these firms, while seeking to mitigate negative news and promote positive information, help companies navigate social media and provide guidance on policies such as having a Facebook page, creating a YouTube channel, and talking with consumers on fan pages or Twitter. Some have dubbed this new, more interactive public relations PR 2.0.

To many journalists, PR is a necessary evil. To others, it's just plain evil. Nevertheless, journalists rely heavily on the information PR firms provide for stories. Public relations is a vital part of the three-way relationship among the media, organizations, and the public, including employees, consumers, shareholders, activists (who might oppose certain corporate policies), and regulators. Edward L. Bernays, the late father of modern public relations, used to say that propaganda was better than "impropaganda." The same might be said of public relations. It all depends on how it's done.

Advertising for children's toys often perpetuates gender stereotypes and promotes unrealistic lifestyles and body images. A recent analysis of Barbie's proportions revealed the world's best-selling doll to be anatomically impossible.

> **DISCUSSION QUESTIONS:** Consider the concept of reputation for companies. How would you define reputation and how do you think it could be measured and given some sort of monetary value? Are there similarities between the concept of reputation with humans and with companies?

THE HISTORICAL DEVELOPMENT OF PUBLIC RELATIONS

Modern public relations has evolved rapidly and in unique ways, informed by the rise of mass communications and technological advances. Some say PR is the world's second-oldest profession. But it was not recognized as a separate activity until the early twentieth century when a number of publishing activities began to be categorized discretely as either journalism or public relations. Thomas Paine's influential pro-Revolution pamphlets in the 1770s, such as *Common Sense*, and the sympathetic newspaper pieces on the Boston Massacre, for example, would be considered public relations or even propaganda by today's standards rather than journalism.

The first stage of public relations occurred during the nineteenth and early twentieth centuries. Getting publicity in the press (or other media) for a client was a central practice in age of **press agentry**. As newspapers developed into a form of mass communication, publicity as part of a news story meant increased exposure for a product or a company without needing to pay for an advertisement. Press agentry flourished as practiced by Phineas Taylor "P. T." Barnum, who entered the world of promotion, press manipulation, and show business in the 1830s, creating the famous American circus in 1870. A great showman, Barnum used various techniques to communicate with the public. His staged events, publicity stunts to attract attention, were particularly successful.

Although the term "public relations" had not yet been coined, former journalist Ivy Ledbetter Lee was perhaps its first true modern practitioner. (Muckraking journalist Upton Sinclair, author of *The Jungle*, called Lee "Poison Ivy.") A master of managing the press, Lee once observed, "Crowds are led by symbols and phrases." Many of his innovations became staples of modern public relations practice, including press conferences and newsreels, known today as video news releases (VNRs), where PR firms provide video footage for television stations to use in their news broadcasts.

One of Lee's most visible clients was John D. Rockefeller Sr., the founder of the Standard Oil Trust and the world's first billionaire, who managed his companies and employees ruthlessly, even by the standards of the day. After Rockefeller had the Colorado state militia put down a miners' strike, resulting in dozens of deaths, Lee produced reports stating that an overturned stove had started a house fire that killed dozens of women and children. Lee was also behind the photographs and newsreels of Rockefeller handing out dimes to poor children wherever he went. So legendary was his ability to manipulate the media, that in the early 1930s, the Nazis hired Lee to present a more favorable face for the "New Germany" in the United States.[14]

Press agentry was known for special events and publicity stunts. In 1928, debutantes were invited to march in the Easter Parade in New York City, holding their "torches of freedom"—that is, lit cigarettes. This performance was intended to attract media attention and build support for women smoking in public at a time when society frowned on it. The American Tobacco Company, manufacturer of Lucky Strike cigarettes, sponsored the event, created by a man many consider the founder of modern public relations, Edward L. Bernays.

Edward L. Bernays managed some of the earliest and most famous PR campaigns of the twentieth century. He trained during World War I as a member of the Foreign Press Bureau of the U.S. Committee on Public Information (CPI), essentially the propaganda arm of the U.S. government. Bernays often dined with his famous uncle, Sigmund Freud, whose theories he mastered and whose first English-language translations he produced. After the war, Bernays applied the principles of both Freudian psychology and social science, a then-budding field, to the strategic influence and shaping of public opinion. His book *The Engineering of Consent*, a collection of essays by him and associates on the theory and practice of public relations, became a classic.

Arthur W. Page was the vice president of public relations for AT&T from 1927 to 1946, the first PR person on the board of a major public corporation. He also served on many boards of charities and other organizations. Page helped create ethical guidelines for public relations with his Page Principles, such as "tell the truth," "prove it with action," and "listen to the customer." Today, the Arthur W. Page Society continues his work through various educational programs, networking events, forums for PR executives, and sponsored PR research initiatives.

press agentry

Getting media attention for a client, often by creating outrageous stunts to attract journalists.

General Tom Thumb achieved widespread fame as a performer with master showman P. T. Barnum.

MEDIA PIONEERS
Doris E. Fleischman

Much has been written about Edward L. Bernays, celebrated as the father of public relations in eulogies upon his death at the age of 103 in 1995. Much less, however, has been published about his wife, Doris E. Fleischman, despite her status as an equal partner in their storied PR firm, whose clients included President Calvin Coolidge, Procter & Gamble, General Electric, the U.S. War Department, the American Tobacco Company, and Sigmund Freud, Bernays's uncle. Although integral to their joint enterprise, her role was played largely behind the scenes, while her husband remained the face and principal name of the business, the man who worked in person with their clients, even on campaigns she had developed or press releases and speeches she had ghostwritten.

Whereas many of her pioneering PR achievements went unnoticed at the time, her earlier feminist activities did not, some even garnering widespread newspaper headlines. She and her husband were members of the Lucy Stone League, a civil rights organization founded in 1921 dedicated to promoting the legal use of a woman's maiden name, a radical initiative for the time. In September, 1922, the newlyweds checked into their hotel as Bernays *and* Fleischman, a first for the Waldorf Astoria register.[15] Three years later, she became the first married woman ever issued a U.S. passport in her birth name.

Young Doris seemed poised to accomplish great things in an era that did not always encourage greatness from women in the public sphere. She received a BA (1913) from Barnard College, where she won varsity letters in softball, basketball, and tennis while a member of Theta Sigma Phi, the national sorority of women in communications. She subsequently worked at the *New York Tribune* as a reporter and an editor for the women's pages and the Sunday edition. Among her more notable assignments were an interview with Theodore Roosevelt and—another first for a woman—covering a prizefight, albeit accompanied by her father, who feared for her safety. Her writings frequently considered the challenges women of her day faced in their domestic and professional lives, a balancing act also suggested by the title of her memoir, "A Wife Is Many Women."

Her essay "Notes of a Retiring Feminist" implies that these tensions, acute for many early feminists, were never fully resolved: "Mrs. stands to the right of me, and Miss stands to the left. Me is a ghost ego nowhere in the middle." For pragmatic reasons later in life, Fleischman, weary of having to explain herself, increasingly adopted the use of Bernays.

TRENDS IN THE DEVELOPMENT OF PUBLIC RELATIONS

One continuing trend as public relations has developed as a profession is establishing a dialog with the public, no longer considered a mute and passive mass audience. In the earliest forms of PR during much of the nineteenth century, communication was largely asymmetric, from the public relations agent through the media to the audience. Audience feedback was not sought. In the early twentieth century, a limited symmetric model of communications was espoused, with the public providing feedback on the efficacy of a campaign. Although this appeared superficially to be dialog, PR representatives still controlled the flow of communications.

Many of the principles espoused by Page and since adopted by most firms belong to a **two-way symmetric model** of public relations, articulated by pioneering PR educator James E. Grunig. This model emphasizes public relations as a system of managing relationships among organizations and individuals and their many publics, internal and external. Mass communication and social media are

two-way symmetric model

Model of public relations that emphasizes the profession as a system of managing relationships among organizations, individuals, and their many publics.

key, and building mutual understanding and good relationships is emphasized as much as influencing public opinion.

Research shows that organizational excellence (as defined in terms of accomplishing both short- and long-term objectives) can be achieved with a two-way symmetric model that incorporates the public relations function into senior management and organizational decision making. The two-way symmetric model formally and informally assesses the attitudes, knowledge, behaviors, and intentions of various publics or stakeholders, and it also places a premium on the ethical practice of public relations.

One of the best examples remains Johnson & Johnson's handling of the infamous Tylenol tampering case in 1982, when seven people died of cyanide poisoning from tainted Extra-Strength Tylenol capsules. After the first reported poisoning in the Chicago, Illinois, area, Johnson & Johnson took immediate steps to prevent further tragedy while maintaining clear and open lines of communication with both the media and the public. Along with its parent, McNeil Consumer Products Company, it offered a $100,000 reward, established a hotline, and opened regional poison-control centers to dispense information and assistance.

After a nationwide recall of all Extra-Strength Tylenol capsules, at a cost of some $100 million to remove and destroy all 31 million bottles, in January 1983, the capsules were successfully reintroduced with a triple-sealed, tamper-resistant packaging warning. Johnson & Johnson and McNeil Consumer Products Co. were cleared of any legal liability, although in 1991, they provided the victims' families with an undisclosed settlement, estimated to be as much as $50 million.

Despite the tragedy, Tylenol sales recovered. Journalists often criticize companies in crisis for hiding information from the press and the public, but Johnson & Johnson was praised for its open and immediate responses. "The public relations people were knowledgeable and available when the media needed to talk to them," said John O'Brien of the *Chicago Tribune*. "They didn't try to sugar-coat anything."

Citizens have been empowered to engage in two-way or multidirectional communication with organizations and their stakeholders, and social media such as Twitter, Facebook, and the blogosphere have nurtured a more organic form of participatory public relations. Launched in 2000, the American Legacy Foundation's national "Truth" campaign, engages the public in an antismoking dialog with edgy mass media messages and social media such as Facebook, Twitter, and YouTube.[16] One study found that smoking rates among teens in Florida dropped significantly as a result of the Truth campaign, with only 6.6 percent of Florida teens reporting smoking in the previous thirty days as compared to the national average of 14.4 percent.[17]

DISCUSSION QUESTIONS: If you were running a PR firm, would you accept a company that makes harmful products, such as tobacco, as a client? What about a political group known for its extreme views? Explain your decisions.

PR AND MEDIA RELATIONS

Although public relations professionals engage in a wide range of activities, they typically devote most of their time to the media, including journalists, producers, and others responsible for content. Developing and maintaining these working

"The Donald" first announced that he might run for president in 1988, a possibility he tantalized the press with again in the 2000, 2004, 2008, and 2012 election cycles. "The only one who can make America truly great again" (his words), he finally made it official for 2016, and even his earlier pseudo-events succeeded in making national and international headlines.

pitch

Request to review a client's new product or do a story about the client or the product.

relationships increases the possibility of obtaining fair or positive coverage of their organizations. When a negative story does occur, the PR professional should be able to communicate clearly and responsibly with the media, and several important tools in the PR toolbox aid in the pursuit of desired media coverage.

Pseudo-Events

One of the most enduring legacies from the early days of modern public relations is the pseudo-event, manufactured by individuals or organizations to capture the attention of the media and consequently the public. Press conferences, protests, parades, and even award ceremonies are all pseudo-events, arguably forms of media manipulation on which the media have become dependent. In fact, as much as 75 percent of news content in even the nation's best newspapers, such as the *Washington Post*, is in some way influenced by pseudo-events. Only occasionally is a story generated through pure enterprise or original reporting without public relations influence.[18]

Distributing News to the Media in the Digital Age

An important development in media relations is the distribution of corporate or other organizational news, information, and data (whether statistical or multimedia, including audio and video) through news releases or press releases. Formerly typed stories sent through the mail, these are now primarily emailed or posted directly to the Web.

Given that influential bloggers and others using social media may be as important as professional journalists in terms of reaching audiences, a press release at times is not even needed. Rather, a well-placed **pitch**, a request to review a client's new product, may be enough to get people writing about it and then get mainstream media attention.

Finding Sources Online

Similar to classified advertising, expert-source clearinghouses that have enhanced the media–PR relationship over the years continue to thrive on the Web, which allows highly efficient targeting of communications and searching. *The Yearbook of Experts, Authorities & Spokespersons* is now available online, greatly facilitating, especially when on deadline, such identifications. Perhaps the largest of these clearinghouses is ProfNet, an online service that connects more than 14,000 news and information officers at colleges and universities, businesses, research centers, medical centers, not-for-profits, and public relations agencies with journalists and bloggers around the world.

PR FIRMS AND THE PR INDUSTRY

Like other American industries, the business of public relations is tied to the general economy. Financial difficulties have caused companies to cut back on advertising and PR, even though this is arguably when they most need such services. In public relations, revenues are based on a combination of sources: primarily fees for consulting and services; income from specialized communications services such as research, interactive communications, and employee communications; and markups for production services and other media materials.

In the 1990s, public relations firms consolidated, but acquisition slowed considerably in the early years of the twenty-first century. Most acquisitions still

Press kits have transitioned from analog to digital multimedia, enabling journalists, bloggers, and other content creators to tell stories interactively.

occurred internationally among European holding companies such as Incepta Group, Havas, Publicis Groupe, and Cordiant. Omnicom is the one major U.S. communications firm that acquired several technology firms for its subsidiary Fleishman-Hillard.

Although most organizations of any size maintain their own internal PR units, many hire firms to aid their efforts with more specialized services. Media relations during campaigns or crises can be extremely complex, requiring extensive experience with local, national, and global media. PR firms are organized into three main areas:

1. *Core practice areas*: stakeholder relationships the client needs managed, including marketing communications or consumer relations; investor relations; public, not-for-profit, and governmental affairs; corporate and employee communications; political communications; and community relations

2. *Services*: activities the firm provides for clients, including media relations, research, interactive or online communications, writing, lobbying, fundraising, and crisis management

3. *Industries*: business sectors within which the clients operate, including utilities, technology, retail, manufacturing, health care, financial services, and consumer products

Many firms specialize in one or more core practice areas, services, or industries. This enables them to focus resources yet achieve sufficient expertise to serve clients operating on a national or global scale. Most of the larger PR firms offer integrated communication programs (sometimes called integrated marketing communications), a comprehensive set of communication management services, including both public relations and advertising activities.

Table 9-4 provides data on the top five independent U.S. public relations firms according to total worldwide revenues for 2014. Some of the PR firms that are part

TABLE 9-4 Top Five Independent Public Relations Firms

FIRM	HEADQUARTERS	NUMBER OF EMPLOYEES	2014 NET FEES	% CHANGE FROM 2013
Edelman	New York, New York	5,308	$797,328,238	+8.6
APCO worldwide	Washington, DC	635	$118,112,600	−1.9
WAGGENER EDSTROM WORLDWIDE	Bellevue, Washington	705	$106,676,000	−9.3
W₂O GROUP	San Francisco, California	402	$82,625,000	+10.1
ruder·finn what's next	New York, New York	522	$73,891,000	+16.8

Source: O'Dwyer's PR Firms Database, 2015, accessed June 12, 2015, http://www.odwyerpr.com/pr_firm_rankings/independents.htm. Used with permission of Jack O'Dwyer, Publisher, O'Dwyer Co.

of the larger agencies include WPP's Hill & Knowlton (approximately $384 million) and Omnicom Group's Fleishman Hillard (approximately $605 million), Ketchum (approximately $505 million), and Porter Novelli (approximately $126 million).[19] These PR agencies are all bigger than any of the independent PR firms except for Edelman. Founded in 1952 by former journalist Daniel Edelman, his firm, now run by his son Richard, has more than 5,000 employees in 65 cities.

Changing Trends in Advertising and PR

Clearly, the professional divisions between advertising and PR are blurring. In the analog age, PR practitioners, unconcerned with brand strategy or other aspects of advertising, dealt primarily with media relations. But today, PR and advertising professionals have to know what the other is doing to maximize the effectiveness of campaigns.

 **integrated communications**

All channels of communication about a company or brand working together to create a cohesive message.

Integrated communications try to determine the best ways to manage a brand's image across media channels while learning what the public is saying

---

 ETHICS IN MEDIA

Fooling Most of the People Most of the Time . . . Digitally

Online shoppers increasingly rely on reviews on websites such as Amazon, Yelp, and TripAdvisor for information about new books, hotels, restaurants, and much more. But how trustworthy are these sources of information? Increasing evidence suggests that many people writing these reviews are in fact paid $5 to $10 to write favorable appraisals by the companies and products being evaluated.[20] Following are two reviews from a Cornell study designed to help ferret out fabricated reviews from honest ones. One is genuine, the other fake. Can you tell which is which?

1. I have stayed at many hotels traveling for both business and pleasure, and I can honestly say that The James is tops. The service at the hotel is first class. The rooms are modern and very comfortable. The location is perfect, within walking distance to all of the great sights and restaurants. Highly recommend to both business travelers and couples.
2. My husband and I stayed at the James Chicago Hotel for our anniversary. This place is fantastic! We knew as soon as we arrived we made the right choice! The rooms are

BEAUTIFUL and the staff very attentive and wonderful!! The area of the hotel is great, since I love to shop—I couldn't ask for more!! We will definitely be back to Chicago and we will for sure be back to the James Chicago.[21]

Don't feel bad if you couldn't tell the real review from the fake one; neither could most people in the study. (Review #2 is the phony one.)

about the brand through blogs, websites, and other social media, called *social media listening*. Advertising agencies are acknowledging what public relations professionals have long known—a company cannot send a message without considering audience response and what it may mean for a company's reputation. Similarly, public relations professionals are understanding that a company or brand exists within a network of relationships and that thinking on a larger, strategic level can help them integrate their messages better to various stakeholders.

Companies are learning—sometimes the hard way—that the online public demands more transparency. Attempts at deception in any manner will likely elicit a strong backlash that will hurt the brand or company. More equitable, symmetrical dialog is occurring as companies learn to talk with their clients or publics through forums, blogs, and social media, a shift from "controlling the message" to "guiding the conversation."

FIGURE 9-1 Salaries for Advertising Account Managers by Experience

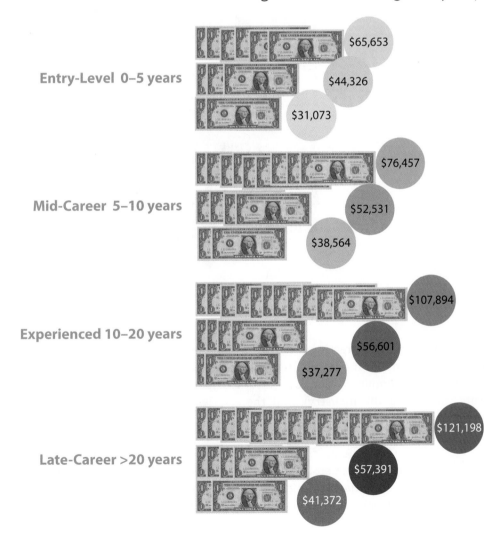

FIGURE 9-2 Salaries for Corporate PR Specialists by Experience

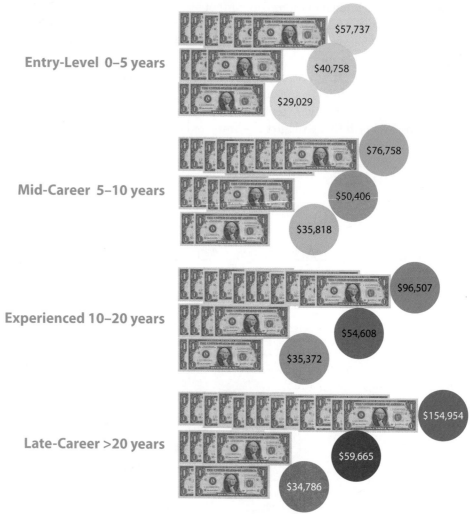

A wide variety of interesting and increasingly overlapping jobs exist in both advertising and PR. The trends in media production and consumption tend to favor strategic communications over fields like journalism (which has seen drastic cuts throughout the industry), and the salaries are generally better than in journalism.

Young people often find rewarding careers in a number of areas in advertising and PR, ranging from the creative side to account management to market research. Larger firms allow greater scope for changing career tracks and industry clients. Someone working in pharmaceuticals for a few years may switch to telecommunications or consumer packaged goods, starting in effect a different career in a new industry.

MEDIA CAREERS

Social media are creating new job opportunities in advertising agencies and PR firms as well as in large companies with internal marketing or PR departments. Keeping track of what is being said about a company and reaching influential members of the audience through social media are increasingly vital. More importantly, knowing what tool to use when, why a company or client should use (or not use) a particular social media tool such as Instagram or Twitter, is a skill companies are actively seeking.

The not-for-profit sector should not be ignored when considering a job in public relations or advertising. Although salaries are generally lower than in corporations, not-for-profit foundations, charities, and research institutes need the skills of strategic communications just as much as for-profit companies, if not more so. The not-for-profit sector is often particularly focused on issues of social responsibility and benefit, although most corporate PR efforts maintain a commitment in this regard as well, especially those practicing symmetrical public relations.

LOOKING BACK AND MOVING FORWARD

Although news and entertainment are the most popular media content, advertising is the most pervasive, and much editorial content and programming are inspired or influenced by public relations. Underlying advertising and PR, both forms of strategic communications, is the desire to persuade an audience to change an attitude or belief or to take some action. Persuasive communication, historically called rhetoric, has long played a role in human affairs, and today dozens of theories attempt to explain how persuasion works.

As public reliance on online and mobile media grows, so does advertising on the Web and via mobile, a substantial part of total advertising spending worldwide, surpassing that of newspapers. Consumer research targeting and tracking media behavior has also increased. Technology allows for greater accountability of response rates to advertisements, and advertising agencies have been trying new types of online advertisements that link advertising with ecommerce and mcommerce better.

Advertising revenues support the majority of content we see today. Advertising helps pay journalist salaries and keeps television studios operating. Historically, few people have been willing to pay the full price for the content they get largely for "free," although this is beginning to change as increasing numbers of consumers pay for subscriptions to media or buy content for digital download.

Of course, content has never been truly free. Consumers pay in the form of higher prices for goods, corporate expenses for advertising and marketing being passed on to consumers. Moreover, digital consumers are increasingly and often unwittingly "selling" their personal information online in exchange for "free" digital content. Because such costs are largely hidden from the public, the adoption of subscription-based or pay-per-use models seems less attractive by comparison.

Social media will continue to greatly affect strategic-communications professionals, who must keep in mind that transparency and engagement with their audiences will enhance their credibility. Monitoring online conversations about companies—and, more importantly, joining those conversations—has become an imperative for advertising and public relations professionals.

One thing is increasingly clear: The democratization of media and the capacity for more people than ever before to create and distribute messages makes it in some ways harder than ever to be heard. Knowing how to speak clearly above the digital din, how to persuade, how to craft powerful messages, and how to understand audiences are all requisite skills in today's fields of advertising and public relations.

MEDIA MATTERS   THE DYNAMICS OF PERSUASION

1. If you participated in a blind taste test with your favorite brand of cola, do you think you could tell which is yours?

2. Identify the main differences and similarities between advertising and public relations. Which field would you prefer to work in and why?

3. What is the difference between SEO, SEM, and social media optimization (SMO)? Why are they important?

4. Which shows do you watch where product placement is apparent? How does it affect your viewing experience when you notice one of these products?

5. Name the five major trends in mobile advertising. Which ads do you find most effective?

6. Compare the branding and advertising for a major consumer brand with that of a large nonprofit organization, noting similarities and differences. Which branding is more effective?

7. How does a viral video work? Identify your top five favorites and explain your selection.

FURTHER READING

The Skinny on the Art of Persuasion: How to Move Minds. Jim Randel (2010) Rand Media Company.

Thank You for Arguing: What Aristotle, Lincoln, and Homer Simpson Can Teach Us About the Art of Persuasion. Jay Heinrichs (2007) Three Rivers Press.

Ad Land: A Global History of Advertising. Mark Tungate (2007) Kogan Page.

A History of Advertising. Stephane Pincas, Marc Loiseau (2008) Taschen.

The Advertising Concept Book. Pete Barry (2008) Thames & Hudson.

Advertising, the Uneasy Persuasion: Its Dubious Impact on American Society. Michael Schudson (1987) Basic Books.

Guerrilla Advertising: Unconventional Brand Communication. Gavin Lucas, Michael Dorrian (2006) Laurence King Publishers.

Ogilvy on Advertising. David Ogilvy (1987) Vintage Books.

The Conquest of Cool: Business Culture, Counterculture, and the Rise of Hip Consumerism. Thomas Frank (1998) University of Chicago Press.

PR! A Social History of Spin. Stuart Ewen (1996) Basic Books.

The Father of Spin: Edward L. Bernays and the Birth of Public Relations. Larry Tye (2002) Holt.

Spin Sucks: Communication and Reputation Management in the Digital Age. Gini Dietrich (2014) Que Publishing.

Unconscious Branding: How Neuroscience Can Empower (and Inspire) Marketing. Douglas Van Praet (2014) Palgrave Macmillan Trade.

The Art of Social Media: Power Tips for Power Users. Guy Kawasaki, Peg Fitzpatrick (2014) Portfolio.

Social Media: Usage and Impact. Hana S. Noor Al-Deen, John Allen Hendricks (eds.) (2012) Lexington Books.

Social Media: Dominating Strategies for Social Media Marketing with Twitter, Facebook, YouTube, LinkedIn and Instagram. Michael Richards (2015) CreateSpace Independent Publishing Platform.

The Daily You: How the New Advertising Industry Is Defining Your Identity and Your Worth. Joseph Turow (2013) Yale University Press.

Return on Engagement: Content Strategy and Web Design Techniques for Digital Marketing, 2nd ed. Tim Frick, Kate Eyler-Werve (2014) Focal Press.

Media Ethics

ong famous for pop culture pieces and music criticism, *Rolling Stone* has more recently developed a reputation for hard-hitting, investigative reporting, articles such as the provocatively titled "A Rape on Campus: A Brutal Assault and Struggle for Justice at UVA." The 9,000-word, in-depth feature, published in November 2014, described the alleged 2012 gang rape of a University of Virginia freshman at a fraternity house party, its subsequent mishandling by the administration, and the pervasive culture of rape on college campuses nationwide.

Author Sabrina Rubin Erdely's story quickly went viral while increasing coveted clicks to rollingstone.com. Three days after the story broke, in response to mounting public outrage, the UVA president suspended all Greek activities and called for an official police investigation.[1] This striking example of news-media agenda setting promoted a national conversation about sexual assault and society's indifference when confronted with what many consider a hidden epidemic of these brutal crimes.

On closer inspection, however, the initially persuasive and compelling exposé began to unravel at the seams as other media professionals advanced critiques that held *Rolling Stone* accountable for a journalistic account that flouted best practices. The essential fabric of the story had been spun from a single thread, relying on one unidentified, uncorroborated source, "Jackie."

At this point, discussion in the public sphere turned swiftly from the subject of sexual assault to the topic of media ethics. More careful reporting, critics argued, would have revealed discrepancies in Jackie's description of events. Yet neither the friends who came to her rescue after the alleged attack nor the alleged attackers were ever interviewed, despite the damning article having quoted them according to Jackie's recollection of what had been said.

Rolling Stone announced that their trust in Jackie had been misplaced, a statement that incited even more controversy for its apparent victim blaming. An independent analysis, subsequently conducted at *Rolling Stone*'s request, blamed

LEARNING OBJECTIVES

>> Define basic elements in media ethics.

>> Outline the major systems of ethical reasoning.

>> Explain the main issues involved in ethical decision making.

>> Discuss the role of commercialism in media ethics.

>> Describe the major ethical issues in journalism, advertising, PR, and entertainment.

"avoidable" lapses in the fundamentals of reporting, editing, and fact checking. It also mentioned "the problem of confirmation bias—the tendency of people to be trapped by pre-existing assumptions and to select facts that support their own views while overlooking contradictory ones."[2] In other words, the reporter's search for an emblematic case became at some point the construction of one.

In April 2015, the magazine published the "painful" findings of a team from the Columbia School of Journalism. No one was fired, but the "anatomy of a journalistic failure" was preceded by an official retraction of the original story and an apology to readers, to the Phi Kappa Psi house, to UVA administrators and students, and to rape victims, who might now be more reluctant to step forward.

Media ethics is not truly a stand-alone subject, for ethical decision-making skills should be part of media professionals' daily practices. Ethical reasoning should be a primary component when considering actions.

To do that, however, requires a solid understanding of ethics and the strengths and weaknesses of various ethical frameworks. This knowledge helps us recognize ethical problems before they arise and deal with them once they do. By focusing on ethics as a separate subject, this chapter gives you the basic tools to make ethical decisions. Anybody working in media should be mindful of how ethics in general and media ethics in particular are integral to our personal and professional lives, and how the decisions of media professionals can have far-reaching consequences for many others.

Ethics, Morals, and Laws

Technically, ethics is a branch of philosophy that examines moral questions, or questions of right and wrong, and thus is also called moral philosophy. There are many specialties within ethics. One of the main branches attempts to answer moral questions in both theory (moral theory) and practice (applied ethics). Another branch, metaethics, deals with nonmoral questions about morality, such as the nature of moral facts and the meanings of moral statements. In this chapter, we will first look at some moral theories and then examine applied ethics as it relates to mass communication and journalism, advertising, PR, and entertainment in particular.

Although ethics actually refers to the branch of philosophy that examines questions of morality, in common usage, the term "ethics" is often used synonymously with "morals." Morals are what we believe to be right or wrong. The question of why we consider an action such as lying to be wrong is a matter for metaethics and not something we address here. Although it may seem impossible to dictate what is right or wrong for a person in a given situation, ethics provides us with a framework and method for good moral reasoning.

Ethics and laws are not the same. Many of our basic laws are based on moral precepts, but many unethical actions are not illegal. Similarly, many laws are not based on moral precepts (consider traffic parking laws, e.g.). Some laws, such as segregation in the United States or apartheid in South Africa, have been deemed immoral and have eventually been reformed, through civil disobedience and other means, to better reflect what is considered right and good.

Major Systems of Ethical Reasoning

There is no single underlying and unified ethical system that all people can follow for complete justice and peace. That does not mean, however, we will not benefit from examining the thinking of philosophers, religious leaders, and scholars, and the different ethical systems that have been developed, some over thousands of years. Various classifications of ethical reasoning and moral theories exist, but here we will use a system employed by William Neher and Paul Sandin in their book *Communicating Ethically*. In some ways matching that of noted media ethics scholar Clifford Christians,[3] their classification also diverges to highlight the role of communication in ethics.

Neher and Sandin group the four major systems within the categories of character, duties, consequences, and relationships. We will look at these and also examine the issue of moral relativism.

CHARACTER, OR VIRTUE ETHICS

Virtue ethics is the oldest of the ethical systems, with roots in some of our earliest religions. The Greeks believed strongly in the notion of virtue and the role of character in living a virtuous life. They aspired to virtues such as courage, modesty, stoicism, and honesty, among other character traits. In virtue ethics, a virtuous character lets you live a virtuous life. Simply acting modest or selfless, when in fact you do not really feel those traits, does not make you virtuous (partly because you are breaking another virtue, that of honesty).

Many great thinkers have given us lists of virtues, sometimes falling short of meeting their own standards. Benjamin Franklin famously made a list of thirteen virtues and vowed to focus on a different item every week, dutifully logging in a notebook how he did each day. He soon gave up, though, after realizing he could not practice the virtue of order, or keeping things in their place, only the third virtue on his list.[4] He was also famous for not following his twelfth virtue, chastity. Virtue ethics can give us a framework for the best way to live our lives, but it does not tell us exactly how to do that.

Although virtue ethics may seem old-fashioned, given its long religious and philosophical history, it has become more important in recent years among media ethicists. Its stress on character touches on fundamental aspects of what makes us human, a compelling emphasis absent in some later ethical systems.

There are two virtue-based ethics you are probably familiar with: the Golden Rule and the Golden Mean.

The Golden Rule

A basic ethical principle in Judeo-Christian belief, which dominates most Western societies, is often cited as "Do unto others as you would have them do unto you." Another way to express the same idea is "Love thy neighbor as thyself."

This principle could be applied by a journalist when interviewing a grieving relative, for example. By treating the person with respect and dignity and asking themselves how they would want to be treated in the same situation, journalists can perhaps avoid some of the charges of invasion of privacy or tastelessness in coverage often leveled at the media. Some journalists, when interviewed in similar situations, have expressed shock at the realization of how insensitive and intrusive the news media can be during trying times of personal grief.

The Golden Mean

One of the oldest ethical principles, the Golden Mean, was espoused in different forms by Aristotle and Confucius, each of whom said that finding a balance between two extremes is the most ethical way. This "middle way" may well shift as the extremes shift, of course, and even this principle has to be taken in moderation. Stealing only half, rather than all, the money from a cash register would not be ethical, for example, because stealing is wrong in the first place.

Applying the Golden Mean to news stories would involve trying to find balance and fairness among all sides of an issue. It does not mean automatically giving each side the same amount of coverage or space in the newspaper, however, because the relative importance of the groups must be judged. For example, an extreme fringe group with only a few hundred vocal members should not receive the same amount of coverage on a controversial issue as a long-standing national organization with tens of thousands of members.

According to Aristotle, the process of deciding on a mean is one way we determine what constitutes virtue, and the mean becomes the standard by which ethical acts are judged. This is part of the reason that acts typically deemed wrong, such as stealing, should not be considered one extreme.

Virtue Ethics in Action

Taking today's much-touted notion of transparency as a virtue, we can see where unethical actions may occur when companies try to hide information or mislead the public. One such case is when the major networks, of which news organizations are a part, fought a proposed regulation that would require television stations to disclose the sources and amounts of political advertising they received. If transparency is a virtue that news organizations demand of other companies, then these networks were acting unethically—if not hypocritically—when trying to keep the information secret. In the end, a kind of golden mean was reached in that only the four major networks and stations in the top markets would have to disclose the information, whereas cable networks and smaller-market stations would not.

DISCUSSION QUESTIONS: Discuss what virtues you think are most admirable in today's world. Why do you think so? How many of those can you honestly say you practice?

DUTIES

As the name suggests, duty-based ethical systems state that we must follow a prescribed set of rules, or duties, regardless of the outcome. It is our moral obligation to follow these duties, no matter what. Duty theories provide basic principles for moral obligations in life. These may spring from religious beliefs (duties to God), but duties to others and oneself may also be embraced.

Duty-based approaches differ from virtue-based ethical systems in important ways. The virtue-based approach emphasizes the individual's choices within a prescribed framework. In a duty-based approach, individual choice is eliminated in favor of a set of rules that apply equally to everybody.

The Categorical Imperative

Immanuel Kant was an influential German philosopher in the eighteenth century whose duty-based ethical system stated that actions should be decided on moral laws that would apply to everyone. Kant said that we should create these moral laws only when we have carefully considered if we would want these laws applied to us at all times. He referred to this unconditional moral obligation as a **categorical imperative**. The categorical imperative cannot depend on a personal inclination, goal, or purpose. It encourages one to act for the benefit of others first and not for personal gain. Treating someone with respect, giving to charity to benefit those in need, and lending a hand to help another with a difficult task are examples of actions that reinforce the inherent value of others.

Media organizations can apply Kant's categorical imperative in many ways. Consider, for instance, an advertising firm's decision to decline clients who sell tobacco or alcohol, or a public relations firm's decision not to accept government clients from nations with poor human rights records. Following categorical imperatives would entail rejecting such clients, no matter how promising the contract.

For news organizations, decisions to publish names of criminal suspects or to cover all serious crimes, for example, would fall under the categorical imperative. In this case, if a newspaper published all names of drivers arrested for drunk driving, it would make no exception for even the mayor or the newspaper publisher.

The strength in duty-based approaches should be clear: Simply by following the rules, you are acting ethically. Nevertheless, obeying certain rules can still complicate many situations. Reporting crime victim names, for instance, seems like a simple policy. But when looking at a stigmatized crime like rape, reporting the victim's name may further harm the victim. Others argue that not treating sexual crimes like other crimes deepens misunderstanding and stigmatization by perpetuating the myth of sexual violence as being somehow intrinsically different than other violent crimes.

> 💬 **categorical imperative**
>
> In ethical thought, Kant's concept of an unconditional moral obligation that does not depend on an individual's personal inclinations or goals.

Immanuel Kant was an influential eighteenth-century German philosopher who developed the notion of the categorical imperative in ethics.

> **DISCUSSION QUESTIONS:** If you believe that telling the truth is always the best course of action, then create a list of cases in which you would lie, ranging from extreme ("I would lie to save my life") to less serious cases ("I would lie not to hurt someone's feelings"). What does this exercise teach about telling the truth as both an ideal and a practical reality?

Discourse Ethics

German social theorist and scholar Jürgen Habermas, most known for his concept of the "public sphere" (see Chapter 14), has proposed what he calls "discourse ethics" as an ethical framework. Habermas claims that communication is integral to how we understand the world, and when practiced without bias or coercion, it becomes an ethical act brought about through the process of rational interaction, or argument. He proposes several actions for participants in discourse, a formalized discussion in which the ideas of all affected parties are heard and considered on their own merits—not outside factors, such as who is more powerful or more persuasive. Discourse ethics prescribes rules but also assumes that justice and equality are most important for a good society.

Principles of discourse ethics could work well when an organization does not agree on the proper course of action. If all affected parties participate in the discussion, they can see other perspectives better, yielding a decision that ideally makes everyone happy. Note that this process is not about finding a compromise simply for the sake of compromise but more about letting people come to a shared and consensual understanding of what is true or correct based on the merits of the argument.

A company promoting a highly unpopular development project may ask a small PR firm to represent them. A discourse-ethics approach to the project could help them decide whether to take on the client. All those in the firm could state their views. They might also solicit opinions from other clients and local citizens whom the project might affect. Bringing in parties normally without a voice would ideally provide new perspectives for all involved and lead to an ethical decision.

Duties-Based Ethics in Action

The *News of the World*, a 168-year-old UK tabloid newspaper with 2.6 million readers, published its last issue on July 10, 2011, with the headline "Thank You and Goodbye." The paper, owned by Rupert Murdoch's News Corp., was at the heart of a shocking scandal involving journalists hacking phones of celebrities, sports stars, politicians, and families of crime victims, all to get material to scoop competing tabloids.

Phone hacking—eavesdropping on private phone calls or messages—is illegal, but a host of ethical issues were also raised by industry experts, the government, and the public regarding whether journalism in the United Kingdom needed further regulation. Further complicating matters, while raising even more legal and ethical concerns, was the revelation that journalists had bribed police officers for information for stories.

In response to public outrage, advertisers promptly pulled their ads from the *News of the World*, which led in part to its sudden closure. Public concern about invasions of privacy, especially by a profession that claims to be the watchdog of government, seriously damaged the reputation of journalism. Fierce competition among Britain's tabloids, which specialize in lurid stories, and the drive to sell more papers, stifled ethical decision making at the *News of the World*. Adhering to the duties of professional journalists and editors, rather than the scoop mentality of daily tabloids, might have prevented such misconduct.

The *News of the World* phone-hacking scandal had massive repercussions in the British press and government.

CONSEQUENCES

We often consider the likely consequences of our actions as we make ethical decisions. Of course, nobody can predict the future, so exact forecasts may be difficult. Nevertheless, some influential ethical systems look primarily at consequences as ways to judge what is ethically good or not.

Utilitarianism

Utilitarianism assumes that the most ethical action does the greatest good for the greatest number. A decision or act that severely hurts someone or a small group is still right if it helps many more people.

This may promote a numbers game, thinking of the greatest good strictly in terms of the number of people who benefit. Another way to look at it weighs a small good for a great number of people against a greater good for a small number. Scientific research on animals operates under a utilitarian principle, with many safeguards to minimize potential suffering and harm of test subjects. A small number of animals suffer or are killed to find cures for diseases that may help much larger numbers of people. It may be harder from a utilitarian ethical perspective to justify testing cosmetics on animals than testing animals to find a cure for cancer—a classic case of how both "greatest number" and "greatest good" must be weighed.

Utilitarianism can often be used to justify media coverage of sensitive or painful events for a small number of people because the coverage can help many others. Examples include investigative reports of government wrongdoing in which a few individuals may go to jail or lose their jobs, but society as a whole benefits, or textbook coverage of professionals who have committed ethics violations. **Social marketing** operates under utilitarian principles because it attempts to do the greatest good for the greatest number of people by changing their behaviors, such as encouraging them not to drive drunk, smoke, or binge drink.

social marketing

Advertising and marketing techniques that persuade people to change bad or destructive behaviors or adopt good behaviors.

Social Justice

Egalitarian philosophers believe that what is ethical is whatever brings about the most social justice or fairness for everyone. In this way, the utilitarian belief of "the greatest good" is interpreted as "the most fairness for everyone."

Philosopher John Rawls argued in his 1971 book *A Theory of Justice* that fairness is the fundamental idea behind justice. Yet establishing what is fair in a complex modern society, where certain groups have greater wealth, power, and advantages, is often difficult. To better understand fairness, Rawls advocates that the parties step behind a "veil of ignorance" and give up their usual roles. They must stake out an "original position" on the issue, not knowing what their role may be after it is decided.

By following this procedure, managers in disputes with workers would have to imagine that they may end up part of the workers after the exercise is finished. If so, would they be satisfied with the result proposed by management? From this framework, Rawls says, the parties would be better able to establish fair practices, for they could more clearly see other viewpoints and those interests.

Understanding other viewpoints is key to effective media communications. Advertising executives may realize that if they were of a different ethnic group or gender, they might find a proposed advertisement offensive. Newsroom editors may reassess the workload of reporters after admitting it

Social marketing campaigns to discourage harmful behaviors employ a utilitarian perspective, trying to achieve the greatest good for the greatest number of people.

would be too onerous for them, which may lead to policy changes. Reporters may choose their words more carefully or write the story more thoughtfully if they imagined themselves as the subject of the piece.

Still, such ponderings may seem unrealistic in today's competitive business world. An editor may realize, on a personal level, that the workload of reporters is unfair but may not be able to do anything about it on a professional or organizational level. Asking those in control to step behind a veil of ignorance or follow certain rules of discourse is also asking them to surrender their power and position. And, as with discourse ethics, the dominant group has little incentive to abandon its ability to coerce others.

Consequence-Based Ethics in Action

Childhood obesity and its accompanying diseases, such as diabetes and high blood pressure, are a growing problem in the United States. The problem is exacerbated in Puerto Rico, where Hispanic cultural norms see a chubby kid as a healthy kid.

As part of an advertising campaign, Subway restaurant let children go grocery shopping while their parents secretly watched on video in another room. The ad showed shocked and horrified parents observing their children fill the shopping carts with junk food. Similar to public service ads in the United States that highlighted the effect of parents' bad shopping habits on children's eating habits, Subway's ads provided a social caution—while also of course reminding viewers that Subway sandwiches are a more healthful option than other fast foods.

A social marketing campaign like Subway's could clearly be seen as using utilitarian principles to promote the greatest good for the greatest number. Even so, it does raise issues of self-interest while downplaying the fact that some of Subway's menu items also are high in calories.

RELATIONSHIPS, OR DIALOGICAL ETHICS

Neher and Sandin call dialogical ethics "a system in which ethics can be judged by the attitudes and behaviors demonstrated by each participant in a communication transaction." In ethical dialogs, the participants are willing to open themselves up and see how the other side views the world and themselves. In dialogical ethics, we do not try to force our own agenda but strive for open and honest dialog that accepts other views without judgment. We do not simply abandon our own views and become uncritical sponges, but we remain open to hearing other views and respecting those we encounter.

Dialog forms the basis of our relations with others. This is especially true with social media because dialog is often the only way we interact with many people online. Further, professions such as advertising and public relations, in which success is measured by how well the audience has been persuaded to buy a product, change a belief, or perform some other action, would seem to be unethical from a dialogical-ethics perspective because they are using people as a means to an end.

These points are valid. Even so, perhaps some of the seemingly unethical issues involving advertising may be mitigated if a dialogical ethical approach is considered. In today's world of social media, where audience members communicate regularly with each other, joining the dialog has become increasingly important for companies. A common mistake of organizations as they enter the social

INTERNATIONAL PERSPECTIVES
Mistaken Identity: One Life Lost, Another Ruined

Social-networking sites such as Facebook and Twitter have played important roles in many recent social movements, including protests in Iran in 2009 as students took to the streets against President Mahmoud Ahmadinejad's government, which banned media coverage.

Despite the media ban, one particularly poignant incident was recorded and sent through social media all over the world. Militia members shot a 26-year-old student, Neda Agha-Soltan, her dying moments captured on video. Her photo quickly became a rallying cry for protesters and a symbol of the extreme repression they opposed.

The only trouble was that the photo they—and all Western media outlets—used was not that of Neda Agha-Soltan. Rather, it was a Facebook photo of Zahra Soltani, who also goes by the name Neda. Nobody was more surprised to see this than Soltani herself as she got friend requests on Facebook and saw her photo appear all over the media.

Iranian authorities contacted Soltani, a 33-year-old English-literature teacher at a university in Iran, and asked her to support the government claim that foreign intelligence agencies had faked the shooting photo to discredit the Iranian government. When she refused, they became more persistent and started asking her questions about her contacts with people overseas, where she was planning to attend a conference. When she was warned by a friend that the government was going to arrest her as a spy, she hastily fled the country with nothing but her laptop computer, a backpack, and the clothes she was wearing.

Soltani first stayed in Germany, where she was granted asylum while she tried to get the media to stop using her picture for Agha-Soltan's. Even after proving to media agencies they were mistaken, she never received

apologies; and some continued to use her picture, as have many websites that have written about the story. Soltani's case demonstrates what can happen when media outlets think of people only as objects for news stories to attract bigger audiences.

According to dialogical ethics, the media should have been willing to listen to Soltani and to correct the misinformation they were spreading about her rather than largely ignoring her. Later Soltani accepted a visiting professorship position at Montclair State University in New Jersey, where she teaches English literature. "Both sides have destroyed my life, the Western media and the Iranian intelligence," Soltani told the *New York Times*. "But I still have the hope that at least the media will realize what they have done."[5]

---

media space is trying to control the dialog and squash dissent rather than truly listening to consumers and trying to understand their viewpoints, as dialogical ethics dictates.

Ethics of Care

The ethics of care challenges many traditional ethical systems and speaks to issues in modern society and communication. This branch of feminist ethics has many variants and has been quite controversial. A number of beliefs characterize feminist thought in general: Women are the equal of men; oppression of women is wrong; categories of male and female and their associated gender roles are socially constructed; the male perspective has dominated throughout history to the detriment of women; and consequently, society has accepted ostensibly male virtues as the standard or highest ideals.

Like dialogical ethics, the ethics of care emphasizes the importance of relationships but places a greater emphasis on improving relationships. In the ethics of care, acting ethically involves caring for oneself and for others within the context of a relationship in real life, not because of abstract principles. It replaces a justice-based ethical system with a caring-based ethical system, the *one caring* and the *cared for*.

Feminist ethics is important in a communication context for a number of different reasons. First, the assumptions that "male" means "normal" has implications for everything from how advertising messages are constructed to who is making the advertisements (and who are simply models within them). Mass communication, in subtle and not-so-subtle ways, helps establish and reinforce the roles of men and women in society. Second, even if women are hardwired differently than men—still a debatable point—promoting caring about others offers a valuable alternative way of conceptualizing communications.

Dialogical Ethics in Action

In 2012, McDonalds launched a Twitter campaign using the #McDStories hashtag, encouraging customers to share their experiences as children with Happy Meals and other fond memories of time spent at McDonalds. The plan would seem to be a perfect case of dialogical ethics at work, with a multinational corporation reaching out on social media and asking its customers to share recollections of good times at their restaurants.

What they received, however, were not the expected Happy Stories of Happy Meals: "One time I walked into McDonalds and I could smell the Type 2 diabetes floating in the air and I threw up"; "Eating a Quarter Pounder Value Meal makes me feel exactly like an hour of violent weeping"; "I ate a @McDonalds cheeseburger

Feminist ethics provide a moral framework that encourages the empowerment of women while protesting discrimination and harassment.

a few years ago and got food poisoning so bad I had to get hospitalized"; and so on.[6] McDonalds realized too late the nature of the beast they had unleashed, a PR monster that crushed subsequent corporate efforts to further dialog by addressing negative consumer comments.

In 2014, Dr. Oz opened similar dialogic floodgates when he solicited questions on Twitter, promising to reply to his favorites on his website. Despite being a highly accomplished cardiothoracic surgeon who has devoted his life to improving the health of others, Dr. Oz is as controversial a brand as allegedly health-impairing McDonalds. So perhaps not surprisingly to anyone but Oz himself, his PR team, and his legions of fans, #OzsInbox, the hashtag he created, was similarly swiftly inundated with vitriol, most notably from practicing physicians who took this opportunity to unload on Dr. Oz for perceived quackery.

The following is from the medical Twitterverse: "When you're doing an internal mammary artery bypass graft, does . . . crap, I forgot, you're not a real doctor anymore, never mind"; "Can you go an entire show without saying the words 'miracle,' 'toxin,' and 'belly fat?'"; "Why have you not been censured or fired from @ColumbiaSurgery for conduct unbecoming a physician, scientist, and gentlemen?"[7] The latter tweet evidently expressed the sentiments of many in the profession who, in April 2015, called for his removal from the Columbia faculty, where Oz is vice chair of Columbia's Department of Surgery.[8]

Public relations nightmares such as these will likely educate other companies about the possible negative consequences of well-intentioned forays into dialogic social media. Perhaps the following tweet best captures this lesson: "Dear, Dr. Oz, at what point today did you realize that the Twitter demographic is different from your show's regular audience?" As these cautionary tales illustrate, social media can be a minefield. Meaningful dialog can still be generated on this platform, though, without setting off explosives. Moreover, these conversations are taking place about brands and companies, formerly accustomed to dictating and controlling their message whether or not they become an active part of the conversation.

MORAL RELATIVISM

Moral relativism suggests that none of the ethical systems can be said to be any better than the others and that traditional ethical principles have historically been used primarily to secure the stature of established social groups. The notion of moral relativism derives from anthropological research that recognizes behaviors deemed wrong in our culture may be considered perfectly normal, even moral, in another culture. This led early researchers to question the basis on which some groups declared their moral codes superior to others.

A weakness of moral relativism is that it leaves no agreed-on rules or principles for discussing ethical issues and reaching conclusions. There is no fundamental component or rulebook for trying to understand the point of view of others, no yardstick of social justice or greatest good, no duties to follow, and no virtues to aspire to that will improve our characters. Each of us is out for himself or herself, with no way (or incentive) to communicate and find common ground for understanding.

Moral relativism makes it impossible to justify from an ethical perspective social marketing campaigns that attempt to change practices or beliefs among others. One example is cockfighting, in which roosters with razor blades attached to their feet fight each other to the death and spectators bet on the outcome. It is practiced legally in many countries in Asia and South America (and illegally in the United States and Europe). Using moral relativism, one could not make a valid moral argument that cockfighting proponents are unethical and must be stopped because they see nothing wrong with an event that remains for many a part of their culture.

> **DISCUSSION QUESTIONS:** If you had to pick just one ethical system by which to live by which would it be? Why?

Issues in Ethical Decision Making

One size does not fit all; that is, no theoretical approach will work for all situations, and conflicts between ethical precepts produce ethical dilemmas in life and in media. The ethics of care may often conflict with the categorical imperative. An editor, for instance, may not want to publish anything about his wife's run-in with the law, whereas the newspaper's policy is always to print names of people arrested. Media accounts of their own business practices and mistakes often lack the vigor of their reports on other businesses, a clear violation of the categorical imperative.

The principle of utilitarianism can be used to run roughshod over rights of privacy. Editors often justify intrusive coverage of famous people as "the public's right to know." But what good does such coverage actually serve? Who actually benefits the most from exposing a shocking celebrity scandal? Does the public get important information that somehow makes them better citizens, or has the paper simply sold more newspapers?

A utilitarian argument might also be used to suppress news coverage. A story on the unsafe practices of a local factory could force it to close down and put hundreds of people out of work. In this case, would keeping quiet about the violations serve the greatest good for the greatest number of people?

Media professionals deal with a number of ethical problems on the job, some of which are discussed throughout this book. Because of the nature of work in mass communication, ethical lapses can have far-reaching repercussions, potentially ruining careers, affecting the public's perception and trust of media in general, and in some instances even ending lives.

Corporate decisions made in executive boardrooms far above the typical media professional's level can also have ethical repercussions. Sometimes media professionals may be willing pawns in unethical practices; other times, they simply try to do their jobs as best they can within the dictates of the larger organizational environment.

According to academic Ronald Howard and business consultant Clinton Korver, authors of *Ethics for the Real World: Creating a Personal Code to Guide Decisions in Work and Life*, three disciplines—legal, prudential, and ethical—are important to keep in mind when assessing ethical actions. They claim that we often confuse these concepts when attempting moral reasoning. In other words, we may present our reasoning within an ethical framework, when our reasons are actually prudential or practical, such as improving the company's bottom line.

Howard and Korver offer several easy self-tests to evaluate whether your decision is truly rational or simply a rationalization couched in ethical terms. These include the "other-shoe test" (how would you feel if the shoe were on the other foot?), the "front-page test" (would you think the same way if what you did was on the front page of the *New York Times*?), the "loved-one test" (how would you feel if the recipient of your action was someone you loved?), the "role-model test" (would you want your children to model your behavior?), and the "mother's test" (what would your mother think?).

A more systematic method of ethical decision making is called the Potter Box, named after social ethics professor Ralph B. Potter. The Potter Box provides a framework for analyzing a situation, separating facts from opinions and taking into account those individuals affected by a given ethical issue. Once one has sorted out the facts, defined the situation, and analyzed it, then values and principles (what we are calling ethical frameworks) can be applied and loyalties to different parties can be considered. Figure 10-1 shows how the Potter Box can be used.

FIGURE 10-1 The Potter Box

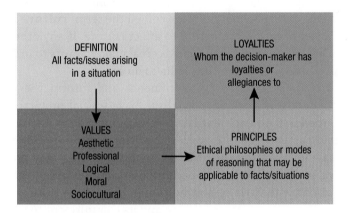

Let us use the Potter Box to examine the *Rolling Stone* case from the beginning of this chapter. Imagine that you are an editor at *Rolling Stone* who has received the story by Sabrina Rubin Erdely of the rape at the fraternity. First, you consider the facts of the situation—is the information being presented supported by corroborating evidence? Second, you would consider the values at work, including the professional values of journalism that discourage publishing articles based on unknown sources or conjecture.

Third, you would select the ethical frameworks that could be applied, each of which may recommend a different conclusion. From a consequences-based approach, you may reason that publishing the story helps others by highlighting a much larger problem of sexual assault on college campuses (a rationale Erdely offered even after the *Rolling Stone* apology). A virtues-based approach would argue that *Rolling Stone* ignored truthfulness and veracity—two fundamental principles of journalism—when it published the story. Feminist ethics, although not condoning the shoddy reporting, would emphasize the relationship of the publication with the victim in helping her tell her story (and would—and did—strongly criticize the victim-blaming that *Rolling Stone* engaged in after the story's flaws came to light).

Fourth, as an editor you would consider your loyalty to *Rolling Stone*, your employer. Would publishing such a titillating and controversial story help sell more copies and enhance your organization's reputation? You may, for example, reason that it would indeed sell more copies, but without considering the other issues with the story, you may not see beyond sales for the magazine to the harm for individuals and institutions featured in the story—and ultimately for *Rolling Stone* itself.

This later step should help you select among the various responses and rationales that the different frameworks recommend. In the case of *Rolling Stone*, key editorial decision makers were likely not thinking about the underlying ethical and professional principles that should have been considered much earlier in the process.

Role of Commercialism in Media Ethics

Whether privately held or publicly traded on the stock market, businesses in a capitalist society are expected to make money for their owners. Members of the public invest in companies that are expected to be successful, which means making profits. Media companies are no different than other types of corporations in that regard.

They are, however, uniquely positioned to influence the public compared to other types of companies because of the "product"—media content—they create. Scholars in the Frankfurt School tradition coined the term "**culture industry**" to describe the power of media companies to affect culture. If any other kind of organization, such as a car manufacturer or a cereal maker, wants to influence public opinion, they have to go through the media to do so.

Because of the media's ability to influence and inform the public, some branches of the industry, such as journalism, have special protection under the Constitution; the First Amendment is a case in point. Partly as a result of these protections and partly through historical traditions, media—and journalism in particular—have had a strong public service mission. This may no longer be a mandate when news organizations become divisions of larger entertainment-media corporations with little or no tradition in the unique culture of the newsroom and its commitment to public service.

At the heart of many media-ethics dilemmas are the conflicting goals of informing the public and maximizing corporate profit. These issues can arise in a number of ways. Commercial interests can take precedence over public interests when powerful advertisers cancel or threaten to cancel their advertising in a media outlet. A blatant example could involve toning down or eliminating an unflattering story on a large local advertiser who has threatened to withdraw advertising revenue. More commonly, advertisers may pull their ads when a media organization covers unpopular issues or takes unpopular editorial stands. Examples of this include Southern newspapers that supported the civil rights movement in losing local advertisers in the 1950s and 1960s. Although controversial news coverage was not directly about the advertisers, they either

culture industry

A term coined by the Frankfurt School to describe how media companies produce or "make" culture in the same way that other companies produce products.

The civil rights movement forced some Southern newspapers to make tough choices when advertisers threatened to pull their ads if the papers appeared to support the movement.

disagreed with or did not want to be associated with the newspaper's content for fear of losing business.

The costs associated with running a modern newsroom have become increasingly problematic ethical concerns. Cutting staff is one of the surest ways to considerably reduce operating costs, but at what expense in terms of news coverage? Fewer staff means less coverage of certain subjects, such as education and city hall, in favor of more wire-service copy or light features. This practice can provide the public with an incomplete picture of local events and issues. Similarly, investigative reports are often time-consuming and expensive and are less likely to be conducted in a media organization intensely aware of maximizing profits.

Professional training and development also often suffer. Many journalists who want to learn how to use computer-assisted reporting tools or digital media must pay their own way to conferences or workshops and use their personal vacation time to attend. This is despite a push by some news organizations for journalists to become multimedia reporters, doing their stories in print, TV, and audio formats. Production costs are reduced when one journalist is doing the work previously done by three.

Real Housewives of Atlanta was Bravo's first show to get more than two million viewers in the coveted 18–49 age range, but has faced criticisms in the past for apparently fabricating portions of their storylines. **CRITICAL THINKING QUESTIONS:** How strictly should "reality TV" stick with real portrayals of people, and is it acceptable for producers to fabricate storylines in order to increase the entertainment value of the shows, even if it portrays some people unfairly in a negative light?

MEDIA TYPES INFLUENCING CONTENT

Various business pressures arise with the various media types. The expense of producing feature-length films, for example, is an important factor for large media companies that want to maximize their profits. A film could have a greater likelihood of getting produced if the media company already owns the rights to the character in the film, for example, and if there is good potential for other media content from within the company, such as music and television shows, to be tied in with the movie to help in marketing.

The individual divisions of a large media company must deal with the demands of the corporate parent to maximize profits. For example, the book-publishing branch may feel pressure to emphasize books from established authors in a popular genre to generate sales, but at the expense of finding new authors or types of books that do not fit established categories.

The need for exciting visual elements has even affected news coverage. *Dateline NBC*'s fifteen-minute segment "Waiting to Explode," which ran on November 17, 1992, was meant to demonstrate the danger of the gas tanks exploding with certain models of General Motors' pickup trucks. Yet the trucks filmed exploding on the segment had been rigged by the production team to ensure a fiery explosion, and some of the information presented was misleading or inaccurate. Only later, through independent investigations and information from sources who were at the initial filming, did the truth behind the segment come out, forcing NBC to make a public apology and settle the lawsuit that GM had brought against it.[9] In this case, the need to have an exciting visual element likely helped cause the ethical breaches.

On a smaller scale, but no less unethical, was the example of *Today* reporter Michelle Kosinski covering flooding in Wayne, New Jersey, in 2005. She is shown paddling a kayak down a flooded street as she gives her report, only to have two people walk right in front of her, revealing that the water is actually only ankle deep. Despite this, she continues with the report and paddles as if nothing happened.

Not every dramatic photograph on the front page of a newspaper or in television news reports is a breach of media ethics, for newsworthiness is always a consideration for news organizations. It is important to ask, though, whether the decision to include certain elements in visual media was driven more by the need to capture the public's attention than true news value.

Ethics in Journalism

Because of journalism's unique role in society, its First Amendment protection, and its public service mission, many ethical dilemmas arise in the course of practicing it. Difficult ethical questions play a role in the entire news-gathering and production process. Ethical issues become even more important with the rise of citizen journalism.

Editors must consider whether headlines and captions accurately reflect the important points of a story or simply titillate. Privacy issues play a role when private citizens are thrust by circumstance into the media spotlight. Reporters must consider fairness and balance in their choice of interview subjects. Photo editors and designers must avoid the temptation to alter elements of photos to make them more dramatic. Societal mores and cultural values of the audience must be considered when determining what qualifies as news and how it is reported, although newspapers must also sometimes take highly unpopular stands on issues when acting as the public's conscience.

> **DISCUSSION QUESTIONS:** Do you think that because news organizations receive extra legal protection not enjoyed by most other types of companies that they should also be held to a higher ethical standard? Is this standard more difficult to meet when one journalist is doing work previously done by three? Defend your views.

PRIVACY RIGHTS VERSUS THE PUBLIC'S RIGHT TO KNOW

Although no actual law states this, the public's "right to know" is often cited as a commonly understood principle when journalists are trying to obtain information that can better inform the public regarding anything from political candidates to corporate wrongdoing to potentially dangerous foods, drugs, or buildings.

Gathering proof of wrongdoing is one of the biggest challenges journalists face. Admissions of guilt are unlikely to come out during an interview—if the subject even agrees to one. Journalists are often barred from the very locations they need to visit to gather information. Employees are forbidden by management to speak to journalists or threatened with losing their jobs if they do; police or public officials refuse to see or talk to journalists or are slow in providing requested documentation, even if the documents are public records.

New technology such as miniature microphones and cameras and the old technique of going undercover may seem easy answers to the journalist's dilemma.

But the ethics and legality of these tools and actions must be considered. Sometimes these techniques are the only ones that will give access to people engaged in illegal or unethical behavior, such as selling drugs or arms.

Federal law prohibits the media or anyone else from intentionally intercepting, or attempting to intercept, anyone's communication by wire, oral, or electronic means. Citizens have a reasonable expectation of privacy for oral, or spoken, communications, via telephone or over the Internet, for example. State laws vary, however, on whether only one person or both people in a conversation must consent to having it recorded.

Regardless of the legality of intercepting communications, is it ethical? It depends on the circumstances, including whether it is print or broadcast media. The FCC generally prohibits the use of wireless microphones to overhear private conversations unless all parties to the communication have given prior consent. Conversations that occur in a public place, such as a restaurant or bar, however, would not be subject to the same prohibition because people in public places cannot expect the same right to privacy. Broadcast television or radio stations may not record telephone conversations without the consent of all parties, and they must notify the parties prior to broadcasting recorded content. Long-distance calls can only be recorded under limited circumstances, including an announcement made at the beginning of the call indicating it will be recorded or possibly broadcast. Violation of these rules can result in the forfeiture of the station's license, fines, or other penalties.

One area of confusion regarding privacy is whether posting material in a blog or on a social media site like Facebook is public or not. Some claim that it is the same as a public space. An offhand comment in a bar, however, disappears once it is said; but an inflammatory blog post written years ago and later deleted still exists somewhere on the Web.

Online conversations have raised new issues of privacy and whether messages are public or private, as posts written years ago can be found and reposted by others.

GOING UNDERCOVER

The legality and ethics of journalists going undercover are also not settled. In many ways, it depends on how ethical or responsible the media professional was in using these techniques. Questions that may be asked in a court of law include the following: Were the media being fair? Does going undercover or using hidden cameras somehow manipulate or distort the situation? Do the undercover techniques help build meaningful information or simply sensationalize the story? If a media professional (or anyone else, for that matter) is convicted of violating the law in going undercover, penalties may include prison terms and fines.

The Internet raises new questions about journalists not announcing their identity. If a journalist participates in a child-pornography online discussion group without revealing her or his identity as a journalist pursuing a story, is it ethical to use others' posts without their permission? Is it ethical to pose as someone other than a journalist to get people to talk as they naturally would in an online forum?

VICTIMIZING THE VICTIMS

Publicizing details of crimes can contribute to copycat crimes. Journalists must always consider which elements of a story are important and which are simply lurid or titillating. Needlessly mentioning race, gender, or sexual orientation can often be unethical, framing a subject in a way that reinforces social stereotypes and makes crime victims feel like they are being victimized again.

Photographs and video can sometimes tell a story more powerfully than words alone. Yet news value alone does not always justify publicizing dramatic photos or footage. In fact, in cases of human tragedy, sadness, or crime, the repeated presentation of pictures or video can violate personal grief.

Citizen-journalists, often unaware of professional norms or laws, may act unethically or find themselves in legal trouble. In a social media world, the question of who is a journalist and thus who gets special First Amendment protections lacks a clear answer.

Some victims of sexual crimes have been victimized further, not by the mainstream media but by peers who have posted videos or photos of their acts on social media. In 2013, 17-year-old Rehtaeh Parsons killed herself. Seventeen months previously, she had reported having been raped at a party. Shortly after the alleged rape, a photo of the incident was posted online, and Rehtaeh received online messages calling her a slut and asking to have sex with her. The Nova Scotia authorities initially claimed there was not enough evidence to arrest the accused rapists. After her suicide gained worldwide attention, the authorities said they were looking into the matter again. Such consequences of cyberbullying have been increasing as teens too readily use social media to hurt others.

After admitting he had overstated the risks he faced while covering conflict in the Middle East, Brian Williams was suspended by NBC in 2015. **CRITICAL THINKING QUESTIONS:** Was NBC's response appropriate? What does their decision say about their ethical values? What factors do you think may have encouraged Williams to exaggerate the dangers he experienced?

MISREPRESENTATION AND PLAGIARISM

Instances of journalists distorting or misrepresenting the facts are sadly legion. Janet Cooke, Jayson Blair, and Stephen Glass became textbook examples, an infamous club of journalistic ignominy that highly esteemed and veteran reporter Brian Williams recently joined when he was suspended from his venerable position as NBC anchor amid allegations of misrepresenting events that had occurred while he was covering the Iraq war a decade earlier.

Another problem occurs when journalists misrepresent their relationship to their work, claiming inappropriate authorship of material. The most common type of plagiarism involves copying the work of others without formal attribution. Authors can also plagiarize themselves, however, by reproducing what they have previously published without citing themselves as the source. In 2012, Jonah Lehrer, 31, a noted journalist and science writer, was castigated for self-plagiarism, a sin compounded by an even worse transgression—fabricating quotes from the likes of Bob Dylan. Such revelations torpedoed his rising star, as publishers pulled his books from stores and Lehrer was fired from his job at *The New Yorker* after only two months on the job.[10]

SOCIETY OF PROFESSIONAL JOURNALISTS CODE OF ETHICS

The Society of Professional Journalists (SPJ) is a large organization of working journalists and student chapters that tries to ensure that journalism is being practiced professionally and ethically as it fulfills its role in society. The SPJ's code of ethics states that journalists should "seek truth and report it" and that "journalists should be honest, fair and courageous in gathering, reporting and interpreting information." These are some of the other principles in the code:

- Test the accuracy of information from all sources and exercise care to avoid inadvertent error. Deliberate distortion is never permissible.
- Diligently seek out subjects of news stories to give them the opportunity to respond to allegations of wrongdoing.
- Identify sources whenever feasible. The public is entitled to as much information as possible on sources' reliability.
- Make certain that headlines, news teasers, and promotional material, photos, video, audio, graphics, sound bites, and quotations do not misrepresent. They should not oversimplify or highlight incidents out of context.
- Never distort the content of news photos or video. Image enhancement for technical clarity is always permissible. Label montages and photo illustrations.
- Avoid misleading reenactments or staged news events. If reenactment is necessary to tell a story, label it.
- Support the open exchange of views, even views journalists find repugnant.
- Avoid undercover or other surreptitious methods of gathering information except when traditional open methods will not yield information vital to the public. Use of such methods should be explained as part of the story.

Ethical Issues in Advertising

Mass media are a powerful vehicle to influence the public's opinions, even when they are simply trying to inform or educate. It is no wonder, then, that companies spend billions of dollars on advertising each year. Yet numerous ethical issues have been raised involving false and deceptive advertising in the mass media.

Advertising is an important part of how goods and services are marketed in a capitalist economy, and some advertising contains useful product information. Advertising is also the economic engine that drives much of the system of mass communication.

The advertising industry has not been entirely successful at regulating itself. Historically, the government has enacted new laws or regulations after receiving consumer complaints—or sometimes after long campaigns regarding certain advertising practices. The Federal Trade Commission (FTC) and the Food and Drug Administration (FDA) enforce regulations regarding deceptive advertising. Industry self-regulation comes from a variety of trade organizations. One of the main ethical issues, from a mass-communication perspective, is false or deceptive advertising.

DECEPTIVE ADVERTISING

Deception in advertising is not always illegal because, in some cases, it does not mislead. For instance, real ice cubes would disappear quickly under the photographer's hot lights. Fake ice cubes, on other hand, do not melt, nor do they deceive anyone regarding the taste or look of the beverage. In other cases, however, deceptive claims do mislead the consumer, offering a "going out of business" sale, for example, when the store intends to remain open.

A court ordered Skechers to pay $40 million to customers because it claimed without substantiation that the design of its Shape-ups sneakers would help people lose weight.

A division of the FTC is assigned responsibility to ferret out deception and can expel such advertising from mass media and even levy fines. The FTC once found a commercial for a toy car misleading, even though it was not false. The toy was filmed in extreme close-up next to the track, making it appear to move rapidly like a blur. After an FTC ruling that children could be deceived by the toy's apparent speed, the ad had to be canceled or modified.

PUFFERY

Nevertheless, the temptation among those selling goods and services, as well as those sponsoring ads, to exaggerate claims is great. **Puffery**, an ethical and legal gray area (sometimes allowed, sometimes not), usually involves an opinion statement about the product. Examples include these familiar advertising slogans:

- "Red bull gives you wings" (Red Bull)
- "Eat fresh" (Subway)
- "For the bold" (Doritos)
- "Now that's better" (Wendy's)

Except for Red Bull, the truth or falsehood of these claims cannot be verified. The FTC permits most puffery, assuming audiences do not perceive these claims as factual. Nobody would actually believe, for example, that wings would grow from drinking Red Bull.

> **DISCUSSION QUESTIONS:** Have you ever felt deceived by a product you bought based on seeing it advertised? How did it make you feel, and did you continue to use the product or brand? Why or why not?

CONFLICTS OF INTEREST IN ADVERTISING

Advertising agencies must be loyal to their clients. It makes little business sense for an agency whose client is a tobacco company to lecture the organization about the harmful effects of smoking. Helping clients sell more product is the advertising agency's professional responsibility, whether they are selling healthy soup or less healthy cigarettes.

Conflicts of interest in advertising can arise in a number of ways. First, employees may find selling harmful products unethical. Some agencies allow employees to choose the organizations they are willing to work with, but making such a choice could ruin a career in other agencies. Second, conflicts of interest occur if an agency works for two competing companies. Even if the teams working for each client are completely separate from each other and based in different cities, confidential information about one client may be divulged to members on the other team. Third, a conflict of interest between loyalty to the client and the actual qualities of the product may arise. An effective advertising campaign can make even a product that lacks the benefits it claims a market leader.

ADVERTISING CODES OF ETHICS

Various advertising and marketing groups have created codes of ethics for their members. Like all codes of ethics, these are largely unenforceable but act instead

CONVERGENCE CULTURE
Forbidden Fruit

Ethical consumerism refers to consumers buying products grown, produced, or manufactured in accordance with their personal ethical standards. Some such ethical concerns include a preference for organic or locally grown produce, fair-trade coffee, and sweatshop-free clothing.

With the rise in popularity of organic foods and fair-trade products, many companies would like their products to seem more environmentally friendly. Although the word "organic" is regulated and may refer to either organic growing practices or the amount of organic ingredients, the word "natural" is not regulated.

Consumers have demonstrated willingness to spend more for products that are good for the environment or produced ethically. For this reason, some companies have engaged in **greenwashing**, inaccurately making products

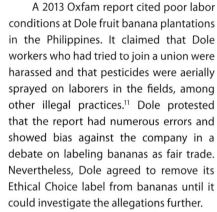

appear to be environmentally friendly or obtained through fair-trade practices.

A 2013 Oxfam report cited poor labor conditions at Dole fruit banana plantations in the Philippines. It claimed that Dole workers who had tried to join a union were harassed and that pesticides were aerially sprayed on laborers in the fields, among other illegal practices.[11] Dole protested that the report had numerous errors and showed bias against the company in a debate on labeling bananas as fair trade. Nevertheless, Dole agreed to remove its Ethical Choice label from bananas until it could investigate the allegations further.

Food companies are not the only ones tempted to greenwash. Some energy companies have tried to make their drilling and production activities seem less detrimental. And lobbyists often promote bills that sound environmentally friendly but are not such in practice.

---

as guiding principles and ideals for how the profession or industry wants to present itself to the world.

The American Marketing Association (AMA) lists three ethical norms: Do no harm, foster trust in the marketing system, and embrace ethical values. Many of the values that it gives sound remarkably like virtues, including honesty, responsibility, fairness, respect, transparency, and citizenship. The first code of the American Advertising Federation (AAF) is that "advertising shall tell the truth, and reveal significant facts; the omission of which would mislead the public." Several other points, such as substantiation, comparison, price claims, and testimonials, also address issues of misleading the public.

Ethics in Public Relations

Public relations people face unique ethical issues compared to journalists, media-entertainment professionals, and advertising people. As with advertising professionals, their loyalties lie with the client; but like journalists, if they present false or misleading information, their credibility and that of their clients can be lost. In addition, although some public relations practitioners like to claim they are the "conscience of the client," they do not always have access to the corporate channels of power to prevent unethical decisions. Often, they are called in to minimize or negate damage already done.

ethical consumerism

A kind of activism in which consumers buy only products that they believe are produced ethically.

greenwashing

The practice of companies making themselves or their products appear to be organic, environmentally friendly, or supportive of free trade when in fact they are not.

MEDIA PIONEERS
Kalle Lasn

Activist, author, editor, and documentarian, Kalle Lasn was born in Tallinn, Estonia, in 1942. His family, having fled the advancing Soviet army near the end of WWII, lived in German refugee camps before relocating to Australia. A graduate of the University of Adelaide who studied theoretical and applied mathematics, Lasn wrote war-games computer code for the Australian military. Subsequently, he founded a lucrative market research company in Tokyo that conducted computer-based studies of ad campaigns for global corporations.

Advertising would continue to define his career, although not in the way one might expect given the earlier positions on his resume. World travel and the rebellious spirit of the sixties had a profound and formative influence on young Kalle, particularly the student uprisings in Paris in 1968. In 1970, he moved to Canada, where he turned his talents to film making; and some twenty years later, he established Adbusters with fellow documentarian Bill Smalz.[12]

Based in Vancouver, BC, this nonprofit organization identifies on their website as "a global network of artists, activists, writers, pranksters, students, educators and entrepreneurs who want to advance the new social activist movement of the information age." Their mission involves reclaiming our mental and physical environments through increased media literacy, public education that promotes an aware and engaged citizenry sensitive to the plight of the planet and its people. Grounded in lefty politics (some might say radically so), the anti-consumerist activism of

Adbusters seeks nothing short of a paradigm shift that topples existing power structures while encouraging lifestyles that harmonize ecology and economy.[13]

To that end, Lasn relentlessly targets what he views as a major culprit in creating and sustaining the ills of consumer culture—advertising. True to their name, the signature media of Adbusters are subversive advertisements, or "subvertisements": Joe Camel, the iconic cigarette mascot, revisited as a patient in a cancer ward; or a smiling Tiger Woods, his grin transformed into Nike's logo, the swoosh stripe synonymous with the company he endorses. These spoof ads function as "culture jams" intended to reassign provocative new meaning to familiar media images, satire that conveys political messages about corporate, commercial, and branded products.

Other controversial Adbusters campaigns include Digital Detox Week, Buy Nothing Day, and Buy Nothing Christmas (whose names speak for themselves), and—most famously—OccupyWallStreet. Conceived on Canada's West Coast and named for Lasn's activist hashtag #OccupyWallStreet, his brainchild rapidly developed into a global movement protesting social and economic inequality.

astroturfing campaign

A movement or campaign that looks as though it was created by concerned citizens as a grassroots movement when in fact it was actually created or controlled by an organization with a vested interest in the outcome.

Some PR firms hire people to attend corporate or government meetings and present testimonials as if they were concerned citizens. They also create faux grassroots campaigns online, **astroturfing campaigns**, designed to present the appearance of citizen support for a company or cause. If people posing at a public forum is unethical, then so too is the online equivalent. Today's 24/7 social-media environment makes damage control difficult, especially when celebrity clients tweet offensive comments. Even when quickly deleted, such posts remain in the public eye, retweeted by the celebrity's many followers.

CONFLICTS OF INTEREST IN PR

Partly because of professional loyalty to their clients, public relations is plagued by many of the same conflicts of interest as advertising. A PR firm may have to manage a crisis communication situation for a disaster caused by a company, even as they see corporate executives take further PR missteps—such as when BP's

CEO at the time, Tony Hayward, said "I'd like my life back," after their oil spill had claimed eleven lives and devastated the environment in the Gulf.

PR professionals may also have clients who believe that anything they release to the media is newsworthy. Clients may also not like having to adjust to a world where their customers can talk and complain with each other in public forums. Although PR agencies claim to manage relationships with a the client's many publics, in truth, many clients do not want an equal relationship with consumers based on dialog and openness. Instead, they want to dictate messages to the public without a response. This dynamic can be difficult for a PR professional who ethically believes in the importance of dialog.

One of the thorniest conflicts of interest occurs when a PR professional is asked to keep material about the client confidential to protect the company's image, such as information about a prescription drug's harmful side effects. Other ethical lapses in PR can have far-reaching consequences, especially when it comes to politics and war.

Hired at a cost of more than half a million dollars by the Kuwaiti government to foster support among the American public and the U.S. Congress, the firm of Hill and Knowlton was widely criticized for clandestine efforts to influence opinion on the Gulf War. They produced and distributed dozens of video news releases (VNRs) to television news operations around the country, aired by many stations without editing and without identifying their source as either the PR firm or the government of Kuwait—propaganda presented as impartial journalism.

Hill and Knowlton also helped organize the "Congressional Human Rights Caucus." In October 1990 at a Capitol Hill hearing, a 15-year-old Kuwaiti girl, known only as Nayirah, spoke tearfully: "I volunteered at the al-Addan hospital. While I was there, I saw the Iraqi soldiers come into the hospital with guns, and go into the room where . . . babies were in incubators. They took the babies out of the incubators, took the incubators, and left the babies on the cold floor to die." For months after her testimony, the media and even President George H. W. Bush repeated the Iraqi soldiers' killing of babies as a rationale for U.S. presence in the region.

Later, Nayirah was revealed to be a member of the Kuwaiti royal family whose testimony had been fabricated. A Hill and Knowlton vice president had even coached her on it. Hill and Knowlton was never penalized or formally reprimanded for their campaign, but the CBC (Canadian Broadcasting Corporation) produced an Emmy Award–winning documentary on the subject, *To Sell a War* (1992).

PUBLIC RELATIONS CODES OF ETHICS

Professional associations such as the Public Relations Society of America (PRSA) and the International Association of Business Communicators (IABC) publish guidelines for ethical public relations practices. According to the PRSA, unethical behavior includes lying by omission, as in failing to release a company's financial information or misrepresenting its performance; deceiving the public by employing people as speakers for public hearings and ostensibly grassroots campaigns; and giving expensive goods or gifts to journalists or politicians to influence their opinion.

On the other hand, their guidelines also state that members must protect the privacy rights of clients and safeguard their confidential information as well as advise appropriate authorities if they discover an employee divulging confidential information. An ethical conflict could easily arise for a PR professional if asked by a company to promote positive news on its financial health rather than report the truth.

Ethics in Entertainment

Media professionals in entertainment do not wrestle with the same issues regarding truth and the public as journalists, advertisers, and public relations professionals do. Entertainment is meant to entertain, and the truth may be immaterial in this pursuit. Documentary films or books and movies based on actual events may be judged on their faithfulness to the facts, but straying from the truth does not usually harm their entertainment value. Because of this, entertainment content is not held to the same ethical standards as, say, a newspaper story or an investigative TV report. But ethics do enter into the world of entertainment because of its ability to shape society's beliefs and influence behavior.

STEREOTYPES IN ENTERTAINMENT

Because entertainment plays such an important part in our lives and is a powerful force for transmitting cultural values, its depiction of stereotypes can be especially hurtful or damaging to groups. At the turn of the twentieth century, minstrel shows were popular in vaudeville, with white actors made up in "blackface" to depict African Americans, often in demeaning or clownish roles. Jewish minstrel shows similarly played on popular stereotypes of the time.

Asians and Asian Americans have faced both positive and negative stereotypes over the years. As many Asians emigrated to the United States in the nineteenth and early twentieth centuries, the mass media often depicted them in negative ways. Today, they are often touted as a "model minority" because of their many academic and professional achievements. However, racist stereotypes still appear in the media, such as the controversial 2013 Day Above Ground video "AsianGirlz," removed from YouTube within days due to critical responses in social media. Taylor Swift's 2014 video "Shake It Off" also engendered controversy for playing with racial stereotypes, notably twerking.

Some may wonder where the harm lies in good-natured jokes or satiric stereotypes, especially those meant to entertain. Yet underlying stereotypes, often taken for granted, help mold beliefs, especially when the media provide our primary exposure to these groups. Italian American stereotypes are a good case in point. According to a 2003 Zogby poll, 78 percent of teenagers associated Italian Americans with either criminal activity or blue-collar work. Another poll showed that 74 percent of adult Americans believed that Italian Americans had some connection to organized crime, likely because of the number of popular movies and shows that depict them as mobbed up. Such misperceptions influence in subtle and sometimes not-so-subtle ways how we interact with the groups stereotyped.

Some Native Americans have protested the use of "tribal" clothing by fashion designers and shoppers.

The debate continues: Does violence in entertainment contribute to violence in society?

DISCUSSION QUESTIONS: Consider a movie or television show that has stereotypes. Replace that stereotyped group with your own ethnicity or gender and consider how you would feel seeing a member of your group depicted in those situations. How might that make you feel about your group?

SEX AND VIOLENCE

Depictions of sex and violence have long been staples of entertainment media, and the old adage "sex sells" is even truer for entertainment than other forms of media. We will look at the legal implications for media and freedom of speech regarding pornography, obscenity, and violence in Chapter 11. Here, we consider the ethical implications of depictions of sex and violence.

At the heart of the issue is the belief that media exposure affects us: Watching too many violent programs can produce violent behavior; people may copy crimes they've seen on television or in movies. Although these media effects will be examined in more detail in Chapter 12, let us assume for now some truth to this claim. If so, then any kind of violent content could be unethical. Within the utilitarian, virtue-based, or another ethical system, would purposely harming others be considered ethical, especially when done simply to profit a company and shareholders?

Another issue arises with sex and violence in the media, even given the fact that most people do not become mass murderers after watching a violent movie. This new issue relates to the earlier points about stereotypes and how they may affect our thinking about certain groups. Consider the double standards about male and female nudity in movies, for example. Rarely do movies show full frontal male nudity, whereas female nudity can be seen much more frequently. Such depictions may give us cues that normalize the treatment of women, but not men, as sex objects.

This parody poster for the movie *Avengers* portrays the male characters as female characters are usually portrayed, drawing attention to the objectification of women in entertainment media.

MEDIA CAREERS

Relatively few firms have ethics officers (independent PR firm Ruder Finn is a notable exception) whose sole job is helping employees make ethical decisions that affect clients, the public, and even their coworkers. Yet as ethical lapses may have serious repercussions for media companies, even playing a role in closing down the business, as was the case for the *News of the World* newspaper, more companies may be looking to establish ethics officer positions.

Some news organizations have an ombudsman or public editor whose job is to analyze, decide on, and respond to ethical problems that the organization faces when working on various stories. The ombudsman or public editor is usually a well-respected editor or columnist who has spent many years building his or her reputation within journalism.

Most media organizations of any size have legal teams or lawyers who can be consulted when needed, but remember that an organization can act legally even if it is not acting ethically. Do not confuse getting advice on the legality of an action with whether it is ethical or not. And as noted earlier in the chapter, media ethics is not a stand-alone subject. These decision-making skills should inform daily practices for all media professionals, even those whose jobs are not formally dedicated to ethics.

LOOKING BACK AND MOVING FORWARD

The issue of ethics, although an integral part of our media environment, is too often ignored, misunderstood, or overlooked in the day-to-day hustle of media professionals. Developing moral-reasoning skills takes time and enduring effort. The sheer variety of situations that arise calling for moral reasoning, especially in the media professions, means that there will always be a new challenge ahead. If, however, you can develop good moral-reasoning abilities, you can build on past experiences and results—right and wrong decisions—and apply that knowledge to new situations.

Understanding the various ethical systems and what they deem right can help you find your own moral compass. You do not have to choose an ethical system and stay with it, but you may feel more comfortable regularly drawing from one ethical system over others. Even so, being able to take elements from each one, as the situation calls for, can help you determine the values in conflict and find answers that help ensure ethical decision making.

Some of the later ethical systems, such as the dialogical and ethics-of-care systems, can be especially fruitful in a social media world where conversations online and perceived relationships become more important. Further, the virtues that they espouse in showing respect to others may help mitigate some of the divisiveness and anger that we see today in our political rhetoric and social lives.

MEDIA MATTERS   HOW MORAL ARE YOU?

Ethical questions can often be difficult because there may not always be a single "right" answer. There are always conflicts between groups and between individuals and society. See if you can come up with ethical solutions to the following scenarios based on real-life incidents:

1. You work in a PR firm whose biggest and most important client is a noted Fortune 500 company. In a meeting with them to discuss future strategy and publishing their annual report, they admit that they have "cooked the books" in some of their divisions to inflate revenues. They say everyone in their industry does it, even as they want promises from everyone at the meeting that they will not divulge that information. What do you do?

2. The TV news crew you are part of is covering an investigative story on a defect in a brand of car. You see other members of the crew wire the car to create a large explosion. Your editor explains that having failed to show the desired results with the first two cars, they are trying to emulate what has been reported to have happened. Do you think this is ethical?

3. While working as a member of the production crew on a reality television series, you befriend one of the cast members. Weeks later, in the editing room, you see the producer piecing together snippets of the hundreds of hours of video and audio to create a loose narrative that puts that cast member in a highly negative light. She has signed a waiver, as is typical, in which she agrees to any depiction of her. Do you think what the producer is doing is ethical?

4. The advertising agency you work for has created an ad campaign for a new soft drink— "The best-tasting orange soda. Ever." You know from the market research and from blind taste tests that the client's soda consistently scored lower than competing brands. Is it ethical to use this phrase in the advertising campaigns?

FURTHER READING

Moral Theory: An Introduction, 2nd ed. Mark Timmons (2012) Rowman & Littlefield.

Communicating Ethically: Character, Duties, Consequences, and Relationships. William W. Neher, Paul J. Sandin (2007) Pearson Education.

Would You Eat Your Cat?: Key Ethical Conundrums and What They Tell You About Yourself. Jeremy Stangroom (2012) W. W. Norton & Company.

Media Ethics at Work: True Stories from Young Professionals. Lee Anne Peck, Guy S. Reel (2012) CQ Press.

The Handbook of Mass Media Ethics. Lee Wilkins, Clifford G. Christians (eds.) (2009) Routledge.

Ethics for Public Communication. Clifford Christians, John Ferre, Mark Fackler (2011) Oxford University Press.

Living Ethics: Across Media Platforms. Michael Bugeja (2007) Oxford University Press.

Ethics for the Real World: Creating a Personal Code to Guide Decisions in Work and Life. Ronald Howard, Clinton Korver (2008) Harvard Business Press.

Lying: Moral Choice in Public and Private Life. Sissela Bok (1999) Vintage.

The Cambridge Companion to Virtue Ethics. Daniel Russell (ed.) (2013) Cambridge University Press.

Virtue Ethics, Old and New. Stephen Gardiner (2005) Cornell University Press.

Moral Understandings: A Feminist Study in Ethics, 2nd ed. Margaret Urban Walker (2007) Oxford University Press.

Habermas: A Very Short Introduction. Gordon Finlayson (2005) Oxford University Press.

A Theory of Justice: Original Edition. John Rawls (2005) Belknap Press of Harvard University Press.

Ethics of Media. Nick Couldry, Mirca Madianou, Amit Pinchevski (eds.) (2013) Palgrave Macmillan.

Disconnected: Youth, New Media, and the Ethics Gap. Carrie James (2014) MIT Press.

The Ethics of Star Trek. Judith Barad, Ed Robertson (2001) Harper Perennial.

Media Ethics Beyond Borders: A Global Perspective. Stephen J. A. Ward, Herman Wasserman (eds.) (2010) Routledge.

Communication Law and Regulation in the Digital Age

L
ook up into the sky. You may just observe what may be observing you: a drone—perhaps the greatest media buzz of the early twenty-first century. Once thought of as the exclusive province of the military, camera-equipped drones have descended from their original heights to become a widespread tool for news gathering, video recording, and general image capture from the air. Such drones have already been deployed around the nation and the world to provide aerial perspectives on everything from activists protesting to whale pods swimming, from X Games competition to volcanic eruption.

Yet drones also represent one of the hottest areas of legal and regulatory upheaval. Although many see drones as important to the future of media reporting, both commercial and civilian, a number of concerns have emerged about their safe operation as well as their implications for privacy.

As of this writing, the Federal Aviation Administration (FAA) is expected to establish national regulations in 2015 regarding the commercial operation of drones in U.S. air space. In the meantime, many local laws have already restricted their use. Los Angeles, for example, requires all commercial drones to comply with ordinances restricting operation to line of sight, limiting altitude to 400 feet, and avoiding operation over people or populated areas. In addition, media enterprises planning drone use must register with a local board to obtain a permit, much as a movie company must obtain a permit to shoot on location in LA.

Outside the United States, policies vary. In the United Kingdom, legal guidelines are already well established, and the BBC employs drones extensively in documentary production. In other parts of the world, drones, especially small ones, have been largely unregulated.

In the United States, media use of drones may largely prove a constitutional battleground between protecting public safety and privacy, a Fourth Amendment concern, and freedom of speech, a First Amendment concern. Although many in law enforcement are rightly concerned about the potential abuse of drones near

LEARNING OBJECTIVES

>> Examine the nature of freedom of speech and press and how media are regulated in the United States.

>> Describe the key legal concepts protecting and restricting freedom of speech and press, including threats to national security, libel, and censorship.

>> Discuss the principal legislation that defines communication regulation in the United States, and the principal federal communications regulatory agency, the Federal Communications Commission.

>> Outline the regulation of content in the United States, especially regarding commercial speech and political speech.

>> Explain intellectual property issues, especially copyright, and how the digital age has affected them.

airports or by terrorists, this must be balanced against the right of citizens or professionals to obtain remarkable aerial views of the environment, public spaces, or anywhere important news may occur.

> Congress shall make no law respecting an establishment of religion, or prohibiting the free exercise thereof; or abridging the freedom of speech, or of the press; or the right of the people peaceably to assemble, and to petition the government for a redress of grievances.
>
> FIRST AMENDMENT TO THE CONSTITUTION OF THE UNITED STATES

The First Amendment is very much an American invention. Most other countries have no such stipulation in their constitutions, which of course has sometimes resulted in vastly different laws and regulations regarding mass communication and journalism.

Governments decide on policies or overarching objectives that they want to accomplish based on a variety of factors. These factors include the political views of the party in power, the type of government (whether elected by citizens or empowered in some other way), and the general social and cultural norms of the nation. Laws are created and enacted to carry out the government's policies, but which laws are created also depends on the form of government. In democracies, even the party in power may not be able to create laws it wants because of opposition-party actions, or bills may be altered as part of compromises to become laws. Laws, once enacted, are forcibly upheld by the state and carry penalties such as fines or imprisonment if broken. Similar to laws, regulations act as tools to enable policies, but if violated, fines or other less severe sanctions serve as penalties rather than imprisonment.

First Amendment

Guarantees that Congress shall make no law restricting freedom of speech, press, or religion.

Although the **First Amendment** guarantees that Congress shall make no law restricting freedom of speech or of the press, interpretations of the courts, elected officials, and legal scholars have permitted some level of regulatory and legal restriction. Some of these laws deal with libel, obscenity, and other media content. Others deal with technical issues related to broadcast-station operation, such as preventing one station from interfering with another's signals; and others pertain to media ownership, intellectual property rights, and fulfilling the requirements of broadcasting licenses. We will look at how these differ and how they relate to media and public policy, primarily in the United States, although other countries will sometimes be examined for comparison.

The Legal Framework

When printing began in Renaissance Europe, political and religious authorities were quick to recognize the power of publishing to spread not only religious teachings but political edicts as well. Political and religious dissidents, however, found printing presses equally useful in disseminating their views against authority. The tension between government control of the press and the press as a means to be free of political or religious control continues to this day.

The reasons underlying the value of freedom from governmental control were perhaps best articulated by U.S. president Thomas Jefferson, who said, "Information is the currency of democracy." When the first U.S. Congress passed the Bill of

Rights in 1789, fewer than three dozen printing presses existed in the country. Despite this small number, the nation's founders recognized the great importance of the press. Jefferson said, "Were it left for me to decide whether we should have a government without newspapers, or newspapers without a government, I should not hesitate a moment to prefer the latter."

The press is a critical watchdog of government and other powerful institutions in society, including business. But as an unofficial "fourth branch" of government, or **fourth estate**, the press must be free from government censorship or control. Although Jefferson referred only to print media, the only form of mass communication during his time, his comments apply equally to electronic mass communication. When we refer to "the press," we include print and electronic media.

In societies where government control over the press, or media, is substantial, as in China or other authoritarian countries where journalists must be licensed to operate, the press cannot criticize the government, its policies, or its representatives. The press usually promotes government positions rather than evaluating them independently. In democratic societies, the press ideally acts as an independent balance of power to government bodies. Yet concentration of ownership and media companies' commercial interests can adversely affect the ability of the press to pursue the public interest impartially. For news organizations, business interests may sometimes outweigh public interests.

Despite the early constitutional admonitions to protect freedom of speech and the press, the government at all levels has frequently tried to infringe on the independence of the press and to censor content. In addition, the government has extended full First Amendment protection only to print media. In *Miami Herald Publishing Co. v. Tornillo* (1974), for instance, the U.S. Supreme Court struck down a Florida statute that required newspapers to give space at no cost to political candidates whose personal or professional character the paper had criticized. Television and radio stations, however, must provide candidates with the opportunity for equal airtime should the station itself editorially endorse or oppose a specific candidate.

Radio, television, cinema, and the Internet have received much less First Amendment protection than print media, and only through extended legal battles have they won a certain degree of freedom. In fact, cinema had no First Amendment protection until the Supreme Court's 1952 *Miracle* decision (*Joseph Burstyn, Inc. v. Wilson*), when the court ruled that the showing of a film could not be prohibited because a censor deemed it sacrilegious.

The historical influences and legal and regulatory decisions on print and electronic media are complex but worth exploring briefly to better understand the restrictions on media content today.

The Foundations of Freedom of Expression

Governments continue to use many means to control media. One heavy-handed method is to jail journalists and editors, not only to silence them but to produce a **chilling effect** on others who may be tempted to write on similar topics.

Yet such tactics can anger the public or damage the government's reputation. More subtle means of control, such as licensing laws for journalists or special taxes on printing equipment, paper, or ink, have been adopted in the past. By controlling the materials needed for printing, governments hoped to be able to

fourth estate

Another term for the press, or journalism, which acts as a fourth branch of government, one that watches the other branches (executive, legislative, and judicial).

Thomas Jefferson's famous quote about his choice between government and newspapers is often cited to show the important role that journalism plays in a democracy.

chilling effect

The phenomenon that occurs when journalists or other media producers decide not to publish stories on a topic after a journalist has been punished or jailed for such a story.

control the free flow of information. Government censors, or bodies that examine and approve all printed material, have also been used.

Although different governmental measures persist in various countries, controlling information has become increasingly difficult. This is partly because vastly more information is available and partly because electronic media, including the Internet, have become important information sources alongside print media. Nevertheless, countries like China maintain strict control over electronic media and the Internet. The government blocks certain websites from appearing on searches performed within the country, and companies like Google have agreed to restrictions they would normally not allow, just so they can do business in China.

Our modern concept of freedom of expression has evolved over time, influenced by several major court decisions that dealt with national security issues, libel, or censorship. These cases have dealt primarily with print media, partly because some occurred before electronic media and partly because print media have traditionally received greater First Amendment protections than electronic media.

NATIONAL SECURITY

In 1798, the Federalist-controlled U.S. Congress passed the **Alien and Sedition Acts** as a response to the possibility of war with France. The acts, which limited freedom of speech, were meant to silence the Jeffersonian Republicans, who supported France. Among other things, the acts prohibited **sedition**, spoken or written criticism of the U.S. government, and imposed penalties of a fine or imprisonment on conviction. Once the threat of war passed, the Sedition Act expired in 1801; but other sedition acts have resurfaced throughout U.S. history, especially during times of war.[1]

💬 Alien and Sedition Acts

A series of four acts passed by the U.S. Congress in 1798 that, among other things, prohibited sedition, or spoken or written criticism of the U.S. government, and imposed penalties of a fine or imprisonment on conviction. Although they expired in 1801, other sedition acts have been passed periodically, especially during times of war.

💬 sedition

Speech or action that encourages overthrow of a government or that subverts a nation's constitution or laws.

The Alien and Sedition Acts of 1798 were an early example of government attempts to clamp down on dissent and to censor the press.

Several important legal concepts have developed with court cases that involved issues of national security, one of the main areas where press freedoms are curtailed.

Clear and Present Danger

The most basic restriction is when the speech in question meets both of the following conditions: (1) It is intended to incite or produce dangerous activity (as with falsely shouting "Fire!" in a crowded theater), and (2) it is likely to succeed in achieving the purported result. This **clear and present danger** test is subject to criminal-law-enforcement authorities and the judicial system rather than regulatory authorities.

The clear and present danger test emerged from *Schenck v. United States* (1919). In that case, the U.S. Supreme Court unanimously upheld the conviction of Charles T. Schenck for violating the Espionage Act of 1917. Schenck had been distributing handbills urging resistance to U.S. involvement in World War I. He was a Communist but had committed no violent acts. The Court based its decision on the beliefs that the First Amendment is not absolute and that ordinary constitutional rules do not apply in wartime.

Prior Restraint

An important ruling came in the 1931 Supreme Court case *Near v. Minnesota*. Minnesota courts had stopped the publication of an anti-Semitic weekly on the basis that it was a "malicious, scandalous and defamatory" periodical in violation of the state's nuisance law. The Supreme Court reversed the decision, saying that **prior restraint**—the government's preventing or blocking the publication, broadcasting, showing, or otherwise distributing of media content, whether in print, over the air, or in movie theaters—must be used only in cases of serious or grave threats to national security.

In the 1971 case of *New York Times Co. v. United States*, the Supreme Court overturned a lower court ruling that had stopped the *Times* from publishing "The Pentagon Papers," a top-secret Pentagon study of U.S. involvement in the Vietnam War. The government failed to prove that national security interests outweighed a heavy presumption against prior restraint.

In 1979, a district court stopped *The Progressive* magazine (*U.S. v. Progressive*) from publishing "The H-Bomb Secret." The magazine had obtained its information from publicly available documents, and six months later the court injunction was lifted after others published similar material.

Although the courts have ruled that freedom of speech is not absolute, especially during wartime, there is, nonetheless, a strong presumption against permitting the government any form of prior restraint on publication or distribution of speech. The government must clearly demonstrate that publication poses a clear and present threat to national security. This framework seems especially relevant in the aftermath of the September 11, 2001, terrorist attack on the World Trade Center and the Pentagon.

It is expected that in 2015 the U.S. Supreme Court will rule on the extent to which the First Amendment applies to social media such as Facebook. In 2014, the Court took up the case involving a man named Anthony Elonis, who posted comments on Facebook threatening his estranged wife and law enforcement.[2] His posts included, "I've got enough explosives to take care of the state police and the

clear and present danger

A restriction on speech when it meets both of the following conditions: (1) It is intended to incite or produce dangerous activity (as with falsely shouting "Fire!" in a crowded theater), and (2) it is likely to succeed in achieving the purported result.

prior restraint

When the government prevents or blocks the publication, broadcasting, showing, or distribution of media content, whether in print, over the air, in movie theaters, or online.

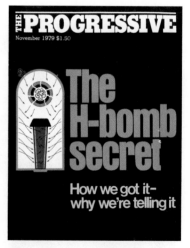

The planned publication by *The Progressive* of instructions for making a hydrogen bomb was a landmark case regarding the government's right of prior restraint.

sheriff's department"; and "enough elementary schools in a ten mile radius to initiate the most heinous school shooting ever imagined. And hell hath no fury like a crazy man in a kindergarten class." Convicted of making threats, Elonis has appealed his conviction, claiming his comments were not intended to frighten and were only therapeutic.

In his book *Mass Media Law*, Don Pember describes a **preferred-position balancing theory**. According to this theory, a balance must be struck between speech and other rights, but speech is given a preferred position (especially in print media), and limitations on freedom of speech in print are usually illegal. The government must demonstrate that certain speech threatens national security rather than journalists and media organizations having to prove that it does not.

> **preferred-position balancing theory**
>
> A legal theory that says that a balance must be struck between speech and other rights, although speech has a preferred position.

DISCUSSION QUESTIONS: Do you think the government should have more or less power to exercise prior restraint and block publication or broadcast of material that it feels might hurt national security interests, even from citizens posting to social media sites?

LIBEL

In the colonial era, the case of John Peter Zenger, a New York printer and journalist, established the relationship between freedom of expression and libel in the United States. Zenger faced a libel suit from the publication of the *New York Weekly Journal*, a political journal. As publisher of the *Journal*, Zenger was responsible for articles that featured scathing attacks on the colonial governor, William Cosby.

Zenger's attorney, Andrew Hamilton, requested that the jury rule on the truth of Zenger's printed statements; and in a surprise ruling in August 1735, Zenger was acquitted of libel. This important precedent established the principle of freedom of the press in early America and departed from the way much of the world considers libel, even today. For example, in England, someone can successfully be sued for libel even if the statements are true and the statements damage a person's reputation.

> **slander**
>
> A type of defamation that is spoken, as opposed to written (libel), and that damages a person's reputation or otherwise causes harm.

The libel case of Peter Zenger in colonial times was a turning point for what defined "libel" in America.

In the United States, libel is a type of written defamation, such as a false attack on a person's character that damages a person's reputation. **Slander** has historically referred to a similar defamation involving the spoken word. In the twentieth century, libel has been extended to broadcasting on television or radio as well as to online communications, even though broadcast media are technically spoken rather than printed.

In the case of *Phipps v. Clark Oil & Ref. Corp.* (1987), the Minnesota court ruled that libel occurs when a publication "tends to injure the plaintiff's reputation and expose the plaintiff to public hatred, contempt, ridicule, or degradation."

New York Times Co. v. Sullivan (1964)

Media historians and legal scholars tend to agree that the most important legal decision to establish a free press in the United States was the 1964 Supreme Court ruling in *New York Times Co. v. Sullivan*.

In 1960, the *New York Times* printed a fundraising advertisement for the civil rights movement that contained minor factual errors. L. B. Sullivan, a Montgomery, Alabama, city police commissioner, said that some of the false statements in the advertisement regarding Montgomery police actions defamed him, even though he was not mentioned by name. A jury agreed and awarded him a half-million dollars. The case eventually went to the Supreme Court, which overturned the lower court ruling.

The Supreme Court ruled that public figures (publicly prominent) and public officials (the makers of public policy) may not sue for libel unless they can prove "actual malice." For nonpublic figures (private citizens), the standard for libel requires merely that the plaintiff show that a "reasonable person" knew or should have known the defamatory statement was false.

The Court defined actual malice in terms of either (1) the defendant's intent being malicious or (2) the defendant's knowing the statement is false but publishing it anyway. The Court ruled that the common law of defamation violated the guarantee of free speech under the First Amendment and that the citizen's right to criticize government officials is too important to be intolerant of speech containing even harmful falsehoods. The ruling has fostered a more robust environment for media to publish criticisms of public figures because they can be found libelous only if they meet the stringent actual-malice test.

Protecting Journalists Against Libel

Most media organizations have libel insurance to protect journalists. Freelance journalists often do not, though, so the threat of libel can have a chilling effect. This is especially true for online journalists, bloggers, and others who operate on a shoestring budget or who are not widely recognized by media organizations as professional journalists.

Moreover, although there is no prior restraint for libel cases, journalists can be imprisoned for contempt in libel or other cases, such as not divulging the identity of a source or not releasing one's notes.

Five steps can help minimize a journalist's chances of committing libel:

1. Engage in thorough research, including investigating the facts and maintaining good records, establishing and adhering to written criteria in deciding when and what to publish, and using reliable sources.

2. Confirm the identity of the target of your report.

3. Use quotations whenever possible and attribute statements to sources.

4. Report only facts and avoid language that draws conclusions.

5. Avoid bias in reports, and strive for balance (i.e., give the different sides in a debate fair play).

Shield Laws

Shield laws are intended to protect journalists from legal challenges to their freedom to report the news. Journalists have received neither blanket protection from the Supreme Court nor a federal shield law. Yet thirty-four states have enacted laws to protect journalists from having to answer every subpoena.[3] In these states, journalists need not testify or produce materials obtained from confidential sources. Most of the states and territories that lack shield laws provide some court protection for journalists.

 shield law

A law intended to protect journalists from legal challenges to their freedom to report the news.

MEDIA PIONEERS
Anthony Lewis

Most of the media pioneers featured throughout these pages have shaped their fields. Few, however, can claim to have actually *created* the field for which they are known.

The late (2013) *New York Times* journalist and columnist Anthony Lewis could make such a claim. Lewis is widely credited for creating legal journalism, which focuses on covering courts and legal issues. "He brought context to the law," said Ronald K. L. Collins, a University of Washington scholar who compiled a bibliography of Mr. Lewis's work. "He had an incredible talent in making the law not only intelligible but also in making it compelling."[4]

Supreme Court judges also admired Lewis's work, with Justice Felix Frankfurter once observing that there weren't two justices sitting on the Court who had more of a grasp of the cases Lewis covered. One of the factors that distinguished Lewis's coverage of court issues was how he brought his own interpretation and opinions into his analysis, going beyond the standard call for objectivity in professional journalism.

Lewis won two Pulitzer Prizes for his coverage of the Supreme Court: in 1955, when he was only twenty-eight, and again in 1963. His published books include *Gideon's Trumpet*, which has been in print since 1964. Another book, *Make No Law*, examined the repercussions of the landmark 1964 case *New York Times v. Sullivan* for libel law in the United States. Despite Lewis's strongly left and liberal views, he did not agree that the press should have a preferred position under the First Amendment. He believed that the First Amendment was meant primarily as a bulwark against government censorship, not as a rationale to give news organizations powers that other groups lacked. Besides writing his column and books, Lewis taught a weekly media-law class at Columbia University's Graduate School of Journalism

for twenty-three years. Through his classes, generations of journalism students experienced his sharp intellect and conversational style that helped bring the law to life.

In May 2013, the public learned that the Department of Justice had secretly seized the phone records of some Associated Press journalists to discover who had been leaking classified information. In response, President Obama called for a federal shield law, which he had first proposed in 2009.

Without shield laws, legal action might exert a chilling effect on journalists, some suggested, including Reed Hundt, former FCC chairman: "Newsgatherers might be less aggressive and cease to pursue confidential sources or information. Whistle-blowers and other sources could be left without any legal protection from discovery."[5] Under a shield law, the Department of Justice would still likely have obtained the Associated Press phone records, but the journalists involved would have been alerted to this when it occurred rather than after the fact.

Evidence suggests that shield laws have limited effectiveness, based on studies done on the number of subpoenas served to journalists in states with shield laws compared to the number in those without. Opponents of shield laws argue that journalists, given the difficulty inherent in defining this profession, should not be given special protections from answering subpoenas. Others worry that trying to explicitly articulate a definition for journalist could lead to official licensing, which most news organizations strongly oppose as a curtailment of their First Amendment rights.

CENSORSHIP

Censorship refers to the act of prohibiting certain expression or content. It targets specific material within a publication, broadcast, film, or website rather than a work in its entirety. Although rarely permitted in the United States, censorship is routine in countries with authoritarian regimes that prohibit criticism of the government.

The case *Hazelwood School District v. Kuhlmeier* (1988) established that people still in school lack full First Amendment protection. In this case, a school principal was permitted to censor school newspaper articles dealing with pregnancy and divorce. The court found that school-sponsored publications are not a public forum and thus may be subject to censorship to protect the young from harm.

In the United States, censorship is most common in two circumstances: (1) during wartime, when content, especially that being reported from the battlefield, may threaten national security; and (2) with pornographic or obscene content, which can sometimes include graphic violence or detailed accounts of criminal behavior. Citizen groups have long criticized media entertainment companies for portrayals of sex and violence. This has led to fights over censorship and new laws and regulations that have affected the kind of media available to the public, or at least some members of the public.

The Censorship of Comics

Both governmental and public critics have long scrutinized comics, popular among children and adults. In the McCarthy-era 1950s, psychologist Fredric Wertham, MD, published his book, *Seduction of the Innocent*, which contended that violent and sexually graphic comic books caused juvenile delinquency and worse. Wertham's book produced intense pressure from the government and other groups to curtail the graphic sexual and gruesome violent content of comic books, especially horror comics such as *Tales from the Crypt, Haunt of Fear*, and *Vault of Horror*.

Wertham based his argument on his own observations of juvenile delinquents. He found that many delinquents read a lot of comic books, especially horror comics. He also found that many of these kids were poor readers. Wertham concluded that reading comics, especially horror comics, caused both juvenile delinquency and illiteracy. Although Wertham's reasoning and methodology were flawed, in response to his claims, the U.S. Senate conducted a full-scale investigation in 1954 into the effects of comics on children.

censorship

The act of prohibiting certain expression or content. Censors usually do not target the whole publication, program, or website but seek to prohibit some part of the content.

According to courts, high school students do not have full First Amendment rights with student publications.

In the 1950s, comic books showing graphic horror and violence were said to cause juvenile delinquency.

The Hays Code, the movie studios' attempt at self-censorship, eventually led to our movie-rating system.

Hays Code

A code established in 1930 by the movie industry to censor itself regarding showing nudity or glorifying antisocial acts. Officials for the Hays Office had to approve each film distributed to a mass audience.

The Senate took no formal legal action against the comics industry. Instead, a consortium called the Association of Comics Magazine Publishers formed the Comics Code Authority (CCA), an industry censorship review board. The CCA read every comic book published and effectively banned sexual content and the most graphic material popular in many horror comics of the day, including torture, sadism, and detailed discussion of criminal acts. A CCA seal of approval appeared on the cover of acceptable comics. The CCA action put many graphic horror comics out of business.

The Hays Code

Some early films, especially prior to 1920, contained considerable nudity or near nudity. Although nudity and sexuality were popular with many filmgoers, some conservative groups were outspoken in their criticism, especially of bare-breasted women or women dressed in revealing clothing. Fearing government censorship, the film industry created the Hays Office, a self-censorship body.

The office produced the **Hays Code** in 1930, outlining many dos and don'ts for the film industry. The Hays Code articulated three general moral principles. First was the intention to prevent production of any motion picture that would "lower the moral standards of those who see it. Hence the sympathy of the audience should never be thrown to the side of crime, wrongdoing, evil or sin." Second, every picture was to present "correct standards of life, subject only to the requirements of drama and entertainment." Third, no picture was to ridicule "natural or human" law.

The code prescribed the proper depiction of content in twelve specific areas, including criminal activity, sex, and religion. By today's standards, many of these prescriptions seem quaint—although well intentioned—and some are offensive, racist, or at least politically incorrect. Still, movies without the Hays Office's stamp of approval might not have received mass distribution by a major studio—a chance most producers were unwilling to take. In the mid-1960s, after a series of Supreme Court cases involving obscenity and a general change in public mores regarding depictions of sexuality, the Hays Code was significantly revised and enforced less stringently. By 1968, the movie-rating system of G, M, R, and X—today modified as G, PG, PG-13, R, NC-17, and X—had replaced the Hays Code. The movie-ratings code has served as a model for industry self-censorship for music, television, and video games.

Indecent Content

Although not prohibited, **indecent speech** is subject to federal regulation. Broadcasters may not air indecent speech when children are likely to be in the audience, or between 6 a.m. and 10 p.m. This has been called a safe harbor period, and concerned groups sometimes request portrayals of violence or sex to be barred from the time period as well.

Federal law defines indecent speech as "language or material that, in context, depicts or describes, in terms patently offensive as measured by contemporary community standards for the broadcast medium, sexual or excretory organs or activities." Exempted from this definition is profanity that is neither indecent nor obscene. "Damn" is an example of a permitted word. Indecent speech was put to the test in a landmark First Amendment case involving comedian George Carlin.

Carlin recorded before a live California audience a twelve-minute monolog titled "Filthy Words." He opened his routine by contemplating "the words you couldn't say on the public airwaves, the ones you definitely wouldn't say, ever." He then listed those words and repeated them in a variety of contexts. The Supreme Court decision in *Federal Communications Commission v. Pacifica Foundation* (1978)

George Carlin's comedy routine "Filthy Words" turned into a landmark case regarding indecent content.

> ### indecent speech
>
> Language or material that, in context, depicts or describes, in terms patently offensive as measured by contemporary community standards for the broadcast medium, sexual or excretory organs or activities.

In 2013, under pressure from women's groups, Facebook toughened its standards against user-generated content that promoted violence against women.

upheld the FCC's power to regulate the airwaves, characterizing the words as indecent but not obscene. The ruling formed the basis for subsequent regulations on indecent speech for broadcasters.

Other entertainers have also pushed the limits of freedom of speech in the electronic media, including shock jock Howard Stern. Before Stern moved to satellite radio, his frequently vulgar on-air commentary drew criticism from citizen groups and government regulators. In 1995, Infinity Broadcasting Corp. (owned by CBS), the producer and broadcaster of Stern's radio show, agreed to pay $1.7 million without admitting guilt to settle a variety of indecency charges that the FCC had leveled against Stern since 1989.

As part of the **Telecommunications Act of 1996**, the first sweeping federal legislation to rewrite the foundation of communications regulation in the United States since 1934, legislators had sought to curb "indecent" speech online while generally opening up the airwaves to greater innovation. Title V of this effort, the Communications Decency Act, made it illegal to "depict or describe" on the Internet anything considered indecent and made no distinctions between scientific or literary works and pornography. In 1997, however, the U.S. Supreme Court in *Reno v. ACLU* struck down its anti-decency provisions as unconstitutional.

Despite the ruling, some organizations have chosen to self-censor. In 2013, women's groups protested Facebook policy allowing groups, pages, and images that glorified or poked fun at violence against women. Protesters pointed out the contrast with Facebook's long-standing policy of removing photos of breastfeeding mothers from member pages. On Twitter, they shared examples of these violent images from Facebook. Thousands of emails asked major advertisers to abandon Facebook, and protesters claimed to have convinced fifteen brands to do so.[6] After a weeklong campaign, Facebook agreed to improve its standards for detecting and removing such content.

Telecommunications Act of 1996

The first major regulatory overhaul of telecommunications since 1934, designed to open the industry to greater competition by deregulating many aspects of it.

DISCUSSION QUESTIONS: Are FCC standards for indecent speech, that is, what a "contemporary community" considers "patently offensive," still tenable in online communities? If not, what new standards could be applied? Do you agree that violent images should be censored on Facebook? If so, what kinds of violent images?

---

obscenity

One of the forms of speech not protected by the First Amendment and thus subject to censorship. Although an exact definition of the term has been difficult to achieve in various court cases, generally a three-part standard is applied for media content: It must appeal to prurient interests as defined by community standards, it must show sexual conduct in an offensive manner, and it must on the whole lack serious artistic, literary, political, or scientific value.

Obscenity

Pornography, or **obscenity**, is deemed unprotected by the First Amendment and is subject to government censorship. A landmark case was *Miller v. California* (1973) in which Miller had been convicted in California of mailing unsolicited pornographic brochures. He appealed his conviction on the grounds that it inhibited his right to free speech, but the Court disagreed and outlined three criteria for determining whether content is obscene:

1. An average individual applying contemporary community standards must believe the content, taken as a whole, appeals to prurient interest.

2. The content must show or describe in an offensive manner sexual conduct.

3. The content on the whole must lack serious literary, artistic, political, or scientific value.

Nevertheless, defining obscenity remains difficult, and some would prefer to simply conclude that "I know it when I see it (or hear it)."

The digital age has produced unique issues for obscenity cases. One is the ease with which pornography can be distributed across national boundaries. Another is computer-generated pornography that includes realistic images. In April 2002, the Supreme Court struck down provisions in the Child Pornography Prevention Act of 1996, which made it a crime to create, distribute, or possess "virtual" child pornography, or computer-generated images of children in sexual acts (as opposed to images of actual children, which are not protected as free speech). Justice Anthony M. Kennedy wrote for the majority, claiming the act "prohibits speech that records no crime and creates no victims by its production." Although the government argued that real children could be harmed and exploited if a market for virtual child pornography were sustained, Justice Kennedy maintained, "The mere tendency of speech to encourage unlawful acts is not a sufficient reason for banning it."[7]

Criticism, Ridicule, or Humor

The U.S. Constitution protects stereotypes and other offensive material, as objectionable as they may be. Criticism, ridicule, and jokes about individuals (including government officials), groups, or institutions based on race, religion, gender, national background, or other factors are protected speech, whether in print or electronic media, and may not be regulated by the FCC. In the case of licensed broadcasters, station owners and operators must offer programming that meets the needs of the communities they serve.

The following discussion of the evolution of electronic-communications regulations will highlight the FCC's origin, its role, how regulations differ from those of print media, and how they have influenced today's programming and communication networks.

Fresh Off the Boat, the first network show in twenty years to feature an Asian American family, debuted in early 2015 to rave reviews and considerable criticism, stirred by some critics who claim it perpetuates stereotypes. **CRITICAL THINKING QUESTIONS:** Do you agree that comical ethnic depictions such as these do more harm than good? Are cultural stereotypes inherently degrading, and is every cultural group equally vulnerable in this regard? Should negative stereotypes be subject to greater regulatory restrictions?

Regulating Electronic Media

The origins of U.S. electronic-communications regulations lie in the development of broadcasting in the early part of the twentieth century, starting with radio and later including television. The approach has evolved as a result of changing technical and economic factors.

EARLY DAYS AND THE RADIO ACT OF 1912 (1911–1926)

The regulation of broadcasting in the United States has included four stages. Prior to 1911, no authority regulated broadcasting, which at the time meant specifically radio transmissions. So little was known about the new medium in its infancy that there was little to regulate. Because radio emerged as a vital technology for ships at sea, especially for making distress calls, the Commerce Department's Bureau of Navigation was put in control of radio and made it a legal requirement in the **Radio Act of 1912** that all large ships maintain radio contact with ships or

 **Radio Act of 1912**

The act assigned frequencies and three- and four-letter codes to radio stations and limited broadcasting to the 360-meter wavelength.

shore stations. Responsibility for radio regulation rested with the Commerce Department until 1927.

During this period, most radio broadcasters were amateur technology enthusiasts, and obtaining a frequency on which to broadcast was an informal process. As broadcast historian Mark Goodman points out, "By mailing a postcard to Secretary of Commerce Herbert Hoover, anyone with a radio transmitter, ranging from college students experimenting in science classes to amateur inventors who ordered kits, to newspaper-operated stations, could broadcast on the frequency chosen by Hoover."[8]

By 1926, there were 15,111 amateur radio stations and 536 broadcasting stations in the United States. Despite geographic separation of radio transmitters and various power restrictions on those transmitters, great interference still occurred between the different stations' signals. As radio became what historian Erik Barnouw calls "A Tower of Babel," the need for regulation grew. In the 1920s, much public attention became focused on the new medium of radio and the government's attempts to regulate it.[9]

INCREASING REGULATION AND THE FEDERAL RADIO COMMISSION (1927–1933)

Radio Act of 1927

An act of Congress that created the Federal Radio Commission, intended to regulate the largely chaotic airwaves and based on the principle that companies had a civic duty to use airwaves, a limited public good, responsibly.

"The airwaves by 1927 were an open forum for anyone with the expertise and equipment to reach a forum with 25 million listeners," explains Mark Goodman.[10] But the rapid and largely uncontrolled growth of the new medium required a new regulatory structure. The **Radio Act of 1927**, signed into law in February of that year and influenced by railroad regulations, stated that anyone who owned a radio frequency and radio should operate for the "public convenience, interest, or necessity"—even though it didn't define those terms.[11]

The act established the Federal Radio Commission (FRC), with five politically appointed commissioners and a limited staff whose mandate was to sort out the mess in radio. They revoked the vast majority of radio licenses and instituted a new system that favored fewer high-powered stations over many low-powered stations.[12] This change effectively favored radio for big companies over educational institutions, religious organizations, and other groups with small radio stations.

In radio's earliest days, anyone could create his or her own radio station simply by setting up a tower and transmitter and sending a postcard to the Commerce Department.

THE COMMUNICATIONS ACT AND SPECTRUM SCARCITY (1934–1995)

In 1934, Congress enacted the Communications Act, which became the foundation of communications law for the next sixty-two years. The act was based on the premise established in the Radio Act of 1927 that the airwaves were a public good, a limited natural resource that belonged to the people. Licenses were granted to broadcast on the airwaves at no cost, but to those considered public trustees and expected to use the airwaves responsibly. Because of the limited nature of the airwaves, the act established regulations based on the notion of "spectrum scarcity," or limited channel capacity. Under this model, news came to meet the public service requirements for radio and television broadcasters.

The Communications Act of 1934 established the Federal Communications Commission (FCC), with five political appointees, including one chair, and a series of bureaus, each assigned responsibility for an area of the growing radio industry. The FCC would eventually assume regulatory responsibility for television, wire, satellite, and cable as well.

THE TELECOMMUNICATIONS ACT AND THE INTERNET (1996–PRESENT)

The technological transformation of the global communication system, including the Internet, led Congress to enact the Telecommunications Act of 1996, the first major overhaul of the Communications Act of 1934. The convergence of telecommunications, computing, and traditional media in a digital, networked environment required a basic reconstruction of the regulatory framework for the media of mass communication.

The act introduced that new framework. Although it preserved the requirement to serve in the "public interest, convenience, and necessity," the act's new mandate was to foster competition in the communications marketplace. The preamble of the act states that it is intended "[t]o promote competition and reduce regulation in order to secure lower prices and higher quality services for American telecommunications consumers and encourage the rapid deployment of new telecommunications technologies." The digital revolution made the premise of channel scarcity obsolete. The public no longer had only three or four network channels to watch—it now had broadcasting choices ranging from cable or satellite television to, increasingly, Internet-based programming.

The Telecommunications Act of 1996 raises issues that affect not just the structure and regulation of the communications industry but the nature of programming and production. The act promotes direct competition among all telecommunications providers, including terrestrial broadcasters, direct broadcast satellite providers, mobile-communication services, cable providers, and the regional Bell telephone companies. Further, the act specifically targets violent or sexual programming and interactive services.

Since passage of the act, media ownership has become dramatically more concentrated. Whether this trend will foster competition or create powerful media cartels has been a subject of some debate. The act does not limit the number of television stations a single person or organization may own in the United States, as long as the combined reach is no more than 35 percent of U.S. households. Eli Noam and Robert Freeman point out that these regulatory, economic, and technological trends have resulted in unprecedented programming diversity at the national level and ever-dwindling diversity at the local level.[13]

Because the act eliminates the legal barriers preventing telephone and television companies from competing in the areas of telephone and video services, consumers have seen an increased array of alternative service providers. These include cable companies providing telephone service, for example. Similarly, consumers have seen an increase in the range of both phone and video services, such as VOD, voicemail, and call waiting. Several attempts have been made in recent years to pass further sweeping legislation on issues such as **Network neutrality** (Net neutrality), voice-over IP (VoIP), and other new technologies that either did not exist or were just emerging in 1996.

> **Network neutrality**
>
> The principle that broadband networks should be free of restrictions on content, platforms, or equipment and that certain types of content, platforms, or equipment should not get preferential treatment on the network.

INTERNATIONAL ELECTRONIC MEDIA REGULATION

In many countries, the development of radio as mass communication was an extension of existing government-run telegraph services. Unlike the United States, where commercial forces tended to dominate, in Europe and European colonies, a public service ethos for electronic media was most prevalent. This limited the number of radio or television networks to a few licensed or run directly by the government. The principle of public service led programming to emphasize news, education, and culture rather than pure entertainment.

The European Union in the last twenty years has seen a steady trend toward privatization and less regulation of radio and television. Consequently, European broadcasters have licensed more U.S. programming, making shows like *Baywatch* and *The Simpsons* global hits. While this trend has varied audience programming, it also raises charges of cultural imperialism (discussed in Chapter 14). Local broadcasters may too easily buy American programming rather than support homegrown productions.

The EU's movement toward more liberalization and privatization will likely increase the concentration of media ownership there. Asian countries each have their own regulations and laws; but, with the exception of Japan, India, the Philippines, and South Korea, most Asian countries have more government control over electronic media than the EU or the United States. For example, owning a satellite

CONVERGENCE CULTURE
The Great Network Neutrality Debate

Network neutrality, or Net neutrality, is a concept based on an Internet that should not discriminate among the types of content that pass through it. Internet pioneers believed equality and openness to be a foundational premise of the Net, and these qualities have been espoused by other, equally influential Net researchers and innovators.

After the FCC passed certain regulations in 2005, however, the leading cable and phone companies began lobbying Congress to change the laws governing the operation of the Internet. Essentially, these companies sought a tiered system in which content providers would pay according to how much content they sent over the Internet.

Critics of the lobbying efforts claimed that this would destroy the democratic nature of the Internet, making telephone and cable companies Internet gatekeepers with the power to decide what type of content would be sent fast and what type sent slow, and from whom, and even whether some sites or content would be blocked completely. The companies countered that certain content providers using most of the bandwidth should pay more.

The companies also claimed they had no desire to censor the Internet or to control content, but during 2007 and 2008, they did exactly that on several occasions. One case involved a company slowing the speed of content delivery from a rival media company. In another case, AT&T censored part of a comment from Eddie Vedder during a Pearl Jam concert when he criticized President George W. Bush.

In 2012, the entertainment industry encouraged the Stop Online Piracy Act (SOPA) and the Protect IP Act (PIPA), proposals that would allow companies to sue Internet service providers that carried illegal material. A huge uproar among various groups and citizens helped block this legislation, leaving politicians who had created the bills (many of whom had received large donations from the entertainment industry) scrambling to "rework" them.

The debate is a complex one but may soon be resolved as the FCC moves in 2015 to settle the matter. FCC Chairman Tom Wheeler has endorsed a proposal by President Obama to reclassify broadband service as a telecommunications, interactive service. This move would prevent large companies from establishing fast and slow lanes online.

INTERNATIONAL PERSPECTIVES
The Rise and Fall of Russian Media

After the demise of the Soviet Union in 1991, great hope arose for a democratic Russia and a free press that would rebuild the country. Russians have enjoyed tremendous growth in available newspapers, magazines, and books as well as an increase in radio and television stations and the type of programming they offer.

Since 2000, however, certain disturbing trends in Russia have raised alarm among journalists and media scholars. One is the concentration of media ownership and owner expectations regarding uncritical coverage of themselves and their interests. Although not as overtly as in the era of Soviet media control, the private owners of many media companies nevertheless exert undue influence over editorial content and programming.

Of even greater concern is how dangerous Russia has become for journalists critical of the government. Since Vladimir Putin first became president in 2000, twenty-six Russian journalists have been killed, with only two of the murders solved. The Committee to Protect Journalists viewed a slight downturn in journalist murders as a potentially good sign. Still, in May 2010, journalist Mark Minin was shot four times as he walked to his car. In November 2010, another Russian journalist, Oleg Kashin, was nearly beaten to death outside his apartment. Both journalists, who had published stories critical of the Russian government, believe the attacks stemmed from their work.[14]

The term "extremism" has recently been broadened to include any criticism of the government. As a result, journalists who criticize the government or its policies face jail time, and the publications they work for can be shut down. In 2014, Putin introduced another expanded press law that classifies interactive media, such as blogs with at least 3,000 readers, as mass communication. Blogs are therefore subject to the same restrictive laws governing newspapers and other heavily regulated Russian media, including criminal penalties for libel and fact-checking errors.

dish in Malaysia is illegal, and countries like Singapore and Indonesia have strict regulations on content, especially material critical of the government.

The Federal Communications Commission (FCC)

The **Federal Communications Commission (FCC)** is the principal communications regulatory body at the federal level in the United States. Some would say the FCC is also a lightning rod for criticism because of its prominent position on the communications regulatory landscape. Oftentimes, regardless of how the commission rules, some group is left unhappy and vocal about its displeasure.

The Federal Communications Commission (FCC)

Established in 1934, the principal communications regulatory body at the federal level in the United States.

The FCC consists of five commissioners appointed by the president for five-year terms, each of whom must be confirmed by the Senate. The commission must include at least two representatives of each of the major parties to help ensure its nonpartisan nature.

Among its principal duties, the FCC allocates new broadcast radio and television stations and renews the licenses of existing stations, ensuring that each licensee is complying with laws mandated by Congress. The FCC does not license TV or radio networks—such as CBS, NBC, ABC, Fox, CW, and PBS—except when they are owners of stations. Cable TV and satellite channels are available only to subscribers and have fewer rules to abide by than network broadcasters.

UNIVERSAL SERVICE

An important item for the FCC is the definition of "universal service," a notion central to, but not defined in, the 1934 act. The act, which identifies universal service as "an evolving level of telecommunications services that the commission shall establish periodically under this section," recognizes six key principles:

1. Quality services at reasonable and affordable rates
2. Access to advanced telecommunications and information services throughout the United States
3. Access in rural and high-cost areas
4. Equitable and nondiscriminatory contributions to the preservation and advancement of universal service
5. Specific, predictable, and sufficient federal and state mechanisms to preserve and advance universal service
6. Access to advanced telecommunications services in elementary and secondary schools and classrooms, health care providers, and libraries

Debates arise from this evolving concept of universal service. One could imagine that it should include fully interoperable high-bandwidth, two-way communication services in homes because during much of the twentieth century, homes were expected to have telephone service. This would create a powerful network engine to drive a new information infrastructure linking wired and wireless technologies and to empower the development of fully interactive, multimedia communications. An alternative perspective, however, would simply mandate that all homes have access to at least two communication-service providers capable of delivering both traditional and new media services (including the Internet). This paradigm reinforces the traditional media producer/consumer divide that characterized mass communications throughout the twentieth century.

THE FCC, LICENSE RENEWAL, AND REGULATORY POWER

The FCC allows stations to operate either as commercial or noncommercial-educational (public) broadcasters for up to eight years, after which the station must renew its license. This is the case for both radio and television broadcasters licensed to transmit their signals via terrestrial frequencies.

At the time of license renewal, a station must meet five basic requirements demonstrating that it has served in the public interest and met all legal requirements. A station must also accept and respond to viewer or listener complaints. Audience members, journalists, or anyone else may also review what is called the station's "public inspection file," which contains a variety of information about the station.

Federal law regulates or prohibits various station activities. The FCC is authorized to levy a fine or even revoke a station's license for violations. Among the programming concerns for which the FCC may impose fines or withdraw licenses are the airing of obscene or indecent language and nudity when children are likely to be viewing. Generally, only the stations themselves are responsible for selecting their material, including coverage of local issues, news, public affairs, religion, sports events, and other subjects.

Among the prohibited activities for stations are knowingly broadcasting a hoax, including false information regarding a crime or catastrophe (defined as a disaster), especially when such a broadcast might cause public harm. This rule resulted largely from the 1938 *War of the Worlds* radio broadcast.

SPECTRUM AUCTION

Since 1994, the FCC has held auctions for available electromagnetic spectrum. The auctions are open to any individual or company that makes an upfront payment and that the FCC deems a qualified bidder. Many countries auction spectrum, which can generate large revenues for governments. Some critics claim that the spectrum tends to be leased too cheaply as essentially a corporate giveaway, considering the profits accrued from the spectrum acquired.

Today's FCC regulates broadcasting and sets Internet policy, including Network neutrality.

A 2008 auction in the United States drew special attention, thanks in part to disagreements and lawsuits among bidders, including Google and several major telecommunications companies. Google requested that the auctioned spectrum be open, meaning that the winning bidder would have to keep the spectrum available to anyone to develop applications and communication tools that could be used by anyone else, along the lines of open-source business models. Google claimed this would give consumers more choices and spur greater innovation in mobile-communication devices.

Open communications like this directly threaten the established business models of telecommunication companies, and Verizon filed a lawsuit against the FCC to prevent the open requirement. In the end, Google was granted two of its four requests, creating a partially open system, and the auction generated close to $20 billion for the government.

Regulating Commercial and Political Speech

Free-speech issues include censorship, national security, and obscenity, although a range of other types of speech that do not fall into these categories may still have government oversight. Examples include commercial speech, political speech, and issues of privacy. The **Federal Trade Commission (FTC)** enforces antitrust and consumer protection laws, including cases of deceptive advertising in print, electronic media, and the Internet. As the Food and Drug Administration (FDA) is responsible for deceptive advertising claims for food and drugs, confusion can sometimes arise regarding which agency enforces

Federal Trade Commission (FTC)

The principal commerce regulatory body, established in 1914, at the federal level in the United States.

regulations about deceptive advertising. The FTC is also responsible for enforcing the 1998 Children's Online Privacy Protection Act (COPPA), which gives parents control over what kinds of information can be collected about their children online.

Although the FTC does not regulate the Internet to the extent that the FCC does with broadcast, cable, wireless, and satellite radio, a mandate to protect consumers against deceptive advertising and business practices confers broad power. With dishonest practices that include spam, phishing, trademark infringement, breaches of consumer privacy, and false advertising claims, to name a few, the Internet has created whole new ways to trick and cheat people while also making many traditional scams cheaper and easier to execute.

One problem for the FTC is its ability to enforce regulations and laws, especially with companies based overseas. Not only may other countries have different laws regarding the legality of spammers or phishing operations, but many such companies frequently relocate their operations and are consequently hard to catch even if the FTC or host country had the resources to do so.

COMMERCIAL SPEECH

Commercial speech, including advertising, has generally been afforded less First Amendment protection than other forms of speech, especially political speech and the news. In a landmark decision, the U.S. Supreme Court ruled in 1942 in *Valentine v. Chrestensen* that "purely commercial advertising" was unprotected by the First Amendment. Chrestensen was a businessman who dispersed leaflets advertising tours for a World War I–era submarine he had on display at a pier in New York City. The police commissioner forbade him from distributing the leaflets, which were becoming litter. Chrestensen claimed violation of his First Amendment rights, but the Supreme Court disagreed.

In the 1970s, the broad powers granted to government regarding commercial speech were restricted somewhat by cases that allowed some First Amendment protection, although not on par with other forms of speech. In 1976, the Court ruled in *Virginia State Board of Pharmacy v. Virginia Citizens Consumer Council, Inc.* that speech that does "no more than propose a commercial transaction" is entitled to at least some First Amendment protection. This was in response to a case brought by some citizens' groups in Virginia that wanted to see pharmacies advertise prices of drugs, which the state legislature had prohibited.

In some cases, however, commercial speech has been afforded more protection than one might expect. An interesting example involves a former New York City mayor. In 1997, Rudolph Giuliani was lampooned on the city buses of New York in an advertising campaign by *New York* magazine, which claimed their magazine was "possibly the only good thing in New York that Rudy hasn't taken credit for." Giuliani, who had boasted he was responsible for everything from drops in the crime rate to a booming economy, found the ads offensive and demanded their removal. In this instance, commercial speech won. Consider the conclusion of United States District Judge Shira Scheindlin, who quipped, "Who would have dreamed that the mayor would object to more publicity?" She ruled that Giuliani's administration violated the First Amendment when it ordered city buses to remove paid ads.

Advertisements for alcohol are allowed on television and radio, although ads for tobacco are not.
CRITICAL THINKING QUESTION: If electronic media ads are not permitted for tobacco, should they be allowed for marijuana in states where its use is legal?

Tobacco, Alcohol, and Marijuana Advertising

Most goods can be legally advertised on electronic media under the jurisdiction of the FCC, with the general exception of one product: tobacco. Advertising cigarettes, small cigars, smokeless tobacco, or chewing tobacco is prohibited on radio, television, and any other electronic medium regulated by the FCC, such as telephony. It is permissible, though, to advertise smoking accessories, cigars, pipes, pipe tobacco, or cigarette-making machines. No federal laws or FCC regulations prohibit the advertising of alcoholic beverages, such as beer, wine, and liquor, on television and radio.

A number of states have recently legalized recreational marijuana and even more have approved its medical sale.[15] This grassroots movement remains presently at odds, however, with federal laws that categorize marijuana as illegal and prohibit advertising the sale of illegal drugs—bans that Facebook, Yahoo, Google, and Twitter strictly enforce to avoid costly fines for such violations. Significantly, the Treasury Department now allows U.S. financial institutions to have marijuana businesses as clients. As cultural acceptance, legal support, and economic revenues for marijuana continue to grow, it will be interesting to see how the FCC responds to pressure from different advocacy groups.

Unclear Regulatory Boundaries

Offensive advertising and subliminal programming are not clearly regulated by any single agency. Presumably, the advertiser would decide either not to run an offensive ad, or if it does and receives negative publicity, it would pull the ad to avoid further damaging its brand. In many cases, companies have abandoned ads in the face of public criticism. For example, in 2013, Mountain Dew discontinued an ad after critics charged it was racist. According to the FCC, subliminal advertising, messages directed to our subconscious perception, is "inconsistent with a station's obligation to serve the public interest." Still, it does not officially prohibit subliminal programming. Research has not provided conclusive evidence that subliminal messages are even understood or have an influence on behavior, and no advertisers have admitted using them.

POLITICAL SPEECH

Historically, the heart of freedom of expression is in political speech, or speech that deals with the political process, government, elected officials, or elections. Some go so far as to contend that the only speech the founders intended when they wrote the First Amendment was political speech. Political speech is also one area where federal regulations have been most extensive.

equal-time rule

The requirement that broadcasters make available equal airtime, in terms of commentaries and commercials, to opposing candidates running for election. It does not apply to candidates appearing in newscasts, documentaries, or news-event coverage.

Equal-Time Rule

Under the **equal-time rule** from the 1934 Communications Act, if a station permits a qualified candidate for public office to use its facilities, including commentaries or paid commercials, the station must "afford equal opportunities to all other such candidates for that office." Two circumstances are exempted from the equal-time provision: when the candidate appears in a newscast, interview, or documentary and when the candidate appears during on-the-scene coverage of a news event. Candidate debates, ruled as "on-the-spot" news coverage, are thus exempt from equal-time-rule provisions. In 1981, the U.S. Supreme Court ruled in support of the equal-time rule, supporting the rights of viewers and listeners, adding that "as defined by the FCC and applied here, [it] does not violate the First Amendment rights of broadcasters by unduly circumscribing their editorial discretion, but instead properly balances the First Amendment rights of federal candidates, the public, and broadcasters."

The equal-time rule says that TV stations must allow equal opportunities for all political candidates to air paid commercials.

Fairness Doctrine

Although often confused with it, the equal-time rule is not the same as the **Fairness Doctrine**. The former deals only with giving political candidates equal time, with the exceptions noted previously. The Fairness Doctrine, adopted by the FCC in 1949, was much broader in scope, requiring broadcasters to seek out and present all sides of a controversial issue. This gave people a chance to respond on air to personal attacks, and it offered candidates airtime to respond to a station's endorsement of another candidate.

In 1969, in *Red Lion Broadcasting Co. v. FCC*, which required Red Lion Broadcasting to provide equal airtime for a politician's response to an attack, the Court held that because of the scarcity of broadcasting frequencies, the government

Fairness Doctrine

Adopted by the FCC in 1949, it required broadcasters to seek out and present all sides of a controversial issue they were covering. It was discarded by the FCC in 1987.

might require a broadcast licensee to share the frequency with others who might not otherwise have a chance to broadcast their views. The Court thus gave the public a right of access "to social, political, esthetic, moral, and other ideas and experiences."

Largely discarded in 1987, the last vestiges of the Fairness Doctrine were suspended by the FCC in 2000, and a federal court overturned it entirely, ruling that the FCC had not demonstrated the value to the public of the doctrine, given the limitation it places on broadcasters' First Amendment rights. Legislative attempts to resuscitate the Fairness Doctrine in 2005 and 2008 failed. The FCC has refrained from supporting such efforts, claiming that the doctrine never really produced more diversity in programming and that channel proliferation has generated more diversity than could have been hoped for when three major commercial networks dominated television.

The prevalence of conservative commentators such as Ann Coulter has led liberals to try to reinstate the Fairness Doctrine.

Children's Programming Protections

Parents, elected officials, and others have long sought to protect children from unwanted or offensive speech and to create a media system that actively nourishes them. Considerable regulation exists to both protect and promote children's welfare in a media environment, especially the electronic media. A ratings system, similar to that used for movies, gives parents a guide to program suitability for children of certain ages. Among the most important pieces of regulation designed to protect children is the Children's Television Act.

THE CHILDREN'S TELEVISION ACT

The **Children's Television Act (CTA)** took effect in 1990. It limits the amount of commercial content in children's TV programming (including broadcast, satellite, and cable) and mandates that each television station provide programming of educational and informational value for children age sixteen and younger. Programming must meet four FCC criteria:

1. Designed primarily to address children's educational and informational needs (i.e., it can't be primarily entertainment, such as a cartoon, and have as a by-product some educational value).
2. Broadcast between 6 a.m. and 10 p.m., hours when children are likely to be viewing.
3. Scheduled regularly each week.
4. Runs at least a half hour.

In addition, commercial stations are required to identify their educational programs for children as such at the beginning of those programs, as well as to publishers of program guides. Moreover, all programs aimed at children twelve and younger may not contain more than 10.5 minutes of advertising per hour on weekends and 12 minutes on weekdays. The FCC also established that at least three hours of core children's programming a week would fulfill station obligations under the CTA, "core" being defined primarily in terms of item number 1 in the list of criteria.

Children's Television Act (CTA)

Created in 1990, it limits the amount of commercial content that programming can carry, forces stations to carry certain amounts of educational programming for children sixteen and under, and includes other provisions to protect children.

VIOLENT AND SEXUAL PROGRAMMING: THE V-CHIP

Violent and sexual programming receives special attention from the FCC because of its potential implications for young viewers. With the Telecommunications Act of 1996, the federal government began regulating televised violent content in addition to sexual content. Seeking to increase parental control over their children's viewing of violent and sexual programming, the act begins by summarizing research that demonstrates the negative impact of television violence on children. It notes, "Parents express grave concern over violent and sexual video programming and strongly support technology that would give them greater control to block video programming in the home that they consider harmful to their children."

To that end, the government mandated that as of January 2000, all television sets thirteen inches or larger come equipped with a **V-chip**, or "violence chip." The V-chip is a computer device that enables parents or any other viewer to program a TV set to prevent access to programs containing violent or sexual content based on the program rating, also called "TV Parental Guidelines." At the request of the government, the television industry agreed to broadcast signals with its own voluntary ratings system, one the V-chip can detect. These ratings appear on the TV screen for the first fifteen seconds of rated programming, permitting viewers to use the V-chip to block those programs from their sets. On the basis of the First Amendment, all news programming is exempted from the V-chip.

In the digital age, the V-chip is no longer the only tool that restricts television viewing. All digital-media systems, including digital cable and satellite television, contain software controls that can block individual programs, entire channels, or classes of programs based on their ratings.

Children's programming has been an area of FCC regulatory focus, which even determines the maximum number of commercial minutes for programs.

V-chip

A computer device that enables parents or any other viewer to program a TV set to block access to programs containing violent or sexual content based on the program rating.

DISCUSSION QUESTIONS: When you were younger, did you ever see movies that you were not supposed to watch because of the rating? Did your parents have parental controls on your television or computer? If so, did you get around the controls, and how did you do so? Do you believe the shows you saw were harmful to you or your friends in any way?

---

intellectual property (IP)

Ideas that have commercial value, such as literary or artistic works, patents, trademarks, business methods, and industrial processes.

copyright

A form of intellectual property law that protects the right to use, publish, reproduce, perform, display, or distribute a literary or artistic work, such as a piece of writing, music, film, or video.

Intellectual Property Rights

Of significant and growing concern to those in mass communication is the protection of their **intellectual property (IP)**. IP refers to ideas that have commercial value, such as literary or artistic works, patents, software programs, business methods, and industrial processes, particularly in the form of copyright protection. A **copyright** ("copyright" refers to the legal right to make a copy of a work) is one form of intellectual property rights protection that deals with specific expressions of ideas. The other two main areas of intellectual property law are patents and trademarks.

Patents are intended to protect a specific form of intellectual property known as inventions. Once granted, a patent prohibits anyone from copying the invention, pattern, or design. Anyone can apply for a patent, as long as the idea is new. **Trademarks** refer to images, designs, logos, or even words or phrases. In March 2004, for instance, Donald Trump, host of *The Apprentice* reality TV show, attempted to trademark his phrase "You're Fired!" so that it could be sold on clothing and other items. The U.S. Patent and Trademark Office turned down his request because it was too similar to "You're Hired!," an educational board game whose phrase had been trademarked in 1997.

In October 2011, organizers of a London conference were forced to change its name from the "Radical Media Conference" to the "Rebellious Media Conference" after a London-based PR firm named Radical Media threatened to sue for copyright infringement, despite the long history of the term "radical media" going back to the nineteenth century. Nevertheless, the PR firm had trademarked the name, and the conference organizers could not afford a costly legal battle, even if they had eventually won the case.

A copyright exists from the moment a work is created in its fixed form, such as being written down or recorded, so simply claiming an idea does not give you a copyright to it. Inserting a © symbol (or a symbol with a P in a circle for a musical recording, ℗), along with a date and the name of the copyright owner, helps indicate that you are copyrighting a work. This is not necessary, however, nor is registration with the U.S. Copyright office, unless at some future point you wish to sue for infringement of a work (in which case, prior registration and public documentation would likely have been prudent).

A copyright is in effect for the lifetime of the author, plus 70 years, although it may be up to 125 years with a work for hire, typically owned by the employer. The rationale of a copyright is to protect not only the intellectual product but also the author/owner's financial interests. In 1989, the United States joined the Berne Convention for the Protection of Literary and Artistic Works, extending copyright protection globally.

Copyright law applies to a wide range of expression, primarily the creations of authors or artists. A copyright, not a patent, protects a nonfiction book or article as well as literary works (including newspapers, books, and magazines); musical works; dramatic works; pantomimes and choreographic works; pictorial, graphic, and sculpture works; motion pictures and other audiovisual works; sound recordings; and architectural works. The **Digital Millennium Copyright Act** extends to digital works, including those on the Internet or other online media, because if something exists on a hard drive it is considered a fixed form.

> **patent**
>
> A form of intellectual property law that protects the right to produce and sell an invention.

> **trademark**
>
> A form of intellectual property law that protects the right to use a particular sign, logo, or name.

The NFL has trademarked the term "Super Bowl," forbidding local restaurants, bars, and other advertisers—even in the host city—from using the term without permission. **CRITICAL THINKING QUESTIONS:** Do you agree with the NFL's claim that the words "Super Bowl" will lose their importance if used too widely? Why or why not?

> **Digital Millennium Copyright Act**
>
> A 1998 act of Congress that reformed copyright law comprehensively to update it for the digital age. Key provisions addressed the circumvention of copyright-protection systems, fair use in a digital environment, and Internet service providers' liability for content sent through their lines.

DISCUSSION QUESTIONS: If you were a young novelist or struggling musician trying to make a living writing stories or making music, would you oppose or support greater government or corporate control of copyright if the technology they used prevented unauthorized copies of your work from being circulated?

FAIR USE

fair use

Allowable use of someone else's copyrighted work that does not require payment of royalties, with a number of factors that determine if something falls under fair use or violates copyright.

Holding a copyright to a work provides the owner with an exclusive right to reproduce, distribute (over any media), perform, display, or license that work. Copyright law recognizes limited exceptions, including primarily for **fair use** of an expression, such as in a movie or book review where the reviewer might include an excerpt, or in criticism or commentary. In general, four factors determine whether the use of another's copyrighted work is legal under the "fair use" provision of the act:

1. Purpose and nature of the use (i.e., it is purely commercial, educational, or for the news, the latter two of which are generally more likely to qualify)

2. Character of the copyrighted work (some works are inherently more protected; this is a subjective matter determined by the courts)

3. Amount and extent of the excerpt, in proportion to the copyrighted work in its entirety (this is determined more qualitatively than quantitatively, however, and there are no exact rules on the permissible number of words one may borrow from a text or the amount of video, audio, or image one may excerpt because even a small clip may represent the most significant creative aspect of the work)

4. Effect of the use on the copyrighted work's market potential (i.e., in dollar terms), especially when the copyrighted work is the basis for a derivative work (e.g., a movie based on a book)

The issue of fair use has become a flashpoint for digital media, especially in relation to content aggregators such as Google News or video search engines. In several recent court cases, copyright holders have sued content aggregators for copyright infringement. If, however, the content aggregator has been able to prove that it has transformed the content sufficiently—for example, by making low-resolution thumbnails of images or video clips—and to show that it is not profiting directly from doing so, it has generally won the case. Other aggregators have arrived at licensing agreements with media companies for displaying or collecting their content. Google, for instance, struck a deal with Associated Press to aggregate its news stories and keep them on Google News for a limited time.

Privacy

We discussed the role of privacy with social media in Chapter 7, but traditional media have a rich history of raising challenging privacy issues. For entertainment media, all members of the public appearing on shows, such as reality shows, game shows, and talk shows, must sign a waiver granting permission to use their image. These people are generally not paid for such appearances, and they are essentially giving away all rights, so broad are the waivers. This protects the show's producers from lawsuits if people dislike how they were depicted. Live sporting events do not require these waivers, in part because they take place in public spaces, where people cannot expect the same right to privacy. This is why spectators' faces are not blurred out when shown at sporting events.

Issues of privacy become more complex in journalism. Journalists often find themselves trying to get information that others wish to keep private. Obtaining records or private information without breaking trespass, eavesdropping, or privacy laws can be difficult. Even secretly recording a conversation can create legal trouble for a journalist, depending on the state. State laws vary as to whether only one party or both must consent to the recording of a conversation. Even more dilemmas arise when journalists acquire private records that someone else has stolen, such as when a whistle-blower provides confidential and damaging company documents.

At the heart of the matter is what is commonly called our "right to privacy." Although this right is not explicitly articulated in the Constitution, different Amendments mention privacy. Over time, the Supreme Court has used especially the Fourteenth Amendment, which addresses equal protection under the law, to develop a concept of privacy a citizen should expect.

The right to privacy differs between private citizens and celebrities or public figures, however. People not normally in the public limelight generally have greater privacy protections than celebrities or political officials. Greater privacy also applies to people who become celebrities through unanticipated circumstances such as rescuing a child from a burning building because they did not seek public attention.

Legal Issues in the Digital World

The courts and legal system have not kept up with the many changes to mass communication that the Internet and digital media have brought. As a result, cases decided by the courts from the mid-1990s through today can have dramatic effects because they establish precedent, becoming the basis for subsequent court decisions and legislation.

One example of just how far the legal system has had to come occurred in a 2000 ruling against Eric Corley (pen name: Emmanuel Goldstein), publisher of *2600: The Hacker Quarterly*. He included links in the online version of the magazine to a site with the code to DeCSS, a computer program that opened encrypted DVDs and allowed them to be copied freely. Corley argued that being forced to remove the hyperlinks was an infringement of his First Amendment rights. The court disagreed, claiming that a hyperlink was not an example of free speech because it acted as a kind of "mechanism" providing access to the site. Posting the URL of a site without a hyperlink, however, would still be considered free speech. An appellate court agreed with this decision in May 2001, and Corley decided not to take the case to the Supreme Court.

Media organizations and writers, artists, and musicians—anyone creating copyrighted media content for a living—want to be fairly compensated for their work. There would be no incentive, the reasoning goes, to create something only to have it rapidly copied and distributed without financial reward for the artist. Several lawsuits currently working their way through the court system could increase control for copyright holders—which are usually media organizations and not individuals.

ETHICS IN MEDIA
Does the Punishment Fit the Crime?

Aaron Swartz was widely hailed as a technological genius and known as an ardent Internet activist. After dropping out of school at age fourteen, he helped create the RSS syndication framework, which made it much easier to follow blogs and

Internet activism has emerged as a vibrant and global force for social movements especially those advocating for civil liberty.
CRITICAL THINKING QUESTIONS: Do you think guerilla tactics are justified when fighting perceived oppression? Do you feel the government shares all or some of the responsibility for Aaron Swartz's suicide because of their pursuit of such severe penalties for his activist actions? Do you think punishments for intellectual property infringement are too harsh, or do they accurately reflect the damage that can be done by stealing intellectual property?

other media content online. He co-created the social news and entertainment site Reddit when he was nineteen; and at twenty-three, he founded Demand Progress, an online advocacy group that campaigned against Internet censorship.

Swartz was an advocate of **open access**. Open-access proponents believe that information should be accessible to everyone and that unjust imbalances in power arise when certain groups have access to information that others do not.

The opening assertion of the Guerrilla Open Access Manifesto, which Swartz wrote in 2008, is "Information is power." Swartz goes on to complain about how scientific publishers have scientists sign away their copyrights and enclose the latest scientific research behind paywalls that only large organizations such as universities can afford; his manifesto contends that companies are blinded by both greed and power.

Employing digital guerilla tactics, Swartz acted on his beliefs. In January 2011, MIT police arrested him on a number of charges, all involving his downloading the entire database of academic journals from the publishing and database site JSTOR. It was unclear what he intended to do with the articles, whether he was planning to release the information to the public or was simply trying to make a point. Nevertheless, he faced combined felony charges that, if convicted, could have meant a $1 million fine and thirty-five years in prison.

On January 11, 2013, a little over two years after his arrest and as prosecutors subpoenaed his friends for the upcoming trial, Swartz hanged himself in his Brooklyn apartment, leaving no suicide note. Eulogies from Internet luminaries came in print and at his funeral, where Web creator Tim Berners-Lee gave a eulogy. Lawrence Lessig wrote an article asking why the prosecutor's office felt they had to bully Swartz and pursue such stringent punishments. Other open-source and open-access advocates also showed their support for what he stood for and protested the heavy-handed tactics of the government.

Swartz's story is told in the 2014 documentary *The Internet's Own Boy: The Story of Aaron Swartz*.[16] Released at the Sundance Film Festival, the film not only features Swartz's short but eventful life but also examines his legacy and impact on the NSA surveillance revelations and the Stop Online Piracy Act (SOPA) protests.

 open access

A system that makes information accessible to all to discourage power imbalances that may arise from unequal access.

DIGITAL RIGHTS MANAGEMENT

File-sharing and royalty issues related to music, and increasingly video, continue to be one of the main areas of contention in the digital space. Record labels have tried various measures to deter free file sharing, including suing customers and having universities hold seminars for incoming students on the matter, but with no decrease in free downloading.

Digital rights management (DRM) is the use of technology to rein in copyright infringement of digital content. Encryption has had some success, although, as the DeCSS example demonstrates, it is not foolproof. A **digital watermark** is computer code (usually invisible but sometimes visible) inserted into any digital content—images, graphics, audio, video, or even text documents—that authenticates the source of that content. Watermarks can protect media assets and intellectual property from theft—or at least make illegal activities easier to track.

For instance, if a media company sends digital video over the Internet, which someone tries to copy and distribute without obtaining permission, the original copyright holder, an end user, or even an intelligent software agent can examine the content for an embedded digital watermark. If the watermark is present and is that of the original copyright holder, then it can easily be demonstrated that the redistributor is in violation of copyright law. In essence, digital watermarking is analogous to cattle branding to deter or catch rustlers.

DRM has faced resistance from some groups, such as the Electronic Frontier Foundation, which claim that media companies want to limit the capabilities of new technologies simply to increase their revenues and force digital media to behave like their analog counterparts. These restrictions anger many consumers and raise serious questions about what exactly a person is "buying" when purchasing a CD and what rights the purchaser has to that content.

Whenever a new secure system is proposed, a method to break the system is not far behind. Rather than deal with this fundamental issue, media organizations have lobbied to change laws to favor copyright holders, and they have taken people to court for merely publicizing the existence of security weaknesses in encrypted or watermark systems, arguably infringing on free speech.

PRIVACY

Privacy issues have become increasingly important with the Internet and digital media. Not only can websites track users in ways impossible with analog media, but they can insert code, called a "cookie," onto computers and track users even after they have left that particular website. Not all cookies track relentlessly, however; and in fact, cookies, as discussed in previous chapters, can also make the Web a more user-friendly environment.

Still, their overuse can be a problem. Just as a website will add a cookie to your computer, so will advertisers on a website. These **third-party cookies** also track your Web usage and send information directly to the advertisers, who can determine how long you've stayed on a page and where you went afterward.

Spyware can be secretly loaded onto computers from websites and can do everything from tracking browsing behavior to recording keystrokes, a technique that can lead to the surreptitious monitoring and recording of a password or other private information by an unseen person on another computer.

In 2013, Edward Snowden, a National Security Agency (NSA) employee, revealed that the NSA had been reviewing the phone records of all U.S. citizens and the digital communications of those in other countries to find potential terrorist activities. The case reminded the public of how easily the government can work with telecommunications companies and Internet media giants to gather information about people.

> **digital rights management (DRM)**
>
> Technologies that let copyright owners control the level of access or use allowed for a copyrighted work, such as limiting the number of times a song can be copied.

> **digital watermark**
>
> Computer code (usually invisible but sometimes visible) inserted into any digital content—images, graphics, audio, video, or even text documents—that authenticates the source of that content.

> **third-party cookies**
>
> Cookies put on a computer by those other than the website being visited, such as advertisers.

Other legal issues involve the status of messages sent by private citizens. Is a posting to a discussion board considered "publishing," and could a poster be sued for libel? What if a person writes something libelous in a private email to a friend and that friend includes the email in a discussion-board topic? Who could be sued for libel? These and many other similar legal issues have yet to be resolved. In other words, the public, as it gains access to a worldwide distribution network, will have to start considering issues of privacy, libel, defamation, and attendant lawsuits—all issues traditional media companies must consider every day.

CONTENT RIGHTS AND RESPONSIBILITIES

Another new area that media companies have had to contend with is the status of user-generated content (UGC). It is virtually impossible for a company to police all the content uploaded to the Internet. The question of who is responsible for the content on a site arises when someone is defamed in a user comment, as opposed to something the company itself wrote.

In general, the courts have made a "safe haven" provision for content providers, protecting them to some extent from libel lawsuits as long as they remove the offending content promptly and make good faith efforts to prevent similar transgressions. Similarly, Internet service providers (ISPs) have been considered largely immune from responsibility for what is sent over their networks, although the threat of a lawsuit can sometimes be sufficient incentive to remove offending content or to ban users, especially those accused by record labels of rampant free file sharing.

 **MEDIA CAREERS**

Legal considerations frame and shape all media careers. Increasingly, anyone pursuing a career in journalism or media must consider the legal and regulatory context for their work on multiple levels. The First and Fourth Amendments are particularly vital concerns. Freedom of speech and privacy are defining legal underpinnings for work in journalism and the media. Yet other laws, once deemed beyond the framework of journalism and the media, are also becoming important. For instance, media professionals now need to be familiar with laws of agencies such as the Federal Aviation Administration, evolving regulations that pertain to new technologies such as drones. Further, journalists and other media professionals must be aware of international laws, including copyright and intellectual property considerations that pertain globally where their content may appear online.

As the work of the great Anthony Lewis exemplifies, journalism reporting on legal issues in the media is a profoundly significant career pathway. Legal journalism in the twenty-first century means much more than covering U.S. laws. Successfully negotiating a global village requires advanced knowledge of the broader legal framework that applies across borders: geographic, political, and cultural.

LOOKING BACK AND MOVING FORWARD

Many legal and regulatory issues complicate Internet media for users and producers, and the legal system generally lags far behind in dealing with these. The global nature of the Internet also raises questions about whose laws should be followed when offensive or illegal content originating in one country can be viewed online in another. The question of whether a hyperlink is protected by the First Amendment can generate heated discussions about the complex nature of digital media. Similarly, the seemingly simple question "Where does publishing occur?" can stir complicated legal debate.

With traditional media, the answer was obvious—publishing occurred in the country where the printing press was located. A book might be legally printed in one country but banned in another; thus, if a copy was smuggled into the country where it was banned, the person caught with book would be penalized, not the printer.

But on the Internet, where something is published is not at all clear. A person may create banned content in his country for his website, which is on a web server in another country where the content is not banned. Someone else may come across the content in a third country where the material is considered harmful, sacrilegious, or defamatory. In this scenario, many questions arise, such as which country's laws will be in effect in a lawsuit and what constitutes libel because it differs from country to country.

A pertinent, highly controversial case was brought forward in 2002. *Dow Jones and Co. Inc. v. Gutnick* involved an article in *Barron's* (published by Dow Jones) in October 2000 that mentioned Melbourne businessman Joseph Gutnick several times. Although the number of print copies of *Barron's* sent to Australia was minuscule, the online readership of the magazine was over half a million, and Gutnick claimed that many more Australians would see the article than just those who subscribed to the print version. He argued his libel lawsuit should be heard in Australia, where he was defamed. Dow Jones countered that the article was actually published in the United States, where its Web servers were located, and thus the case should be heard in the United States (where libel charges are harder to win than in Australia). The Australian High Court agreed with Gutnick, however, and Dow Jones eventually settled with him in 2004.

The case was of serious concern to Internet watchers and media companies because of its potential implications for publishers on the Web. The ruling could mean that people could sue a media company or website according to their own country's laws, which may more severely restrict acceptable content than regulations where the material was published. On the other hand, it is arguably not fair to impose another country's views of acceptable free speech on foreign content simply because it was published on the Internet. The question remains open and will likely come up again in the future.

MEDIA MATTERS   LEGAL LIMITS

Test your legal knowledge as it relates to the First Amendment, media regulations, and copyright.

1. "Libel" refers to defaming someone in print or broadcast, whereas "slander" is defamation that occurs through the spoken word. How do you think defamation should be classified if it appears in a YouTube video?

2. Do you think a hyperlink that takes a user to an illegal site is protected as free speech by the First Amendment? Why or why not?

3. National security issues are one of the few cases in which the government can possibly stop publication or broadcast of information. Should the government be able to use the "national security" rationale to censor videos in a situation such as occurred following the Boston Marathon bombing in 2013 when the public pored over video footage and made inaccurate claims about identifying the suspected bombers?

4. If I tell my friend my idea for a novel and he then writes a novel based on my idea, can I sue him for copyright infringement? Why or why not?

5. (T/F) Camera-equipped drones have emerged as a potential battleground pitting First Amendment rights against concerns over national security and privacy, or Fourth Amendment rights.

ANSWERS: 1. Even though defamation appears on video or television as spoken words, it is still considered libel. 2. First Amendment protection does not apply to a link, deemed by the courts to act like a mechanism that takes a person to a specific place. 4. Copyright covers only works that are recorded in some form, so simply talking about an idea does not protect it as copyrighted. 5. True.

FURTHER READING

Digital Media Law, 2nd ed. Ashley Packard (2012) Wiley-Blackwell.

Major Principles of Media Law: 2015 Edition. Genelle Belmas, Wayne Overbeck (August 12, 2014) Cengage Learning.

Freedom for the Thought That We Hate: A Biography of the First Amendment. Anthony Lewis (2008) Basic Books.

Perilous Times: Free Speech in Wartime: From the Sedition Act of 1798 to the War on Terror. Geoffrey R. Stone (2005) W. W. Norton.

Born Secret: The H-Bomb, the Progressive Case, and National Security. Gerald Marsh, Alexander De-Volpi, George Stanford, Ted Postol (2011) Kindle edition.

Make No Law: The Sullivan Case and the First Amendment. Anthony Lewis (1992) Vintage.

The Associated Press Style Book and Briefing on Media Law. Associated Press (2013) Basic Books.

We're All Journalists Now: The Transformation of the Press and Reshaping of the Law in the Internet Age. Scott Gant (2007) Free Press.

Insult to Injury: Libel, Slander and Invasions of Privacy. William Jones (2003) University Press of Colorado.

Rethinking Global Security: Media, Popular Culture, and "The War on Terror." Andrew Martin, Patrice Petro (eds.) (2006) Rutgers University Press.

Who Controls the Internet? Illusions of a Borderless World. Jack Goldsmith, Tim Wu (2006) Oxford University Press.

Intellectual Property Law and Interactive Media: Free for a Fee. Edward Lee Lamoureux, Steven Baron, Claire Stewart (2009) Peter Lang.

Intellectual Property and Open Source: A Practical Guide to Protecting Code. Van Lindberg (2008) O'Reilly Media.

Censored 2014: Dispatches from the Media Revolution; The Top Censored Stories and Media Analysis of 2012–13. Mickey Huff (ed.) and Project Censored (contributor) (2013) Triangle Square.

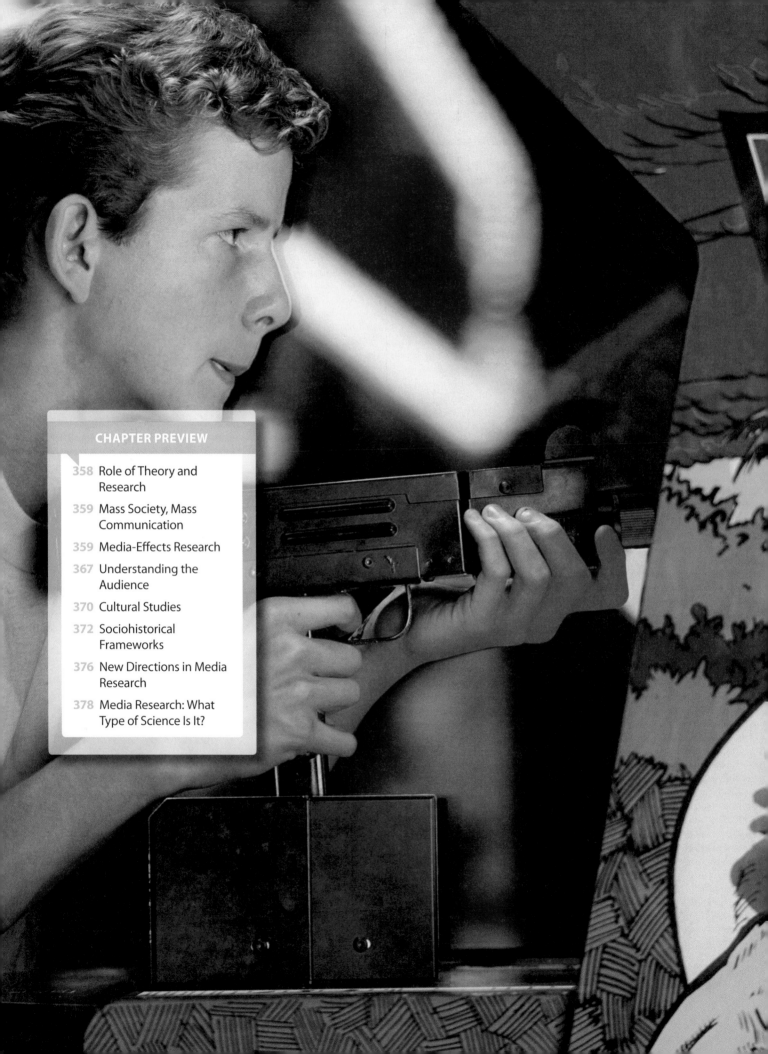

Media Theory and Research

"Guns don't kill people," National Rifle Association (NRA) Executive Vice President Wayne LaPierre said at a press conference one week after the mass shooting at Sandy Hook Elementary School on December 14, 2012. "Video games, the media, and Obama's budget kill people." LaPierre elaborated: "There exists in this country, sadly, a callous, corrupt and corrupting shadow industry that sells and stows violence against its own people through vicious, violent video games with names like Bulletstorm, Grand Theft Auto, Mortal Kombat, and Splatterhouse."[1]

The video game industry has long confronted charges from across the political spectrum that violent games increase violence among children and teens, concerns that have only intensified with the rise in popularity of video games and advanced technology creating hyperrealistic graphics. And the fact remains that the incidence of gun-related deaths in the United States is higher than that of any other industrialized country.

Yet the results from numerous studies on gaming and violence are inconclusive as to whether violent video games or TV programs increase the likelihood of aggressive or violent behavior in real life. Some studies demonstrate a correlation while others do not. And even correlation cannot prove causation. Furthermore, Americans play violent video games at the same rate as people in countries with little gun violence, such as South Korea and the Netherlands.[2]

Nevertheless, people looking for explanations for inexplicably brutal acts continue to blame the simulated brutality of video games. In September 2013, after "Navy Yard shooter" Aaron Alexis killed twelve people and injured three others in Washington, DC, early reports were quick to cite his apparent obsession with violent video games. Subsequent inquiry, however, revealed that he might have been delusional as the result of an undiagnosed mental illness. As Alexis was fatally shot by an officer at the scene, the mystery of what drove him to mass murder will likely never be resolved.

Research findings on media and violence can have a tremendous impact on media industries in the form of government censorship or regulations and sales of media products such as games, movies, and books. Media effects have been an area of keen interest since the dawn of the mass-communication era. Theories about media and communication attempt to explain the underlying processes of media, how we interact with media, and how media affect our cultures, societies, attitudes, and lives. This research takes on special importance given how much time we spend with media, demonstrated by the following findings from years of research:

Americans spend an average of just over five hours a day watching television. By age 75, the average American will have spent nine years of his or her life watching television.[3]

By age eighteen, a child has seen on TV two hundred thousand acts of violence, including forty thousand acts of murder.[4]

Half (47 percent) of violent actions include no depiction of pain.[5]

Fifty-four percent of children in the mid-1990s had a television set in their own bedroom and often watched with a friend, unsupervised.[6]

Media research is the systematic and scientific investigation of communication processes and effects that often bases its explorations on theories of media and communication. Some types of media research, such as that conducted by market research firms, are more oriented to answering practical questions, such as whether audience members remember a particular advertisement, their impressions of a product or brand, or their media use and consumption habits.

Media-research methodology, or how research is carried out, takes many forms. It can entail social scientific research using quantitative tools and statistical analysis of data, such as surveys and experiments; or it can involve critical studies using qualitative methods, such as ethnography or focus groups.

Role of Theory and Research

For media professionals, research may seem more important than theory. Someone planning to work in journalism or advertising may see practical inquiry as more significant than academic theory. Yet media theories have had a number of profound effects. They play a foundational role, providing cognitive constructs that help us organize and make sense of the world. They also play a key role in research agendas, which then affect the questions asked during the course of investigation, the findings or discoveries, and the funding for such projects.

Research findings in turn shape public policies on the media and media industries, decisions about what and how items should be regulated, such as ratings systems for movies, music, and video games. This of course has important implications for the organization and operation of media companies, which affects everything from content development to job creation.

Media research carried out specifically for business purposes helps determine audience numbers for particular shows or networks (thus determining advertising rates and kinds of shows produced). It also helps identify which media campaigns have been more effective and which messages more persuasive, and consequently, which areas are of most interest to businesses, not-for-profit organizations, and politicians.

In short, media theories not only help media professionals better predict or explain various phenomena, they also help us better understand the world we live in and the forces at work in it. As we will see, questions about the fundamental nature of communication and media are not new.

Mass Society, Mass Communication

A number of larger social, political, cultural, and scientific factors throughout the course of history have greatly influenced the study of mass communication and media theories. Here we will explore some of these historical and sociopolitical forces.

The dramatic societal and political changes that took place in Europe and the United States during the nineteenth and twentieth centuries, thanks largely to industrialization, provide the backdrop for early theorizing on mass communication. The new demands of factory work and mass migrations to the quickly growing cities changed traditional ways of life that had remained largely the same for generations. Harsh working and living conditions produced clashes between workers and authorities, leading to various social and political movements that called for greater democracy and workers' rights.

Elites threatened by these developments found various rationales for why they should lead and most should simply follow, such as the notion of "the masses": people were largely uneducated, lacking in culture, and not intelligent enough to rule themselves. Others opposed elitism, claiming that more participation, better education, and greater distribution of wealth were necessary to create a more democratic and just society.

During these debates, which still echo today, film was starting to be recognized as an important medium of mass communication. Literacy was not needed to understand the stories in silent films, and moving images were regarded as powerful influencers, especially for the uneducated, passive masses, or other supposedly vulnerable groups such as women and children. Messages in various media could help educate, persuade, or control the masses; the question then became how best to do accomplish these goals.

Media-Effects Research

The obvious way to study media influence was to identify effects of media exposure. The notion that media could harm people was already well established, dating back to the ancient Greeks. With new and powerful communication technologies that could reach millions at once, such as film, radio, and, later, television, it was not hard to imagine the power that mass communication could have over people.

Media effects have been a dominant concern in the history of media research and continue to be important today. Findings from these studies have influenced the creation of the movie-rating system, dictated regulations for the television industry, and determined what types of advertisements we view. Although earlier assumptions of direct and powerful media effects have been scaled back as newer, more complex theories developed, the idea that media affect us directly (usually

Propaganda posters during World War I led researchers to hypothesize how persuasion worked on the public.

negatively) is still prevalent. The history of effects research reveals the interesting roles of communication technologies in relation to social issues and norms deemed important.

PROPAGANDA AND THE MAGIC BULLET

Some of the earliest media-effects research was conducted to better understand how mass communication persuaded people. During World War I, both the United States and Germany employed film and other media (including posters) as instruments of propaganda to generate public support for their positions in the war.

Attempts to influence an audience through mass communication, **propaganda** usually involves total control of the transmission of information, often without the audience knowing who is controlling the message. Although perhaps hard to imagine today, many people through much of the twentieth century had extremely limited sources of information—perhaps only a government radio station or a single government television station broadcasting a few hours a day.

Political scientist Harold Lasswell, during his analysis of World War I propaganda efforts, used the term "hypodermic needle" to describe the concept that media can act like a drug being injected into a passive audience. The **hypodermic-needle model** assumes that messages have a profound, direct, and uniform impact on individuals. This model has also been called the "magic bullet" model of communication and derives largely from learning theory and simple stimulus–response models in behavioral psychology.

As film became more popular and began to share space with radio as a form of mass communication in the 1920s, research about both mediums looked beyond specific political or propaganda uses and examined effects on the general public, especially children.

propaganda

The regular dissemination of a belief, doctrine, cause, or information, with the intent to mold public opinion.

hypodermic-needle model

A model of media effects, also called the "magic bullet," that claims media messages have a profound, direct, and uniform impact on the public.

DISCUSSION QUESTIONS: Do you think propaganda is more or less likely to happen today with social media? Why or why not?

PAYNE FUND

Between 1928 and 1933, some of the most prominent psychologists, sociologists, and educators of the day conducted the Payne Fund studies. Published in 1933, they included a twelve-volume report on the impact of film viewing on children.[7] The studies provided a detailed examination of the effects of film in wide-ranging areas, including sleep patterns, attitudes about violence, delinquent behavior, and knowledge about foreign cultures.

The Payne Fund studies concluded that the same film would influence children differently depending on their backgrounds and characteristics, including age, sex, life experience, predispositions, social environment, and parental influence.

The Payne Fund studies in the 1920s examined the effects of violence and sex in movies on young people.

One study of movies, delinquency, and crime, for instance, found that the impact of film on criminal behavior may vary with the range of themes presented as well as the social context, attitudes, and interests of the viewer. Contrary to the original assumption about largely negative effects, the Payne Fund research also revealed that children could learn some positive lessons from film and that information retention was a function of grade in school.[8]

The Payne Fund studies also created a "school of the air" that would use radio to educate children on a variety of subjects.[9] This led to the formation of the National Committee on Education by Radio (NCER) as well as the allocation of some $300,000 in the early 1930s to support U.S. broadcasting reform, which at that time meant radio.

RADIO'S WIDER IMPACT

Radio's social effects reached far beyond children, as dramatically illustrated by events that unfolded on October 30, 1938, when Orson Welles broadcast a radio program created to sound like a news event. At 8 p.m., the Columbia Broadcasting System's *Mercury Theater of the Air* began its radio broadcast from a New York City studio. Regular listeners and others who heard the introduction understood perfectly well what was about to follow, a radio adaptation of the famous 1897 novel *War of the Worlds* by science fiction writer H. G. Wells.

Those who missed the introduction tuned in to a supposedly live orchestra, a performance whose calm ambiance was abruptly interrupted by breaking news—an announcement that Martians had landed at a farm near Grovers Mill, New Jersey. The frequent and increasingly disturbing news flashes sounded very much like reports by Walter Winchell, the radio standard of the day. As the invasion ensued so did the panic. When it became apparent that the Martians had vastly superior weaponry, numerous residents of the eastern seaboard, especially in the New York and New Jersey area, opted to hide in their basements or even flee their homes.

Orson Welles and his *War of the Worlds* radio broadcast had many listeners believing that Martians were actually invading the East Coast.

A study by a psychologist showed that one in six listeners—1 million people—believed the broadcast and the Martian invasion to be real, although not all 1 million panicked and fled. Studies of the *War of the Worlds* broadcast and other radio programming demonstrated that media effects could be dramatic but were not uniform. Certain factors, including individual personalities, demographics, and psychological variables such as good critical-thinking ability, could mediate responses to media exposure.

This event focused American attention on the power of mass communication and triggered one of the first major investigations of a media program on the subject of social panic and mass hysteria as well as a debate about the government's control over the radio industry. As spectacular and strange as these incidents may be, by far the major concerns of researchers have been depictions of sex and violence, particularly since the advent of television.

TELEVISION AND VIOLENCE

Much television programming is educational and entertaining, and much is peppered with violence, sex, and profanity. Consequently, many adult viewers and policy makers have pondered the effects of extended television viewing on the next generation. Are children learning to be overly aggressive, imitating what they see on the television screen? Are they learning more about the Three Stooges than the three branches of government?

Bobo doll studies

Media–effects experiments in the 1950s that showed children who watched TV episodes that rewarded a violent person were more likely to punch a Bobo doll than children who saw episodes that punished a violent person.

Hundreds of studies have been conducted and millions of dollars spent to investigate how TV violence affects children. Among the first was a study that claimed television had become the new Pied Piper, providing a model (often not a good model) for children to imitate. Yet few early analyses could provide conclusive evidence that exposure to TV violence would have negative consequences in the real world.

Laboratory research in the 1950s by psychologist Albert Bandura and others demonstrated that children exposed to TV violence were more likely to repeat the behavior they had witnessed (e.g., beating a "Bobo doll") as well as become more aggressive—while they were still in the laboratory. Although these studies suggested that children learned by watching others, effects were documented in a laboratory setting only. Researchers who conducted the **Bobo doll studies** could not confirm that the children remained more aggressive once they left the laboratory.

Social unrest and violence in public, much of it politically motivated, rose dramatically in the 1960s. Concerned about a broad range of violence and its social causes, President Lyndon B. Johnson convened the National Commission on the Causes and Prevention of Violence in 1968. *Violence and the Media*, a report by the commission's media task force, focused not only on the quantity of violence on entertainment television but also on its quality. How did

Depictions of violence on television continue to be a concern among many groups.

the media portray violence? Who used which weapons to kill whom? What motivated these acts? What were the consequences? Were aggressors rewarded or punished?

Professor George Gerbner of the Annenberg School for Communication at the University of Pennsylvania, who oversaw this content analysis and follow-up research, defined violence as "the overt expression of force intended to hurt or kill." Overall, Gerbner and his colleagues found the consequences of television violence unrealistic. There was rarely much pain or blood. Good guys, often as violent as bad guys, did not suffer negative consequences for their actions. And bad guys were usually punished by cops rather than courts. Whites were often the victims, while young black males and other people of color, as well as immigrants, were typically the perpetrators.

Research on TV violence continued in the eighties and nineties. In 1992, the American Psychological Association issued its TV violence report, *Big World, Small Screen: The Role of Television in American Society*: "The accumulated research clearly demonstrates a correlation between viewing violence and aggressive behavior. Children and adults who watch a large number of aggressive programs also tend to hold attitudes and values that favor the use of violence." Correlation is not causation, however: A relationship between television-violence viewing and aggressive behavior does not mean one necessarily causes the other.

A team of researchers at UCLA led by Jeffrey Cole conducted one of the most important studies of TV violence in the 1990s, research that indicated American network television series had become somewhat less violent while the number of "shockumentary" reality-based specials had increased dramatically. Funded by the networks themselves, the *UCLA Television Violence Report* found that overall violence decreased on ABC, CBS, Fox, and NBC during the 1994–1995 season. But reality-based programs, most commonly encountered on Fox, were especially violent, featuring real and recreated footage of police shootouts, car chases and crashes, and animals attacking people, in some cases killing them on air.

LIMITED EFFECTS

Conducted by Wilbur Schramm, Jack Lyle, and Edwin Parker, *Television in the Lives of Our Children*, a 1960 landmark investigation of the impact of television on children in North America, concluded that some children under some conditions were likely to exhibit some negative consequences of exposure to television violence. But there was no magic bullet of media effects. From these results and similar findings developed various kinds of limited-effects models.

In this view, media are a component in a much larger and more fundamental system of influences to which we are all subject. Institutions such as the family, school, and religion are much more influential forces that shape individual tastes, attitudes, and behaviors. Media exposure contributes to and often reinforces the individual's worldview but is clearly secondary.

Cultivation Analysis

George Gerbner's research on the long-term impact of television watching generated the theory of **cultivation analysis**, which argues that television cultivates in audiences a view of reality similar to the world portrayed in TV programs. Rather than emphasizing the impact of individual programs on individual

cultivation analysis

A theory of media effects that claims television cultivates in audiences a view of reality similar to the world portrayed in television programs.

CONVERGENCE CULTURE
How Free Is Academic Freedom?

The open and free-wheeling nature of social media would seem a natural forum for academics to exchange a variety of ideas grounded in their research, assertions that challenge our perceptions and enrich our dialog about society and culture. In recent years, however, a number of incidents on social media involving politically insensitive tweets, inappropriate comments about students or colleagues, and hoaxes have raised questions about academic freedom and have even cost some professors their jobs.

In fall 2014, two weeks before Professor Steven Salaita was to start a new position, the University of Illinois at Urbana-Champaign rescinded their job offer because of inflammatory tweets Salaita had made regarding Israeli settlers in the West Bank. Salaita has authored a number of books on Arab Americans, including *Arab American Literary Fictions, Cultures and Politics*; and *Anti-Arab Racism in the USA: Where It Comes from and What It Means for Politics Today*. Salaita sued, arguing the university had violated his free speech rights and "trampled on principles of academic freedom,"[10] and students at the school marched to protest his dismissal, a decision trustees nevertheless reaffirmed in January 2015.

Early in 2015, the Marquette administration began the process of terminating political science professor John McAdams's tenure after he criticized a philosophy teaching assistant on his blog for her handling of student comments she considered homophobic. McAdams has spent some forty years in academe, most of them at Marquette. His case raises issues of academic free speech and shines a spotlight on a university's apparent inclination to strip faculty of tenure, a power that would have a chilling effect on open debates.

In November 2013, a satirical blog reported that in his final class before retirement, Massachusetts College of Art and Design Professor Noel Ignatiev, author of *How the Irish*

Became White, stated, "If you are a white male, you don't deserve to live. You are a cancer, you're a disease. White males have never contributed anything positive to the world. They only murder, exploit and oppress non-whites."[11] Ignatiev was not retiring, nor did he make this over-the-top, inflammatory statement, a direct quote falsely ascribed to him, but with a disclaimer acknowledging the material was satire. Even so, several conservative talk shows, including Rush Limbaugh, picked up this fiction and ran with it as fact. This "true story" occasionally resurfaces in social media, a hoax that generates new rounds of vitriolic hate mail for Ignatiev.

💬 **mean-world syndrome**

A syndrome in which people perceive the world as more dangerous than it actually is, the result of viewing countless acts of media violence.

viewers, cultivation analysis stresses cumulative effects. Coined by Gerbner, **mean-world syndrome** can result from viewing countless acts of media violence that make viewers perceive the world as more dangerous than it actually is. Designed as mainstream entertainment that is easy to understand, TV programs are powerful instruments of socialization, especially for children.

According to research by Gerbner and others, not only are those who watch more television more likely to consider the real world a more dangerous place, they are also more likely to support a more powerful system of law enforcement. Senior citizens who watch more television are more inclined to stay at home, fearful of perceived dangers. Cultivation effects are not uniform, however.

Watching too much television over years, especially news shows, can lead viewers to believe the world is more dangerous than it actually is. **CRITICAL THINKING QUESTIONS:** Do you feel more fearful in public places after viewing news like that on the Boston Marathon bombing? Is your fear greater if the violent event seems to be everywhere in the news?

Spiral of Silence

German communication scholar Elisabeth Noelle-Neumann developed the **spiral of silence** as a theoretical construct to explain why people may be unwilling to publicly express minority opinions. Derived from her observations of Germans during the Nazi regime in the 1930s and 1940s, the spiral of silence has been tested widely and shown to be valid in a variety of circumstances. It is based on three premises:

1. People have a natural fear of isolation.
2. Out of fear of isolation, people are reluctant to publicly express views that they feel are in the minority.
3. A "quasi-statistical organ," a sort of sixth sense, allows people to gauge the prevailing climate of opinion and determine majority views on matters of public importance.

A number of factors affect how people assess public opinion, particularly the media as well as their experiences and interactions with others. If a person feels a point of view matches the prevailing one, then that person will feel more comfortable expressing it publicly. If, on the other hand, a person feels out of step with public opinion, then that person will be less likely to express that opinion, thus producing a spiral of silence. In some instances, even a majority opinion, if perceived to be a minority position (possibly through biased media reporting), may not be expressed publicly.

Third-Person Effect

Among the most interesting of media effects is the **third-person effect** of communication, the tendency for people to underestimate the effect of a persuasive message on themselves while overestimating its effect on others. This tendency sometimes encourages one group to shield another from messages it thinks will harm them.

spiral of silence

A theoretical construct that explains why people may be unwilling to publicly express opinions they feel are in the minority.

third-person effect

The tendency for people to underestimate the effect of a persuasive message on themselves while overestimating its effect on others.

Although many researchers have demonstrated the widespread and varied impact of the third-person effect, W. Phillips Davison first identified this communication phenomenon when examining World War II records. The Japanese had dropped propaganda leaflets to black servicemen who were going to take part in the invasion of Iwo Jima (at that time whites and blacks were segregated in the military). Stating that the Japanese were fighting white imperialists and had no ill will toward blacks, the leaflets encouraged them to surrender or desert—to no effect, however, according to records. The campaign did persuade white officers of these black troops, though, to transfer them from the combat area to avoid any potential loss of morale.

CRITICISMS OF MEDIA-EFFECTS RESEARCH

Although subsequent research quickly discredited the direct-effects assumptions and hypodermic-needle model of media power, many members of the public and policy makers continue to believe in these effects. When tragedies occur such as the shootings at Columbine High School in 1999; Virginia Tech in 2007; Sandy Hook Elementary School in Newtown, Connecticut, in 2012; or the DC Navy Yard in 2013, the killer's media use is always discussed. Experts may not blame comic books and radio anymore, but television, movies, the Internet, and video games are all fair game when trying to explain violent or antisocial actions.

Much media-effects research is flawed by the belief that the audience has no will of its own. The assumption that the audience is a passive dupe easily manipulated by media messages derives directly from the belief that the masses are incapable of governing themselves. Although researchers today do not believe that people can be programmed by media messages to behave a certain way, even some of the limited-effects models perceive audiences as more passive than active.

A further complication in media-effects research is how to measure media exposure. Self-reporting, a common research technique, has been unreliable because people either intentionally or unintentionally under- or overreport media exposure. Furthermore, simply measuring exposure does not really capture how we interact with media and how it may influence us.

Media-effects researchers may use new ways of assessing audience interactions. Tracking Facebook Likes, tweets, or re-tweets, for example, helps quantitatively measure audience engagement in different situations. New developments in social-media listening software are helping researchers measure media consumption and interaction, although concepts like sentiment and engagement are still often open to interpretation.

Even if we accept the premise of media influence, separating intertwined social, cultural, psychological, and other factors and identifying clear cause-and-effect explanations remain difficult. That certain programs, songs, or video games produce predictable and widespread behaviors or attitudes has largely been disproven, given all the other influences in our lives and the different circumstances in which each of us interact with media.

Examining the wrong dimension of the communications process is another arguable fault in media-effects research. Some scholars claim that we have to understand the processes and economics of media products to understand the role of media in our lives. Others, such as audience-focused researchers, focus less on what media may or may not do to us and more on what we may or may not do with media.

DISCUSSION QUESTIONS: Do you think that a highly interactive medium like video games could have greater effects on media users than a more passive medium such as television? Why or why not?

Understanding the Audience

To a certain extent, mass-communications research has always been about trying to understand the audience. For advertising and public relations, knowing how the audience thinks and how to persuade it can make or break a campaign or new brand. For political communication, the audience, broadly conceived, is essentially the public and public opinion. For media companies, knowing what shows, books, music, and films audiences will like is a vital element. In scholarly communications research, the trend in audience studies in recent years has been toward seeing the audience as increasingly active in how it makes sense of the world and uses media.

Teaching children media and computer literacy will help them succeed in the twenty-first century.

AUDIENCES CREATING MEANING

The idea that audiences create new meaning from the media content they consume may seem odd. Yet scholars who use new audience-studies approaches question the assumption that a media product comes with a predetermined and unchangeable meaning that audiences simply ingest like fast food. Earlier discussion in this book about semiotics indicated that a given meaning of a sign or symbol, once learned, tends to be taken for granted. In the following section, however, we focus on active participation in the creation of new meaning around the media we encounter and among an audience. Some approaches look at psychology, others focus on the social aspects of creating meaning, and still others examine broader cultural issues and power relations.

Uses and Gratifications

Uses-and-gratifications research looks at *why* people use particular media. It examines what people do with media rather than what media do to people. Popular in the 1970s and 1980s, uses-and-gratifications research posits that people have certain needs, especially psychological needs, which they seek to satisfy through media usage. This research makes three basic claims:

1. People use the media actively for their own purposes.
2. People know what those purposes are and can articulate them.
3. Despite individual differences in media use, basic common patterns exist among people.

Modeled on an audience more active than passive, whose members hope to satisfy certain needs through the media they seek out, uses-and-gratifications research may lend itself to research on the Internet and interactive media.

uses-and-gratifications research

A branch of research on media effects that examines why people use media, what they do with media rather than what media do to them.

Uses-and-gratifications research has its detractors, however. It has been criticized for being hard to test empirically and for circular reasoning. In other words, it's hard to know which came first—the social/psychological need or the media use. Other criticisms include its focus on psychological needs while ignoring social forces and the assumption that audiences always do know (and can articulate) why they are using media.

Encoding/Decoding

💬 **encoding/decoding**

A theoretical model that states media producers encode media products with meanings, decoded in various ways by various audiences.

The **encoding/decoding** model, developed by Stuart Hall in the 1970s, launched what is known as the active-audience approach. A response to dissatisfaction with previous media-effects research, it tries to examine audiences within larger sociocultural contexts. The model is complex but essentially states that media producers encode media products with meanings, decoded in various ways by various audiences.

There is no guarantee the producer's preferred meaning will be accepted. Audience members have three basic options when decoding. They can choose the dominant, or hegemonic, reading, the one that the media producer likely intended and the one most people would recognize as common sense or natural. They can select an oppositional reading in which they recognize the codes being used but reject them for their own meanings. They can also choose a negotiated reading, largely accepting the dominant meaning but adding certain variations. Decoding skills and tendencies will vary with background, education, identity, and other social factors.

Studying pop culture can often reflect aspects of a society that other forms of media, such as news, cannot explain adequately.

Reception Analysis

Reception analysis was a major break in audience research in a number of respects. First, it assumed that audience members actively make meaning from the media they consume. Second, researchers looked at popular entertainment such as soap operas, women's magazines, and romance novels rather than the traditional news or other "serious" programming studied in earlier years. Third, the areas of study allowed feminist and other scholars to study women in media and women as active consumers of media.

The 1980s findings challenged long-held assumptions about why women read romance novels or watch a soap opera such as *Dallas*, or how teen girls perceived Madonna. Contrary to some prevailing feminist arguments that maintained these forms of popular culture demeaned women, encouraging them to see themselves from a patriarchal viewpoint as sex objects, scholars found that women actively and freely chose a variety of meanings for such content.

Reception analysis attempts to fill the holes in previous theorizing and research by looking at cultural and social patterns of media production and power relations between different groups. Some critics object, however, to the active nature it ascribes to audiences, claims that make media seem almost powerless.

DISCUSSION QUESTIONS: Identify your three favorite television shows or films in recent years, along with a brief sentence on why you like(d) each one. Compare lists with classmates, and discuss your choices. What do your similarities and differences tell you about each other?

FRAMING

We discussed **framing** briefly in Chapter 2, noting that the presentation of a message colors perceptions of it. The concept of framing appears widely in media studies and in other social sciences, such as sociology and psychology, sometimes in conjunction with media-studies research.

> **framing**
>
> The presentation and communication of a message in a particular way that influences our perception of it.

We use frames to make sense of the world in which we live, a set of filters that help us categorize and understand our social reality. Frames emerge through our daily interactions with media and are shaped by our culture and social norms. Often our exposure to certain issues and people is solely through media in various forms (news, entertainment, advertising, etc.), framing our perceptions even more.

Message framing can have a profound effect on behavior, depending on whether a message is framed as a gain or a loss. In 1984, psychologists Daniel Kahneman and Amos Tversky presented two different scenarios to different groups of participants who were asked to make a choice regarding a hypothetical disease outbreak expected to kill six hundred people. The "gain-framed" scenario emphasized saving lives: Option A would save two hundred people, whereas option B specified a one-third probability of saving everyone but a two-thirds probability of saving no one. Overwhelmingly, participants chose option A, which seemed the less risky choice.

Other participants were given "loss-framed" choices that emphasized lives lost: Option A would kill four hundred people, while option B had a one-third probability of killing no one but a two-thirds probability of killing everyone. A large majority of participants chose option B, the risky option. This difference in selection can be explained only by how the messages were framed because identical scenarios were presented to both groups.

The aspects of framing messages are more numerous and complex than one experiment can suggest. Still, Kahneman and Tversky's research has special implications for social marketing campaigns and strategic communications. When messages are framed in terms of potential gain, people choose what seems to be the safer option to pursue a guaranteed gain. When framed in terms of losses, however, people choose the riskier option to avoid a guaranteed loss.

Consider framing's role in a social marketing campaign for reducing a sexually transmitted disease like AIDS. If the message is framed in terms of potential loss rather than potential gain, people may actually opt for the riskier behavior (unprotected sex) than what sounds like a safer option. For example, a campaign that discusses the chances of dying from AIDS without using a condom may actually encourage unprotected sex, whereas a campaign that focuses on the benefits of condom use could promote that behavior. Of course, many more factors are involved in social marketing that targets public behavior, but a poorly chosen frame could doom a campaign from the start.

Another strand of research on mass communications, cultural studies, looks at media through broad cultural and social frameworks and media production.

Cultural Studies

The focus on culture and broader societal issues in relation to media, seen in reception-analysis research and the encoding/decoding model of Stuart Hall, falls within a category of scholarly research developed in the 1970s called **cultural studies**. Difficult to define concisely because of its wide range of research interests, this field has seen tremendous growth from the 1990s into the early part of the twenty-first century. More and more universities have created cultural-studies departments in recent years.

Cultural-studies approaches largely reject the media-effects research tradition and examine how meaning is produced not only among audiences but also among media producers. By looking at popular culture in its many facets and with a critical eye toward issues of power, dominance, and subordination, researchers hope to better understand the role of media in perpetuating these social relations.

European versions of cultural studies tend to be Marxist and highly critical of existing politics and culture, whereas North American versions are inclined to be less critical, even celebratory, of consumer culture and media. Despite these differences, cultural-studies research is typically more normative than descriptive. In other words, it seeks to improve society rather than simply describe it.

IDEOLOGY AND THE CULTURE INDUSTRY

The normative focus of cultural studies stems from its origins in **critical theory** and the Frankfurt School scholars who created critical theory in the 1930s and 1940s in Germany at the Institute for Social Research based in Frankfurt. Theodor Adorno, Max Horkheimer, Herbert Marcuse, and Walter Benjamin were German Marxist scholars with research interests ranging from music theory and philosophy to sociology.

The Frankfurt School coined the term "**culture industry**" to refer to how media businesses created mass-produced "cultural products" that were then consumed by the masses. They distinguished between "high art" (opera, classical music, etc.) and "popular art" (jazz, film, etc.), which they deemed crass, partly because of its commercial nature.

Although their particular views on art may be considered artistic snobbery, they advanced a larger political argument in that the culture industry propagates an **ideology** that helps maintain the status quo. In other words, it makes existing power relations and inequality seem natural while discouraging critical reflection among people—which they believed high art, on the other hand, encourages. In this view, media production is not simply a by-product or reflection of popular tastes and desires; it actively creates those desires and suppresses freedom.

The Frankfurt School scholars were not simply talking about authoritarian governments such as Nazi Germany, although their theory applied to these kinds of governments. They claimed that even supposedly "free market" democratic systems of government were not free at all because the media of mass communications promoted capitalist ideology while ignoring or downplaying the negative consequences of capitalist economies.

cultural studies

An interdisciplinary framework for studying communication that rejects the scientific approach while investigating the role of culture in creating and maintaining social relations and systems of power.

critical theory

A theoretical approach broadly influenced by Marxist notions of the role of ideology, exploitation, capitalism, and the economy in understanding and eventually transforming society.

culture industry

A term coined by the Frankfurt School to describe how media companies produce or "make" culture in the same way that other companies produce products.

ideology

A comprehensive and normative body of ideas and standards held by an individual or a group.

Max Horkheimer was a prominent member of the Frankfurt School and one of the founders of critical theory.

MEDIA PIONEERS
danah boyd

Looking at the intersection of technology and society in her research, as well as online youth culture and identity, media scholar danah boyd has enough academic titles to make her studies on identity seem like a personal quest. A senior researcher at Microsoft Research, a faculty affiliate at Harvard's Berkman Center for Internet & Society, and a visiting professor at New York University's Interactive Telecommunications Program, boyd divides her time equally among Redmond, Washington (Microsoft headquarters), Cambridge, Massachusetts, and New York.

She is also a prolific writer on social media, a frequent blogger, and a committed activist for a number of causes, especially with groups that focus on ending violence toward women. Social media are a primary focus as not only a participant but also a scholar who studies how young people incorporate social media such as Twitter and blogging into their everyday lives and practices. She is coauthor of *Hanging Out, Messing Around, and Geeking Out: Kids Living and Learning with New Media* (2010) and author of *It's Complicated: The Social Lives of Networked Teens* (2014).

Her research interests on identity are reflected in her legally changing her name, taking her maternal grandfather's last name and not capitalizing any letters. She has observed that English is one of the few languages to capitalize the personal pronoun "I" rather than keeping all pronouns lowercase or capitalizing other pronouns like "you" and "we." She maintains that a name is just another descriptor for someone; it is not the person herself.

"It's *my* name and i should be able to frame it as i see fit, as my adjective, not someone else's," she writes.[12] "Why must it follow some *New York Times* standard guide for naming? The words that i choose to describe myself should be framed in writing and in speech in a way that feels as though i own them, as though i can relate to them."

CRITICISMS OF CULTURAL STUDIES

Cultural studies, despite its popularity in academia, still has its detractors and faults. One common complaint is the often impenetrable, jargon-laden writing of many researchers, a style that excludes almost everyone but academics. This is at odds with their broad goal of transforming society by enlightening the public about its oppression and the part the media play in that oppression.

The writing style is also criticized for hiding muddled thinking and masking mundane ideas behind grandiose jargon. In 1996, a physicist at New York University, Alan Sokal, published an article in the postmodern journal *Social Text* entitled "Transgressing the Boundaries: Toward a Transformative Hermeneutics of Quantum Gravity." (Cultural studies is often situated under the larger rubric of postmodernism, a sprawling movement defined later in the chapter.) The title and prose were typical of many journal articles penned from a postmodern perspective, but Sokal's article was a hoax purposely composed to be nonsensical, suggesting the dangers of adopting merely fashionable or trendy schools of thought in general, and applying less-than-scientific perspectives to the physical sciences in particular.

In the same vein, other critics of cultural studies say that because it largely rejects scientific tenets such as the use of reason in finding truth, it cannot actually be called a science. And without any shared and consensual basis for measuring the validity of viewpoints, the cultural-studies perspective cannot actually prove or refute ideas in the same way and with the same authority of traditional scientific methods.

Sociohistorical Frameworks

Other theories draw on a variety of schools of thought, especially Marxism or critical theory, as well as a number of disciplines, such as sociology, anthropology, psychology, and even economics. These tend not to emphasize audiences as much as previous frameworks but examine instead the entire media system within larger social, political, and historical contexts. Some researchers claim that a primary focus on audiences neglects many of the most fundamental questions and answers regarding media and their effects on our world today.

INFORMATION SOCIETY

information society

A society where information production has supplanted industrial production, dramatically transforming cultural, economic, and political activity.

Social scientists continue to debate the meaning and nature of the **information society**, sometimes also labeled the network, knowledge, or postindustrial society. Information-society theories posit that the prominence of communications and media has ushered in a new era that breaks drastically from the industrial society. Networks become hugely important as they bring the world closer together; and economic value lies not so much in the old manufacturing centers, as it once did, but in knowledge centers. Education and training are key for workers, valued not for manual labor but for ideas, knowledge, and creativity that enable them to make sense of and create information.

The often-utopian picture painted by information-society theorists has elicited much criticism. Some scholars, especially those influenced by Marxism or critical theory, claim that the information society actually strengthens established relations of dominance as global media corporations control more media channels, including those on the Internet. They point to earlier media types such as radio that also initially promised to be emancipatory and chronicle the relentless governmental and corporate control that rendered new media claims to increased freedom and democracy largely hollow. One example of the enduring domination of elite interests is when companies barred WikiLeaks from receiving online donations after it released secret U.S. government diplomatic cables.

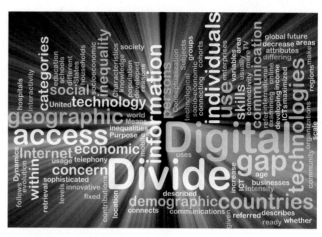

According to the Pew Research Center's "Fact Tank: News in the Numbers," 84 percent of U.S. households own a computer, but 21 percent of households have no regular access to the Internet at home or elsewhere.

A criticism of information-society theories is how they extrapolate from a small segment of the world's population. One does not have to look far to see that much of the world lives in conditions where access to clean water is rare, let alone the Internet or even electricity. This generates discussions regarding the **digital divide**, one of the most important Internet-audience issues today.

Research indicates that from the early days of public Internet, access tended to be much higher among society's economically advantaged—those with a higher education and with a legacy of higher overall print-media use. Economically disadvantaged groups, especially minority groups and the rural poor, enjoyed less Internet access and usage. With certain groups, this gap has closed dramatically if not disappeared. Women, for example, now make up the majority of Internet users in the United States—across economic lines. Problems of equity of access to online media will not be eliminated soon, however, especially among the economically disadvantaged and those in the developing world.

digital divide

The gap between regions and demographics that have access to modern, digital-communications technology and those that have limited or no access.

POLITICAL ECONOMY

Another area of media research inspired by Marxism and influenced by critical theory is **political economy**. These communication scholars examine the production and ownership of media that determine our media environment and its effects on our social and political systems.

Robert McChesney, for example, studies the history and current status of media ownership, regulations, and laws, especially how ownership conglomeration has affected types of media. Challenging claims of increased democracy and freedom, he argues that since the 1990s, corporate interests that influence government regulations and policy decisions have controlled the Internet at the expense of public interests.

According to political-economy scholars, examining media production—who owns what media companies, how their business decisions determine types of media, how they are delivered, to whom, and in what way—reveals the underlying forces that inform power relations and dominance. Unlike other forms of audience-studies research, a political-economic viewpoint can explore areas where an audience does not actually yet exist. For example, an audience-studies researcher would not be able to study Spanish-language newspaper readership in an area that is without a Spanish-language newspaper. But the question, "Why isn't there a Spanish-language newspaper in this market when 20 percent of the population is Hispanic?," would be a legitimate area of study for a political economist, as would exploring the content likely to be found in such a newspaper.

political economy

An area of study inspired by Marxism that examines the relationship between politics and economics with media ownership and the influences they all have on society and perpetuating the status quo.

MEDIA ECOLOGY

media ecology

The study of media environments and their effects on people and society.

Media ecology, as its name suggests, is the study of media environments and their effects on people and society. Just as an ecological system in nature is complex and can be studied from a number of perspectives or specialties (a chemist studying soil samples will see an ecosystem very differently than a biologist studying bear habitats), so too is media ecology. Media ecology examines how our media environment influences our thinking and how specific types of media affect our perceptions (medium theory).

Perhaps the most famous proponent of medium theory was Canadian scholar Marshall McLuhan, who coined the phrase "The medium is the message," arguing that the medium itself was more critical to our perception of the message than its content or its manner of production. His claims that electronic media had

INTERNATIONAL PERSPECTIVES
Theories Old, Theories New, Theories Borrowed . . .

Tracing the intellectual history of currently popular media research can be a fascinating exercise that improves our understanding of how theories may influence our thinking. Some widely believed theories in the past have since been proven false or flawed, but some older theories that never caught on have also been revived when it is later discovered they have a lot to offer current research.

One example concerns early sociologists who tried to study social behavior in relational, rather than objective, terms. For decades, much of this research was ignored, but now several sociological theories rely on relational or network-oriented ways of looking at the world. The terms early sociologists used may differ from those in current research, but many of the concepts can be surprisingly similar.

Most of the theoretical frameworks in media research derive from European schools of thought in the humanities or social sciences. The American-made school

Noted French sociologist Pierre Bourdieu wrote widely for the mainstream media in France.

of philosophical thought, pragmatism, was largely superseded by European schools of thought after the early part of the twentieth century, although some social theories still feature important aspects of pragmatism.

Many ostensibly "new" theories actually have deep roots in combinations of much older theories or are combinations of different theoretical schools, with unique insights introduced for greater relevance. Some of Europe's most interesting thinkers draw from a wide variety of sources to tackle social issues and the role of media in society, including philosophy, literary theory, history, economics, political theory, social theory, and cognitive science.

Scholars in some European countries are much more visible than their American counterparts. In France, for example, social theorists Michel Foucault and Pierre Bourdieu were virtually media celebrities in their own right, appearing on television to discuss theoretical issues and writing regularly on political and social topics for popular newspapers.

transformed the world into a "global village," free of the hierarchical and rigid power relations created by the culture of print media, echo what we hear about the Internet, even though he was speaking only of radio and television.

He has been faulted for espousing a form of **technological determinism**, the belief that technology causes certain human behaviors—a charge that some forms of media ecology must still address. Others also argue that by celebrating technology, he ignored (and thereby left unchallenged) the relations of power and dominance technological communication creates and perpetuates.

Despite these and other arguable weaknesses in his theories, McLuhan offered important and novel insights into how modern media affect our lives, particularly our sense of time and space. Some of his claims become even more important when considering digital media. Although technology may not be the most important component of media theory, the consequences of mass media's capacity to immediately send mass audiences the same messages are considerable.

technological determinism

The belief that technology causes certain human behaviors.

AGENDA SETTING

Agenda setting does not take as broad a view as the frameworks just mentioned, although this concept does relate directly to media messages and industries. In 1948, Paul F. Lazarsfeld and Robert K. Merton proposed that conferring status is one of the primary functions of the media. Singling someone out from the masses bestows prestige and authority on the person so identified: "The audiences of mass media apparently subscribe to the circular belief that if you matter, you will be at the focus of mass attention and, if you are at the focus of mass attention, then surely you must really matter."[13]

This assertion rings truer than ever today due to our growing mix of social and mass media. As agenda setters, the media can determine which issues are perceived as important and to what degree, depending on how prominently they present them. Political scientist Bernard Cohen clearly articulated the agenda-setting model: "The press may not be successful much of the time in telling people what to think, but it is stunningly successful in telling its readers what to think about."[14]

agenda setting

Media's role in deciding which topics to cover and consequently which topics the public deems important and worthy of discussion.

Television news shapes people's sense of which of the day's issues and events matter most, setting the agenda for public debate. In June 2015, a video of a police officer detaining a young girl at a pool party in McKinney, Texas sparked allegations of racism and fueled national conversation about police tactics.

In the 1970s, Max McCombs and Donald Shaw demonstrated that the media are especially effective at influencing public views on the importance of various issues. Moreover, McCombs and Shaw's research showed that different media play different roles in the agenda-setting process. Newspapers in particular have historically set the general agenda of public issues, determining which topics the public is likely to see as important, such as taxes, education, crime, or health care. Meanwhile, the electronic media of television and radio are especially effective at shaping the public's views on which of these issues are most important.

New Directions in Media Research

As digital and social media become fully integrated in our lives, new strands of research in the social sciences emerge in business communication, organization science, and library science, among many other fields.

Recent research has focused on the role of social media in activism and democracy. **CRITICAL THINKING QUESTIONS:** Have social media prompted you to participate in activist discussions or action? Would you record a protest event as it unfolds to post later on social media? In what circumstances might this make you feel vulnerable?

Scholarship on digital media is often complicated by the fact that technologies may change rapidly, transforming user behavior or making certain topics of study less relevant or obsolete. For instance, research on user behavior on Usenet may not have much to offer researchers examining identity formation and interactions through social media today. Research can become dated during the long lead time for publication in most peer-reviewed academic journals, typically twelve to eighteen months between submission and publication.

While scholars continue to study traditional media companies, more and more are researching aspects of digital and social media. Although classifying these diverse research areas is difficult, we can briefly survey some of the broad topics of current study.

Since the origin of the Internet, researchers have studied the impact of time spent online on both children and adults. Launched in 1999, the World Internet Project, the most comprehensive and longest-running study of its kind, examines the social, cultural, and commercial impact of the Internet. Funded by a consortium of major companies interested in online communication—such as Microsoft, America Online, Disney, and Sony—the study is headed by Jeffrey Cole, current director of the Center for the Digital Future at the USC Annenberg School for Communication and Journalism and former director of the UCLA Center for Communication Policy.

These researchers are following a group of subjects over twenty years to explore various questions such as how Internet use influences family time, political leanings, and social life. This **longitudinal study** also examines online banking, credit-card purchases, buying habits, and other issues related to ecommerce. International representatives have been added to the initial panel including two thousand people selected from a national sample.[15]

longitudinal study

A study that gathers data on subjects over a long period of time.

ETHICS IN MEDIA
Advertising's Negative Effects on the Sexes

Advertising is designed to persuade people in various ways to do various things. Usually, it encourages us to buy some product or service, but it can also aspire to change attitudes and beliefs about everything from practices such as smoking to the suitability of political candidates.

A large body of academic research examines the dark side of advertising, particularly its many unintended consequences. Author and filmmaker Jean Kilbourne has studied the image of women in advertising for over three decades, linking prevalent depictions to a number of public health issues such as eating disorders, addiction, and violence against women. Studies indicate that advertising can profoundly affect women's attitudes about their bodies and behavior. The beauty industry is particularly notorious for its almost exclusive use of ultra-thin models and other images airbrushed to perfection, unattainable ideals that make many women feel inadequate.

But what about men—are they equally affected by advertising? A growing body of research indicates they are. Whereas women are often depicted as dependent or submissive (or primarily sexual), men are usually portrayed as strong, confident, and independent, sending persuasive messages about how men should perform their gender roles.

Advertising often portrays men too as sex objects. Ads both promote sexual prowess and highlight sexual deficiencies (with the promise that the product advertised will fix those problems). And just like the largely unobtainable female bodies in ads geared toward women, men regularly

see ads featuring males with hairless chests, six-pack abs, and chiseled muscles.

If they are only advertisements—which most of us don't really notice—how seriously could they affect us? Consider, however, the 360,000 television commercials that a young adult has seen by the age eighteen and the ease with which we all recognize popular commercial jingles and tag lines.[16] Perhaps we absorb more than we realize. Consequently, advertisements and other media images, particularly those that objectify men and women or play on certain gender or ethnic stereotypes, raise important ethical questions about media effects and advertisers' responsibilities.

The Pew Research Center also frequently publishes insightful research on the Internet and social media in America, typically in the form of a **cross-sectional study** on attitudes and patterns of behavior with various technologies. In April 2015, for instance, they published reports on the use of smartphones and teen use of social media. Pew conducts certain surveys repeatedly over the years, providing interesting data about how behavior and attitudes have changed over time.

The evolving role of the audience in an interactive communication environment has also spurred research. The prevalence of user-generated content challenges the traditional relationship between the audience and media producers. This movement from viewer to user or produser affects media organizations and the presentation and prevalence of different kinds of news and entertainment.

 cross-sectional study

A study that gathers data on subjects at a specific point in time.

Scholars interested in politics have found a rich source of new material to study online. Early optimism about the democratizing potential of the Internet has been tempered by more realistic views, notably the recognition that the Internet also aids governments and corporations in surveillance of citizens and consumers. In 2013, game-changing documents leaked by former NSA analyst Edward Snowden made the extent of this surveillance shockingly clear. Further revelations in the media involved Internet and telecommunications giants like Google and AT&T secretly sharing consumer data with the government.

Research on social media in social movements has become popular, thanks in part to the Arab Spring, the Occupy Wall Street protests, and popular protests in Turkey and Brazil in 2013. Activists draw inspiration from other parts of the world, sharing information and encouragement while promoting solidarity and common goals. Still, the initial enthusiasm for the empowering aspects of social media has waned in recent years, as many social movements failed to achieve their stated goals in the face of various forms of government oppression.

Recent media research has examined issues surrounding social-networking sites. Areas of study include identity formation and presentation: issues related to privacy, anonymity, and the use of fake names or usernames. Some research relates to perceptions of the self, including the idea of the "networked self" in which we see ourselves as part of communities connected by networks of communication rather than as individuals largely unaffected by our communication and social interactions.

Researchers are studying how the increasing popularity of video games may reinforce gender or racial stereotypes, how they may affect our sense of identity, whether we can learn better through game playing than traditional means, and other facets of the gaming world. The effect of violent video games on children has been studied less, though, than the impact of violent television programming.

All these areas of research draw from a broad swath of humanities and social science disciplines, including literary theory, history, ethics, political communication, psychology, sociology, anthropology, and economics. Because media research crosses multiple disciplines, media scholars today must become familiar with a broad range of knowledge, a trend likely to continue.

> **DISCUSSION QUESTIONS:** In which online communities do you experience a networked self connected to other members through social communication? Do you think a requirement to use real names enhances a sense of genuine connection among members? What do you think constitutes a real or authentic identity online?

Media Research: What Type of Science Is It?

epistemology

A study or theory of the limitations and validity of knowledge; more simply, a way of, or framework for, understanding the world.

Asking what type of science media research provides may seem odd, but this question raises several important issues about media studies. At the heart of the matter is whether the social sciences, such as psychology, sociology, and anthropology, can (and should) be conducted according to the rules of the natural or physical sciences.

For most of their histories as individual disciplines, the social sciences have tried to emulate the rules and methods of hard sciences, but whether this can be done properly or at all remains debatable. Is it possible to discover the same kind of natural laws for communication and media that we see in the natural sciences, such as a law of gravity? More importantly, in trying to copy scientific models that may be inappropriate for the social sciences, are we missing the point and asking the wrong questions about our social world?

The confusion about where to locate media-studies research as a form of inquiry is also reflected in the range of schools and departments where it can be found. Sometimes media studies reside within a school of journalism; other universities may locate it in a school of communications or even in an English department. To further complicate matters, scholars trained in sociology and psychology or other fields such as literary theory are responsible for much important research and theorizing on mass media and communication. Mathematicians actually developed the hugely influential transmission model of communication (discussed in Chapter 1) to help solve an engineering problem.

Broadly speaking, the debate on the type of science media research should entail can be divided into two main camps, each with a different way of understanding the world, a distinct **epistemology**. **Positivism,** the dominant epistemology throughout the twentieth century, assumes an objective reality that can be observed, measured, and explained by a neutral observer. Rigorous testing and experimentation following the scientific method can prove or disprove hypotheses based on observations. Related theorizing may improve our understanding of the world and our ability to predict behaviors or alter phenomena with predictable results.

Several other epistemologies reject positivism in varying degrees. **Postpositivism** largely agrees with most positivist claims but also recognizes knowledge that cannot be understood through scientific means, such as religious faith.

Social constructionism argues that all meaning and truth are derived from social interactions, especially those involving symbols and signs, whose meanings are relativistic and change with context. Language is not simply a transparent medium that describes the world; it creates the world as we know it.

Postmodernism, although it has many variants, largely eschews grand theorizing and what it calls "metanarratives," overarching narratives that try to explain the world, because any such metanarrative essentially favors one worldview over others. It, like social constructionism, questions the formation of knowledge and challenges the assumption of positivist science that it is a better (or the only) way to find and establish truth.

Some of the basic elements of constructionist and postmodern thought are not entirely new or simply a reaction to the dominance of positivist science in the twentieth century. Their histories can be traced back to early philosophical traditions and later influential schools of thought in the nineteenth and early twentieth centuries, like **pragmatism,** which affirms truth in actions that work and rejects overarching or purely objective notions of truth. In some ways, such thinking is a return to the roots of theorizing about the role of media and communication.

The debate about what type of science media-studies research falls under can also be roughly mapped to the two main types of current research methodologies: **quantitative research** and **qualitative research**.

positivism

A view, common among scientists in the physical or natural sciences and many social sciences, that affirms an objective reality to be discovered and explained through rigorous scientific research.

postpositivism

A view that agrees largely with positivism but also recognizes knowledge that may not be revealed through scientific inquiry.

social constructionism

A view that claims much or all of what we know and understand about the world, including scientific knowledge, is constructed through social interactions and language.

postmodernism

A broad category of viewpoints that rejects grand narratives attempting to explain the world and absolute truths because truth is relative and unknowable.

pragmatism

A school of thought affirming truths found in actions that work and rejecting the possibility of overarching or purely objective notions of truth.

quantitative research

A method of inquiry favored in the physical sciences that focuses on numerical data and statistical measures to describe phenomena. Researchers often attempt to prove or disprove a hypothesis through the empirical method, particularly controlled experimentation.

qualitative research

A method of inquiry favored in the social sciences that explores typically unstructured phenomena through interviews, focus groups, and participant observation among other techniques that produce descriptive rather than predictive results.

QUANTITATIVE RESEARCH

Researchers relying heavily on quantitative techniques tend to have a positivist perspective. They assume that their research will better predict behavior, find causal effects for certain phenomena, and support or weaken certain media theories.

Quantitative studies include the familiar methods of experiments, surveys, and statistical analyses. The exact method depends on several factors, especially the goals or purposes of the research. If a study intends to suggest causality, such as whether watching violent TV programming increases violence among children, then experimental or quasi-experimental methods could be appropriate. If a study means to document the amount of violence on television, then a content analysis should be conducted. If an investigation is designed to determine how much televised violence children can recall, then a survey may be in order.

In any case, research methods are never perfect indicators, and the design of the study as well as the particular method can affect results. For example, conducting a laboratory experiment with children on the effects of television violence not only raises important ethical questions, it also creates an unrealistic media environment that makes accurate measurements problematic. The laboratory, no matter the extent to which it is altered to look and feel like a home, still cannot capture the range of environmental factors in a normal viewing experience.

Analyzing data using statistics raises its own set of problems, including incomplete or missing data that may skew results, **sampling error** that does not accurately reflect the entire population, and faulty study design that yields misleading findings. Consider a simple example of sampling error. Let's say you want to learn what students at your school think about a certain issue. You stand in the quad during the day, stopping every fifth person to ask your questions. This may seem like a **random sample**, in which every person has an equally probable chance of being selected, but in fact you have not accurately captured a sample that represents the entire student body. What about students who do not pass by the quad to get to their classes, such as those in other campus locations, or those who take only night classes?

These and other methodological difficulties with quantitative research have encouraged the growth and acceptance of qualitative research methods.

QUALITATIVE RESEARCH

Qualitative researchers may reject the assumptions behind quantitative research, or they may simply appreciate the limitations of such research and prefer other means to explore their areas of interest. They are generally not trying to make predictions but are focusing on description to gain a better understanding of the world as the participants see it. Qualitative research can include in-depth interviews, focus groups, and ethnography, among other techniques.

Ethnography involves a technique developed in anthropology in which researchers immerse themselves in a culture to observe it directly in its natural state while disrupting it as little as possible. An ethnographer might enter a household, a newsroom, or an advertising agency and spend hours, days, weeks, or even

sampling error

Error in a statistical analysis that results from selecting a sample that does not represent the entire population.

random sample

A sample in which every person has an equally probable chance of being selected, intended to represent the entire population of study.

ethnography

A variety of qualitative research techniques that involve immersion of a researcher in a particular culture to allow interaction with participants through observation, participation, interviews, or a combination of methods.

Focus-group research can provide rich insights into consumer opinions of products or issues.

months directly observing media behaviors of those involved, documenting these in note and transcript form and likely video and audio recordings. A detailed analysis would follow. The results might be used in isolation or in combination with other methods, such as interviews or even quantitative techniques such as content analysis of conversations or written memos.

A variation of ethnography is **participant-observation**. In this technique, researchers join the group they are studying, such as a fan club or an online multiplayer video game. The researcher's status as a participant not only helps better understand the world that researcher is observing but also encourages participants to disclose more than they might otherwise to an outsider.

Focus groups are widely employed by media researchers. Often, how such participants interact and discuss what is being studied provides important insights that the researcher would not glean from individual interviews or surveys. Marketers testing consumer reactions to their brand or products favor focus groups.

Qualitative research raises its own ethical concerns and is not without weaknesses. One question is whether participants should be informed of the researcher's true role. Many would consider posing as a genuine member of a group to gain the trust of others and generate research material unethical behavior. Transparency is especially important when researching groups online where the researcher's identity may not be obvious. Another ethical issue arises when researchers see participants engaging in risky or dangerous behavior. Do they try to intervene, thus altering research findings, or simply continue to observe?

Qualitative research makes no claims, of course, to being generalizable to the larger population or being reliable in the sense of getting the same results if conducted by another researcher or with another group, even under similar circumstances. Researchers need to identify the limitations of their qualitative research and avoid, for example, representing data from a particular set of interviews like that from a quantitative random sample.

participant-observation

A qualitative research technique in which researchers participate as members of the group they are observing.

focus group

A small group of people assembled by researchers to discuss a topic. Their interactions are closely observed, recorded, and analyzed to determine people's opinions.

QUALITATIVE AND QUANTITATIVE RESEARCH WORKING TOGETHER

Each methodology has its place in media research, and each methodology has its strengths and weaknesses. Ignoring one methodology over another because of a philosophical disagreement can create a blind spot for a researcher seeking comprehensive knowledge. A screwdriver can pound a nail, but a hammer works much better. Selecting the right tool from the methodological toolbox is the first step to research success.

Qualitative techniques often provide greater depth or texture to quantitative studies. In designing a survey, for example, you may not really know what issues your research subjects find important or even how they talk about certain things. Common themes may emerge from qualitative research that can then help you design a better survey. Simple observation of certain media behaviors often yields fertile insights that generate even more interesting research questions. Noting, for example, who controls the remote control in the living room may reveal something more significant about television viewing habits than specific program preferences.

Qualitative research, if conducted properly, helps you see the world creatively from other perspectives in ways foreign to quantitative research. Quantitative research, on the other hand, with its statistical techniques and its claims to represent a much larger population than that studied, is extremely powerful. People can often be persuaded of the veracity of results by simply viewing data presented in a seemingly authoritative chart or graph.

> **DISCUSSION QUESTIONS:** Have you ever been involved in a study involving media or some other field such as psychology? Identify whether this was qualitative or quantitative inquiry and, more specifically, what type: a survey, a focus group, or an experiment, for example. Describe your experience and why you decided to participate.

MEDIA CAREERS

Those interested in media research can choose from two main paths: corporate or academic. Teams of researchers work with various clients at large advertising and PR agencies, and media research underlies many important organizational decisions when determining everything from what shows to produce to which ads were most effective. In corporate research, various quantitative and qualitative methods are used to achieve fairly specific goals. In other words, you are generally trying to find answers to specific questions such as which campaign generated higher sales or better product recall.

Academic research also has goals, of course, but these can be more open-ended and exploratory, allowing the pursuit of knowledge for the sake of simply learning and sharing new insights within the scholarly community. Most academic media researchers have doctorate degrees and also teach at the schools where they conduct research. A PhD is helpful in corporate research but not necessary. For students interested in media research, even the academic track, some professional communications experience can prove invaluable, fostering a general understanding of media industries while generating particular questions of interest and relevance to media research.

LOOKING BACK AND MOVING FORWARD

As may be expected of a relatively new medium, large gaps remain in research and theory about digital media and the Internet. Early euphoria about the positive transformative effects of the Internet for society and democracy have given way to more measured, cautious statements that also recognize dangers or weak spots. The concerns about exposure to television and movie violence could be amplified when considering the amount of fictionalized and actual violent acts on the Internet.

Some scholars claim that nothing has fundamentally changed with the rise of the Internet and digital media; from a theoretical perspective, existing conceptual frameworks remain perfectly adequate for researching and explaining new media. Although true in some cases, this position creates large blind spots in a research agenda that should attempt to address the evolving nature of mass communication.

Researchers who focus on digital media tend to draw heavily from research traditions in media studies, sociology, information science, and communication studies, among other disciplines. These research frameworks correspond more or less to those applied to traditional media, ranging from the broad sociocultural perspectives to the more narrow use-and-effects research. Researchers also study how characteristics of the medium itself, such as interactivity, may affect our relation with content.

Curiously, some pre-Internet scholars could experience a revival of interest in certain lines of their work. Marshall McLuhan, for example, may have much to offer digital-media scholars, particularly his examination of the ways electronic media implode space and time and affect social relations. Uses-and-gratifications principles may prove especially fruitful in an interactive medium where users largely control what content they can get and how they get it. Political economy raises even more important questions about how powerful media companies can actually increase their control over public media systems, even as popular ideology claims that we have more freedom than ever.

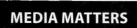

MEDIA MATTERS   THEORY AND PRACTICE

1. What does the term "information society" mean to you?

2. Do you think advertising affects your decisions? Why or why not? Do you think it affects other people? If so, who is most affected, and why?

3. Do you feel that media can influence us? Why or why not? Which types of media are most influential, and why?

4. Do you believe there is an objective reality "out there" that we can describe and all agree on, or do you believe that each of us creates his or her own reality? Explain your response.

5. How and to what extent did your parents or guardians supervise your television viewing? Your time on the computer?

FURTHER READING

Critical Media Studies: An Introduction, 2nd ed. Brian Ott, Robert Mack (2014) Wiley-Blackwell.

Media Studies: Theories and Approaches. Dan Laughey (2010) Oldcastle Books.

Media Effects Research: A Basic Overview, 4th ed. Glenn G. Sparks (2012) Cengage Learning.

Media Effects: Advances in Theory and Research, 3rd ed. Jennings Bryant, Mary Beth Oliver (eds.) (2008) Routledge.

Quantitative Research Methods for Communication: A Hands-On Approach. Jason Wrench, Candice Thomas-Maddox, Virginia Peck Richmond, James McCroskey (2008) Oxford University Press.

Understanding Media Theory. Kevin Williams (2003) A Hodder Arnold Publication.

Understanding Media Cultures: Social Theory and Mass Communication. Nicholas Stevenson (2002) Sage.

Anthropology and Mass Communication: Media and Myth in the New Millennium. Mark Allen Peterson (2003) Berghahn Books.

Orality and Literacy. Walter J. Ong (2002) Routledge.

Manufacturing Consent: The Political Economy of the Mass Media. Edward S. Herman, Noam Chomsky (2002) Pantheon Books.

Media and Cultural Studies: Keyworks, 2nd ed. Meenakshi Gigi Durham and Douglas Kellner (eds.) (2012) Wiley-Blackwell.

Critical Theories of Mass Media: Then and Now. Paul Taylor, Jan Harris (2007) Open University Press.

More Than Meets the Eye: Watching Television Watching Us. John J. Pungente, Martin O'Malley (1999) McClelland & Stewart.

Understanding Media: The Extensions of Man. Marshall McLuhan (1994) MIT Press.

Communication, Media, and American Society: A Critical Introduction. Daniel W. Rossides (2002) Rowman & Littlefield.

Theories of the Information Society, 2nd ed. Frank Webster (2002) Routledge.

A Networked Self: Identity, Community, and Culture on Social Network Sites. Zizi Papacharissi (ed.) (2010) Routledge.

An Invitation to Social Construction, 2nd ed. Kenneth Gergen (2009) Sage.

E-Crit: Digital Media, Critical Theory, and the Humanities. Marcel O'Gorman (2007) University of Toronto Press.

Ethnography: A Way of Seeing. Harry F. Wolcott (1999) Rowman & Littlefield.

Netnography: Doing Ethnographic Research Online. Robert V. Kozinets (2010) Sage.

Dark Fiber: Tracking Critical Internet Culture. Geert Lovink (2003) MIT Press.

Mass Communication and Politics in the Digital Age

A lthough a new kind of political action committee (PAC) came into existence in July 2010, it wasn't until the 2012 presidential and congressional election that people really started talking about so-called Super PACs and their potentially harmful effects on the election process.

Technically called an independent expenditure-only committee, a Super PAC differs from a regular PAC in that it can accept unlimited donations from individuals, corporations, unions, and associations. Traditional PACs can accept only limited funds from individuals and nothing from the other groups. Also, unlike a traditional PAC, a Super PAC cannot contribute directly to a politician's campaign. Consequently, it can spend the money any way it sees fit to advocate for a favored candidate.

Even though Super PACs cannot give directly to candidates and are supposed to operate independently from the candidate or staff, many are run by former staff members or aides who have other close ties to the candidates they support. On *The Colbert Report*, Stephen Colbert famously mocked these relationships—and some of the legal loopholes that Super PACs enjoy—as he "transferred" his Super PAC power to Jon Stewart (the episode won a Peabody Award). Colbert actually did create a Super PAC called Americans for a Better Tomorrow, Tomorrow, which had raised $1.2 million by election day, even though he spent only a fraction of the money.[1]

But other Super PACs did spend, for a total of $1.3 billion during the presidential and congressional election in 2012. Despite two-thirds of Super PAC funds supporting Republican candidates in various races, the results proved disappointing for many of those so invested. Karl Rove's Super PAC, American Crossroads, endorsed eight Republican Senate candidates to the tune of $104.7 million; only two won their races. The National Rifle Association spent $11 million; none of their candidates prevailed.[2]

In the 2014 election cycle, Super PACs had received more than $688 million and spent about $344 million as reported in January 2015, according to the

Center for Responsive Politics. About 67 percent of the advertising expenditures were for negative ads.[3]

How Super PACs might influence the 2012 presidential election was a source of great concern. Yet the dramatic amounts they spent—and the barrage of negative advertising they funded—apparently did little to produce winners.

Stephen Colbert's Super PAC illustrates some of the recent dramatic changes in media and politics. Since the earliest days of the republic, the media have been intimately involved in our political process. The colonial newspapers were a **partisan press**, typically aligned with a particular political party and presenting information that helped its cause, with no sense of objectivity or balance in news coverage. Media also aided the Revolutionary cause. Fiery pamphlets such as Thomas Paine's *Common Sense* helped persuade colonists that they were fighting for a just and noble cause.

Yet more than journalism drives the engine of media and politics. Political advertising, particularly on television, is how most candidates, particularly presidential candidates, reach most voters most often. Negative political advertising, a mainstay of politics in the United States, has been extensively researched. Political advertising also provides substantial income for media organizations and has made it necessary for political candidates to raise large sums of money from donations.

Entertainment has played an increasingly important role in helping political candidates create a more down-to-earth image. Appearances on late-night talk shows and even comedy shows like *Saturday Night Live* are now becoming the norm; and "fake news" shows, such as *The Daily Show* and *The Colbert Report,* often provide political news, particularly for young people.

The Internet and social media have also transformed politics and political elections. Some candidates have used these effectively to fundraise and communicate their messages directly to the public rather than through the media. Social media and the Internet are not only important sources of information, they also a means by which members of the public can organize quickly and effectively regarding causes or candidates.

Entertainment plays a powerful role in creating likable, down-to-earth images of our political figures. Michelle Obama quickly became a YouTube sensation after performing "The Evolution of Mom Dancing" on *Late Night with Jimmy Fallon,* receiving over 16 million views.

Journalism and Political Coverage

Journalism has long considered itself the main conduit of political information for the public and therefore key to democratic processes. Journalism claims to be the mechanism for obtaining public unbiased and impartial information about candidates for office, sitting elected officials, the agencies they represent and operate, and relevant contemporary political issues—in other words, journalism aspires to be an engine of democracy.

Consider the words of Joseph Pulitzer, the former publisher of the *New York World* and the founder of the Pulitzer Prize, the highest award for journalistic excellence. In his proposal for founding a school of journalism, Pulitzer summarized his credo: "Our Republic and its press will rise or fall together. An able, disinterested, public-spirited press, with trained intelligence to know the right and courage to do it, can preserve that public virtue without which popular government is a sham and a mockery. A cynical, mercenary, demagogic press will produce in time a people as base as itself. The power to mold the future of the Republic will be in the hands of the journalists of future generations."[4]

Although most journalists aim to report the news fairly and in a balanced way, media critics contend the media are anything but unbiased. They claim that media companies can hardly be considered disinterested, given they, like most for-profit companies, have vested self-interests in pro-business government regulations and policies.

Like other industries, the media industry lobbies politicians to vote in favor of laws or regulations that favor the industry or key players. During the debates about the Stop Online Piracy Act (SOPA) and Protect Intellectual Property Act (PIPA) of 2012, many of the biggest media and telecom companies—such as Comcast, Disney, and News Corp., who own networks NBC, ABC, and Fox, respectively—spent tens of thousands of dollars on lobbyists.

In another example, dozens of news organizations, including the *Washington Post, Politico*, Fox News, NBC News, ABC News, and *USA Today*, vigorously lobbied the FCC to prevent greater transparency regarding political spending on advertisements. In April 2012, the FCC approved greater access to databases of such information, but with several restrictions. The rule would apply only to the big four television networks (NBC, ABC, CBS, and Fox) in the top fifty media markets and would expire after two years.

Given that news organizations frequently call for more transparency from the government and organizations they cover, critics find it hypocritical that these same organizations do not want the same level of scrutiny regarding advertising revenues they receive from political campaigns. Their stated reasons for opposing the measure ranged from difficulties and added costs of compiling and posting the information to creating an atmosphere that might hurt their deals with other advertisers.

Critics also see **media bias** in political news coverage and in the types and the coverage of news stories in general. The critics say that complex topics often do not get the airtime or depth of treatment required to truly inform the public. Instead, the media focus more on simpler topics, features on political personalities or exposés of scandals. Existing coverage of policy issues and other important matters often lacks context and historical information that aid public understanding.

Budget cuts have also affected news coverage of politics, with many big-city newspapers closing their Washington bureaus and relying for their political news on wire services. The more general wire-service coverage can miss important specific points that a Washington-based local reporter might otherwise be able to report on. Even for small-town newspapers, cuts in staff may mean less or even no coverage of politics at the state or even local level, leaving the public less informed on local issues that often affect them most directly.

> **media bias**
>
> A real or perceived viewpoint held by journalists and news organizations that slants news coverage unfairly, contrary to professional journalism's stated goals of balanced coverage and objectivity.

DISCUSSION QUESTIONS: Do you agree with Joseph Pulitzer's statement on the importance of the press in preserving American democracy? Why or why not? What trends and events both historical and current support your views?

Politicians often use journalists and their need for scoops to test proposals or to hurt opponents.

POLITICIANS USING THE NEWS

Public figures such as politicians are media savvy and use the news media to their advantage. If possible, many officials will not, for example, announce bad news until late Friday afternoon, the end of a workweek when most people do not following the news as closely. Media organizations will also have more trouble contacting sources for interviews and accessing information over the weekend to follow up on the story. The hope is that by Monday morning, their bad news will be largely forgotten and new stories will be of greater interest. Of course, this strategy does not always work. Sometimes stories have enough weight to carry through the weekend and become even bigger if more information is uncovered.

A public figure may use a **news leak** for many purposes. Giving a journalist exclusive and secret information helps build the relationship between a journalist and the official as a good source of information. More importantly, it can strategically damage opponents or even halt certain programs or projects. Providing news leaks is a dangerous game, however, for giving someone confidential or classified information often entails breaking the law. If the person giving the information is discovered, he or she can be sentenced to prison, depending on the severity of the case.

Similar to news leaks, politicians may use a **trial balloon** to test **public opinion** on proposals they are considering. A politician may announce plans for a new industrial park, even though no plans have been finalized. The subsequent media coverage and public discussion may reveal who might oppose the plan and whether it would be politically damaging to move forward with it.

Journalists are not naive about these techniques, of course. A journalist may fully realize why a politician is providing an exclusive scoop on a new budget proposal, but publishing the story also helps the news organization beat its competition, and the story itself may be newsworthy.

The symbiotic relationship between politicians and journalists is especially evident during elections, with both parties in the public eye. Television has changed political campaign coverage in important ways, as have polls.

news leak

Secret information deliberately given to journalists with the hope that they will publish the item.

trial balloon

Leaking information to the press about a proposed plan or idea to see how the public will respond.

public opinion

The notion that the public, as a group, can form shared views or ideas about topics and that these ideas guide the public's actions.

SOUND BITES AND HORSE RACES

With the rise of electronic media in the past half-century, especially television, political communication and debate in the media have become increasingly superficial. More often than not, the horse-race aspect of the campaign—chronicling who's ahead, who's behind, and what their latest campaign tactic might be to move ahead in the polls—becomes the whole story, at the expense of coverage of issues. Critics claim news coverage of campaigns essentially disenfranchises voters, making them jaded about politics and less willing to participate politically. Emphasizing campaign strategies and depicting politicians as those who will do and say anything just to get elected increases public cynicism and apathy.

Another highly criticized aspect of campaign coverage has to do with the nature of television. In 1968, Kiku Adatto of Harvard University did a study on political **sound bites**—specifically, how long a source in a television news story was allowed to speak without editing. In 1968, the average sound bite was 42.3 seconds. Nearly a quarter of all political sound bites were at least a minute in length, providing considerable room for context. Twenty years later, in 1988, the average TV sound bite of a political candidate had shrunk by some 80 percent to just 9.8 seconds, and virtually none were a minute or longer—in fact, entire stories were often not a minute in length.[5] This greatly reduces the context news can provide, let alone adequate facts about complex political issues.

> **sound bite**
>
> The length of time a news subject is allowed to speak without editing. It also has come to refer to short, catchy utterances designed to capture media attention.

THE CHANGING TONE OF TELEVISION POLITICAL COVERAGE

The overall tone of television political coverage has also changed. Consider the research findings of Syracuse University political scientist Thomas Patterson, author of *Out of Order*. He found that in the 1960 presidential election, three-quarters (75 percent) of the news reports about leading candidates John F. Kennedy and Richard M. Nixon were positive in tone; only a quarter (25 percent) were negative. Thirty-two years later, in the 1992 presidential election, news reports had become predominantly negative. More than half (60 percent) of the reports about then-candidate Bill Clinton and then-president George H. W. Bush were negative, and less than half (40 percent) were positive. Patterson's research also shows that the length of candidate statements in election stories on the front page of the *New York Times* had shrunk. In 1960, the average quote was fourteen lines. In 1992, it was less than seven lines.

Has the rise of online news changed this situation? Not much. Although research evidence is still scant, much of the online political coverage is lifted and repurposed from other media, including television, radio, newspapers, and magazines. The sound bites and quotes are the same.

Many of the better online news operations, such as CBS News online, typically augment stories adapted from on-air coverage, turning the text of a sixty-second video clip (less than two hundred words perhaps) into a five-hundred-word or longer report with greater depth. More quotes may be added, or quotes repeated from the broadcast text may be extended. Much of the additional reporting is drawn from wire-service copy (e.g., Reuters, the Associated Press) pulled off the Internet or sometimes from original interviews conducted via telephone or email. Increasingly, graphics such as maps are integrated as well.

OPINION POLLS

Increasingly, **opinion polls** drive campaign coverage. Patterson's research indicates that news becomes more favorable as poll support rises markedly or a candidate's lead widens. Conversely, media coverage becomes more negative if the candidate trails significantly or his or her poll standing drops.

Media organizations usually use one of several professional polling organizations, such as Gallup, to conduct polls. These organizations try to take random samples of the public to assess what the population as a whole is feeling about a candidate or an issue. Lower telephone response rates in recent years, as people screen calls to avoid telemarketers, have made conducting telephone polls more

> **opinion poll**
>
> Usually conducted by a professional polling organization, a poll asking members of the public their opinions on issues or political candidates.

:The Upshot Senate Forecasts   Overview   Other Forecasts   Changes   About

Who Will Win The Senate?

According to our statistical election-forecasting machine, the **Republicans** have a moderate edge, with about a **75% chance** of gaining a majority.

Tweet or Share on Facebook

Final update Tuesday, November 4 at 2:13 PM EST.
Visit elections.nytimes.com for results.

The Upshot from *The New York Times* used a statistical model, including poll data, to correctly predict Republicans would win a majority in the Senate in the 2014 midterm elections. **CRITICAL THINKING QUESTIONS:** Do you think polls influence election results? Are you less likely to vote if polling data indicate your candidate is unlikely to win?

expensive. In contrast to the more random telephone sample, online polls represent only users who have visited the website and choose to answer the poll. And, although not considered scientifically valid, they appear increasingly on news websites, and their results may be mistakenly assumed to accurately represent the point of view of the general populace.

Although the profile of the average Internet user is evolving as demographic diversity increases, a higher percentage of Internet users are likely to be white, male, and more affluent than average. Moreover, an online poll taken by a politically conservative entity, such as Fox News, will usually show vastly different results than the same poll taken by a politically liberal entity, such as MSNBC. Some polling organizations, such as Harris Interactive, conduct online polls, efforts that other organizations and the American Association for Public Opinion Research (AAPOR) typically deride as nonscientific.

Sometimes telephone "polls," called **push polls**, are actually political advertising. Push polls try to sway voters by giving them false or misleading information about opposing candidates under the guise of conducting a poll, or they try to make a candidate look good by asking leading questions. Push polls ask deliberately misleading questions such as "Would you support the policies of a candidate who will curtail some of our freedoms and raise taxes?" Few would answer "yes" to such a question, but the respondent may not realize that the pollster was referring to a certain candidate when asking it. Nevertheless, the publicized poll results would indicate that "90 percent of the people polled say they do not support Candidate Y."

push poll

A type of political advertising that appears to be a telephone poll but is actually a telemarketing campaign to sway voters by making a favored candidate look good or by misrepresenting the opposition.

DISCUSSION QUESTIONS: Compare two or three online political polls from organizations with different political positions, such as Fox News and MSNBC. How much did polling results on similar issues differ? Can you detect any bias in how the questions were framed? Which poll do you find more credible, and why?

Political Advertising

Candidates have historically employed a wide variety of techniques to reach as many people as possible directly, from whistle-stop speeches to political rallies. Partly due to the shrinking sound bite; the poll-driven, horse race, media coverage of campaigns; and a growing desire to control their own messages, candidates have turned increasingly to paid advertising. Campaigning has become increasingly expensive in the United States, as campaigns and technology become more complex and candidates attempt to reach voters through the media.[6]

The 2012 presidential election was the second in which the candidates raised more than $1 billion (the first was 2008), although in 2012 that also counts Super PACs, not immediately connected to the campaigns. As Table 13-1 shows, official campaign (not Super PAC) media expenditures represented more than half of all expenditures. Print media were the big loser in 2012, down from 2008

TABLE 13-1 2012 Presidential Campaign Expenditures

Media expenditures	Media consultants		$323,482,876
	Broadcast media		$307,484,203
	Internet media		$104,694,680
	Miscellaneous media		$27,382,641
	Print media		$2,380,760
		Total for media	$765,425,160
Nonmedia expenditures	Salaries and benefits		$93,996,097
	Travel		$73,701,465
	Postage/shipping		$36,089,762
	Rent/utilities		$13,063,452
	Campaign events		$34,519,202
	Polling/surveys/research		$32,391,152
	Fundraising direct mail/telemarketing		$95,518,174
	Other nonmedia		$213,613,251
		Total for nonmedia	$592,892,555
		Overall total	$1,358,317,715

Source: OpenSecrets.org, http://www.opensecrets.org/pres12/expenditures.php, July 26, 2013.
Note: Based on Federal Election Commission data released electronically on Monday, March 25, 2013.

expenditures, and broadcast media also had lower expenditures compared to 2008. However, the $1.3 billion spent by Super PACs, much of it on advertising, could account for the lower expenditures by the campaigns themselves.

The money candidates need to run for national or even state offices is so great partly because of the cost of political advertising. Although many criticize the way campaigning has changed in U.S. elections, with huge costs being one major complaint, many media companies benefit greatly from political advertising. They are unlikely to lobby to change a system that helps their bottom line, especially when advertising revenues in general have been down.

Political campaign expenditures will only increase over time. In the 2014 midterm elections, candidates and PACs spent nearly $1 billion (more than $933 million), what would in the past have been an "off" year in campaign spending. If Hillary Rodham Clinton, former first lady, senator, and secretary of state, runs for president in 2016, her campaign spending could top a whopping $1.7 billion.[7]

IMPACT OF NEGATIVE ADVERTISING

Some claim that political advertising is no different than other product advertising, except that a political campaign precedes a one-day sale—the election. This mentality drives the industry, and many candidates gravitate toward negative advertising. Based on an examination of more than 1,100 political commercials, political-communications scholar Larry Sabato concluded the following:

> Even when television is used to communicate political truth (at least from one candidate's perspective), the truth can be negatively packaged—attacking the opponent's character and record rather than supporting one's own. If there is a single trend obvious to most American consultants, it is the increasing proportion of negative political advertising. . . . At least a third of all spot commercials in recent campaigns have been negative, and in a minority of campaigns half or more of the spots are negative in tone or substance.[8]

Although some paid political spots on television simply provide information about the candidate and her or his position on the issues, most criticism and research have addressed ads that attack the opposing candidate. The rise of negative political advertising has also led news media to focus more of their coverage on the candidates' advertising.

Negative political advertising has been problematic for a number of reasons. One of the biggest concerns, Kathleen Hall Jamieson points out, is that many ads promote falsehoods or encourage the audience to make false inferences.[9] President Obama had no qualms about running negative advertising against Republican candidate Mitt Romney in the 2012 election. Negative summer ads, which helped frame Romney as a corporate raider and wealthy elitist, are credited with raising unfavorable impressions of Romney 6 percentage points, at a time when his campaign lacked sufficient funds to respond. Romney's campaign eventually fired back with ads that portrayed Obama as a failed manager of the economy.

EFFECTIVENESS OF NEGATIVE ADVERTISING

Researchers Richard Lau and Lee Sigelman tested three hypotheses regarding negative political advertisements: (1) that they work (i.e., they get voters to

ETHICS IN MEDIA
Can Imagery Lead to Action?

On January 8, 2011, U.S. Representative Gabrielle Giffords (D-AZ) was holding a "Congress on Your Corner" meeting in front of a Safeway in Tucson, Arizona, an informal gathering on a Saturday morning, intended to promote discussion of relevant issues and citizen interaction with Giffords in her daily settings.

But in the space of only a few minutes, the brief time it took Jared Loughner to approach the meeting, shoot Giffords in the head, then fire randomly at the crowd with his semiautomatic pistol, this familiar and harmless setting outside the local grocery morphed nightmarishly into a scene of inconceivable carnage. By the time he was subdued, thirteen people were wounded and six lay dead, including a federal judge and Christina Taylor-Green, 9, who was born on September 11, 2001.

Soon after the shooting, the media began to question Sarah Palin's use of gun crosshairs and terms like "targeted" and other inflammatory language on her website, "takeback-the20," dedicated to winning back seats from Democrats. Critics of the vitriol expressed by both parties in the 2010 Congressional elections wondered if such imagery and rhetoric helped spur someone like Loughner to violent action.

Although the controversial content quickly disappeared from Palin's website, she continued to defend her position, arguing that metaphors, similes, and imagery could not be blamed for the actions of individuals. She further fanned the fires of debate by claiming critics had committed "blood libel" against her, yet another controversial word choice the media were quick to seize on, which originally referred to the false claim that Jews murdered Christian children for religious rites.

Loughner pleaded guilty to nineteen counts of murder or attempted murder, but whether the violent imagery and language deployed by conservatives against politicians like Giffords influenced his actions will likely never be known. Nevertheless, the tragic incident did serve as a powerful reminder to politicians and the public that hateful partisanship

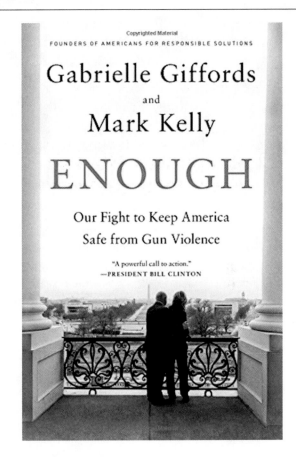

and "politics as usual" rhetoric can be lethal for democracy. It also helped motivate Giffords and her husband, Mark Kelly, a retired NASA astronaut, to organize their own efforts for gun control. In 2014, they published a book, *Enough: Our Fight to Keep America Safe from Gun Violence*, and organized Americans for Responsible Solutions, a Super PAC opposing gun violence. As of July 2014, the group had raised $17.5 million and spent more than $2.5 million in the 2014 midterm elections.[10]

endorse the attacking candidate), (2) that voters dislike negative ads, and (3) that negative ads have an unintended side effect of disenfranchising the electorate.[11]

Regarding the first hypothesis, Lau and Sigelman found in a study of voters in 1997 that negative ads did not work and actually decreased the favorability of voters' attitudes toward the candidate whose campaign ran the negative ad. Conversely, the favorability of voters' attitudes toward the target of the ads increased.

Negative political advertising is controversial, with some research indicating that it turns off voters and actually hurts the politician making the negative ad.

A study of multiple campaigns similarly revealed that candidates who initiated negative ads lost eighteen out of twenty-five elections. They also found no strong preponderance of evidence indicating that negative political ads were more memorable than positive ads.

With respect to the second hypothesis, that voters dislike negative ads, their results were clear again: "Six of the nine studies found negative political ads being rated less ethical, less fair, and otherwise less liked than positive political ads, while two studies came to the opposite conclusions and one uncovered no significant differences."

For the third hypothesis, that negative ads contribute to voter apathy or disenfranchisement, their findings were mixed: "Of the twenty relevant findings, ten report no significant differences and two associate positive outcomes with negative political ads (e.g., higher turnout), but eight report significant negative consequences."

Some research indicates that alienating young viewers from the political process is one of the most significant effects of negative political advertising, which increases cynicism and decreases interest among young viewers.

> **DISCUSSION QUESTIONS:** What type of political advertisements do you consider negative? Do your reactions vary depending on your prior views of the candidate? Can you find any examples in these ads of factual information framed in unjustly negative ways? Do ads that attack a candidate's platform affect you in the same way as ads that attack a politician's character?

Politics and Entertainment

"Politics is showbiz for ugly people" is a popular saying that succinctly captures the dynamics of the campaign trail where politicians have long utilized elements of show business and entertainment to attract voters.

POLITICAL CAMPAIGNS AND ENTERTAINMENT

Throughout the nineteenth century, election campaigns and elections themselves were very public spectacles, with parades, speeches from local leaders, music, and a generally festive atmosphere. Until well into the nineteenth century, voting occurred publicly, making it easy to see who voted for whom. The political parties created well-organized groups of supporters who persuaded others to vote for their candidates, often with promises of plum government jobs if their candidate was elected.

Songs and pithy catchphrases have long played a part in political campaigns, going back to Andrew Jackson's campaigns in 1824 and 1828. In the 1840 presidential campaign, the song and phrase "Tippecanoe and Tyler Too" became popular and helped get William Henry Harrison elected president. The use of campaign songs continued into the twentieth and twenty-first centuries, although in the past thirty years or so candidates generally adopt pop hits rather than creating original campaign songs. One exception is will.i.am's "Yes We Can," which features various artists with lyrics consisting entirely of select clips of Barack Obama speeches during the 2008 presidential primaries.

There have also been some ironic and humorous uses of songs that have caused some politicians mild embarrassment. Republicans and Democrats alike have used Bruce Springsteen songs at campaign events, until the Boss specifically forbade the use of his songs at Republican events. In the 2012 election, Republican vice presidential candidate Paul Ryan raised eyebrows when he said one of his favorite bands was Rage Against the Machine—a band whose angry lyrics attack much of what conservative Republicans stand for.

Catchy slogans and symbols have also been widely used in political campaigns. Although an eye-catching logo would likely not be responsible for electing a president, a bad one could hurt a candidate's image in subtle but powerful ways, especially for undecided voters who may not keep up with political issues and rely more heavily on peripheral cues when deciding whom to vote for, such as how the candidate looks.

Political campaigns in the nineteenth century often used entertainment such as bands and popular music to attract the public to campaign events.

POLITICAL DEBATES

Although not intended to be entertainment, political debates today have many of the trappings of show business, including the backdrops, the positioning of candidates, and the careful selection of live audience members. Carefully choreographed aspects aside, the actual debate remains one of the most important areas of political communication. Debates have been a proving ground for candidates to test their mettle against an opponent and to reveal their character and platform to the public.

Early debates were quite different from today's televised debates. For instance, a debate between Abraham Lincoln and Stephen A. Douglas during the 1858 Senate race lasted more than five hours, with each candidate offering detailed commentary of an hour or more on a single issue, such as abolition, their first debate topic. Further, because television or radio did not yet exist, these exchanges were not heard by anyone other than those present for the live event, although the public could read about them in newspapers. Today, a five-hour televised debate between political candidates is hard to imagine.

Arguably the most important debate between U.S. presidential candidates in the twentieth century occurred in 1960, when for the first time presidential candidates debated live on broadcast television and radio. Research conducted at the time showed that viewers of the televised debate rated John F. Kennedy, who was handsome and well groomed, as clearly superior. Nixon, whose dark stubble and "shifty" eyes gave him a more sinister look (the debate was scheduled for the evening and Nixon had not shaved since the morning), was deemed to have lost.

In 2013, President Obama apologized for calling Kamala Harris "the best looking attorney general in the country." Some research indicates that focus on a female politician's appearance, even in ways that stress her physical attractiveness, damages her overall appeal to voters. **CRITICAL THINKING QUESTIONS:** Why do you think compliments about a female politician's appearance might hurt her chances of being elected? Do you think this may be true for male politicians too?

The 1960 Kennedy–Nixon presidential debate showed how powerfully television could influence public perceptions of candidates.

Meanwhile, on radio, with listeners only able to hear what the candidates said, Nixon was judged the clear winner for his more convincing arguments. Kennedy ultimately won the presidential contest in an extremely close election, and it is not clear whether the debate was the deciding factor. But it has been the touchstone for televised campaigning ever since. Today, it is a given that one's television persona is essential for winning an election.

Social Media and Political Campaigns

going viral

The phenomenon in which a media item spreads rapidly from person to person via the Internet.

Twitter is often a medium for pithy, snarky comments from the public and politicians.

Electronic media have been increasingly significant in political elections ever since the first use of radio in political campaigning in 1924, and the Internet and social media have created even greater changes in recent years.

In the early years of radio, Democrats employed radio effectively in the elections of both 1936 and 1940. The majority of newspapers throughout the United States openly endorsed Republican candidates for office, but the Democrats did better in the elections. Democratic President Franklin Roosevelt was masterful in his use of radio to reach the masses, providing his regular "Fireside Chats" during the 1930s and 1940s. This ushered in an era in which radio, and later, television, had the personal qualities of candidates, rather than their political-policy stances, take center stage in the campaign process.

The Internet further transformed the political communication landscape, especially regarding elections. Voters can go to a candidate's website to obtain information about a candidate's stance on an issue, make a campaign contribution, or volunteer to help the candidate's party.

Although a candidate website may have been considered groundbreaking in 1998, by 2012, it was only a part of much more robust communication strategies that included YouTube, Facebook, and Twitter. Social media allowed candidates to communicate in more informal ways with voters than they could via other media channels; and social media can also generate more media attention, particularly if an item **goes viral**. In the 2012 election, President Obama famously tweeted a response the day after Clint Eastwood's bizarre performance at the Republican National Convention in which he spoke to an invisible President Obama in an empty chair. The tweet—a simple picture of the back of President Obama's chair (with him in it) saying, "This seat's taken"—perfectly fit the terse and snarky mode

CONVERGENCE CULTURE
Image Is Everything

Although the obsession with a politician's image did not begin with television, it certainly took on much greater

importance than it ever had in the age of print. Even so, politicians then were hardly fashion icons. Presidential portraits show that after a spate of presidents with facial hair in the latter 1800s, the fashion for men at the time, the last president with a beard or mustache was William Howard Taft (1909–1913). Today, except perhaps for Sinn Fein president and Irish MP Gerry Adams, almost no Western politicians have facial hair. Of course, no correlation exists between the ability to govern and the presence of facial hair, yet it has been considered a political taboo for at least eighty years. The increasing role of women in positions of political leadership may also be a contributing factor.

It has been claimed that several presidents would have never been elected had television had been available to broadcast their looks or disabilities. These include Abraham Lincoln, with his gawky, awkward appearance; William Howard Taft, weighing in at three hundred pounds; and wheelchair-bound Franklin Delano Roosevelt, stricken by polio at age thirty-nine. FDR would never be able to get the press today to agree, as they did then, not to publish images of him getting in and out of his wheelchair.

Today, image consultants help political candidates look the part, advising on shirts, ties, and hairstyles, among other fashion concerns. These style choices can sometimes backfire, however. In late September 2012, Mitt Romney drew criticism when he appeared on the Hispanic TV network Univision looking unnaturally tanned. Romney almost cancelled the interview until Univision bussed in Hispanic Republicans to fill the hall. "Fake tan. Fake fans. Really sad," wrote one Facebook commenter. The expected prominence of female candidates in the 2016 U.S. presidential campaign may shine the spotlight on image even more brightly, the question of facial hair notwithstanding.

---

so characteristic of Twitter. Eastwood's comical exchange also inspired one of the most famous **memes** from the election and even spawned its own verb "Eastwooding," the act of speaking to an empty chair.

Every social media user is a potential media producer, or "produser," of text and images that may be created and distributed with equal ease, two social media trends that can conspire by accident or by design to derail or even ruin a political career. Congressman Anthony Weiner became the poster boy for sexting scandals in 2011, and again in 2013, as a NYC mayor hopeful. In December 2014, Elizabeth Lauten, a congressman's aide, was also the digital architect of her own demise after a snarky post to her Facebook page about Malia and Sasha Obama went viral and public backlash prompted her resignation. A 2006 clip from the campaign trail of Virginia senator George Allen recorded him publicly calling an opponent's campaign worker of Indian descent "macaca," a European racial slur for African immigrants. The video circulated widely on the Internet and left indelible impressions that no amount of subsequent press-release apologies could successfully whitewash or counter.

 meme

A media item of cultural interest that spreads through repetition and replication via the Internet.

A video of Virginia senator George Allen repeatedly using the racial slur "macaca" at a campaign stop in 2006 was widely circulated on the Internet and credited in part with his defeat.

But digital media can, of course, disseminate more significant items than witty retorts or embarrassing videos. Obama's social media team proved masterful at fundraising and increasing voter registration and turnout in both the 2008 and 2012 elections. So successful was Obama's 2008 campaign at getting small donations from many people that he was the first presidential candidate to refuse taxpayer funding (and, not coincidentally, the spending restrictions that went with that). Some even claim that President Obama owed his first election win to the Internet. Joe Trippi, Howard Dean's presidential campaign manager in 2004, said that the extent and kind of Obama's Internet activity would have required "an army of volunteers and paid organizers on the ground."[12]

In 2012, Obama once again tapped this network, even though the media often commented as the race tightened in the fall that Obama supporters lacked the enthusiasm of 2008. Nevertheless, in election postmortems, many commentators observed that part of the credit for Obama's win went to his well-organized campaigns, especially in swing states, with organizing facilitated by social media and online communication between campaign managers and volunteers.

CHANGES WITH SOCIAL MEDIA

Social media were more prominent in the changed media landscape of 2012. An October 2012 study by the Pew Internet & American Life Project found that 39 percent of Americans used social media to discuss politics. In 2012, over 10 million tweets were sent during the first presidential debate between Obama and Romney; whereas in 2008, only 1.8 million tweets were sent on Election Day itself. President Obama's speech at the Democratic National Convention initiated over 2.5 million online conversations.

In the 2008 election, YouTube proved key in promoting Obama, according to Arianna Huffington, founder of the *Huffington Post*. It purposely positioned itself to play a potentially important role in the elections by launching the YouTube You Choose '08 campaign, which gave presidential candidates their own YouTube channels. In posted videos that the public could watch when they wanted, without commercials, candidates could speak at greater length than the sound-bite culture that dominates the mainstream news allows. YouTube also allowed people to repeatedly watch and share these videos with friends.

The transformations produced by social media are even more remarkable when we consider that neither YouTube nor Twitter even existed during the 2004 election. Yet within eight years, they had become integral components of the electoral process. Scholars and political consultants continue to study and analyze the implications for future campaigns of this evolution in mass communications, one that has recast expectations and interactions of American voters with their political candidates.

CHANGING RULES FOR POLITICIANS

The changes in political campaigns produced by YouTube, Facebook, and other social media technologies are still not fully understood and will likely continue to develop as technologies continue to evolve. Certain fundamental shifts, however, can already be identified from the 2008 and 2012 presidential campaigns.

Candidates seem not to have yet learned that there is no such thing anymore as an "off the record" event. In another era, journalists attending fundraisers or other gatherings that were off the record respected that whatever was said there by a candidate could not be reported. But today's citizen-journalists and bloggers often ignore these unwritten rules. When damaging material can be readily redirected to the public sphere via the Internet, the assumption that those present constitute a partisan audience wholly sympathetic to one's cause or sensitive to a remark's context is a dangerous supposition.

At a private fundraiser for wealthy donors in May 2012, Romney infamously characterized 47 percent of Americans as government freeloaders who paid no taxes and who considered themselves victims. A bartender catering the event, who explicitly invoked his Boston blue-collar roots when explaining his actions to ABC News, surreptitiously taped and subsequently released the "47 percent video" to the media months later as the election campaigns were heating up. It further reinforced negative perceptions of Romney as elitist, someone who if elected would be more concerned about the rich rather than the middle class.

Campaign gaffes also generate a life of their own on social media. During the first televised presidential debate in 2012, Mitt Romney claimed that he would cut funding of public television if president but added, "I love Big Bird," generating more than 200,000 tweets that mentioned the beloved *Sesame Street* character. In the days that followed, people posted humorous, and often profane, photos and videos of Big Bird "responding" to Romney's comments.

Social media have allowed some topics to thrive in online conversations long after they would have disappeared from the regular news cycle. One example is

After his 2012 election victory, President Obama turned his campaign's highly successful online component into a means of organizing popular support on key issues.

The different seating formats in the three presidential debates between President Obama and Mitt Romney affected the candidates' interactions. The second debate, in which they could walk around, was considered the most aggressive; and the third debate, in which they were seated, was seen as much calmer and more reasoned.

Missouri Senate Republican candidate Rep. Todd Akin's comments in August 2012 that in cases of "legitimate rape," women could control whether they got pregnant or not. This statement, and similarly controversial assertions from other conservative Republican candidates about abortion and a woman's right to choose, became the subject of closer scrutiny and extended discussion on social media.

A more prominent Internet presence in campaigns has made the electoral landscape more attractive to young people, a demographic that has recently proven a powerful force in helping to organize and volunteer. This bucks a trend, going back at least thirty years, of steadily declining youth participation in elections. Realizing much of his voter base was comprised of young people, Obama campaigned on college campuses days before the election in battleground states such as Ohio and Virginia. Often he appeared with Bruce Springsteen, who gave free concerts to support Obama.

Not only do the Internet and social media help politicians communicate better and organize more efficiently, they also provide the public with media and informational tools to organize their efforts more effectively and improve their communication with the government.

INTERNATIONAL PERSPECTIVES
Crowdsourcing Election Monitoring

Some historical election practices in the nineteenth century in the United States look downright fraudulent to us today—political parties offering voters free trans-

portation to polling places, providing free turkeys to families, and ballot stuffing (putting false names in ballot boxes or people voting in more than one district under different names). In the past, however, they were not considered so. Over time, more stringent rules and laws helped ensure fair elections and reduce voter fraud, incidents of which are now rare in U.S. elections. In certain foreign countries, charges of election fraud are frequent and include not only vote buying but also intimidation and actual physical violence against voters.

Election monitoring can be time consuming and difficult, for accusations must be investigated and evidence gathered at each polling site. Social media and crowdsourcing, using raw data gathered from the public, make this process a little easier. The Venezuelan presidential election of April 2013 saw a close result between the incumbent, President Nicolás Maduro, who took over after Hugo Chávez's death, and the challenger, Henrique Capriles Radonski. Venezuela's Citizen Election Network challenged President Maduro's victory, using Twitter to document charges of election fraud in various polling stations. Follow-up investigation of the tweets confirmed dozens and in some cases hundreds of instances of election fraud and misconduct.

In Kenya's 2013 election, a company that had previously created an interactive mapping tool to track election violence reworked it to allow for crowdsourcing of the country's election. Posting updates to Uchaguzi via Twitter, SMS, mobile phones, email, and the Web, citizens documented 4,500 cases of both good and bad acts during voting, and nearly 60 percent of the cases were investigated.[13]

In 2014, Indonesia's electoral commission (KPU) took steps to ensure extensive crowdsourcing of elections by putting large volumes of voting data online, such as scanned images of every polling station's final report. Citizens can access the data, compare it to their own experience with local polling places, and report any irregularities or potential fraud.

Social Media and Civic Engagement

With the Internet, never before have candidates and the public had such ability to communicate directly with one another. The public can see online databases that indicate how much their neighbors have contributed to which candidates. They can look at fact-checking sites, sometimes in real time, via social media to see whether candidates are telling the truth during political debates. In the 2012 election, several media organizations had post-debate fact-checking stories that analyzed various claims and their degree of truthfulness.

Email initially seemed to promise a faster, more efficient way for constituents to communicate directly with their members of Congress. A study released in 2004 by the Congress Management Foundation as part of the Communicating with Congress series of reports revealed this to be the case, although not without some pitfalls. In 2004, the House received 10.4 million communications by post and over 99 million over the Internet, while the Senate received 7.9 million communications by post and 83 million over the Internet. Overall, Congress received four times as many communications from citizens than in 1995, all due to the Internet. Staff, however, had not increased during this time, meaning offices of the same size now had more work.

According to the report, almost 80 percent of congressional staffers believe that the Internet has made it easier for people to become involved in public policy, and over half believe it has increased public understanding of what takes place in Washington. A plurality of nearly half also believes that it makes politicians more responsive to the public.

Mass email petitions and form letters created by sites like change.org do have their weaknesses, however. Politicians said that original, individual communications hold more weight for them. In general, a personal written letter or telephone call is given more priority than a prewritten form email in which a constituent simply clicked a button to forward to her representative. That is why online petition sites encourage people to write about the issue in their own words, even if they can provide a form letter.

DATABASES AND GOVERNMENT TRANSPARENCY

Online databases and sites that provide direct information about political donations, voting records, and other political activities have become especially useful tools for journalists and citizens. Visitors to such sites can customize information on demand about any community in the United States or any person who may have contributed to a candidate, using data from the Federal Election Commission. The user simply enters a zip code and immediately obtains a list of everyone in that geographic area who has contributed to federal campaign committees. Alternatively, entering the first three or more letters of a last name will produce a detailed inventory of that person's contributions during any election cycle dating back to 1990.

OpenSecrets.org maintains the database and offers online a wide range of other political information, such as details on the activities of political action committees (PACs), the spending of lobbyists (which can be extremely revealing about organizations' or industries' efforts to shape the nation's political agenda), and the fundraising and spending on various political races. Not everyone agrees these public records should be widely available on the Internet.

The Sunlight Foundation offers a number of social media tools to make government more transparent and accountable.

Government transparency has become increasingly important in the digital age, as citizens want to see how their elected leaders and government operate. The Sunlight Foundation is one of the leaders in to the movement to make government more open and accountable. This not-for-profit, nonpartisan organization has created a range of apps and online tools to enable citizens to do everything from search for deleted tweets by U.S. politicians (Politwoops) to track influence of political donations at the federal and state levels (Influence Explorer) to search for organizations buying ads or using other forms of political communication (Follow the Unlimited Money). One of Sunlight Foundation's projects includes Churnalism U.S., a web tool and browser add-on that highlights articles whose similarities to press releases or other material suggest plagiarized content.

DISCUSSION QUESTIONS: Use one of the tools on the Sunlight Foundation's website to learn something about a bill or your local politician that you have not seen in the news. Discuss what you learned and whether it has altered your view of how the news business does its job.

SMART MOBS

smart mob

A term coined by author Howard Rheingold to define a group of people communicating with each other via text messaging or wireless networks to coordinate their activities.

Digital media can also facilitate physical gatherings, dubbed **smart mobs** by author Howard Rheingold. Some political activists use cellular phones and wireless networks to organize groups and communicate rapidly with each other. Smart mobs contributed to the 1998 overthrow of President Suharto in Indonesia and to the 2001 ousting of Philippine President Joseph Estrada, orchestrating protests via cell phone text messages. With wireless technology, mass demonstrations in various parts of a city can be roughly coordinated in real time, affording protestors a communication network almost as effective as that of police or the military. In 2011, social media tools helped the Occupy Wall Street protestors masterfully coordinate protests and attract many participants.

Handheld video- and audio-recording equipment has also aided activism. Protestors at the Republican National Convention in New York City in 2004 were encouraged to record what was happening around them, especially as police started arresting people. Hundreds of protestors were arrested; and in some of the subsequent trials, video footage that directly contradicted authorities' testimony about activists' behavior was presented in their defense.

DISCUSSION QUESTIONS: What are your perceptions of social movements that protest at national conventions or at international meetings like those of the World Trade Organization (WTO)? What influenced these perceptions?

Political Polarization and Media Habits

Those unfettered by concerns about evidence or logic can simply rely on their gut response to a politician's claims, what Stephen Colbert on *The Colbert Report* would often invoke as the "truthiness" of a matter. For others, tools, such as the aptly named PolitiFact, can help determine the veracity of political assertions. Another group may not follow their instincts alone yet feel little need to seek out independent fact checkers when they have trusted news sources they consider credible.

Not surprisingly, where people look for truth, which news sources they trust, may be influenced by their political ideology, especially for those at both the far right and the far left of the spectrum, about 20 percent of the overall public. According to an October 2014 Pew report entitled "Political Polarization and Media Habits," nearly half of consistent conservatives identify Fox News as their main news source (see Figure 13-1). No other outlet comes close, although conservative talking heads Sean Hannity, Rush Limbaugh, and Glenn Beck also ranked high on the dimension of trust. Consistent liberals tend to gather news from a broader array of sources, trusting more media to

Occupy Wall Street protesters used social media effectively to organize activists and to inform the public about their actions.

FIGURE 13-1 Political Polarization and Media Habits

Trusted News Sources		Main Source of Government and Political News		Trusted News Sources
NPR 72%		CNN 15%	Fox News 47%	Fox News 88%
PBS 71%	Consistent Liberals	NPR 13%	Consistent Conservatives	Hannity 62%
BBC 69%		MSNBC 12%		Limbaugh 58%
The N.Y. Times 62%	ABC News 52%	*The N.Y. Times* 10%		Glenn Beck 51%
NBC News 56%	MSNBC 52%			
CNN 56%	CBS News 51%			

Source: Pew Research Center (October 21, 2014)

provide information on politics and the government. Their main news sources are CNN, NPR, MSNBC, and the *New York Times*; yet a majority also trust PBS, BBC, and the national networks NBC, ABC, and CBS.

MEDIA PIONEERS
Bill Adair

In this multimedia, multisource world, it is increasingly difficult to sort through the competing claims of politicians, government officials, and advocacy groups. Journalist fact checking helps people evaluate these claims and, ideally, encourages those making claims to be more careful in their public pronouncements.

PolitiFact arose from an assessment by Bill Adair, Washington correspondent for the *Tampa Bay Times* (formerly the *St. Petersburg Times*), that too little had been done to address distortions perpetrated in the 2004 presidential election.[14] Adair gathered a team of reporters to fact check statements by public figures and groups and report their truthfulness on the PolitiFact.com website. By 2008, PolitiFact was operational, and it was soon awarded the Pulitzer Prize for distinguished reporting on national affairs.[15] Adair's creative efforts to popularize such reporting include the Truth-O-Meter, a six-category scheme that assesses a claim's accuracy, ranging from true to pants-on-fire false. PolitiFact also features a Flip-O-Meter and an evaluation of whether presidential promises have been kept.[16] This journalistic form is growing. PolitiFact now has affiliates in ten other states and most recently Australia.[17]

In 2014, the Truth-O-Meter shed valuable light on the contentious matter of the Common Core curriculum transforming American schools. The Truth-O-Meter revealed that the following claim by U.S. Senator Kay Hagan (D-North Carolina) was "mostly true": "The Common Core was not put together by the Department of Education in Washington. It was put together by governors and by states." In sharp contrast, Wisconsin State Sen. Joe Leibham (R) asserted that Common Core is a federal mandate, a claim the Truth-O-Meter determined to be false.

Working in various journalistic endeavors while majoring in political science at Arizona State University, Adair naturally gravitated toward political journalism. Covering the Washington beat for the *Times*, he was a 1997 recipient of the Everett Dirksen Award for Distinguished Coverage of Congress, among numerous other awards. In April 2013, Duke University appointed him their Knight Professor of Computational Journalism, where his goal at the Reporters' Lab in the Sanford School of Public Policy is to develop new tools and forms of journalism to address public policy and political arenas.[18]

Adair notes, "This is a time of great promise in journalism, when we can reinvent how we tell stories and how we hold government accountable." He advises students in the digital age "to learn not only journalism but also how to code—to build websites and mobile apps."[19] Bill Adair's career demonstrates the potential reward for developing the skill set to work in today's convergent media environment.

MEDIA CAREERS

Media jobs in the political field as traditionally conceived are increasingly rare. Pursuing a career in journalism and politics requires more today than a questioning mind and advanced knowledge of politics and political processes, although these are still essential. Increasingly critical is an understanding of data and of algorithms that can analyze the data. Political and electoral process are increasingly defined by so-called Big Data, massive data sets often based on social media and voter information, and the analytics used in their interpretation.

News organizations such as *The New York Times*, Politico, and Huffington Post now have extensive staff led by data scientists devoted to quantitative, or numerical, inquiry, particularly political analysis. Digital companies such as Google, Facebook, and Twitter similarly employ social media and data analytics and analysts, especially during political campaigns. The emergence of computational journalism in both academy and industry underscores the increasing importance of data and its digital analysis in the tool kit of political journalists and other media professionals.

For those who may not have a penchant for data, another career possibility lies at the intersection of media and politics—satire. As the tragic terrorist attack on *Charlie Hebdo* in 2015 reveals, this pathway is not without its risks.[20] But, for those who want to provide humorous observations about institutions and public figures such as elected officials, writing satire for TV shows or other media, online or off, is an option to consider.

LOOKING BACK AND MOVING FORWARD

As we have seen, political communication is not simply about elections and political campaigns. Media companies employ lobbyists just like other industries to influence political and regulatory decisions that may harm their business yet protect the public.

Citizens should be knowledgeable about how the media work within our political system and how they may affect basic rights such as privacy or determine the kinds of stories we see. The role of mass communication in democracies will likely be even more important in the future as the focus moves from a perceived need to inform the public to that of engaging the public in dialog. To that end, social media will also play an important part, facilitating conversations between members of the public and between the public and its elected officials.

Fostering more dialog may be one of the biggest shifts in political campaigns and elections. Encouraging participation may engage more people than ever before in these democratic processes. Something as simple as tweeting about what took place at a school board meeting or blogging for a local news organization could affect the way leaders govern as they observe citizens becoming more responsive to policy issues. Maintaining our rights to privacy while keeping governance as transparent as possible will be ongoing efforts. Many government leaders may see the greater transparency that social media in part represent as a threat to standard ways of conducting political business.

Transparency will also be vital in the international arena, where the policy decisions of a growing number of international organizations, such as the World Bank and the International Monetary Fund (IMF), can affect entire nations and the global economy. Whereas leaders within democratic nations may face increased pressure to be more transparent, the heads of these international groups, who may arguably have more power to affect national policies than elected officials do, will not be beholden to any specific public and have little incentive to make their decision-making processes transparent.

Activist groups call for closer monitoring of the increased powers of certain organizations such as the World Trade Organization (WTO). To raise public awareness about the WTO's policy decisions on global business and trade, they routinely stage demonstrations that sometimes turn violent. These social movements adopt organizing and protest tactics similar to those of antinuclear and environmental groups in the 1970s and 1980s while exploiting the power of new social media to communicate with each other and to attract media attention for their causes.

MEDIA MATTERS   PLAYING POLITICS

1. Consider a political candidate in the most recent election. What are your impressions of the candidate, and what policies does he or she stand for? Now consider where you got most of this information—was it from news sites, from appearances on entertainment shows such as a late-night talk show or *The Daily Show*, or from ads? What implications do these main sources have for your impression of the candidate and important political issues?

2. Media companies fought an FCC ruling that would require them to be more transparent about the sources of their political advertisers and how much they spent. Why do you think they would fight such a ruling, and what implications do you think greater transparency might have for media organizations?

3. Have you ever volunteered or participated in a government election campaign? If so, in what way, why did you participate, and what was your impression of the experience?

4. Have you ever participated in a protest or some other form of activism, such as signing a petition online or offline or posting a political message on social media? What was the campaign or issue, and what persuaded you to participate? Did it have the desired effect?

FURTHER READING

The Myth of Digital Democracy. Matthew Hindman (2008) Princeton University Press.

Mosh the Polls: Youth Voters, Popular Culture and Democratic Engagement. Tony Kelso, Brian Cogan (eds.) (2008) Lexington Books.

Into the Buzzsaw: Leading Journalists Expose the Myth of a Free Press. Kristina Borjesson (ed.) (2002) Prometheus Books.

Media Spectacle and the Crisis of Democracy: Terrorism, War, and Election Battles. Douglas Kellner (2005) Paradigm Publishers.

Media Politics: A Citizen's Guide, 2nd ed. Shanto Iyengar (2011) W. W. Norton.

unSpun: Finding Facts in a World of Disinformation. Brooks Jackson, Kathleen Hall Jamieson (2007) Random House Trade Paperbacks.

Tuned Out: Why Americans Under 40 Don't Follow the News. David Mindich (2005) Oxford University Press.

The Press Effect: Politicians, Journalists, and the Stories That Shape the World. Kathleen Hall Jamieson (2004) Oxford University Press.

The Obama Victory: How Media, Money, and Message Shaped the 2008 Election. Kathleen Hall Jamieson, Kate Kenski, Bruce Hardy (2010) Oxford University Press.

The Nightly News Nightmare: Network Television's Coverage of U.S. Presidential Elections, 1988–2000. Stephen J. Farnsworth, S. Robert Lichter (2002) Rowman & Littlefield.

Mass Media and American Politics, 9th ed. Doris A. Graber (2014) CQ Press.

Bloggers on the Bus: How the Internet Changes Politics and the Press. Eric Boehlert (2009) Free Press.

Entertaining Politics: Satiric Television and Political Engagement, 2nd ed. Jeffrey Jones (2009) Rowman & Littlefield.

Cyberprotest: New Media, Citizens, and Social Movements. W. Van De Donk (ed.) (2004) Routledge.

Blowing the Roof Off the Twenty-First Century: Media, Politics, and the Struggle for Post-Capitalist Democracy. Robert W. McChesney (2014) Monthly Review Press.

Global Media in the Digital Age

The gruesome images and graphic stories in the global media about the Islamic State or Islamic State of Iraq and Syria (ISIS)—beheadings of Western hostages, mass executions, and other human rights violations in territory they control—certainly have not painted an appealing picture of ISIS.

Yet despite regular news reports of their atrocities, a small but steady stream of Westerners—3,400, including 200 Americans, according to counterterrorism officials—have traveled abroad to join ISIS. Many have responded to recruitment efforts that involve encrypted communications on what officials call the "dark space" of the Web, an apt location for campaigns to expand an Islamist state of the darkest nature.[1]

Counterterrorism officials and media experts, while decrying these media campaigns as ISIS propaganda, admit these media-savvy efforts have been remarkably effective. Advanced marketing techniques commonly used by cutting-edge advertising and PR agencies have supplemented their social media campaign with professionally produced online magazines and high-quality videos depicting life in the Islamic State.

ISIS is just the latest, yet perhaps the most successful, example of terrorists utilizing the Internet. In the early 2000s, the FBI reported that groups such as Al Qaeda were communicating online to organize and coordinate activity within and between cells. The suspects in the lethal Boston Marathon attack allegedly learned about bomb making from Al Qaeda material available on the Web.[2] Swaying disaffected people within Western countries, encouraging and guiding them to commit terrorist acts at home in the name of ISIS, is a greater concern for law enforcement and counterterrorism officials than a mass exodus to ISIS-controlled territory.

Despite Western experts' grudging acknowledgment of extremists' strategic success employing media, terrorism, like other human enterprises, is fallible. A colossal error occurred in mid-2015 when a militant posted a selfie on social media, a photo of him at a command and control center inside ISIS territory, with boastful comments about their military capabilities. This item on social media quickly became

LEARNING OBJECTIVES

>> Describe the role of mass communication in democratic and nondemocratic countries.

>> Define the public sphere and public opinion.

>> Discuss the implications of the digital divide for citizen participation in the public sphere.

>> Explain the concept of hegemony and its relevance to media in an age of globalization.

>> Outline the role of developed and developing nations in a global flow of news and entertainment media.

>> Assess the importance of indigenous media to local and global culture.

>> Explain how the rise of digital media has affected national and international security.

intelligence information for the U.S. Air Force, unwittingly supplied by the enemy himself, whose building was identified and destroyed with a missile airstrike—a mission accomplished within 24 hours of the original post.

Global media, interconnected either technologically or economically and often in real time or near real time, developed in the mid-nineteenth century. Since the mid- or late 1800s, most countries have had printed media, such as newspapers and books; and since the early to mid-1900s, many have had systems of electronic broadcasting and motion picture production, albeit generally on a smaller scale than in the United States.

Before the rise of mass electronic communication in the twentieth century, print journalism was a primary driver of media globalization. In the 1840s, Paul Julius Freiherr von Reuter (Baron de Reuter), founder of the Reuters News Agency in the French city of Aachen, used carrier pigeons to deliver news to Brussels. This gave him a competitive edge over other international news agencies, which used trains, slower than pigeons, to transport the news across borders. By 1851, the carrier pigeon was superseded by the newly invented electric telegraph, which could spread the news from country to country at the speed of light.

Carrier pigeons provided state-of-the-art international news delivering in the 1840s for Baron de Reuter, until surpassed by the electric telegraph.

The convergence of television and the communications satellite with the launch of the Telstar satellite in 1962 enabled delivery of television programming in real time between Europe and the United States. The growth of the Internet, broadband communications, and mobile digital devices has only expanded interconnection among the world's media. Government regulations around the world have increasingly favored media globalization. Ownership of media on a global scale has grown dramatically since the 1970s as technology enabled broadcasters and publishers to extend their reach worldwide. At the same time, however, it appears that some executives of publicly owned global media conglomerates have become more concerned with company revenue and stock value than with the quality of the media products themselves.

Yet even in an era of increasing globalization, media operations around the world are diverse. Variations in local regulations and culture shape media practice and content, whether in the form of news or entertainment. In this chapter, we examine the global media system and the issues it raises for an increasingly interconnected world. We begin with an examination of four enduring theories about the nature and function of international mass communication.

DISCUSSION QUESTIONS: Why do you think ISIS media strategies have been so successful? How can Western countries counter ISIS media campaigns to recruit young men and women?

Four Theories of International Mass Communication

In 1956, social scientists Fred S. Siebert, Wilbur Schramm, and Theodore Peterson presented four theories of international mass communication.[3] These theories explain how the press operates in different political, historical, and cultural environments around the world. Although the authors referred specifically to "the press," we can apply their four theories to all mass communication, including television, radio, and the Internet:

1. Authoritarian theory
2. Libertarian theory
3. Social responsibility theory
4. Soviet theory

AUTHORITARIAN THEORY

Authoritarian theory describes the oldest system of mass communication whose roots extend to sixteenth- and seventeenth-century England. This system exists in authoritarian states whose governments exert direct control over the mass media. Countries governed by a small ruling class are especially likely to have an authoritarian media system.

Media in authoritarian systems are not permitted to print, broadcast, or webcast anything the government feels might undermine its authority. Content that threatens or challenges the existing political system and its values is prohibited. Anyone who violates the rules is subject to harsh punishment, including imprisonment, expulsion, or even death.

Government uses the media not only to inform the public of important events but also to shape public opinion in support of its policies. Although ownership of media can be private or public, media professionals lack editorial independence within their organizations. Foreign media are also subordinate to governmental authority. Countries where the authoritarian theory most accurately describes current systems of mass communication include China, Cuba, North Korea, Saudi Arabia, and to slightly lesser extents Singapore and Russia.

LIBERTARIAN THEORY

Libertarian theory, also called free press theory, rests on the belief that the individual should be free to publish whatever she or he likes. Its roots lie in the work of seventeenth-century philosopher and writer John Milton, who argued in *Areopagitica* (1644): "And though all the winds of doctrine were let loose to play upon

authoritarian theory

A theory of international mass communication that contends authoritarian governments exert direct control over the media.

libertarian theory

A theory of international mass communication that supports the individual's right to publish whatever she or he wants, even material critical of the government or of government officials.

Watchdog group Reporters Without Borders ranked Singapore 153 out of 180 countries in its World Press Freedom Index, the lowest ranking the country has ever received. Pictured here is the cover of *The Straits Times*, a newspaper closely monitored by the Singaporean government. **CRITICAL THINKING QUESTIONS:** Do you approve of authoritarian governmental control of the media as long as a country's citizens are safe and happy? What kind of penalties should these governments be able to impose for media transgressions?

the earth, so Truth be in the field, we do injuriously by licensing and prohibiting to misdoubt her strength. Let her and Falsehood grapple; who ever knew Truth put to the worse, in a free and open encounter?"

In libertarian theory, criticism of the government and its policies is accepted and even encouraged, and the import and export of media messages across national borders is not restricted. Media professionals have full autonomy within their organizations. Although the libertarian model is an ideal that does not realistically apply in full anywhere, elements of the theory are clearly in practice in the media of many countries.

social responsibility theory

A theory of international mass communication that perhaps best describes the media's role in democratic societies. It asserts that the media should be free from most governmental constraints to provide the most reliable and impartial information to the public.

SOCIAL RESPONSIBILITY THEORY

Social responsibility theory best describes the systems of mass communication in most democratic societies. It holds that to provide the most reliable and impartial information to the public, the media in a democracy should be free from most governmental constraints. To operate effectively in this environment, however, the media must act responsibly. In 1947, the Commission on Freedom of the Press (known as the Hutchins Commission) articulated the media's obligations to society, which included truth, objectivity, balance, and diversity. The commission

ETHICS IN MEDIA
J-Ethinomics—Teaching Ethics and Economics in Journalism

Bhutan, tucked into the eastern Himalayas and bordered by India and China, held its first national parliamentary elections in 2008. Officially the Kingdom of Bhutan, the constitutional monarchy was among the last countries to introduce television and to allow the Internet, entering the world of digital media in 1999. This new democracy sought to develop an effectively functioning local news media. To help achieve this goal, twenty Bhutanese journalists attended a workshop in J-Ethinomics, a unique media ethics program developed by the Center for International Media Ethics (CIME). J-Ethinomics addressed the challenge of training a largely inexperienced group of reporters, editors, and Bhutanese media owners in the fundamental principles of media freedom and responsibility.

The CIME program seeks to balance truth-telling and ethics with profitability and other critical media influences on culture, environment, and business. J-Ethinomics teaches reporters and editors to frame every story, especially those involving economics, with journalistic ethics in mind. Rather than report stories uncritically, reporters learn to ask questions about business activities and

Bhutanese journalists attend a CIME workshop addressing journalism ethics, especially truth-telling, and the economic demands of profitability.

their potentially harmful consequences, such as their effects on the environment. Ethical reporting increases public trust as it enhances media credibility.

argued that a responsible media system must do more than simply report the facts. It must place them in context. This means the media must provide analysis, explanation, and interpretation.

Although social responsibility theory may best describe the system of mass communication in democracies such as the United States, Canada, France, and the United Kingdom, prioritizing public good over corporate profit both at home and abroad is a challenge in the age of global media expansion. Siebert, Peterson, and Schramm cautioned, "The power and near monopoly position of the media impose on them an obligation to be socially responsible, to see that all sides are fairly presented and that the public has enough information to decide; and that if the media do not take on themselves such responsibility it may be necessary for some other agency of the public to enforce it."

They added, "Freedom of expression under the social responsibility theory is not an absolute right, as under pure libertarian theory.... One's right to free expression must be balanced against the private rights of others and against vital social interests." A socially responsible news organization would exercise extreme care in reports about terrorist activities, for example, especially ones that might detail how bioterrorism is conducted or specify a city's disaster plans, information terrorists might use to plan future attacks.

SOVIET THEORY

The **Soviet theory** of the press is based on a specific ideology: the communist system of government practiced in the former Soviet Union. Siebert traced the roots of this theory to the 1917 Russian Revolution and the views of Karl Marx and Friedrich Engels. According to the Soviet theory, media should serve the interests of the working class and should be publicly, not privately, owned.

Despite certain similarities between the Soviet and authoritarian systems, notably, the media being subordinate to the government, there are also important differences. In particular, the Soviet theory asserts that the media should recognize their responsibility to the people and self-regulate their content. Government censorship is not the norm. With the demise of the Soviet Union in the 1980s, this theory is now most useful as a historical reference point. One can see some elements of its philosophy, however, in the media-reform movement that argues for-profit media have been harming democracy and claims some news organizations should be publicly funded.

Soviet theory

A theory of international mass communication that states that the media should be publicly owned and used to further the needs of the working class.

The Soviet Union's main newspaper was *Pravda,* meaning "truth."

DISCUSSION QUESTIONS: Visit a website for a non-U.S. media enterprise, such as Canada's *The Globe and Mail* (www.theglobeandmail.com), the British Broadcasting Corporation (www.bbc.com/news), or *The Times of India* (http://timesofindia.indiatimes.com/international-home). What value, if any, do you see in visiting internationally produced news websites and in the content they present?

The Public, the Public Sphere, and Public Opinion

"The public" and "public opinion" are surprisingly complex concepts whose definitions are still debated by scholars today. In some ways, the public can be considered an audience for governments or politicians, but this description would be an oversimplification that fails to consider exactly how the public has evolved throughout history, how it differs today from the public in the Middle Ages, for example.

Most scholars agree that the notion of the public did not come about until the late sixteenth or early seventeenth century, when Europe was beginning to enter the modern era and governments were changing from monarchies to more representative forms of government. A new middle class arose, the **bourgeoisie**, which began to recognize the differing economic and political interests of business, government, and citizens. More importantly, the bourgeoisie recognized themselves as a separate group, apart but also a part of government and economics. Through media of the day, primarily newspapers, pamphlets, journals, and other periodicals, the bourgeoisie were able to communicate with each other about common interests and challenge government policies that did not suit them.

The forums in which the bourgeoisie debated matters of public interest included popular coffeehouses in England and salons in France, where material disseminated in print publications inspired conversation and where a sense of conventional wisdom developed through discussion among peers. The **public sphere**, as first described by German social theorist and philosopher Jürgen Habermas, was an arena for rational-critical debate, where the best argument won the day and where rank or privilege took a backseat to the quest for knowledge and truth. This ideal was not realized, of course, for a number of reasons. Women, for example, played an integral role in French salons but were excluded from discussion in bourgeoisie English coffeehouses.

Despite its many flaws in practice, the public sphere remains a rich concept in theory, a popular subject in media and mass-communication research today. Many scholars take a critical view, some arguing that commercial media have taken over the public forum and imposed new forms of (often hidden) control over what is discussed and how it is discussed. Hope still exists, though, for the Internet to rejuvenate the public sphere as a forum where users discuss subjects of mutual concern civilly and openly without fear of government censure or commercial manipulation. Nevertheless, a coherent public sphere in which all participants abide by shared rules of rational argument and civic-mindedness, the Habermasian gold standard, has proven elusive, particularly given the diversity of people online and their various, often conflicting, interests and perspectives.

bourgeoisie

A class of society that translates approximately to "middle class," distinguished from the aristocracy above and the proletariat (or workers) below.

public sphere

An idealized conversational forum in which people discuss and debate mutual interests and societal issues.

Coffeehouses and salons in the eighteenth century were important locations for development of the public sphere. **CRITICAL THINKING QUESTION:** How might gender have affected the substance and style of discussions in the coffeehouse compared to the salon?

The public sphere is key to the formation of **public opinion**, itself a contested concept, which can nevertheless be broadly defined as "what the public thinks." Public opinion pertains directly to efforts to define who exactly "the public" is and how a commonly shared opinion is formed and advanced. Is public opinion simply the aggregate of individual beliefs, writ large, or does it become something greater than the sum of its parts? If so, how does it change? And what are the effects of such changes?

The public is more complex than a mere mass of people, to which the enduring debates over proper definitions attest. Many contemporary scholars question the premise of a sole and united public, positing instead a multiplicity of publics and spheres whose interests, agendas, and access to mainstream media vary. The more recent theoretical concept of **counterpublics** recognizes a public forum of resistance for those who "perceive themselves to be excluded from or marginalized within mainstream or dominant publics and communicate about that marginality or exclusion."[4]

Public opinion, however it may be defined, is a foundational concern of democracies, and consequently so too are the media that create, shape, and spread ideas that inform and influence public opinion. Few major policy decisions are made without first testing the public waters to gauge their reaction. This is not to suggest, however, that the government is controlled by what French political historian Alexis de Tocqueville referred to in *Democracy of America* (1835) as the **tyranny of the majority**. Various groups can manipulate public opinion for their own ends, and an entire media industry—public relations—exists for the primary purpose of swaying public opinion with campaigns that cast their clients and their policies in the most attractive light possible.

PR professionals are not the only ones who can influence the masses. Just as the bourgeoisie in eighteenth-century coffeehouses found themselves with powerful new tools of mass communication, the range of media platforms people enjoy today has expanded, the result of advanced digital technology. We can start online petitions on any topic we choose, create sites that complain about products or parody politicians, post news scoops on blogs or videos of embarrassing moments in the lives of public and private figures, and act as citizen-journalists reporting injustices that other media may choose to ignore. Examples of this include the 2011 revolutions in several Arab countries. During the Arab Spring, people posted powerful images that the government-controlled media in those countries would not publish, for fear—proven correct—that it would sway public opinion.

Clearly, democratic countries are not the only nations that use social media to advance political and humanitarian causes. When a major earthquake hit China's Sichuan province on April 20, 2013, killing 20,000 persons, China's social-networking communities instantly went into action. One microblogger, Zuoyeben, who had some 5.6 million followers, posted a call for help for victims. Followers retweeted his post, prompting a wave of volunteerism and donations. A similar appeal from Li Chengpeng, a Chinese sportscaster with 7 million followers on Sina Weibo (a Chinese site similar to Twitter), yielded five hundred tents and more than twelve hundred blankets, all within two days of the quake.

Social media have also provided a forum to expose local corruption in China, even leading to the prosecution of some public officials. The government only allows citizens a voice, however, when it aligns with governmental interests, such as President Xi Jinping's anti-corruption campaign. In March 2015, for example, a documentary appeared on YouTube entitled *Under the Dome* about the severe air

public opinion

The notion that the public, as a group, can form shared views or ideas about topics and that these ideas guide the public's actions.

counterpublics

Public forums of resistance created by those who consider themselves to be excluded from or marginalized within dominant media and communication.

tyranny of the majority

A situation in which governmental laws and policies benefit the majority without concern for the welfare or rights of other groups or individuals.

pollution in many Chinese cities that forces school children to play "outside" under plastic domes. The video struck a nerve with the Chinese public and quickly went viral. The Chinese government, despite initially approving the content, subsequently decided the topic could undermine its authority and removed the video from websites, effectively sending a clear message that the subject was not to be discussed publicly.

Political and Socioeconomic Issues with Global Media

Radio and television are frequently used to reach remote agricultural regions in developing countries with information on health issues, agricultural techniques, and government policies. Broadcast stations are often among the first places taken in a coup because those in power—or those wishing to gain power—recognize the importance of controlling the distribution of information. Print media often foster business development in a region, although their effectiveness is limited in countries with low literacy rates or many different languages. In the networked, digital age, authoritarian governments increasingly monitor media, censoring or shutting down digital and mobile communications seen as threats to the existing regime or social order.

Foreign governments tend to control the content of their mass-communication organizations, especially television and radio, as well as online and mobile communications, far more than in the United States. In some cases, broadcasting stations are entirely government owned or run, and access can be limited by licensing restrictions for television sets or media devices such as satellite dishes.

MEDIA IN DEVELOPING COUNTRIES

The media and companion communication technologies are instruments of economic development throughout the world. Western companies hoping to take advantage of cheap labor costs in other nations look for developed infrastructure, including transportation routes and communication networks—in addition, of course, to stable governments and corporate-friendly policies, such as low taxes.

Countries like India have become sources of relatively cheap software and computer-programming workers as well as home to database and information-processing centers. India's generally well-educated workforce who speaks English makes it well positioned to profit from meeting low-end information-economy needs such as scanning documents, transcribing documents, and providing technical support for computer makers and software companies. It has also become a major producer of content, especially recorded music, motion pictures, and news media.

Some countries in Africa have been making similar moves toward fulfilling the information-processing needs of industrial countries. A data-processing company in Ghana, for example, inputs minor violations that occur in New York City, ranging from parking tickets to jaywalking. For Ghanaian workers, the pay and the working conditions are better than many other industries can offer, although hours are long and breaks short by Western standards.

Critics argue that moving information-processing work overseas is no different than sending factories there to obtain cheaper labor and avoid

CONVERGENCE CULTURE
Through a PRISM of Global Surveillance

Breaking news has become a global media phenomenon with worldwide repercussions. In the late spring of 2013, the United Kingdom's *Guardian* news site published a story that affected people and politics around the globe, riveting the public, pundits, and politicians for months. It involved the existence and nature of the U.S. government's top-secret surveillance program known as PRISM.

The *Guardian* revealed that the National Security Agency (NSA) had tapped into the servers of major digital communications and media enterprises—including Google, Apple, and Microsoft—to monitor the online communications and activity of many foreign nationals and some U.S. citizens. Although many had suspected that governments conducted online surveillance, few if any foresaw the extent of the NSA program and the far-reaching consequences of a project whose stated purpose was specifically the detection of terrorist plots.

When the *Guardian* reported that former NSA contractor Edward Snowden had provided top-secret documents detailing the massive digital surveillance program,[5] reaction around the world was swift. Some applauded Snowden for blowing the whistle on the top-secret program perceived as an egregious intrusion into citizens' privacy. Others called for his arrest along with those who had published the story, alleging they were coconspirators, spies, and traitors who had violated federal law.

Media around the world subsequently tracked the whereabouts of Snowden, who fled the United States to seek asylum abroad. Relegated to five weeks of limbo in a Russian airport, Snowden was finally allowed to remain in Russia, a decision that caused a rift in U.S./Russia relations.[6] Snowden has since been granted three-year residency there, with the possibility to apply for citizenship after five years.

The media question whether privacy can exist in an age of ubiquitous digital communications and whether it should in an age of international terrorism. Years later, journalists and academics continue to examine this epic leak of top-secret documents, particularly its impact on international relations and future governmental surveillance and counterterrorism efforts.

pollution problems and employee-benefits costs. Others who support this trend, however, respond that the information technology (IT) industry is not like industrial-era factories: It is generally nonpolluting. It can be created using existing buildings. And employees receive training and education on the job that makes them qualified for other jobs within information societies. The hope is that developing countries can avoid the worst effects of the industrial age as they move directly into the information age, although this remains to be seen.

Some factors hinder the growth of IT in these countries. Excessive government regulation often impedes the creation of telecommunication infrastructure that could better

Outsourcing IT services to developing countries has provided new job opportunities for workers in those countries.

reach all citizens within a country. A lack of other infrastructure, such as regular electrical power, political instability, and policy changes—all these can hurt the development of telecommunication technologies.

To attract Western businesses, Singapore, Malaysia, and other Southeast Asia nations have been promoting themselves as high-speed Internet ecommerce zones. They promise a broadband infrastructure enabling the production and distribution of video and other media content, especially to mobile users. Yet from a cultural or political perspective, rather than a technical one, the free flow of information raises important concerns. Singapore strictly controls most forms of media, even banning certain Western newspapers critical of the government; and it attempts to control citizens' access to the Internet, restrictions that Western companies, especially media organizations, may not abide.

SEARCHING FOR TRUTH: SELF-CENSORSHIP IN CHINA

China has also become increasingly attractive to Western media as growing numbers of this massive market go online. Similar to Singapore, however, China's restrictions on the press and Internet access remain at odds with Western practices and policies. China blocks a wide range of websites, those that publish pornography or that criticize the government, mentioning, for example, the 1989 protests and deaths in Tiananmen Square or the banned group Falun Gong.

Reporters Without Borders publishes an annual index highlighting obstacles to and violations of press freedom of information around the world. Scores on the World Press Freedom Index are based on a weighted scheme of seven different indicators: pluralism, media independence, environment and self-censorship, legislative framework, transparency, infrastructure, and abuses. (See Figure 14-1.) In 2015, it reported a decline on all fronts.

The 2015 World Press Freedom Index ranks China 176 out of 180 countries, continuing to identify it as one the worst violators of press freedom. Earlier, Reporters Without Borders noted that since Xi Jinping took office, "the authorities have arrested more journalists and bloggers, cracked down harder on cyber-dissidents, reinforced online content control and censorship and stepped up restrictions on the foreign media."[7] Vietnam, ranked in 2015 only one rung above China, introduced a law in 2013 that banned sharing developments in the news on blogs and social media. Reporters Without Borders describes Decree 71 as part of "an all-out offensive against the new-generation Internet, which [Vietnam] sees as a dangerous counterweight to the domesticated traditional media."[8]

In 2006, Google was roundly criticized when the company chose to censor itself to enter the Chinese search engine market. Many observers noted the irony in Google's "Don't Be Evil" mantra regarding its business philosophy and wondered how the search engine giant could rationalize its decision not to include full access to sites on the Internet. Google responded that providing some access, with the hope that it might help China open its media system more, was better than offering nothing at all. Despite compromises made to enter to the Internet market in China, Google still remains less popular there than homegrown search engine company Baidu.

FIGURE 14-1 2015 World Press Freedom Index

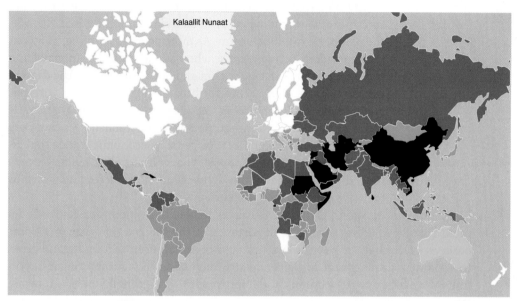

Scores range from 0 to 100, with 0 representing the highest degree of press freedom and 100 the lowest. The world map divides 180 nations into five categories:

White: good situation, from 0 to 15 points (21 countries)

Yellow: satisfactory situation, from 15.01 to 25 points (31 countries)

Orange: noticeable problems, from 25.01 to 35 points (62 countries)

Red: difficult situation, from 35.01 to 55 points (46 countries)

Black: very serious situation, from 55.01 to 100 (20 countries)

Source: Reporters Sans Frontières, http://index.rsf.org/#!/

Rank	Country	Country Score
1	Finland	7.52
8	Canada	10.99
18	Poland	12.71
34	United Kingdom	20.0
42	Botswana	22.91
49	United States	24.41
57	Argentina	26.11
73	Italy	27.94
101	Israel	32.09
122	Afghanistan	37.44
136	India	40.49
152	Russian Federation	44.97
164	Saudi Arabia	59.41
176	China	73.55
180	Eritrea	84.86

Yahoo faced heavy criticism from the press a year earlier when the company provided user information requested by the Chinese government that helped put a Chinese journalist in jail for ten years. As long as the Communist government in China maintains strict controls over media access and the types of content allowed, Western media companies will have some difficult ethical choices to make if they do business in China.

DISCUSSION QUESTIONS: Find the most recent World Press Freedom Index on the website for Reporters Without Borders. Guess the ranking for your country before looking closely at the index, then discuss why it might be ranked higher or lower than where you expected. Do you agree with the reasons cited by the index?

Baidu is the homegrown search engine rival of Google in China.

💬 **digital divide**

The gap between regions and demographics that have access to modern, digital-communications technology and those that have limited or no access.

Providing affordable technology to access the Internet is only part of solving the digital divide; the other part involves teaching users how to be critical consumers of information.

THE DIGITAL DIVIDE

Nearly 80 percent of people in developed nations have Internet access. For some countries, such as Iceland, Sweden, and Norway, the number is over 90 percent. As more people get online, however, the gap widens between those who have access to the Internet and those who don't. Existing within and between nations, the **digital divide** is particularly acute for broadband, high-speed, wireless, and mobile Internet access. Because Internet access generally has a cost attached—in equipment and establishing a network connection—this gap reflects larger socioeconomic trends that already separate citizens. Some experts and policy makers worry that, if ignored, the digital divide could have increasingly serious negative consequences for society.

In the United States, early Internet users tended to be more wealthy and educated than later users. Given the importance of the information economy, some observers fear that the poor or less educated could fall even further behind given the distinct advantages of being connected, increasing the capacity to get important information, make decisions, and improve social and economic status. Internationally, Internet usage has grown, particularly among consumers of mobile media. Yet the digital divide persists, for those with low incomes are hard pressed to afford even the least expensive smartphone, tablet computer, or wireless service.

The digital divide is apparent when looking at the different rates of Internet penetration across global regions and countries, as seen in Figure 14-2. Although the world average for Internet penetration is 42.4 percent, rates vary significantly from region to region. Consider, for example, North America's 86.9 percent and Africa's 27.5 percent. But such percentages tell only part of the story. Another perspective on Internet access addresses the actual number of people who are using the Web in different countries. There are now more users in Asia than Europe, North America, and Latin America combined, despite having an Internet penetration of only 34.8 percent, slightly below the world average. This suggests that Asian users will truly dominate Internet access across the globe once users in Asia reach the percentages now shown for North America and Europe.

These figures are always increasing, although at different rates. Africa has shown remarkable growth in Internet penetration since 2000, growing nearly 7,000 percent. Expansion in the Middle East has also been considerable, more than 3,300 percent since 2000. Asia has grown more than 1,100 percent in Internet penetration during the same period, and even developed countries have increased their Internet penetration rates since 2000 by between 450 percent (Europe) and 187 percent (the United States). Yet even with this pervasive growth, many people still lack Internet access.

Access to the Internet is one component, but access to high-quality information is also important. Lowbrow entertainment does little to inform or educate the public. Mere access, therefore, will not bridge the digital divide if users lack the critical-thinking skills to discern high-quality information and employ it for helpful purposes, or if access is limited to a barrage of reality or game shows that do little to further public knowledge of important issues and events in the world.

Thus, the digital divide issue has two major components. The first factor is technological: providing communications technologies and access to the Internet. Computers, software, and other tools need to be purchased, and a relatively small

FIGURE 14-2 World Internet Users and Penetration Rates

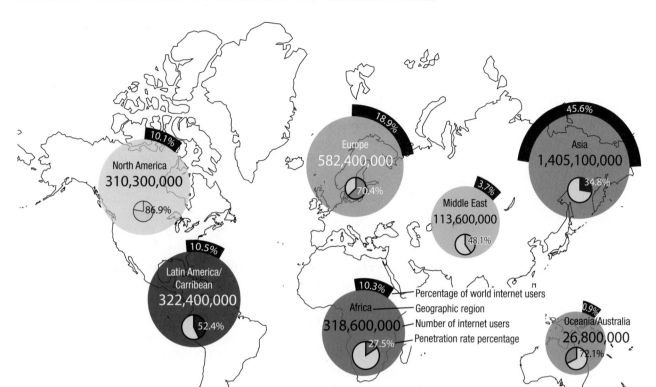

Source: Internet World Stats; www.internetworldstats.com/stats.htm

Internet subscription fee for someone in the West may constitute an entire month's wages for someone in a developing country. The second factor is educational: teaching people how best to benefit from the online communication tools available to them. Entertainment will always be an attractive category of online media, but it is not the sole genre available to the more affluent, nor should it be for the less privileged.

Complex political and socioeconomic issues such as the digital divide and the role of the Internet in society require long-term commitments to widespread dialog. Such discussions must also consider larger quality-of-life issues such as basic health care, clean water, and education. Corporate concerns may ultimately prevail over public interests, particularly if companies feel such discussions threaten profits. Media will help (or hamper) this inquiry, although their role may not always be apparent.

Global Media, Local Values

Media content that exposes audiences to different lifestyles and cultures provides access to new worlds and new ways of thinking. The Web has further expanded the possibilities for exploration, especially with video-sharing sites such as

YouTube and a proliferation of other social media. But given the impact of concentrated media ownership on the production of media content, questions arise regarding the actual diversity of voices heard. Yes, there are more cable channels than ever, but how fundamentally diverse are many of the police crime shows or reality TV programs, and how many DIY (do-it-yourself) channels such as HGTV do viewers need?

DISCUSSION QUESTIONS: Most media organizations rely increasingly on digital paywalls for revenue, but is it fair to expect the economically disadvantaged to pay for news and entertainment content? What might be done to address the problem of the global digital divide?

NEW WORLDS—OR CULTURAL IMPERIALISM?

The global reach of media giants and their ability to promote their programming in foreign markets raises the issue of **cultural imperialism**: when a foreign country dominates a domestic media market through an influx of its products. The large viewership for current and past shows imported from the United States, such as *NCIS*, *House*, *Grey's Anatomy*, and *The Simpsons*, suggests that this programming meets some need unfulfilled by domestic television fare.

This may be true to some extent because many countries that cannot afford to create shows with high production values air local programs that appear relatively amateurish in visual quality. Precisely because of the flood of media imports, however, many domestic television and movie production companies may not get a chance to develop fully. Countries with small populations can also discourage the growth of robust movie and television industries, as high production costs cannot be recouped in limited markets, especially when the local language is not widespread.

Of great concern from an ethical perspective to many in these countries is the possibility that citizens are absorbing alien cultural values in conflict with domestic ones. People in a conservative Muslim nation, for instance, may object to the frequently explicit content in many American television shows or movies. Although such exposure can encourage viewers to question governmental positions on freedom and democracy, shows such as *Grey's Anatomy* do not necessarily deal with political topics in any meaningful way. Still, critics argue that appreciation of and pride in traditional culture may be undermined with a slickly produced, idealized version of what it is to be American. People may lose touch with native traditions and values as they adopt distorted values based on skewed, unrealistic images of the United States.

Hegemony is the claim that the ideas of the ruling class translate into the ideas that rule the masses in society. **Media hegemony**, as explained by scholars such as Italian Antonio Gramsci, is a concept that asserts the dominant class in society control the mass media, largely through ownership. A Marxist economic concept, hegemony is rooted in the belief that the content of the mass media in the United States is designed to cater to the interests of the capitalist ruling elite and maintain the status quo, keeping those with wealth and in power wealthy and powerful. Hegemony suggests that a U.S.-driven global media system will turn the world into a giant commercial marketplace, and there is some evidence to support this view.

cultural imperialism

A condition that occurs when a powerful foreign country dominates a domestic media market through an influx of its products.

media hegemony

A condition that occurs when dominant groups in society control the mass media, largely through ownership.

A contradictory body of research exists regarding the hegemonic nature of media content. The work of professional journalists, socialized according to certain widely held guidelines and routines, is increasingly being complemented and often contested by that of citizen reporters, freelancers, and public service journalists with diverse methods, procedures, and perspectives. And although some news stories may resonate around the world, reports vary, with different accounts that are not perceived as equally credible. For instance, during the early days of the most recent war in Iraq, most mainstream U.S. news media supported the position that the distinct possibility of weapons of mass destruction in Iraq justified military action. Yet at the same time, media beyond American borders challenged this claim, which proved ultimately to be false.

There is also little evidence that most journalists around the world tend to present pro-American positions and negative coverage of other countries. Since the early 2000s, independent international reporting has grown, and sources such as the British Broadcasting Corporation (BBC), Japan's *Asahi Shimbun*, and Argentina's *Clarín* have featured voices emanating from diverse perspectives free of American influence.

Moreover, global media production and viewership in the entertainment and sports realms have grown dramatically in the digital age as production costs have fallen and distribution possibilities have increased. Consider the success of India's Bollywood, the Hindi-language movie industry based in Mumbai. While the name evokes America's Hollywood, Bollywood movies have their own distinct character and flavor that have proven to be hugely popular with both Indian and non-Indian audiences around the world. The 2014 film *PK*, the top-grossing film of all time in India, has made over $110 million worldwide in box office receipts, only half of which were generated domestically in India. Of course, Bollywood, like Hollywood, is a highly commercial system of motion picture entertainment, although its stories may differ.

Still, scholars such as Robert McChesney maintain that American hegemony shapes global digital media.[9] Google and Facebook are Internet corporate giants. Apple also plays a leading role on the world stage, with iTunes and its hugely popular mobile devices. Yet there are countervailing trends and forces. In 2014, for example, South Korea's Samsung sold more smartphones than Apple.[10] In 2012, the year not coincidentally that London hosted the Summer Olympics, Great Britain topped *Monocle* magazine's list of the most culturally influential nations, beating the United States for the first time.[11]

Britain is also known for world-famous cultural products such as the Beatles, James Bond, Adele, the 2012 Summer Olympics, and the royal family.
CRITICAL THINKING QUESTIONS:
When do cultural exports become a form of cultural imperialism? How would your media consumption be affected if you were to limit it to American products only?

DISCUSSION QUESTIONS: How powerful a force is American hegemony in global digital media? What specific cultural products, trends, and events, both historical and current, support your view?

CONVERGENCE AND ITS DISCONTENTS

In *Civilization and Its Discontents*, Sigmund Freud, the famous Viennese creator of psychoanalysis, articulated what he saw as the basic tension between the individual and civilization.[12] This tension, according to Freud, stems from the instinctive desire of the individual for freedom that conflicts with civilization's inherent need for order and stability achieved through the imposition of standard norms of behavior, or social conformity.

Similar tensions arise between global media and local culture. At its best, local culture provides a rich tapestry of diverse ideas, customs, and behaviors that can be presented on the world stage. Because of its global reach and impact, media convergence can provide unprecedented access to this richness but also generate conflict among diverse values. Ultimately, media convergence may also encourage increased cultural homogeneity, particularly given the common ownership of various media types (horizontal integration), such as book publishers, newspaper chains, and TV station groups.

MEDIA PIONEERS
Steve Chen, Chad Hurley, and Jawed Karim

Only since 2005 have we been able to see events global and local, past and present, historic and mundane, whenever we choose. Whether it be the coronation of Queen Elizabeth II, a Beyoncé concert, an interview with Russian President Vladimir Putin, or just "me at the zoo" (the first YouTube video uploaded), YouTube has forever changed our capacity to observe the activities of others and to display our own. In any month this year, more than 1 billion individuals will view a YouTube video, and more than a hundred hours of video will be uploaded in less time than it takes you to read this box.[13]

In 2013, YouTube became "the leading source of Internet traffic in the entire world."[14] That some 60 percent of YouTube views come from outside a creator's country is apt,

given its international founders.[15] Chad Hurley was born and raised in Pennsylvania. Steve Chen, born in Taiwan, emigrated to the United States when he was 15. Jawed Karim was born in Germany, the son of a Bangladeshi father and a German mother, who emigrated to America in 1992.

Like so many digital innovations, YouTube was a collaborative effort of young people: Its founders were in their late twenties when it launched. Chen and Karim studied computer science at the University of Illinois, leaving there to join PayPal, a new venture in California. Hurley, a graduate of Indiana University of Pennsylvania, became a designer at PayPal. After profiting from eBay's $1.5 billion purchase of PayPal in 2002,[16] they sought out new projects. The universal difficulty in sharing video online was their inspiration for YouTube, and the rest is global history.

In less than two years after its inception, YouTube was sold to Google for $1.65 billion in stock.[17] After YouTube, Chen and Hurley founded AVOS. Chen then left to join Google Ventures as an entrepreneur in residence, while Hurley focused AVOS efforts on developing video-sharing service MixBit.[18] Karim left shortly after the sale, earning a master's degree in computer science at Stanford University. Subsequently, he founded Y Ventures that seeks to "help talented teams with innovative products to take the next step."[19]

On the other hand, digital technology can also disempower companies that have traditionally controlled media production and distribution. Authors, for example, can self-publish and sell their works on sites such as Amazon, bypassing traditional publishers and bookstores. Digital technology also offers the potential for new players (such as Apple and Google) to enter the field of media production and distribution. It is important to consider who benefits financially from these transformations and what cultural consequences may ensue.

Digital music distribution is another domain where media convergence may create cultural conflict. For example, within months of Apple's 2003 launch of the iTunes Store, music distribution to its iPod helped Apple achieve dominance in the music market through downloads, subscriptions, and other services. By 2005, Apple's iTunes store branched out into the delivery of video; and by 2013, iTunes had begun delivering other forms of media content including books, newspapers, and magazines. The cultural consequences of a dominant horizontally integrated digital media distribution system could be profound. Such a system could increasingly foster a consumer culture worldwide as it shapes global tastes. The fundamental question remains: Does media convergence foster greater cultural uniformity, or does it advance cultural variety by enabling diverse groups to produce and consume cultural products (such as a book, a movie, or a website) of their choice?

GLOBALIZATION OF MEDIA PRODUCTION

Media production has increasingly become an international phenomenon. One of the principal forms this takes is the international coproduction of movies and television shows, which has become much more common since the early 1990s. For example, the blockbuster film *Iron Man 3* was coproduced in China by the Walt Disney Company and China's DMG Entertainment Group. Coproductions allow companies with differing strengths and capabilities to combine creative, financial, and technological resources across countries. They also offer international locations for storytelling.

Typically, such coproductions involve international treaties and regulations, with host countries often providing tax incentives to the companies involved. They also often receive public funding that can enhance production budgets. As a result, movies and television shows coproduced internationally have significant economic benefits for both American and foreign media companies. Coproductions were once conceived as a means to increase collaboration between countries with large and small production industries.[20] Ideally, coproductions feature material intended for and generated by local markets whose lone funding is inadequate to support the high production values seen in American movies and television shows that typically dominate the market. In the case of *Iron Man 3*, four minutes of extra footage of Chinese actors with whom local viewers could identify were added to the Chinese version of the film.

Rather than creating culturally relevant or authentic programming, however, coproductions often recreate common Hollywood media derived from popular genres. These include reality series, adventure shows, situation comedies, science fiction, and the like. In the end, economics drives global media program production and distribution. Increasingly, Hollywood executives make movies with a global market in mind, shaping both the selection of subject matter and the manner in which stories are told. Local, authentic culture tends to take a backseat. Kathleen Kennedy, president of Lucasfilm, identifies the globalization of audiences and the industry as one of the greatest challenges currently confronting Hollywood. As countries increasingly and rightly want to create their own content and tell their own stories, "it puts the pressure on the creative community to acknowledge and recognize that it's a bigger world and you need to tell many, many different kinds of stories."[21]

GLOBAL MEDIA FLOW

In the mid-1970s and 1980s, the United Nations Education, Scientific, and Cultural Organization (UNESCO) led a global examination of the flow of news and media entertainment around the world, dubbed the New World Information and Communication Order (NWICO). The UNESCO-sponsored discussion and debate identified a number of important issues, such as long-standing concerns about the dominant influence of media from the developed world and media coverage of the developing world. Another matter was the role of new technologies with important military and commercial uses, including satellite and computer technologies.

Advances in digital technology since the 1970s have altered the debate about intercultural communication, regional coexistence, and the relative dominance of the developed world. Mass-media content, including movies and television shows, has tended to move from the developed world, particularly the United States, to less-developed countries. Moreover, the launch of satellite and cable systems around the world has facilitated a multichannel viewing environment in many places, enabling international viewing on an extraordinary level.

Research also indicates that Western news agencies have historically produced as much as 80 percent of the news distributed globally. Some observers fear that this reporting often reflects the priorities of news agencies based in New York, London, or Paris and focuses on topics such as natural disasters and military coups rather than the basic realities of poverty, pollution, and unemployment. This situation has improved more recently, however, with the growth of social media, citizen reporting, and regional news agencies such as Al Arabiya in the Middle East.

Advertising agencies and marketers of goods and services in the developed world also tend to dominate the world's global media system, with commercial messages from the West often featuring significantly in many international markets. Since the 1980s, most companies, recognizing the cultural diversity and sensitivities in various markets, adapt their messages to the local market. But the process is not seamless. In 2012, Ikea apologized for digitally removing women from its product catalog for distribution in Saudi Arabia.[22] The global company believed it had been appropriately adapting its commercial message for local Islamic sensibilities regarding the representation of women in photographs. Once the newspaper *Metro* in Ikea's native Sweden reported these alterations, though, the story stirred such controversy in the West that the company backtracked, stating it regretted this editorial decision not in keeping with its corporate values.

Western backlash forced Ikea to apologize for having digitally removed images of women from its catalog produced for and distributed in Saudi Arabia.

PROTECTING LOCAL VOICES

Many media critics argue that Western media, typically profit-driven and privately owned and operated, not only dominate the global flow of news and entertainment media but also carry a commercial or corporate bias. To counterbalance the influx of foreign commercial media, many countries around the world have sought to develop internally more authentic, culturally relevant media programming and content for their citizens. Although these initiatives to promote national media content often involve government funding and other incentives to buy or, as the case may be, broadcast locally, these media efforts may also succeed in attracting a more global audience.

Some Developing Nations

Many alternative sources of local media content now exist in developing countries to help redress the historical dominance of Western information and entertainment, especially from American media companies. In Asia, examples include India's Bollywood, films that tend to reflect indigenous culture and traditions. In Africa, GhanaWeb reports local and national news and information.

In Australia or Brazil, for example, indigenous peoples, who often live in rural areas, promote a message of environmental stewardship and respect for the earth. Yet people of indigenous heritage often suffer disproportionately from poverty and other social ills, their marginalized voices drowned out by dominant world media. "Consider that indigenous peoples make up just 5 percent of the world's population," explained Kanavo F. Nwanze, president of the International Fund for Agricultural Development (IFAD). "But they are 15 percent of those living in poverty."[23]

Genghis Khan's empire took over much of Asia at the speed of his mounted armies, but today the world can reach even remote areas in Mongolia at the speed of light.

IFAD financed the 2012 launch of the first community radio station in Malaysia. Bario Radio enables indigenous Malaysians to make vital contributions to the local and global dialog on environmental sustainability and poverty with stories about the environmental impact of development on Central Borneo, for example, and the disastrous consequences of global warming. Bario Radio also confronts stereotypes and affirms indigenous peoples' rights and identities.

Indigenous, noncommercial media complement the dominant, for-profit media channels from the West. They tell seldom-heard stories of those frequently marginalized by the economically powerful institutions that sponsor and control most commercial media. Known globally for rich oral traditions, indigenous voices are especially well suited to the use of community radio, online video, and social media. These tools have allowed them to inform and educate local audiences while reaching global ones.

A Neighbo(u)ring Nation

Many governments fund the internal production of music and other media arts as well as news and information sources. Although the United States provides limited funding for such endeavors through the National Endowment for the Arts (NEA) and the Corporation for Public Broadcasting (CPB), its neighbor to the north has extensive programs. In 1957, Canada created the Council for the Arts to "foster and promote the study and enjoyment of, and the production of works in, the arts."[24] Production grants are awarded in a variety of artistic fields, including media arts, writing, and publishing. Such initiatives help offset commercial influences in imported mainstream media while promoting artistic innovation and expression at home.

In 1968, a broadcasting act was also passed that ensured Canadian voices and stories access to Canadian airwaves. Radio and television broadcasts must feature a high percentage of "CanCon"—Canadian content created primarily by Canadian talent. At least 35 percent of the popular music broadcast on commercial radio stations between 6:00 a.m. and 6:00 p.m. Monday to Friday must be Canadian. On CBC (Canadian Broadcasting Corporation), the national public radio and television broadcaster, 50 percent Canadian popular music content is required.[25]

The digital distribution of media content, though, is circumventing these and similar long-standing regulations intended to strengthen Canada culturally, socially, and economically. American provider Netflix proved an attractive option for Canadians once it crossed the border, although the content Canadians may choose to stream is more limited. Canadians engage more with video than Americans, however, spending 5.1 more hours per month watching videos online.[26] "The competition in digital is, more or less, borderless," says Neil McEneaney, interim executive vice-president of CBC's English Services, "and many of those competitors have access to vast content resources and deep pockets."[27]

PROMOTING GLOBAL VOICES

Farther abroad, similar initiatives have also been implemented. The Doha Film Institute in the Middle East, for example, receives arts funding from the government, with financial support from the Qatar Foundation. Also based in Qatar is the Al Jazeera Network, a pan-Arab news service and media company launched in 1996 with $137 million in funding from the emir of Qatar. Al Jazeera was the only international news organization with correspondents in Iraq during Operation Desert Fox in 1998, a U.S. military operation.[28] By 1999, Al Jazeera had begun broadcasting 24 hours daily, and it became increasingly well known for its coverage of the wars in Iraq and Afghanistan.

In January 2013, it acquired former vice president and Nobel Laureate Al Gore's Current TV. Paying an estimated $500 million for the cable channel, Al Jazeera almost instantly gained a significant foothold in the American television market. Al Jazeera English, which debuted in 2006, reached only 4.7 million U.S. households. Launched in 2013, Al Jazeera America (AJAM), their new English-language 24-hour cable and satellite news channel, is available in over 64 million U.S. households. The new AJAM channel, headquartered in New York City, has some two hundred journalists with several news bureaus around the country to build news programming content. It competes with other cable and satellite news channels, such as CNN, Fox, and MSNBC.

Al Jazeera has positioned itself as an impartial news source. Yet some contend the network offers a pro-Arab slant, while others claim its perspective is anti-Arab. "The network's weaknesses," notes observer Everette E. Dennis, dean of Northwestern University in Qatar, "are a lingering reputation that conjures up images of Al Qaeda videotapes, mostly a thing of the past if still etched in memory; suspicions about the network's obligations to the Qatari government;

With its 2012 acquisition of Current TV, Al Jazeera brings news and other types of programming in the Middle East and beyond to an increasingly global audience. **CRITICAL THINKING QUESTION:** What concerns, if any, do you have about the increasing presence of Al Jazeera programming in the United States, and why?

and a general anti-Arab bias which is still something of an 'acceptable' prejudice in the U.S."[29]

Criticism notwithstanding, Al Jazeera has developed a reputation for quality journalism, specifically, according to the Index on Censorship, for combatting censorship and contributing to the free and open exchange of news and information in the Arab world. Al Jazeera has also won numerous American awards for news coverage, such as the Peabody Award, the Columbia University Journalism Award, and the People's Choice Award.

The Al Jazeera Network operates multiple sports channels, a children's channel, and a documentary channel. Other international Al Jazeera channels include Al Jazeera Balkans (a Bosnian/Croatian/Serbian-languages channel that debuted in 2011) and Al Jazeera Turk. Al Jazeera English is known for *The Stream*, a TV and online program based on social media, especially Twitter. Competition for regional news coverage in the Arab world has grown, however, since the Arab Spring of 2011. For example, Al Arabiya, founded in 2003 by a group of Saudi investors, has captured a significant share of the region's audience.

DISCUSSION QUESTIONS: Compare and contrast treatment of a global issue or recent big news event as reported by Al Jazeera America and another news site such as CNN or Fox News. What are some of the key differences in how the story is presented and told?

CYBERSECURITY AND MEDIA

Media convergence—technological, economic, and cultural—continues to bring countries and peoples closer together and in so doing produces new challenges, not only for local cultural identity but also for global national security. Backlash against American foreign policy sometimes takes the form of cybercrime. Hackers from various countries have attempted to break into Western computer networks, often with considerable success. In early 2013, cybercriminals hacked the systems of several digital-media companies. A Chinese-based group hacked Apple, Facebook, and even Google, according to the FBI. The same or a related group also attacked news organizations, including the *Washington Post* and the *New York Times*.[30] In late 2014, North Korea hacked Sony Pictures, and the ensuing scandal rocked Hollywood. In mid-2015, a hacking group based in China accessed the private information of four million U.S. federal employees.

In St. Petersburg, Russia, a group called the Internet Research Agency has been known to coordinate complex disinformation campaigns using social media, fake websites, doctored news footage, and multiple Twitter accounts that target influential Twitter users to maximize the spread of their messages. These techniques promote pro-Kremlin messages but also to try to provoke panic by claiming (and ostensibly showing) supposed terrorist acts, such as a bombing of a chemical plant in Louisiana on the anniversary of 9/11, an incident that did not in fact occur.[31]

As the nature of online cybercrime has evolved to include cyberterrorism, the United States has made cybersecurity a top national defense priority. The Commerce Department is working with both technology and media companies to develop rules and protocols for sharing online-threat information with the government as well as strategies for cyberdefense. President Obama defended the PRISM surveillance program as vital in the war against terrorism, while others praised NSA whistle-blower Edward Snowden as a champion of the individual's rights to civil liberty and privacy.

For the media and for society, the truth likely lies somewhere in between. United States Supreme Court Justice Hugo Black argued that constitutional protection was necessary to empower a free press that should hold the government publicly accountable for secrets and deceptions.[32] Yet, without the tools to combat terrorist threats, the government cannot protect its citizens. A sustainable balance must be struck between the competing interests of freedom, security, and public accountability.

 **MEDIA CAREERS**

As the fields of journalism, advertising, PR, and entertainment media are all practiced all over the world, opportunities abound for people with foreign-language skills. Fluent professionals can successfully navigate the local media in the region's native language while working in English-language media abroad or operate exclusively in the local language.

The United Nations (UN) and a variety of nongovernmental organizations (NGOs) need people with good professional communication skills in the field of development communication, an enterprise intended to improve the lives of locals. These campaigns focus on health communication, education, and environmental or wildlife conservation, among other areas. Communication students who major or minor in political science, international relations, foreign languages, sociology, anthropology, education, or one of the life sciences could be well-positioned for jobs with NGOs in foreign countries.

Typical PR functions also exist in this field, such as media relations, publicity and promotion, and donor and volunteer recruitment. These jobs could take you to developing nations but are just as likely to be based at an NGO's main office in a developed country. With field offices throughout the world and many large regional offices in big cities, besides its New York headquarters, the UN strongly encourages employees to request postings in various locations every few years to expand their range of knowledge and skills.

In addition to the obvious interest in foreign cultures, a successful development-communication professional must be able to readily adapt to local customs. This career is ideally suited to people who love to travel and experience foreign cultures in depth but who are also willing to accept hardships, sometimes dangerous living conditions, and often a lower standard of living (e.g., everything from regular electricity to flush toilets may be considered a luxury, depending on the country).

LOOKING BACK AND MOVING FORWARD

Globalization is transforming media as digital and networking technologies enable media empire building. These conglomerates can overwhelm local media enterprises and stifle indigenous voices. While government funding for international coproductions may help support authentic, local media, it does little to improve access for the masses who lack the means to buy an iPad, iPhone, Android, or Windows mobile device or subscribe to broadband telecommunications service.

The consequences of this problem, especially acute in developing nations, include reduced access not only to entertainment but also to ecommerce, public affairs news, and educational content. Although nearly 80 percent of the world's population has Internet access, the digital divide is widening between those with access and those without. As media have become more digital and networked, costly broadband or high-speed Internet service has become near ubiquitous in developed nations, exacerbating this disparity. Moreover, a growing number of digital-media enterprises on the global stage are implementing digital paywalls, an additional financial obstacle to media access.

The forms and functions of mass communication are evolving in the digital age. Siebert, Schramm, and Peterson's four theories of the press are still relevant but are best seen as ideal types and not exact models for twenty-first-century media. Traditional media are converging with social media and global ownership, and international coproduction and digital distribution are increasingly common.

Media play a critical role in political and social-cultural systems around the world. Western media have tended to dominate the worldwide flow of news and entertainment, generating pressures and tensions resulting from hegemony. Yet at the same time, digital and networked technologies have dramatically lowered the cost and other barriers to media production and distribution, enabling more global and widespread movie, television, and news production. Alternative voices are being heard more frequently on the global stage, including those of indigenous peoples and local producers. Social media and mobile technology are also enabling citizen reporters around the world to cover breaking news, from Tahrir Square to Timbuktu, through photos, video, and tweets.

Global terrorism has expanded from the physical to the virtual realm, with cyberterrorism a growing threat. While the digital landscape holds great promise for global communication, it also presents many hazards and dangers. Cybercitizens will need to be vigilant to ensure that the benefits of globally networked digital media continue to outweigh the risks.

MEDIA MATTERS   GLOBAL MEDIA

1. Identify a country that follows the authoritarian theory of communication. If offered some kind of media position there, would you consider it?

2. Which theory of communication do you think is best equipped to most effectively utilize digital and social media? Why do you think so?

3. Define the concept of the public sphere. Where online do you feel this ideal has the greatest possibility of being realized?

4. Which form of mass communication—print, radio, or television—is most effective in reaching a broad cross section of the population in a developing country? Why do you think so?

5. What role have social media played in the aftermath of disasters like the 2013 Ya'an earthquake in China or the 2015 Yangtze River ship sinking?

6. Which do you think are more susceptible to cyberattacks, established multinational media corporations or media companies in developing countries that have recently been using the Internet to reach the global stage?

FURTHER READING

The Myth of Digital Democracy. Matthew Hindman (2008) Princeton University Press.

Into the Buzzsaw: Leading Journalists Expose the Myth of a Free Press. Kristina Borjesson (ed.) (2002) Prometheus Books.

Media Spectacle and the Crisis of Democracy: Terrorism, War, and Election Battles. Douglas Kellner (2005) Paradigm Publishers.

(Un)Civil War of Words: Media and Politics in the Arab World. Mamoun Fandy (2007) Praeger.

Cyberprotest: New Media, Citizens, and Social Movements. W. Van De Donk (ed.) (2004) Routledge.

Religious Broadcasting in the Middle East. Khaled Hroub (ed.). (2012) Hurst & Company.

Arab Media: Globalization and Emerging Media Industries. Noha Mellor, Muhammad Ayish, Nabil Dajani, Khalil Rinnawi (2011) Policy Press.

Real-Time Diplomacy: Politics and Power in the Social Media Era. Philip Seib (2012) Palgrave Macmillan.

Global Media, Culture, and Identity: Theory, Cases and Approaches. Rohit Chapra and Radhika Gajjala (2011) Routledge.

Detecting Bull: How to Identify Bias and Junk Journalism in Print, Broadcast and on the Wild Web, 2nd ed. J. H. McManus (2012) Unvarnished Press.

The Ethics of Reality TV: A Philosophical Examination. W. N. Wyatt, K. Bunton (2012) Continuum.

After Broadcast News: Media Regimes, Democracy, and the New Information Environment. Bruce A. Williams, Michael X. Delli Carpini (2011) Cambridge University Press.

American Indians and the Mass Media. Meta G. Carstarphen, John P. Sanchez (eds.) (2012) University of Oklahoma Press.

Communication for Development and Social Change, 2nd ed. Jan Servaes (ed.) (2008) Sage.

The Handbook of Development Communication and Social Change. Karin Gwinn Wilkins, Thomas Tufte, Rafael Obregon (eds.) (2014) Wiley-Blackwell.

The International Television News Agencies: The World from London. Chris Paterson (2011) Peter Lang "Media and Communication" Series.

Public Relations in Global Cultural Contexts: Multi-Paradigmatic Perspectives. Nilanjana Bardhan, C. Kay Weaver (eds.) (2011) Routledge.

Glossary

actualities Edited audio clips from interviews with people.

ad-agency commission A percentage amount of the cost of an advertisement taken by the advertising agency that helped create and sell the ad.

advertising An ancient form of human communication designed to inform or persuade members of the public with regard to some product or service.

advertorial Display advertisement created to look like an article within the publication, although most publications have the words "advertisement" or "paid advertisement" in tiny print somewhere nearby.

agenda setting Media's role in deciding which topics to cover and consequently which topics the public deems important and worthy of discussion.

Alien and Sedition Acts A series of four acts passed by the U.S. Congress in 1798 that, among other things, prohibited sedition, or spoken or written criticism of the U.S. government, and imposed penalties of a fine or imprisonment on conviction. Although they expired in 1801, other sedition acts have been passed periodically, especially during times of war.

amplitude modulation (AM) Radio carrier signal modified by variations in wave amplitude.

Associated Press Founded in 1848 as a not-for-profit members' cooperative by a group of six New York newspaper publishers to share the costs of gathering news by telegraph. Today, some 1,500 newspapers and 5,000 television and radio stations are members.

astroturfing Creating a movement controlled by a large organization or group designed to look like a citizen-founded, grassroots campaign.

astroturfing campaign A movement or campaign that looks as though it was created by concerned citizens as a grassroots movement when in fact it was actually created or controlled by an organization with a vested interest in the outcome.

asynchronous media Media that do not require the audience to assemble at a given time, such as printed materials and recorded audio or video.

augmented reality Digital overlays of information on a screen that correspond to what is being looked at in the real world through the screen.

auteur Director as storyteller.

authoritarian theory A theory of international mass communication that contends authoritarian governments exert direct control over the media.

balance Presenting sides equally and reporting on a broad range of news events.

bandwidth The carrying capacity and speed of telecommunication networks that determine how much information can be sent and how fast it can travel over the networks.

banner ad Original form of advertising on the Web, it appears across the top of a website.

beat Reporter's specialized area of coverage based on geography or subject. Common beats in large or medium-sized newspapers include education, crime, and state politics.

behavioral targeting Advertisers tracking individuals' Web-browsing behavior to provide ads that closely match the topics of sites visited or searches made.

Benjamin Day Publisher of the New York Sun who originated the penny press in 1833 by offering his paper on the streets for a penny.

big data A collection of data sets too large for traditional analytic techniques to sort, analyze, and visualize.

blog Short for weblog, a type of website in which a person posts regular journal or diary entries, with the posts arranged chronologically.

Bobo doll studies Media–effects experiments in the 1950s that showed children who watched TV episodes that rewarded a violent person were more likely to punch a Bobo doll than children who saw episodes that punished a violent person.

bourgeoisie A class of society that translates approximately to "middle class," distinguished from the aristocracy above and the proletariat (or workers) below.

branding Process of creating in the consumer's mind a clear identity for a particular company's product, logo, or trademark.

broadband A network connection that enables a large amount of bandwidth to be transmitted, which allows for more information to be sent in a shorter period of time.

broadcast Originally a reference to casting seeds widely in a field that was subsequently applied to the fledgling electronic medium of radio and later television.

camera obscura A dark box or room with a small hole that allows an inverted image of an outside scene to be shown on the opposite inner wall.

categorical imperative In ethical thought, Kant's concept of an unconditional moral obligation that does not depend on an individual's personal inclinations or goals.

catfish Someone who fakes an online profile, usually to encourage another to fall in love with the false persona.

cathode-ray tube (CRT) Device in older televisions and computers using electron beams to transmit images to the screen.

censorship The act of prohibiting certain expression or content. Censors usually do not target the whole publication, program, or website but seek to prohibit some part of the content.

Children's Television Act (CTA) Created in 1990, it limits the amount of commercial content that programming can carry, forces stations to carry certain amounts of educational programming for children sixteen and under, and includes other provisions to protect children.

chilling effect The phenomenon that occurs when journalists or other media producers decide not to publish stories on a topic after a journalist has been punished or jailed for such a story.

circulation Number of newspaper copies sold or distributed.

citizen journalism The gathering and sharing of news and information by public citizens, particularly via mobile and social media, sometimes via traditional media.

classified advertising Advertising traditionally found in print media, especially newspapers but also in some magazines and now increasingly online, that consists of messages posted by individuals and organizations to sell specific goods or services.

clear and present danger A restriction on speech when it meets both of the following conditions: (1) It is intended to incite or produce dangerous activity (as with falsely shouting "Fire!" in a crowded theater), and (2) it is likely to succeed in achieving the purported result.

click-through rate (CTR) Rate at which people click on an online advertisement to access more information.

codex Manuscript book of individually bound pages.

community antenna television (CATV) Cable television developed in 1948 so communities in hilly or remote terrain could still access television broadcasts.

consolidation A process whereby traditional media companies have grown fewer and much larger in the past fifty years through mergers and acquisitions.

convergence The coming together of computing, telecommunications, and media in a digital environment.

cookies Information that a website puts on a user's local hard drive so that it can recognize when that computer accesses the website again. Cookies also allow for conveniences like password recognition and personalization.

copyright a form of intellectual property law that protects the right to use, publish, reproduce, perform, display, or distribute a literary or artistic work, such as a piece of writing, music, film, or video.

cord-cutters Those who have switched from cable or other connections to Internet-delivered TV.

cord-nevers Those who have known only mobile or wireless Internet-delivered TV.

correlation Media interpretation ascribing meaning to issues and events that helps individuals understand their roles within the larger society and culture.

cost per thousand (CPM) Standard unit for measuring advertising rates for publications based on circulation.

counterpublics Public forums of resistance created by those who consider themselves to be excluded from or marginalized within dominant media and communication.

critical theory A theoretical approach broadly influenced by Marxist notions of the role of ideology, exploitation, capitalism, and the economy in understanding and eventually transforming society.

cross-sectional study A study that gathers data on subjects at a specific point in time.

crowdsourcing Using raw data gathered from the public and citizen-journalists to help create a news report.

cultivation analysis A theory of media effects that claims television cultivates in audiences a view of reality similar to the world portrayed in television programs.

cultural imperialism A condition that occurs when a powerful foreign country dominates a domestic media market through an influx of its products.

cultural studies An interdisciplinary framework for studying communication that rejects the scientific approach while investigating the role of culture in creating and maintaining social relations and systems of power.

cultural transmission The process of passing on culturally relevant knowledge, skills, attitudes, and values from person to person or group to group.

culture industry A term coined by the Frankfurt School to describe how media companies produce or "make" culture in the same way that other companies produce products.

daguerreotype Photograph created by exposing a positive image on a metal plate.

David Sarnoff Head of RCA, he promoted the development of television as a mass medium yet blocked the development of FM radio for years because RCA produced and sold AM radio receivers.

daypart A segment of time radio and television program planners use to determine their primary audience during that time of day or night.

digital divide The gap between regions and demographics that have access to modern, digital-communications technology and those that have limited or no access.

digital immigrant An individual who grew up in the analog media era and who generally has more trouble adapting to new digital technologies, despite perhaps a desire to use and understand them.

Digital Millennium Copyright Act A 1998 act of Congress that reformed copyright law comprehensively to update it for the digital age. Key provisions addressed the circumvention of copyright-protection systems, fair use in a digital environment, and Internet service providers' liability for content sent through their lines.

digital native A term coined in 2001 by author Marc Prensky for a member of a younger generation who has grown up with and is consequently very comfortable using digital media and adapting to rapid technological changes.

digital rights management (DRM) Technologies that let copyright owners control the level of access or use allowed for a copyrighted work, such as limiting the number of times a song can be copied.

digital television (DTV) Television system in which all information broadcast by cable or through the air is in digital, or computer-readable, form.

digital watermark Computer code (usually invisible but sometimes visible) inserted into any digital content—images, graphics, audio, video, or even text documents—that authenticates the source of that content.

digitization The process that makes media computer readable.

dime novel First paperback form whose cost of ten cents made it accessible even to the poor.

direct effects model Model of mass communication that claims media have direct and measurable effects on audiences, such as encouraging them to buy products or to become violent.

display advertising Advertising in print media that usually consists of illustrations or images and text that can occupy a small section of a page, a full page, or multiple pages.

distributed computing Individual, autonomous computers that work together toward a common goal, typically a large, complex project that requires more computing power than that of any individual computer.

earned media Favorable publicity prompted by a public relations source rather than advertising, such as a news conference, an event, or a press release; the opposite of paid media, such as advertising or product placements.

echo effect A phenomenon that occurs when people surround themselves with online voices that echo their own, reinforcing their views and the belief that those opinions are in the majority when in fact they may not be.

Edward R. Murrow A radio and, later, television journalist and announcer who set the standard for journalistic excellence during TV's golden age.

Edwin Howard Armstrong Columbia University engineering professor who invented FM radio transmission.

electronic news-gathering (ENG) equipment Tools such as video cameras and satellite dishes that allow journalists to gather and broadcast news much more quickly.

encoding/decoding A theoretical model that states media producers encode media products with meanings, decoded in various ways by various audiences.

entertainment Providing or being provided with amusement or enjoyment.

epistemology A study or theory of the limitations and validity of knowledge; more simply, a way of, or framework for, understanding the world.

equal-time rule The requirement that broadcasters make available equal airtime, in terms of commentaries and commercials, to opposing candidates running for election. It does not apply to candidates appearing in newscasts, documentaries, or news-event coverage.

ethical consumerism A kind of activism in which consumers buy only products that they believe are produced ethically.

ethnography A variety of qualitative research techniques that involve immersion of a researcher in a particular culture to allow interaction with participants through observation, participation, interviews, or a combination of methods.

fair use Allowable use of someone else's copyrighted work that does not require payment of royalties, with a number of factors that determine if something falls under fair use or violates copyright.

fairness News reporting on all relevant sides of an issue that allows representatives of those various sides the same coverage.

Fairness Doctrine Adopted by the FCC in 1949, it required broadcasters to seek out and present all sides of a controversial issue they were covering. It was discarded by the FCC in 1987.

fear appeal Advertising technique that attempts to persuade the audience by scaring them, such as antismoking ads that show disfigured former smokers.

Federal Communications Commission (FCC) Established in 1934, the principal communications regulatory body at the federal level in the United States.

Federal Radio Commission (FRC) Formed by the Radio Act of 1927, the commission, the precursor to the FCC, created a policy that favored fewer high-power radio broadcasting stations rather than more numerous low-power stations.

First Amendment Guarantees that Congress shall make no law restricting freedom of speech, press, or religion.

focus group A small group of people assembled by researchers to discuss a topic. Their interactions are closely observed, recorded, and analyzed to determine people's opinions.

folksonomies Collection of tags created by users that provide metadata (data about data) regarding information.

fourth estate Another term for the press, or journalism, which acts as a fourth branch of government, one that watches the other branches (executive, legislative, and judicial).

frame Structure or angle given a news story that influences reader understanding covering the event.

framing The presentation and communication of a message in a particular way that influences our perception of it.

free and open-source software movement (FOSS) A movement that wants software to be freely available and the source code open to anyone to make modifications and improvements.

freemium Subscriptions that provide some content for free but require a monthly subscription to take advantage of all the site has to offer.

frequency modulation (FM) Radio carrier signal modified by variations in wave length/frequency.

gamification The use of game-like mechanics in nongame settings, such as earning points, badges, or rewards for performing certain actions.

genres Topical categories.

going viral The phenomenon in which a media item spreads rapidly from person to person via the Internet.

gramophone Developed by inventor Emile Berliner, it used a flat disc rather than a cylinder to record sound.

Granville T. Woods Inventor of railway telegraphy in 1887, a type of wireless communication that allowed moving trains to communicate with each other and with stations, greatly reducing the number of railway collisions.

graphical user interface (GUI) Computer interface that shows graphical representations of file structures, files, and applications in the form of folders, icons, and windows.

graphophone An improvement on Thomas Edison's phonograph in recording audio, it used beeswax to record sound rather than tinfoil. Developed by Alexander Graham Bell and inventor Charles Tainter.

greenwashing The practice of companies making themselves or their products appear to be organic, environmentally friendly, or supportive of free trade when in fact they are not.

Guglielmo Marconi Italian inventor and creator of radio telegraphy, or wireless transmission, in 1899.

Gutenberg Bible Bible printed by Johannes Gutenberg in Europe in 1455, considered one of the first mechanically printed works.

Hays Code A code established in 1930 by the movie industry to censor itself regarding showing nudity or glorifying antisocial acts. Officials for the Hays Office had to approve each film distributed to a mass audience.

Heinrich Hertz Demonstrated the existence of radio waves in 1885, setting the stage for the development of modern wireless communications. The measurement unit of electromagnetic frequencies was named for Hertz.

high-definition television (HDTV) Modern television technology that produces a much higher-resolution image, sharper color, a wider aspect ratio, and superior audio. Ultra-high definition is next-generation TV with even higher resolution video. 4K TVs can display video at 4,000 lines of resolution, compared to the 420 lines of standard definition TV.

human–computer interaction Any interaction between humans and computers, either through devices such as keyboards, mice, and touch screens or through voice recognition.

hyperlink Clickable pointer to other online content.

hypertext Text online linked by HTML coding to another Web page or website or to a different part of the same Web page.

Hypertext Markup Language (HTML) A coding format that describes how information should look on the Web.

Hypertext Transfer Protocol (HTTP) A protocol that enables the standardized transfer of text, audio, and video files, as well as email, from one address to another.

hypodermic-needle model A model of media effects, also called the "magic bullet," that claims media messages have a profound, direct, and uniform impact on the public.

ideology A comprehensive and normative body of ideas and standards held by an individual or a group.

indecent speech Language or material that, in context, depicts or describes, in terms patently offensive as measured by contemporary community standards for the broadcast medium, sexual or excretory organs or activities.

independent films Films made by production companies separate from the main Hollywood studios.

independent labels Small companies that produce and distribute records. Not part of the three major-label corporations, they include those producing only one or two albums a year as well as larger independents such as Disney.

infomercial Also called "paid programming," a thirty- or sixty-minute television show that seeks to sell a product and that usually involves a celebrity spokesperson and customer testimonials.

information overload The difficulties associated with managing and making sense of the vast amounts of information available to us.

information society A society where information production has supplanted industrial production, dramatically transforming cultural, economic, and political activity.

instant messaging Often abbreviated IM, a form of real-time communication through text typed over a computer network.

integrated communications All channels of communication about a company or brand working together to create a cohesive message.

intellectual property (IP) Ideas that have commercial value, such as literary or artistic works, patents, trademarks, business methods, and industrial processes.

interactivity For digital-media purposes, it consists of three main elements: (1) a dialog that occurs between a human and a computer program, (2) a dialog that occurs simultaneously or nearly so, and (3) the audience has some measure of control over what media content it sees and in what order.

interpersonal communication Communication between two or more individuals, often in a small group, although it can involve communication between a live speaker and an audience.

interpretive reporting Reporting that places the facts of a story in a broader context by relying on the reporter's knowledge and experience.

interstitial ad Online advertisement that opens in a new window from the one the user was in.

James Carey Communications scholar and historian who has shaped a cultural-studies approach to communication theory.

James Gordon Bennett Founder of the *New York Herald* in 1835. He initiated features found in modern newspapers including a financial page, editorial commentary, and public-affairs reporting.

Johannes Gutenberg German printer credited with creating the first mechanical printing press in 1455.

joint operating arrangement (JOA) Legal agreement permitting newspapers in the same market or city to merge their business operations for economic reasons while maintaining independent editorial operations.

Joseph Pulitzer American newspaper magnate whose publications competed vigorously with those of Hearst. After 1900, Pulitzer retreated from sensational journalism, favoring instead more socially conscious reporting and muckraking. He founded the Pulitzer Prizes, annual awards for outstanding journalism.

laugh track A television sitcom device that generates prerecorded laughter timed to coincide with punch lines of jokes.

Lee de Forest Considered the father of radio broadcasting because of his invention that permitted reliable voice transmissions for both point-to-point communication and broadcasting.

libertarian theory A theory of international mass communication that supports the individual's right to publish whatever she or he wants, even material critical of the government or of government officials.

listservs Automated mailing-list administrators that allow for easy subscription, cancellation, and delivery of emails to subscribers.

long tail The principle that selling a few of many types of items can be as or more profitable than selling many copies of a few items, a practice that works especially well for online sellers such as Amazon and Netflix.

longitudinal study A study that gathers data on subjects over a long period of time.

Louis Daguerre Inventor of the daguerreotype, an early type of photography.

lurking Only reading what others write in online discussion boards but not contributing to the discussions.

machinima A combination of machine and cinema that uses 3-D animation techniques and characters from popular video games to make movies.

major labels Universal Music Group, Sony Music, and Warner Music Group—the three biggest recording-arts companies, which control much of the music industry partly through their powerful distribution channels and ability to market music to mass audiences.

mass communication Communication to a large group or groups of people that remain largely unknown to the sender of the message.

mass-market paperback Inexpensive, softcover books small enough for a back pocket and sold in bookstores, supermarkets, drugstores, and other public places.

Mathew B. Brady Nineteenth-century photographer acclaimed for his Civil War images and portraits of famous people.

mean-world syndrome A syndrome in which people perceive the world as more dangerous than it actually is, the result of viewing countless acts of media violence.

media bias A real or perceived viewpoint held by journalists and news organizations that slants news coverage unfairly, contrary to professional journalism's stated goals of balanced coverage and objectivity.

media ecology The study of media environments and their effects on people and society.

media grammar The underlying rules, structures, and patterns by which a medium presents itself and is used and understood by the audience.

media hegemony A condition that occurs when dominant groups in society control the mass media, largely through ownership.

media literacy The process of interacting with and critically analyzing media content by considering its particular presentation, its underlying political or social messages, and its ownership or regulation issues that may affect what is presented and in what form.

media oligopoly A marketplace in which media ownership and diversity are severely limited and the actions of any single media group affect its competitors substantially, including determining the content and price of media products for both consumers and advertisers.

medium A communication channel, such as talking on the telephone, instant messaging, or writing back and forth in a chat room.

meme A media item of cultural interest that spreads through repetition and replication via the Internet.

mods Short for "modifications," user-created code changes that alter how video games are played or look.

muckrakers Journalists, particularly magazine journalists, who conduct investigative reporting on major corporations and government; they were dubbed muckrakers in the early twentieth century for the "muck" they uncovered.

multicast Simultaneous transmission of multiple channels of compressed content or the same content but at different times.

multitasking In a computer environment, doing several activities at once with a variety of programs, such as simultaneous word processing, spreadsheet, and database work while conducting real-time chat through an instant-messenger service.

Network neutrality The principle that broadband networks should be free of restrictions on content, platforms, or equipment and that certain types of content, platforms, or equipment should not get preferential treatment on the network.

news hole Amount of total space available after advertisement space has been blocked out, typically in newspapers.

news leak Secret information deliberately given to journalists with the hope that they will publish the item.

Newspaper Preservation Act Created in 1970 to preserve a diversity of editorial opinion in communities where only two competing, or independently owned, daily newspapers exist.

objectivity Journalistic principle that says reporting should be impartial and free of bias. Because of the difficulties involved in complete objectivity, this principle has largely been replaced by the concepts of fairness and balance.

obscenity One of the forms of speech not protected by the First Amendment and thus subject to censorship. Although an exact definition of the term has been difficult to achieve in various court cases, generally a three-part standard is applied for media content: It must appeal to prurient interests as defined by community standards, it must show sexual conduct in an offensive manner, and it must on the whole lack serious artistic, literary, political, or scientific value.

oligopoly An economic structure in which a few very large, very powerful, and very rich owners control an industry or collection of related industries.

open access A system that makes information accessible to all to discourage power imbalances that may arise from unequal access.

opinion poll Usually conducted by a professional polling organization, a poll asking members of the public their opinions on issues or political candidates.

opt in When consumers choose to receive mailings or marketing material, usually by checking a box on a website when registering for the site.

outdoor advertising Billboards and other forms of public advertising, such as on buses or taxis.

participant-observation A qualitative research technique in which researchers participate as members of the group they are observing.

partisan press A press, such as colonial newspapers, typically aligned with a particular political party and presenting information to help its cause, with no sense of objectivity or balance in news coverage.

patent A form of intellectual property law that protects the right to produce and sell an invention.

payola Cash or gifts given to radio disc jockeys by record labels in exchange for greater airplay of the label's artists or most recent songs. After several scandals in the 1950s, the practice is now illegal.

peer-to-peer (P2P) The basis of file-sharing services, a computer communications model and network whose computers are considered equal peers who can send, store, and receive information equally well.

penny press Newspapers that sold for a penny, making them accessible to everyone. Supported by advertising rather than subscriptions, they tried to attract as large an audience as possible.

performance-based advertising Any form of online ad buying in which an advertiser pays for results rather than paying for the size of the publisher's audience or the CPM.

phonograph First patented by Thomas Edison in 1877 as a "talking machine," it used a tinfoil cylinder to record voices from telephone conversations.

pitch Request to review a client's new product or do a story about the client or the product.

place shift Viewing TV from anywhere using the Internet to access video originally delivered digitally to the home (or another location).

political economy An area of study inspired by Marxism that examines the relationship between politics and economics with media ownership and the influences they all have on society and perpetuating the status quo.

positivism A view, common among scientists in the physical or natural sciences and many social sciences, that affirms an objective reality to be discovered and explained through rigorous scientific research.

postmodernism A broad category of viewpoints that rejects grand narratives attempting to explain the world and absolute truths because truth is relative and unknowable.

postpositivism A view that agrees largely with positivism but also recognizes knowledge that may not be revealed through scientific inquiry.

pragmatism A school of thought affirming truths found in actions that work and rejecting the possibility of overarching or purely objective notions of truth.

preferred-position balancing theory A legal theory that says that a balance must be struck between speech and other rights, although speech has a preferred position.

press agentry Getting media attention for a client, often by creating outrageous stunts to attract journalists.

print-on-demand (POD) Publication of single books or tiny print runs based on customer demand using largely automated, nontraditional book-printing methods such as the color laser printer.

prior restraint When the government prevents or blocks the publication, broadcasting, showing, or distribution of media content, whether in print, over the air, in movie theaters, or online.

product placement A form of advertising in which brand-name goods or services are placed prominently within programming or movie content that is otherwise devoid of advertising, demonstrating the convergence of programming with advertising content.

produsers Audiences who no longer are simply consumers but also produce content.

propaganda The regular dissemination of a belief, doctrine, cause, or information, with the intent to mold public opinion.

pseudo-events Events staged specifically to attract media attention, particularly the news.

public information campaign Media program funded by the government and designed to achieve some social goal.

public opinion The notion that the public, as a group, can form shared views or ideas about topics and that these ideas guide the public's actions.

public service announcement (PSA) Advertising-like message from an organization with a worthy purpose that ostensibly benefits the public and for which the media donate time or space.

public sphere An idealized conversational forum in which people discuss and debate mutual interests and societal issues.

puffery A type of advertising language that makes extravagant and unrealistic claims about a product without saying anything concrete.

push poll A type of political advertising that appears to be a telephone poll but is actually a telemarketing campaign to sway voters by making a favored candidate look good or by misrepresenting the opposition.

qualitative research A method of inquiry favored in the social sciences that explores typically unstructured phenomena through interviews, focus groups, and participant observation among other techniques that produce descriptive rather than predictive results.

quantitative research A method of inquiry favored in the physical sciences that focuses on numerical data and statistical measures to describe phenomena. Researchers often attempt to prove or disprove a hypothesis through the empirical method, particularly controlled experimentation.

Radio Act of 1912 The act assigned frequencies and three- and four-letter codes to radio stations and limited broadcasting to the 360-meter wavelength.

Radio Act of 1927 An act of Congress that created the Federal Radio Commission, intended to regulate the largely chaotic airwaves and based on the principle that companies had a civic duty to use airwaves, a limited public good, responsibly.

random sample A sample in which every person has an equally probable chance of being selected, intended to represent the entire population of study.

rate card List of advertising rates by size, placement, and other characteristics, such as whether ads are black and white or full color. Frequency discounts are also usually offered, and the listed rates are usually negotiable, especially for large advertisers.

rating Used in broadcast media to explain the number of households that watched a particular show.

readership Number or percentage of newspaper readers.

rhetoric One of the ancient arts of discourse that focuses on the art of persuasion.

sampling error Error in a statistical analysis that results from selecting a sample that does not represent the entire population.

scrolling Simply repeating the same message in a chat room, which quickly draws the ire of other participants.

search-engine marketing Paying for certain keywords to show up high in rankings in a search engine, such as Google or Bing.

sedition Speech or action that encourages overthrow of a government or that subverts a nation's constitution or laws.

semiotics The study of signs and symbols.

sensational journalism News that exaggerates or features lurid details and depictions of events to increase its audience.

serious games Games created to be fun and educational that use game dynamics to instruct players on topics.

shield law A law intended to protect journalists from legal challenges to their freedom to report the news.

simplified communications model Developed by Wilbur Schramm in 1954 and based on the mathematical theory of communication. It includes a source who encodes a message, or signal, which is transmitted (via the media or directly via interpersonal communication) to a destination where the receiver decodes it.

six degrees of separation Notion that everyone in the world is separated from all other individuals by at most six additional nodes in a social network.

slander A type of defamation that is spoken, as opposed to written (libel), and that damages a person's reputation or otherwise causes harm.

slashdot effect When a smaller news site's Web server crashes because of increased traffic after its mention on popular websites, named for a frequent occurrence on the very popular technology news site Slashdot.org.

small world Tight-knit social network with many strong ties.

smart mob A term coined by author Howard Rheingold to define a group of people communicating with each other via text messaging or wireless networks to coordinate their activities.

social constructionism A view that claims much or all of what we know and understand about the world, including scientific knowledge, is constructed through social interactions and language.

social games Online or mobile games that are played in real time with others or that encourage simultaneous group playing.

social marketing Advertising and marketing techniques that persuade people to change bad or destructive behaviors or adopt good behaviors.

social responsibility theory A theory of international mass communication that perhaps best describes the media's role in democratic societies. It asserts that the media should be free from most governmental constraints to provide the most reliable and impartial information to the public.

soft news day A day in which not much has happened that is newsworthy, entailing the addition of features with less real news value, such as human-interest stories.

sound bite The length of time a news subject is allowed to speak without editing. It also has come to refer to short, catchy utterances designed to capture media attention.

Soviet theory A theory of international mass communication that states that the media should be publicly owned and used to further the needs of the working class.

spam Unwanted mass emailing from advertisers.

spiral of silence A theoretical construct that explains why people may be unwilling to publicly express opinions they feel are in the minority.

subliminal advertising Persuasive messages that have supposedly unconscious effects on the audience, such as an image or word flashed almost imperceptibly on a screen.

superstation A local TV station that reaches a national audience by beaming its programming nationwide via satellite to local cable systems.

superstitial ad Online advertisement that covers part of the existing screen or moves over part of it without opening a new window.

surveillance Primarily the journalism function of mass communication, which provides information about processes, issues, events, and other developments in society.

swarming The process used by some P2P systems in which multiple downloads of the same file are temporarily coordinated to accelerate the downloading process.

synchronous media Media that take place in real time and require the audience to be present during the broadcast or performance, such as live television or radio.

tagging Using searchable keywords to define a piece of information, file, image, or other type of digital media in a nonhierarchical system.

technological determinism The belief that technology causes certain human behaviors.

Telecommunications Act of 1996 The first major regulatory overhaul of telecommunications since 1934, designed to open the industry to greater competition by deregulating many aspects of it.

The Federal Communications Commission (FCC) The principal communications regulatory body, established in 1934, at the federal level in the United States.

The Federal Trade Commission (FTC) The principal commerce regulatory body, established in 1914, at the federal level in the United States.

theory of cognitive dissonance Theory of persuasion that states we act first and then rationalize our behavior afterward to make our actions consistent with self-perceived notions of who we are.

third-party cookies Cookies put on a computer by those other than the website being visited, such as advertisers.

third-person effect The tendency for people to underestimate the effect of a persuasive message on themselves while overestimating its effect on others.

Thomas Alva Edison His inventions included the electric light, the phonograph, and the Kinetoscope. Edison's lab in Menlo Park, New Jersey, had over sixty scientists and produced as many as four hundred patent applications a year.

time shift Recording of an audio or video event for later listening or viewing.

trademark A form of intellectual property law that protects the right to use a particular sign, logo, or name.

Transmission Control Protocol (TCP) A part of the main protocol for the Internet that allows computers to easily communicate with each other over a network.

trial balloon Leaking information to the press about a proposed plan or idea to see how the public will respond.

trolling Posting deliberately obnoxious or disruptive messages to discussion groups or other online forums simply to get a reaction from the participants.

two-way symmetric model Model of public relations that emphasizes the profession as a system of managing relationships among organizations, individuals, and their many publics.

tyranny of the majority A situation in which governmental laws and policies benefit the majority without concern for the welfare or rights of other groups or individuals.

usenet One of the earliest discussion forums in use today in which participants discuss topics in categories called newsgroups.

user-generated content (UGC) Content created by the general public for distribution by digital media.

user interface (UI) Junction between a medium and the people who use it.

uses-and-gratifications research A branch of research on media effects that examines why people use media, what they do with media rather than what media do to them.

V-chip A computer device that enables parents or any other viewer to program a TV set to block access to programs containing violent or sexual content based on the program rating.

viral marketing Promoting a product, service, or brand online through word of mouth, usually via online discussion groups, chats, and emails.

virtual reality The replacement of the real world with a digitized, virtual one, a mainstay of science fiction stories hyped in the late twentieth century.

voice-over An unseen announcer or narrator talking while other activity takes place, either on radio or during a television scene.

wiki Website that lets anyone add, edit, or delete pages and content.

William Randolph Hearst American newspaper magnate during the late nineteenth and early twentieth centuries whose newspapers across the United States were noted for sensational journalism and political influence.

word-of-mouth marketing Marketing that takes place among customers through discussions with one another.

yellow journalism Style practiced notably by publishers Pulitzer and Hearst during the late 1890s in which stories were sensationalized and often partly or wholly fabricated for dramatic purposes.

Notes

CHAPTER 1

1. Lance Liebl, "The Interview Becomes Sony's #1 Online Film of All Time," *Gamezone* (January 8, 2015), accessed January 8, 2015, http://www.gamezone.com/news/the-interview-becomes-sony-s-1-online-film-of-all-time-2231-jrrl.
2. "Apple Wins Big in Patent Case," *Wall Street Journal*, August 25, 2012, accessed February 19, 2013, http://www.wsj.com/articles/SB10000872396390444358404577609810658082898.
3. Irving Fang, *A History of Mass Communication: Six Information Revolutions* (Boston: Focal Press, 1997).
4. Malcolm Gladwell, "Creation Myth," *The New Yorker*, May 16, 2011.
5. Walter Isaacson, "American Icon," *Time*, October 17, 2011.
6. Adam Lashinsky, "Insights on the Writing of *Steve Jobs*," *Fortune*, December 27, 2011, http://fortune.com/2011/12/27/insights-on-the-writing-of-steve-jobs/.
7. Xiyun Yang, "China's Censors Rein in 'Vulgar' Reality TV Show," *New York Times*, July 18, 2010, accessed April 12, 2012, http://www.nytimes.com/2010/07/19/world/asia/19chinatv.html?pagewanted=all.
8. Kevin Widdop, "Desperate Chinese Boy, 17, Sells Kidney for £2000 to Buy an iPad and iPhone," *Mail Online*, April 7, 2012, accessed April 12, 2012, http://www.dailymail.co.uk/news/article-2126172/Chinese-boy-sells-kidney-buy-iPad-iPhone.html.
9. Jon Krakauer, *Into Thin Air* (New York: Anchor Books, 1999).
10. "Social TV and second-screen viewing: The stats in 2012." TheGuardian.com, October 29, 2012, accessed February 19, 2013, http://www.theguardian.co.uk/technology/appsblog/2012/oct/29/social-tv-second-screen-research.
11. Speedtest.net. Retrieved January 11, 2015 from http://www.netindex.com/download/allcountries/.
12. Harold D. Lasswell, "The Structure and Function of Communication in Society," in *The Communication of Ideas*, ed. Lyman Bryson (New York: Institute for Religious and Social Studies, Jewish Theological Seminary of America, 1948), 37.
13. Claude E. Shannon and Warren Weaver, *The Mathematical Theory of Communication* (Urbana: The University of Illinois Press, 1971), 7.
14. Wilbur Schramm, "How Communication Works," in *The Process and Effects of Mass Communication*, ed. Wilbur Schramm (Urbana: The University of Illinois Press, 1961), 5–6.
15. J. W. Carey, "A Cultural Approach to Communications," *Communication* 2 (1975): 1–22.
16. Werner J. Severin and James W. Tankard Jr., "Introduction to Mass Communication Theory," in *Communication Theories: Origins, Methods, and Uses in the Mass Media*, 5th ed. (New York: Addison Wesley Longman, 2001), 16.
17. "Wired, Zapped, and Beamed, 1960's through 1980's," FCC website, accessed October 20, 2011, http://transition.fcc.gov/omd/history/tv/1960–1989.html.
18. Gary Gumpert and Robert Cathcart, eds., *Inter/Media: Interpersonal Communication in a Media World*, 3rd ed. (Oxford: Oxford University Press, 1986).
19. World Internet Project, accessed February 19, 2013, http://www.worldinternetproject.net/.

CHAPTER 2

1. Chase Goodbread, "Michael Sam, NFL Draft Prospect, Announces He's Gay," NFL.com, Feb. 9, 2014, accessed February 9, 2015, http://www.nfl.com/news/story/0ap2000000324603/article/michael-sam-nfl-draft-prospect-announces-hes-gay.
2. Chase Goodbread, "Reaction to Michael Sam News Explodes on Twitter," NFL.com website, February 9, 2014, accessed Feb. 9, 2015, http://www.nfl.com/news/story/0ap2000000324616/article/reaction-to-michael-sam-news-explodes-on-twitter.
3. "Tennis Star Martina Navratilova, Among First 'Out' Pro Athletes, Congratulates NBA's Jason Collins," *Democracy Now!*, May 1, 2013, accessed May 15, 2013, http://www.democracynow.org/2013/5/1/tennis_star_martina_navratilova_among_first.
4. W. James Potter, *Media Literacy*, 2nd ed. (Thousand Oaks, CA: Sage Publications, 2001), 4–7.
5. Tom Gormley, "'Ruination Once Again': Cases in the Study of Media Effects," theory.org.uk, 1998. Retrieved November 4, 2002, from http://www.theory.org.uk/effec-tg.htm.
6. Terence Gordon, "Marshall Who?" Marshall McLuhan, July 2002, accessed December 20, 2014, http://www.marshallmcluhan.com/biography.
7. Lisa Rein and Michael Horowitz, "Timothy Leary and Marshall McLuhan, Turned On and Tuned In," Boingboing, accessed January 24, 2015, http://boingboing.net/2014/06/03/timothy-leary-and-marshall-mcl.html.
8. "Essay: The Playboy Interview: Marshall McLuhan," March 1969, Next Nature, accessed December 15, 2014, http://www.nextnature.net/2009/12/the-playboy-interview-marshall-mcluhan/.

9. David McKnight, "Rupert Murdoch and His Influence on Political Life," theguardian.com, August 7, 2013, accessed January 10, 2015, http://www.theguardian.com/commentisfree/2013/aug/07/rupert-murdoch-australian-election-2013.

10. Christopher Mims, "31% of Kenya's GDP Is Spent Through Mobile Phones," *Quartz*, February 27, 2013, accessed May 18, 2013, http://qz.com/57504/31-of-kenyas-gdp-is-spent-through-mobile-phones/.

11. Nmachi Jidenma, "How Africa's Mobile Revolution Is Disrupting the Continent," CNN.com, Jan. 24, 2014, accessed February 9, 2015, http://edition.cnn.com/2014/01/24/business/davos-africa-mobile-explosion/.

12. W. Lance Bennett, *News: The Politics of Illusion*, 9th ed. (Boston: Longman, 2012).

13. Hannibal Burress, "Hannibal Burress's Bill Cosby Rant," *Boston Magazine*, n.d., accessed February 9, 2015, http://bostonmagazine.magnify.net/video/Hannibal-Burress%E2%80%99s-Bill-Cosby-.

14. Bill Carter, Graham Bowley, and Lorne Manly, "Comeback by Bill Cosby Unravels as Rape Claims Re-emerge," *New York Times*, Nov. 19, 2014, accessed February 9, 2015, http://www.nytimes.com/2014/11/20/business/media/bill-cosby-fallout-rape-accusations.html?hp&action=click&pgtype=Homepage&module=photo-spot-region&region=top-news&WT.nav=top-news&_r=1.

15. Ken Wheaton, "Children Mystified by Racial Outcry Over Cheerios Ad," AdAge.com, July 17, 2013, accessed July 18, 2013, http://adage.com/article/the-big-tent/children-mystified-racial-outcry-cheerios-ad/243136/.

16. Heather Kelly, "Syrian Group Cited as New York Times Outage Continues," CNN.com, August 29, 2013, accessed February 9, 2015, http://edition.cnn.com/2013/08/27/tech/web/new-york-times-website-attack/.

CHAPTER 3

1. Brett Molina, "Apple Settles E-books Price-Fixing Suit for up to $400M," *USA Today*, July 16, 2014, accessed May 4, 2015, http://www.usatoday.com/story/tech/2014/07/16/apple-ebooks-prices/12734921/.

2. Polly Mosendz, "Amazon Has Basically No Competition Among Online Booksellers," The Wire, May 30, 2014, accessed May 4, 2015, http://www.thewire.com/business/2014/05/amazon-has-basically-no-competition-among-online-booksellers/371917/.

3. Drew DeSilver, "Overall Book Readership Stable, but E-books Becoming More Popular," Pew Research Center, January 21, 2014, accessed April 10, 2015, http://www.pewresearch.org/fact-tank/2014/01/21/overall-book-readership-stable-but-e-books-becoming-more-popular/.

4. Marshall McLuhan, *The Gutenberg Galaxy: The Making of Typographic Man* (Toronto, Canada: University of Toronto Press, 1962), 293.

5. DBW, "Self-Publishing Maturing, Up 17% Last Year in the U.S.," Digital Book World, October 8, 2014, accessed April 10, 2015, http://www.digitalbookworld.com/2014/self-publishing-maturing-up-17-last-year-in-the-u-s/.

6. "Entertainment and Media," pwc website, accessed June 22, 2013, http://www.pwc.com/gx/en/entertainment-media/index.jhtml.

7. International Publishers Association, "Annual Report, October 2013 / October 2014," October 2014, accessed April 11, 2015, http://www.internationalpublishers.org/images/reports/2014/IPA-annual-report-2014.pdf.

8. Association of American Publishers, "US Publishing Industry Annual Survey Reports $27 Billion in Net Revenue, 2.6 Billion Units for 2013," June 26, 2014, Association of American Publishers website, accessed April 11, 2015, http://publishers.org/news/us-publishing-industry-annual-survey-reports-27-billion-net-revenue-26-billion-units-2013.

9. "The World's 56 Largest Book Publishers, 2014," *Publisher's Weekly*, accessed May 5, 2015, http://www.publishersweekly.com/pw/by-topic/industry-news/financial-reporting/article/63004-the-world-s-56-largest-book-publishers-2014.html.

10. Laura Hazard Owen, "Department of Justice Clears Random House-Penguin Merger," February 14, 2013, accessed June 22, 2013, http://paidcontent.org/2013/02/14/department-of-justice-clears-random-house-penguin-merger-in-the-u-s/.

11. IBISWorld, "Book Publishing Industry Performance," 2015, IBISWorld.com, accessed April 27, 2015, http://clients1.ibisworld.com/reports/us/industry/currentperformance.aspx?entid=4579.

12. Lauren Indvik, "Ebook Sales Surpass Hardcover for First Time in U.S.," June 17, 2012, Mashable website, accessed April 27, 2015, http://mashable.com/2012/06/17/ebook-hardcover-sales/.

13. Lauren Indvik, "EBook Sales Expected to Reach $9.7 Billion by 2016 [Study]," December 1, 2011, Mashable website, accessed June 22, 2013, http://mashable.com/2011/12/01/ebook-sales-10-billion-2016/.

14. Audio Publishers Association, "The Audiobook Industry Continues to Grow," October 2014, APA website, accessed May 6, 2015, http://www.audiopub.org/October_APA_2013_Survey_Press_Release.pdf.

15. Alison Flood, "Printed Book Sales' Decline Slowed in 2012," January 9, 2013, *theguardian*, accessed June 22, 2013, http://www.guardian.co.uk/books/2013/jan/09/printed-book-sales-2012.

16. Angie Han, "J.K. Rowling's 'The Casual Vacancy' Being Adapted for the BBC," December 3, 2012, SlashFilm website, accessed June 22, 2013, http://www.slashfilm.com/j-k-rowlings-the-casual-vacancy-being-adapted-for-the-bbc/.

17. "Number of Sunday Newspapers in the United States from 1985 to 2011," 2013, Statista website, accessed June 23, 2013, http://www.statista.com/statistics/183416/number-of-us-sunday-newspapers/.
18. Metro website "About" page, accessed April 12, 2012, http://www.metro.lu/about.
19. "Ruben Salazar Project," accessed January 30, 2015, directed by Phillip Rodriguez. http://rubensalazarproject.com/.
20. *Ruben Salazar: Man in the Middle,* PBS, April 29, 2014, directed by Phillip Rodriguez.
21. Steve Mariotti, Debra DeSalvo, and Tony Towle, *The Young Entrepreneur's Guide to Starting and Running a Business* (New York: Three Rivers Press, 2000).
22. MPA Factbook 2014, "Magazine Media," MPA: The Association of Magazine Media, accessed April 22, 2015, http://www.magazine.org/sites/default/files/MPA%20Magazine%20Media%20Factbook-%202014.pdf.
23. Randall Stross, "A Shopper's Companion, Still Going Strong," *New York Times,* December 11, 2011, accessed June 23, 2013, http://www.nytimes.com/2011/12/11/business/media/consumer-reports-going-strong-at-75-digital-domain.html?_r=0.

CHAPTER 4

1. Steve Knopper, "Taylor Swift Abruptly Pulls Entire Catalog from Spotify," November 3, 2014, *Rolling Stone,* accessed February 9, 2015, http://www.rollingstone.com/music/news/taylor-swift-abruptly-pulls-entire-catalog-from-spotify-20141103.
2. Rebecca Davison, "Taylor Swift Is Surprised with IFPI Award After Being Named World's Most Successful Artist of 2014," February 23, 2015, *Daily Mail,* accessed March 1, 2015, http://www.dailymail.co.uk/tvshowbiz/article-2965721/Taylor-Swift-surprised-IFPI-award.html.
3. Christine Hansen and Ranald D. Hansen, "Music and Music Videos," in *Media Entertainment: The Psychology of Its Appeal,* eds. Peter Vorderer and Dolf Zillmann (Mahwah, NJ: Lawrence Erlbaum Associates, 2000), 179–181.
4. Ed Christman and Glenn Peoples, "Album Sales Hit a New Low," *Billboard* website, August 28, 2014, accessed February 9, 2015, http://www.billboard.com/articles/business/6236365/album-sales-hit-a-new-low-2014.
5. Richard Smirke, "IFPI Music Report 2014: Global Recorded Music Revenues Fall 4%, Streaming and Subs Hit $1 Billion," *Billboard* website, March 18, 2014, accessed February 9, 2015, http://www.billboard.com/biz/articles/news/global/5937645/ifpi-music-report-2014-global-recorded-music-revenues-fall-4.
6. Jon Ronson, "Amanda Palmer: Visionary or Egoist?," *theguardian,* June 22, 2013, accessed January 30, 2015, http://www.theguardian.com/music/2013/jun/22/amanda-palmer-visionary-egotist-interview.
7. Max Read, "Amanda Palmer's 'A Poem for Dzhokhar' Is the Worst Poem of All Time," *Gawker,* April 22, 2013, accessed January 29, 2015, http://gawker.com/amanda-palmers-a-poem-for-dzhokhar-is-the-worst-poem-476820444.
8. Amanda Palmer, "The Art of Asking," filmed March 2013, TED video, accessed February 4, 2015, https://www.ted.com/talks/amanda_palmer_the_art_of_asking/transcript?language=en.
9. Tyler Hayes, "Digital Music Prices: Is Cheaper Better," Hypebot, June 4, 2012, accessed February 9, 2015, http://www.hypebot.com/hypebot/2012/06/digital-music-prices.html.
10. Adrian Covert, "A Decade of iTunes Singles Killed the Music Industry," CNN.com, April 13, 2013, accessed February 9, 2015, http://money.cnn.com/2013/04/25/technology/itunes-music-decline/.
11. Ed Christman, "SoundScan's Third Quarter Numbers in One Word: Bleak," *billboard,* October 10, 2014, accessed February 9, 2015, http://www.billboard.com/biz/articles/news/retail/6281506/soundscans-third-quarter-numbers-in-one-word-bleak.
12. Eriq Gardner, "Robin Thicke Admits Drug Abuse, Lying to Media in Wild 'Blurred Lines' Deposition," *Hollywood Reporter,* September 15, 2014, accessed February 9, 2015, http://www.hollywoodreporter.com/thr-esq/robin-thicke-admits-drug-abuse-732783.
13. Alan Duke, "Marvin Gaye Heirs Sue 'Blurred Lines' Artists," CNN.com, November 1, 2013, accessed February 9, 2015, http://www.cnn.com/2013/10/31/showbiz/blurred-lines-lawsuit/.
14. Gaius Chamberlain, "Granville Woods," The Black Inventor Online Museum, May 23, 2013, accessed August 3, 2009, http://www.blackinventor.com/pages/granvillewoods.html.
15. Bob Lochte, "The Life and Legend of Nathan B. Stubblefield: A Chronology," accessed May 17, 2002, http://campus.murraystate.edu/academic/faculty/bob.lochte/NBSDates.htm.
16. "NPR Stations and Public Media," NPR website, accessed February 9, 2015, http://www.npr.org/about-npr/178640915/npr-stations-and-public-media.
17. "PRI Fact Sheet," Public Radio International website, accessed June 28, 2013, http://www.pri.org/pri-facts.html.
18. MarketingCharts staff, "US Radio Ad Revenues, 2006-2018," Marketing Charts website, April 4, 2014, accessed February 9, 2015, http://www.marketingcharts.com/traditional/us-radio-ad-revenues-2006-2018-41795/5.
19. Albert N. Greco, "The Structure of the Radio Industry," in *The Media and Entertainment Industries,* ed. Albert N. Greco (Boston: Allyn & Bacon, 2000).
20. David Carr, "'Serial,' Podcasting's First Breakout Hit, Sets Stage for More," *New York Times,* Nov. 23, 2014, accessed February 9, 2015, http://www.nytimes.com/2014/11/24/business/media/serial-podcastings-first-breakout-hit-sets-stage-for-more.html?_r=0.

21. "Serial Podcast," WBEZ Chicago, 2014, accessed February 9, 2015, http://serialpodcast.org.

22. Matt Petronzio, "The Enduring Power of Radio in the Digital Age," Mashable website, Feb. 13, 2013, accessed February 9, 2015, http://mashable.com/2013/02/13/radio-in-the-digital-age/.

23. UNESCO, "World Radio Day 2015, 13 February, 2015," accessed February 9, 2015, http://www.unesco.org/new/en/world-radio-day.

24. "The Infinite Dial," Edison Research and Triton Digital 2014, accessed March 1, 2015, http://www.edisonresearch.com/wp-content/uploads/2014/03/The-Infinite-Dial-2014-from-Edison-Research-and-Triton-Digital.pdf.

CHAPTER 5

1. Robert Leggat, "The Beginnings of Photography," A History of Photography website, accessed May 15, 2002, http://www.rleggat.com/photohistory/.

2. Ibid.

3. "Sprocket Holes: The Lumière Brothers," accessed June 3, 2002, presscard.com, www.presscard.com/sprocket-holes2.html; Gerald Beals, "The Biography of Thomas Alva Edison," accessed August 3, 2009, ThomasEdison.com, http://www.thomasedison.com/biography.html.

4. VICE News, "Raw Coverage from the Streets of Ferguson," November 24, 2014, accessed February 10, 2015, https://news.vice.com/article/raw-coverage-from-the-streets-of-ferguson.

5. Stephen J. A. Ward, "Trauma and Journalists," Center for Journalism Ethics, School of Journalism & Mass Communication, University of Wisconsin–Madison, n.d., accessed July 9, 2013, http://ethics.journalism.wisc.edu/resources/global-media-ethics/trauma-and-journalists/.

6. Erik Barnouw, *Documentary: A History of the Non-Fiction Film*, 2nd rev. ed. (New York: Oxford University Press, 1993).

7. Netflix, "Statistics and Facts About Netflix," Sept. 24, 2014, accessed February 10, 2015, http://www.statista.com/topics/842/netflix/.

8. Michael Cieply, "Streaming Lifts Home Entertainment Spending," *Media Decoder* (blog), *New York Times*, January 8, 2013, accessed July 9, 2013, http://mediadecoder.blogs.nytimes.com/2013/01/08/streaming-lifts-home-entertainment-spending/?ref=media.

9. Rebecca Ford, "CinemaCon: Kathleen Kennedy Honored with Pioneer of the Year Award," *The Hollywood Reporter*, April 17, 2013, accessed August 4, 2013, http://www.hollywoodreporter.com/news/cinemacon-kathleen-kennedy-honored-pioneer-441625.

10. "Our Team: Kathleen Kennedy: President," Lucasfilm Ltd. website, accessed February 8, 2015, lucasfilm.com/our-team/kathleen-kennedy.

11. Kathleen Kennedy, email message to Mary Ann McHugh, August 7, 2013.

12. Barry R. Litman, *The Motion Picture Mega-Industry* (Boston: Allyn & Bacon, 1998), 74–88.

13. Statista, "Box office revenue* in North America from 1980 to 2014 (in billion U.S. dollars)," Jan. 1, 2015, accessed February 10, 2015, http://www.statista.com/statistics/187069/north-american-box-office-gross-revenue-since-1980/.

14. "Yearly Box Office," Box Office Mojo.com, accessed July 25, 2011, http://boxofficemojo.com/yearly/?view2=domestic&view=releasedate&p=.htm.

15. "Curtains Rise Halfway on Digital Cinema," *Business 2.0* (May 29, 2001): 32–33.

16. Megan Geuss, "Celluloid No More: Distribution of Film by Celluloid to Cease by 2013 in the US," *Ars Technica*, June 9, 2012, accessed February 13, 2013, http://arstechnica.com/gadgets/2012/06/the-silver-screen-no-more-distribution-of-film-to-cease-by-2013-in-the-us/.

17. David J. Hill, "Movie Theaters Ramp Up for the Next Big Thing: Satellite Delivery of Digital Films," *Singularity HUB*, April 27, 2012, accessed February 13, 2012, http://singularityhub.com/2012/04/27/movie-theaters-ramp-up-for-the-next-big-thing-satellite-delivery-of-digital-films/.

18. Stephen Zeitchik, "Popularity of 3-D Is Affecting How Screenplays Are Written," *Los Angeles Times*, April 25, 2010, accessed May 16, 2012, http://articles.latimes.com/2010/apr/25/entertainment/la-ca-3ddirector-20100425.

19. Les Brown, *Les Brown's Encyclopedia of Television*, 3rd ed. (Detroit, MI: Gale Research Inc., 1992), 528.

20. Kenneth Olmstead, Mark Jurkowitz, Amy Mitchell, and Jodi Enda, "How Americans Get TV News at Home," October 11, 2013, accessed February 10, 2015, http://www.journalism.org/2013/10/11/how-americans-get-tv-news-at-home/.

21. TiVo, "Estimated Subs for Top 25 US Cable MSOs (GCI is high here, as we have 122K in GCI's latest filing)," March 21, 2013, accessed February 10, 2015, http://www.investorvillage.com/smbd.asp?mb=3928&mn=117816&pt=msg&mid=12644072.

22. Christopher Zara, "Comcast, Time Warner Cable Bleeding Cable Subscribers In Pay-TV's Worst Third Quarter Ever," *International Business Times* website, November 14, 2014, accessed February 10, 2015, http://www.ibtimes.com/comcast-time-warner-cable-bleeding-cable-subscribers-pay-tvs-worst-third-quarter-ever-1723870.

23. Brian Stelter, "Customers Up, Profit Up at Comcast," CNN.com, October 23, 2014, accessed February 10, 2015, http://money.cnn.com/2014/10/23/media/comcast-third-quarter-earnings/.

24. Jamal Carnette, "The Average American Pays This Amount For Cable, How Do You Compare?" *The Motley Fool*, February 1, 2015, accessed February 10, 2015, http://www.fool.com/investing/general/2015/02/01/the-average-american-pays-this-amount-for-cable-ho.aspx.

CHAPTER 6

1. Taylor Clark, "How Palmer Luckey Created Oculus Rift," Smithsonian.com, November 2014, accessed January 19, 2015, http://www.smithsonianmag.com/innovation/how-palmer-luckey-created-oculus-rift-180953049/?no-ist.

2. Eddie Makuch, "Minecraft Console Sales Pass PC, Series Nears 54 Million Copies Sold," *Gamespot*, June 25, 2014, accessed February 9, 2015, http://www.gamespot.com/articles/minecraft-console-sales-pass-pc-series-nears-54-million-copies-sold/1100-6420724/.

3. Sheizaf Rafaeli, "Networked Interactivity," *Journal of Computer Mediated Communication*, accessed August 3, 2009, http://jcmc.indiana.edu/vol2/issue4/rafaeli.sudweeks.html#Interactivity.

4. Elaine Mcmillion and Alissa Quart, "Hollow: The Story of a Dying County in West Virginia," June 2013, accessed January 19, 2015, http://hollowdocumentary.com/.

5. David Dufresne, "Fort McMoney: An Interactive Game Based on an Oil Boomtown," November 2014, accessed January 19, 2015, http://www.fortmcmoney.com/#/fortmcmoney.

6. Romain Jeanticou and Charles-Henry Groult, "Le Mystere de Grimouville: A Mystery in a French Community (requires French)," May 19, 2014, accessed January 19, 2015, http://grimouville.francebleu.fr/#/.

7. Nadine Pequeneza, "Inside Disaster Haiti," Insidedisaster.com, 2011, accessed January 19, 2015, http://insidedisaster.com/haiti/.

8. "Internet World Users by Language: Top 10 Languages," Internet World Stats (May 20, 2013), accessed May 20, 2013, http://www.internetworldstats.com/stats7.htm.

9. John Carey, *Winky Dink to Stargazer: Five Decades of Interactive Television* (Dobbs Ferry, NY: Greystone Communications, 1998).

10. Lisa Napoli, "A Gadget That Taught a Nation to Surf: The TV Remote Control," *New York Times*, February 11, 1999, accessed January 10, 2002, http://www.nytimes.com/library/tech/99/02/circuits/articles/11howw.html.

11. "Control Data Corporation Historical Timeline," Charles Babbage Institute Collections website, accessed August 3, 2009, http://www.cbi.umn.edu/collections/cdc/histtimeline.html.

12. Judith Newman, "Ray Tomlinson: Inventor of E-Mail, a New Discourse," *Intelligent Systems* 9, no. 2 (July 2002), accessed August 3, 2009, http://www.chenaultsystems.com/articles/Intell33.htm.

13. Robert Hobbes' Zakon, "Hobbes' Internet Timeline," version 5.6, Zakon.org, accessed July 24, 2013, http://www.zakon.org/robert/internet/timeline.

14. Robert Hobbes' Zakon, "Hobbes' Internet Timeline," version 12, Zakon.org, accessed February 17, 2015, http://www.zakon.org/robert/internet/timeline.

15. Emil Protalinski, "Internet Explorer Continues Growth Past 55% Market Share Thanks to IE9 and IE10, as Chrome Hits 17-Month Low," *The Next Web*, March 1, 2013, accessed July 25, 2013, http://thenextweb.com/insider/2013/03/01/internet-explorer-continues-growth-past-55-market-share-thanks-to-ie9-and-ie10-as-chrome-hits-17-month-low/.

16. P. William Bane and Stephen P. Bradley, "The Light at the End of the Pipe," *Scientific American* (October 1999): 110–115.

17. Wikipedia, s.v. "Microvision," accessed July 28, 2013, http://en.wikipedia.org/wiki/Microvision.

18. "Video Game Timeline (1967–present)," Education Database Online website, accessed June 20, 2013, http://www.onlineeducation.net/videogame_timeline.

19. Ibid.

20. Jimmy Thang, "The Sims 3 Set for Global Launch in 2009," *IGN*, March 19, 2008, accessed July 28, 2013, http://www.ign.com/articles/2008/03/19/the-sims-3-set-for-global-launch-in-2009.

21. "Video Game History Timeline," National Museum of Play website, n.d., accessed June 20, 2013, http://www.icheg.org/icheg-game-history/timeline/.

22. Josh Wolford, "Halo 4 Breaks Records, Sees $220 Million in Sales in First 24 Hours," *WebProNews*, November 12, 2012, accessed July 25, 2013, http://www.webpronews.com/halo-4-breaks-records-sees-220-million-in-sales-in-first-24-hours-2012-11.

23. Angela Moscaritolo, "Angry Birds Space Hits 10M Downloads in Three Days," *PCMag*, March 26, 2012, accessed July 28, 2013, http://www.pcmag.com/article2/0,2817,2402092,00.asp.

24. Scott Lowe, "OUYA Review: The Mediocre Beginning to a Promising Idea," *IGN*, July 26, 2013, accessed July 28, 2013, http://www.ign.com/articles/2013/07/26/ouya-review.

25. Rus McLaughlin, "IGN Presents: The History of Super Mario Bros," *IGN*, September 13, 2010, accessed July 25, 2013, http://www.ign.com/articles/2010/09/14/ign-presents-the-history-of-super-mario-bros.

26. Barbara Ortutay, "How Mario Saved the World of Video Games," *Mail Tribune*, November 22, 2009, accessed July 25, 2013, http://www.mailtribune.com/apps/pbcs.dll/article?AID=/20091122/LIFE/911220314.

27. "Top 100 Video Games of All Time," *G4*. Retrieved July 25, 2013, from http://www.g4tv.com/top-100/478/super-mario-bros/.

28. "List of Games by Date," Mario Wiki, July 15, 2013, accessed July 25, 2013, http://www.mariowiki.com/List_of_Mario_games_by_date.

29. William D'Angelo, "Top 10 in Sales—Mario Franchise, 500M Games Sold—News," *VGChartz*, December 24, 2012, accessed July 25, 2013, http://www.vgchartz.com/article/250637/top-10-in-sales-mario-franchise-500m-games-sold/.

30. Nick Statt, "For Video Game Industry, 2014 Couldn't Escape Slumping Game Sales," Cnet.com, January 15, 2015,

accessed February 17, 2015, http://www.cnet.com/news/for-video-game-industry-2014-couldnt-escape-slumping-software-sales/.

31. Ian Williams, "Chinese Gamer Dies after 15-Day Session," V3.co.uk, March 1, 2007, accessed May 14, 2012, http://www.v3.co.uk/v3-uk/news/1998377/chinese-gamer-dies-day-session.

32. Mike Futter, "Video Gaming Changes Adolescent Brains, May Cause Addiction," gameinformer website, June 23, 2014, accessed January 19, 2015, http://www.gameinformer.com/b/news/archive/2014/06/23/video-gaming-changes-adolescent-brains-may-cause-addiction.aspx.

33. Kimberly Stern, "Colorado State University Study Examines Potential Positive Effects of Video Games," Colorado State University News & Information website, April 4, 2011, accessed May 14, 2012, http://www.news.colostate.edu/Release/5653.

34. Gerry Shih, "Zynga Slashes Workforce by a Fifth, Shares Dive," Reuters, June 3, 2013, accessed June 13, 2013, http://www.reuters.com/article/2013/06/03/us-zynga-cuts-idUSBRE95211320130603.

35. Amy Kraft, "Video Game Play Sharpens Elderly Minds," *Scientific American*, May 3, 2013, accessed June 20, 2013, http://www.scientificamerican.com/podcast/episode.cfm?id=video-game-play-sharpens-elderly-mi-13-05-03.

36. Jenna Pitcher, "Games Industry Revenue May Hit $100 Billion by 2018, Says Research Firm," Polygon.com, June 25, 2014, accessed January 19, 2015, http://www.polygon.com/2014/6/25/5840882/games-industry-revenue-hit-100-billion-by-2018-dfc-Intelligence.

CHAPTER 7

1. Jon Ronson, "How One Stupid Tweet Blew Up Justine Sacco's Life," *The New York Times Magazine*, February 12, 2015, accessed April 10, 2015, http://www.nytimes.com/2015/02/15/magazine/how-one-stupid-tweet-ruined-justine-saccos-life.html?_r=2.

2. Katie Kindelan, "Boy Behind Viral Birthday Plea Gets 'GMA' Surprise Party," ABC News.go.com, March 7, 2014, accessed April 10, 2015, http://abcnews.go.com/blogs/headlines/2014/03/boy-behind-viral-birthday-plea-gets-gma-surprise-party/.

3. John Jantsch, "The Definition of Social Media," *Duct Tape Marketing* (blog), September 25, 2008, accessed February 20, 2009, http://www.ducttapemarketing.com/blog/2008/09/25/the-definition-of-social-media/.

4. Brian Solis, "Defining Social Media," Brian Solis website, June 28, 2007, accessed August 19, 2015, http://www.briansolis.com/2007/06/defining-social-media/.

5. Anvil Media, "SEM Glossary of Terms," n.d., Anvil Media website, accessed February 20, 2009, http://www.anvilmediainc.com/search-engine-marketing-glossary.html.

6. Clay Shirky, *Here Comes Everybody: How Change Happens When People Come Together* (New York: Penguin Group, 2009).

7. Jessica Clark and Patricia Aufderheide, "Public Media 2.0: Dynamic, Engaged Publics," February 2009, accessed March 17, 2009, http://www.cmsimpact.org/future-public-media/documents/articles/public-media-20-dynamic-engaged-publics.

8. Benny Evangelista, "Social Media Sites Become No. 1 Online Activity," SFGate.com, August 3, 2010, accessed July 14, 2011, http://articles.sfgate.com/2010-08-03/business/22010227_1_online-activity-zynga-game-network-mafia-wars.

9. Twitter (2015), About, www.twitter.com, accessed May 15, 2015 from https://about.twitter.com/company.

10. Erin Kutz, "Just a Few on Twitter Do All the Tweeting: Study," Reuters, June 5, 2009, accessed June 5, 2009, http://tech.yahoo.com/news/nm/20090605/wr_nm/us_twitter_study_3.

11. Tumblr. Tumblr website, accessed May 15, 2015, http://www.tumblr.com/about.

12. Abby Liu, "Is WeChat the Next Sina Weibo in China?" Global Voices Online, July 12, 2013, accessed July 20, 2013, http://globalvoicesonline.org/2013/07/12/is-wechat-the-next-sina-weibo-in-china/.

13. Steven Levy, "The Many Sides of Jack Dorsey," Wired, June 22, 2012, accessed July 15, 2013, http://www.wired.com/business/2012/06/ff_dorsey/all/.

14. Seth Stevenson, "Simplicity and Order for All," *Wall Street Journal,* October 26, 2012, written in conjunction with WSJ's Innovator of the Year Award 2012 (in technology), accessed July 15, 2013, http://www.wsj.com/articles/SB10001424052970204425904578072640691246804.

15. Gina Chon, "Square CEO Jack Dorsey Picks Up San Francisco Trash on Fridays," *Quartz* website, July 5, 2013, accessed July 15, 2013, http://qz.com/100997/payments-company-square-jack-dorsey-clean-up-trash/.

16. danah m. boyd and Nicole B. Ellison, "Social Network Sites: Definition, History, and Scholarship," *Journal of Computer-Mediated Communication* 13, no. 1 (2007): article 11, accessed April 4, 2009, http://jcmc.indiana.edu/vol13/issue1/boyd.ellison.html.

17. Stan Schroeder, "Study: More Teens Are Fleeing from Facebook," Mashable.com, December 19, 2014, accessed May 17, 2015, http://mashable.com/2014/12/19/study-teens-fleeing-facebook/?utm_campaign=Feed%3A+Mashable+%28Mashable%29&utm_cid=Mash-Prod-RSS-Feedburner-All-Partial&utm_medium=feed&utm_source=feedburner.

18. Joshua Barrie, "Nobody Is Using Google+," Business Insider, January 20, 2015, accessed May 17, 2015, http://www.businessinsider.com/google-active-users-2015-1.

19. Axel Bruns, *Blogs, Wikipedia, Second Life, and Beyond: From Production to Produsage* (New York: Peter Lang, 2008).

20. Sameer Hinduja, "Cyberbullying on Instagram," Cyber Bullying Research Center, May 21, 2013, accessed June 18, 2013, http://cyberbullying.us/cyberbullying-on-instagram.

21. Amanda Holman and Alan Sillars, "Talk About 'Hooking Up': The Influence of College Social Networks on Nonrelationship Sex," *Health Communications* 27, no. 2 (2012): 205–216.

22. Shayne Hughes, "I Banned All Internal Emails at My Company for a Week," *Forbes*, October 25, 2012, accessed July 21, 2013, http://www.forbes.com/sites/for besleadershipforum/2012/10/25/i-banned-all-internal-e-mails-at-my-company-for-a-week/.

CHAPTER 8

1. Sheri Fink, "The Deadly Choices at Memorial," Pulitzer website, accessed May 16, 2012, http://www.pulitzer .org/works/2010-Investigative-Reporting-Group2. Originally published in *The New York Times Magazine*, August 30, 2009.

2. Pulitzer Prizes, "The 2012 Pulitzer Prize Winners: National Reporting," pulitzer.org, accessed April 17, 2012, http://www.pulitzer.org/citation/2012-National-Reporting.

3. David Wood, "Beyond the Battlefield: From a Decade of War, an Endless Struggle for the Severely Wounded," *Huffington Post*, October 10, 2011, accessed May 16, 2012, http://www.huffingtonpost.com/2011/10/10/bey ond-the-battlefield-part-1-tyler-southern_n_999329 .html?ncid=edlinkusaolp00000003.

4. Jeremy W. Peters and Verne G. Kopytoff, "Betting on News, AOL Is Buying the Huffington Post," *New York Times*, February 7, 2011, accessed July 26, 2013, http:// www.nytimes.com/2011/02/07/business/media/07aol .html.

5. "Hugo Chavez Dead: Venezuela's President Dies at 58," *Huffington Post*, March 5, 2013, accessed June 30, 2013, http://www.huffingtonpost.com/2013/03/05/hugo-chavez-dead_n_2296423.html.

6. The Write Site Newsroom, "Tracing the Story of Journalism in the United States," accessed October 20, 2011, http://www.writesite.org/html/tracing.html.

7. "About Us" (2013), Associated Press website, accessed July 26, 2013, http://www.ap.org/company/about-us.

8. "AP's History" (2013), Associated Press Website, accessed July 26, 2013, http://www.ap.org/company/history/ap-history.

9. "AP News Values & Principles" (2013), Associated Press website, accessed July 26, 2013, http://www.ap.org/ company/news-values.

10. Michael G. Robinson, American Culture Studies, "1890s" course, spring 1996, accessed October 20, 2011, http:// www.bgsu.edu/departments/acs/1890s/yellowkid/ yellow1.html.

11. Joseph Pulitzer, "The College of Journalism," *North American Review* (May 1904).

12. George Seldes, "Farewell: Lord of San Simeon," in *Lords of the Press* (New York: Julian Messner, 1938).

13. Anna Bahr, "Latinos Onscreen, Conspicuously Few," *The New York Times*, June 18, 2014, accessed February 23, 2015, http://www.nytimes.com/2014/06/19/upshot/lati nos-onscreen-conspicuously-absent.html?_r=1&abt= 0002&abg=0.

14. Andrew Tyndall, *Who Speaks for America? Sex, Age and Race on the Network News* (Washington, DC: 10th Annual Women, Men, and Media Study, conducted by ADT Research in conjunction with the Freedom Forum, October 20, 1998).

15. The PEW Research Center's Project for Excellence in Journalism, "Key Findings," *The State of the News Media 2013: An Annual Report on American Journalism*, March 18, 2013, accessed July 28, 2013, http://stateofthemedia .org/2013/overview-5/key-findings/.

16. The PEW Research Center's Project for Excellence in Journalism, "Overview," *The State of the News Media 2013: An Annual Report on American Journalism*, March 18, 2013, accessed July 28, 2013, http://stateofthemedia.org/2013/ overview-5/.

17. Nick Porter, "Top Op-Ed Pages Offer Choice of Elites: On Reigning Issues, Convergent Perspectives," April 1, 2012, FAIR website, accessed July 26, 2013, http:// fair.org/extra-online-articles/top-op-ed-pages-offer-choice-of-elites/.

18. Lee B. Becker, Tudor Vlad, and Holly Anne Simpson, "2013 Annual Survey of Journalism & Mass Communication Graduates," University of Georgia (December 2013), accessed on January 15, 2015, http://www.grady.uga.edu/ annualsurveys/Graduate_Survey/Graduate_2013/Grad_ Report_2013_Combined.pdf.

CHAPTER 9

1. Louis Bien, "A Complete Timeline of the Ray Rice Assault Case," SB Nation, November, 28, 2014, accessed April 11, 2015, http://www.sbnation.com/nfl/2014/5/23/5744 964/ray-rice-arrest-assault-statement-apology-ravens.

2. Alexia Elejalde-Ruiz, "Cover Girl, 'Game Face' Ad Becomes Part of NFL Scandal," *Chicago Tribune*, September 16, 2014, http://www.chicagotribune.com/business/breaking/ chi-game-face-cover-girl-ad-black-eye-viral-20140916-story.html.

3. Sandra L. Calvert, "Children as Consumers: Advertising and Marketing," *The Future of Children* 18, no. 1 (Spring 2008), accessed August 9, 2013, http:// futureofchildren .org/publications/journals/article/index.xml?journalid= 32&articleid=62&sectionid=306.

4. "Emergence of Advertising in America: 1850-1920," A project of the Digital Scriptorium, Rare Book, Manuscript, and Special Collections Library, Duke University.

Copyright 2000 Duke University, accessed October 31, 2002, http://scriptorium.lib.duke.edu/eaa/timeline.html.

5. Kathleen Hall Jamieson, *Dirty Politics* (New York: Oxford University Press, 1992), 54–55.

6. "Mark Ritson on Branding: Norse Fire Smokes Out Bland Brands," *Marketing Magazine*, November 1, 2006, accessed September 25, 2013, http://www.marketingmagazine.co.uk/news/534969/Mark-Ritson-branding-Norse-fire-smokes-bland-brands/?DCMP=ILC-SEARCH.

7. Robin Wauters, "Study: In-Game Video Advertising Trumps TV Advertising in Effectiveness," March 24, 2009, accessed March 10, 2013, TechCrunch website, http://techcrunch.com/2009/03/24/study-in-game-video-advertising-trumps-tv-advertising-in-effectiveness/.

8. Patrick Walsh, Matthew H. Zimmerman, Galen Clavio, and Antonio S. Williams, "Comparing Brand Awareness Levels of In-Game Advertising in Sport Video Games Featuring Visual and Verbal Communication Cues," *Communication & Sport* (May 8, 2013).

9. Lindsay D. Grace, *"Player Performance and In-Game Advertising Retention,"* Digital Library, ACM website, 2011, http://dl.acm.org/citation.cfm?id=2071492.

10. Richard Shears for Mail Online, "British Man Who Put His Life Up for Sale on eBay Finally Sells the Lot for £193,000," *Daily Mail* website, June 30, 2008, accessed August 9, 2013, http://www.dailymail.co.uk/news/article-1030391/British-man-life-sale-eBay-finally-sells-lot-193-000.html.

11. Steve Lohr, "Algorithms Get a Human Hand in Steering Web," *New York Times*, March 10, 2013, accessed March 10, 2013, http://www.nytimes.com/2013/03/11/technology/computer-algorithms-rely-increasingly-on-human-helpers.html?_r=0.

12. Matt Krantz, "Has Facebook Figured It Out?," *USA Today*, July 25, 2013, accessed August 9, 2013, http://www.usatoday.com/story/money/markets/2013/07/25/facebook-mobile-revolution-winner/2587117/.

13. eMarketer, "Adspend Tool," accessed June 10, 2015, http://www.emarketer.com/adspendtool.

14. Stephen Millies, "The Ludlow Massacre and the Birth of Company Unions," *Workers World*, January 26, 1995, accessed October 31, 2002, http://www.hartford-hwp.com/archives/45b/030.html.

15. Anne Bernays, "Doris Fleischman: 1891–1980," *Jewish Women's Archive: Encyclopedia*, accessed June 12, 2015, http://jwa.org/encyclopedia/article/fleischman-doris.

16. Kim Krisberg, "Anti-Smoking Campaign Lowers Youth Smoking Rates with 'Truth' Funding Threatened," *Medscape* (2005), accessed March 10, 2013, http://www.medscape.com/viewarticle/502009.

17. Jeff Niederdeppe, Matthew C. Farrelly, and M. Lyndon Haviland, "Confirming 'Truth': More Evidence of a Successful Tobacco Countermarketing Campaign in Florida," *American Journal of Public Health* 94, no. 2 (February 2004): 255–257, accessed September 25, 2013, http://www.ncbi.nlm.nih.gov/pmc/articles/PMC1448237/.

18. Daniel J. Boorstin, "From News-Gathering to News-Making: A Flood of Pseudo Events," in *The Modern World: The Image* (New York: Vintage, 1961), 7–44.

19. "Agency Family Trees," *Ad Age*, accessed June 12, 2015, http://adage.coverleaf.com/advertisingage/20150504?pg=71#pg72.

20. David Streitfeld, "In a Race to Out-Rave, 5-Star Web Reviews Go for $5," *New York Times*, August 19, 2011, accessed May 14, 2012, http://www.nytimes.com/2011/08/20/technology/finding-fake-reviews-online.html.

21. Myle Ott, Yejin Choi, Claire Cardie, and Jeffrey T. Hancock, "Finding Deceptive Opinion Spam by Any Stretch of the Imagination," in *Proceedings of the 49th Annual Meeting of the Association for Computational Linguistics*, Portland, Oregon, June 19–24 (Association for Computational Linguistics, 2011), 309–319, accessed May 14, 2012, http://aclweb.org/anthology/P/P11/P11-1032.pdf.

CHAPTER 10

1. Margaret Hartmann, "Everything We Know About the UVA Rape Case [Updated]," *New York Magazine*, accessed April 15, 2015, http://nymag.com/daily/intelligencer/2014/12/everything-we-know-uva-rape-case.html.

2. Sheila Coronel, Steve Coll, Derek Kravitz, "Rolling Stone and UVA: The Columbia University Graduate School of Journalism Report," *Rolling Stone*, April 5, 2015, accessed April 15, 2015, from, http://www.rollingstone.com/culture/features/a-rape-on-campus-what-went-wrong-20150405.

3. William W. Neher and Paul J. Sandin, *Communicating Ethically: Character, Duties, Consequences, and Relationships* (Boston: Pearson, 2007); Clifford G. Christians, Mark Fackler, Kathy Brittain Richardson, Peggy J. Kreshel, and Robert H. Woods Jr., *Media Ethics: Cases and Moral Reasoning*, 8th ed. (Boston: Allyn & Bacon, 2008), 1–34.

4. H. W. Brands, *The First American: The Life and Times of Benjamin Franklin* (New York: Doubleday, 2000).

5. Souad Mekhennet, "Mistaken as an Iranian Martyr, Then Hounded," *New York Times*, July 31, 2010, accessed June 24, 2013, http://www.nytimes.com/2010/08/01/world/middleeast/01neda.html.

6. *HVNews*, "10 Funniest Tweets From the #McDstories Disaster," *Hypervocal*, January 25, 2012, accessed June 24, 2013, http://hypervocal.com/news/2012/mcdonalds-tweets-twitter-mcdstories-fail/.

7. Greg Matthews, "The World's Doctors Pile on Dr Oz' Twitter Hashtag," MDigital Life website, November 14, 2014, accessed May 30, 2015, http://mdigitallife.com/the-worlds-doctors-pile-on-dr-oz-twitter-hashtag/.

8. Corey Stern, "Doctors Call for Removal of Penn Graduate Dr. Oz from Columbia Faculty," *The Daily Pennsylvanian*, April 20, 2015, accessed May 31, 2015, http://www.thedp.com/article/2015/04/doctors-call-

for-removal-of-penn-graduate-dr-oz-from-colubmia-faculty.

9. William A. Henry III, "Where NBC Went Wrong," *Time*, Monday, Feb. 22, 1993, accessed August 16, 2011, http://www.time.com/time/magazine/article/0,9171,977814,00.html.

10. Joe Nocera, "How to Monetize Plagiarism," *New York Times*, June 7, 2013, accessed June 24, 2013, http://www.nytimes.com/2013/06/08/opinion/nocera-how-to-monetize-plagiarism.html.

11. "Dole Cans Banana Label After Oxfam Claims," 3News/NZN, May 28, 2013, accessed June 24, 2013, http://www.3news.co.nz/Dole-cans-banana-label-after-Oxfam-claims/tabid/421/articleID/299462/Default.aspx.

12. Jeff Sommer, "The War Against Too Much of Everything," *The New York Times*, December 22, 2012, accessed June 1, 2015, http://www.nytimes.com/2012/12/23/business/adbusters-war-against-too-much-of-everything.html?pagewanted=all&_r=1.

13. Adbusters [Siobhan McGuirk], "The Aesthetics of Activism," Adbusters.com, October 27, 2010, accessed June 1, 2015, https://www.adbusters.org/blogs/adbusters-blog/aesthetics-of-activism.html.

CHAPTER 11

1. Dwight L. Teeter Jr. and Don R. Le Duc, *Law of Mass Communications: Freedom and Control of Print and Broadcast Media* (Westbury, NY: The Foundation Press, 1992).

2. M. K. Mallonee and Pamela Brown, "Facebook Threats Case Heard at Supreme Court," CNN.com, December 1, 2014, accessed January 19, 2015, http://www.cnn.com/2014/12/01/politics/supreme-court-elonis-vs-u-s-free-speech/.

3. "Shield Laws and Protection of Sources by State," Reporters Committee for Freedom of the Press website, accessed August 19, 2015, https://www.rcfp.org/browse-media-law-resources/guides/reporters-privilege/shield-laws.

4. Adam Liptak, "Anthony Lewis, Supreme Court Reporter Who Brought Law to Life, Dies at 85," *New York Times*, March 25, 2013, accessed May 26, 2013, http://www.nytimes.com/2013/03/26/us/anthony-lewis-pulitzer-prize-winning-columnist-dies-at-85.html?pagewanted=all&_r=0.

5. Chairman Reed E. Hundt, Federal Communications Commission, "Not So Fast," [speech, Museum of Television and Radio, New York, New York, June 3, 1997], accessed November 8, 2002, http://www.fcc.gov/Speeches/Hundt/spreh729.txt.

6. Doug Gross, "Under Pressure, Facebook Targets Sexist Hate Speech," CNN.com, May 30, 2013, accessed August 5, 2013, http://www.cnn.com/2013/05/29/tech/social-media/facebook-hate-speech-women.

7. Linda Greenhouse, "'Virtual' Child Pornography Ban Overturned," *New York Times*, April 17, 2002, accessed August 19, 2015, http://www.nytimes.com/2002/04/17/us/virtual-child-pornography-ban-overturned.html.

8. Mark Goodman, "The Radio Act of 1927 as a Product of Progressivism," *Media History Monographs* 2, no. 2 (1998–1999), accessed November 8, 2002, http://www.scripps.ohiou.edu/mediahistory/mhmjour2-2.htm.

9. Erik Barnouw, *A Tower of Babel: A History of Broadcasting in the United States*, vol. 1, *A History of Broadcasting in the United States to 1933* (New York: Oxford University Press, 1966).

10. Mark Goodman, "The Radio Act of 1927 as a Product of Progressivism," *Media History Monographs* 2, no. 2 (1998–1999), accessed November 8, 2002, http://www.scripps.ohiou.edu/mediahistory/mhmjour2-2.htm.

11. M. S. Mander, "The Public Debate About Broadcasting in the Twenties: An Interpretive History," *Journal of Broadcasting* 28, no. 2 (1984): 167–185.

12. Alan B. Albarran and Gregory G. Pitts, *The Radio Broadcasting Industry* (Boston: Allyn & Bacon, 2001), 27–29.

13. Eli Noam and Robert Freeman, "Global Competition," *Television Quarterly* 29, no. 1 (1998): 18–23.

14. Contributor, "Combating the Dangers of Journalism," *RustyBee*, March 21, 2011, accessed August 19, 2015, http://rustybee.com/combating-the-dangers-of-journalism/.

15. Cheryl Lee, "Will FCC Bend Rules for Marijuana Internet Advertising?" Wordpress website, January 7, 2015, accessed February 17, 2015, https://wjlta.wordpress.com/2015/01/07/will-fcc-bend-rules-for-marijuana-internet-advertising/.

16. Brian Knappenberger, "The Internet's Own Boy Documentary 2014," Internet Archive, June 27, 2014, accessed August 19, 2015, https://archive.org/details/TheInternetsOwnBoyTheStoryOfAaronSwartz.

CHAPTER 12

1. Erik Kain, "The Truth about Video Games and Gun Violence," *Mother Jones*, June 11, 2013, accessed June 22, 2013, http://www.motherjones.com/politics/2013/06/video-games-violence-guns-explainer.

2. Ibid.

3. "Statistic Brain: Television Watching Statistics," BLS American Time Use Survey, A.C. Nielsen Co., March 27, 2015, accessed May 24, 2015 http://www.statisticbrain.com/television-watching-statistics/.

4. Rolf Wigand Lichter, "Communication and Violent Behavior," *ICA Newsletter* 2, no. 5 (July 1999): 5.

5. "Facts About Media Violence and Effects on the American Family," National Television Violence Study, issued by Mediascope Inc., February 1996.

6. Statistics compiled by TV-Free America, Washington, DC, 1996.

7. Garth S. Jowett, Ian C. Jarvie, and Kathryn H. Fuller, eds., *Children and the Movies: Media Influence and the Payne Fund Controversy* (Cambridge: Cambridge University Press, 1996).

8. P. W. Holaday and G. D. Stoddard, *Getting Ideas from the Movies* (New York: Macmillan, 1933).

9. Garth Jowett et al., "Payne Fund Radio Broadcasting Research, 1928–1935," in *Children and the Movies: Media Influence and the Payne Fund Controversy* (Cambridge: Cambridge University Press, 1996).

10. "Professor Fired Over Anti-Israeli Tweets Sues University of Illinois," RT.com, January 30, 2015, accessed May 28, 2015, http://rt.com/news/227791-israel-professor-sues-university/.

11. Stacey Patton, "A Professor Tries to Beat Back a News Spoof That Won't Go Away," *Vitae* website, May 21, 2015, accessed May 26, 2015 https://chroniclevitae.com/news/1014-a-professor-tries-to-beat-back-a-news-spoof-that-won-t-go-away?cid=wc&utm_source=wc&utm_medium=en.

12. danah boyd, "what's in a name?" danah boyd website, n.d., accessed June 23, 2013, http://www.danah.org/name.html.

13. Paul F. Lazarsfeld and Robert K. Merton, "Mass Communication, Popular Taste and Organized Social Action," in *The Communication of Ideas*, ed. Lyman Bryson (New York: Institute for Religious and Social Studies, Jewish Theological Seminary of America, 1948), 95–118.

14. Bernard Cohen, *The Press and Foreign Policy* (Princeton, NJ: Princeton University Press, 1963), 13.

15. Jeffrey Cole, "Surveying the Digital Future: A Longitudinal International Study of the Individual and Social Effects of PC/Internet Technology," accessed November 5, 2002, http://www.digitalcenter.org/wp-content/uploads/2014/12/2014-Digital-Future-Report.pdf.

16. Pat Hartman, "Television Advertising and Childhood Obesity, Part 5," *Childhood Obesity News*, December 13, 2010, accessed April 16, 2012, http://childhoodobesitynews.com/2010/12/13/television-advertising-and-childhood-obesity-part-5/.

CHAPTER 13

1. "Super PACS," OpenSecrets.org, accessed May 8, 2012, http://www.opensecrets.org/pacs/superpacs.php.

2. Michael Isikoff, "Karl Rove's Election Debacle: Super PAC's Spending Was Nearly for Naught," accessed on November 8, 2012, http://openchannel.nbcnews.com/_news/2012/11/08/15007504-karl-roves-election-debacle-super-pacs-spending-was-nearly-for-naught?lite.

3. "Super PACs," Sunlight Foundation Reporting Group website, accessed January 19, 2015, http://reporting.sunlightfoundation.com/outside-spenders/2014/super-pacs/.

4. Joseph Pulitzer, "The College of Journalism," *North American Review* 178, no. 570 (May 1904).

5. Daniel C. Hallin, "Sound Bite News: Television Coverage of Elections 1968–1988," *Journal of Communication* 42, no. 2 (June 1992): 5–24.

6. Herbert E. Alexander, "Financing Presidential Elections Campaigns," *Issues of Democracy, Electronic Journals of the U.S. Information Agency* 1, no. 13 (September 1996), accessed November 7, 2002, http://usinfo.state.gov/journals/itdhr/0996/ijde/alex.htm.

7. Rachel Streitfeld, "Hillary Clinton 2016 Campaign Could Cost $1.7 Billion," CNN.com, March 12, 2014, accessed January 19, 2015, http://politicalticker.blogs.cnn.com/2014/03/12/a-hillary-clinton-2016-campaign-could-cost-1-7-billion/.

8. Larry Sabato, *The Rise of Political Consultants: New Way of Winning Elections* (New York: Basic Books, 1981), 165–166.

9. Kathleen Hall Jamieson, *Dirty Politics* (New York: Oxford University Press, 1992), 19–20.

10. Susan Page, "Gabby Giffords' Comeback: Word by Word, Step by Step," *USA Today*, September 28, 2014, accessed January 19, 2014, http://www.usatoday.com/story/news/politics/2014/09/28/day-in-the-life-of-gabby-giffords/16281013/.

11. Richard Lau, Lee Sigelman, and Ivy Brown Rovner, "The Effects of Negative Political Campaign: A Meta-Analytic Re-Assessment," *The Journal of Politics* 69, no. 4 (November 2007): 1176–1209.

12. Claire Cain Miller, "How Obama's Internet Campaign Changed Politics," *New York Times*, November 7, 2008.

13. Tom Pepinsky, "Crowdsourcing Election Monitoring," *Cornell University*, July 14, 2014, accessed January 19, 2014, http://tompepinsky.com/2014/07/14/crowdsourcing-election-monitoring/.

14. Andrew Phelps, "Inside the Star Chamber: How PolitiFact Tries to Find Truth in a World of Make-Believe," Nieman Journalism Lab website, August 21, 2012, http://www.niemanlab.org/2012/08/inside-the-star-chamber-how-politifact-forges-truth-in-the-world-of-make-believe/.

15. The Pulitzer Prizes, http://www.pulitzer.org/citation/2009-National-Reporting.

16. "About PolitiFact," *Tampa Bay Times* Politifact.com, http://www.politifact.com/about/.

17. Brendan Nyhan, "Bill Adair, Setting Pants Ablaze No More," *Columbia Journalism Review,* April 8, 2013, http://www.cjr.org/united_states_project/bill_adair_setting_pants_ablaze_no_more.php.

18. Caroline O'Donovan, "Tuesday Q&A: Bill Adair on Leaving PolitiFact for Academia and the Simon & Garfunkel Theory of Presidential Coverage," Nieman Journalism Lab website, April 9, 2013, http://www.niemanlab.org/2013/04/tuesday-qa-bill-adair-on-leaving-politifact-for-academia-and-the-simon-garfunkel-theory-of-presidential-coverage/.

19. Interview with Mary Ann McHugh and George Watson, July 24, 2013.

20. Editorial Board, "Wrong Responses to Charlie Hebdo," *The New York Times*, January 16, 2015, accessed January 19, 2015, http://www.nytimes.com/2015/01/16/opinion/after-paris-attacks-wrong-responses-to-charlie-hebdo.html?hp&action=click&pgtype=Homepage&module=c-column-top-span-region&region=c-column-top-span-region&WT.nav=c-column-top-span-region.

CHAPTER 14

1. Ray Sanchez, "ISIS Exploits Social Media to Make Inroads in U.S.," CNN.com, June 5, 2015, accessed June 7, 2015, http://www.cnn.com/2015/06/04/us/isis-social-media-recruits/.

2. Cristina Corbin, Mike Levine, and The Associated Press, "Boston Bombing Suspects Built Explosives with Help of Online Al Qaeda Magazine, Official Says," Fox News website, April 23, 2013, accessed July 16, 2013, http://www.foxnews.com/us/2013/04/23/marathon-attack-suspect-communicating-by-writing-sources-say-with-faith-seen-as/.

3. Fred S. Siebert, Wilbur Schramm, and Theodore Peterson, *Four Theories of the Press: The Authoritarian, Libertarian, Social Responsibility, and Soviet Communist Concepts of What the Press Should Be and Do* (Champaign: University of Illinois Press, 1956).

4. Daniel C. Brouwer, "Communication as Counterpublic," in *Communication as Counterpublic: Perspectives on Theory*, eds. G. J. Shepherd, J. St. John, and T. Striphas (Thousand Oaks, CA: Sage, 2006), 195–208.

5. Glenn Greenwald and Ewen MacAskill, "NSA Prism Program Taps in to User Data of Apple, Google and Others," *theguardian*, June 6, 2013, accessed July 16, 2013, www.guardian.co.uk/world/2013/jun/06/us-tech-giants-nsa-data.

6. Steven Lee Meyers and Andrew E. Kramer, "Defiant Russia Grants Snowden Year's Asylum," *The New York Times*, August 2, 2013, A1.

7. "World Press Freedom Index 2014," Reporters Without Borders, http://rsf.org/index2014/en-asia.php.

8. Ibid.

9. Robert W. McChesney, *Digital Disconnect: How Capitalism Is Turning the Internet Against Democracy* (New York: New Press, 2013).

10. "Gartner Says Smartphone Sales Surpassed One Billion Units in 2014," Gartner website, March 3, 2015, accessed June 13, 2015, http://www.gartner.com/newsroom/id/2996817.

11. Tom Kelly, "Britain Ousts the U.S. as World's Most Influential Nation: Country Tops Rankings for 'Soft Power'," *Daily Mail*, November 18, 2012, accessed July 15, 2013, http://www.dailymail.co.uk/news/article-2234726/Britain-tops-global-soft-power-list.html.

12. Sigmund Freud, *Civilization and Its Discontents*, reprint ed. (New York: W. W. Norton & Company, 2012).

13. "Statistics," YouTube, accessed August 13, 2013, http://www.youtube.com/yt/press/statistics.html.

14. Sandvine, "Global Internet Phenomena Report," http://www.sandvine.com/downloads/documents/Phenomena_1H_2013/Sandvine_Global_Internet_Phenomena_Report_1H_2013.pdf.

15. "Statistics," YouTube, accessed June 13, 2015, http://www.youtube.com/yt/press/statistics.html.

16. Miguel Helft, "It Pays to Have Pals in Silicon Valley," *New York Times*, October 17, 2006, accessed August 13, 2013, http://www.nytimes.com/2006/10/17/technology/17paypal.html?pagewanted=all.

17. Miguel Helft, "YouTube's Payoff: Hundreds of Millions for the Founders," *New York Times*, February 7, 2007.

18. Nitasha Tiku, "YouTube Cofounders Break up the Band After Second Act Flops," *ValleyWag* (blog), June 6, 2014, http://valleywag.gawker.com/youtube-cofounders-break-up-the-band-after-second-act-f-1587208160.

19. Y Ventures, accessed August 13, 2013, http://www.youniversityventures.com/.

20. Paul W. Taylor, "Co-productions—Content and Change: International Television in the Americas," *Canadian Journal of Communication* 20, no. 3 (1995): 411–416.

21. Marco R. della Cava, "Lucasfilm's Kathleen Kennedy Has Produced Quite a Career," *USA Today*, June 6, 2013, accessed August 5, 2013, http://www.usatoday.com/story/life/movies/2013/06/05/kathleen-kennedy-innovators-and-icons-lucasfilm/2164285/.

22. Ben Quinn, "Ikea Apologises Over Removal of Women from Saudi Arabia Catalogue," October 1, 2012, accessed July 16, 2013, http://www.guardian.co.uk/world/2012/oct/02/ikea-apologises-removing-women-saudi-arabia-catalogue.

23. International Fund for Agricultural Development, "Indigenous Media Amplify the Voices of Marginalized Rural Communities," July 31, 2012, accessed July 16, 2013, http://www.ruralpovertyportal.org/topic/voice/tags/indigenous_peoples/ipday.

24. Canada Council for the Arts, accessed August 13, 2013, http://www.canadacouncil.ca/.

25. "Canadian Content Requirements for Music on Radio," Canadian Radio-television and Telecommunications Commission website, accessed August 5, 2013, http://www.crtc.gc.ca/eng/cancon/r_cdn.htm.

26. "2015 Canada Digital Future in Focus," comScore website, March 27, 2015, accessed June 13, 2015, http://www.comscore.com/Insights/Presentations-and-Whitepapers/2015/2015-Canada-Digital-Future-in-Focus.

27. Dan Fricker, "How Digital Distribution Is Transforming the Canadian Television Industry," *Huffington Post*, July 26, 2013, accessed August 5, 2013, http://www.huffingtonpost.ca/dan-fricker/how-netflix-changed-everything_b_3654983.html.

28. Department of Defense, "Desert Fox," accessed August 13, 2013, http://www.defense.gov/specials/desert_fox/.

29. Everette E. Dennis, "Al Jazeera America—A New Voice as a Business Proposition," *Arab Business*, February 2013.

30. Haley Tsukayama, "Apple Confirms Attack by Same Hackers Who Hit Facebook," *Daily Times News*, February 20, 2013, accessed July 16, 2013, http://www.delcotimes.com/general-news/20130220/apple-confirms-attack-by-same-hackers-who-hit-facebook.

31. Adrien Chen, "The Agency," *New York Times Magazine*, June 2, 2015, accessed June 7, 2015, http://www.nytimes.com/2015/06/07/magazine/the-agency.html?emc=edit_th_20150607&nl=todaysheadlines&nlid=69673382.

32. *New York Times Co. v. United States*, 403 U.S. 713 (1971).

Credits

CHAPTER 1

Page 2 © Snap Stills/Rex/REX USA; 5 isaravut/Shutterstock; 6 Bon Appetit/Shutterstock; 9 MAStock/Shutterstock; 10 Bloomberg/Getty Images; 11 AFP/Getty Images; 12 PHOTOCREO Michal Bednarek/Shutterstock; 17 AP Photo/Brendan Smialowski; 23 arek_malang/Shutterstock; 26 The Granger Collection, New York; 26 AP Photo/Marcio Jose Sanchez; 27 Syda Productions/Shutterstock; 31 © 2015, The Poynter Institute for Media Studies

CHAPTER 2

Page 36 AP Photo/Rick Scuteri; 39 Kheng Guan Toh/Shutterstock; 40 © 2015 C. Herscovici/Artists Rights Society (ARS), New York; 42 AP Photo/Ben Margot; 44 Takis Tsafos/picture-alliance/dpa/AP Images; 45 Bill Pugliano/Getty Images; 46 Everett Collection/Rex Shutterstock; 48 © Bettmann/Corbis/AP Images; 49 AP Photo/Tom Roberts; 50 Sipa via AP Images; 53 AP Photo/Charles Sykes; 55 Jonathan Leibson/Getty Images; 59 iStock/zoliky

CHAPTER 3

Page 62 Bloomberg/Getty Images; 65 Saul Loeb/AFP/Getty Images; 66 AP Photo/Bram Janssen; 66 Library of Congress, Asian Room; 67 Universitatsbibliothek, Gottingen, Germany/Bildarchiv Steffens/Bridgeman Images; 68 © Bettmann/Corbis/AP Images; 69 American Treasure of the Library of Congress; 69 AP Photo/Ben Margot; 70 © Iain Masterton/Alamy Stock Photo; 73 iStock/Yuri_Arcurs; 74 © Studio Works/Alamy Stock Photo; 76 Front cover of newspaper reproduced courtesy of The Yomiuri Shimbun; 77 PD-US; Special Collections, Stanford University Libraries; 84 Photo by Petteri Sulonen/Flickr/CC BY 2.0: https://creativecommons.org/licenses/by/2.0/; 85 Bloomberg/Getty images; 87 © Bettmann/Corbis/AP Images; 89 PD-US; Special Collections, Stanford University Libraries; 93 © Oleksiy Maksymenko Photography/Alamy Stock Photo

CHAPTER 4

Page 96 Helga Esteb/Shutterstock; 98 Crollalanza/REX USA; 100 iStock/faruk_tasdemir; 101 Culver Pictures/The Art Archive at Art Resource, NY; 101 Michael Ochs Archives/Getty Images; 101 © Granamour Weems Collection/Alamy Stock Photo; 102 Brian Rasic/Rex Shutterstock; 102 Adam J. Sablich/Shutterstock; 105 Jude Domski/Getty Images; 108 Electronic Frontier Foundation; 109 iStock/pressureUA; 109 MediaPunch/REX USA; 110 © Ole Spata/dpa/Corbis; 110 JUPITERIMAGES/ABLESTOCK/Alamy; 111 © Renee Jones Schneider/Minneapolis Star Tribune/ZUMA Wire; 111 © Joe Bangay/Lebrecht Music & Arts; 112 Science and Society Picture Library/Getty Images; 115 © Corbis; 121 AP Photo/Karel Prinsloo; 121 L. Busacca/WireImage/Getty Images

CHAPTER 5

Page 124 Yap.tv, © AF archive/Alamy Stock Photo, AMC-TV/THE KOBAL COLLECTION/ART RESOURCE; 126 Penguin Random House; 127 Library of Congress, Prints & Photographs Division LC-B811-557; 130 iStock/ferrantraite; 130 © Rolling Stone LLC 2013. All Rights Reserved. Used by Permission; 131 Everett Collection/Rex Shutterstock; 132 © AF archive/Alamy; 134 © Bettmann/CORBIS; 135 RKO/THE KOBAL COLLECTION/KAHLE, ALEX/ART RESOURCE; 136 © Sunset Boulevard/Corbis; 136 Tom Kingston/WireImage/Getty Images; 136 FIRST NATIONAL/WARNER BROTHERS/THE KOBAL COLLECTION/ART RESOURCE; 137 © Everett Collection Inc./Alamy; 137 © AF archive/Alamy Stock Photo; 139 © Ted Soqui/Corbis; 141 Used with permission of Kathleen Kennedy; 142 © Moviestore collection Ltd/Alamy Stock Photo; 144 Moviestore/Rex/REX USA; 145 Bloomberg/Getty Images; 146 MacFormat Magazine/Getty Images; 146 Bettman/Corbis; 147 CBS/Landov; 150 © John McCoy/Los Angeles Daily News/ZUMAPRESS.com; 150 Mike Hewitt/Getty Images; 151 Everett Collection/Rex Shutterstock; 153 Chris Pizzello/Invision/AP; 156 CBS Photo Archive/Getty Images; 157 Everett Collection/Rex Shutterstock

CHAPTER 6

Page 160 Rex Features via AP Images; 163 Elaine McMillion Sheldon/Hollow Documentary; 165 iStock/haneck; iStock/rouzes; 167 August Dvorak and William Dealey; 168 © Gary Reyes/TNS/ZUMA Wire; 170 Press Association via AP Images; 171 Maridav/Shutterstock; 173 Used with permission from Microsoft.; 175 FlickrVision; 177 © Jake Charles/Alamy Stock; 179 Robee Shepherd/Moment/Getty Images; 179 Stefano Tinti/Shutterstock; 180 © Mike Margol/PhotoEdit — All rights reserved.; 181 iStock/Christopher Futcher; 182 AP Photo/Damian Dovarganes; 184 © ALBERT GEA/Reuters/Corbis

CHAPTER 7

Page 190 © Ikon Images/Masterfile; 194 Bloomberg/Getty Images; 200 Photo by Aaron Parecki/Flickr/CC BY 2.0: https://creativecommons.org/licenses/by/2.0/; 200 Denis Rozhnovsky/Shutterstock; 201 Aleksandra Gigowska/Shutterstock; 202 Tim Robberts/Getty Images; 204 AP Photo/Mark Lennihan; 206 AP Photo/Jeff Chiu; 208 iStock/FLDphotos; 211 Michael Tran/Getty Images; 214 QUT Media; 221 ©iStockphoto.com/pearleye

CHAPTER 8

Page 226 Kazuhiro Nogi/AFP/Getty Images; 229 © IanDagnall Computing/Alamy Stock Photo; 230 iStock/stocksnapper; 232 Used with permission, Library Archives of Canada; 232 The Granger Collection, New York; 233 Hulton Archive/Getty Images; 234 Hulton Archive/Getty Images; 235 Hulton Archive/Getty Images; 236 Getty Images; 238 iStock/Juanmonino; 240 MUSA AL-SHAER/AFP/Getty Images; 241 © Bill Gentile; 242 AP Photo/Brad Barket; 245 Joe Raedle/Getty Images; 247 rmnoa; 357/Shutterstock; 252 AP Photo/Jose Luis Magana; 254 Paul Sakuma Photography

CHAPTER 9

Page 258 © epa european pressphoto agency b.v./Alamy Stock Photo; 260 iStock/Yuri_Arcurs; 261 Everett Collection/

Shutterstock; 262 Anthony Behar/Sipa Press; 263 Stuart Wilson/Getty Images; 265 A'Lelia Bundles/Madam Walker Family Archives; 269 iStock/ABDESIGN; 271 Borderlands/Alamy; 273 Everett Collection/Rex Shutterstock; 273 © Bill Aron/PhotoEdit — All rights reserved.; 276 © J Emilio Flores/The New York Times/Redux; 277 Marcos Mesa Sam Wordley/Shutterstock; 282 Bloomberg/Getty Images; 283 © Corbis; 284 © Bettmann/Corbis/AP Images; 286 Dennis Van Tine/STAR MAX/IPx; 286 © Blend Images/Alamy Stock Photo

CHAPTER 10

Page 294 AP Photo/The Daily Progress, Ryan M. Kelly; 299 DEA Picture Library/Getty Images; 300 © Jeff Gilbert/Alamy Stock Photo; 303 MARK RALSTON/AFP/Getty Images; 304 The Washington Post/Getty Images; 308 © Everett Collection Inc./Alamy; 309 © ZUMA Press, Inc. / Alamy Stock Photo; 312 Brad Barket/Invision/AP; 313 © WENN UK / Alamy Stock Photo; 316 Photo by Eviatar Bach/Creative Commons CC 1.0 Universal Public Domain Dedication; 318 Michael Stewart/FilmMagic/Getty Images; 318 © BSIP SA/Alamy Stock Photo; 319 Kevin Bolk

CHAPTER 11

Page 322 Hindustan Times/Getty Images; 325 Stock Montage/Getty Images; 326 © Everett Collection Historical/Alamy Stock Photo ; 327 © 2009, The Progressive Magazine; 328 The Granger Collection, New York; 330 Matthew Peyton/Getty Images; 331 © Aurora Photos/Alamy; 332 Ted Streshinsky/Corbis; 332 American Stock Archive/Getty Images; 333 Kevin Statham/Getty Images; 335 Fierce Baby Productions/Detective Agency/20th Century Fox/The Kobal Collection/Art Resource; 336 Deutsche Kolonialgesellschaft; 339 Anatoli Zhdanov/UPI/Landov; 341 Mark Van Scyoc/Shutterstock; 344 Gabriel Buoys/Getty Images; 345 Christopher Halloran/Shutterstock; 346 Angela Waye/Shutterstock; 350 © ZUMA Press, Inc./Alamy

CHAPTER 12

Page 356 Kevin Beebe/Getty Images; 360 The Granger Collection, New York; 361 First National/Warner Brothers/The Kobal Collection; 361 CBS/The Kobal Collection; 362 AllStar Picture Library; 364 marekuliasz/Shutterstock; 367 Rob Marmion/Shutterstock; 368 Everett Collection/Rex Shutterstock; 370 Fred Stein/picture-alliance/dpa/AP Images; 371 Christopher Lane/Contour/Getty Images; 373 Kheng Guan Toh/Shutterstock; 374 Louis Monier/Gamma-Rapho/Getty Images; 376 © M. Scott Brauer/Alamy; 377 Richard Baker/In pictures/Corbis/AP; 381 © Marmaduke St. John/Alamy

CHAPTER 13

Page 386 AP Photo/Comedy Central, Kristopher Long; 388 NBCU Photo Bank via Getty Images; 390 MEDIA RIGHTS CAPITAL/THE KOBAL COLLECTION/ART RESOURCE; 392 From The New York Times, November 4, 2014 © 2014 The New York Times; 395 Simon & Schuster, Inc., The Washington Post/Getty Images; 396 © Neno Images/PhotoEdit – All rights reserved.; 397 Fotosearch/Getty Images; 398 Ed Clark/Getty Images; 398 AP Photo/Damian Dovarganes; 399 The Washington Post/Contributor/Getty Images; 400 Alex Wong/Getty Images; 401 iStock/andrearoad; 405 Mario Tama/Getty Images; 406 ©Duke Photography, Used with permission of Bill Adair

CHAPTER 14

Page 410 Joe Raedle/Getty Images; 412 © blickwinkel/Alamy; 415 STF/AFP/Getty Images; 416 Mary Evans Picture Library; 419 John Macdougall/AFP/Getty Images; 419 Atul Loke/Panos Pictures; 422 © M4OS Photos/Alamy; 423 wavebreakmedia/Shutterstock; 425 Sipa via AP Images; 427 © ZUMA Press, Inc./Alamy Stock Photo; 429 HENRIK MONTGOMERY/AFP/Getty Images; 429 iStock/Bartosz Hadyniak; 431 © Shawn Baldwin/Corbis

Index

T

tablet computers, 16–17, *17*, 91, *93f*
tagging, 198
The Talk, 53
talk shows, 149
TCP. *See* Transmission Control Protocol
Technicolor Motion Picture Corporation, 131, 134
technological convergence, 8–9, *8f*
technological determinism, 375
Telecommunications Act of 1996, 116, 154, 158, 334, 337
telegraphy, 5, 6, 112, 231
telemarketing, 274
telephony, 4. *See also* mobile telephony
    cable television and, 158
    cell phones, 4–5, 7, 221
    compatibility, 6
    convergence in, 4–8
    developing world and mobile, 50
    as early radio, 6
    government or privately run, 6
    lines, 5
    transmission model of communication and, 29
television, 4, 125–26, 144–46. *See also* broadcasting; cable television; *specific networks*
    advertising, 125, 142, 156, 260, 266–67, 278, *278t*
    audience, 145, 146, 149, 153, 156
    color, 147
    commercial, 266–67
    convergence and, 31–33, 152
    cultural transmission and, 146
    dating shows, 11
    digital, 152, 157
    distribution of, 153–54, *155t*
    first systems, 146
    flat-panel displays, 152–53
    functions, 146
    HDTV, 152
    history of, 146–53
    industry of China, 11
    interactive, 32–33
    interfaces, 165–66
    Internet and, 125, 146, 153, 157, 158
    media grammar of, 46
    modern, 146–47
    movies and, 32, 137, 142
    Nielsen ratings, 156
    objectivity of, 54
    ownership, 154, *155t*
    politics and, 391, 398–99
    remote controls, *165*, 166
    risk-averse network, 149, 156
    satellite, 154, 155, *155t*, 157
    social media and, 193
    subscription services, 138, 139, 154, 155, 157
    surveillance functions of, 146
    3-D, 32, 153
    time shifting and place shifting, 25, 145

    viewing habits, 31
    violence and, 357, *362*, 362–64, *365*
television industry
    business models, 156–57
    outlook for, 157
    today, 154–55, *155t*
television programming
    cable, 128, 148–49, 156
    children's, 345–46, 361–64
    daytime, 149
    genres and, 147–52
    Internet, 157
    news, 234–35, 242, 309–10, *375*
    prime-time network, 149–50, 157
    pushing envelope of, 148
    reality shows, 151, *151*
    sports, 150–51
Te'o, Manti, 219
terrorism, 411–12
    cyberterrorism, 432, 434
textbooks, 66, 68
theories. *See also* research and theory; *specific theories*
    cognitive dissonance, 263
    communication, 28–31
    international mass communication, 413–15
A Theory of Semiotics (Eco), 41
Thicke, Robin, 111, *111*
third-party cookies, 274, 351
third-person effect, 365–66
"This is not a pipe," *41*
Thomson Reuters, 72
3-D
    movies, 32, 145, *145*
    television, 32, 153
Thumb, General Tom, *283*
Time Inc., 89
time shifting, 25, 145
Time Warner, 13, 52, 89, *140t*, 154, *155t*
Tin Pan Alley, 100
TMZ, 259
tobacco advertising, 343
Today, 310
Tornberg, Pelle, 85
To Sell a War, 317
touch screens, 167
trademarks, 269, 347
traditional mass-communication model, 24
traditional media
    digital media absorption of, 20
    privacy and, 348–49
    social media compared to, 192–95, 197, 199, 222, 223
Transmission Control Protocol (TCP), 169
transmission model of communication, *24t*, 28–30
transparency
    government, 403–4, 407
    international organizations, 408
    media, 21
    social media and, 217–18
trial balloon, 390
Tribune Media Company, *82f*

trolling, 186
trolls, 207
Trump, Donald, *286*, 347
trust, 214–15
    on Internet, 21
Tsarnaev, Dzhokhar, 130, *130*, 217
Tumblr, 205
Turkle, Sherry, 220
Turner, Ted, 32
Twitter, 25, 37, 57, 104, 191, 205, 206, 250, 303
    fake accounts, *217*, 218
    fake tweets, 18, 218
    McDonalds campaign on, 304–5
    political campaigns and, 398, *398*, 398–99, 401, 402
two-way symmetric model, 284–85
typewriters, 166
tyranny of the majority, 417

U

Ubisoft, 180
UGC. *See* user-generated content
UI. *See* user interface
UMG. *See* Universal Music Group
Undercover Brother, 138
United Nations, 428, 432
United States v. Paramount Pictures, 135, 139
Universal Music Group (UMG), 102
universal service, 340
University of Virginia (UVA), *294*, 295–96
USA Today, 75, 76
Usenet, 203
user-generated content (UGC), 18, 19, 151, 352
user interface (UI), 162, 165
    computer, 165
    GUI, 167–68, *170*
    historical development of, 165–68
    intuitive, 166–67
    television, 165–66
uses-and-gratifications research, 367–68
utilitarianism, 301
UVA. *See* University of Virginia

V

Valentine v. Chrestensen (1942), 342
values
    changes, 20–23
    global media and local, 423–32
    of journalism, 230–31
    news, 230–31
V-chip, 346
Venezuela election, 402
Vergara, Sofia, *150*
Verizon, 154, 158
Vice News, 130
victims, journalists victimizing, 311–12
Victor Talking Machine Company, 99, 100